Classification/Division

Comparison

Cost–Benefit Analysis

Definition

Description

Narration

Problem–Solution

Process Analysis

Becoming an Active Reader

Second Edition

Becoming an Active Reader

A Complete Resource for Reading and Writing

Eric Henderson

OXFORD
UNIVERSITY PRESS

OXFORD
UNIVERSITY PRESS

Oxford University Press is a department of the University of Oxford.
It furthers the University's objective of excellence in research, scholarship,
and education by publishing worldwide. Oxford is a registered trade mark of
Oxford University Press in the UK and in certain other countries.

Published in Canada by
Oxford University Press
8 Sampson Mews, Suite 204,
Don Mills, Ontario M3C 0H5 Canada

www.oupcanada.com

Database right Oxford University Press (maker)

First Edition published in 2013

Library and Archives Canada Cataloguing in Publication
Henderson, Eric, 1951–, author
Becoming an active reader: a complete resource for
reading and writing/Eric Henderson.—Second edition.

Includes bibliographical references and index.
ISBN 978-0-19-901906-9 (paperback)

1. English language—Rhetoric—Textbooks. 2. Academic
writing—Textbooks. 3. Report writing—Textbooks. 4. Reading
comprehension—Textbooks. 5. College readers. I. Title.

PE1408.H3853 2016   808'.042   C2016-900311-6

Cover image: © iStock\DragonImages

Oxford University Press is committed to our environment.
Wherever possible, our books are printed on paper which comes from
responsible sources.

Printed and bound in the United States of America
1 2 3 4 — 19 18 17 16

Contents

PART II | READING   99

READINGS

PART III | HANDBOOK   359

Preface

Becoming an Active Reader is a multi-purpose textbook designed primarily for first-year college and university students in Canada. It is divided into a rhetoric and research guide (Part I), a reader with 39 academic and non-academic readings (Part II), and a writing handbook (Part III). It is essential that today's textbooks reflect the needs of both instructors and their students. *Becoming an Active Reader* aspires to this goal by providing a review of composition principles and practices in Chapter 1 and by including common forms of first-year student writing: the summary, the rhetorical analysis, the argumentative essay, and the research paper are discussed thoroughly in Chapters 2–5. Points are amply illustrated by examples from student writing and excerpts from the readings in Part II, making *Becoming an Active Reader* a practical, integrated text.

The stress on argument in Part I reflects a trend in composition pedagogy: the use of argument to introduce students to research. To this end, Chapter 4 features a student argumentative essay that employs research, with more specific information on research following in Chapter 5. Chapter 4 begins with the introduction of three models of argument before breaking down argument into various purposes, giving students a wider-than-usual frame of reference. Similarly, students are encouraged to think beyond Aristotle's three appeals—important as these are—in planning an argument.

Many assignments at the college level involve writing about texts. Although reading a text usually precedes writing about it, the writing and thinking skills discussed in Part I are designed to maximize these skills—both general writing skills and those associated with specific assignments—making it more likely that texts will be read efficiently and understood thoroughly—a main goal of Part II. Much of Part II (Chapters 6–10) focuses on areas neglected by traditional textbooks, which often present readings without concrete strategies for approaching and analyzing them. However, knowing the techniques and strategies of academic and non-academic writers, as well as where important information is located, can make challenging essays more accessible and increase confidence (not to mention enjoyment) in the reading process—as well as promote class discussion.

Chapter 6 begins with general reading strategies and concludes with close reading techniques to ensure understanding of challenging material. Reinforcing the chapter on argument (Chapter 4), Chapter 7 helps students connect good argument with critical thinking. Too often, critical thinking remains an abstract concept as well-meaning instructors simply encourage students to exercise their critical thinking faculties, without explaining how this can be done. In this chapter, critical thinking is defined, then broken down through the use of concrete examples, exercises, and questions designed to engage students deeply and practically in the process of critical thinking.

In their academic careers, students will be exposed to various kinds of writing; through examples and clear explanation, Chapters 8–10 introduce students to the distinctive features of non-academic and academic prose. Whereas Chapter 8 orients the student by explaining basic similarities and differences, the two subsequent chapters identify features of both non-academic and academic writing, discussing them within the context of the student's own writing aims and practices.

The readings in Part II introduce students to a variety of types of written discourse, including across-the-disciplines writing and different essay types, from personal and reflective essays to non-academic (journalistic) and academic essays, including scientific papers and review essays. Introductions to each section as well as each essay promote students' active reading and critical thinking skills at all stages of the reading and writing process. The eight scholarly essays in Section VI, "Voices from the Academy," were chosen for their interest and accessibility—all are relatively short and discuss topics of interest to many students; they also illustrate key features discussed in Chapter 10.

Part III provides the basic resources for clear, grammatical writing. The stress falls on common, everyday errors, but more comprehensive information is also included (often in summary form, such as tables). Students are encouraged to analyze their own sentences rather than memorize a set of rules. For example, rather than dividing the section on punctuation into the comma, the colon, and the semicolon followed by lists of rules and common errors. Part III teaches students to recognize specific contexts in their own writing and to approach "correctness" according to these contexts. In addition, the many examples from student writing (rather than "made-up" examples) are designed to help students see clear and correct prose as relevant to the various kinds of writing they do in college or university.

Of course, such comprehensiveness can be achieved only by some omissions. For example, exhaustive information on citation styles can be found on college and university library websites, so only the more common formats appear in the research guide (Chapter 5). Students can further test their knowledge of grammatical rules (Chapters 11–13) by accessing the companion website for this book or the many other online sources sponsored by educational institutions.

Highlights

Oxford University Press is delighted to bring you *Becoming an Active Reader*, an accessible, student-friendly approach to reading and writing effectively. With a guide to rhetoric and research, a reader, and a grammar handbook together in one volume, augmented by the following special features, students can be assured they have everything they need for success in their post-secondary classrooms and beyond at their fingertips.

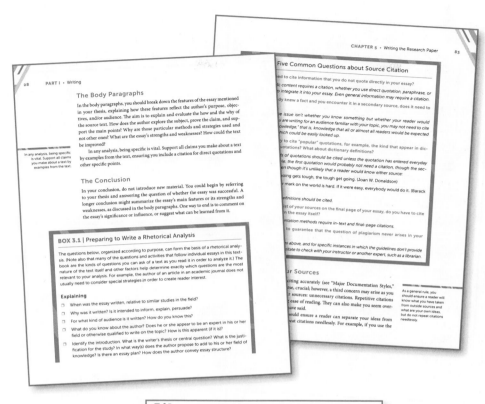

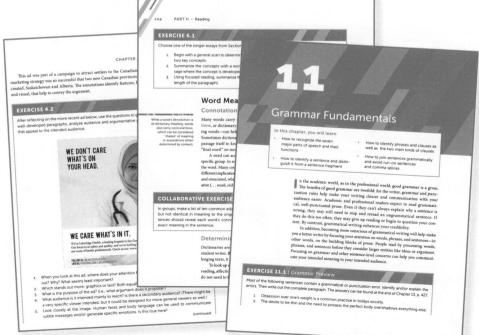

Special-topic boxes offer checklists, FAQs, and review tools for quick reference.

Individual and collaborative exercises provide ample opportunity for practising skills.

Part 3 hints give useful prompts for remembering grammatical structures and functions.

Annotated sample student essays illustrate important techniques for good writing and rhetorical styles.

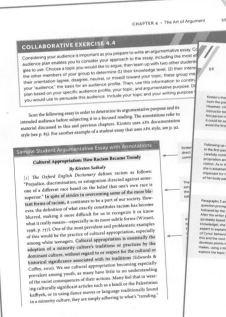

PART II • Readings   348

Comprehension

1. What is the potential problem with self-confidence, according to the author (see par. 4)?
2. Using the information in paragraph 5, come up with concise definitions of "me experiences" and "bigger-than-me experiences."
3. According to the author, why might arts classes be well suited to the development of "bigger-than-me experiences"?

Organization and Style

1. a. Identify, then paraphrase the thesis statement.
   b. Identify, then summarize the paragraph in which Tepper makes the transition between pointing out the problem with "me experiences," as he sees it, and solutions to the problem.
2. Discuss the role of experts in Tepper's essay, drawing on two examples in order to show how they are used to support the author's points.

Critical Thinking

1. Do you think that Tepper is offering mostly constructive criticism in his essay, or is he more concerned with pointing out the failures or inadequacies of the present generation? Support your answer by specific references to the text.
2. Taking one of the four strategies discussed in paragraphs 8–13, come up with a concrete application of your own that would produce a "bigger-than-me experience" in the classroom. (This could be done individually or as a collaborative project that is tried out in class.)

Joanna Pachner, "Do You Have the Brain of a CEO?"

Joanna Pachner begins her essay "Do You Have the Brain of a CEO?" with a title and opening designed to intrigue the reader, but her use of first-person experience has a more complex aim (though attracting interest is one aim). Synthesizing personal experience with the evidence of experts, she provides a look at leadership qualities and the tests that are given to detect them.

Preparing to Read

1. By the time you get to college, there is a good chance you have been interviewed for a job. What was the experience like? How did/did you judge your performance? Reflect

---

SECTION VI • Voices from the Academy   325

Harold Herzog, "The Impact of Pets on Human Health and Psychological Well-Being: Fact, Fiction, or Hypothesis?"

"The Impact of Pets" illustrates the need for clear organization in academic review articles. Diverse studies on a topic need to be carefully categorized and logically connected to one another. Using critical thinking, the author begins by questioning the common perception that pets provide physical and psychological benefits for their owners. In his review, he underscores a vital principle: findings can be taken as reliable only if experimental results can be replicated.

Preparing to Read

Have you and/or your family owned a pet? Consider the pros and cons of pet ownership from your own perspective (you could freewrite on the topic).

The Impact of Pets on Human Health and Psychological Well-Being: Fact, Fiction, or Hypothesis?

Harold Herzog

Current Directions in Psychological Science,
August 2011
(2300 words)

1   Many people are deeply attached to companion animals. In the United States, over two-thirds of households include a pet, most of which are regarded by their owners as family members. Considering that the lifetime costs of owning a pet are about $8000 for a medium-sized dog and $10,000 for a cat (cats tend to live longer than dogs), devoting resources on a crea-

ture with whom you share no genes and who is unlikely to ever return the favour seems to make little evolutionary sense. Aside from the expense, there are other downsides to companion animals. In the United States, a person is 100 times more likely to be seriously injured or killed by a dog than by a venomous snake, and over 85,000 Americans are taken to emergency rooms each year because of falls caused by their pets. Further, people can contract a cornucopia of diseases from companion animals, including brucellosis, roundworm, skin mites, *E. coli*, salmonella, giardia, ringworms, and cat-scratch fever. And, pets are second only to late-night noise as a source of conflict between neighbors.

2   Although not culturally universal, pet keeping exists in most societies, and an array of theories have been offered to explain why people bring animals into their lives (Herzog, 2010). Among these are the misfiring of parental instincts, biophilia (a hypothetical biologically-based love of

---

Thirty-nine accessible and engaging readings on an array of topics demonstrate high-quality professional and academic writing and are accompanied by pre- and post-reading questions.

CHAPTER 5 • Writing the Research Paper   85

(CMS). Here we will discuss the two styles most commonly used in academic essays: APA and MLA. (CMS isn't discussed here but can be found in the "student study guide" and at www.oupcanada.com/Becoming2e).

MLA is widely used in the humanities, including English literature. APA style is used in many social science and science disciplines, as well as in education and business. Both are parenthetical styles, meaning that a brief citation including the author's name and page number (MLA) or name and publication year (APA) follows the reference in the text of an essay. (Both these styles also require an end-of-essay listing of sources alphabetically by last name.)

In the parenthetical styles, there are two methods to integrate source material:

1. Give the name of the author(s) and (APA style only) the publication year in a signal phrase (which includes the author's last name and a "signal verb," such as *states*, *explains*, or *argues*) *before* the information from the source. You do not repeat the author's name (MLA) or the author's name and year (APA) in the end citation.

   APA: **Pilon (2005)** explains that in strategic voting, people often have to compromise their vote to ensure an undesirable candidate does not win **(p. 14)**.

2. Give the name of the author, page number, and (APA style only) publication year *after* the information from the source.

   MLA: In strategic voting, people often have to compromise their vote to ensure an undesirable candidate does not win **(Pilon 14)**.

Many of the main features of the MLA and APA styles are given below. Examples of the most common citation formats are then provided.

Electronic formats in all styles should include as much information as is available. If an author's name is not given, use the name of the organization or sponsoring group in its place. If there is no sponsor, use the work's title alphabetized by the first major word. MLA style requires you to include date of access for Internet citations; APA does not. Paragraph number or section heading can sometimes be used to identify location, if necessary, in the absence of standard page numbering (APA style only). APA style also requires you to use digital object identifier (DOI) if it is available for journal articles.

APA (American Psychological Association) Style

In-Text Guidelines

- APA uses an "author-year" referencing format. One basic format includes the author's last name and year of publication (used for general reference).

CHAPTER 5 • Writing the Research Paper   89

Website

Statistics Canada (2010, March 26). Gasoline and fuel oil, price by urban centre. Retrieved from www.40.Statcan.ca/ 101/cst01/econ154a.htm

Film/Video

Joffe, J. (Producer & Director). (2012). Burlesque assassins. [Motion picture]. Canada: Joe Media Group.

Video Post

Broken Rhythms. (2013, August 9). *Grim promo*. [Video file]. Retrieved from http://youtube.com/dAe5b7vUXgU

Podcasts and blog posts follow a similar format; URL is preceded by "Podcast retrieved from" and "Message posted to," respectively.

MLA (Modern Language Association) Style

In-Text Guidelines

- MLA uses an "author/number" referencing format. The basic parenthetical format includes author's last name and page number with no punctuation in between. (Slotkin 75); (Rusel and Wilson 122).
- With a signal phrase, only the page number is in parentheses. The page number follows the reference.

  Arango et al. found that a large proportion of children who exceed the recommended number of TV-viewing hours per day have low HRQOL scores (71).

- No signal phrase

  A large proportion of children who exceed the recommended number of TV-viewing hours per day have low HRQOL scores (Arango et al. 71).

- No author: Use the name of the organization in place of author's name (e.g., Canada Wildlife Federation). If there is no author or organization, for example some encyclopedia entries, use the title in place of author (or a shortened version if the title is long).
- Indirect source: Author A (where you found the quote) quotes Author B (indirect source). Name Author B in your sentence (list Author A (the indirect

---

Expanded coverage of documentation styles provides students with valuable guidance on APA and MLA citation methods.

Supportive pedagogy, such as learning objectives, a running marginal glossary, and chapter-end review questions, guide readers through each chapter.

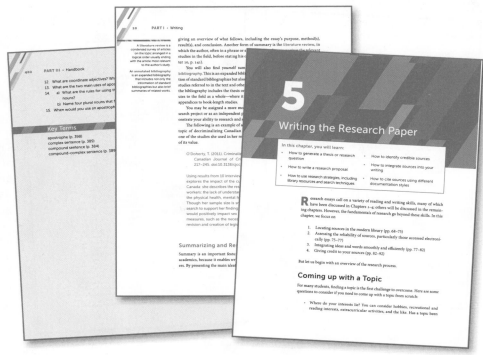

Online Resources

For Instructors

- An **instructor's manual** offers answer keys to post-reading questions for selected readings and to the exercises in Part 3 of the book.
- **PowerPoint slides** are available for each chapter.

For Students

- A **student study guide** includes grammar exercises, interactive quizzes, activities to address writing challenges, and further documentation guidelines (APA and MLA).

COMPANION
WEBSITE

Eric Henderson

Becoming an Active Reader, Second Edition
ISBN 13: 9780199019069

Inspection copy request

Ordering information

Contact & Comments

About the Book

Becoming an Active Reader offers a three-in-one approach that combines a comprehensive guide to rhetorical writing, an engaging reader, and a detailed grammar handbook, all in a single volume. The advice and exercises found throughout help students understand and apply the most effective reading and writing strategies, while the 39 thought-provoking readings encourage meaningful interaction with the written word.

Sample Material

Get Adobe PDF reader [US | UK]

Instructor Resources

You need a password to access these resources. Please contact your local Sales and Editorial Representative for more information.

Student Resources

 www.oupcanada.com/Becoming2e

Acknowledgements

As always, I wish to gratefully acknowledge the editorial staff at Oxford University Press Canada for their confidence in my work, as well as their enthusiasm and expertise in this, my fifth textbook with the Press. I would particularly like to thank Leah-Ann Lymer for her excellent editorial guidance, Shelly Stevenson for her thorough copyediting, and Steven Hall for making the production stages virtually stress-free.

Thank you also to reviewers Mark Feltham, Fanshawe College; Terry B. Jackson, College of New Caledonia; Matt Kavanaugh, Okanagan College; Teresa MacVicar, Conestoga College; Raj Mehta, Camosun College; Beth Ann Wiersma, Lambton College; Robert Ackroyd, Northern Alberta Institute of Technology; Trevor Arkell, Humber College; Tim Chamberlain, Camosun College; Jennifer Chambers, Sheridan College; Dorritta Fong, Douglas College; Julie Morris, Sheridan College; Karen Pike, Conestoga College; and others who gave feedback anonymously, whose comments helped to shape this second edition of *Becoming an Active Reader*.

For their generosity, I am indebted to Christine Walde and other University of Victoria librarians for updates to sections in Chapter 5. I also acknowledge the many students who allowed their writing to be represented here.

I am most grateful to my family for all manner of intellectual and creative stimulation, along with their support, love, and personal affirmation.

PART I | Writing

Students today are writing more than they ever did before. Much of that writing is casual and unstructured, but the tasks you will be assigned at college or university will require a different approach: following procedures and guidelines will be key to your success in this writing environment. Chapter 1 reviews the writing process and then breaks down a typical assignment (such as an essay) into distinct stages, discussing the characteristics of each. From there, we turn to specific types of assignments and their formats, beginning with the summary in Chapter 2. The rhetorical analysis is the focus of Chapter 3. The skills of summarizing and analyses are crucial when taking on longer, more complex assignments, such as the argumentative essay (Chapter 4) and the expository research essay (Chapter 5).

1

Essay Writing Basics

In this chapter, you will learn:

- How to take a step-by-step approach to essay writing

- How to write an introduction with a strong thesis statement

- How to write unified, coherent, and developed paragraphs

- How to support your claim through evidence

- How to write a conclusion

This chapter focuses on the basic conventions of the student essay. Later chapters will consider the specific forms that student writing can take, such as a summary, a critical response, a rhetorical analysis, an argumentative essay, and a research paper. Although there are many differences among these, in most cases they will draw on the elements discussed in this chapter.

An essay, like most projects, is written in stages. Academic writing may emphasize revising and editing the rough draft or research more than you are used to. However, it's important to understand that students approach academic writing knowing that it is a chronological process that usually begins with a broad topic.

From Blank Page to Thesis

A **thesis** includes the main point of your essay or what you will attempt to prove. It is placed at the end of your introduction.

Using pre-writing techniques, you explore the topic, asking what you know and what you want to find out about it. The goal is to narrow the topic to discover your specific focus or approach, which you express as your thesis. Some students find this the most difficult stage: intimidated by a blank page or screen, they may feel frustrated. Fortunately, there are several pre-writing techniques to ease the transition from blank to written page.

Step One: Pre-Writing Techniques

The process of pre-writing is an important preparation stage before beginning to write a research paper. It is at this point that you can consider and organize the ideas that you want to write about. Here we will discuss freewriting, questioning, brainstorming, and clustering.

Freewriting uses your thought associations. To freewrite, begin with a blank piece of paper or a blank screen and start recording your associations with a subject. A good starting point is a sentence that includes the subject you want to explore. Do not stop to reflect on your next thought or to polish your writing. Simply write continuously for a predetermined time—such as five minutes.

After you are done, look back at what you have written. You may find much of it repetitive. You may have started thinking about one thing and suddenly switched to something else. That is to be expected. But it is likely that your writing will reveal thoughts you had not considered before, or were not aware of when you were writing. Underline potentially useful points. You can take the best ones and use them as starting points for other freewriting sessions. You could also summarize a significant section of text in one sentence and use that sentence as a new starting point.

In the questioning technique, you list questions about the topic. Initially, these questions could be the basic *who, what, where, when, why, how.*

Brainstorming and clustering (mapping) work by generating associations. In brainstorming, you list your associations with a topic, writing down words and phrases until you feel you have covered the topic. Then you look for connections among the items.

While brainstorming works linearly, clustering is a spatial technique that generates associations and seeks connections among them. You begin by writing a word or phrase in the middle of a blank page and circling it. As associations occur to you, you write them down and circle them. Then connect each by a line to the word/phrase that gave rise to the association. As you continue this process beyond the first words/phrases surrounding the original word/phrase, some clusters will become larger than others. The larger clusters may suggest the most promising ways to develop your topic.

Your thesis statement should always reflect your purpose in writing. For example, if you were writing a personal essay as part of your application to study a new language in another country, it would be very different from a research essay on the value of studying abroad. See p. 8 for examples of thesis statements.

Step Two: Finding Support

In the next stage, you back up your thesis. A thesis statement is a claim or assertion that you want your reader to accept. This is where your support comes in. For

Freewriting is a pre-writing technique in which you write on a subject without stopping to edit.

Questioning is a pre-writing technique in which you list questions about the topic.

Brainstorming is a pre-writing technique in which you list your associations with a subject in the order they occur to you.

Clustering is a pre-writing technique that works spatially to generate associations with a subject and connections among them.

Support consists of evidence to help prove a claim.

example, although you could claim that the dog ate your homework, your instructor is not likely to take such a claim seriously. But if you produced your vet bill, the claim would have some support. If you were writing a critical analysis of a poem, the support would need to come from the poem itself (primary source). If you were writing a research paper, you would need to find out what other people have said or written about the topic as it relates to your thesis (secondary sources).

Your general claim (thesis statement) must be supported by more specific claims (main points), which, in turn, require support such as examples: references to primary sources (English or history essay) or factual information such as statistics or secondary sources (research essay). If it becomes clear that you cannot support your thesis, consider adapting the thesis to be in line with the support you have found, or come up with a new thesis.

Step Three: Organizing

When you have found enough support, you can begin thinking about how you will connect the general claim (thesis statement) to the specific claims (main points) and their support. With this in mind, begin organizing claims and support in a logical and consistent way that clearly expresses the relationship between each claim and its support. One way to clarify these relationships is to construct an **outline**, which is a schematic representation of the essay and a plan you can use in the composing stage to keep yourself on track.

An outline can be a brief listing of your main points or a longer, more complete version. A *scratch* or *sketch outline* is often used for in-class or exam essays, when you do not have much planning time. With a longer essay, however, a *formal outline* should be used. This kind of outline should be more thorough and specific. A formal outline should include levels of sub-points (developments of main points), along with details and examples, and use a number/letter format to represent the essay's complete structure. Here is an example of the conventional outline format.

> An **outline** is a linear or graphic representation of main points and sub-points, showing an essay's structure.

I. First main point (topic sentence of paragraph)
   A. First sub-point (development of main point)
      1. First sub-sub-point (development of sub-point: detail or example)
      2. Second sub-sub-point
   B. Second sub-point
      1. First sub-sub-point
      2. Second sub-sub-point

This example represents a paragraph with a three-level outline—that is, one main point and two sub-points.

When you are considering your outline, especially if it is a formal outline, remember that it serves as the blueprint for the essay itself. Therefore, to construct a useful outline, you should ask questions like the following:

- How do the main points in my outline relate to my thesis statement?
- How do the sub-points relate to my main points?
- Do I have enough main points to support my thesis?
- Do I have enough sub-points (at least two) for each main point?
- Are there any points that seem either irrelevant or out of place? If the latter, where do they belong?
- What is the most effective order for my points? Are my points logically connected? What kinds of transitions would help connect them?
- Can points be expanded? Have I covered everything my reader would expect me to cover?

It's important that you consider your outline an "essay in the works" that can be adapted as you proceed. Even the most polished and detailed outline can be changed if you find a better way to organize your ideas or find new, important approaches to your topic.

Step Four: Composing

Making the commitment to the first draft is difficult for students and non-students alike. Approaching the composing stage should be similar to approaching the organizing stage: a significant step toward the final version in which second thoughts may surface. However, record your thoughts fully—imperfectly expressed as they may be. See below, pp. 7–17, for strategies for drafting the introduction, middle paragraphs, and conclusion.

Step Five: Revising and Editing

In composing the first, "rough" draft, your focus is on getting ideas down, explaining, clarifying, integrating, and ordering. During the revision stage, however, you should not expect to be just looking for minor errors. The word *revise* means to "see again."

One useful method is the "top-down" approach. With this approach to revision, you start with large-scale concerns, such as essay organization, and finish by checking and rechecking grammar, spelling, and presentation. To begin then, take a hard, objective look at your essay's purpose and audience, its structure, and its main points and their relation to your thesis. Review these areas as if you are seeing them for the first time. It is sensible to wait several hours after you have completed a rough draft before revising it. Then ask yourself the kinds of questions you

In the "top-down" approach to revision, you begin with large-scale concerns, such as essay organization, and finish by checking and rechecking grammar, spelling, and presentation, ensuring you allot plenty of time for all stages in the revising process.

originally asked when you were creating an outline (see above, p. 3). Are you are satisfied with the results?

Next, turn to individual paragraphs and check that each paragraph contains a main idea (claim) with sufficient support. Thoroughly check for correct grammar, clear expression, and concise wording. *Then*, it will be time to check for spelling errors and typos, ensuring that the essay conforms to the format your instructor requires.

Don't underestimate the importance of these end-stage activities. Try to see your essay through the eyes of your instructor. What often strikes a marker first are the very things you may have glossed over as your deadline approached: grammatical errors, lack of coherence, faulty word choice, poor or missing transitions, wordiness, typos, and mechanical errors that could easily have been fixed.

Though nothing replaces careful attention to every detail, Box 1.1 provides a checklist that will help you "re-see" your essay. All of the points listed can be found detailed in this chapter.

Concise writing is effective writing in which you use only the words that are essential to express your meaning and do not waste words.

BOX 1.1 | Revising an Essay

Content and Structure

☐ Is the essay's purpose clear? Is it stated in the introduction, consistent throughout the middle paragraphs, and reinforced in the conclusion? (see pp. 7, 11, and 17)

☐ Is it written for a specific audience? What would show a reader this? For example, is the level of language, voice, or tone aimed at your particular audience? (see p. 118)

☐ Is the thesis statement in line with the focus of the essay and its main points? If not, consider adjusting the thesis—sometimes just changing a word or phrase will help. (see pp. 8–9)

☐ Are all paragraphs well developed and focused on one main idea? Are they logically connected to your thesis? (see p. 11)

☐ Are any paragraphs noticeably shorter or longer than others are? If so, can you combine short paragraphs, ensuring a logical transition between them? Should you break up longer paragraphs, while ensuring that each can stand on its own? (see p. 11)

☐ Have different kinds of evidence been used for support? Does any part of the essay seem less well supported than other parts? (see p. 16)

☐ Would an example, illustration, or analogy make an abstract point more concrete or a general point more specific? (see p. 16)

☐ Will a reader misunderstand any part of the essay due to the complexity of a point or the way it is expressed? If your draft has been edited by a peer, pay attention to passages noted as unclear. If one reader has difficulty understanding it, others may too. (see p. 12)

Drafting the Essay

Virtually any essay you read is divided into an introduction, middle or body paragraphs, and a conclusion. Each part contributes in a unique way to the essay and requires a unique focus. The same is true for the essays you will be asked to write.

Writing an Introduction

The introduction is more than just a starting place. Its primary function is to inform the reader about the essay's purpose and topic, and the writer's approach to the topic (usually through the thesis statement). Sometimes, it also mentions the essay's main points. As well, the introduction may indicate the primary organizational pattern for the essay. In all these ways, the introduction previews what is forthcoming.

The introduction previews the essay by announcing its purpose, topic, and thesis. A good introduction interests a reader and establishes the writer's credibility.

Grammar and Style

Give particular attention to

- ☐ Sentence structure (e.g., no sentence fragments) (see pp. 371–9)
- ☐ Punctuation (see pp. 384–402)
- ☐ Apostrophes (see pp. 398–401)
- ☐ Agreement (see pp. 403–11)
- ☐ Pronoun consistency and reference (see pp. 403–17)
- ☐ Misplaced and dangling modifiers (see pp. 418–21)
- ☐ Parallelism (see pp. 421–5)
- ☐ Clear, direct, and concise prose (see pp. 138–9)

Mechanics

- ☐ Have all references been cited correctly? Have you used the documentation style preferred by your instructor or by your discipline? (see p. 82)
- ☐ Have you met word length, essay/page format, and other specific requirements?
- ☐ Have you proofread the essay at least twice (once for content and flow, and once for minor errors such as typos)? Breaking each word into syllables and reading syllabically throughout is the best way to catch minor errors.

A good introduction is persuasive. It must sufficiently interest the reader, encouraging him or her to read on, perhaps by conveying the importance of the topic. The introduction introduces not only the essay but also you, the writer. Therefore, you must come across as credible and reliable.

When should you write your introduction? One reason for writing it last is that you may not know how the topic will develop until the body of the essay is written. On the other hand, you may like to have a concrete starting point. If this is the case, you should return to the introduction after you have completed drafting your middle paragraphs to ensure that it fits well with them.

The Thesis Statement

The Greek word *thesis* refers to the act of placing or setting down. A **thesis statement** sets down a generalization that is applicable to the entire essay. However, this generalization can take different forms depending on purpose and audience. Student and academic writers usually place the thesis statement in the introduction; journalistic writers often do not (see pp. 142 and 127).

The thesis announces the topic and includes a comment about the topic (*simple thesis statement*). The thesis statement may also include the major points to be discussed in the essay (*expanded thesis statement* or *essay plan*). The thesis statement usually embodies a **claim**, which depends on the essay's purpose. Typical argumentative claims are ones of *value* or *policy*. *Fact-based* claims are common in expository essays in the sciences and social sciences, while *interpretive* claims are used in many humanities essays in which the writer sets out to interpret one or more primary sources.

The following statements illustrate the different forms that a thesis can take.

> *Simple thesis statement from an expository student essay (fact-based claim):* Social and economic pressures of the twenty-first century have given rise to what some experts are terming a new anxiety disorder, nomophobia, a fear of being without our cell phones and computers. (student writer Celeste Barnes-Crouse)

> *Expanded thesis statement from an argumentative student essay (policy claim):* Decriminalizing prostitution in Canada would increase safety for Canadian sex workers; at the same time, tax payers would benefit from a decrease in health care and legal costs incurred by sex workers due to the inordinate stress and violence they experience at their jobs. (student writer Annika Benoit-Jansson)

Using an *expanded* thesis statement, as in the second thesis statement, puts your main points before the reader, which is often a strong way to begin an

---

A **thesis statement** sets down a generalization that is applicable to the entire essay (simple thesis) or includes the essay's main points (expanded thesis, or essay plan).

A **claim** is an assertion about the topic appearing in the thesis statement and topic sentences. Claims require support.

argumentative essay. This kind of thesis is also called an essay plan because it lays out the essay's organization, or plan.

> *Thesis in the form of a question:* Given the severity of the personal debt crisis in Canada, research into the extent and the reason for its occurrence is both timely and necessary. How far do our elevated levels of personal debt extend? How did we borrow ourselves to the brink of crisis? (student writer Sam Kerr)

Using a question as a thesis often creates interest and suggests a more open, or explorative approach to the topic.

Creating Reader Interest

Readers need to be convinced at the outset that your essay is worth reading. The most traditional way to generate interest and persuade your reader of the topic's importance is to use a logical opening. This type of opening begins with a general statement that becomes more specific and ends with the most specific claim, the thesis itself. This method is referred to as the inverted triangle method.

However, if you make the first sentence too broad or familiar, it might not interest the reader. Therefore, consider using a dramatic opening (see Chapter 10 for examples of dramatic openings). In the first example below, the writer uses a logical opening while in the second, the writer uses a dramatic approach. In both cases, however, the paragraph ends with a clear thesis statement (italicized).

> *Logical:* At the end of the twentieth century, society was rocked by the creation of the Internet and the beginning of the digital age, giving rise to the era of instant communication with unlimited information and interaction. The first generation with access to this technology now makes up the world's student body, and it is becoming clear that conventional teaching techniques may not be effective with this group. As a result, today's educators have looked to this new technology, with many successful results. The next step in integrating technology is immersive interaction, such as the use of video games. Although challenges exist in their use, research has shown that, *if implemented properly, video games can be an effective supplement in teaching grade school and post-secondary students.* (student writer David Stephen)

> *Dramatic:* What does it mean to say that one is a perfectionist? Does it mean that one does everything perfectly? In common language, the term "perfectionist" carries the connotation that the perfectionistic individual does everything perfectly, but according to perfectionism experts in social psychology, perfectionism is a term referring to a mentality, or set of cognitions, that are characteristic of certain people.

Sidebar notes:

A **logical opening** is a technique for creating reader interest by beginning with a generalization and narrowing to the thesis.

A **dramatic opening** is a technique for creating reader interest by beginning with a question, illustration, anecdote, quotation, description, or other attention-grabbing technique.

The writer makes a general statement about the creation of the Internet.

The writer introduces the topic: the use of the new technology in education today.

The thesis statement follows logically from the preceding sentences and shows the writer's specific approach.

Two questions are used to evoke the reader's interest while introducing the topic.

The definition of perfectionism, as cited by an authority, answers the previous questions.

Referring again to the common perception of perfectionism, the writer introduces her specific approach to her topic and follows in the next sentence with the thesis.

According to Hollender (as cited in Slade & Owens, 1998), perfectionism refers to "the practice of demanding of oneself or others a higher quality of performance than is required by the situation" (p. 384). Although the name suggests to the layperson that perfectionism would be a desirable trait, this quality is in fact often unrecognized for its harmful effects on the lives of some people. *For these people, perfectionism is associated with mental illness and can contribute to problems in areas of life such as academic success and intimate relationships.* (student writer Erin Walker)

EXERCISE 1.1

In the following paragraphs:

- Identify the method for creating interest.
- Discuss how the writer establishes his or her credibility.
- Identify the thesis statement, deciding if it is a simple thesis or an expanded one.

You can also pre-read "Rhetorical Patterns and Paragraph Development," p. 13, to determine the essay's main organizational method.

1. The North American Free Trade Agreement (NAFTA) was a much-heralded accomplishment when it was ratified in January 1994, eliminating most of the trade barriers between Canada, the United States, and Mexico. While some citizens feared that economic integration in the trilateral area would disrupt cultural independence, polls showed that most people believed free trade would be beneficial. When ratified, NAFTA became the world's largest free trade agreement (MacPherson 2054). The removal of restrictions on trade opened up vast new markets for the three countries, creating more competition among firms and growth opportunities for companies. However, despite NAFTA's potential to benefit consumers and workers alike, the legalities of the agreement have created many negative consequences. In particular, the adverse effects of the Agreement pose a threat to the average Canadian, Mexican, and American: poor labour conditions, agribusiness, and the unprecedented power of corporations are key issues resulting from NAFTA that must be renegotiated. (student writer Kourtney Lane)

2. As you dive into the beautiful, crystal-clear Pacific Ocean, you descend slowly among Hawaii's glorious underwater reefs. As you look around you, you see other divers in the . . . water. But they are not admiring spectators; they are equipped with large syringes, nets, and crowbars. They are cyanide divers, engaging in the illegal practice of cyanide fishing. This practice does more than kill fish: it damages the environment, killing many species, destroying underwater reefs, and negatively affecting the economy worldwide. According to Charles Barber of the World Resources Institute, "this multimillion dollar industry is what drives many individuals to do some damaging acts and continue with such cruel practices" (39). Despite the millions of fish that are killed and the miles of underwater reef that end up looking like the aftermath of a category nine earthquake, thousands continue to cyanide fish every day, while governments do little to stop it. (student writer Ryan Campbell)

Writing Middle Paragraphs

The structure of middle paragraphs is often said to mirror that of the essay itself. Each paragraph begins with a general statement that is supported by the sentences that follow. In its structure and function, the essay's thesis statement is equivalent to the topic sentence of a paragraph, which announces the main idea (topic) of that paragraph. This is a useful analogy because it stresses the importance of a predictable order, for both essays and paragraphs, which helps a reader understand what is coming next.

> A **topic sentence**, usually the first sentence, states the main idea in the paragraph.

When a writer uses a topic sentence to announce the central idea, the rest of the paragraph provides support, such as examples, reasons, statistical data, or other kinds of evidence. In some way, it illustrates, expands on, or reinforces the topic sentence.

In the following paragraph, student writer Leslie Nelson expands on the main idea, first by explaining the function of talking therapies and then by dividing them into three different subcategories and explaining the function of each (the topic sentence is italicized).

Talking therapies—especially when combined with medication—are common to treatment of adolescent depression. There are several kinds of talking therapies, including cognitive and humanistic approaches, and family and group sessions. Each of these therapy types confronts depression in a different way, and each is useful to adolescent treatment. Cognitive therapies confront illogical thought patterns that accompany depression; humanistic therapies provide support to the patient, stressing unconditional acceptance. Group therapies, on the other hand, encourage depressed patients to talk about their feelings in a setting with other people who are undergoing treatment for similar problems. This therapy can inspire different coping strategies, and it allows people to realize that they are not alone in their problems. (student writer Leslie Nelson)

Writing Strong Paragraphs

Effective paragraphs are unified, coherent, and well developed. A unified paragraph focuses on only one main idea; when you move to another main idea, you begin a new paragraph. If, however, a paragraph is long, you should consider dividing it into two paragraphs even if each contains the same idea. Look for the most logical place to make the division, for example, where you begin an important sub-point.

> A **unified** paragraph focuses on developing only one main idea.
>
> A **coherent** paragraph is constructed with ideas that are logically laid out with clear connections between them.
>
> **Reader-based prose** is clear, accessible writing designed for an intended reader.

A coherent paragraph is easy to follow. It is both clear and carefully arranged to place the emphasis where you want it. In reader-based prose the writer focuses on the concerns of the reader (specific audience) by using carefully designed, understandable, and well-organized prose. In this way, the writer stresses what is most important and omits what is irrelevant, while clarifying the relationships among the points and sub-points. You can make your paragraphs easy to follow by considering the following points:

1. *Logical sentence order:* One sentence follows naturally from the preceding one; there are no sentences out of order or off-topic (an off-topic sentence would not result in a unified paragraph); and there are no gaps in thought.

2. *Organizational patterns:* You can order the paragraph according to a specific pattern. (See "Rhetorical Patterns and Paragraph Development," pp. 13–15.)

3. *Precise language:* Word choice is not always a case of the right word versus the wrong word. Choose the *best word* for the given context. Whenever you use a word that is not part of your everyday vocabulary, you should check its meaning by looking it up in a dictionary. A misused word could make the meaning of an entire sentence—even a paragraph—unclear.

4. *Appropriate adverbial transitions:* Transitional words and phrases enable you to convey precise relationships between one idea and the next.

5. *Selective rephrasing:* Being aware of the knowledge level of your audience helps you determine whether you should rephrase in order to clarify a difficult concept.

6. *Repetition of key words/phrases or the use of synonyms:* You can use repetition to emphasize important ideas. Of course, needless repetition should always be avoided.

7. *Parallel/balanced structures:* Employing parallel/balanced structures creates coherence, partly because of familiar word order. Balanced structures have a pleasing rhythm, making them more easily understood—and even remembered.

In the excerpt below, after defining the term *nanotechnology*, student writer Jeff Proctor makes effective use of transitions (italicized) to help explain a difficult concept to general readers. He uses a balanced structure in sentence [4] to make a comparison understandable and repeats the key word *precision* at strategic points in the paragraph (the beginning, middle, and end). Other words, too, can be considered near-synonyms for *precision* (synonyms and repetition are underlined).

[1]Nanotechnology will allow the construction of compounds at nanometre precision. [2]*Essentially*, this capability would allow scientists to form a substance one atom at a time and to put each atom exactly where it needs to be. [3]*Consequently*, any chemical structure that is stable under normal conditions could theoretically be produced. [4]In comparison to semiconductor lithography, which could be imagined as the formation of electrical circuits by joining large heaps of molecules, the techniques of nanotechnology could be imagined as the careful

arrangement of molecules with a pair of tweezers. [5]With this incredible degree of <u>precision</u>, electrical circuits could be designed to be smaller than ever before. [6]*Currently*, each component in a computer is the size of thousands of atoms; *however*, if nanotechnological processes were used to produce it, one component could be on the scale of several atoms. [7]This fact alone emphasizes the potential efficiency of next-generation computer circuits, for smaller components are closer together and, *thus*, able to communicate with each other in less time. [8]*Furthermore*, it could be guaranteed that products are reproducible and reliable as a result of the absolute <u>precision</u> of these formation processes.

Transitions in the paragraph above convey various relationships: *essentially* (transition of summary), *consequently, thus* (cause/effect), *currently* (time), *however* (contrast), *furthermore* (addition). See Table 1.1 for common transitions.

Striving for coherence throughout the writing process should not just enable a reader to follow you but also help you clarify your own train of thought as you write. It can be useful to consciously rephrase ideas and specific passages as you write. Without crossing out what you wrote, follow it with transitions like *in other words, in short, in summary, to reiterate,* or *that is,* and a paraphrase or expansion of the original. If your "second attempt" is clearer—and it often is—you can then consider crossing out the original to avoid needless repetition.

For information on reading challenging paragraphs, see Chapter 6 and Chapter 10, pp. 143–6.

Rhetorical Patterns and Paragraph Development

A **rhetorical pattern** is a systematic way to organize and present information. All the claims you make in your essay, regardless whether they're your general claims,

> A **rhetorical pattern** is a method for organizing and presenting information in essays and paragraphs. Examples include cause and effect, classification, comparison and contrast, cost–benefit analysis, and definition.

TABLE 1.1 Some Common Transitions	
Types of Transitions	**Words or Phrases**
Transitions of limit or concession	admittedly, although, it is true that, naturally, of course, though
Transitions of cause and effect	accordingly, as a result, because, consequently, for this reason, if, otherwise, since, so, then, therefore, thus
Transitions of illustration	after all, even, for example, for instance, indeed, in fact, in other words, of course, specifically, such as
Transitions of contrast or qualification	after all, although, but, by contrast, conversely, despite, even so, however, in spite of, instead, nevertheless, nonetheless, on the contrary, on the one hand . . . on the other hand, otherwise, rather (than), regardless, still, though, whereas, while, yet
Transitions of summary or conclusion	in conclusion, in effect, in short, in sum (in summary), so, that is, thus

specific claims, or theses, must be well supported or they will not be convincing. When drafting your essay, you should consider not just what kinds of evidence to use but also how to organize it. In this way, you utilize specific patterns to organize and develop individual paragraphs, which in turn will support the specific claims in the topic sentences. Part of an essay's success lies in choosing the most appropriate rhetorical pattern(s) to develop a claim.

TABLE 1.2   Organizational (Rhetorical) Patterns

Purpose	Rhetorical Pattern	Description/Explanation
To create an image or picture of something	Description	Uses images of sight or the other senses to create immediacy and involve the reader; uses modifiers (adjectives and adverbs) to add detail
To tell a story	Narration	Relates an occurrence, usually in chronological order; stresses action through the use of strong verbs; provides anecdotes or brief narratives that illustrate a point
To show how something works or is done	Process analysis	Breaks down a process into a sequence of steps, making it more understandable; provides instructions or directions
To explain what something is	Definition	Explains the attributes or key features of something, usually in order to apply it in some way
To discuss similarities and/or differences	Comparison and contrast (sometimes referred to as comparison, even if differences are focused on)	Looks at similarities and differences; can be organized by block method (all points of similarity and difference of Subject A, followed by all points relevant to Subject B) or point-by-point method (points relevant to each subject discussed separately)
To show the way something changed/developed	Chronology	Uses time order; can be applied to people, objects (like technology), or events
To particularize the general or concretize the abstract	Example	Gives particular instances of a larger category, enabling readers to better understand the larger category; gives immediacy and concreteness to something abstract
To analyze why something happened or a result/outcome	Cause and effect	Uses inductive methods to draw conclusions; for example, to determine whether smoking leads to (causes) heart disease or to determine whether heart disease results from (is an effect of) smoking
To account for or justify something	Reasons	Uses deductive methods that draw on one's knowledge or experience; for example, "you should not smoke because it often leads to heart disease" (reason derived through empirical evidence)
To analyze by dividing into subcategories	Classification/division	Classification: groups items or ideas by shared characteristics (e.g., types of bottled water: purified, mineral, or sparkling). Division: separates large category into parts (e.g., the essay into introduction, middle paragraphs, conclusion)

TABLE 1.2 *(continued)*		
Purpose	**Rhetorical Pattern**	**Description/Explanation**
To look at two sides/views of something	Cost–benefit analysis	Weighs the pros and cons of an issue, question, or action, usually to decide which is stronger
To identify a problem or solve/resolve it	Problem and solution	Analyzes or explains a problem or proposes a solution; may incorporate other methods, such as reasons, cause and effect, or cost–benefit analysis
To better understand something	Analogy	Shows how one subject is similar to another to clarify the nature or a feature of the first subject

Most topics can be developed by using one or more of the methods above. For example, if you were looking for ways to develop the topic "fighting in hockey," you could use description or narration to convey the excitement of a hockey brawl. Conversely, you could use either method to convey it as an unseemly spectacle. You could use the process analysis pattern to illustrate the step-by-step procedures officials use to break up a fight, the chronological pattern to trace the history of rules governing fighting, or the pattern by example to call attention to notorious fighting incidents in recent years.

The examples below illustrate two rhetorical patterns that help develop individual paragraphs. In the first example, after summarizing common perceptions about the negative effects of gaming (costs), the writer introduces one surprising benefit, which he analyses in the paragraphs that follow.

Cost–benefit analysis:

While urban environments restrict access to nature and the virtualized environments of many video games seem like caricatures of the physical world (for now), gaming provides an interactive experience that can support learning and awareness of the otherwise inaccessible natural world. (See Nik Harron, "Fully Destructible: Exploring a Personal Relationship with Nature through Video Games," p. 213.)

The next example breaks a process into successive stages (all stages of the process are given in the essay).

Process analysis:

To behave ethically is not a one-step process: Do the right thing. It is a sometimes arduous eight-step process. To behave ethically, you must:

1. Recognize that there is a situation that deserves to be noticed and reflected upon.
2. Define the situation as having an ethical component . . .

(Continued on p. 274, in "Slip-Sliding Away, Down the Ethical Slope," Robert J. Sternberg.)

For examples of essays in this textbook that employ different rhetorical patterns, see "Classification by Essay Type and Organizational Pattern," located on the inside front cover of this textbook.

Kinds of Evidence

Although it is good to use various kinds of evidence in your essay, some are likely going to be more important than others are. The choices you make depend on your purpose, audience, topic, and claim, and the type of essay you are writing. For example, if you are writing a rhetorical analysis, it will focus on the essay you're analyzing as a primary source. If you are writing a research essay, you will focus on secondary sources.

Common kinds of evidence may vary from discipline to discipline:

Humanities writing often uses direct quotation from primary sources. Social sciences writing tends to focus on statistics, interviews, questionnaires, case studies, and interpersonal observation. The sciences rely on direct methods that involve experimentation.

- Humanities writing often uses direct quotation from primary sources.
- Social sciences writing tends to focus on statistics, interviews, questionnaires, case studies, and interpersonal observation.
- The sciences rely on direct methods that involve experimentation.

Some kinds of evidence can be more authoritative than others. In fact-based writing, "hard" evidence—facts, statistics, and the findings of empirical research—provides the strongest support. "Soft" evidence, such as expert opinion, examples, illustrations, and analogies, may also be important to help explain a concept but will likely be less important than "hard" evidence. Argumentative essays may use analogies, precedents, expert opinion, anecdotal evidence, and even, perhaps, personal experience. (See pp. 41–3 for the kinds of evidence commonly used in an argument.)

Issues of Credibility

Credibility is essential for all writing. Appearing credible involves showing knowledge as well as coming across as trustworthy and fair.

Credibility factors include *knowledge*, *reliability*, and *fairness*. You exhibit your knowledge by appearing well informed about your topic and supporting each claim with solid and substantial evidence. You convey reliability in many ways:

- by using the accepted conventions of the discipline in which you are writing; this includes using the correct citation style, being aware of the specialized language of the discipline, and following format requirements, such as the use of an abstract and formal sections (science writing and report writing);
- by writing effectively and following the rules of grammar, punctuation, and spelling; writing efficiently, using words that express exactly what you want them to;
- by using credible and authoritative sources (research essays); and
- by reasoning logically and avoiding logical fallacies (argumentative essays).

Although fairness applies particularly to argumentative essays, it can also be important in a research essay. For example, if you find sources whose findings contradict your claim or hypothesis, you will increase your credibility if you try to account for inconsistent results. In argument, you convey fairness in several ways:

- by using an objective voice and not showing bias;
- by acknowledging and accurately representing the opposing view;
- by looking for common ground; and
- by avoiding slanted language and emotional fallacies.

Writing a Conclusion

While a conclusion is always a vital part of an essay, it can perform different functions. The conclusion may refer back to the thesis statement, rephrasing it and reasserting its importance. It may also look ahead by considering a way that the thesis can be applied or the need for further research.

Although a conclusion may both look back to the thesis statement and look ahead to the thesis's implications, the stress often falls on one or the other. A circular conclusion primarily reminds the reader of your thesis and reinforces it. Even so, if you want to emphasize these functions, you should not repeat the thesis word for word, nor should you simply summarize what you have already said in your introduction. *You should draw attention to the significance of the body paragraphs in which you have developed your topic.*

A spiral conclusion looks beyond the thesis. In an argumentative essay, you may want to make an emotional or ethical appeal. Other spiral conclusion strategies include ending with a relevant anecdote or personal experience (informal essay) or a question that extends from your findings or that of the research you have used (expository essay). If you have focused on a problem, this may be the time to briefly suggest solutions. You can suggest how the topic is relevant to the reader.

The following paragraph uses the spiral pattern, though, like most conclusions, it also includes information from the introduction. However, in the second half of the conclusion, the writer considers the challenges and speculates on the future of video games as an educational tool. You can compare the conclusion to the introduction illustrated earlier (see p. 9).

> Video games bring many benefits to educators, including, significantly, an increase in student academic achievement. However, there are financial and social challenges to meet if the use of video games is to be effectively implemented. The next step is the creation of a unified system that can be tested and modeled in schools across the globe; education also has its role to play in overcoming a prejudice against the use of this promising teaching tool. If the challenges can be met, it may be only a matter of time until games become a staple of our education. (student writer David Stephen)

A **circular conclusion** reminds the reader of the thesis and reinforces it.

A **spiral conclusion** suggests applications or further research.

Chapter 1 Review Questions

1. What are the five chronological stages of essay writing?
2. Choose one pre-writing method (as discussed on p. 3) and, in your own words, explain how it works. (It might be good to choose a method that works well for you or one that you would like to try.)
3. Explain the difference between editing and revising. Why are these important activities for the writer?
4. Name four functions of an introduction and three forms that a thesis statement could take.
5. When might a dramatic opening be a better choice than a logical opening?
6. a) What is the difference between unified and coherent paragraphs?
   b) Rank the strategies for coherence in order of importance and explain why you have chosen the ones you did (see p. 12).
   c) Choose a paragraph from a piece of your own writing and suggest how you can make it more coherent.
7. Pick a topic other than hockey and suggest ways that you could use specific rhetorical patterns to develop that topic (see pp. 13–14). Give at least three examples of suitable patterns.
8. What could influence your decision to use mostly "hard" or mostly "soft" evidence in an essay?
9. What factors can influence your credibility as a writer?
10. Answer true or false:
    a) A circular conclusion repeats your thesis word for word.
    b) A spiral introduction is usually superior to a circular introduction.
    c) In a spiral introduction, you do not refer to your thesis.

Key Terms

brainstorming (p. 3)
circular conclusion (p. 17)
claim (p. 8)
clustering (p. 3)
coherent (p. 11)
concise (p. 6)
credibility (p. 16)
dramatic opening (p. 9)
freewriting (p. 3)
logical opening (p. 9)

outline (p. 4)
questioning (p. 3)
reader-based prose (p. 11)
rhetorical pattern (p. 13)
spiral conclusion (p. 17)
support (p. 3)
thesis (p. 2)
thesis statement (p. 8)
topic sentence (p. 11)
unified (p. 11)

2

Writing Summaries

In this chapter, you will learn:

- What the different kinds of summaries are
- How stand-alone summaries are used
- How to use strategies for successful summarizing

ummaries are a major part of research-related writing. Research never occurs in a vacuum; it is a collaborative effort. Even original theories and innovative research must be placed within the context of what has been thought and written before. And that is often where summarization comes in.

Times and Places for Summaries

Summarization is a general term for representing the ideas of a writer in a condensed form, using your own words. You will find a variety of scenarios where you will need to summarize:

- When you are writing a review, of a book, movie, and the like, you will need to summarize its plot or characters before you begin your analysis.
- When you are critiquing a text in order to argue for or against the author's position, you will need to summarize the author's arguments before replying with your own points.
- When you are writing a critical analysis, you will likely need to write a brief summary before applying your critical thinking skills to it.
- You will also need to summarize when using sources in your research (see Chapter 8, p. 75).

In addition, specialized summaries have various functions. In many academic essays, a concentrated summary called an **abstract** precedes the essay,

Summarization is a general term for representing the ideas of a writer in a condensed form, using your own words.

An **abstract** is a condensed summary used in empirical studies. It is placed before the study begins and includes its purpose, method(s), result(s), and conclusion.

A **literature review** is a condensed survey of articles on the topic arranged in a logical order usually ending with the article most relevant to the author's study.

An **annotated bibliography** is an expanded bibliography that includes not only the information of standard bibliographies but also brief summaries of related works.

giving an overview of what follows, including the essay's purpose, method(s), result(s), and conclusion. Another form of summary is the literature review, in which the author, often in a phrase or sentence for each, summarizes the relevant studies in the field, before stating his or her own thesis or hypothesis (see Chapter 10, p. 141).

You will also find yourself summarizing when you write an annotated bibliography. This is an expanded bibliography that includes not only the information of standard bibliographies but also brief summaries of related works, including studies referred to in the text and other significant studies. Typically, each entry in the bibliography includes the thesis or finding and a comment on what it contributes to the field as a whole—where it fits in. Annotated bibliographies may form appendices to book-length studies.

You may be assigned a more modest annotated bibliography as part of a research project or as an independent project. In either case, the purpose is to demonstrate your ability to research and summarize relevant works on a topic.

The following is an example of an entry in an annotated bibliography on the topic of decriminalizing Canadian prostitution laws. The student summarizes one of the studies she used in her research essay and provides a brief assessment of its value.

O'Doherty, T. (2011). Criminalization and off-street sex work in Canada. *Canadian Journal of Criminology and Criminal Justice, 53*(2), 217–245. doi:10.3138/cjccj.53.2.217

Using results from 10 interviews with off-street sex workers, O'Doherty explores the impact of the current Criminal Code prostitution laws in Canada: she describes the resulting separation between police and sex workers: the lack of understanding of the laws among sex workers; and the physical health, mental health, [and] legal and social implications. Though her sample size is small, O'Doherty incorporates external research to support her findings that the decriminalization of prostitution would positively impact sex workers; she also includes precautionary measures, such as the necessity of practising sex workers input in the revision and creation of legislation.

(student writer Annika Benoit-Jansson)

Summarizing and Research

Summary is an important feature of research, whether practised by students or academics, because it enables writers to connect their own points to those of others. By presenting the main idea(s) of your sources and relating them to your own ideas, you are developing your thesis. Writers of academic essays rely on this form of development to

- elaborate on their own point,
- disagree with a relevant study,
- explain a concept or theory related to their topic, and
- compare/contrast a study's findings with those of other studies.

The amount of space you devote to a summary depends on how you want to use it and on its importance. For a book or movie review, you want to provide enough plot to enable your reader to grasp what the work was about. If you are summarizing an author's position with which you disagree, you do not want to do more than briefly sketch the main arguments on the other side, unless your purpose in arguing is to reach a compromise. If one source is particularly important to your research essay, that summary should be longer than those of less important sources. Summaries, then, can range greatly in length as well as in purpose.

The Stand-Alone Summary: The *Précis*

A summary can also serve as an end in itself. A stand-alone summary, sometimes called a *précis* (meaning something precise), represents the main points in a complete work or section(s) of a work. It follows the same order of points as the original but omits most sub-points and all detail. The specific guidelines that apply to stand-alone summaries do not apply to all types of summaries, but learning these guidelines and practising them is the best way to learn the art of summary writing. The important skills required in *précis* writing include the following:

Précis is a term for a stand-alone summary. It is usually 20–25 per cent the length of the original.

- **Comprehension skills:** Because a *précis* summary, like most summaries, requires you to change the wording of the original, you focus more closely on comprehension than if you quoted the words of the source directly. You have to be clear on content in order to write a successful summary.
- **Prioritizing skills (establishing a hierarchy of importance):** Separating the main ideas from the less important ideas is a fundamental part of the reading process. In order to know what to include when summarizing, you need to think about the importance of a point relative to other points, the importance of a sub-point relative to other sub-points, and so on. Including a less important sub-point and omitting a more important one would make your summary misrepresentative.
- **Concision skills:** A crucial principle applies to *précis* writing: the more efficient your writing, the more content you can include, and the more informed

Stand-alone summaries help develop three main skills basic to reading and writing at the college and university level: comprehension, prioritizing, and concision skills.

your reader will be. In addition, focusing on conciseness serves you well in any writing you do, making you a more disciplined writer.

Pointers for *Précis* Writing

To write an effective summary, pay attention to the guidelines below:

1. Follow the exact order of the original. Begin with the thesis or first main point, not a generalization about the essay as a whole (e.g., why it was written).
2. Include only the most important points. If space is limited, you may be able to only include the most important sub-point(s) or developments.
3. Avoid detail. Do not include examples unless they are very important.
4. Avoid repetition. Although ideas stressed in the original should also be stressed in your summary, do not repeat needlessly.
5. Do not repeat the author's name or the work's title any more than necessary.
6. Do not analyze, interpret, or give your opinions.
7. Use your own words and avoid direct quotations. If, however, you need to quote directly, be sure to use quotation marks. This will show the reader that those exact words occured in the original. Common everyday words from the original do not have to be placed in quotation marks unless they occur in a phrase of four words or more. (The number of successive words requiring quotation marks can vary. It is best to check with your instructor.)
8. Write efficiently. Rephrase the original concisely and check that you use no more words than you must. Use basic nouns, verbs, adjectives, and adverbs, with minimal modifiers. Use transitions sparingly to connect ideas.
9. Use verbs that reflect the author's rhetorical purpose. For example, if the writer is arguing rather than explaining a point, use a verb that reflects this: The author *argues . . . claims . . . criticizes . . .* (argument); the author *states . . . explains . . . discusses . . .* (exposition).

For a summary, space is at a premium, so remember to be **SPACE** conscious. Be:

Specific
Precise
Accurate
Clear
Efficient

A How-To of *Précis* Writing

Reading to summarize means you should use the forms of selective reading appropriate for this activity. Begin by scanning the text to understand the core ideas (thesis and main points), and to determine how the author has divided the text (structure). See Chapter 6 for more on selective reading and scanning. Here are four steps for summarizing, using an outline to help you order your points:

1. Identify main ideas with distinctive underlining, such as double underlining. In *paragraphs*, pay attention to topic sentences. In *sentences*, look for independent clauses, which usually contain the main idea in the sentence.

2. Identify the most important sub-points (developments) by single underlining. For information about using contextual cues, such as transitions and prompts to lead you to main ideas, see pp. 145–6.

3. Prepare an outline with all main points and important sub-points. If you wish, indent sub-points as in a formal outline.

4. Write your summary from the outline, using your own words as much as possible, and adding transitions to create coherent prose. If the summary exceeds the allowable length, omit the least important sub-point(s).

BOX 2.1 | Some Summary Writing Strategies

In addition to the summarization guidelines listed in this chapter, you might find the following strategies helpful:

☐ Read through the essay at least twice before beginning to identify main points and important sub-points.

☐ If you find it difficult to identify what is important in a passage, ask if or how it contributes to the thesis or controlling idea.

☐ Pay attention to paragraph structure. For example, does the author use topic sentences?

☐ Put parentheses around what you know are unimportant details and examples. This will leave you with less to work with.

☐ For longer works, pay particular attention to the writer's own summaries, which may occur in the introduction, in the conclusion, or toward the end of detailed or complex sections.

☐ Not all paragraphs are equally important, and not all contain main ideas. In much non-academic writing, for example, opening paragraphs may serve to attract the reader's interest and not contain an important point.

A Sample Summary

The following is a section from an essay in Part II, "The Impact of Pets on Human Health and Psychological Well-Being," by Harold Herzog (see p. 323). Important points are explained in the margin. The passage is 300 words. A 60-word summary would represent 20 per cent of the original; a 75-word summary would represent 25 per cent.

Point 1: The importance of this study is suggested by the writer's phrasing: it was "[t]he first demonstration"; "[t]hese findings generated a flurry of research."

Details, such as examples, are usually omitted in summaries.

Point 2: The writer mentions the most notable study. In your summary, you should not include the detail given here.

Point 3: Much less space is given to psychological effects, suggesting their lesser importance.

Point 4: Clear organization helps the reader. Here, the writer introduces the topic of the paragraph in the first sentence.

The Evidence That Pets Are Good for People

[1] The first demonstration of an association between pets and health was an early study of 92 heart-attack victims in which 28 per cent of pet owners survived for at least a year as compared to only 6 per cent of non-pet owners (Friedmann, Katcher, Lynch, & Thomas, 1980). These findings generated a flurry of research on the positive impact of interacting with companion animals (see review by Wells, 2009a). For example, stroking dogs and cats, watching tropical fish in an aquarium, and even caressing a pet boa constrictor have been reported to reduce blood pressure and stress levels. The most convincing of these studies was a clinical trial in which hypertensive stockbrokers were randomly assigned to either pet or no-pet conditions. Six months later, when put in a stressful situation, subjects in the pet group showed lower increases in blood pressure than did those in the non-pet control condition (Allen, Shykoff, & Izzo, 2001). Researchers have also reported that psychological benefits accrue from living with animals. These include studies showing that pet owners have higher self-esteem, more positive moods, more ambition, greater life satisfaction, and lower levels of loneliness (El-Alayli, Lystad, Webb, Hollingsworth, & Ciolli, 2006).

[2] Epidemiologists have also connected pet ownership to better health and well-being (see review by Headey & Grabka, 2011). For example, among 11,000 German and Australian adults, pet owners were in better physical condition than non-pet owners, and they made 15 per cent fewer doctor visits, a potential savings of billions of dollars in national health expenditures. And an epidemiological study of Chinese women found that pet owners exercised more, slept better, felt more physically fit, and missed fewer days from work than women without pets. Further, these effects were particularly strong for individuals who reported that they were very closely attached to their pets.

The following 75-word summary includes the points identified above, but focuses more on the first two points. If you were going to write a shorter summary of 60 words, what would you leave out?

Summary of "The Evidence That Pets Are Good for People," by Harold Herzog

In 1980, researchers found that pet owners who suffered a heart attack were over four times more likely to survive for at least a year than non-pet owning victims. This study led to further research. For example, stockbrokers with pets were found to experience less of a blood pressure increase in a stressful situation than those without pets. Other studies revealed that people with pets experience better psychological health and are in better physical condition.

Of course, there is more than one way to summarize this section. To check the effectiveness of this summary, you can refer to the pointers on page 22.

Chapter 2 Review Questions

1. Identify three different kinds of summaries and their main purposes.
2. Explain the importance of summarizing in the research process.
3. What three important skills are tested in a stand-alone (*précis*) summary? Why might these skills be crucial in other kinds of writing you do at college or university?
4. Answer true or false:
    a) A *précis* summary should begin with a generalization.
    b) A summary should be specific, but avoid detail.
    c) A summary should include both your own words and direct quotations.
5. What steps can you take to ensure that your summary includes all the main points of the original?

Key Terms

abstract (p. 19)

annotated bibliography (p. 20)

literature review (p. 20)

précis (p. 21)

summarization (p. 19)

3

Rhetorical Analyses

In this chapter, you will learn:

- What the differences are between a rhetorical analysis and a critical response

- How to organize a rhetorical analysis

- How to use questions to generate a rhetorical analysis

Analyzing Texts

In-class and out-of-class assignments often require you to analyze an essay you have never seen before. To do so, you need to exercise your active reading skills, especially critical thinking. A rhetorical analysis, usually called a critical analysis when you are analyzing an argument, demonstrates your ability to analyze such elements as the writer's purpose, audience, techniques, and, in critical analyses, reasoning strategies.

A critical response requires some of the same skills, as well as relating your observations and experiences to the topic of the essay you are responding to. In this chapter, we focus on the more objective rhetorical and critical analyses. However, Table 3.1 on p. 30 compares analyses and responses, and there is a brief student critical response on p. 32.

When you analyze a work, you break it down in order to examine its parts. In this way, the rhetorical analysis assumes you are familiar with how such texts are written and can evaluate the author's success in achieving his or her objectives. The main purposes of a rhetorical analysis are (1) to explain how the text is put together and (2) to evaluate or critique the author's use of rhetorical strategies. An analysis needs to be planned carefully. For example, it is often a good idea to outline your points before beginning your draft.

Writing a rhetorical analysis makes you more conscious of the ways that texts are written, that is, the kinds of techniques and strategies used to make content clear and accessible. In this sense, you critically analyze a text in order to see what works and what does not—and why. Honing your analytical abilities in this way helps you use the essays you analyze as models for your own writing.

A **rhetorical analysis** focuses on the text you have read. In a rhetorical analysis, you break down a work in order to examine its parts and the author's rhetorical strategies, using your critical thinking skills and your knowledge of texts themselves.

A **critical analysis** focuses on the text you have read. In a critical analysis, you break down the writer's argument, evaluating its effectiveness for its intended audience while considering the use of reason and specific argumentative strategies.

A **critical response** focuses on your own opinions or observations about an issue raised in a text. Although a response is usually more informal than a rhetorical analysis, it should clearly demonstrate critical thinking.

Rhetorical Analysis and Essay Type

Analysis of Literary Works

One kind of rhetorical analysis, a literary analysis, applies to literary works. The literary analysis breaks down the elements of the text—in fiction, such elements include plot, character, setting, point of view, and language—showing their interconnections. (Of course, such texts contain no thesis but rather themes.) Like other kinds of texts, literary texts can be analyzed according to their conventions, which vary by genre (poetry, drama, fiction, creative non-fiction) and by subgenre (lyric, dramatic, and narrative poetry, for example). Some non-fiction essays, like those on pp. 155 and 162, can also be analyzed for their point of view, language, tone, and techniques, like metaphors.

Analysis of Arguments

Argumentative claims are debatable—for example, one writer might claim that social media advocacy is a good thing, while another could argue it is not. Therefore, arguments make a good source for analysis. In a rhetorical analysis of an argumentative essay, or critical analysis, you might question the validity of an author's premise or question the use of argument. Such analyses should focus on the hows and whys of the author's use of reason and argumentative strategies. It should *not* be used as a forum for expressing your personal agreement or disagreement with the author's opinions. Instead, it should be used for evaluating the logic and effectiveness of the argument itself. (See also "Argumentative Strategies" in Chapter 4, p. 47.)

A **premise** is based on many kinds of thinking, especially deductive reasoning in which conclusions can be drawn from specific assertions.

Organizing a Rhetorical Analysis

The Introduction

A typical rhetorical analysis begins with an introduction that includes a generalization about the essay and/or the topic, such as its importance or relevance in today's world. It must also include a summary of the author's thesis. If a reader of your analysis isn't familiar with the source text, you could briefly summarize its main points. However, rhetorical analyses are much more than simple summaries.

At the end of your introduction, include your thesis statement. The form of the thesis depends on the kind of text you are analyzing and your purpose. Essentially, though, it should address whether the text successfully fulfills its purpose and supports its own claims. This can be accomplished by discussing the most relevant features, those that stand out most in the text. If the essay is argumentative, your thesis might evaluate the author's use of reason and argument. As in most essays, your body paragraphs provide support for your thesis.

The Body Paragraphs

In the body paragraphs, you should break down the features of the essay mentioned in your thesis, explaining how these features reflect the author's purpose, objectives, and/or audience. The aim is to explain and evaluate the how and the why of the source text. How does the author explore the subject, prove the claim, and support the main points? Why are those particular methods and strategies used and not other ones? What are the essay's strengths and weaknesses? How could the text be improved?

In any analysis, being specific is vital. Support all claims you make about a text by examples from the text, ensuring you include a citation for direct quotations and other specific points.

> In any analysis, being specific is vital. Support all claims you make about a text by examples from the text.

The Conclusion

In your conclusion, do not introduce new material. You could begin by referring to your thesis and answering the question of whether the essay was successful. A longer conclusion might summarize the essay's main features or its strengths and weaknesses, as discussed in the body paragraphs. One way to end is to comment on the essay's significance or influence, or suggest what can be learned from it.

BOX 3.1 | Preparing to Write a Rhetorical Analysis

The questions below, organized according to purpose, can form the basis of a rhetorical analysis. (Note also that many of the questions and activities that follow individual essays in this textbook are the kinds of questions you can ask of a text as you read it in order to analyze it.) The nature of the text itself and other factors help determine exactly which questions are the most relevant to your analysis. For example, the author of an article in an academic journal does not usually need to consider special strategies in order to create reader interest.

Explaining

- ❐ When was the essay written, relative to similar studies in the field?

- ❐ Why was it written? Is it intended to inform, explain, persuade?

- ❐ For what kind of audience is it written? How do you know this?

- ❐ What do you know about the author? Does he or she appear to be an expert in his or her field or otherwise qualified to write on the topic? How is this apparent (if it is)?

- ❐ Identify the introduction. What is the writer's thesis or central question? What is the justification for the study? In what way(s) does the author propose to add to his or her field of knowledge? Is there an essay plan? How does the author convey essay structure?

❐ What are the essay's main points?

❐ What format does the essay follow? How does the text reflect the conventions of the discipline for which it was written? Does it follow these conventions exactly, or does it differ from them in any way?

❐ What kinds of evidence does the author use? Which are the most important?

❐ Is there a stress on either analysis or synthesis in the essay? (See p. 124.) Or is there stress on both equally?

❐ What inferences are readers called on to make?

❐ How is the essay organized? Is there a primary rhetorical pattern? What other kinds of patterns are used?

❐ What level of language is used? Does the author include any particular stylistic features (e.g., analogies, metaphors, imagery, and unusual or non-standard sentence structure)?

❐ Is there a conclusion? What is its primary purpose?

Evaluating/Critiquing

❐ In the introduction, does the author successfully prepare the reader for what is to follow?

❐ Does the author manage to create interest in the topic? How is this done? Would other strategies have worked better?

❐ Main points: Are they identifiable (in topic sentences, for example)? Are they well supported? Is supporting detail specific and relevant?

❐ If secondary sources are used, are there enough? Are they current?

❐ What kinds of sources were used? Books? Journal articles? Websites? Other?

❐ What kinds of strategies and techniques does the author use to facilitate understanding? Are they effective? Are there other ways that organization or content could have been made clearer?

❐ What makes the conclusion effective/ineffective?

The following questions are applicable to a critical analysis:

❐ Does the essay appear free of bias? Is the voice as objective as possible? Has slanted language been avoided?

❐ Does the author appear reasonable? Has he or she used reason effectively, establishing a chain of logic throughout? Are there failures in logic (logical fallacies)?

❐ Does the author make the issue relevant to the reader? Does he or she appeal to the reader's values? Does he or she use other argumentative strategies?

❐ Does the author make emotional or ethical appeals? Are any of the appeals extreme or manipulative? Are there any emotional fallacies? For more information on argumentative strategies, see Chapter 4, "The Art of Argument."

TABLE 3.1	Main Features of a Rhetorical Analysis and a Critical Response		
Type of Assignment	**Purpose**	**Style and Audience**	**Typical Activities/ Structure**
Rhetorical analysis	To examine how a text is constructed and assess its importance or influence; to better understand types of texts and arguments, their uses, and their effectiveness	Uses formal style and objective voice for readers knowledgeable about rhetorical practices and argumentative strategies	Focused reading; comprehension and critical thinking; analyzing and evaluating; breaking down text and its arguments to provide support for thesis; focusing on source text
Critical response	To explore your views on a topic and share them with others	Uses semi-formal style, perhaps from first-person point of view, for readers interested in the topic who might also have opinions and observations about it	Critical thinking; expressive and/or personal writing; synthesizing the author's and your own views/observations

Sample Critical Analysis

The analysis below, on Andrew D. Pinto's "Denaturalizing 'Natural' Disasters: Haiti's Earthquake and the Humanitarian Impulse" (see p. 307), highlights some of the main features of the source text, using summary, explanation, and evaluation of the writer's use of reason. The annotations refer to some of the points discussed above.

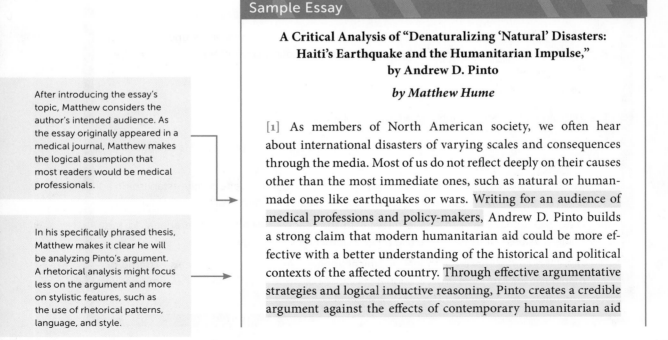

Sample Essay

A Critical Analysis of "Denaturalizing 'Natural' Disasters: Haiti's Earthquake and the Humanitarian Impulse,"
by Andrew D. Pinto

by Matthew Hume

After introducing the essay's topic, Matthew considers the author's intended audience. As the essay originally appeared in a medical journal, Matthew makes the logical assumption that most readers would be medical professionals.

In his specifically phrased thesis, Matthew makes it clear he will be analyzing Pinto's argument. A rhetorical analysis might focus less on the argument and more on stylistic features, such as the use of rhetorical patterns, language, and style.

[1] As members of North American society, we often hear about international disasters of varying scales and consequences through the media. Most of us do not reflect deeply on their causes other than the most immediate ones, such as natural or human-made ones like earthquakes or wars. Writing for an audience of medical professions and policy-makers, Andrew D. Pinto builds a strong claim that modern humanitarian aid could be more effective with a better understanding of the historical and political contexts of the affected country. Through effective argumentative strategies and logical inductive reasoning, Pinto creates a credible argument against the effects of contemporary humanitarian aid

and its supposed benefits. Use of ethical appeals, comparisons, and concessions, along with a range of primary sources and concrete proposals contributes to his argument's success.

[2] The topic itself encourages an ethical stance on the part of the reader, reminding him or her of the internal obligation to help those in need, especially those less fortunate on the global scale. Such an appeal, strategically placed at the end of Pinto's introduction, generates an incentive to continue reading the article.

[3] Pinto shows the severity of Haiti's 2010 earthquake by using a comparison. Specifically, he compares the earthquake in Haiti with the much less deadly but higher magnitude quake in Chile that occurred on February 2010. The comparison conveys the idea not only that the earthquake in Haiti was obviously deadly but also that there must have been other factors that led to a death toll and displacement so much higher than in Chile. The author believes such factors might be rooted in historical and political influences, and Pinto next uses the chronological rhetorical pattern along with historical facts to help paint a vivid picture of the hardships and exploitation of the nation over the course of more than 500 years. Furthermore, these facts come from many different sources, adding to Pinto's credibility.

[4] After building historical and political background for his argument by outlining Haiti's past, Pinto uses a concession, acknowledging that many non-governmental organizations should be given credit for the humanitarian accomplishments in their immediate responses to the Haiti earthquake, which he says "succeeded in many ways" (p. 309). The concession enables him to transition to rebuttal as he then cites several sources to outline how the long-term effects of the humanitarian aid response is problematic, such as the priority given to military over supply flights to the country (p. 310). Pinto keeps a logical hold on his claim through to his conclusion where he again concedes that the humanitarian aid has been "laudable" (p. 311).

[5] Pinto uses both deductive and inductive reasoning effectively in his essay. First, by questioning the assumption that humanitarian aid from developed nations is always good, he is able to challenge the general claim as superficial at best. Throughout the essay he supports his claim inductively by using a variety of primary sources, including statistics in paragraphs 6, 9, and 12, and the ideas of political philosopher Thomas Pogge in paragraph 13. Pinto refers to Pogge's concept of "relational justice," which looks for underlying causes of disparities

> Although much of the paragraph that follows analyzes Pinto's use of a comparison, Matthew also considers his use of chronology in the paragraph. A more effective topic sentence might have been to mention both rhetorical patterns.

> Matthew cites the text three times in this paragraph, supporting his point about Pinto's use of concessions, an argumentative strategy (see p. 47) that demonstrates the writer's objectivity and fairness toward the other side.

In pointing to the use of Thomas Pogge to set up Pinto's "strongest statement," Matthew goes beyond just stating his importance; he explains how and why he is important. Later in this paragraph, Matthew similarly analyzes Pinto's use of practical solutions. Successful rhetorical and critical analyses focus on the hows and whys of texts, using critical thinking to show what makes them successful (or unsuccessful).

between rich and poor countries while acknowledging "complicity," to set the grounds for the strongest statement in his essay: "[A]ctual histories should replace the more palatable fictional histories that attempt to explain away wealthy nations' past contributions to the persistent poverty in the world" (pp. 310–11). Following up this statement with concrete proposals and practical solutions is an effective way to conclude the essay, as it enables Pinto to be more positive about a depressing situation. Although some of the proposals may be idealistic, giving Partners in Health as an example of an NGO that has made a difference in Haiti shows that acknowledging actual histories can be beneficial for the affected country. Pinto's argument is logical and effective.

[6]   Although it is written for policy-makers and medical professionals, his claims can be grasped by the general reader. His credibility is seen through the use of comparisons, concessions, ethical appeals, and strong inductive support. In "Denaturalizing 'Natural' Disasters," Pinto successfully raises our awareness concerning an issue of international importance. Only by creating awareness of an injustice or wrongdoing can we move forward to address the injustice.

In his conclusion, Matthew mentions the author's purpose and audience, and summarizes Pinto's strategies, touching briefly on the essay's possible significance.

Sample Critical Response

In the following critical response, student writer Josie Gair uses critical thinking, her knowledge of indigenous groups, and her own reflections to respond to two issues raised by Pinto.

Sample Essay

**A Critical Response to "Denaturalizing 'Natural' Disasters,"
by Andrew D. Pinto**

by Josie Gair

[1]   Pinto suggests that once a natural disaster occurs and a relief fund is established for the affected area, the focus then must shift to the long term redevelopment. He argues that even with an organization or outside government's best intentions, the affected community must be involved from the beginning of the reconstruction process. I believe that he is correct in stating that the indigenous people must be highly involved because if we incorporate more

After identifying the point to which Josie is going to respond, she states the reason for her agreement and provides an example from the Canadian experience. Unlike rhetorical or critical analyses, the use of first person in responses is usually acceptable.

historical examples of Europeans trying to help indigenous people, we know now that they have often done more bad than good. For example, the Canadian indigenous peoples did not wish to be stripped of their identities and assimilated into European culture. We all know the severe cultural and political repercussions of those choices made by the Canadian government almost a hundred years ago. Therefore, Pinto is correct in saying the less interference, the better. Haiti has been trying to self-govern for hundreds of years, and it should continue to do so even after the initial disaster.

[2] Pinto states that only 5% of the earthquakes rubble has been removed in the past two years and that only about ten percent of the $5.3 billion pledged has been used. Those arguments were the strongest in my opinion because I found it very hard to believe and sad; Pinto made me ask "why?" Pinto's purpose for writing the essay was to make people wonder "why" and thereby question the long-term humanitarian efforts going on in Haiti, and I found his essay very effective in this respect.

Josie uses the first person to respond to Pinto's use of facts. Notice that she does not just give her reaction to the statistics but connects the feelings she experienced to the essay's purpose.

Chapter 3 Review Questions

1. Compare and contrast rhetorical analyses and critical responses in their:
   a) Purpose
   b) Kinds of skills involved
2. A rhetorical analysis can best be compared to which one of the following?
   a) A summary
   b) A literary analysis
   c) An argumentative essay
   d) A research paper
3. Explain two features of the introduction of a rhetorical analysis.
4. Answer true or false:
   a) Examples are a crucial part of successful body paragraphs in a rhetorical analysis.
   b) Approximately half of the rhetorical analysis should be spent on summary.
5. How important is it to consider intended audience in a rhetorical analysis of a work? Explain your answer.

Key Terms

critical analysis (p. 26)
critical response (p. 26)

premise (p. 27)
rhetorical analysis (p. 26)

4

The Art of Argument

In this chapter, you will learn:

- What the three different argumentative models are and how they are used

- What the goals of argument are

- What the different types of argumentative claims are

- How to use different kinds of evidence

- How to identify effective and ineffective uses of reason

- How to use strategies for effective arguments

- How to use rebuttal techniques

Classical argument had its origins among the ancient Greeks, but the development of a scholar's rhetorical skills remained a vital part of Western education up to the end of the nineteenth century and beyond. These abilities were considered ideal vocational training. Specifically, the formal debate was thought to develop life skills such as mental and verbal sharpness.

Argument and Aristotle

Although rhetoric has taken on a range of meanings today, the Greek philosopher Aristotle (384–322 BCE) uses "rhetoric" to stress a speaker's choices available to persuade an audience. He believed that readers or listeners would need to be persuaded—that showing knowledge alone was not enough. Aristotle identifies specific *topoi*, or strategies, that could help persuade an audience. Two such strategies are definition and comparison (see p. 49).

Aristotle, who laid much of the groundwork for classical argument in his book *Rhetoric*, divides arguments into three kinds: those founded on reason (logos), on morality (ethos), and on emotion (pathos). The most important appeal is usually to a reader's reason. Ethical appeals play a major role, too, mostly in establishing the arguer's credibility and understanding of morality. To use emotional appeals

Rhetoric refers to the structure and strategies of argumentation and language use to persuade a specific audience.

An **audience** is the reader or readers for whom most writing is designed. Being aware of your audience will help you decide what to include or not include or, in the case of argument, what strategies to use to help convince this audience.

Aristotle divides arguments into three kinds: those founded on reason (**logos**), on morality (**ethos**), and on emotion (**pathos**).

successfully, Aristotle believed that you needed to know the audience's "hearts" and be able to understand the causes of different emotions and the way they work. The stress on knowing your audience and adapting your words accordingly remains a fundamental aspect of a successful argument. Such knowledge can also be used in making emotional appeals, arousing the feelings of an audience in order to strengthen an argument.

Aristotle named and categorized certain kinds of logical errors and realized that faulty reasoning could seem convincing and even sway the uncritical reader; however, it does not produce a good argument. It fails not only the test of logic but also the test of fairness. (For more about fallacies in argument, see p. 45.)

Aristotle's stress on knowing your audience and adapting your words accordingly remains a fundamental aspect of a successful argument.

Two Modern Models of Argument: Rogers and Toulmin

Aristotle's model heavily influenced the development of rhetorical theory through to the twentieth century. But as modern arguers tried to make argument more relevant to real-life situations, two new approaches developed. First, we will discuss the importance of Carl Rogers' ideas and then turn to a widely used approach today, that of Stephen Toulmin.

Carl Rogers' Approach to Argument

The approach of Carl Rogers emerges out of communication theory and involves "see[ing] the expressed idea and attitude from the other person's point of view." Rogerian strategies include framing your argument in terms that are acceptable to the other person. Rogers' approach, too, focuses on one's audience; it works best when your reader disagrees with you but is willing to listen.

In classical arguments, concerned mostly with victory, arguers may be encouraged to anticipate counterpoints in order to sharpen their *own* points, and not to genuinely engage with one's critics, as the Rogerian model invites. The Rogerian approach encourages establishing common ground—points of agreement—with your audience and discourages a "winner takes all" approach.

The Rogerian argument uses objective language, pointing out differences between the positions of the arguer and the reader, and stresses fairness and consciousness of the reader's position—for example, the arguer may make concessions as a way of showing the reader that compromise is possible (see p. 47).

Of course, most arguments are not *either* Aristotelian *or* Rogerian, but combine features of both: effective arguments may rely on Aristotle's logical, emotional, or ethical appeals and strategies yet include many features of the Rogers approach. For example, student writer Kirsten Saikaly presents a forceful "classical" argument while occasionally using the Rogerian approach by including concessions and appeals to common ground in her essay. Otherwise, her points might strike some as harsh or critical of those she hopes to change (see p. 55). (See also "Argumentative Strategies," p. 47.)

Stephen Toulmin's Approach to Argument

Stephen Toulmin's ideas are a direct response to the limitations of classical (Aristotelian) argument. The Toulmin model, based on the way lawyers present their cases before courts, was designed for many kinds of arguments, from complex to casual ones. In particular, Toulmin realizes that claims alone aren't enough but must also have a foundation, a means of linking the evidence to the claim. One of Toulmin's important contributions is the concept of the warrant, the foundation of an argumentative claim.

The Role of Warrants in Argument

Strong arguments do not simply consist of an arguable claim and supporting evidence. They also need to show why the evidence is relevant or that it supports the claim. Toulmin called this the **warrant**. If the warrant is obvious, it does not have to be announced. The following warrant is clear without being stated.

A **warrant** provides the foundation of a claim, linking the evidence to the claim that is being made.

> *Claim:* I have to buy a new watch.
>
> *Evidence:* My current watch says the same time as it did 30 minutes ago.
>
> *Warrant:* My watch is broken.

The evidence is sufficient support for the claim because the reader would infer the link ("My watch is broken"). On the other hand, if someone used the same claim and offered as evidence "I just bought a new outfit to attend a wedding," a reader or listener might ask what link existed between the evidence and the claim of having to buy a new watch. The speaker might then reply, "I could never show up at a wedding with an accessory that didn't match the rest of my outfit!" which would be an attempt to link the claim to the evidence—for most people, a less convincing one!

A warrant can arise from physical laws, human laws, assumptions, premises, common knowledge, ethical principles, or, in the case of the fashionable wedding guest above, aesthetic values. For an argument to be successful, the reader must agree with the warrant, whether stated or implied. Again, then, it is important to know your audience.

The underlying assumption of Bruce M. Hicks in "The Undiscovered Province" (p. 294) is based on an ethical principle: self-government for Aboriginals is an important goal for all Canadians as it would make Aboriginal representation a part of the Canadian democratic process. If readers didn't agree with the warrant, the author's claim would likely be rejected.

Claim: Create a new, eleventh province made up of Aboriginal lands.

Evidence: Hicks presents several points to support his claim.

Warrant: Aboriginal self-government is necessary for a fully functioning Canadian democracy.

Kirsten Saikaly makes several claims in her essay about racism (see p. 55). If readers did not acknowledge the ethical principle that all forms of racism are unacceptable, they would be less likely to acknowledge her claim and her supporting evidence.

Toulmin also believed that arguers should avoid overly general statements. A qualified claim is more acceptable to a reader, who may simply reject a claim that is too broad. With or without a qualifier, though, a claim, says Toulmin, must have something behind it to justify it, to make it reasonable and acceptable to its audience. If arguers ask themselves "Will readers accept my statement?" and "Why is this true and/or what makes it true?" they will be encouraged to consider the foundation for their claim, the warrant. Looking at *if* and *how* a claim is justified helps prevent the kind of reasoning that sees argument simply as stating an opinion and backing it up—an oversimplified approach.

Table 4.1 summarizes the major features of the influential argumentative models of Aristotle, Rogers, and Toulmin.

> If arguers ask themselves, "Will readers accept my statement?" and "Why is this true and/or what makes it true?" they will be encouraged to reflect on the basis of their claim, the warrant. Looking at *if* and *how* a claim is justified helps prevent the kind of reasoning that sees argument simply as stating an opinion.

TABLE 4.1   Summary of Major Features of Argumentative Models

Argumentative Model/Theory	Original Uses	Key Concepts/ Terms	Uses in Argumentative Essays
Aristotle	Oratory/public Speaking	Logical, ethical, and emotional appeals and other strategies	Understanding inductive and deductive kinds of reasoning; using reason effectively; establishing authority and trustworthiness; appealing to audience emotions
Rogers	Psychology/ interpersonal communication	Common ground, consensus	Acknowledging opposing views; laying grounds for trust and acceptance; reaching consensus and mutual understanding
Toulmin	Law	Claim, warrant, data (support)	Providing foundation for/developing a claim to make it convincing; tying claim to support; qualifying claim to avoid generalizations

Purposes for Arguing

From the above, it is evident that argument today cannot be simplified to an "us versus them" approach. Indeed, it can serve various purposes:

- To state or defend your point of view
- To seek to change a situation
- To critique a viewpoint, position, or text, etc.
- To expose a problem or raise awareness of an issue
- To solidify an opinion
- To reach a compromise

The most straightforward purpose for arguing is defending your point of view. By contrast, arguing to reach a compromise involves objectively analyzing both sides of the debate, which is a more realistic approach than just defending your point of view. An example of this is in student writer Daniella Gudgeon's essay on a section of the Criminal Code that permits corporal punishment under "reasonable circumstances," In her essay, Gudgeon appeals to those who want the law upheld and those who want it abolished. Her middle position makes it likely that an audience on both sides will consider her points, making her argumentative goal more attainable.

> Section 43 of the Criminal Code has a social utility for both teachers and parents, but it is an old law that must be amended to reflect society's progression. The addition of clear guidelines to the law regarding the severity of discipline and the use of objects as weapons will create a distinction between abuse and discipline. This will prevent subjectivity within the courts and discourage future abuse, while affording parents the option of disciplining their children. (student writer Daniella Gudgeon)

In "Jazzwomen: The Forgotten Legacies," student writer Danica Long makes it evident in her thesis statement that she is arguing to draw attention to a neglected topic, to make her audience more aware of something:

> Where are all the classic female jazz musicians? In fact, they have excelled on every instrument, in every era, and in every style, yet they have been overlooked or underrated in the history of the jazz profession. (student writer Danica Long)

Opinions versus Arguments

An *opinion* is not the same as a *fact*. Facts can be confirmed by observation or research, while opinions are challengeable.

An *opinion* is not the same as a *fact*. Facts can be confirmed by observation or research, while opinions are challengeable.

As you will see, you cannot "argue" a position on a topic with no opposing view that cannot be challenged. Yet, facts can be interpreted in various ways and, therefore, can be used to support the thesis of an argumentative essay. However, effective arguers are always clear about when they are using facts and when they are using opinion. In reading, use your critical thinking skills to ask if the writer always clearly separates facts from opinion. If not, he or she might be guilty of faulty reasoning (see p. 45).

As suggested above, the *interpretation of facts* may be challenged by a reader. Interpreting facts to support your claim is an important strategy in argument. For example, the fact that just over 50 per cent of lung transplant recipients have a five-year survival rate could be used to support a claim that more resources should be allocated to boost this rate. The same statistic could be used to support a claim that fewer resources should be allocated to this procedure since the result is less promising than for other kinds of transplants in Canada.

Claims in Argument

We have been using the word *claim* in this chapter, rather than *thesis* or *point*. Claims are particularly appropriate to argument: a claim is an assertion that you attempt to support through logic and evidence in the body of your essay. However, simply claiming something does not entitle you to it: you must convince people that the claim is valid, which is what you do when you argue effectively. (See Chapter 1, pp. 3–4.)

An argumentative claim is usually one of value or policy. In a **value claim**, you argue that something is good or bad, right or wrong, fair or unfair, and so on. A **policy claim** advocates an action. In this sense, a policy claim goes further than the value claim. However, value claims can be used to make your audience consider something in a more positive light. For example, if you argue in favour of euthanasia to an audience of opponents you might not want to use a policy claim, one that focuses on changing laws. A value claim instead would focus on changing attitudes, getting the reader to see, as a first step, that euthanasia relieves the suffering of a terminally ill patient. Value claims can be used if you are critiquing a viewpoint or text (as book or movie reviews do), raising awareness, or trying to reach a compromise (i.e., to arrive at a middle ground).

A **value claim** is an assertion about a topic that appeals to its ethical nature (e.g., good/bad or fair/unfair).

A **policy claim** is an assertion about a topic that proposes an action (e.g., to fix a problem or improve a situation).

Effective Argumentative Claims

In writing an academic argument, ensure that your claim is *arguable*, *specific*, and *realistic*.

Arguable Claims

It is difficult for facts themselves to serve as the basis of an **arguable claim**, though they may be used to support that claim. For example, you could not easily argue

An **arguable claim** has an opposing viewpoint and has objective evidence to support it.

against the fact that the closest star to Earth is 4.2 light years away. However, you could use this fact as evidence to support a policy claim, say, for allocating more financial resources to the space program.

In addition, a belief—for example, that God exists—is not arguable in a formal way, although you could argue the merits or interpretation of something within a given belief system, such as the meaning of a passage from the Quran or other religious text. Similarly, you could not logically argue that one religion is *better* than another since there are no clear and objective standards that everyone would agree with. *Arguable claims must be supported through objective evidence, not just opinion.*

Where general agreement exists about a value, for example, the value of a safe environment or a healthy diet, you will find yourself arguing in a vacuum. You do not have a meaningful claim if your audience accepts an idea as obvious and not in need of proving. *If you cannot think of a strong opposing view to the one you want to argue, consider revising the topic so that it is arguable, or choose another topic.*

If, however, you are arguing to raise awareness, there may not be another "side." Even so, it is essential that you support your claim by objective evidence.

Specific Claims

Claims can be too broad: "we need to change our attitude toward the environment" or "we need to do something about terrorism." One way to narrow a general claim is to think about how it might apply to a subject that you know something about.

If you have come up with a broad topic, you can ask how it might affect people you know. For example, if you wanted to argue that the media promotes unhealthy weight loss in teenagers—a very big topic—and you were an athlete, you could consider what rules or procedures can lead to unhealthy weight loss in your sport. Many sports, such as rowing, have weight categories. In some provinces, the junior female lightweight category is 135 pounds and under. As a rower, you might be aware of unhealthy eating habits that rowers can develop seeking to remain in a lower weight category in order to be competitive. Your thesis statement might take this specific form: *To help prevent unhealthy and dangerous activities in young rowers, junior lightweight categories should be eliminated from provincial regattas.*

> If a claim is too vague or general, it will be hard to support and to research. Narrow broad claims so that they are specific.

A broad claim can also be made more specific if you can apply it to a particular group. It might be unwise to apply an anti-smoking claim to Canada or even to an entire province since municipalities may have their own smoking bylaws. You might therefore restrict the focus to your city or even your campus. (See Chapter 1, p. 3, for more information about narrowing topics.)

Realistic Claims

Some policy claims are unrealistic because they have little chance of being implemented. You may be able to come up with some points in favour of decriminalizing illegal substances to increase government revenues, but since such arguments would not take account of social conditions today, the claim would not be realistic.

Be careful not to use an exaggerated or weak claim as the basis for your argument—for example, that all cellphones should be banned in public places because they are distracting when they go off. A stronger argument would be for banning cellphone use in your classrooms because it distracts other students.

Kinds of Evidence in an Argumentative Essay

Although an effective argument can be built around reasonable points with logical connections between them, specific kinds of evidence can strengthen a claim. Some are more common to argument than to exposition, but most can be used in both.

COLLABORATIVE EXERCISE 4.1

In discussion groups, evaluate the five claims below, determining whether they would make good thesis statements for an argumentative essay. Are the claims arguable, specific, and realistic? If not, consider what changes would need to be made to make them arguable. Revise them accordingly.

1. The media has had a negative effect on the self-perceptions of young women.
2. In order to represent the interests of voters more accurately, give voters a wider selection of candidates, and provide a stronger voice for minority issues, the government should adopt the single transferable vote (STV) electoral model.
3. *The Hunger Games: Mockingjay–Part 1* was the best of *The Hunger Games* movies.
4. Text messaging should be prohibited because it interferes with the ability to use correct English.
5. Internet dating services are an innovative, convenient, and affordable alternative to the singles scene.

Experts

Most likely, experts will be directly involved in the issue you are arguing. It's important to use both experts who support your claim and experts you disagree with because it will result in a more accurate and balanced argument. If you use experts who favour the other side, ensure you represent them accurately and fairly.

Examples and Illustrations

Using examples—specific instances or cases—can make a general claim more concrete and understandable, enabling the reader to relate to it. An illustration could take the form of an *anecdote* (a brief informal story) or other expanded example. Joe Castalado begins "Steal Your Success" by giving an example of a CEO who was unconcerned when a rival imitated one of his company's innovations (p. 256). Castalado then uses a reversal strategy to suggest that he *should*, in fact, have been concerned.

Anecdotal Evidence

Although anecdotal evidence is not "hard evidence," it can be convincing. For instance, if you are arguing that fighting in hockey should be banned but cannot find enough studies on this topic, you may seek the opinions of coaches or hockey players who can comment on their own situations or others they have heard about. Sometimes, anecdotal evidence is combined with hard evidence to give a human dimension to which the reader can relate.

Anecdotal evidence is suggestive rather than conclusive. It is often based on reliable observation.

Precedents

In law, a precedent is an important kind of example, a ruling that can apply to subsequent cases that involve similar facts or issues. To *set a precedent* means to establish a method for dealing with future cases. In argument, using a precedent—the way something was done in the past—can be particularly effective in policy claims. To use a precedent, you must show that:

A **precedent** is a specific example that refers to the way a situation was dealt with in the past in order to argue for its similar use in the present.

1. The current situation (what you are arguing) is similar to that of the precedent.
2. Following the precedent will be beneficial.

For example, when arguing for the use of renewable energy sources, Jim Harris in "The UnAtomic Age" refers to programs known as Feed-In-Tariff [FIT] that reward creators and users of efficient alternative energy sources. He argues that its proven benefits in more than 50 countries are reasons why such a program could be implemented in Canada (p. 203). Of course, you can use a precedent as a negative example as well, showing that what you are proposing has not produced benefits in the past.

Precedents can be used effectively in arguing controversial issues, such as decriminalizing marijuana or prostitution, providing universal access to post-secondary education, or justifying safe injection sites in urban areas.

If you use personal experience, you should stress the ways that it has been a learning experience for you and, therefore, could be for the reader, too. Personal experience alone will not usually produce a good argument.

Personal Experience

The occasional use of personal experience in argumentative essays can be a way to involve your reader. In some cases, it can also increase your credibility. For example, if you have worked with street people, you may be well qualified to argue a claim about homelessness.

Personal experience could be direct experience, observing something first-hand or reporting something that happened to a friend. However, simply announcing that you experienced something and benefited by it does not necessarily make your argument stronger. For example, saying that you enjoyed physical education classes in high school is not going to convince many people that it should be a required subject in schools.

If you use personal experience, you should stress the ways that it has been a learning experience for you. The following introduction serves as a compelling set-up for the carefully phrased value claim (italicized).

> To most people, my brother, Terry, is just another face on a bus. For me, he is both the inspiration for this paper, and my brother and friend. When Terry was a child, he was diagnosed with autism, a disorder within the Autism Spectrum Disorders (ASDS). While all the other children were stuffing themselves with candy, Terry was "getting his fix" from hockey cards and statistics. At a very young age, he had memorized the statistics of all the major NHL players; for him, hockey was a form of escape. Terry is one of many in North America, where autism is one of the fastest growing but least known developmental disorders. A central question for parents and caregivers of autistic children is the type of education that offers the greatest benefits, an inclusive or exclusive one. Each system has its advantages and drawbacks, making this choice far from simple. However, *an inclusive educational system offers the best hope for those with the disorder to become well-adjusted individuals as well as contributing members of society.* (student writer Alex McLeod)

Facts, Statistics, and Scientific Studies

Policy claims often benefit from factual support. Make sure, however, that all factual data are accurate and clearly presented. Use the most current statistics from the most reliable sources. Referring to an outdated fact, statistic, or study can damage your credibility. Be wary of sources that do not reveal where the facts they cite come from or the methods used to obtain them (see pp. 76–77). Sources need to be acknowledged in your essay. (See "Documenting Your Sources," p. 83).

Two Kinds of Reasoning

Two methods of reasoning are inductive and deductive reasoning. Knowing the differences between them will help you understand how a writer is using reason. Similarly, using one method—or, more likely both—will help you build a stronger argument.

In **inductive reasoning**, you arrive at a conclusion by observing and recording occurrences. Flaws in inductive reasoning can occur if (1) not enough observations have been made—that is, if there is not enough evidence to draw a conclusion, or (2) if the method for gathering the evidence is faulty.

> **Inductive reasoning** relies on facts, details, and observations to form a conclusion.

Researchers, therefore, try to include as large a sample as possible within the population they draw from, making their findings more reliable. Similarly, researchers reveal the details about their experiment. They need to show that their evidence-gathering methods are unbiased.

While inductive reasoning works from detail to generalization, **deductive reasoning** begins with a generalization, a major premise assumed to be true. A second premise, which is a subset or instance of the major premise, is then applied to the major premise. If both statements are true and logically related, the conclusion follows as true.

> **Deductive reasoning** is based on a generalization, which is applied to a specific example or subset to form a conclusion.
>
> A **syllogism** is a logical three-part structure that can illustrate how deductive conclusions are made.

The deductive reasoning method can be set up as a **syllogism**, a three-part structure that illustrates how deductive reasoning works in forming conclusions. Syllogisms have very complex applications in logic and mathematics. However, in its simple form, the syllogism can show the validity of a conclusion. The conclusion of the following two premises is true because both premises are true and logically related.

Major premise: All students who wish to apply for admission to the college must submit their grade transcripts.

Minor premise: Saki wishes to apply for admission to the college.

Conclusion: Saki must submit her grade transcripts.

Using Reason in Arguments

Whatever the purpose in arguing—whether to defend your view, expose a problem, or reach a compromise—getting the reader to agree with your premises, or claims, is vital. It is also vital to make a neutral or hostile reader consider what you have to say. This is why it is important to use specific strategies like concessions and appeals to common ground. Emotional and ethical appeals are useful argumentative strategies as well (see below, p. 48). *But most successful arguments begin and end with your effective use of reason.*

However, reason can be misused in arguments. Consider the following statements: the first illustrates the misuse of inductive reasoning because there isn't enough evidence to justify the conclusion; the second illustrates the misuse of deductive reasoning because a false premise has resulted in a faulty conclusion. Avoiding logical fallacies (failures in reasoning) in your own essays and pointing them out in the arguments of others makes your arguments stronger and more credible.

> Avoiding logical fallacies (failures in reasoning) in your own essays and pointing them out in the arguments of others make your arguments stronger and more credible.

1.   The premier broke a promise he made during his election campaign.
     He is a liar, and his word can no longer be trusted.

Should you distrust a politician because he broke one pre-election promise? If the premier broke several promises, there would be much stronger grounds for the conclusion. In most people's minds, therefore, there is not enough inductive evidence to prove the claim.

2.   Eduardo is the only one in our family who has an MA. He's obviously
     the one who inherited all the brains.

Does having an MA always indicate intelligence? Possessing an advanced degree *could* be a measure of intelligence. It could also indicate persistence, a fascination with a particular subject, a love of learning, inspiring teachers, an ambitious nature, strong financial and/or familial support, and so on. The general claim—that having an MA shows your intelligence—is therefore misleading or flawed.

Using your critical thinking skills will help you identify faulty arguments. (See below and Chapter 7 on critical thinking.)

Failures in Reasoning

Just as we engage in different kinds of argument every day—from arguments over whose turn it is to clean up to arguments about sports, politics, or other topics we are passionate about—so we often make errors in our reasoning. The most common kind is rationalizing. Indeed, procrastination is a form of rationalizing in which you constantly make delays appear reasonable.

When you rationalize, you construct a framework for argument to hide the absence of one, substituting a convenient or invalid claim (see the "straw man fallacy" in Table 4.2, which uses similar reasoning)—for example, "I can't babysit my young brother tonight because I have an important test tomorrow." Perhaps you did not intend to study much for the test—or you could easily study while babysitting your brother, an option you don't consider. The claim, then, masks the simple fact that you don't want to babysit.

Logical Fallacies

In writing, logical errors tend to be more subtle. They fall into several categories, termed logical fallacies. It is not necessary to be able to categorize every failure in logic in order to argue effectively or spot weak arguments. Most errors are the result of sloppy or simplistic thinking—the failure to do justice to a complex issue. Developing your critical thinking skills will alert you to errors of logic. Ten examples of faulty reasoning follow.

Logical fallacies are categories of faulty reasoning.

TABLE 4.2   Ten Common Logical Fallacies

Term	Description	Examples
Certain conse-quences ("slippery slope")	A common fallacy (with other names) concluding that a result is inevitable based on an oversimplified cause–effect relationship	"If we legalize marijuana, other, more dangerous drugs are going to end up being legalized as well."
Circular argument	An argument based on an unproved assumption, as if it didn't need proving	"If *Sesame Street* was such a good show, where is the wave of geniuses out there?" The unproven assumption is that the program was designed to create geniuses instead of to stimulate children's interest in learning.
Either/or (false choice)	Asks reader to choose between two possibilities, one obviously better than the other	"If you don't get a college degree, you might as well resign yourself to low-paying jobs."
False analogy	Compares two things that are, in fact, not alike (while true analogies can provide support for a point, to draw a true analogy, there must be a real basis for comparison)	"How can people complain about circuses that use wild animals in their acts? We keep animals, such as cats, that were once wild in small spaces in our homes."
False cause (post hoc)	A cause–effect fallacy that asserts that simply because one event preceded another, there must be a cause–effect relationship between them	"I've lost two items in the last week, which is when our new roommate arrived. He must have stolen them." Here the recent arrival of a roommate is judged cause for suspicion. If one of the items was found in the roommate's room, such a conclusion would be more reasonable.
Confirmation bias	Selects evidence solely on the basis that the results or argument matches one's own, ignoring contradictory results or arguments (sometimes called "cherry-picking")	"I found three sources who argue that 9/11 was really a US government conspiracy; that should be enough to prove my thesis." Here the writer has looked for extreme arguments on one side of the issue and ignored contrary explanations. The best arguer looks at opposing views and explains their weaknesses.
Straw man	Misrepresents an opponent's main argument by putting a minor or simpli-fied argument in its place, then attacks the minor argument	"My roommate doesn't go out on Friday nights. He doesn't know how to enjoy his life at college, and I'm going to enjoy mine!"
Hasty generalization	Uses too few examples or other evidence to support a conclusion (generalization)	"This is the coldest January in five years. So much for the threat of global warming."
"It does not follow"	Suggests that there is a logical connection (such as cause–effect) between two unrelated areas	"I worked hard on this essay; I deserve at least a B+." Working hard at some-thing does not guarantee success, even if it makes it more likely.
Red herring	A fallacy of irrelevance that attempts to distract or sidetrack the reader, often by using an ethical fallacy	"My honourable opponent's business went bankrupt. How can we trust him to run the country?"

[handwritten: Propter hoc]

Emotional and Ethical Fallacies

Fallacies may also make exaggerated or unfair appeals to a reader's emotions or sense of ethics. They are very different, then, from legitimate appeals to emotion. Similarly, using highly charged language often attempts to inflame, rather than inform and convince the reader.

Emotional and ethical fallacies are statements that appeal to a reader's emotions in a manipulative or unfair way, such as a partisan appeal, name-calling (*ad hominem*), guilt by association, or dogmatism (simply asserting something without offering proof—often, over and over). The *bandwagon* fallacy argues in favour of something because it has become popular. It is sometimes used to support an ethically questionable practice, such as "Illegal downloading is okay; everyone does it."

> *Emotional fallacy:* You have to buy the latest iPhone app. Everyone else has it.

The *ad hominem* fallacy directly attacks the arguer rather than the argument, while the *guilt by association* fallacy argues that something is unacceptable because a supposedly disreputable person or group favours it.

> How bad can whale hunting be when an extremist group like Greenpeace opposes it?

Effective arguers also avoid slanted language, negative language used to dismiss an opponent's claims. Simply characterizing an opponent as "ignorant" or "greedy" serves no constructive purpose. Of course, you may be able to show through unbiased evidence that the opponent has demonstrated these characteristics.

Argumentative Strategies

Although effective arguments depend on reasonable claims supported by convincing evidence, logic alone will not necessarily convince readers to change their minds or adopt the writer's point of view. You should consider using the following strategies, depending on topic, purpose, and audience, to shape a logical and appealing argument, one that will make readers accept your claim.

1. **Dramatic introduction:** A dramatic introduction may enable the reader to relate to a human situation (see Chapter 1, p. 9). The introductory paragraph in the essay on autism (see p. 43) illustrates a dramatic introduction.
2. **Establishing** common ground: Getting your readers to see that you share many of their values enables you to come across as open and approachable.

Emotional and ethical fallacies appeal to the emotions in a manipulative or unfair way, such as a partisan appeal, guilt by association, name-calling, or bandwagon.

Slanted language is extreme or accusatory language, which can make an arguer seem biased.

Establishing **common ground** is an argumentative strategy in which you show readers that you share many of their values, making you appear open and approachable.

Although familiarity with your audience is important in knowing where your values and those of your audience intersect, you can assume that most readers value generosity, decency, security, and a healthy and peaceful environment. Rogerian arguments stress areas of agreement between arguer and audience (see p. 35).

3. **Making a concession:** When you acknowledge the validity of an opposing point, you show your fairness. After conceding a point, you should follow with a strong point of your own. In effect, you are giving some ground to get your reader to do the same. The concession can be made in a dependent clause and your own point in the independent clause that follows.

> "Although it is valid to say . . . [concession is made], the fact is . . . [your point]."

Concessions can be vital in cases in which there is strong opposition or in which you wish to reach a compromise. Knowing that most people associate antibiotics with saving lives, Aviva Romm begins her essay "Stop Killing the Good Guys!" by conceding their benefits before pointing out their dangers (p. 231).

4. **Emotional and ethical appeals:** While dramatic openings can be successful in many argumentative essays, the success of an opening that includes an appeal to emotion depends on your audience. Beginning an essay on animal testing by describing a scene of caged animals at a slaughterhouse may alienate neutral readers. If you do use such an opening, you need to ensure that a typical reader will respond in the way you wish.

Emotional and ethical appeals, however, are commonly used in essay conclusions, enabling the audience to reflect on the topic. The following conclusion, from an essay about the riots in Vancouver after a Stanley Cup final game, includes both emotional and ethical appeals. The final two sentences also demonstrate the common ground strategy.

> Wouldn't it be preferable to live in a society in which we actually knew our neighbours to begin with? To know and trust the people around us to act like responsible individuals? To enjoy a culture of mutual respect rather than suspicion, hyper-competition, and meaningless interaction mediated through our phones and iPads?
>
> . . . There was a beautiful outpouring of love and support for our fair city this morning as hundreds of volunteers took to the streets to help clean up the terrible mess from last night. We do have the capacity to be kind, gentle, thoughtful individuals, and, hopefully, we can begin to repair the damage to our tarnished reputation. (Adrian Mack and Miranda Nelson, "Vancouver Hockey Riot Is a Symptom of a Larger Problem," p. 186)

Making a concession is an argumentative strategy in which you concede or qualify a point, acknowledging its validity, in order to come across as fair and reasonable.

Emotional and ethical appeals call forth the emotions and morals of your reader. They work best when they are subtle and not extreme.

In the cases of neutral or opposing viewpoints, emotional and ethical appeals work best when they are subtle, not extreme.

5. **Definition:** Value claims often rely on definition (i.e., explaining what you mean by something). Carefully defining something may give it authority. Then, using logic and various kinds of evidence, you can show that your claim is valid because it supports the definition. More subtly, Nik Harron begins his essay, "Fully Destructible," by citing a brief, somewhat humorous definition of video gaming as "the voluntary attempt to overcome unnecessary obstacles." This leads into a discussion of the pros and cons of gaming before Harron introduces one surprising benefit of gaming (p. 214).

6. **Comparisons:** Some topics have a compare–contrast component built in, for example, arguing that it is better to live on campus than off campus or vice versa. For other topics, comparisons can provide strong support for a claim. Remember that comparisons require a valid basis. If you are arguing that professional athletes today are overpaid, comparing today's multi-million dollar salaries to the salaries of North American athletes in the 1920s would not be valid, owing to many factors, including inflationary ones and the additional income available today in endorsements. However, it could be valid to compare an average athlete's salary to the average salary of another working professional today, such as a doctor or lawyer.

In her essay, "Giving up the Ghost," Lynn Cunningham compares the attitude toward smoking in her youth to the attitude today.

> At the time, nearly half of Canadian adults were smokers, and in that *Mad Men* era you could light up just about anywhere—planes, banks, movie theatres, even doctors' offices and hospital rooms . . . . These days, though, the 16 per cent of us who still smoke daily are the ones beyond the pale. (p. 171)

(For a list of essays using comparison, see the inside front cover.)

7. **Appeal to reader interests:** When you appeal to the interests of your readers, you show how they might be affected by your claim. In a policy claim, you might highlight the practical advantages of adopting the policy or the disadvantages of not adopting it. For example, arguing for a costly social program may be a hard sell to those whose support is vital, such as business leaders. Therefore, you could explain how the program could help them by preventing a bigger problem, such as increased health-care costs. If you know the values and motivations of your readers, you may be able to use this knowledge to make your points directly relevant to them.

A way to appeal to the interests of an undecided reader is to offer acceptable options. While not conceding your point, you show that you are flexible and open to alternatives. For example, after arguing against the routine use of antibiotics, Aviva Romm proposes what she considers healthier alternatives in "Stop Killing the Good Guys!" (see p. 231).

When you appeal to the interests of your readers, you show how they might be affected by your claim.

Visual Arguments

Arguments do not always take a verbal form. If you spend much time on social media or just browsing the Internet, you are likely exposed to dozens or more visual arguments a day.

The variety of visual arguments is considerable, but so is the possibility of manipulation or even outright dishonesty. Everyone today—traditional readers and Internet users alike—needs to use their knowledge of how arguments work in order to interpret them correctly to avoid being "taken in" by emotional or logical fallacies. The need for critical thinking is imperative.

Advertisements are examples of arguments that are partly or, sometimes, entirely comprised of images designed to persuade members of their target audience. Like all arguments with policy claims (see p. 39), they seek to change behaviour or advocate a specific action. A common strategy, then, is appeals to reader (viewer) interests, as in the first example below.

"Last Best West" was a catchy phrase used to market the Canadian west to European immigrants, including the British, in the early 1900s. The use of "Homes," rather than "Land for Millions," makes a subtle emotional appeal to those, perhaps, who currently lack a true home, the kind of people who might consider immigration.

The viewer's eye naturally goes to the idyllic image at the centre of the ad, and to the approaching team of horses. The orderly hayricks (middle left) suggest productivity, while the standing grain to the right conveys potential. In the distance farm buildings are glimpsed. The concept of infinite space would appeal to immigrants, possibly living in crowded cities.

More subtly, the image is framed by an oval mirror or looking glass, inviting the viewer to infer a connection between an image seen in a mirror (i.e., of one's self) and the prosperity suggested by the scene itself. The image and frame are designed to appeal to viewer interests.

The maple leaf has long been a Canadian icon. Here, the cluster of leaves suggests abundance, while the diagonal gives depth and dimension to an otherwise flat perspective. Finally, the base of the mirror might suggest an Aladdin's lamp of desire.

Photo National Archives of Canada C-30620

This ad was part of a campaign to attract settlers to the Canadian west. The marketing strategy was so successful that two new Canadian provinces were soon created, Saskatchewan and Alberta. The annotations identify features, both verbal and visual, that help to convey the argument.

EXERCISE 4.2

After reflecting on the more recent ad below, use the questions to guide you, and, in at least one or two well-developed paragraphs, analyze audience and argumentative purpose, as well as specific features that appeal to the intended audience.

Lakeridge Health, lakeridgehealth.on.ca

1. When you look at this ad, where does your attention first go? What other parts of the ad stand out? Why? What seems least important?
2. Which stands out more: graphics or text? Both equally?
3. What is the purpose of the ad? (i.e., what argument does it propose?)
4. What audience is it intended mainly to reach? Is there a secondary audience? (There might be a very specific viewer intended, but it could be designed for more general viewers as well.)
5. Look closely at the image. Human faces and body language can be used to communicate subtle messages and/or generate specific emotions. Is this true here?

(continued)

6. Look closely at the text. How does it reflect audience and purpose? How does it work with the graphic element?

7. An ad may directly or indirectly challenge opposing viewpoints and, therefore, act as a rebuttal (see below, p. 52). Does this ad do this? How?

8. Does the ad make logical, emotional, or ethical appeals? Are other argumentative strategies used, such as appeals to reader interests or common ground?

COLLABORATIVE EXERCISE 4.3

The controversial image below, used by the Vancouver Humane Society shortly before the start of the 2012 Calgary Stampede, depends both on its impact and its verbal impact. Analyze the effectiveness of the argument. You could begin by looking at which of the strategies (above) are used and then considering questions like the following:

1. What are the strengths of the argument?
2. What are its weaknesses—e.g., fallacies?
3. How could audience affect the way the "message" is received?
4. Overall, does it satisfy the requirements of a successful argument as discussed in this chapter? Why or why not?

Vancouver Humane Society

Rebuttal Strategies

Since the existence of an opposing viewpoint is usually needed for an argumentative claim, you should refer to it directly in your essay—otherwise, it may appear that you are avoiding it. Although you may use concessions as part of your argument, you will mostly be concerned with refuting the competing claims. In your rebuttal, or *refutation*, you show the weaknesses or limitations of these claims.

> **Rebuttal** is an argumentative strategy of raising opposing points in order to counter them with your own points.

Here are three general strategies to consider. Which one you use depends on the three factors that you need to take into account when planning your argumentative essay: your topic, purpose, and audience. There may be additional factors involved too, such as essay length.

Strategy 1: Acknowledgement

If the argument on the other side is straightforward or obvious, you may need to do no more than acknowledge it. For example, acknowledgement would be a natural choice if the claim argued against the use of pesticides in lawn maintenance. The opposing view is obvious: lawn owners use pesticides to make their lawns look attractive. After acknowledging the competing claim, the writer would go on to raise counter points without necessarily referring to the other side again.

> Rebuttals can range from simply acknowledging the opposing viewpoint, to focusing on one or two main opposing points, to presenting a point-by-point critique. The rebuttal strategy you choose depends on your topic, your purpose in arguing, and your audience.

Occasionally, there may not be a recognizable opposing view to acknowledge. For example, if your argumentative purpose is to raise awareness of an important issue, as Andrew D. Pinto does in "Denaturalizing 'Natural' Disasters" (p. 307), there may be no clear view to refute. He is not refuting the importance of international aid but arguing that developing countries need to acknowledge historical realities before Haiti's problems can be addressed.

Strategy 2: Limited Rebuttal

In a limited rebuttal, you raise and respond to some major point(s) on the other side, then follow with your own points. This strategy may be appropriate if the strength of the opposing view depends on one or two major claims. You would not want to undermine your claim by raising and refuting less important issues unless you are trying to reach a compromise when both strengths and weaknesses might be considered. When you analyze the main argument on the other side, however, it is important to do so fairly.

Whether you adopt the limited rebuttal strategy can depend on your audience and purpose for arguing. For example, if your audience is not very knowledgeable about an issue, mentioning less important points on the other side might be counterproductive since the readers might not have been aware of them.

Strategy 3: Full Rebuttal

There are two ways to organize a full rebuttal:

1. You may raise competing claims and respond to them one at a time (*point-by-point rebuttal*).
2. You could summarize the competing claims—after your introduction, for example—before you present the support for your claim (*block rebuttal*).

Point-by-point rebuttals can be very effective if the opposing points are well known, such as essays debating common topics like capital punishment or legalizing marijuana, or if your readers strongly disagree with you. For example, since Bruce M. Hicks expects many to see his proposal of an "11th province" for Aboriginal peoples as radical or extreme, he carefully anticipates objections and responds to them separately (see pp. 296–7).

If you are responding to a viewpoint in a specific text or if your argumentative purpose is to reach a compromise, you might also choose to use the point-by-point strategy. In the last instance, however, you would attempt to reach out to the other side (or both sides), showing that you understand their points. This strategy would demonstrate your knowledge and fairness.

Organizing Your Argument

Before you begin an outline, you should decide on the order of your points. For most argumentative essays, this means choosing between two orders: the **climax order** or a **mixed order**. In the first, you begin with the weakest point and build toward the strongest. In the second, you could begin with a strong point—but not the strongest—follow with weaker points, and conclude with the strongest. It may not be advisable to begin with the weakest point, if your audience opposes your claim, since an initial weak point may make your readers believe your entire argument is weak.

Other orders are also possible. For example, if you are arguing to reach a compromise, you might need to focus the first part of your essay on one side of the debate, the second part on the opposite side, and the third on your compromise solution. Whatever order you use, it should be identical to the order of points in your thesis statement.

A good strategy is to outline the points on the other side before writing your essay. In particular, consider how someone who disagrees with your claim might respond to your main points. This could reveal the strengths on the other side and any weaknesses in your own argument. More important, perhaps, it will keep the opposing view in focus as you write, causing you to reflect carefully on what you are saying and how you say it.

The most thorough rebuttal is a full rebuttal in which you raise opposing views before countering them. In a limited rebuttal, you raise only the major claims on the other side, ignoring minor claims the reader may not be aware of.

Climax order is the order of points that proceeds from the weakest to the strongest. Other orders include inverse climax order and **mixed order**.

COLLABORATIVE EXERCISE 4.4

Considering your audience is important as you prepare to write an argumentative essay. Constructing an audience plan enables you to consider your approach to the essay, including the most effective strategies to use. Choose a topic you would like to argue, then team up with two other students and interview the other members of your group to determine (1) their knowledge level, (2) their interest level, and (3) their orientation (agree, disagree, neutral, or mixed) toward your topic; these group members serve as your "audience," the basis for an audience profile. Then, use this information to construct an audience plan based on your specific audience profile, your topic, and argumentative purpose. Discuss strategies you would use to persuade this audience. Include your topic and your writing purpose in the plan.

Scan the following essay in order to determine its argumentative purpose and its intended audience before subjecting it to a focused reading. The annotations refer to material discussed in this and previous chapters. Kirsten uses APA documentation style (see p. 85). For another example of a student essay that uses APA style, see p. 92.

Sample Student Argumentative Essay with Annotations

Cultural Appropriation: How Racism Became Trendy

By Kirsten Saikaly

[1] *The Oxford English Dictionary* defines racism as follows: "Prejudice, discrimination, or antagonism directed against someone of a different race based on the belief that one's own race is superior." In spite of strides in overcoming some of the more blatant forms of racism, it continues to be a part of our society. However, the definition of what exactly constitutes racism has become blurred, making it more difficult for us to recognize it or know what it really means—especially in its more subtle forms (Winant, 1998, p. 757). One of the most prevalent and problematic examples of this would be the practice of cultural appropriation, especially among white teenagers. Cultural appropriation is essentially the adoption of a minority culture's traditions or practices by the dominant culture, without regard to or respect for the cultural or historical significance associated with its traditions (Edwards & Coffey, 2010). We see cultural appropriation becoming especially prevalent among youth, as many have little to no understanding of the racist consequences of their actions. Many feel that in wearing culturally significant articles such as a bindi or the Palestinian kaffiyeh, or in using dance moves or language traditionally found in a minority culture, they are simply adhering to what's "trending."

Kirsten's title is informative and direct. It uses the two-part format common in academic essays.

The brief concession here also serves as a transition linking the sentences that precede and follow.

Kirsten defines two terms in her introduction. Why do you think she might have used direct quotation for the first term and paraphrase for the second one? (For the differences between direct quotation and paraphrase, see Chapter 5, pp. 77–80.)

Kirsten's thesis follows logically from the preceding sentences. However, check with your instructor before you use the first person in your thesis. Here it could be easily rephrased to avoid the first person.

Following up on definitions in the first paragraph, Kirsten carefully contrasts cultural appropriation and cultural appreciation. As in the first paragraph, she is establishing key concepts important for the development of her body paragraphs.

Paragraphs 3 and 4 begin with question prompts (see p. 144) followed by the topic sentence. After the writer gives an example (probably based on her own knowledge), she leaves it to an expert to explain the significance of Cyrus' behaviour. Throughout this and the next paragraph, she develops points that the expert makes, using critical thinking to explore the topic thoroughly.

In reality, participation in these acts can serve to propagate a culture of casual racism. Through the analysis of trends in popular culture and fashion as well as academic literature on the subject, I will examine how both a lack of education and awareness about the implications of cultural appropriation create a culture of casual racism among many of today's youth.

[2]   When discussing cultural appropriation, it is important to note the difference between appropriation and appreciation. Whereas cultural appropriation is an act of ignorance and disregard for the importance associated with a specific culture, cultural appreciation, also known as cultural exchange, comes from a place of respect. For example, if a member of a minority culture invites you to participate in a culturally significant occasion or event, and you do so in a respectful manner which does not undermine the traditions of the culture, this would be considered cultural appreciation, and thus would not be considered a racist act (*Everyday Feminism*, 2013). Unfortunately, many instances we see in youth culture are closer to appropriation than appreciation.

[3]   How does cultural appropriation arise? Celebrities tend to be some of the most common offenders when it comes to appropriation. Miley Cyrus recently came under fire after the release of her music video for the song "We Can't Stop" and its blatant appropriation of black culture. In an interview with *Vice* in 2013, Ohio University's African American Studies professor Akil Houston stated that "within commodity culture, ethnicity becomes like spice seasoning. It is used to liven up the dull dish that is mainstream/white culture. The distinction is important, as I think authentic images and references affirm, acknowledge, and embrace a particular culture." Houston also discussed Cyrus' use of the black actors who appeared in the video as accessories rather than as people. This dehumanization is another key aspect of cultural appropriation: by stripping those whose culture is being appropriated of their status as equals, it becomes easier to convince oneself that what they are doing is not damaging. Youth can be particularly sensitive to the behaviour of celebrities, especially with the attention the media gives celebrities today. With messages similar to the one being sent by Cyrus in the forefront of the minds of today's youths, it is understandable that many teens become influenced by this behaviour.

[4]   So what is the key to preventing the spread of this kind of racism among youth? Houston has what is perhaps the easiest and

most controversial answer: acknowledge white privilege. When youth are taught about racism in school, it is almost exclusively seen as an issue that creates disadvantages for those who are oppressed by it. What is not discussed, however, is the way that racism puts white people at an advantage. These advantages are reflected in almost every aspect of life, including the ability to move to a new area without fear of feeling unwelcome, the constant portrayal of white people in a positive light in the media, and the advantages white people often have in hiring decisions and in access to higher education. These advantages are classified as white privilege, and, frequently, white people are not taught to recognize it (McIntosh, 1990). In this way, a lack of awareness, especially among youth, is the driving force that allows cultural appropriation to continue. However, it is clear that when youth are educated about white privilege, they are significantly more likely to make positive changes that can promote the realities of racial inequality.

[5]   A concept associated with white privilege is the ideology of "colour-blindness." Jason Rodriquez (2006) explains colour-blind ideology as "abstract, liberal notions of equality ('equal opportunity for all') to disconnect race from the power relations in which inequality and racial discourses are embedded" (p. 646). Both white privilege and colour-blindness allow white youth to participate in minority cultures as much or as little as they might like. It might be described as a sort of "à la carte" type of minority status in which they are able to choose to adopt the portions of the minority culture that they consider trendy and leave those which would put them at a disadvantage in our society. An efficient example of young people using their white privilege to appropriate a part of another culture manifested itself recently at the popular music festival Coachella. One of the most popular fashion "trends" at the festival was wearing bindis, which are traditionally worn by those from countries in parts of southeast region Asia. Many young celebrities were spotted wearing them, including Kendall and Kyle Jenner, Vanessa Hudgens, Kate Bosworth, and Sarah Hyland (CBC, 2014). The appropriation of bindis by young, non-minority celebrities illustrates how these young people are unable to recognize their own white privilege. While for the Jenner sisters wearing a bindi to a festival such as Coachella represents no more than a fashion choice and has no other repercussions, for those to whom it is culturally significant, wearing a bindi in public goes far

In this well-developed paragraph, Kirsten refers to two different kinds of sources, the first an academic one and the second non-academic. The absence of citations in the last two sentences shows that the points are Kirsten's own, a product of her critical thinking skills.

beyond fashion into their traditions and cultural values. Also, for those of southeast heritage, wearing a bindi in public is likely to bring about racist or race-centric comments or sentiments from those around them, perpetuating the cycle of racism.

[6]   Cultural appropriation and white privilege as well as the colour-blind ideology have contributed to the creation of the state of "casual racism" we currently live in. Casual racism, also known as "racism lite" or "racism with a smile," denotes a type of racism that is not outwardly violent or hateful, yet is still oppressive and stems from the same root sentiments associated with what we traditionally think of racism of the past (Zamudio & Rios, 2006, p. 483). Through cultural appropriation, racial jokes, and other seemingly harmless methods of oppression, white people are able to continue benefiting from their privilege while still maintaining the stance that racism is an issue of the past that we need not be concerned with today. This pattern of seemingly "harmless" racism presents itself among youth not only through cultural appropriation but also through a general lack of sensitivity to how their actions are perceived. In "Five Young Teens Talk about Racism," by Andrea Neblett (cited in O'Neil, 2005), a 14-year-old boy from Quebec stated,

> Sometimes I don't think kids are trying to be mean; they're trying to be funny. Most people are racist or bullies because it comes from TV or the media. They don't necessarily believe black people are stupid or ghetto rappers—but those are the images they see on TV. (p. 1)

[7]   This statement suggests, first, that the media and the actions of those in the public eye, such as Miley Cyrus or those who made culturally appropriative fashion choices at Coachella, have a direct influence on the perception and implementation of casual racism among youth. Second, it suggests that youth fail to understand how damaging casual racism can be, or that they are partaking in it at all. The boy's statements can be applied to many different situations if you replace the word "funny" with words like "fashionable" or "cool." It is imperative that teens need to be better educated about cultural appropriation and what underlies it if we have any hope of putting an end to this cycle of casual racism.

[8]   In many ways, we live in a more enlightened age than those of previous generations. For example, we have made strides as a nation in acknowledging issues related to the colonial appropriation of Aboriginal peoples—though we still have far to go. Although physical appropriation is clear to see, embedded in outdated institutions and

---

Having explained concepts related to cultural appropriation and given examples, Kirsten now focuses on its wider significance and relevance in contemporary culture.

The writer makes an ethical appeal highlighting the need for education to help end casual racism.

Kirsten begins her conclusion with a concession. She uses other argumentative strategies in this paragraph, including ethical and emotional appeals. She ends by trying to establish common ground with the reader, getting him or her to acknowledge that cultural diversity is a goal to which Canadians aspire.

attitudes, cultural appropriation is more subtle. Its rise in recent years, however, is not difficult to explain: the notion of colour-blind ideology as well as the unwillingness to recognize white privilege fosters an environment of casual racism in which appropriation thrives undetected. In order to prevent these behaviours from trickling down to the next generation, it is imperative that we educate our youth in the realities of white privilege and racism, and that we show them that no matter how harmless their intentions may be, racism is racism, whether or not it is fashionable. The result will be a more prominent cultural diversity in which we view our neighbours as equals in all senses, uniquely contributing to the fabric of our everyday lives.

> In her conclusion, Kirsten stresses two terms given importance in the body paragraphs. This shows she is concerned with much more than simply rephrasing her thesis, in which neither of these terms appear.

References

Cooper, W. (2013, June 27). Miley Cyrus needs to take an African American studies class. Retrieved from www.vice.com/en_ca/read/miley-cyrus-needs-to-take-an-african-american-studies-class

Edwards, C. L., & Coffey, D. (2010). Cultural appropriation: A rose by any other name. *PsycCRITIQUES*, *55*(15). doi:10.1037/a0018623

McIntosh, P. (1990). White privilege: Unpacking the invisible knapsack. *Multiculturalism*, *49*, 30–36. doi:10.1080/14725880701859969

Neblett, A. (2005, 11). Five young teens talk about racism. *Today's Parent*, *22*, 120–126. Retrieved from http://search.proquest.com.ezproxy.library.uvic.ca/docview/232892690?accountid=14846

O'Neil, L. (2014, April 14). Celebrity bindis at Coachella: Fashion trend or cultural appropriation? *Your Community*. Retrieved from www.cbc.ca/newsblogs/yourcommunity/2014/04/celebrity-bindis-at-coachella-fashion-trend-or-cultural-appropriation.html

Rodriquez, J. (2006). Color-blind ideology and the cultural appropriation of hip-hop. *Journal of Contemporary Ethnography*, *35*, 645–658. doi:10.1177/0891241606286997

Uwujaren, J. (2013, September 30). The difference between cultural exchange and cultural appropriation. Retrieved from http://everydayfeminism.com/2013/09/cultural-exchange-and-cultural-appropriation/

Winant, H. (1998). Racism today: Continuity and change in the post-civil rights era. *Ethnic and Racial Studies*, *21*(4), 755–766. doi:10.1080/014198798329856

Zamudio, M. M., & Rios, F. (2006). From traditional to liberal racism: Living racism in the everyday. *Sociological Perspectives*, *49*, 483–501. doi:10.1525/sop.2006.49.4.483

Chapter 4 Review Questions

1. Describe two features applicable to argument that have been developed by each of the following:
    a) Aristotle
    b) Rogers
    c) Toulmin

2. Choosing two of the argumentative purposes listed on p. 38 and two topics, come up with a simple thesis statement for each that reflects the argumentative purpose.

3. Explain the differences between an opinion, a fact, and the interpretation of a fact.

4. a) Why might *claim* be a better word than *thesis* in argument?
    b) Identify two kinds of claims in argument.

5. What is needed for a valid claim (thesis) in an argumentative essay? What two other factors could affect the validity of your claim?

6. When might you choose to use the following in an argumentative essay?
    a) Anecdotal evidence
    b) Personal experience

7. What two steps are necessary to ensure that you use a precedent effectively?

8. The kind of reasoning that depends on the truth of a general statement is called _____ reasoning. The kind of reasoning that depends on observation and measurement is called _____ reasoning.

9. a) In your own words, define *logical fallacy*.
    b) For two of the logical fallacies discussed in Table 4.2 (p. 46), come up with one example of your own that illustrates the fallacy.

10. How is an emotional or ethical fallacy different from an emotional or ethical appeal?

11. Write a sentence that contains an example of slanted language. Suggest two substitutes for the word or phrase that would result in a sentence without bias.

12. Answer true or false:
    a) Making a concession weakens your argument.
    b) When you appeal to reader interests, you try to get the reader interested enough to read on.
    c) Emotional and ethical appeals usually work best when they are not extreme or exaggerated.

13. What is a rebuttal, and when is it needed in an argument? In which case(s) might it be unnecessary?

14. Explain the difference between a limited and a full rebuttal. When might a limited rebuttal be a better choice than a full rebuttal?

15. What does the order of points in an argument refer to?

Key Terms

anecdotal evidence (p. 42)

arguable claim (p. 39)

audience (p. 34)

climax order (p. 54)

common ground (p. 47)

concession (p. 48)

deductive reasoning (p. 44)

emotional and ethical fallacies (p. 47)

ethos (p. 34)

inductive reasoning (p. 44)

logical fallacies (p. 45)

logos (p. 34)

mixed order (p. 54)

pathos (p. 34)

policy claim (p. 39)

precedent (p. 42)

rebuttal (p. 53)

rhetoric (p. 34)

slanted language (p. 47)

syllogism (p. 44)

value claim (p. 39)

warrant (p. 36)

5

Writing the Research Paper

In this chapter, you will learn:

- How to generate a thesis or research question
- How to write a research proposal
- How to use research strategies, including library resources and search techniques
- How to identify credible sources
- How to integrate sources into your writing
- How to cite sources using different documentation styles

R esearch essays call on a variety of reading and writing skills, many of which have been discussed in Chapters 1–4; others will be discussed in the remaining chapters. However, the fundamentals of research go beyond these skills. In this chapter, we focus on

1. Locating sources in the modern library (pp. 68–75)
2. Assessing the reliability of sources, particularly those accessed electronically (pp. 75–77)
3. Integrating ideas and words smoothly and efficiently (pp. 77–82)
4. Giving credit to your sources (pp. 82–92)

But let us begin with an overview of the research process.

Coming up with a Topic

For many students, finding a topic is the first challenge to overcome. Here are some questions to consider if you need to come up with a topic from scratch:

- Where do your interests lie? You can consider hobbies, recreational and reading interests, extracurricular activities, and the like. Has a topic been discussed in another class that stimulated your interest? If so, this might be a good opportunity to explore it further.

- Is there something you have a unique perspective on? For example, Alex McLeod began his essay on autism and the education system after thinking about the school experience of his brother, who has autism (see p. 43).

- What would you like to learn more about? Curiosity is a good motivator. Writing a research essay is a good chance to satisfy that curiosity.

- What topic do you think readers might like to learn about? Thinking of *other* people's interests can guide you to a worthwhile topic. What topic could benefit society or a specific group in society (for example, students at your college/university or workplace)? Bethany Truman decided to write on relational bullying when she recalled how people around her reacted to hurtful words and gestures (see p. 66).

- Can you think of a new angle on an old topic? Neglected areas of older topics can be new opportunities for exploration or updating. Checking out "what's trending" and similar "hot" topics online can be useful at this early stage, though such topics may not have been well researched yet.

Preparing for Research

Research often begins after you have come up with a research question or a statement of a problem to be investigated. However, your question or thesis will likely not be clear until you have done some preliminary research.

Typically, this begins with narrowing a general topic. If you began with a topic like "energy sources in today's world," you will soon find that the topic is too large and the information available is overwhelming. However, you can use the pre-writing strategies discussed on p. 3 to make the topic more manageable.

One way to narrow the topic of energy sources is to focus on alternatives to fossil fuels—for example nuclear power, with its safety and environmental concerns, or thermo-mechanical energy, which is often considered a less viable long-term energy source. Most of this research can be done either in the library or online using your library's electronic resources.

Your reading will narrow the topic further. It could lead you to three specific energy sources: bio-diesel, solar energy, and hydrogen. However, if you wrote on all three sources in one essay, you would not be able to include much detail or thoroughly explore the topic. These energy sources *all* offer a potential global solution to the energy crisis, but which offers the *best* potential? Now focusing your research on comparing the costs and benefits of these three energy sources, you might decide

After completing preliminary (exploratory) research, you should be able to phrase your main idea or question as a thesis statement. Remember that while a thesis or research question represents a solid starting point, it can change as you continue your research.

that the most promising is hydrogen. After completing your preliminary research, you might come up with the following thesis:

> Current research into the development of alternative fuels provides hope for an oil and nuclear-free future, but of the different types of alternative fuels, hydrogen is the most promising because it satisfies the requirements for a long-term energy plan.

You could also phrase your thesis as a research question:

> Among the various alternative fuels being promoted today, does hydrogen live up to the claims of its advocates by being able to satisfy the requirements for a long-term energy plan?

Note that if you use a research question as a thesis, you do not answer your question yet. The answer(s) will be revealed as you explore the topic in your body paragraphs, and summarized in your conclusion. (See, for example, Bethany Truman's essay on p. 92.)

Now, with a tentative thesis and organizational pattern (cost–benefit analysis in the case of the topic discussed above), you can conduct further research by turning to specific journals, especially a **peer-reviewed journal** in which academics, scientists, and researchers publish their findings. This is where library search skills enter the picture. Knowing how the modern library works will save you a lot of time and help you find high-quality sources. By following the guidelines in "Research Resources for Today's Student," p. 68, you will be able to locate sources directly relevant to a topic like energy in peer-reviewed journals.

What if you can't find many academic sources during your preliminary research? It might be acceptable to use reliable non-academic sources, such as articles in newspapers, magazines, and websites. In fact, if your topic is very current, such sources may be the only ones available. Always be clear on what kinds of sources are permissible by checking the exact wording of the assignment, or ask your instructor for clarification.

As well as academic and non-academic sources, consider the potential value of questionnaires and surveys, along with interviews with experts or others involved in the field you are investigating.

Research Proposals

Before you undertake your major research, it is useful to write a research proposal. The main purpose of a proposal, whether for your instructor or the kind of proposal used

---

In a **peer-reviewed journal**, submissions are reviewed (critiqued) by experts before publication.

Always be clear on what kinds of sources are permissible by checking the exact wording of the assignment, or ask your instructor for clarification.

A successful proposal will persuade your instructor that you have done adequate preparation and are on the right track to a successful research paper. At a minimum, research proposals need two parts: (1) a description of what you are undertaking and (2) your methodology.

in the workplace, is to convince the reader that your project is worth doing and that you can do it. A successful proposal will persuade your instructor that you are well prepared and on track to a successful research paper.

At a minimum, research proposals need two parts: (1) a description of what you are undertaking (the "what") and (2) your methodology (the "how").

1. Description

What are you proposing to do? Begin by providing background information about the topic. This could include what you already know or have recently learned, such as any controversy related to the topic, the kind of research being done, relevant definitions, and the like. You could also mention how you became interested in the topic or its importance to others.

The proposal represents a *probable* plan: your thesis and main points can be revised as you learn more about the topic. At the end of this section, include your thesis/research question. You may also include your main points or other questions related to the topic.

2. Methodology

How will you approach your topic and conduct research? Here you should include the sources you have found useful so far and the kinds of sources that you will be looking at as you continue your research. Be specific. Give names of books, journals, websites, and so on, along with article titles. If you are planning other kinds of research, such as interviews or questionnaires, mention them too. The more detail you provide, the more your reader will be convinced. Being specific makes your proposal credible.

For you, the researcher, the proposal serves as a plan to follow; it solidifies your approach to the topic in your own mind. A proposal may even include projected dates, such as the date you plan to begin your major research and the date you plan to complete it.

Research proposals have two main functions: (1) they should convince the reader that you will do a good job (e.g., by showing you are interested in the topic and have done preliminary work); and (2) they should give you a plan to follow for your research.

Sample Proposal

The sample research proposal below is by the writer of the essay on bullying (see p. 92). While an outline represents your essay's structure, a proposal usually precedes the outline and has an exploratory function. Therefore, not all the points in the proposal below were included in the essay itself; furthermore, while the student's title suggests that she will look at both relational and physical aggression, she likely found this approach too broad, and she ended up discussing mostly relational bullying. (See her essay on p. 92.)

Research Proposal for "The Impacts of Relational Bullying on School-Age Children in Comparison to Physical Bullying"

By Bethany Truman

Description

[1]   Bullying can come in many forms and affect people in different ways. While groups of girls tend to utilize "relational" bullying (that is, spreading rumours, gossiping about others behind their backs, verbal abuse, threats, etc.), boys usually implement more straightforward, obvious forms of physical aggression. Without doubt, both kinds of bullying can inflict serious harm on the victims, but is one ultimately more damaging than the other? With such differing impacts—damaged self-esteem versus a broken nose—it can be hard to determine. I chose the topic of relational bullying because it is something that has impacted both me and many people around me growing up. It has always struck me how words can sometimes be even more powerful than physical violence and how something as simple as a particular gesture or facial expression can be tremendously hurtful.

[2]   Early in my essay, it will be important to clearly define the term "relational aggression," so readers have a clear idea of how it can be compared to more overt forms of physical aggression, such as hitting and kicking. I will focus on why this form of bullying attracts more girls than it does boys, as well as how it utilizes its "weapon of subtlety" to internalize self-doubt and insecurity in its victims. Since I will be analyzing the issue within a specific age group (school-age), I will look at possible motivations behind this form of bullying, primarily the attainment of social status. This essay will be organized using a cause-and-effect method, as it will describe various relational bullying tactics and their impacts.

[3]   Central research question/thesis: What are the impacts of relational bullying compared to physical bullying, and what makes this more subtle version of aggression so powerful?

Methodology

[4]   Most of the credible research in this field has taken place within the last two decades. My sources will consist of recent issues of peer-reviewed journals focused on the issue of relational aggression and its effects on school-age children. Using a library database, I have found several promising articles, including "It's 'Mean,' But What Does It Mean to Adolescents? Relational Aggression Described by Victims, Aggressors, and Their Peers," by Pronk and Zimmer-Gembeck; "Relational Aggression Among

Students," by Young, Nelson, Hottle, and Warburton; and "Network Ties and Mean Lies: A Relational Approach to Relational Aggression," by Neal. Each of these articles explores the potential motives behind this form of bullying, the effects it has on targeted individuals, and possible sociological explanations as to why this method of bullying appeals more to some groups than others.

Recording Important Information

Keeping accurate records during the research phase of the essay-writing process allows you to read material efficiently as well as save time (and your sanity) when you write your paper. You should record notes as you research, ensuring that they include the following information:

- A direct quotation, a summary, or a paraphrase of the writer's idea (if it is a direct quotation, make sure you put quotation marks around it)
- The complete name(s) of the author(s), ensuring correct spelling
- The complete name(s) of any editors or translators
- The complete name of the book, journal, magazine, newspaper, or website
- The title of the specific article, chapter, section, or webpage
- Full publication details, including date, edition, and translation (if appropriate)
- The name of the publisher and the company's location (including province or state) for books
- In the case of an article accessed electronically, the day you viewed the page and either the URL or the digital object identifier (DOI); the date of the site or its most recent update should also be recorded
- The call number of a library book or bound journal (to help you find it again if necessary)
- The page numbers you consulted, both those from which specific ideas came and the full page range of the work (or some other marker, such as section headings and paragraph numbers, for Internet documents without page numbers)

A **digital object identifier** (DOI) is a number–alphabet sequence often found on journal articles and begins with the number 10; it serves as a permanent link for digital material.

Organizing Research Notes

There are many ways to organize information from your research in order to use it later. The manual method is probably the most familiar to students: notecards, for example, are portable and practical. You can also record notes in a notebook or journal and use tabs to divide the book, using distinct subject headings. In addition, a number of software programs are designed to help with planning and organization. For example, RefWorks (www.refworks.com) is an Internet-based

Keep your research notes, such as summaries and direct quotations, separate from your personal notes. Use a method that clearly distinguishes between the two; otherwise, you could end up plagiarizing by failing to attribute the idea or words of a source, thinking they were your own.

"citation manager" that allows you to import references from popular databases like Academic Search Complete, MLA Bibliography, and EconLit.

Others are databases, such as EndNote (www.endnote.com), Bibliographix (www.bibliographix.com), and Nota Bene (www.notabene.com). Students can usually take a tutorial for these programs on their websites or even through their own institution if it has purchased licences allowing students to use them. These programs offer many benefits, such as automatic formatting for a variety of citation methods.

Research Resources for Today's Student*

The twenty-first-century academic library can seem overwhelming to the student researcher. In addition to the traditional materials found in the library's online catalogue, there are numerous other online resources available, including databases, journals, e-books, and other digital formats and media. The sheer volume of information resources in today's academic library need not be intimidating. On the contrary, an effective research strategy will enable you to take full advantage of the print and electronic information resources available to you.

An effective strategy should include three important considerations:

1. Your *research topic* (see below)
2. The *information resources* most relevant to your topic (p. 69)
3. The *search strategy* you will use to obtain information from those resources (p. 71)

When you understand how to choose a well-defined research topic, where to look for information on that topic, and how to construct an effective search in a library catalogue or database, you will have the basic tools required for most research projects at the first-year level. As you become a more confident researcher, you can expand on these basic skills and strategies by exploring more specialized resources and experimenting with advanced search methods.

> When you understand how to choose a well-defined research topic, where to look for information on that topic, and how to construct an effective search in a catalogue or database, you will have the basic tools required for most research projects at the first-year level.

The Research Topic

The starting point for your research will be your topic. When choosing your own topic, make sure to select one that is neither too broad nor too narrow. If your

---

*The material on pp. 68–75 (from "Research Resources for Today's Students" to "Using Credible Sources") is based on information compiled by Danielle Forster and updated by Justin Harrison, Caron Rollins, and Christine Walde, University of Victoria librarians.

topic is too broad, you will have difficulty focusing your research and writing. Alternatively, if your topic is too narrow or obscure, you may not be able to find enough relevant information to support your research question.

For instance, if you wanted to write about *homelessness* or *the homeless*, it would be difficult to write a focused paper on such a broad topic. To narrow your focus, you might want to research homelessness in a particular age group, such as teenagers. However, this would probably still be too broad. You could narrow your focus further by looking at particular health problems of homeless teens, or risk factors associated with homelessness in teens, such as poverty, addiction, or abuse.

Selecting Resources for Your Research Topic

Subject or Research Guides

Once you have decided on a research topic, you must choose your resources. This usually means using your institution's library. Most academic libraries provide subject or research guides on their website. These guides are prepared by subject librarians with specialized knowledge in their subject areas. Most subject guides provide direct links to relevant online databases, scholarly websites, and primary source materials for the subject, as well as valuable information on reference resources such as dictionaries, encyclopedias, biographies, and bibliographies, including subject headings and call number ranges.

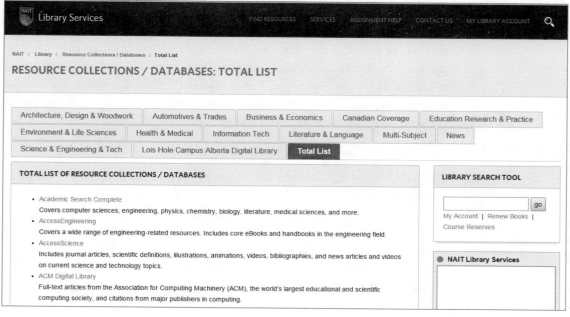

Courtesy of the Northern Alberta Institute of Technology

Primary and Secondary Sources

Your research may require that you investigate both primary and secondary source information. The meaning of primary and secondary sources can vary across the disciplines, but in the humanities and social sciences, primary sources generally provide *first-hand* information or data. This may include original works such as autobiographies, interviews, speeches, letters, diaries, unpublished manuscripts, data sources, government records, newspapers, and government policy papers, among others. Secondary sources are works that analyze or interpret a primary work, source or experience from a *second-hand* perspective. These can include scholarly journal articles, textbooks, or collections of critical essays, biographies, historical articles, or films.

The Library Catalogue

Use your library's subject guides and catalogue to guide you to general sources, such as encyclopedias, dictionaries, and books where you will learn the key concepts relevant to your topic. They can also suggest more specific research sources.

The library catalogue is the most important tool for finding secondary print sources like books, encyclopedias, dictionaries, and journals in your library, as well as electronic versions of these materials. Unlike an Internet search engine such as Google, the library's catalogue is a bibliographic index, and provides a list of the most relevant scholarly and non-scholarly sources related to your research topic through its combined use of subject headings and descriptors.

For concise, general information on your topic, the academic library can also provide you with encyclopedias and dictionaries, which are more scholarly sources of information than Wikipedia, and can help you to narrow your focus by highlighting key academic issues and concepts, as well as providing suggestions for further research. Scholarly books relevant to your topic are also important sources to explore. In addition to covering a subject in more depth than a journal article, they often provide important historical, biographical, literary, or cultural context that may not be available elsewhere. Books also feature images or tables of contents that can help you to identify important aspects of the subject that you may want to explore further and bibliographies to help you locate other resources. E-books are especially useful for browsing tables of contents and bibliographies and for keyword searching within the full text of a book.

Online Databases

Online databases and indexes are your main tools for finding journal articles in both print and online formats. Although books offer an in-depth approach, the most *current* research is usually found in academic journals.

Scholarly journal articles are a key secondary source for your research. Journal articles review what other scholars have said about your topic and often provide important supportive or alternative perspectives relevant to your thesis. Online databases and indexes are your main tools for finding journal articles in both print and online formats. Your library's home page may provide a discovery search tool, such as Summon, for searching for information sources. In a single unified search box, the system retrieves a number of relevant articles from your

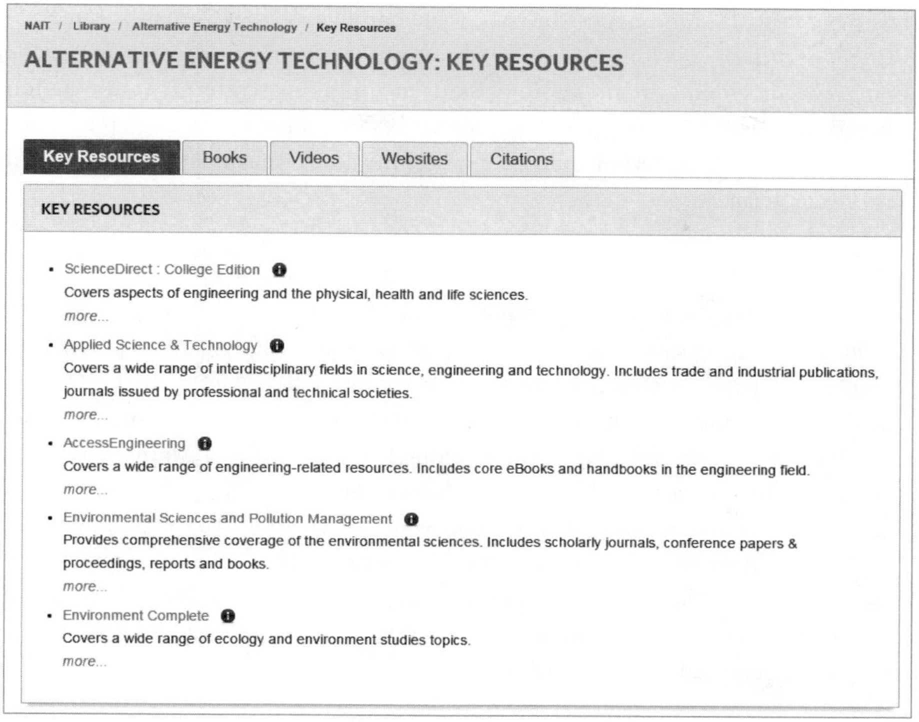
NAIT / Library / Alternative Energy Technology / Key Resources
ALTERNATIVE ENERGY TECHNOLOGY: KEY RESOURCES
Key Resources
Books
Videos
Websites
Citations
KEY RESOURCES
ScienceDirect : College Edition
Covers aspects of engineering and the physical, health and life sciences.
more...
Applied Science & Technology
Covers a wide range of interdisciplinary fields in science, engineering and technology. Includes trade and industrial publications, journals issued by professional and technical societies.
more...
AccessEngineering
Covers a wide range of engineering-related resources. Includes core eBooks and handbooks in the engineering field.
more...
Environmental Sciences and Pollution Management
Provides comprehensive coverage of the environmental sciences. Includes scholarly journals, conference papers & proceedings, reports and books.
more...
Environment Complete
Covers a wide range of ecology and environment studies topics.
more...

Courtesy of the Northern Alberta Institute of Technology

library's catalogue and journal subscriptions, and allows you to limit your search, save or export your results, or link to the full text. This method is useful for quickly finding information on your topic, and can be further refined by using filters and limiters.

A good multidisciplinary online database like Academic Search Complete provides relevant information on most topics for student researchers. As well, subject and specialized databases are available, depending on your discipline. If your library has subject guides, these will list the core databases or "best bets" for each subject. Most libraries will also allow you to select databases by subject in addition to providing an A–Z list.

Modern libraries now offer options for accessing journal articles and other research sources, including library search engines and metasearch tools. They may also let you locate "core" databases which index journals most relevant to your discipline or field of research.

Having a plan is essential. What type of information do you require? For example, statistical information is found in a statistical database. The specialized subject guides, with help from your subject librarian if necessary, will help you determine the right information resources you need for your research topic.

Search Strategies

Determining Keywords

Your next step is to identify the key concepts from your topic to use as keywords or search terms. For instance, if you want to search for information on risk factors associated with homelessness in youth, you can identify keywords that embody the concepts *risk factors*, *homelessness*, and *youth*. Some risk factors might be *poverty*, *addiction*, or *abuse*. Using *risk* or *factors* as search terms would be too broad and would not provide good search results. Similarly, using *risk factors* combined as a single term would not find results unless the books or articles used this exact term.

Boolean Operators

To be effective, the actual search process should employ some form of Boolean strategy. The most common Boolean operators, AND, OR, and NOT are used to combine, expand, or eliminate keywords in your search. For instance, AND combines the two different terms *homelessness* AND *youth*, allowing you to narrow your results. This is more effective than searching for each of the keywords separately, since your sources retrieved will include both terms.

The OR operator is used to expand your search results by including other concepts—either the same concepts or different aspects of a broader concept. In this example, you could use the keywords *youth* OR *teens* OR *adolescents,* which are synonymous concepts. Or you may want to search for *poverty* OR *abuse* OR *addiction* as different aspects of the risk factors.

The NOT operator is used to eliminate results with that given keyword, such as *children* if you don't want results that discuss young children. The NOT operator should be used cautiously, however, because you may eliminate an article that discusses both children and teens, which may be relevant to your topic.

Many databases now let you combine your keywords without using the Boolean operators at all. You simply enter your terms and choose the correct search mode. Using Basic Search in Academic Search Complete as an example, the search mode *Find all of my search terms* is equivalent to AND, and the search mode *Find any of my search terms* is equivalent to OR. Many other databases and catalogues now work similarly, including Google Scholar. When using Google Scholar, however, remember to access it through your academic library website, so that you can directly link to online resources in your library's catalogue, including open-access journals.

Truncation and Wildcards

Boolean search strategy is often used with truncation and/or wildcard symbols. Truncation symbols enable you to include all variants of a search term. Using the asterisk as the truncation symbol in *teen** will return search results for *teen, teens,* and *teenager.* Wildcards are used within a word, for instance in *colo#r* to search for an alternative spelling (*colour* and *color*) or *wom?n* to search for any unknown characters (*woman* and *women*). Most databases and catalogues use the asterisk (*)

Once you have chosen some relevant resources for your subject, the next step will be to identify the key concepts from your topic to use as keywords or search terms.

Boolean operators help you refine your search by defining relationships between different words or phrases. The most common Boolean operators are AND, OR, and NOT.

or a question mark (?) for the truncation or wildcard symbol. Some databases may also use the pound sign (#) or another symbol.

Basic or Advanced Search

Online catalogues and databases usually feature simple or basic search and advanced search options. The basic search field can be used to enter single terms, as described above, or more complex search statements using Boolean operators. However, to construct a search statement using Boolean strategy in a basic search field, you must use parentheses to separate the OR terms from the AND terms as indicated below. The database will search for the terms in parentheses first, then from left to right.

(*Homeless** OR *runaway**) AND (*teen** OR *adolescen** OR *youth*) AND (*poverty* OR *abuse* OR *addict**)

Also, if you want to use a combined term such as *"risk factors,"* you must use quotation marks unless the field provides the option to search two or more words as a phrase.

The advanced search option is set up to allow you to insert your terms and then select AND, OR, or NOT to combine the fields and to add additional fields, if necessary. Advanced search also allows you to search for terms in various fields, such as *All Text, Abstract, Author, Title,* or *Subject Terms*. By selecting a specific field, you limit the search to that field alone. It is often best to try a search in the default field first, and then try other advanced strategies to refine your results, if necessary.

The advanced search option is set up to allow you to insert your terms and then select AND, OR, or NOT to combine the fields and to add additional fields, if necessary. Advanced search also allows you to search for terms in various fields, such as *All Text, Author, Title, Subject Terms,* etc.

Subject Headings or Descriptors

Subject headings or descriptors are very useful for refining your search strategy. In academic libraries, subject headings have been applied to each bibliographic entry to describe what it is about. A subject heading is not merely a keyword found in the article or abstract, and some online databases will enable you to search the subject directly to show related subject headings. Sometimes, subject headings within the results list are linked, so you can either expand or narrow the results of your current search to all of the related records in the database with that subject term.

Another strategy is to take note of the subject headings in your initial keyword searches. Combining these terms again in the *Subject Terms* field will often yield more relevant results. Most online library catalogues will also provide related subject headings to other resources with the same heading. Additionally, there may also be a link to other items in the same immediate call number range. This will enable you to easily "browse" the collection for other relevant materials.

Limiters

Limiters can be used in advanced searches to narrow your results or restrict them to a specific date range, article type, format, or publication.

Another search strategy is using the limiters available to you in a particular database. This strategy is generally used to limit your results if there are too many, or to limit to a particular date range, article type, format, or publication.

One very useful limiter found in many databases is the scholarly or peer-reviewed limiter. Peer-reviewed articles have been reviewed by experts who recommended their publication. They are usually the most reliable source of information for your research. Academic Search Complete provides a *Scholarly (Peer Reviewed) Journals* check box to the right of your search results list, or you can check the *Scholarly (Peer Reviewed) Journals* box in the *Limit your results* field before you execute your search, and the database will only retrieve scholarly articles.

Marking and Saving

It is important to start your library research early. This will allow you enough time to determine a manageable topic, explore as many resources as possible, refine your search strategy as necessary, and obtain any materials that are not readily available online or in your library.

Most online databases and library catalogues provide a marking and saving feature. You can select your most relevant results, mark them by checking a box or adding them to a folder, and then choose from several options—usually print, email, save, or export. Export often includes an option to download or export to the citation management software of your choice, such as RefWorks, EndNote, or Zotero.

These citation management tools allow you to create a customized personal account so you can store and organize your citations, as well as create a bibliography based on your citation style, such as APA or MLA. These tools can help you keep track of your search history, as well as store links to previously searched databases and full-text articles; they often include areas where you can write your own comments. As you scan abstracts and articles, and later during your readings, be sure to note the points and ideas you wish to quote and paraphrase. Remember, crediting sources is an essential part of academic writing.

Refining your Strategy

One final consideration for effective academic library research is refining your strategy throughout the process. It may be necessary to re-evaluate your topic, choice of resources, or search strategy if your initial searches are unsuccessful. Do not feel frustrated: this is not an indication that your strategy is not a good one or that you have failed. Conducting academic research is a naturally evolving process, and knowing how to access the resources at your academic library is a part of the learning experience. In the end, your goal is a strong research topic with thoughtful, meaningful research accompanied by accurate citations. Therefore, it is important to start your library research early. This will allow you enough time to determine a manageable topic, consult your subject librarian, explore as many resources as possible, refine your search strategy as necessary, and obtain any materials that are not available online or in your academic library.

Using Credible Sources

Although research sources accessed through your library are likely reliable, some Internet sources may also be useful to flesh out your topic, especially if recent developments have occurred. In addition, if your topic is controversial, you may want to gauge popular opinions through the Internet.

The criteria below apply particularly to open-access resources, from Google Scholar to the range of commercial, governmental, and personal websites that anyone sitting in front of a computer screen can view. The way you use open-access resources depends on what kind of information you are looking for.

Are you looking for reliable information from an objective source that explains where its facts and figures come from (for example, Statistics Canada), or do you want to learn about a particular viewpoint? If the latter, it might be acceptable to use a website that advocates a position or supports a cause. If you were writing an essay on animal rights, you might want to access People for the Ethical Treatment of Animals (PETA) or Animal Rights Canada, since their position on animal rights is clear (although this does not guarantee that their information is always factual or accurate).

Not all websites, however, acknowledge their true stake in an issue, nor do all websites use quality control to ensure accurate content. Even seemingly reliable and objective websites, such as those affiliated with governments, may contain misleading or outdated information.

Open-access resources are available to the public without charge and can normally be accessed without passwords or other safeguards.

Ask yourself why you want to use an open-access resource for your research. Are you looking for reliable information from an objective source that explains where its facts and figures come from, or do you want to learn about a particular viewpoint?

BOX 5.1 | Assessing the Credibility of Sources

In determining whether to use a source in your research essay, bear in mind the four *Re*'s of research sources: *re*putable, *re*liable, *re*cent, and *re*levant. The first two apply particularly to Internet sources.

Reputable

Reputable sources are usually associated with well-known organizations or experts. To determine reputation, ask

- ❒ What is the purpose of the website? Who are its sponsors?
- ❒ Is the website associated with an official group/recognized organization?
- ❒ Are details available about the site's purpose, sponsors, or administration? This information can often be found in "About Us" or "Mission Statement."

Reliable

Information from reliable sources can be trusted as accurate and free of bias. To determine reliability, ask

- ❒ Can the information be relied on? Is it accurate? Where does it come from?
- ❒ Are sources given (names, dates)? Do they appear to be experts in their field?
- ❒ Are claims backed up by objective evidence?
- ❒ If opinion exists, is it clearly separated from fact? Are other points of view represented? How are they treated?
- ❒ If you have doubts about accuracy, confirm the information through a second source that you know is reliable.

Recent

Although currency is more important to some topics than to others, recent information is generally superior to older information. A site may be reputable but not current if its information is no longer valid. To determine currency, ask

- ❒ What is the date of the website or most recent update? How current does the information on the site appear to be?
- ❒ Is currency essential to your topic? In certain scientific and technological fields, information that is six months old might be outdated; in some humanities topics, older information can still be useful.

Reputable sources are usually associated with well-known organizations or experts.

Information from reliable sources can be trusted as accurate and free of bias.

Recent sources are generally preferable to older ones, but there are exceptions, especially in the humanities.

Relevant

The information in relevant sources is directly related to your thesis and/or main points. To determine relevance, ask

- ☐ How is the information related to your essay? Does it directly support your thesis or one of your points?

- ☐ Does the source provide the best support for your claim? Are there other sources that address your topic more directly?

Other factors may also be important in determining the credibility of a website:

- ☐ How has statistical information been calculated (e.g., through censuses, surveys, questionnaires by reliable organizations)? How are statistical information and other factual data being used?

- ☐ Are there links to other sites? Do these sites appear reliable?

- ☐ Does content primarily consist of text, or do images and graphics dominate?

- ☐ Is the information on the website easy to access? Does it appear well organized? What specific resources are designed to enhance accessibility or ease of site navigation?

> The information in relevant sources is directly related to your thesis and/or main points.

EXERCISE 5.1

Choose two websites devoted to a topic that you're interested in and knowledgeable about. Using the criteria discussed above, along with other criteria you believe relevant, compare the two sites for their credibility, using at least three bases for comparison.

Writing the Rough Draft: Integrating Sources

As you researched your topic, you decided on sources and how they would be used in your essay, that is, how they contributed to your thesis or helped answer your research question. During outlining, you decided on the best order for your points. As you compose, you should integrate these sources, combining the information and, in some cases, the exact words, with your own thoughts and words. Three main ways to integrate information are discussed below.

> When you **integrate** sources during the composing stage, you combine their ideas and/or words with your own ideas/words.
>
> When you **summarize**, you include the main idea (or ideas) from a source, expressing it in your own words.

Summary and Paraphrase

When you **summarize** a source, you use your own words to express a main idea, discarding detail. You could summarize the main idea from a sentence, a paragraph,

When you **paraphrase**, you put someone else's ideas in your own words, keeping the length of the original.

or an entire article. While a summary is selective, a paraphrase includes *all of the original in your own words*. Whereas a summary is an efficient method for integrating material, a paraphrased passage is about as long as the original. Because you include so much in a paraphrase, you must be careful to use different wording or you may unknowingly be plagiarizing. Changing the order of the original will also help you avoid plagiarism (see "Plagiarism," p. 82).

In the example below, a sentence from "The Impact of Pets on Human Health and Psychological Well-Being," p. 327, is summarized, then paraphrased.

Original: And our attitudes and behaviours toward and relationships with other species offer a unique window into many aspects of human nature. [21 words]

Summary: Studying our interactions with other species allows us to explore our own nature. [13 words]

Paraphrase: We can achieve striking insights into human nature by examining how we think about, act toward, and relate to other species. [21 words]

Direct Quotation

When you quote a source directly, you use exactly the same words as the original, putting quotation marks around them.

When you summarize or paraphrase, you show the reader you've understood the material well enough to put it in your own words.

When you quote a source directly, you use exactly the same words as the original, putting quotation marks around them. However, while direct quotation is often essential in a literary analysis, summary or paraphrase is often the better choice for secondary sources. When you summarize or paraphrase, you clearly show you understand the material because you've put it in your own words.

Direct quotation unnecessary or inappropriate: "Twelve per cent of American teens are now battling anorexia nervosa and associated disorders, states a US organization on eating disorders" (Gomez, 2001, p. 76).

Statistical detail does not need be quoted directly.

Paraphrase: According to an American organization studying eating disorders, more than 10 per cent of US adolescents are afflicted by an eating disorder like anorexia nervosa (Gomez, 2001, p. 76).

If facts can be easily put in your own words, prefer summary or paraphrase to direct quotation.

Direct quotation unnecessary: "Beer and spirit producers tend to advertise in magazines with more young adult readers, men, and black people" (Nelson 40).

Paraphrase: Young adults, males, and blacks are typical readers of magazines that contain advertisements for alcoholic beverages (Nelson 40).

You can use direct quotation if you want to define something or if the exact wording is otherwise important—for example, to lend authority to your point or if the wording of the source is significant.

But how do we define our Canadian democracy? "The genius of a free and democratic people is manifested in its capacity and willingness to devise institutions and laws that secure fairness and equitable opportunities for citizens to influence democratic governance" (Royal Commission on Electoral Reform and Party Financing).

Using direct quotation is appropriate because the writer wants to stress the authority of the source.

Combining Summary/Paraphrase with Direct Quotation

Using summary or paraphrase with direct quotation can be an efficient way to integrate sources. In the example below, the writer includes a significant phrase that reveals discrimination against Asians in the first decade of the twentieth century in Canada.

> Combining summary or paraphrase with direct quotation is an efficient way to integrate sources.

According to Sir Clifford Sifton, Prime Minister Wilfrid Laurier's interior minister, Canada was to be "a nation of good farmers," meaning Asian immigration was discouraged (Royal Commission 24).

Integrating Quotations

When you incorporate direct quotations into your essay, you must do so grammatically and smoothly. You must also provide enough context for the reader to grasp their significance. The following shows a poorly integrated quotation and its well-integrated alternative:

> When you incorporate direct quotations into your essay, you must do so grammatically and smoothly. You must also provide enough context for the reader to grasp their significance.

Poorly integrated: An unloving parent–child relationship can be characterized as "unaccepted, unacknowledged, or unloved" (Haworth-Hoeppner 216).

Well-integrated: An unloving parent–child relationship exists when the child feels "unaccepted, unacknowledged, or unloved" (Haworth-Hoeppner 216).

Using Commas and Periods with Quotations

Do not automatically place a comma *before* a direct quotation or precede the quotation by an ellipsis (see "Omitting Words," below).

> *Incorrect:* Cyberbullying can be defined as, ". . . the use of electronic communication technology as a means to threaten, harass, embarrass, or socially exclude" (Hinduja & Patchin, 2008, p. 5).

> *Correct:* Cyberbullying can be defined as "the use of electronic communication technology as a means to threaten, harass, embarrass, or socially exclude" (Hinduja & Patchin, 2008, p. 5).

If the writer included punctuation, such as a comma or period, *after* the last word in the quoted material you use, do not include it.

> *Incorrect:* Kate Moss' emphasis on thinness was "immediately condemned by campaigners," (Poulter).

> *Correct:* Kate Moss' emphasis on thinness was "immediately condemned by campaigners" (Poulter).

Making Changes to Direct Quotations

When you quote directly, you must take care to quote accurately; mistakes in direct quotations may look like carelessness and reduce your credibility. However, altering direct quotations is sometimes a good idea—or even essential.

Omitting Words

If you want to omit unneeded or distracting words from a direct quotation, you must show the reader what you have done by using ellipses, which means "omission."

If you omit one or more words in a single sentence, show this omission by using three spaced dots. However, if you leave out all the words *to the end of the sentence*—and if you leave out the following sentence(s) as well—add a fourth dot, which represents the period at the end of the sentence(s).

> *Original:* "McKinsey & Company, one of the world's preeminent management consulting firms, has identified $2-trillion worth of energy efficiency initiatives not currently being pursued worldwide" (Harris, p. 205).

If you wanted to leave out "one of the world's preeminent management consulting firms," you must replace the words by an ellipsis.

> *Revised:* McKinsey & Company . . . has identified $2-trillion worth of energy efficiency initiatives not currently being pursued worldwide" (Harris, p. 205).

Be very careful when using ellipses that the words you omit are not essential to the meaning of the complete statement. For example, if you replaced "not currently being pursued worldwide" by four dots in the example above, you would be changing the meaning of the statement and misrepresenting the author.

Using three spaced dots in a direct quotation shows you have left out one or more words of the original and that the sentence continues after the third dot. Four spaced dots shows you have left out all words to the end of the sentence.

Adding and Changing Words

If you add to or change quoted material, you need to indicate this by using square brackets (or just brackets). Changes can be made for grammar, style, clarification, or explanation. The following examples from student essays illustrate some of the different reasons for using brackets to add or change words:

> *Grammatical (change* is *to as, in order to create a grammatical sentence):* Many people see "male sporting superiority [as] the 'natural' order of things" (Hargreaves, 1994, p. 6).

> *Stylistic (lowercase the letter* s *in order to avoid a capital letter in the middle of a sentence):* A recent study found that "[s]urfing the Internet at work for pleasure actually increases our concentration levels" ("Researcher Says").

> *Clarification (in order to indicate that a word was added to original):* "With increasing frequency, the term [creativity] is used . . . in fields of endeavour as diverse as science, the arts, education, politics and business" (Prentice 146).

Brackets are used to show a change or addition to a direct quotation or to indicate parentheses inside parentheses.

You can also use brackets to indicate a parenthesis inside a parenthetical statement:

> (I develop this more fully in an essay included in *Ignoring Nature No More*, ed. by Marc Bekoff [Chicago, IL: University of Chicago Press, 2013]).

Table 5.1 summarizes the main features of the integration methods discussed above. Note that whatever method you use, documentation is usually required. See Box 5.2, "Five Common Questions about Source Citation."

TABLE 5.1	Main Features of Integrating Research	
Method	What It Includes	When and How to Use It
Summary	Only main ideas or most important points; is in your words	When you want to refer to main idea in a paragraph, findings of a study, and similar uses; you can summarize as little as part of a sentence, as much as an entire article
Paraphrase	All of the original in your own words, with the structure changed if possible	When you want to refer to important material directly relevant to your point; paraphrases are used for small but significant passages
Direct quotation	Words and punctuation taken directly from the source; put in quotation marks	When material both is important to your point and is memorably phrased or difficult to paraphrase; must be integrated grammatically and smoothly, using brackets and ellipses as required
Combining method	Significant words from source with your own words (i.e., summary or paraphrase)	When you want to include only the most significant or memorable words, omitting the inessential; integrate words from the source grammatically and smoothly with your own prose, using brackets and ellipses as required

Writing the Final Draft: Documenting Sources

Documentation style refers to guidelines for documenting sources put forth in style manuals and handbooks for researchers and other academic writers.

Documenting sources enables a reader to sort your ideas from someone else's and makes it possible for a reader to access the source itself, either to ensure its accuracy or to focus on its content. Documentation formats (called documentation styles) enable scholars to communicate with other scholars. As researchers-in-training, students must use correct documentation formats in their essays.

Plagiarism

It is considered **plagiarism** if you use any outside material—whether you quote directly, summarize, paraphrase, or just refer to it in your essay—without acknowledging it. It also is considered plagiarism if you use the exact words of the source without putting them in quotation marks, or if you follow the structure of the original too closely.

To avoid plagiarism, carefully study the passage you want to use; then, close the text, and write the passage from memory in your own words. Look to ensure that the passage is different in its structure as well as in its language—and that you have accurately restated it.

Plagiarism is an extremely serious academic offence. Most students know that when they use another's exact words, they must acknowledge their source. But plagiarism encompasses more than this: you plagiarize if you in any way use material that is not your own—whether you quote directly, summarize, paraphrase, or refer to it in passing in your essay—without acknowledging it. Finally, you plagiarize if you use the exact words of the source and do not put them in quotation marks, even if you acknowledge their source. You also risk plagiarizing if you follow the structure of the original too closely.

However, if a fact or idea is *common knowledge* (i.e., a typical reader knows it), you may not need to cite it. Further, if the fact or idea is *easily obtainable*, a citation may also be unnecessary. (You may be told a specific number of sources that satisfies the "easily obtainable" factor—often three.) If in doubt, make the citation.

The questions about source citation in Box 5.2 are often asked by first-year student researchers.

BOX 5.2 | Five Common Questions about Source Citation

1. **Do you need to cite information that you do not quote directly in your essay?**

   Yes. Specific content requires a citation, whether you use direct quotation, paraphrase, or summary to integrate it into your essay. Even general information may require a citation.

2. **If you already knew a fact and you encounter it in a secondary source, does it need to be cited?**

   Probably. The issue isn't whether you know something but whether your reader would know it. If you are writing for an audience familiar with your topic, you may not need to cite "common knowledge," that is, knowledge that all or almost all readers would be expected to know or which could be easily looked up.

3. **Is it necessary to cite "popular" quotations, for example, the kind that appear in dictionaries of quotations? What about dictionary definitions?**

   Yes, these kinds of quotations should be cited unless the quotation has entered everyday use. For example, the first quotation would probably not need a citation, though the second would—even though it's unlikely that a reader would know either source:

   When the going gets tough, the tough get going. (Joan W. Donaldson)

   Making your mark on the world is hard. If it were easy, everybody would do it. (Barack Obama)

   Yes. Dictionary definitions should be cited.

4. **If you provide a list of your sources on the final page of your essay, do you have to cite the sources within the essay itself?**

   Yes. Most documentation methods require in-text and final-page citations.

5. **What can you do to guarantee that the question of plagiarism never arises in your essay?**

   Follow the guidelines above, and for specific instances in which the guidelines don't provide the answer, don't hesitate to check with your instructor or another expert, such as a librarian.

Documenting Your Sources

Knowing what to cite and citing accurately (see "Major Documentation Styles," starting on p. 84) are, of course, crucial; however, a third concern may arise as you integrate and document your sources: unnecessary citations. Repetitive citations can clutter an essay, affecting ease of reading. They can also make you seem over-reliant on what other people have said.

As a general rule, you should ensure a reader can separate your ideas from someone else's, but do not repeat citations needlessly. For example, if you use the

> As a general rule, you should ensure a reader will know what you have taken from outside sources and what are your own ideas, but do not repeat citations needlessly.

same source for two consecutive points with no other source intervening, you usually include only the page number in the second citation.

In the following body paragraph from an essay on creativity, student writer Taryn Burgar uses three sources to help develop the main idea. Although the sources of her information are clear, she does not repeat unnecessary information. In particular, she does not repeat the name of the source if she has named the author(s) as part of the previous citation. Taryn uses MLA documentation style. (For an example of efficient citations in an essay that uses APA documentation style, see Bethany Truman's essay on p. 92; in particular, paragraph 3, pp. 93–4.)

Sample Student Body Paragraph with Annotations

> The benefits of teaching students methods that improve their creativity can be seen in all the stages of the educational system. With pre-school and kindergarten children, imaginative activity assists in their growth into intellectually stimulated adults (Prentice 151–52). Such activity comes from play and the direct manipulation of materials and is often associated with creative endeavours, such as making new objects and artistic projects. Connecting physical material to ideas will resonate with young children as they have had less practice in understanding abstract concepts (154). Art should have a central focus in the elementary school curriculum as children are likely to develop an attachment to a specific type of art at this time in their lives. Even if they develop simply an appreciation for art, this will still allow for creative insights (De Backer et al. 63). Post-secondary education systems often focus on a class lecture format; however, Livingston argues that problem solving should become the driving pedagogy (59–60). Today's college students learn to be adept at research, which provides a playground for creative interaction, inquisition, and imagination. Focusing the last formal stage of education on "learning," instead of "teaching," encourages the next generation of teachers to perpetuate this creative cycle (59).

Taryn begins her paragraph with a topic sentence that announces the paragraph's main idea. By referring to "the stages of the educational system," a reader assumes she will develop the paragraph using the division method, where she applies the topic to different stages of a child's education.

In her first citation, Taryn gives the author's last name and the page numbers. Note that she drops the second (redundant) hundreds digit for the second number, as required by MLA style.

Because she includes only the page number, the reader assumes that the information comes from the previous source (Prentice).

Taryn needs to provide complete details because she is citing this material for the first time. A reader could turn to the Works Cited page and see that this source has five authors. The phrase "et al." following the first author's name is used for sources that have more than three authors.

The citation consists only of page numbers because the author's name has been given in a signal phrase (i.e., "Livingston argues").

Because the final point is taken from the same as the preceding source, the author's name is not repeated.

Major Documentation Styles

There are three major documentation styles but many variants on these styles: The Modern Language Association (MLA) style, the American Psychological Association (APA) style, and the Chicago Manual of Style

(CMS). Here we will discuss the two styles most commonly used in academic essays: APA and MLA. (CMS isn't discussed here but can be found in the "student study guide" and at www.oupcanada.com/Becoming2e.)

MLA is widely used in the humanities, including English literature. APA style is used in many social science and science disciplines, as well as in education and business. Both are parenthetical styles, meaning that a brief citation including the author's name and page number (MLA) or name and publication year (APA) follows the reference in the text of an essay. (Both these styles also require an end-of-essay listing of sources alphabetically by last name.)

In the parenthetical styles, there are two methods to integrate source material:

1. Give the name of the author(s) and (APA style only) the publication year in a **signal phrase** (which includes the author's last name and a "signal verb," such as *states*, *explains*, or *argues*) *before* the information from the source. You do not repeat the author's name (MLA) or the author's name and year (APA) in the end citation.

   > *APA:* Pilon (2005) explains that in strategic voting, people often have to compromise their vote to ensure an undesirable candidate does not win (p. 14).

2. Give the name of the author, page number, and (APA style only) publication year *after* the information from the source.

   > *MLA:* In strategic voting, people often have to compromise their vote to ensure an undesirable candidate does not win (Pilon 14).

> A **signal phrase** introduces a reference in a phrase that names the author(s) and usually includes a "signal verb" and, in APA style, year of publication.

Many of the main features of the MLA and APA styles are given below. Examples of the most common citation formats are then provided.

Electronic formats in all styles should include as much information as is available. If an author's name is not given, use the name of the organization or sponsoring group in its place. If there is no sponsor, use the work's title alphabetized by the first major word. MLA style requires you to include date of access for Internet citations; APA does not. Paragraph number or section heading can sometimes be used to identify location, if necessary, in the absence of standard page numbering (APA style only). APA style also requires you to use digital object identifier (DOI) if it is available for journal articles.

APA (American Psychological Association) Style
In-Text Guidelines

- APA uses an "author–year" referencing format. One basic format includes the author's last name and year of publication (used for general references).

The other basic format adds page number (used for specific references, such as direct quotations and paraphrases).

General reference:
Krahn (2007) questions embryo screening. (applies to the entire work)

Specific reference:
Krahn (2007) concludes his argument with an analogy (p. 1446). (applies to a specific page)

- Commas separate author's name from year and year from page number (if required); "p." (for a single page) or "pp." (for more than one page) precedes page number(s). e.g., (Huyer, 1997, p. 43); (Bryson & de Castell, 1998, pp. 542–544).
- With a signal phrase, the year follows the author's name in parentheses. If a page number is required, it is placed in parentheses after the reference:

  Gentile (2011) suggests that there are at least five factors that combine to affect players of video games: content of play, frequency of play, game context, game structure, and mechanics (p. 75).

- No signal phrase:

  At least five factors combine to affect players of video games: content of play, frequency of play, game context, game structure, and mechanics (Gentile, 2011, p. 75).

- An ampersand (&) is used rather than *and* for two or more authors (e.g., Saul & Curtis, 2012).
- No author. Use the name of the organization in place of author's name (e.g., Canada Wildlife Federation). If there is no author or organization, for example some encyclopedia entries, use the title in place of author.
- Indirect source: Author A (where you found the quote) quotes Author B (indirect source). Name Author B in your sentence (list Author A on the References page—i.e., Jones) followed by the phrase *as cited in* along with Author A's last name, year, and page number in parentheses:

  Bechard says embryo testing will produce "a culture of intolerance" (as cited in Jones, 2010, p. 88).

- You can provide more than one source in a single citation. Separate them by semicolons—e.g., (Nadelmann, 2011, p. 25; Long, 2013, p. 44).
- Works by the same author(s) from the same year are assigned different letters—e.g., 2004a, 2004b—in alphabetical order by title. They are listed in this order in "References."
- Block quotations should be used for important passages more than 40 words long. They are indented 1.3 cm (half an inch) from the left margin and double spaced, and do not include quotation marks. The end period precedes the parenthetical citation.

Final Page (References) Guidelines

- Entries are double spaced with the first line flush left and successive lines indented 1.3 cm (half an inch).
- The final page, titled "References," alphabetically lists by author's last name all works used in the essay.
- Authors' initials are used, not given names. Publication year in parentheses follows the last name.
- In article and book titles, only the first letter of first words, first words following colons, and proper nouns, along with all letters in acronyms, are capitalized.

APA Sample Formats on References Page

Book (One Author)

Embry, J. L. (1987). *Mormon polygamous families: Life in the principle.* Salt Lake City, UT: University of Utah Press.

Book or Journal (Multiple Authors)

Plester, B, Woods, C., & Bell, V. (2008). Txt msg n school literacy: Does texting and knowledge of text abbreviations adversely affect children's literacy attainment? *Literacy, 42*(3), 137–144. doi: 10.1111/j.1741-4369.2008.00489.x

- All authors' names begin with the surname followed by initial(s).
- *Two to seven authors:* List all authors.
- *More than seven authors:* List the first six authors followed by three points of ellipsis (. . .) and the last author's name.
- *Two or more works by same author:* Listed chronologically, beginning with the earliest work.

- *Organization as author:* Organization name is used in place of author's name:

American Board for Plastic Surgery. (2010). National average for physician/ surgeon fees per procedure. Retrieved from www.cosmeticplastic-surgerystatistics.com/costs.html

Selection in Edited Work

Chesney-Lind, M. & Brown, M. (1999). Girls and violence: An overview. In D. Flannery & C. R. Huff (Eds.), *Youth violence: Prevention, intervention and social policy* (pp. 171–199). Washington, D.C.: American Psychiatric Press.

Journal Article (Print or Online)

The volume number is italicized; the issue number (required if each issue begins with page number "1") is not italicized. (Do not italicize the punctuation.) If available for print and electronic articles, include the DOI (digital object identifier) as the last item; it is not followed by a period.

Cheung, C., Chiu, P., & Lee, M. (2001). Online social networks: Why do students use Facebook? *Computers in Human Behavior, 27,* 1337–1343. doi:10.1016/j.chb.2010.07.028

If there is no DOI, for articles retrieved electronically, include the URL of the home page of the journal as in the example below.

Priess, H.A., Lindberg, S.M., & Hyde, J.S. (2009). Adolescent gender-role identity and mental health: Gender intensification revisited. *Child Development, 80*(5) 1531–1544. Retrieved from http://srcd.org/publications/child-development

Magazine Article

Aglukkaq, Leona. (2014, December). To the Inuit: Traditional knowledge helped find the lost Franklin ship. *Canadian Geographic, 134*(6), 58–59.

Government Report (Group Author)

Public Health Agency of Canada. (2011). *Family violence in Canada: A statistical profile* (Catalogue number: 85-224-X). Retrieved from www.statcan.gc.ca/pub/85-224-x/85-224-x2010000-eng.pdf

A print version of a report includes place of publication and government ministry in place of the URL.

Website

Statistics Canada (2010, March 26). Gasoline and fuel oil, price by urban centre. Retrieved from www40.Statcan.ca/ 101/cst01/econ154a.htm

Film/Video

Joffe, J. (Producer & Director). (2012). Burlesque assassins. [Motion picture]. Canada: Joe Media Group.

Video Post

Broken Rhythms. (2013, August 9). *Grim promo*. [Video file]. Retrieved from http://youtube.com/dAe5b7vUXgU

Podcasts and blog posts follow a similar format; URL is preceded by "Podcast retrieved from" and "Message posted to," respectively.

MLA (Modern Language Association) Style

In-Text Guidelines

- MLA uses an "author/number" referencing format. The basic parenthetical format includes author's last name and page number with no punctuation in between. (Slotkin 75); (Rusel and Wilson 122).
- With a signal phrase, only the page number is in parentheses. The page number follows the reference.

  > Arango et al. found that a large proportion of children who exceed the recommended number of TV-viewing hours per day have low HRQOL scores (71).

- No signal phrase

  > A large proportion of children who exceed the recommended number of TV-viewing hours per day have low HRQOL scores (Arango et al. 71).

- No author: Use the name of the organization in place of author's name (e.g., Canada Wildlife Federation). If there is no author or organization, for example some encyclopedia entries, use the title in place of author (or a shortened version if the title is long).
- Indirect source: Author A (where you found the quote) quotes Author B (indirect source). Name Author B in your sentence (list Author A (the indirect

source) on the Works Cited page—i.e., Jones) followed by the phrase *qtd. in*, then Author B (last name and page number) in parentheses.

> Bechard says embryo testing will produce "a culture of intolerance" (qtd. in Jones 88)

- You can provide more than one source in a single citation. Separate them by semicolons—e.g., (Nadelmann 25; Long 44).
- Block quotations should be used for important passages at least four typed lines long. They are indented 2.5 cm (1 inch) from the left margin and double spaced, and do not include quotation marks. The end period precedes the parenthetical citation.

Final Page (Works Cited) Guidelines

- Entries are double spaced with the first line flush left and successive lines indented 1.3 cm (half an inch).
- Each major word in a title begins with a capital letter.
- Names of books and journals are italicized: names of shorter works, such as essays, short stories, and poems, are enclosed by quotation marks.
- The medium of publication is usually included at the end of the entry. (In electronic sources, it comes before access date.)

MLA Sample Formats

Book (One Author)

> Westoll, Andrew. *The Chimps of Fauna Sanctuary*. Toronto: Harper-Collins, 2011. Print.

Book or Journal (Multiple Authors)

- *Two authors*: Separate the names with *and*.

> Bolaria, B. Singh, and Peter S. Li. *Racial Oppression in Canada*. 2nd edn. Toronto: Garamond Press, 1988. Print. [only the first author's names are reversed]

- *More than three authors*: The name of first author may be given, followed by a comma and "et al."
- *Two or more works by same author*: List titles of works chronologically beginning with the earliest work. Begin second and any successive entries with - - - (three hyphens) rather than author's name. Follow with a period and continue entry with title of work.

- *Organization as author:* Use organization name in place of author's name:

> United Nations Development Program. *Recovering from the Ebola Crisis*. International Labor Organization, 9 Apr. 2015. Web. 28 Apr. 2015.

For in-text citations, use the full name the first time it's used with the abbreviation in brackets (e.g., United Nations Development Program [UNDP] 37); then use the abbreviation alone for subsequent citations.

Selection in Edited Work

> Wright, Austin M. "On Defining the Short Story: The Genre Question." *Short Story Theory at a Crossroads*. Ed. Susan Lohafer and Jo Ellyn Clarey. Baton Rouge: Louisiana State UP, 1989. 46−63. Print. [UP is the abbreviation for *University Press*]

Journal Article (Print or Online)

> Sugars, Cynthia. "Notes on a Mystic Hockey Puck: Death, Paternity and National Identity in Wayne Johnston's *The Divine Ryans*." *Essays on Canadian Writing* 82.2 (2004): 151–72. Print.

Include both the volume and the issue number.

For electronic articles in a database, include the database name in italics before "Web." End with date of access.

> Orth, Robert J., et al. "A Global Crisis for Seagrass Ecosystems." *BioScience* 56.12 (2006): 987–96. *Oxford Journals*. Web. 29 Mar. 2015.

Magazine Article

> Bingham, John. "A League of Their Own: One Man's Experience at an All-Women's Marathon." *Runner's World* Feb. 2006: 58. Print.

Government Report (Group Author)

> British Columbia. Office of the Auditor General. *Salmon Forever: An Assessment of the Provincial Role in Sustaining Wild Salmon*. Victoria: Office of the Auditor General of British Columbia, 2009. Print.

The electronic version would follow the guidelines for electronic citations and include website title and publisher (the appropriate ministry, for example) as well as "Web" and format and date of access.

Website

"10 Things You Should Know About Climate Change." *Canada's Action on Climate Change*. Government of Canada, 16 Jan. 2012. Web. 6 Apr. 2012.

The first date is that of the article's publication on the website; next, the publication medium is given, followed by the access date. Use angled brackets (<>) to enclose a website address only if the source would be hard to find or read without it or if your instructor requires it.

Film/Video

The Battle of Burgledorf. Dir. Richard Olak. Perf. Krista Mitchell, Matthew Graham, and Nico Santini. Brotherhood, 2015. Film.

Dir. is director, while *Perf.* should be followed by the major performers. Distributor name precedes year.

Video Post

Prosper Canada. "Youth on Credit and Debt." Online video clip. *YouTube*. YouTube. 24 Apr. 2014. Web. 12 Sep. 2015.

Sample Student Expository Essay (APA)

The following essay uses APA documentation style.

Sample Student Expository Essay with Annotations

Relational Aggression: Patterns and Motives Underlying Bullying and Its Impact on Students

by Bethany Truman

[1]   Aggression disguises itself in many different forms, some more obvious and blatantly physical, others more subtle and emotions-based. Most people have had experience with some form of aggression in their lifetime, most likely during their late childhood/ early teenage years. Emotions-based, or relational aggression, a very common kind of bullying, is unique in its subtlety, its common motives, its prominence among girls as opposed to boys, and its impacts on both the aggressors and the victims. In what ways does

relational aggression differ from physical aggression? How harmful is relational aggression when compared with physical violence, and what makes this more subtle version of aggression so powerful?

[2] Relational aggression, consisting of verbal abuse, gossip, rumour-spreading, and exclusion tactics, has the capacity to damage its victims just as thoroughly as some types of physical aggression (Archer & Coyne, 2005, p. 212). Although this form of bullying is subtle by nature, often resembling such passive aggressive behaviours as ignoring classmates in order to isolate and victimize them, it can occasionally manifest itself in more overt forms, such as verbal threats and outright name-calling (Radcliff & Joseph, 2011, p. 172). In its more subtle and manipulative form, relational aggression may not present itself as typical aggressive behaviour, thereby concealing itself from parents and educators. Unfortunately, this means that bullying of this form often gets overlooked in schools, as "overt physical violence is better understood, more readily observed, and more easily confronted" (Young, Nelson, Hottle, Warburton & Young, 2011, p. 25) than the subtle violence of relational aggression. Moreover, kids are often able to conceal their behaviours even more effectively by using nonverbal bullying tactics, such as eye-rolling, giving dirty looks, or turning their backs on individuals. Note-passing and cyber-bullying via email and Facebook are also common methods employed by relational aggressors which can be exceptionally hard to detect (Pronk & Zimmer-Gembeck, 2009, p. 187). This covert form of aggression is predominant among students in middle school, possibly as a result of shifting adolescent relationships, a larger student body, and less monitoring by adults (Werner & Hill, 2010, p. 834).

[3] What, then, are the central motives behind these students' aggression towards their peers? According to Pronk and Zimmer-Gembeck (2009), there are three broad categories that explain the use of relationally aggressive behaviours: social dynamics, the emotional state of the aggressor, and characteristics of the victim. Included within social dynamics is the issue of social dominance, the most common reason for the use of relational bullying among students. Aggressive individuals see their manipulations of their peers as a necessity in order to climb the social ladder, become the centre of attention, and gain more friends (pp. 189–190). Werner and Hill (2010) agree with the notion that

---

Although short, Bethany's introduction succeeds in its purpose. She begins by making a general statement about aggression and becomes more specific in the next two sentences: in the second sentence, she mentions the age that people usually first experience aggression. It becomes obvious in the third sentence that she will be discussing "relational aggression, a very common kind of bullying." Her thesis is in the form of questions that her research will attempt to answer.

Note Bethany's careful placement of her citation, showing exactly what information she got from her source and separating it from her own words.

In this paragraph, which introduces readers to key characteristics of relational bullying, Bethany uses five different sources, effectively synthesizing with the help of transitions such as *unfortunately* and *moreover*, as well as subtle rephrasing (e.g., "This covert form of aggression," in the last sentence, refers to the examples in the previous sentence).

Bethany begins this body paragraph with a question prompt. The next sentence announces the topic of the paragraph, showing that it will be developed by breaking a large subject into three smaller categories: division. What follows is a lengthy paragraph, which makes clear organization crucial.

Bethany cites the study before providing the information from the study. In this format, the study's year follows authors' name. The specific page is given when the reference is complete.

Bethany refers to several sources in this paragraph, giving author names *before* following with the information, thus clearly showing what comes from where.

If Bethany wished, she could have divided her long paragraph here, providing a clear transition from the previous material to what follows.

Note that in the APA documentation style, you do not repeat the year of the source if you have already given it in the same paragraph.

In this paragraph, Bethany summarizes a lot of material from page 193 of Pronk and Zimmer-Gembeck, and includes the page number after she finishes with this source.

relational aggression is used primarily as a means to gain popularity and status, remarking that "strong associations between relational aggression and perceived popularity [indicate] that relational aggression is increasingly reinforced in the peer group with age, via benefits incurred from high status" (p. 827). Pronk and Zimmer-Gembeck describe how the internal emotional state of the aggressor, primarily that of jealousy, is another significant determining factor for the use of relational aggression among students. Aggressors often use relational bullying tactics in order to compensate for their own negative internal emotions, which at times serve to increase positive feelings about themselves. In addition to jealousy, anger and revenge were sometimes reported as motivating factors behind relational aggression (pp. 191–192). The final category described by Pronk and Zimmer-Gembeck is characteristics, both positive and negative, of the victim. Negative traits could include shyness, unattractiveness, boringness, or general submissiveness. Individuals possessing these traits often find themselves easy targets for relational bullying as they tend to be easily upset, and may be perceived as socially undesirable and therefore readily isolated. By contrast, individuals may be ostracized based on their own positive traits, such as popularity and attractiveness; in this case, such individuals are targeted because they are seen as a threat to the aggressor and must be excluded so as to protect the social status of the aggressor. Finally, relational aggression is sometimes also used to create drama and excitement within a group of friends, alleviating boredom and contributing to the attention-seeking behaviours of the aggressor (p. 193).

[4]   While the motives mentioned above apply to both boys and girls, there is a general tendency for boys to have a more central focus on social hierarchies and the attainment of power, whereas girls are more likely to focus primarily on the social isolation of the victim in order to feel important within their friendship group (Pronk & Zimmer-Gembeck, 2009, p. 180). Gender differences have also been noted in relation to the specific methods students use to relationally bully their peers. Boys tend to use more direct tactics, such as excluding individuals when picking sporting teams and teasing. Moreover, while they are more prone to becoming physically aggressive when they get angry with an individual, they are also more likely to forgive and forget more quickly

than girls (p. 188). Girls, in addition to holding grudges, tend more towards giving dirty looks, gossiping behind people's backs, and maintaining a type of friendship exclusivity in which "three is a crowd" (p. 187). While girls often threaten physical violence when bullying other girls, they rarely follow through; boys, on the other hand, commonly use verbal and physical aggression concurrently (p. 186). Relational aggression often has exceedingly damaging impacts on girls as opposed to boys, as their relationships tend to have a greater emotional component; this causes their use of relational aggression with their peers to be much more prominent, whereas the same behaviours among boys are more likely to be overlooked (p. 196). According to Archer and Coyne (2005), girls rate relational aggression as more harmful than physical aggression, whereas boys generally believe that physical aggression has more damaging effects (p. 224).

[5] Relational bullying inflicts much of its damage by internalizing negative feelings of self-doubt and lowering self-esteem, resulting in a depletion of mental health and "other aspects of child and adolescent socio-emotional functioning" (Pronk & Zimmer-Gembeck, 2009, p. 176). As mentioned above, girls may be particularly damaged by relational aggression since social status and friendship groups seem all important to them during adolescence. Girls who find themselves victims of relational bullying often respond with "self-destruction" strategies, such as smoking, doing drugs, or even committing suicide. In middle school, when relational bullying is most common, this form of aggression has many psychologically-damaging consequences, including high levels of depression, loneliness, anxiety, and peer rejection (Archer & Coyne, 2005, p. 224). Victims of relational aggression may also experience a lowered sense of self-worth, become more reluctant to initiate peer interactions for fear of rejection, and avoid social situations in general because of anxiety or fear of negative consequences (Young et al., 2011, p. 25). Victims also report feeling more lethargic and impulsive when they are being relationally bullied, often describing how time seems to pass more slowly and life appears meaningless (Archer & Coyne, 2005, p. 224). The aggressors, too, experience consequences to their actions, such as "more negative life satisfaction, negative and unsatisfying relationships, and emotional instability over time" (Young et al., 2011, p. 25). However, unlike the victims, the subtle nature of this form

This paragraph is developed through the compare and contrast organizational pattern. Note the various words and phrases showing differences: *While . . . , as opposed to, whereas.* Other transitions also guide the reader: *also, moreover, in addition to.*

Here Bethany may have made an unwise word choice. Can you think of a better word than *depletion*?

of aggression can work to the aggressors' advantage. Whereas outright physical aggression has been linked to risk factors such as unpopularity and lower academic performance, relational aggression has been related to being viewed as more attractive, being better at sports, and being regarded more favourably by teachers as assertive individuals; this suggests that those who use more obvious, direct forms of social manipulation end up being rejected, whereas those aggressors who are more subtle and keep their actions disguised can remain unnoticed and possibly even improve their social standing (Archer & Coyne, 2005, p. 225). Unfortunately, this means that such behaviour, especially when undetected, may be self-reinforcing, perpetuating the cycle by leading to more—and perhaps more intense—bullying.

[6] Relational aggression differs from physical aggression in many respects: it is the most common weapon of choice among middle school-aged students; the motives behind its use are very particular and centre mostly on social status; it predominates among girls and can inflict harsh consequences on its victims while simultaneously sheltering its aggressors and rewarding them with high social status. Furthermore, it has the capacity to be just as damaging as physical aggression by virtue of its subtlety. The covert nature of this form of aggression makes it exceptionally hard to detect, and therefore all the more effective at making its victims feel isolated and alone. It is of the utmost importance that parents and educators make an effort to identify the use of this form of bullying, and recognize that it can be just as harmful as physical aggression. It may be harder to see damaged self-esteem in comparison to a broken nose, but it is just as broken, and just as much in need of healing.

Bethany concludes her final body paragraph by considering the negative consequences of relational bullying, looking beyond her sources to briefly explore the long-term effects. This sentence, then, provides a link to the last two sentences of her conclusion in which she reiterates the importance of stopping the cycle of bullying.

Bethany has correctly formatted her References page and been careful to precisely follow the requirements of the APA documentation system as given in the sixth edition of *Publication Manual of the American Psychological Association* (see p. 87).

References

Archer, J., & Coyne, S. M. (2005). An integrated review of indirect, relational, and social aggression. *Personality and Social Psychology Review, 9*(3), 212–230. doi:10.1207/s15327957pspr0903_2

Pronk, R. E., & Zimmer-Gembeck, M. J. (2009). It's "mean" but what does it mean to adolescents? Relational aggression described by victims, aggressors, and their peers. *Journal of Adolescent Research, 25*(2), 175–204. doi:10.1177/0743558409350504

Radcliff, K. M., & Joseph, L. M. (2011). Girls just being girls? Mediating relational aggression and victimization. *Preventing School Failure:*

Alternative Education for Children and Youth, 55(3), 171–179. doi:10.1080/1045988X.2010.520357

Werner, N. E., & Hill, L. G. (2010). Individual and peer group normative beliefs about relational aggression. *Child Development, 81*(3), 826–836. doi:10.1111/j.1467-8624.2010.01436.x

Young, E. L., Nelson, D. A., Hottle, A. B., Warburton, B., & Young, B. K. (2011). Relational aggression among students. *Education Digest, 76*(7), 24–29. Retrieved from www.eddigest.com/

Chapter 5 Review Questions

1. What are some strategies for coming up with a topic from scratch?
2. What does it mean to "narrow" a broad topic? Why is it necessary, and how could you do it?
3. What is the difference between a thesis statement and a research question?
4. What is a peer-reviewed journal? Who would a typical reader be?
5. Choose the best statement among the following:
    a) Academic sources are always better than non-academic sources.
    b) Academic sources tend to be more reliable than non-academic sources.
    c) Research essays should always use a combination of academic and non-academic sources.
    d) No generalizations can be made about academic versus non-academic sources.
6. What are two functions of research proposals?
7. What three factors should you take into account before beginning your major research?
8. Answer true or false:
    a) You would typically use subject guides, dictionaries, and encyclopedias early in your research.
    b) The library catalogue includes only print sources contained within the library.
    c) Online databases are the best source for the most current research available.
    d) Using limiters in your searches produces more results than not using them.
9. The following questions apply to searches using your institution's databases:
    a) Why is it crucial that you choose your database carefully?
    b) Identify two ways that using an advanced search could make your results more precise.
    c) Name two Boolean operators and explain when you would use one and when the other.
    d) What are wildcard and truncation symbols used for?
10. Identify the four "Re's" of research and explain the importance of each.
11. Explain the differences between a summary and a paraphrase.
12. When should you use direct quotations and when should you avoid using them?

13. You can show the reader that you have omitted one or more words from a direct quotation by using _____. You can show the reader that you have made a change to a direct quotation by using _____.

14. Describe three writing situations that could result in plagiarism. When might it not be necessary to provide a citation for an outside source?

15.   a) What are documentation styles?
     b) What is a "parenthetical style"?
     c) Define *signal phrase* and explain how the use of a signal phrase changes the form of the citation you would use (you can use APA or MLA style to illustrate this change).

Key Terms

brackets (p. 81)
digital object identifier (DOI) (p. 67)
documentation styles (p. 82)
ellipses (p. 80)
integrate (p. 77)

paraphrase (p. 78)
peer-reviewed journals (p. 64)
plagiarism (p. 82)
signal phrase (p. 85)
summarize (p. 77)

PART II | Reading

To some, reading might seem to be a more straightforward activity than writing. However, this is not always the case. An overly simplistic approach to reading texts (e.g., by beginning with the first sentence and reading steadily all the way through) could waste both time and effort, leaving you with only a vague knowledge of what you read. Instead, using a systematic approach will help you read more efficiently.

In this chapter, we look at matching the purpose of reading to the strategy of reading, while learning techniques to comprehend challenging words. In Chapter 7, we examine the close connection between reading, writing, and critical thinking. In Chapter 8, we discuss the conventions of academic and non-academic writing—analyzing their similarities and differences. Finally, in Chapters 9 and 10, we look at developing the specific skills applicable to the kinds of texts you will encounter in your academic career. Concluding Part II, we look at 39 "Readings" that will help test these skills in a wide variety of contexts across the disciplines.

6

Interacting with Texts

In this chapter, you will learn:

- How to read actively and annotate what you read

- How to approach a text by considering your reading purpose and other pre-reading activities

- How to use specific strategies for understanding challenging texts

- How to determine meaning through word connotations

- How to determine meaning through context

Reading at the post-secondary level is not a passive process but an *interactive* one involving a relationship *between* you and the text you are reading (*inter-* is a prefix meaning "between").

The nature of the text itself, the author's purpose for writing, the intended audience and the reason for reading it all play a role in the way you interact with a text.

Reading at the post-secondary level is not a passive process but an *interactive* one involving a relationship *between* you and the text you are reading, which often changes as you read and apply critical thinking skills. Your ideas, beliefs, and specific knowledge about the topic reflect who you are as well as your unique experiences. You therefore interact with the text in a unique way.

Likewise, the nature of the text itself, the author's purpose for writing, its audience, and the reason for reading it, all play a role in your approach to a text. The author's own ideas, beliefs, and background—as well as the specific choices in diction, style, and tone that he or she makes—additionally play a key role.

All these factors do not necessarily come into play *every* time you read a text. For example, when you respond to a text, your own ideas, observations, and experiences may well play a role. However, when you write a rhetorical analysis, you use objective standards to determine whether the essay is successful. (Rhetorical/critical analyses and critical responses were discussed in Chapter 3.) What is important to almost all reading at the college level is that you adopt the strategies that match your reading purpose.

Active Reading

Active reading is an ongoing process that deepens and evolves over time. It refers to an approach to reading in which you take an active rather than a passive role. While simply being able to understand what you are reading is a crucial first step, active reading refers also to reading at a more complex level, which is done by questioning, evaluating, re-evaluating, and using critical thinking skills. Finally, it means approaching a text as a learning experience and asking what it can teach you.

Active reading refers to an approach to reading in which you take an active rather than a passive role—by approaching a text as a learning experience. You do this first by considering your purpose for reading, then, by questioning, evaluating, and using critical analysis to develop your understanding of the text at a more complex level.

> ## BOX 6.1 | A Note on Annotation
>
> Following up on your pre-reading and reading(s) of the text itself, you can take a vital step toward active reading by making annotations (notes) in the margins of an essay or in the text itself. (For more on pre-reading and reading academic essays, see Chapter 10.)
>
> Annotating can have many purposes: to identify main ideas, to help in word or context comprehension, and to clarify your thoughts about the text. Importantly, annotating enables you to return to the text later and have your questions and responses fresh in your mind. When you annotate—translating abstract ideas and impressions into concrete language and solidifying those ideas—you are *beginning* your actual work on the assignment. What form the annotation takes depends on several factors, including your reading purpose.

An **annotation** explains, expands, or comments on a written text. It can refer to the comments themselves or to the process of making notes.

Reading Purpose

There are many different reasons for reading a text—beyond the obvious one of satisfying a course requirement. Are you reading it to

- Determine whether the text is related to your topic?
- Identify the main ideas?
- Use the text as a secondary source in your essay?
- Write a critical response to the text?
- Write a rhetorical or critical analysis?

Knowing the answer to such questions affects your reading strategies, many of which are discussed in this and following chapters. The chart below outlines questions and strategies relevant to four major reading purposes.

TABLE 6.1	Summary of Reading Purposes	
Reading Purpose	**Questions to Ask**	**Strategies**
To explore	What is it about? What kind of book or essay is it? Why was it written? How is it divided? What is the function of each section? How is it related to your topic?	Use general scan: scan title, abstract, and headings for content and writing purpose (see below). Use target scan on introduction, looking for specific features (see p. 103). Note bibliographic information (title, author name[s], publication details).
To summarize (see Chapter 2)	What are the main ideas? How are they related to each other?	Use target scan to identify thesis, topic sentences, and important sub-points (see p. 103). Use focused reading (see p. 103) on main points in order to put them in your own words.
To respond or analyze (see Chapter 3)	What is the writer's thesis? What are the main points? *Response:* Do you agree/disagree with the writer's points? *Analysis:* How is the text put together? What are its main features? How is reason used? What rhetorical/argumentative strategies are used?	Use target scan to identify main points. Use focused reading on points of agreement/disagreement and annotate these passages. Use focused reading to identify conventions and other features of similar texts.
To synthesize	How is the text related to my thesis? How does the text's thesis or findings relate to other theses/findings?	Use scan and focused reading to identify thesis, findings, and points relevant to your topic.

Selective Reading: Scanning and Focused Reading

In **selective reading**, your reading strategy is determined by your pre-reading choices, which can depend on what you are reading (book chapter, academic essay, book review) and your purpose for reading (as discussed above). It is therefore very different from reading every word from beginning to end simply and closely. Unlike reading for pleasure, selective reading is planned, conscious reading. Selective reading can be divided into scanning and focused reading.

Scanning

In a **general scan**, you read to get the gist of a text, looking for content markers, such as headings and places in which the author summarizes material (in experimental studies, this summary could include tables, graphs, and other visuals). You identify main ideas by locating topic sentences within major paragraphs but ignore examples and other detail.

In a target scan, you look for specific content, such as its title, abstract, and headings. You might use this method if you are trying to determine whether a text is useful. If, after reading the work's title and abstract, you're not sure if you should spend more time on it, you can investigate further by doing a target scan on the entire text for specific content—words or phrases related to your topic.

If you are looking for information in a book, you can locate it by referring to the subject index (or author index), a standard feature of most full-length reference and scholarly texts. These indexes, found at the back of a book, may give you many page references, so you may have to scan several pages in order to access the information you seek. If you are accessing a text online, you can use your browser's "Find" function under "Edit" to locate significant words or phrases in the text. In a library database, you can search by keywords.

> A **target scan** looks for specific content, such as a subject or keyword.
>
> A *general scan* can give you an overview of content. A *target scan* can help you find relevant content. You can then apply another method of selective reading, such as *focused reading*.
>
> A **subject index** is a list of important words in a text, ordered alphabetically and usually placed at the end of the text.

Focused Reading

Selective reading often involves both scanning and focused reading. **Focused reading** can be time-consuming. Therefore, scanning the essay beforehand to find the most relevant portions of the text can be helpful. This method will help you find the sections that contain the most relevant information to your research, which you then can read in detail.

As the term *focused reading* implies, you read the text closely line by line and word by word. If you are writing a rhetorical or critical analysis, you may look for rhetorical strategies, tone, or stylistic elements. You may also test the author's claims (premises) or question his or her conclusions. Many of the strategies for target scanning and focused reading are discussed in this chapter. Critical thinking is discussed in Chapter 7.

> In **focused reading**, you often concentrate on short- or medium-length passages and relate them to a main idea or to other sections of the work. You often read the text closely line by line and word by word.

In focused reading, you often concentrate on short- or medium-length passages and relate them to a main idea or to other sections of the text. For example, if you are writing an essay for a history class, you might concentrate on specific passages from a primary text—such as a historical document like the Indian Act (1876)—in order to connect key ideas in the passage to a historical event or other historical element. The purpose of analyzing each specific passage is to support your thesis about the significance of the event.

However, before you proceed to analyze, summarize, or synthesize texts, as discussed in earlier chapters, you need to understand the text you are reading. Writers of both academic and non-academic texts may use words whose meanings seem unfamiliar. The following pages focus on helping the reading process by adopting a strategy of understanding words through their connotations and their context.

EXERCISE 6.1

Choose one of the longer essays from Section VI ("Voices from the Academy," p. 299) of this textbook.

1. Begin with a general scan to determine the general meaning of the essay; then identify at least two key concepts.
2. Summarize the concepts with a word or short phrase. Using a target scan, identify one passage where the concept is developed throughout the paragraph.
3. Using focused reading, summarize this paragraph in one to two sentences (depending on the length of the paragraph).

Word Meanings

Connotations and Denotations

> While a word's **denotation** is its dictionary meaning, words also carry **connotations**, which can be considered "shades" of meaning or associations (often determined by context).

Many words carry **connotations**, or implications, beyond those of its **denotations**, or dictionary meanings. Paying careful attention to context—the surrounding words—can help you determine a word's connotation and intended meaning. Sometimes dictionaries suggest a word's connotations, but you need to look at the passage itself to know exactly how it is being used. Dictionaries are often not the "final word" on meaning, but necessary starting places.

A word can acquire different connotations through its use over time or within a specific group. In some cases, positive or negative values have become associated with the word. Many common words have several connotations. Consider, for example, the different implications of the words *slender, slim, lean, thin, skinny, underweight, scrawny,* and *emaciated*, which suggest a progression from positive (*graceful, athletic* . . .) to negative (. . . *weak, sickly*). Sometimes only context makes a word's connotation clear.

COLLABORATIVE EXERCISE 6.2

In groups, make a list of ten common adjectives. Then, for each word, come up with five words similar but not identical in meaning to the original word, and use one of them in a sentence. The ten sentences should reveal each word's connotation, so ensure that you provide adequate context for its exact meaning in the sentence.

Determining Word Meanings through Context

Dictionaries are an indispensable tool whether you are a professional writer or a student writer. But while a good dictionary is part of the key to understanding challenging texts, it is not the only one.

To look up every unfamiliar word would be time-consuming and interrupt your reading, affecting your understanding and retention of the material. Thankfully, you do not need to know the precise meaning of every word you read. Rather, you need to know the exact meanings of the *most important* words but only approximate meanings for others.

Since relying *only* on a dictionary is both inefficient and unreliable, you should develop reading practices that minimize—not maximize—the use of a dictionary. Before using a dictionary, first try to determine meanings through contextual clues.

Context Clues

Important nouns, verbs, adjectives, and adverbs are often revealed through context— the words around them. Writers may define difficult words or may use synonyms or rephrasing to make their meanings easy to grasp. Such strategies are used if the author thinks the typical reader may not know them. On the other hand, authors may use an unfamiliar word in such a way that the meanings of the surrounding words clarify the meaning of the unfamiliar word. In the examples, below, the challenging word is italicized, and the words that can help with meaning are underlined.

For clarification, terms may be explained or defined.

> Here we focus on studies that measure accuracy using a *correlational* approach—that is, by comparing judgments by the self and others to a criterion. (Simine Vazire & Erika N. Carlson, "Others Sometimes Know Us Better Than We Know Ourselves," p. 332)

Challenging words that are not explained can often be determined by the words immediately preceding or following. In the first example, below, the meaning of *enigma*, object of *solve*, can be inferred as something unknown, a puzzle. In the second example, the word following *edict* reveals that it must refer to some kind of order. It is stated that an emperor has made the order, so clearly an edict is an official order or proclamation.

> These results help solve an *enigma* about whether playing "hard to get" increases one's attractiveness to others (Erin R. Whitchurch, Timothy D. Wilson, & Daniel T. Gilbert, "'He Loves Me, He Loves Me Not . . .': Uncertainty Can Increase Romantic Attraction," p. 341).

> In the year 213 BCE, the Chinese emperor Shih Huang-ti issued an *edict* ordering that all books in his realm should be destroyed (Alberto Manguel, "Burning Mistry," p. 292).

If a writer uses examples, they can sometimes be used to infer the meaning of a previous word. In the following sentence, the author gives two examples of "travesties," according to seventeenth- and eighteenth-century thinking, in which undesirable role reversals are involved. (If you are not familiar with *gallants* or *breeches*, you might also guess them from context. That is, since it can be inferred that *effeminate gallants* refers to "womanly" men, it can similarly be inferred that *women in breeches* refers to "manly" women):

Develop reading practices that minimize the use of a dictionary. Use a dictionary if you have to, but first try to determine meanings by utilizing contextual clues. Of course, a dictionary is always the best resource to check your spelling.

> In the seventeenth and eighteenth centuries, bourgeois consumption qualified as "good," if it did not encourage *travesty*—men as effeminate gallants, for instance, or women in breeches (Ulinka Rublack, "The Birth of Power Dressing," p. 192).

A reader can sometimes infer a word's meaning by using nearby information to clarify the word. In the following sentence, the writer includes a word after *fetishizing* that can be used to infer the meaning of *fetishizing* as a *yearning*, a strong desire or obsession.

> But if that kind of empty *fetishizing* of technology is one of the more unfortunate side effects of a broader consumerist culture, I'd venture it also expresses a specific kind of yearning (Navneet Alang, "Stop Believing in the 'World-Changing' Power of Every New Gadget," p. 212).

Family Resemblances

> You may be able to infer the meaning of a new word by recalling a known word with the same word element.

If context does not help you determine a word's meaning, another strategy is to look for resemblances—recalling words that look similar and whose meanings you know. Many words in English come from Greek or Latin. A "family" of words may arise from the same Latin or Greek root. Therefore, you may be able to infer the meaning of a new word by recalling a known word with the same word element. For example, you can easily see a family resemblance between the word *meritocracy* and the familiar word *merit*. You can take this a step further by looking at the second element and recalling that *meritocracy* and *democracy* contain a common element. In a *democracy*, the *people* determine who will govern them. In a *meritocracy*, then, *merit* determines who governs.

Specialized Language

> **Jargon** is discipline- or subject-specific language used to communicate among members.

The strategies discussed above for understanding unfamiliar words apply to all kinds of writing. However, academic disciplines have their own specialized vocabularies that scholars use to communicate with each other. This type of language, known as jargon, is used by groups organized around a common purpose or activity. For example, in rowing, *to crab* is to lose an oar; in medical jargon, *coding* means a patient is experiencing cardiac arrest.

When you take courses in a particular discipline, like psychology, commerce, or exercise science, you begin to acquire its specialized vocabulary, which has developed along with the discipline itself. To learn about a subject is to learn its language simultaneously, in addition to the other conventions of the discipline.

Although some very technical articles may use jargon that is beyond the reach of the student, all readers can use the variety of discipline-specific dictionaries, encyclopedias, and research guides accessed through many libraries. For example,

Oxford University Press publishes a series of subject dictionaries in art and architecture, the biological sciences, classical studies, computing, earth and environmental sciences, and many other disciplines.

EXERCISE 6.3

Using contextual or word resemblance clues, determine the meanings of the italicized words in the following passages, all of which are taken from readings in Part II of this book:

1. Although a *laudable* humanitarian impulse has driven relief efforts in Haiti, it alone is insufficient for the task of rebuilding the nation. (Andrew D. Pinto, "Denaturalizing 'Natural' Disasters: Haiti's Earthquake and the Humanitarian Impulse," p. 307.)
2. The outspoken IPCC chair Rajendra Pachauri has endured a *barrage* of false claims of fraud and corruption from climate deniers. (Danny Chivers, "Debunking the Myths," p. 280.)
3. Yet imitation is *derided* and seen as distasteful. (Joe Castaldo, "Steal Your Success," p. 256.)
4. The brain is *malleable*. Just as it can be trained to be distracted, so can it be trained to pay attention. (Brian Appleyard, "Distraction" p. 223.)
5. Limited budgets are driving individuals and small teams of developers to experiment with *minimalistic* styles and explore themes and taboos that would normally be considered beyond the *purview* of mere games, such as mortality, morality, economics, and abuse. (Nik Harron, "Fully Destructible," p. 213.)

Chapter 6 Review Questions

1. a) What factors could affect the way you interact with a text?
   b) In what ways does an "active reader" read a text?
2. Why is it important to annotate a text you read for class or for an assignment?
3. a) What is the difference between a general scan and a target scan?
   b) Identify one reading purpose for each of the strategies in 3a).
   c) What is focused reading and when should you use it?
4. Answer true or false:
   a) Context clues refer to determining a word's meaning by looking at the words around it.
   b) A word's connotations are its associations or shades of meaning.
   c) You should always use a dictionary to look up every word you're unsure of.
5. What is jargon? Give an example of jargon in an area that interests you (for example, a sport or activity you're familiar with, or a hobby).

Key Terms

active reading (p. 101)
connotation (p. 104)
denotation (p. 104)
focused reading (p. 103)
general scan (p. 102)

jargon (p. 106)
selective reading (p. 102)
subject index (p. 103)
target scan (p. 103)

7

Critical Thinking

In this chapter, you will learn:

- How to apply critical thinking skills to your reading

- How to use inference in critical thinking

- How to use critical thinking to develop an argument

- How to use critical thinking to respond to and analyze a text

Critical thinking can be defined as a series of logical mental processes, including evaluating and weighing the evidence, that lead to a conclusion.

As mentioned in the previous chapter, using your critical thinking skills will help you become a more active reader. But **critical thinking** doesn't mean merely thoughtful consideration of an author's ideas, though that is certainly one of its aims. Critical thinking covers a range of activities to use when approaching a challenging text.

Writing at the post-secondary level also requires readers to make inferences— to draw valid conclusions based on evidence. Reaching a conclusion could involve

- Analyzing
- Questioning
- Recollecting
- Hypothesizing
- Evaluating
- Comparing

- Connecting
- Reconsidering
- Synthesizing
- Weighing the evidence
- Generalizing

If you look up the words *critical*, *critic*, and *criticism* in a dictionary, you will see that they have several meanings. One meaning of *critical* is "negative, finding fault." However, the root of *critical* comes from a Greek word that means "to judge or discern, to weigh and evaluate evidence." The term *critical thinking* implies judging and weighing up in order to make decisions or draw conclusions.

Much of what we do today is done quickly. This is true not only of video games, text messages, Twitter, and email but also in business, where "instant" decisions are often needed. However, because critical thinking involves many related activities, speed is not usually an asset. In fact, since critical thinking is a process, the best way to succeed is to slow down, to be more deliberate in your thinking, so you can complete each stage of the process.

Inferences and Critical Thinking

We make an inference when we form a conclusion based on the evidence or ideas that a writer presents. Writers do not always openly state their conclusions but sometimes leave it to the readers to infer meaning. (Also, context clues can be used to infer the meaning of an unfamiliar word—see Chapter 6, "Word Meanings," p. 104).

Many research methods rely on inferences: astronomers, for example, study black holes by observing the behaviour of the matter that surrounds them. They know that before matter is swallowed up by a black hole, it is heated to extreme temperatures and it accelerates. In the process, X-rays are created, which escape the black hole and reveal its presence. Scientists cannot actually *see* black holes, but they can *infer* their existence through the emission of X-rays.

We practice critical thinking every day, inferring probable causes or consequences from what we observe—the evidence—and our interpretation of this evidence. For example, let's say you arrive at your workplace to see that all the staff are wearing red. After a pause, the wheels begin to turn (a sure sign you are thinking critically!): you realize it is Valentine's Day and that the email from your manager you ignored must have asked everyone to dress in red that day. You might further infer that it is not a good idea to ignore emails from your manager.

More than one inference might be possible in a given situation—an inference could be a *possible* conclusion, but not the *most probable* one. An inference that is more probable is usually a better one. However, an inference can also be incorrect. You might draw a hasty conclusion without thinking something through or if you had a bias (for example, if you prejudged someone based on first impressions). In

An **inference** is a conclusion based on what the evidence shows or points to, without the author stating that conclusion. More than one inference might be possible in a given situation, but the most *probable* one is said to be the *best* inference.

> ## BOX 7.1 | Inferences across the Disciplines
>
> *Humanities:* Literary writers in the humanities don't announce the meanings, or themes, in their works but leave it to the reader to infer meaning by weighing the important elements in the work. It stands to reason that some readings are better than others because they take more into account of theme, character, and other elements.
>
> Sciences and Social Sciences: Researchers in the sciences and social sciences make inferences based on their knowledge of phenomena or human behaviour as well as previous research. They also make inferences about the numerical data generated through an experiment. That is, they draw conclusions about their significance.

reading, you might make an incorrect inference if you failed to read the instructions for an assignment or read them too quickly.

We receive messages today in many different forms—for example, visual ones, like a documentary film, a commercial, a photograph, or artwork. Choices we make in our clothing may also give a message about ourselves, such as how we want others to see us. Using critical thinking to make correct inferences may be vital in certain situations, such as responding to visual clues that indicate someone isn't interested in what we're saying. As well, responding correctly or sensitively to a documentary film may increase our cultural awareness or change our beliefs about a social or political issue, offering a learning opportunity we could otherwise miss.

Everyone has seen cartoons that, through humour or irony, draw attention to a controversial issue. What message does the cartoon below communicate to you? Do you infer that:

a)   society is becoming obsessed with guns;

b)   there are too many guns in Toronto;

c)   Toronto is becoming a dangerous city due to the number of guns; or

d)   guns are ruining Toronto's reputation?

Making the best inference can help us adapt to an unfamiliar situation or enable us to take advantage of a learning opportunity.

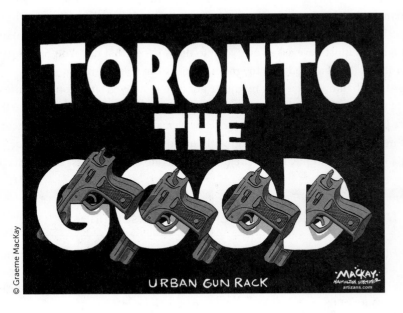

Clearly, the best inference is not "a" because nothing is being said about society. The best inference here is a more specific one. Although the statements in "b" and "c" are possible inferences, critical thinking would likely lead you to "d" as the best, or most probable, conclusion. Even if you are unfamiliar with the expression "Toronto the Good," you likely realized that the message was not only about guns but also about what was happening to Toronto's "good" reputation as a result of gun-related crimes.

Critical Thinking as a Process

Academic and non-academic writers ask questions about a topic and, using some of the methods listed in this chapter, come to a reasoned conclusion. Look at the article in Section IV, "When a Cellphone Beats a Royal Flush," for example. When Doug Saunders read that more people have cellphones than have access to a toilet, his immediate response was like most people's: it seemed ridiculous. But after evaluating, comparing, and weighing the evidence, Saunders concluded that a cellphone might be more useful than a toilet for people who are economically disadvantaged (see p. 269).

In practice, critical thinking leads us to increasingly complex thoughts that evolve the more we think about the situation or text that triggered our original thought.

Similarly, academic studies often arise from a question about prior research or about a misperception. For example, Harold Herzog questions the common perception that pets provide physical and psychological benefits (p. 323).

Critical thinking, then, isn't simply a case of responding reflexively to a trigger, such as a situation or a statement in a text and concluding something about it. In practice, critical thinking leads us to increasingly complex thoughts that evolve the more we think about that situation or statement.

Breaking Down Critical Thinking: An Example

To better understand the process of critical thinking, consider the situation described by Dorothy Woodend in "Generation Velcro" (pp. 181–2).

> The other day I took my seven-year-old son Louis to buy some running shoes. "Pick something with Velcro," I said, as he trotted off to roam the racks.
>
> A clerk, hovering nearby, gave me a jaundiced look; "You know we get high school kids in here who have to buy Velcro because they never learned to tie their shoes. Every year their parents would just buy them Velcro because it was easier than making them learn how to tie laces."
>
> I stared at him and he went on.
>
> "The other day we had to special order a pair of shoes for this kid's high school graduation because he couldn't tie his laces, and he needed a pair of Velcro formal shoes."
>
> I put the shoes Louis had chosen back on the shelf, and picked out a pair of lace-up running shoes. It wasn't just that I'd been shamed into compliance by the salesman, but something Jane Jacobs had written about in her last book about the coming dark ages hit home. The loss of knowledge, she said, once vanished, is so difficult to regain—even if it's something as mundane as tying your shoes.

Woodend claims that she was not simply "shamed into compliance by the salesman," a reflexive response unconnected to critical thinking. Instead, various ways of thinking critically led her to a more complex perception. The process can be represented in three stages by a diagram (though we can't know for certain which activities Woodend did in the second stage).

Trigger   ⟶ clerk's comment about Velcro shoes

Activity   ⟶ connecting, recollecting, analyzing, generalizing . . .

Conclusion ⟶ inability to tie shoelaces related to loss of knowledge

Of course, to be convincing, Woodend must do more than simply state a conclusion and expect the reader (especially the critical thinker) to agree. She needs to present evidence to support her claim, as all arguers do. She refers to a newspaper article and a book by a neuroscientist who comments on the phenomenon of knowledge loss and its possible significance.

If her critical thinking ended here, her essay would only show one stage in the process of critical thinking (recall that critical thinking can best be defined as a *series* of logical mental processes that lead to a conclusion). However, later in her essay, she reconsiders the original situation that triggered her perception about the loss of knowledge and, by asking a question, reaches a second, more significant conclusion.

Which brings me back to the question that has me tied up in shoe knots.
　　If the lights start to go out sometime in the near future, and the Walmart closes its doors, who would really be useful? The answer changes, but basically it comes down to people who know how to do things, farmers, carpenters, doctors, people with a body of knowledge that can be applied directly, physically to the real world. (p. 183)

Trigger   ⟶ her original conclusion

Activity   ⟶ reconsidering, questioning, generalizing . . . other activities?

Conclusion ⟶ Those with practical knowledge and skills will be badly needed in a future "dark age"

Critical thinking, then, involves a chain of logic, a process that can lead you far beyond your original response or question to broader and more complex responses. In this way, the critical thinking process could lead to a new way of looking at the situation and its larger significance. In the example, Woodend's chain of logic begins with Louis' inability to tie his shoes, but ends with questions that are more complex about her own parenting, and that of her entire generation.

As a reader, you may find yourself questioning the critical thinking processes of a writer. Conclusions can often be challenged, especially in an argument. For example, you could ask whether the writer, such as Woodend, sufficiently backs up the claims she makes or whether there is a flaw in the reasoning. You might ask if there is a gap between shoelace-tying ability and problems with coping during a dark age or, indeed, whether such a dark age is inevitable, as the writer seems to think. Critically connecting with a writer, who is critically connected with his or her topic, is a feature of critical thinking at the college and university level. In fact, this is what you do when you write a rhetorical analysis or a research paper (see Chapters 3 and 5).

> Critically connecting with a writer, who is critically connected with his or her topic, is a feature of critical thinking at the college and university level.

Critical Situations for Critical Thinking

When you read a text, you might stop to question a statement. A writer might make a claim that directly contradicts what your knowledge or common sense tells you—for example, that cats are more intelligent than humans. Another example might be a writer making a claim about a topic that experts have been debating for years—for example, that cats are smarter than dogs. Although you would probably just dismiss the first claim, the second claim would probably cause you to use critical thinking to evaluate the following:

- **The writer's credibility:** Who is the intended audience? Has the writer written for this audience? What shows you this? Who is the writer and what is his or her interest in their topic? Is the writer an expert? What kind? Is he or she a researcher into animal behaviour? A veterinarian? An animal trainer? Someone who has owned both dogs and cats? Someone who has owned dogs only? Could the writer have a bias? Are there examples of false reasoning? Has fact been carefully distinguished from opinion? Other factors also affect credibility (see "Support," below).
- **Nature of the claim (thesis):** Specific claims are stronger than general ones and often are easier to prove. Since variability has been found among dog breeds, it would be difficult to generalize about the intelligence of *all* dogs.
- **Basis of the claim:** Some claims are more straightforward than other ones are. There are different ways to define and measure intelligence: physiologically (e.g., the weight of the brain in proportion to the weight of the body) and behaviourally (e.g., trainability, adaptability, independence). Those favouring a dog's intelligence may point to trainability as the intelligence factor, while advocates of cat intelligence may point to adaptability or independence. Both are valid criteria in an argument but could be challenged.
- **Method:** How does the writer attempt to prove the claim? Is the method appropriate? Intelligence can be measured. Therefore, a method that measured

intelligence scientifically would be more credible than one that relied on personal observation—especially since many pet-lovers are quite opinionated about their pets' intelligence and may not always separate fact from opinion. How many measurements were made? (More measurements will likely create more valid results than fewer ones.)

- **Support:** A credible writer needs to provide more than opinion to back up a claim. In critical thinking, you must evaluate the nature of the evidence and the way the writer uses it. Typical questions might include the following: What kind of evidence did the writer use? Has the writer relied too much on one kind of evidence or one source? How many sources were used? Were they current sources (recent studies may be more credible than older ones)? Did the writer provide relevant details from the source(s)? Did he or she ignore some sources (e.g., those that found dogs more intelligent than cats)?

- **Conclusion:** Conclusions result from the *incremental process of reading critically*. In arriving at a conclusion, you weigh the various factors involved in your analysis of the text. Obviously, some points are more important than others, and some evidence is more effective than other evidence. You might consider how weaker points affect the validity of the findings. Were there any gaps or inconsistencies in the use of reason? Was the writer's conclusion logically prepared for? Ultimately, your goal is to determine whether the weight of evidence supports the writer's claim.

EXERCISE 7.1

The specific statements in each passage below can lead to inferences either about the information presented or about the writer's attitude toward the subject. Choose the best (most probable) conclusion:

1. After missing the previous class, you are surprised to see your instructor enter the classroom and, without saying anything, take a seat in the back row. You ask the student beside you why she is not standing at the front preparing for class, but he just shrugs.
   a) The instructor has decided to take the day off from teaching.
   b) The instructor is just sitting down while she catches her breath.
   c) The instructor forgot to tell the class that there would be a guest speaker today.
   d) The instructor told the class there would be a guest speaker the next day, but the student beside you missed the previous class too.

2. Jen was hired as the manager of Cilantro due to her proven competence and high ethical standards. It was a stressful time because a new staff team had been hired to complete a company project. Jen, who was in charge of the project, was annoyed on Monday when a team member told her they needed two more weeks to work on samples before they could begin production. After listening to team concerns, she left the room saying, "Well, if we keep

going at this pace, we're not going to complete production in the projected three weeks." In her end-week report to her supervisors, she indicated that the project was running smoothly.
  a) She lied in the report to protect her job with the company.
  b) She has decided to change her team and hire new members.
  c) She found a solution to the problem and did not want to complain needlessly.
  d) No inference is possible about the reason for Jen's statement.

3. In your women's studies class, you have been asked to write a response on the ways that gender is shaped by socio-economic factors. When handing out the assignment page, your instructor says that she does not expect you to be an expert yourself but that your response must include the view of at least one expert on this topic.
  a) Your instructor expects you to rely mostly on your own opinion.
  b) Your instructor expects you to rely mostly on research sources.
  c) Your instructor expects you to rely on your critical thinking skills.
  d) You do not need to worry about the instructor's comment as the assignment page includes all the information you need to write a successful essay.

4. It was Todd's roommate's turn to cook dinner, but when Todd got home, his roommate was glued to the TV and the kitchen looked untouched. "Wow! Something smells great," enthused Todd.
  a) Todd has a poor sense of smell.
  b) Todd is sarcastically voicing his displeasure.
  c) Todd is trying to give his roommate a hint that he should start dinner.
  d) No inference is possible.

5. Lara works at the city's tourist centre, and she is often asked to recommend whale-watching tours. However, her boss has told her she should provide the relevant brochures and not make personal recommendations. She often tells tourists, "I've heard that Whales Galore is awesome, but I've heard a few good things about Spouting Off, too."
  a) Lara favours Whales Galore over Spouting Off.
  b) Lara favours Spouting Off over Whales Galore.
  c) Lara is careful to praise both companies equally in order to satisfy her boss.
  d) No inference is possible.

Chapter 7 Review Questions

1. Which of the following activities is not usually associated with critical thinking?
  a) Questioning
  b) Comparing
  c) Memorizing
  d) Reconsidering

2. What meaning of the word *critical* is implied in the term *critical thinking*?

3. Define *inference* in your own words. Give an example of an inference you made recently and what led you to this inference (it can be a correct or incorrect one).

4. Explain how inferences differ across the disciplines.

5. The best inference in a given situation is (choose one):
    a) The most probable one
    b) The least probable one
    c) The one most people accept as true
    d) The most recent one

6. Describe two situations which could result in an incorrect inference (they could be general or specific situations) and what would make them incorrect.

7. The situation that often begins the critical thinking process is called the _____.

8. In which of the following three assignments would critical thinking likely not play a major part?
    a) Rhetorical analysis
    b) Summary
    c) Research paper

9. What questions could you ask to determine whether a writer is credible?

10. Answer true or false:
    a) Specific claims are weaker than general claims.
    b) In drawing a conclusion, you should weigh all the evidence equally.

Key Terms

critical thinking (p. 108)   inference (p. 109)

8

An Introduction to Reading Texts

In this chapter, you will learn:

- How writers consider their audience

- How to identify two common kinds of writing—their formats and purposes

- How to distinguish between academic and non-academic texts

- How writers use analysis and synthesis in the writing process

Many tasks you undertake in your academic career will require you to read texts. Through careful reading, you can inform yourself on issues relevant to your world. Perhaps more important, by incorporating your reading experiences into your writing, you can inform others and shape the way they understand these issues.

Most forms of communication, including writing, assume the existence of an **audience**, a community of potential readers. Who are these readers? For researchers, they are other researchers, as well as decision makers who hope to make use of the research—from local school board members and administrators to national governments. For journalists, they are members of the public they hope to reach. Each writer is aware of his or her audience and uses the most effective methods possible to reach this audience.

For student writers, the reader may be an instructor or, possibly, another student who will respond to your writing. Learning to write for your audience prepares you for any public writing you might do.

Most texts, whether written, oral, or visual, are directed to an intended **audience**— for writing, a group of readers. Each writer is keenly aware of his or her audience and uses the most effective methods possible to reach this audience.

Kinds of Texts

For years, you have been developing a variety of reading-related skills—whether you were conscious of them or not. The pages that follow will help you extend and adapt these skills to new situations so you can become a more conscious and capable reader—and writer.

Although reading at the post-secondary level may be more diverse and challenging than you are used to, it helps to know that texts fall into one of two broad categories:

1. academic (usually research-oriented) texts written by experts for knowledgeable readers; and
2. non-academic texts, written by non-experts for general, interested readers.

In turn, these two categories can be subdivided (see p. 120).

The 39 readings in Part II reflect this division. Although non-academic texts are usually written for general readers, they often depend on outside sources, such as government publications or academic studies, even if they do not cite these sources.

In the two previous chapters, we discussed general reading and thinking strategies. In this and the following two chapters, we discuss specific characteristics of writing—non-academic and academic—that will help you read a wide variety of texts differing in their reading level, complexity, and conventions.

> Texts can be divided into academic, written by experts for other experts, and non-academic, written often by non-experts for general readers.

The Reading–Writing Connection

As a student, becoming one of a community of readers makes you part of a community of writers. One reason is that you will inevitably be asked to read something and respond to or analyze it, often in writing.

The more you think about your reading process, the better you will read, and the more you will think about what you read and ask appropriate questions. Considering these questions will help you to write successfully about what you have read.

> The more you think about your reading process, the better you will read, and the more you will think about what you read.

Most students know that the way they write on a friend's Facebook "wall" is very different from the kind of writing they do for their instructor. Much of the writing we encounter online is too informal or subjective to serve as a model for academic writing. Similarly, as you will see in the examples of writing in this textbook, academic and non-academic writing have different purposes, and each is designed for different audiences (see "Purposes," below). Each can therefore serve as a writing model depending on your writing purpose and intended audience.

Academic versus Non-Academic Writing
Formats and Audience

It is usually not difficult to determine whether a piece of writing is intended for an academic or a non-academic audience. To begin with, you can consider *where* academic and non-academic writing are found. If you wanted a casual read, you might scan a magazine rack at a local store or an online list of the top 10 bestsellers. You would not use a specialized database or seek out the publications of a university press. In short, experts and non-experts know where to find the material they're interested in.

Publishers design their covers with specific readers in mind. For example, a popular magazine displays colourful photos or other graphics with, perhaps, captivating quotations or tag lines to catch the reader's interest. Many academic journals include the titles of articles on their cover, stressing their knowledge-based approach.

Purposes

Academic and non-academic writing also differ in purpose. Articles in books and academic journals usually attempt to

- interpret texts in new ways,
- generate new knowledge or confirm/disprove old knowledge, or
- review related studies on a particular topic.

In contrast, articles in magazines, newspapers, and other informal sources usually attempt to

- inform,
- persuade, or
- entertain.

Of course, many non-academic articles combine these purposes in various ways—for example, to inform *and* entertain.

Figure 8.1 summarizes some of the different classifications of academic and non-academic writing, showing the formats, purposes, and audience of each. However, the categories are not always clear-cut. For example, some academic journals include material intended for a more general audience. A periodical is a general term for the kind of publication that is issued periodically—at regular or semi-regular intervals.

Although various kinds of periodicals are represented in the selection of journalistic essays in Part II, many could be considered "ideas" magazines in which professional writers, including some with academic affiliations, address compelling issues in today's world. The mandate of such magazines could be summed up by that of *Inroads*, a 20-year-old Canadian periodical that aims to publish "content [that] is well-researched but not academic."

Articles from mass-circulation magazines or newspapers usually are written for an audience with varied interests and knowledge levels. However, specific sections of newspapers and large-circulation magazines could be written for a narrower audience (e.g., the books section, which is part of the more general arts or lifestyles section, or the stock market quotations, part of the business section).

Academic writing is usually intended to interpret texts, generate new knowledge, or review knowledge about a topic for specialists. Non-academic writing is usually intended to inform, persuade, or entertain general readers.

A **journal** is a kind of periodical designed for readers with specialized interests and knowledge. A journal contains original research, reviews, and editorials—but little, if any, advertising. It may be issued in print and/or online format.

A **periodical** is a general term for the kind of publication that is issued at regular intervals.

In this text, essays written mainly for an audience of scholars, researchers, and professors are referred to as *academic* or *scholarly essays*, whether they are in book or journal format. Essays written for an audience of non-specialists who share certain interests, beliefs, or ideologies are referred to as *non-academic* or *journalistic essays*.

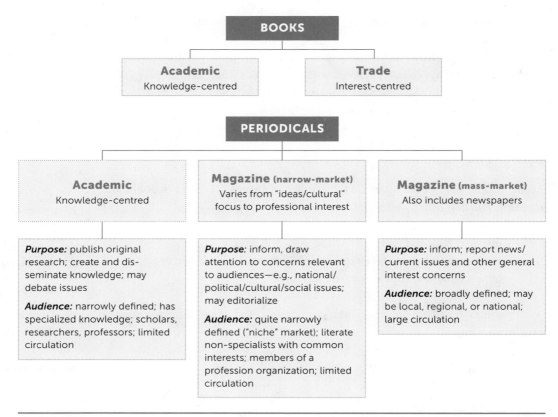

FIGURE 8.1 Published Texts Can Be Divided into Categories Depending on Their Purpose and Audience

Other Differences

In addition to format, audience, and purpose, academic and non-academic writing differ in various ways, as shown in Table 8.1.

The following paragraphs taken from two essays in Part II—one from a non-academic article and one from an academic article—differ in their language, style, and sentence structure.

Non-Academic: Selfish genes, survival of the fittest, competition, hawk, and dove strategies. Like all theories, Darwinism has its own distinct vocabulary. So distinct, in fact, that we end up asking how else we can talk about evolution. After all, isn't competitive evolution the only possible context for explaining the biological facts? The drama implied by competition, war, and selfishness passes unnoticed because people are used to this rather hyped-up, way of talking even about current scientific beliefs. (Mary Midgley, "The Selfish Metaphor," p. 271)

The author begins with a sentence fragment: the list of four recognizable phrases quickly attracts the reader's attention.

A short sentence is followed by another fragment.

Asking a question directly involves the reader.

Colloquialisms, like hyped-up, are common in non-academic prose.

TABLE 8.1 Academic versus Non-Academic Writing		
	Non-Academic	**Academic**
Structure	Varies; may be loosely structured	Tight and logical structure
Introduction	Dramatic introduction common; designed to attract attention	Dense; designed to give information
Thesis	May not be included in introduction	Found in the introduction
Paragraphs	May be short to maintain interest	Vary; tend to be well-developed
Argument/persuasion	Opinion may be evident throughout	Essays may offer recommendations but personal opinion minimized
Conclusion	May end with appeal or stress importance of topic; may be brief and informal	Important part of essay; may suggest further research
Style	Informal; may use *I, you*, etc.; contractions; occasional slang	Formal
Language	Geared to non-specialist; stimulates reader interest	Geared to specialist; conveys knowledge
Sentence structure	Sentence variety; short to medium-length sentences; occasional use of fragments	Varies, but sentences may be long and complex

Academic: The causal role of forbidden desires in ironic effects is clear in experimental research on the effects of imposed secrecy.[32] People randomly paired to play "footsie" under the table in a laboratory study reported greater subsequent attraction to their assigned partner when they had been asked to keep their contact secret from others at the table, and survey respondents revealed similar effects of tainted love: a greater desire for past romantic partners with whom relationships had first started in secret.[33] (Daniel M. Wegner, "How to Think, Say, or Do Precisely the Worst Thing for Any Occasion," p. 317)

Authors of academic essays refer to related studies to support their points. Notes 32 and 33 are placed at the end of the essay. Full details there enable other researchers to access these studies.

Informal (conversational) language is indicated by quotation marks. In a non-academic essay, "footsie" would likely not be placed in quotation marks.

Sixty-word sentences are uncommon in essays aimed at a general reader. However, use of a clear structure, appropriate joining words (*when, and*), and correct punctuation help the reader connect the thoughts.

EXERCISE 8.1

Choose a sample paragraph from an essay in Section V (non-academic essays) and one in Section VI (academic essays) and compare them in two paragraphs. Use three of the following as your points of comparison: (a) language, (b) style, (c) sentence structure, (d) paragraph structure.

Since paragraphs are generally longer in Section VI essays, you may choose part of a paragraph, but ensure it is about the same length as the paragraph of the essay you choose from Section V. (Depending on the essay, you may need to choose two consecutive paragraphs in Section V to come up with three points of comparison.)

Breaking Down and Putting Together

When you write an **analysis**, you are breaking something down in order to look more closely at its parts. When you write a **synthesis**, you are "putting together" in order to reach a conclusion.

Two important terms in almost all writing are analysis and synthesis. When you use your skills for analysis—from the verb *analyze*—you closely examine something. You analyze when you "break down" an essay or paragraph, an argument or point. Critical thinking involves the use of reason in breaking down ideas in order to reach a conclusion (see Chapter 7).

Different methods or patterns can be used to break something down—for example, you can look at causes and effects, pros and cons, or similarities and differences. A literary analysis could involve breaking down a poem's stanzas or a novel's narrative to study smaller units, such as metre (in a poem) or point of view (in a novel). There are many other methods as well (see Chapter 1, pp. 14–15).

Synthesis is the activity of "putting together" in order to reach a consensus or a conclusion. In a student research essay, you combine your own ideas with ideas, facts, and/or findings from other sources. Therefore, it is sometimes called a synthesis essay. In a successful synthesis essay, the writer organizes sources logically, connects them to a central thesis, and clarifies the unique contribution of each source.

Chapter 8 Review Questions

1. The person or persons you are writing to is called your _____. Why is it important to be aware of this person or group before writing?

2. In your own words, explain the "reading–writing connection" and its importance to your development as a reader and writer.

3. Choose the one answer that doesn't apply: Academic writing usually attempts to
    a) Inform and entertain the reader
    b) Review research on a common topic
    c) Generate new knowledge
    d) Interpret a text in a new way

4. Choose three of the following five writing features and explain the difference(s) between academic and non-academic writing for each feature chosen:
    a) The introduction
    b) Paragraphs
    c) The conclusion
    d) Language
    e) Sentence structure

5. What are the differences between analysis and synthesis?

Key Terms

analysis (p. 122)
audience (p. 117)
journal (p. 119)

periodical (p. 119)
synthesis (p. 122)

9

Conventions of Non-Academic Writing

In this chapter, you will learn:

- How non-academic writers use analysis and synthesis

- How personal experience can be used in non-academic texts

- How to read and write different kinds of introductions, including introductions that create interest and introductions that state a thesis

- How to recognize features of language and style in non-academic texts

- How to understand the relationship between the journalistic and scholarly communities

Conventions (from the Latin for "come together") are practices that help direct the actions and thinking of specific groups of people. You can think of them as a set of instructions to help us communicate. For example, in formal letters and emails, it is conventional to use a salutation like *Dear* before the name of the recipient. However, in emailing a friend, a more appropriate salutation might be *Hi*. Conventions depend on audience, along with other factors. Both academic and non-academic writing have their conventions, or "usual practices," that help direct the reader, organize the essay, and open up a channel of communication between writer and reader.

In this chapter, we consider "usual practices" of non-academic writing, including techniques you may use in your own writing. In Chapter 10, we turn to "usual practices" of academic writing. Studying the conventions of non-academic and academic writing will help you locate information and understand how it is being used, making you a better (and more confident) reader. Applying some of these conventions to your writing assignments will also help you to be a better (and more confident) writer.

Conventions are practices that direct the actions and thinking of specific groups. You can consider them a set of instructions that help us communicate with one another.

Analysis or Synthesis?

Although non-academic essays, like student essays, usually combine analysis and synthesis, they can be divided into two main types:

1. Those whose main purpose is to analyze
2. Those whose main purpose is to synthesize

Non-academic writers may use both analysis and synthesis, but the stress is usually on one or the other. Essays seeking to persuade their readers usually focus on analysis, while those seeking mainly to inform focus on synthesis.

Analysis

Some kinds of journalistic essays—such as those seeking to persuade readers—stress analysis over synthesis. Here, *the writer's* opinion and ideas count for more than evaluating and integrating what *others* have said. However, the writers of a persuasive essay may also synthesize the ideas and words of others if this makes the argument more convincing. In "Slip-Sliding Away, Down the Ethical Slope," p. 274, Robert J. Sternberg uses process analysis, breaking down ethical behaviour into eight steps, while Alberto Manguel, in "Burning Mistry," p. 291, mostly analyzes causes and effects that led to an incident of book-burning, with some synthesis as well. (For more information on persuasive or argumentative essays, see Chapter 4.)

Synthesis

Journalistic essays whose main purpose is to inform use synthesis more than analysis. This information comes from what others have discovered or said. Journalistic writers, then, often use other people's words and ideas, synthesizing them in an interesting and entertaining way for their audience. For example, Joe Castaldo in "Steal Your Success" (p. 256) uses mostly synthesis to "put together" the views of entrepreneurs and business leaders to support his thesis that innovators are often less successful than those who take their ideas and use them for their own purposes.

Journalistic writers synthesize by using a combination of summary and direct quotations, especially those that will make the greatest impact on the reader, to explain complex material. Technical information is almost always simplified, or omitted if unimportant.

In contrast to academic writers, non-academic writers often use personal experience for various purposes, including the common ones of attracting the reader's interest and enabling the reader to relate to the author's experience.

Personal Experience in Non-Academic Writing

In contrast to most academic essays, human interest is often a focus in journalistic essays. Writers may interview those most directly affected by an event, as well as observers, often shaping the story around the emotions of those involved.

While academic writers seldom refer directly to themselves—except in the role of objective researchers—a common practice of non-academic writers is to "write themselves" into their essays, enabling their readers to relate to the writer's experience. For example, Joanna Pachner, in "Do You Have the Brain of a CEO?" (p. 248), uses her experiences and self-reflection as a means to question her leadership abilities. Many members of her target audience would likely ask the same kinds of questions as she does.

However, personal experience and observation may play a much larger role throughout the essay. For example, Madeline Sonik (p. 155) and Ian Brown (p. 165) write from their own experiences, whereas Andrew Irvine (p. 162) uses a personal experience to introduce his reflective essay on scientific progress. These types of essays are discussed in the next section.

Personal and Reflective Essays

Other non-academic essays tend to be literary or philosophical, rather than journalistic. The personal or expressive essay, creative non-fiction, the literary essay, and literary journalism are all terms that suggest that the focus is on elegant prose and thoughtful reflection. Their writers may use common fictional techniques, such as irony, imagery, dialogue, and metaphoric language. They may also use narration or description to render an incident or a scene.

Such essays tend to stress the writer's life or experience, but their ultimate purpose is to show us the large picture, to invite us to consider our own world in a new way. Although the distinctions between the many sub-forms are subtle, they can be divided into

1. the personal essay, in which the writer's *life experience* is key; and
2. the reflective essay, in which the writer's *observations and thoughts* are key.

It is important to remember that successful personal and reflective essays are never self-indulgent. They use personal experience or observation to reveal something universal.

The use of personal experience or observation in non-academic essays highlights a key difference between these and academic essays, which seldom include first-hand experience. If they do, it will usually be to provide support through "anecdotal evidence" or to enhance writer credibility. For example, Harold Herzog states that his conclusions should not be taken "as a condemnation of pet keeping. Indeed, companion animals have always been a part of my own life . . . ." Making this statement clarifies the author's intentions by drawing a line between his life and his research subject, the contribution of pets to human health (see p. 327).

> Successful personal and reflective essays are never self-indulgent. They use personal experience or observation as a means to reveal something of greater significance.

> Academic essays, unlike non-academic ones, seldom use personal experience unless it is to directly provide support or increase credibility. Although non-academic essays sometimes do employ the first-person voice, it should have a specific purpose.

In addition to their use of analysis, synthesis, and personal experience, non-academic essays share other features, some of which may apply to the kinds of essays you will write.

Features of Non-Academic Writing

Non-academic writers use various conventions and strategies to create reader interest, beginning with the introduction. An interest-based introduction contrasts with the knowledge-based introduction in academic writing.

Non-academic writers often try to engage their readers directly in their introductions. Interest-based introductions are less common in academic writing.

Interest-Grabbing Introductions

Like the kinds of introductions you may be asked to write (see Chapter 1, p. 7), introductions in journalistic writing are designed to attract the attention of readers and draw them into the essay. There are many ways to interest readers. A typical method is to sketch a familiar scenario to which the reader can relate, or one that is striking because it is unfamiliar. In a variant on this method, the writer makes a common observation or draws a familiar scene, only to use the reversal strategy to counter it.

Other common methods include the following:

- Narrating a personal experience or story that introduces the topic
- Describing a scene
- Using an example that represents a problem or issue central to the essay
- Narrating a brief anecdote
- Posing a provocative question
- Inserting a relevant quotation
- Citing a curious fact or making a challenging statement

Reversal: A sign at the [West Point War] Museum's entrance states, "Unquestionably, war-making is an aspect of human nature which will continue as nations attempt to impose their will upon each other." Actually, this assertion is quite questionable. (John Horgan, "Does Peace Have a Chance?" p. 277.)

Narrating personal experience: Mavis Gallant showed me what's wrong with most online content. I don't think that was ever her goal, of course. But that's what I like about good fiction: it's a bunch of made-up stories that tell you important things when you least expect it. (Shannon Rupp, "I'll Take My Coffee with Fiction, Thanks," p. 151.)

Narrating an anecdote and posing a question: You see your roommate at his computer, writing a paper. You notice him transferring text from

an online document to the paper he is writing without attribution . . . .
Is there a problem here? (Sternberg, "Slip-Sliding Away," p. 275.)

Quotation: I had become the embodiment of T.S. Eliot's great summary of the modern predicament: "Distracted from Distraction by Distraction." (Appleyard, "Distraction," p. 224.)

Curious fact/challenging statement: About a third of the world's people have no toilet. (Saunders, "When a Cellphone Beats a Royal Flush," p. 269.)

Using a Thesis

Thesis statements are less common in journalistic essays than in the kinds of essays that students are usually asked to write and in academic essays. Why? A thesis statement is designed to inform the reader of the essay's content, especially its main point. In most interest-centred writing, announcing a thesis can work against the writer, deflecting the reader's interest where it is most needed, just before the body of the essay begins. In an essay you write, a thesis statement serves to inform the reader. In early drafts, it also ensures that you, the writer, are clear on your purpose and main point.

Instead of making a clear thesis statement, the journalistic writer may continue to draw out the reader's interest throughout the introduction, adding detail about the topic. Many successful journalistic essays contain no announced thesis or delay the thesis until later in the essay. Instead, the writer relies on rhetorical or literary devices to lead the reader on, using linguistic resources, evoking a distinct tone or mood, or seizing on a human connection.

The fact that a non-academic essay may not include a thesis statement in its introduction means that you need to read it differently and be open to the possibility that the thesis will be delayed or not directly stated.

In many cases, especially when literary techniques are used, it would be more precise to speak of a theme than of a thesis. You probably are familiar with themes from literary analysis. A theme—an overarching meaning or universal aspect—is seen through a work's basic elements (such as plot, setting, and characters in fiction), as well as literary devices (such as images, diction, and figurative techniques like metaphors). A writer of this kind of essay evokes a theme, rather than "announces" a thesis.

> A thesis statement is designed to inform the reader of the essay's content, its main point(s). A thesis statement may be omitted in a non-academic essay in order to sustain interest in the topic.

> A **theme** is an overarching meaning or universal aspect, seen through a work's basic elements, such as plot, setting, character, images, language, and figurative techniques.

Organization

Journalistic writing is organized logically, often with the use of organizational patterns common to all writing. For example, a writer could organize points chronologically (time order), beginning with the oldest and ending with the most recent. Journalistic writers often use description and narration to organize information, and all writing benefits from the use of examples to clarify abstract concepts. Paragraph organization tends to be looser than in academic writing, and paragraphs may be short.

Language

In much non-academic writing, diction (word choice) serves the practical function of communicating information directly. The exception is literary writers, who may use words that have more than one connotation (association) in order to invoke richness, even ambiguity, through their language, rather than directness.

Language level is one of the main differences between academic and non-academic writing. Journalistic writers try to substitute common words for less common ones, especially technical terms or jargon. However, to describe journalistic writing as "simple" can be misleading. Writers of specialty or "interest" magazines may use words that only an educated audience would understand. All writers should know their audience well, and one way this knowledge is reflected is in the writer's level of language.

Although non-academic writing is not necessarily simple, it is sometimes colloquial and informal. For example, writers may use colloquial language, which is conversational in nature, or even slang to relate to their readers. Using contractions is another informal method of writing and is commonly favoured as a space-saving approach (see "Space-Saving Techniques," p. 130). As a rule, you should not use colloquialisms or contractions in your own writing, unless you are using dialogue in a narrative.

Tone

Writers can convey their attitude to their subject by their tone. One of the ways that you can infer a writer's tone—and understand what he or she is really saying—is by using critical thinking skills to read "between the lines," paying particular attention to the way language is being used. A writer could use a tone that is serious or solemn, light or comic, mocking or earnest, intimate, thoughtful, or ironic.

Determining an author's tone will help you know how to respond to the essay itself. For example, if a writer uses an ironic tone, he or she is directing you beyond the literal surface meaning. In irony a second, or "deeper," meaning exists below the literal one, which contradicts, or is inconsistent with, the literal meaning. If you fail to notice an ironic tone, you may misread the essay, taking the surface meaning for the intended one. Irony can usually be detected through the writer's language or the subject matter, or both.

Side notes:

All writers should know their audience well, and one way this knowledge is reflected is in the level of language that the writer uses.

Colloquial language is conversational in nature and is a typical feature of some non-academic writing.

Tone can be defined as the use of language to convey the writer's attitude toward the subject or the audience.

In **irony** a second, or "deeper," meaning exists below the literal meaning, which contradicts, or is inconsistent with, the literal meaning.

In the second half of the following sentence, language and subject matter convey the writer's irony (or, perhaps, sarcasm).

"[The current government has] dragged its feet to renew and increase graphic labelling on cigarette packages—and thank goodness, because having to look at images of lung and oral cancers is just *such* a downer when you want a hit of nicotine." (Daniel Rosenfield et al., "Canadian Lifestyle Choices: A Public Health Failure," p. 344.)

In sarcasm, a writer or speaker states something as its opposite.

EXERCISE 9.1

How would you define tone in the following passages? Identify specific features that reveal tone. For each, come up with at least two adjectives that describe the author's tone.

1. My friends and I mordantly joked that every cigarette we smoked would shorten our lives by ten minutes. Because we were immortal, this didn't seem like a big deal.

   At school, I belonged to the science club and entered fairs with projects like "The Miracle of Rayon." I was an A student in home economics; my pocket money came from babysitting. In short, I was something of a nerd, and desperately wished for an edgier image, which I believed smoking bestowed. (Cunningham, "Giving up the Ghost," p. 171.)

2. Kaliouby is totally psyched about the potential of the "emotion economy"—so maybe we should be, too. Think of all that will change. Now when hackers swipe data from the cloud, they'll get your credit card information, your buck-naked selfies, and evidence that you cried at the ending of *Transformers 2*. And who among us doesn't look forward to a day when corporations can quietly monitor the emotional state of their employees? (Feschuk, "The Future of Machines with Feelings," p. 229.)

3. We raised him on our own for 10 years, and the experience almost shattered everything I valued— my family, my marriage, my healthy daughter's life, my finances, my friendships, life as I wanted to live it.

   There was no genetic test for his syndrome when he was born (there still isn't). For a long time, not a day went by when I didn't wish there'd been one. Today, I'm glad no test existed then—that I never had to decide, based on a piece of paper damp with my wife's blood, whether my strange and lonely boy ought to exist. (Ian Brown, "I'm Glad I Never Had to Decide Whether My Strange, Lonely Boy Ought to Exist," p. 167.)

Irony is often used in satire, a genre that mocks or criticizes institutions or commonly held attitudes. One way that satirists "tip off" their readers is through exaggeration. For example, in the thesis of the famous satire "A Modest Proposal" (1729), Jonathan Swift proposes the sale of infants to Ireland's rich to be served up for dinner! The false thesis is so extreme that readers are able to see beneath the literal meaning and realize that Swift is actually attacking the callous attitude of the rich toward the poor. In his argument, he is really making an indirect plea to Ireland's wealthy classes to help combat poverty, his "true" thesis.

Satire is a genre that mocks or criticizes institutions or commonly held attitudes.

Stylistic and Rhetorical Techniques

Repetition

Using **emphasis** helps focus the reader's attention on specific passages through repetition in language or structure, or other techniques, such as diction or rhythm.

A device of emphasis often used in non-academic writing is repetition. Of course, needless repetition wastes words, but occasionally writers may repeat words or phrases to reinforce a point's significance. Repetition is a common device in argument because repeated ideas are more likely to be considered important and be remembered.

Repetition could also extend to repeated structures, such as balanced phrases. For example, Shannon Rupp uses repetition in both her language and structure to create emphasis and make her point more memorable.

> It's a shabby way to treat your audience, but then it's a shabby audience they're after. They lure the gullible with schlock and novelty because they're not in the business of journalism; they're in the business of marketing. ("I'll Take My Coffee with Fiction, Thanks," p. 152)

Sentence Length and Construction

In a **periodic sentence**, the writer builds toward the main idea, which is expressed at the end of the sentence.

In a **cumulative sentence**, the writer begins with the main idea and follows with words, phrases, or clauses that extend this idea.

Writers may vary the length and rhythm of their sentences. A succession of short sentences can create a dramatic effect, while longer, more flowing sentences can be used to expand on an idea. In a periodic sentence, the writer builds toward the main idea, which is expressed at the end of the sentence. In a cumulative sentence, the writer begins with the main idea and follows with words, phrases, or clauses that extend this idea.

In the examples below, note the different rhetorical effects created by these two sentence types. The main idea is italicized in each example.

> *Periodic:* In colleges and universities across the country, in individual blogs and in the public press, *readers expressed their outrage at both the burning and the banning.* (Manguel, "Burning Mistry," p. 293)

> *Cumulative: There was general disdain of slovenly dress*, a strong theme, for example, in the writing of the Dominican priest Thomas Aquinas (1225–1274), who thought that wives needed to look their best to keep their husbands faithful. (Rublack, "Power Dressing," p. 190)

Space-Saving Techniques

Writing concisely is vital to journalistic writers who could lose their reader's attention with lengthy, inefficient sentences. The use of contractions is one example of a space-saving technique. Because efficiency is important in most prose, the two techniques below may find a place in your own writing.

In phrasal sentence openings, the sentence begins with a phrase—words acting as a unit of speech—that modifies a part of speech that follows. The adverbial phrases, modifying the verb *help*, are italicized below. Note that the sentence ends with balanced predicates (*break . . . get . . . have*). Balance at the beginning and end of the sentence makes it appealing to the reader (see "Sentence Length and Construction," p. 130).

> *By playing with unusual juxtapositions, changing the context of learning, and adding an element of surprise to the classroom*, we can help students break with routine, get outside of themselves, and have "bigger than me" experiences. (Tepper, "Thinking 'Bigger than Me' in the Liberal Arts," p. 247.)

An appositive is a word or phrase placed parallel to the noun before it, serving to name, specify, or explain that noun. Any new information the appositive gives is considered non-essential to the basic meaning of the sentence. Although appositives are common in all writing, they are used routinely in articles designed for the mass market, because they enable the writer to express information quickly. (For more information about appositives, see p. 362.)

In the examples below, the first passage contains the same information as the second passage. In the second one, however, the writer uses an appositive combined with the clause *who*, followed by non-essential information. [Note the black commas in the second passage that separate the non-essential information from the main idea in the sentence.]

1. According to Emma Crawley, empowering kids to direct their own learning makes them more confident. Emma Crawley is a primary school teacher in Gateshead, England. She has been using Mitra's method since 2009.

2. According to Emma Crawley**,** a primary school teacher in Gateshead, England**,** who has been using Mitra's method since 2009**,** empowering kids to direct their own learning makes them more confident. (Mendleson, "Raising Young Einsteins," p. 263.)

Journalistic and Scholarly Writing: A Symbiotic Relationship

Although most traditional media—newspapers, magazines, and television—provide their readers and viewers with information about the news of the day, they also communicate new knowledge generated through research. Because many people today get their daily news from the Internet, search engines usually include stories

A **phrase** is a group of words acting as a unit of speech. Therefore, a group of words modifying a noun is an adjectival phrase while one modifying a verb is an adverbial phrase.

An **appositive** is a word or phrase that names, specifies, or explains the previous word or phrase in a different way.

about recent research along with their general interest categories. For example, on a typical day, Google featured the following and other research-generated stories on its news home page:

- Fossil discoveries by researchers uncovering a new species of dinosaur and a clue to the evolution of the sperm whale
- The latest research findings on the value of gluten-free diets
- Data from a space probe showing there might be ice caps on Pluto
- A report on sexual misconduct in the Canadian military

The connection between scholarly research and the popular press is affirmed through short articles that summarize the most significant findings for everyday readers.

Translating the findings of research into everyday language is often the work of media agencies: "wire services" like the Canadian Press, which locate significant studies and rewrite their findings for media outlets. Academic articles are written for those with similar expertise and interest—their peers. The media, however, makes this knowledge known to the people whom it will directly affect the most—for example, those who may benefit from new medical or scientific discoveries. In this way, the connection between scholarly research and the reporting of this research to the public is reinforced every day.

EXERCISE 9.2

As described above, the role of the popular press is a vital one. However, a challenge for the journalist lies in translating the complexities of a study's findings into everyday language and writing an accurate story, in simplifying but not *over*simplifying. Three passages from online sources follow. Each reports on the same topic—the new guidelines for physical activity, which call for lowering the recommended hours of exercise for Canadians in order to encourage the most sedentary Canadians to exercise. The Canadian Society of Exercise Physiology (CSEP) made the recommendations to the Canadian government in 2011. Read the openings below and determine which is the most accurate; then justify your answer. (Using your critical thinking skills, you should be able to explain your choice without seeing the CSEP report (see www.csep.ca/en/guidelines/get-the-guidelines).

1. "Canadians are so inactive that even small amounts of exercise will make a difference in their risk for chronic disease, two fitness promotion groups said Wednesday. But they're still urging people to do more to get healthy and avoid illnesses like diabetes and heart disease."
2. "Canada is expected to take a 'less is more' approach with physical activity guidelines. The new fitness targets should make getting the recommended amount of exercise a little easier."
3. "It's OK, sit your butt back down on the couch. Canadians can get by with less exercise than previously thought, two national fitness groups say."

EXERCISE 9.3

Take a short section from one of the essays in Part II, Section VI of the Reader ("Voices from the Academy") and rewrite it for the general reader. You should condense it but ensure you cover the main points. Like professional writers, you may need to look up unfamiliar words or concepts, but make sure the rewritten version is understandable to a typical (i.e., non-specialist) reader.

Chapter 9 Review Questions

1. Analysis is often more important in non-academic essays whose main purpose is to _____. Synthesis is more important in non-academic essays whose main purpose is to _____.
2. Explain how personal experience can be used effectively in different types of non-academic writing.
3. a) What are some differences between personal/reflective essays and non-academic essays that do not rely on personal experience?
   b) Why might academic writers use personal experience?
4. What are some strategies that non-academic writers might use to get readers interested in their essays? Why are they less likely to be used by academic writers?
5. Answer true or false:
   a) Non-academic writers always include a thesis statement in an introduction.
   b) Writers who use literary techniques may include themes rather than a thesis.
6. Choose the best statement among the choices below:
   a) Non-academic writing is simple and unchallenging.
   b) Non-academic writing is of moderate difficulty.
   c) Non-academic writing uses mainly personal experience.
   d) Non-academic writing varies in difficulty depending on audience and other factors.
7. Define tone and give some examples of different kinds of tones. Why is it important that a reader be able to identify an ironic tone?
8. How could the device of repetition be successfully used in non-academic writing?
9. What is the difference between a periodic and a cumulative sentence?
10. Explain the interdependency of academic and non-academic writing. In your answer, discuss the ways that popular news outlets make use of the findings of academic researchers.

Key Terms

appositive (p. 131)
colloquial language (p. 128)
conventions (p. 123)
cumulative sentence (p. 130)
emphasis (p. 130)
irony (p. 128)

periodic sentence (p. 130)
phrase (p. 131)
satire (p. 129)
theme (p. 127)
tone (p. 128)

10

Conventions of Academic Writing

In this chapter, you will learn:

- How knowledge is defined across the disciplines

- How to tell a primary from a secondary source

- How to identify the features of voice and style in an academic essay

- How to use strategies to pre-read an academic essay

- How to identify important features of an academic introduction, including literature review and thesis

- How to recognize features of body paragraphs to retrieve information, including the use of topic sentences, prompts, and rhetorical patterns

- How to use transitions and other features to understand the relationship between ideas

Among the writing and reading challenges that lie ahead, you will undoubtedly be asked to analyze researched and documented essays by experts who seek to advance knowledge in their discipline. In addition, you may be asked to include their findings in your own research paper.

What Is Academic Writing?

Successful academic writing is not intended to confuse but is written for an audience familiar with a given discipline's conventions, its central ideas, and its ways of presenting them.

Conventions are practices that direct the actions and thinking of specific groups. You can think of them as a set of instructions that help us communicate with one another (see p. 123).

For some people, *academic writing* is a euphemism for difficult or highly technical writing. However, successful academic writing is not intended to confuse. Rather it is written for an audience familiar with a given discipline's conventions, its central ideas, and ways of presenting them.

Like most other writing, academic writing has a distinct purpose, in this case, to advance knowledge in a discipline. It is also intended for a specific audience: knowledgeable and interested readers. However, much academic writing is accessible to a wider audience than you might think. Most of the "barriers" of academic discourse can be overcome by paying careful attention to its conventions.

BOX 10.1 | Knowledge across the Disciplines

Although academic writing is generally written for knowledgeable readers, knowledge itself differs somewhat across the disciplines, as the following definitions suggest.

Humanities: *The branch of knowledge concerned with examining the tools that humans use to express and represent themselves.* Humanities writing focuses on how ideas and values are used to interpret human experience. Typical humanities disciplines are classical studies, history, linguistics, literature, modern languages, indigenous studies, philosophy, and religious studies, among others.

Social sciences: *The branch of knowledge concerned with collective human behaviour and the systems humans create to study this behaviour* (e.g., social, psychological, or political ones). Social science disciplines include anthropology, economics, geography, political science, psychology, and sociology, among others.

Sciences: *The branch of knowledge concerned with the study of natural phenomena using empirical methods to determine or validate their laws.* The natural and applied sciences include biology, chemistry, engineering, environmental sciences, health sciences, mathematics, and many more.

Audience: Who Reads Academic Writing?

It will come as no surprise that the largest audience for academic writing is scholars, people with knowledge of and interest in the subject. However, academic journals and many academic presses vary in their readership, from highly knowledgeable readers to those with a general knowledge.

The most reliable academic journals are peer-reviewed (refereed). As part of the editorial process, articles are read by experts in the field (peers), who decide whether an article should be published.

The aims of academic publications are well summarized by John Fraser, a columnist for *The Globe and Mail*.

> Peer-reviewed (refereed) journals contain articles that have been reviewed by experts. These "peers" suggest whether the article meets the exacting standards in their discipline and may recommend that the article be published, published with revisions, or rejected.

[T]he best academic publications extend our understanding of who we are in ways that trade publications and magazines and newspapers have largely abandoned. Canada's collective memory, our understanding of our social and economic conditions, [A]boriginal challenges to national complacency, the actual consequences of de-linking ourselves from the realities of our past . . . all find provocative and highly useful resonances from our academic publishers. (John Fraser. "Academic Publishers Teach Mainstream Ones a Lesson." *The Globe and Mail* 4 June 2005: F9.)

Features of Academic Writing

Some of the conventions of academic writing described below apply more to scholarly journal articles than books, but likely you will encounter more articles than books (other than textbooks) in your courses during the early years of your academic career.

Length and Complexity

Academic essays vary in length. Scientific studies may be as short as two or three pages; concise writing is a characteristic of such studies. Essays in some humanities disciplines, such as philosophy, history, and English, are often longer, focused on detailed analyses. Writers in the humanities explore new subtleties in and variations on texts and concepts long debated. In addition, writers in the humanities usually refer to primary sources, quoting often from these texts to support their points (see "Research Sources," below).

Length is often a function of the depth and detail expected in academic writing. Many science and social science essays use visual material, such as tables, graphs, and photos, to summarize results.

Research Sources

When you are asked to write a research paper, you must do more than summarize your sources.

Academic writers rely on the writing of other scholars. However, this does not mean that academic writing is concerned only with what has been written before in academic journals/books or delivered at academic conferences. Nor does academic writing consist mostly of summaries of other scholars' work. Therefore, when you are asked to write a research paper, you too must do more than summarize your sources.

Primary sources are original, or first-hand, material in a field of study.

Most research, whether conducted by scholars or by scholars-in-training like you, involves analysis, which is often centred on first-hand or **primary sources**, *original material in a field of study*. Much research begins with primary source material. For example, it would be logical to study a literary work (primary source) before you looked at what other people had to say about it (secondary source). "Primary," then, means *first in order*, not necessarily first in importance. **Secondary sources**, by contrast, are *commentary on or interpretation of primary material*.

Secondary sources comment on, interpret, or analyze primary sources.

Kinds of primary sources vary from discipline to discipline. Here are a few examples from various disciplines:

- **Anthropology and archaeology:** Artifacts, fossils, original field notes, reports resulting from direct observations
- **Literature:** Poems, plays, novels, diaries/letters of writers

- **Fine arts:** Sheet music, recordings, photographs, sketches, paintings, sculpture, films
- **History:** Contemporary documents from the period being studied—e.g., newspaper accounts, letters, speeches, photographs, treaties, diaries, autobiographies
- **Natural sciences:** Data from experimentation, field/laboratory notes, original research reports
- **Sociology:** Interviews, questionnaires, surveys, the raw data from these sources

Of course, it is not just writers of scholarly articles who use research. Non-academic writers may interview experts, pore over archives, or read books. But a journalist, unlike a scholarly writer, does not usually provide a citation for the source, whether primary or secondary. *Documenting sources by using citations is a feature of academic writing.*

Voice and Style

The voice in an academic essay, especially in the sciences, is objective, detached from the subject of the experiment or the object of the analysis. An academic study often sets out to investigate a real-life problem, and its author may propose solutions to the problem at the end of the study. This may take the form of recommendations or suggestions for future research.

However, academic writing can be considered persuasive in that it seeks to convince its reader of the validity of the findings. And, of course, academic writers do have opinions and a stake in what they are investigating. Therefore, they must ensure that their conclusions are free of bias or faulty reasoning.

To show their detachment, academic writers may use **passive construction**, in which the subject of the sentence is the receiver of the action, rather than the person or thing performing the action. Students are told to avoid the passive voice in their writing—with good reason as an unnecessary passive often results in a weaker sentence. However, if the purpose is to de-emphasize the performer of the action, such as the researcher, or to stress the receiver of the action, such as that which is being studied, then a passive construction may be preferable. Note the difference between passive and active in the following example.

Active construction: The "tosser" may allow the coin to fall to the floor, or the "tosser" may catch it.

Tosser is the active subject, but in this case, *coin* (object of the verb) is more important than the generic subject, *tosser*; after all, the researchers are interested in the results of the coin toss, not the fact it was tossed by the subject. Note that in

Academic writers do not usually stress their involvement in their research, especially if that involvement might make them seem biased.

In a **passive construction**, the subject of the sentence is the receiver of the action.

passive constructions, the active subject may not even be expressed. In the sentence below, the original, unimportant subject is shown by brackets.

> *Passive construction:* The coin may be allowed [by the "tosser"] to fall to the floor . . . . (Clark & Westerberg, "How Random Is the Toss of a Coin?" p. 354)

A writer might also substitute *this study shows* or *the research confirmed* to emphasize the study itself—not the researchers. When the article has several authors, as often is the case in the sciences, the writers may refer to themselves in the first-person plural, *we*. Academic writers do not use the first-person without a sound reason for doing so—for example, in order to be direct and concise.

In addition to a passive construction, science writers may also use constructions that stress the study rather than the author(s). However, for concision, they may sometimes refer to the first-person (e.g., *I, we*).

In the following examples from readings in Part II, the writers use the passive voice (italicized), direct phrasing (black), and/or the first-person (underlined) to help explain their studies. In the last sentence in the first example, the authors use an active construction, which you can compare to the passive in the preceding sentence.

> <u>We performed</u> a comparison of proportions. The statistical calculations *were performed* on the basis of how many coin tosses the individual would have to perform to show a significant manipulation. Therefore, any participant who achieved this level would have a significant result. (Clark & Westerberg, "How Random Is the Toss of a Coin?" p. 354)

> **The goal of this article is** not to bring readers to despair of self-perceptions. (Vazire & Carlson, "Others Sometimes Know Us Better than We Know Ourselves," p. 332)

Language

An **analogy** is a systematic comparison between one item and another one.

Compared to much literary writing, academic writing lacks ornamentation. Scientific writing, in particular, is direct, straightforward prose with few modifiers (adjectives and adverbs). Academic writers are also much less likely to use figurative language, such as metaphors, similes, personification, and the like, than are literary writers. They may, however, use analogies to help explain a point. An **analogy** is a systematic comparison between one item and another one that is similar in the point being discussed, but otherwise unlike the first one. An analogy can make the first item more easily understood.

Jargon and language level as well as other elements of style, such as complex sentence and paragraph structure, and intrusive documentation, can make academic writing hard to understand. (See "Specialized Language," Chapter 6, p. 106.) Many of these obstacles can be overcome, though, by exposure to this kind of writing. Although inexperienced readers must read complex material more closely, more slowly, and more consciously than simpler material, new reading habits can be formed by adopting specific strategies (discussed below in "Finding Information in Academic Essays") and patiently practising them.

It is expected that most writers strive for clarity in their work; however, academic writers in particular use deliberate techniques to make their writing clear and accessible.

Finding Information in Academic Essays

Although it may be fine to "begin at the beginning" when you are idly browsing or reading for pleasure, preparing to read an academic essay can be broken into stages (for general strategies related to reading purpose, see Chapter 6, p. 101).

Stage 1: "Pre-Reading" or Previewing Content

Strategy

Look closely at the title, the article's abstract (if present), and the headings (if present) to determine the essay's subject and the writer's approach to the topic, along with organization and other important features.

Title

In contrast to the titles of non-academic articles, academic titles are often

- lengthy and informative;
- divided into two parts with a colon separating them; and
- composed of nouns, most relevant to the essay's content and/or method.

The title of a scholarly article is designed to give the reader important information about content at a glance. This is helpful not only for experts, but also for students because it enables them to scan the contents page of a journal to find potentially useful articles. Typically, key terms in the article appear in the title. Therefore, searching by "title" or "keyword" in an electronic database often yields useful entries.

Many titles include two parts separated by a colon. In this example from the *Journal of Clinical Child and Adolescent Psychology*, the first part summarizes the study's finding while the second part reveals the method: "School connectedness is an underemphasized parameter in adolescent mental health: Results of a community prediction study." If you check the titles of the academic essays included in this textbook, you can see that about half use this structure.

Abstract

Next, locate the abstract: it appears after the title and author names/affiliations and before the actual essay begins. It usually is labelled "Abstract" or "Summary" but

The title of a scholarly article is designed to give the reader important information about content at a glance. This is helpful not only for experts but also for student researchers because it enables them to gauge an article's potential usefulness by a scan of a journal issue's contents. Typically, key terms in the article appear in the title.

An abstract is a kind of summary or condensed version of an article. Abstracts precede most journal articles in the sciences and social sciences, giving a preview of content by focusing on the study's purpose, method, results, and conclusion.

sometimes has no label. An abstract is a condensed version of an article, giving a preview of content by focusing on the study's purpose, method, results, and conclusion. The abstract is usually written by the study's author(s) and is one paragraph long; sometimes, it includes brief headings. (See also, "Abstract" in Chapter 2, p. 19.)

Section Headings

Because of the complex organizational scheme of many academic essays, academic writers often announce upcoming content by using headings. (Non-academic writers may also use headings, especially if the essay is long.) There are two main types of headings, depending on the kind of essay: formal headings and descriptive headings (content-focused).

Empirical studies, such as experiments, use formal headings, which divide the essay into the experiment's stages:

1. The **Introduction** announces the topic and includes summaries of previous research. It ends with a hypothesis, research question, or statement of intent (essay plan).
2. The **Method(s)** explains how the experiment was conducted—for example, *who* took part, *how* it was designed, and *what* procedures were used.
3. The **Result(s)** presents the raw data generated by the experiment, often with accompanying tables and figures.
4. The **Discussion** includes a summary of the results and relates them to similar studies. The section ends by suggesting directions for future research and, often, practical applications of the findings.

> **Formal headings** divide the essay into an experiment's stages; **descriptive headings** summarize section contents.

This structure can be abbreviated as IMRAD (introduction, method(s), result(s), and discussion) and is found in most essays of this type—for example, see pp. 336 and 353. If you are writing a scientific, engineering, or business report, you may be required to use formal markers to divide the major sections of your report.

> **IMRAD** stands for Introduction, Method(s), Result(s), and Discussion, the sections that compose an empirical study.

In other kinds of academic studies, the markers serve a *descriptive function*, enabling readers to preview content. Descriptive section markers are one way that writers can clarify essay structure for their readers. Descriptive headings are especially useful in orienting the reader of a long academic essay or one that deals with complex material. Because the essays students write for class are usually much shorter, such markers are seldom necessary.

Such headings are usually brief, consisting of a key phrase that sums up the section. In Daniel Wegner's "How to Think, Say, or Do Precisely the Worst Thing for Any Occasion" (p. 314), each heading helps the reader find specific information. For example, the following headings suggest content related to thoughts and emotions, respectively: e.g., "Taboos and Faux Pas: Worst Thoughts and Utterances," "Yips and Worries: Worst Movements and Emotions."

In sum, examining the title, abstract, and headings can give you crucial information before you begin reading the essay in detail (see Chapter 6, "Selective Reading," p. 101) or if you need to quickly review it.

Stage 2: After "Pre-Reading"—Introductions in Academic Writing

Strategy

After pre-reading, look at the essay's introduction, identifying its main features. A scholarly introduction is usually designed to do most or all of the following:

1. Introduce the topic by providing background information and/or discussing the topic's importance.
2. Situate the study in relation to work that has been done on the same topic.
3. Justify the need for the study.
4. Summarize the study's approach and/or content, lay out its structure, and, sometimes, include what the authors expect to find or the questions they hope to answer.

These features are described in more detail below.

1. Introduce the Topic

Like most essays, an academic essay begins with an introductory section. It may be titled "Introduction" or "Background," or have no heading, but its purpose is to set the scene for the body of the essay by addressing the topic's significance or by introducing important concepts. Academic writers assume most of their readers are interested in and somewhat knowledgeable about the topic, so do not usually craft openings with a "hook" to draw readers in.

2. Situate the Study

An academic introduction often reviews previous studies on its topic. An experimental study usually includes this review in one section near the beginning of the essay. By including a literature review, the author demonstrates where his or her contribution fits in and how it furthers knowledge about the subject. Here, the writer summarizes the findings of scholars, often but not always in chronological order, and ends with either the most recent studies or those most closely related to the author's approach (see p. 336 for example).

Other essays, such as those designed *primarily to review* the available literature, focus on review throughout the essay, rather than just in the introduction (see pp. 314, 323, and 329 for examples).

Literature review is the term for the section of the introduction that summarizes related studies on the topic. Some essays are devoted entirely to reviewing related studies rather than placing the review in one section of the essay.

3. Justify the Study

An academic essay, unlike a student essay, usually includes a justification. In other words, the author directly or indirectly states the reason for the study. While students generally write essays to become better planners, researchers, and writers (as well as to satisfy a course requirement and receive a grade, of course), academic authors need to convince their peers that their essays are worth reading. The justification answers questions like the following: Why was the study undertaken? Why is it important? What can I learn from it? What does it contribute to scholarship?

A typical justification for a study is a gap in knowledge—the absence of studies in an area of scholarship, according to the author.

4. Summarize the Essay's Approach and/or Content

Student writers are familiar with the common practice of including a thesis statement in the introduction. (See Chapter 1, "The Thesis Statement," p. 8.) Like students, academic writers refer to the thesis near the end of the introduction, but the form that the thesis takes can vary. Two common forms are discussed below:

Thesis as Essay Plan

An essay plan is what it sounds like: an announcement of the essay's structure. It outlines the way the topic will be developed throughout the essay. The plan may be phrased directly through the first-person voice as in the following example: "In this paper, we report data that explore . . ." Students, however, may be discouraged from using the first-person in phrasing a thesis.

An **essay plan** includes the main points or main sections of the essay's development. It may use the first-person voice.

Thesis as Hypothesis

A **hypothesis** is a prediction or probable outcome of an experiment.

In experiments, the thesis may consist of a hypothesis, which is a prediction to be tested by the experiment. In the "Discussion" section, the researcher discusses the results of the experiment, beginning with whether the hypothesis is supported by the results.

The following excerpt from the introduction of an academic essay on bullying reveals most of the characteristics of an introduction discussed above.

The essay begins directly as the writers introduce their topic by defining a key term.

In the second sentence, the authors become more specific, discussing their understanding of the true nature of bullying. They further establish credibility by mentioning their 15 years of research.

> Bullying has been defined as negative actions—physical or verbal—that have hostile intent, are repeated over time, and involve a power differential between the bully and the victim (Olweus, 1993). Through the past 15 years of our research program on bullying, we have come to understand bullying as a relationship problem—because it is a form of aggression that unfolds in the context of a relationship in which one child asserts interpersonal power through aggression. The power that bullies hold over others can arise from their individual characteristics, such as superior size, strength, or age (Olweus, 1993); and from

knowledge of others' vulnerabilities (Sutton et al., 1999). The power in bullying can also arise from a position in a social group, either in terms of generally high social status (Olweus, 1993) or by membership in a group of peers who support bullying (Salmivalli et al., 1997).

In this paper, we examine bullying from a developmental perspective with a cross-sectional study from early through late adolescence. . . . Few studies examine the developmental pattern in the prevalence of bullying others beyond early adolescence . . . . (Debra, J. et al. "A Developmental Perspective on Bullying." *Aggressive Behavior, 32* (2006): 376–384.)

> The authors begin their literature review in the first paragraph. In its entirety, the review demonstrates their knowledge and shows where their own study fits in.

> The authors state the purpose of their essay. At the end of their introduction, they are more specific and detailed, phrasing their thesis as a series of hypotheses, or predictions about their subject (this excerpt does not include the end of the introduction).

> The authors directly justify their essay, showing the gap in the scholarship that they will attempt to fill.

EXERCISE 10.1

Identify the key features of the introductions of two or three academic essays in this textbook. (See Part II, Section VI of the Readings, "Voices from the Academy," p. 299.) In particular, show:

a) Where and how the topic is introduced
b) The study's justification
c) The literature review (if applicable)
d) The thesis and the form it takes. (See also Chapter 1, "The Thesis Statement," p. 8.)

If one or more of these features is missing, try to determine why it was not needed.

Stage 3: Reading Paragraphs

The guidelines below will help you locate important information quickly in the paragraphs of academic essays, enabling you to ignore less relevant information. (Of course, when you practise focused reading, p. 103, you will read more closely.) Although the advice given here applies mostly to academic writing, much of it can be applied to challenging texts in general—both academic and non-academic ones.

Sentence and paragraph length and complexity might make it hard for inexperienced readers to distinguish important from less important information. Thankfully, academic writers often use predictable paragraph construction. For example, they usually announce the paragraph's topic early in the paragraph; they may also use clear and recognizable patterns to organize their paragraphs.

By contrast, non-academic writing may be less structured, with topic sentences appearing later in the paragraph. Some paragraphs do not contain topic sentences but may simply expand on the previous paragraph. Simple transitions, like *and* or *but*, may be preferred to precise transitions, like *in addition* or *in contrast*, showing the relationship between two ideas.

Using Structural Cues

Structural cues show how the paragraph is organized and where to find information.

Topic Sentences

Scanning paragraphs for important information is not just a mechanical process. A paragraph in academic texts may be full of detail; sentences may be long and complex. Therefore, it is helpful to know that important information often occurs in the topic sentence of body paragraphs. (See Chapter 1, "Writing Middle Paragraphs," p. 11.) The topic sentence states the main idea of the paragraph and is usually the most general statement, which is developed by examples or analysis. Although the topic sentence is often the first sentence of the paragraph, a writer may build *toward* the central idea, in which case the topic sentence may be in the middle or even at the end of the paragraph.

Prompts

A **prompt**, which can be as lengthy as a sentence or two, can help you locate important information.

When the topic sentence is not the first sentence of the paragraph, the paragraph may contain a **prompt**, which directs the reader ahead to important information. Common prompts take the form of questions or statements that set up the paragraph but do not actually announce the main idea. A prompt can also appear at the end of a paragraph, setting up the paragraph that follows.

In the paragraph excerpt below, the writer begins by referring to the previous paragraph: the sentence acts as a prompt, leading the reader to find the topic sentence in the following sentence (italicized).

> In many cases, however, blind spots are not so innocent—they are the result of motivated cognitive processes. *One motive that has a strong influence on self-perception is the motive to maintain and enhance our self-worth* . . . (Vazire & Carlson, "Others Sometimes Know Us," p. 331)

Rhetorical Patterns

It is useful to scan first sentences of paragraphs, not just because they may contain the main idea or a prompt, but also because they may suggest each paragraph's development. Information can often be organized by specific rhetorical patterns; identifying these patterns makes the text easier to follow. For example, in the chronological method, the writer traces a development over time, usually from old to new. In process analysis, the stages of a process are broken down and analyzed. (See Chapter 1, "Rhetorical Patterns and Paragraph Development," p. 14.)

Concluding Sentences

Much variety exists in paragraph conclusions. The last sentence of a body paragraph could provide further development or it could summarize the paragraph's main idea. In that case, the sentence does not usually repeat this idea verbatim but connects it to the paragraph's development. Concluding sentences that function as summaries are called paragraph wraps.

In the short paragraph below, it is clear in the first (topic) sentence that the paragraph focuses on effects of television on language skills (cause–effect pattern). After the paragraph is developed by referring to research findings on short-term effects, it concludes by highlighting what the authors thought was significant in the findings.

> Since 1999, [three] studies have evaluated the effects of heavy television use on language development in children 8 to 16 months of age. In the short-term, children younger than [two] years who watch more television or videos have expressive language delays,[12, 43, 44] and children younger than [one] year with heavy television viewing who are watching alone have a significantly higher chance of having a language delay.[44] Although the long-term effects on language skills remain unknown, the evidence of short-term effects is concerning. ("Media Use by Children Younger than 2 Years." *Pediatrics* 128.5 [2011]: 1040–1045.)

Contextual Cues: Using Transitions and Repetition

Topic sentences, prompts, and rhetorical patterns are examples of structural cues since they help structure the paragraph, showing the reader where key information is located or how the information is organized. Writers use contextual cues to show the relationship between ideas and to stress words, phrases, and concepts that are critical in understanding the paragraph.

Transitions

Transitional words and phrases can indicate whether an idea is going to be expanded on or whether there will be a shift from one idea to another one. Transitions can occur between one paragraph and the next, between one sentence and the next, or between clauses within a sentence (see the annotated example below). Paying attention to transitions can help you break down an essay, a paragraph, or a sentence into smaller and more manageable units.

The following body paragraph illustrates use of transitions and other cues. For more about the role of transitions in writing, see Chapter 1, "Writing Strong Paragraphs," p. 11.

> Of course, not all others are created equal—the relationship between the judge and the target matters. While too much intimacy can lead to the same biases that distort self-perceptions (e.g., one's self-worth can be threatened as much by the knowledge that one's spouse is incompetent as it is by the thought of one's own incompetence), closeness is

Paragraph wraps are concluding sentences that function as summaries.

Contextual cues show the relationship between ideas and stress words, phrases, and concepts critical in understanding the paragraph.

The topic sentence introduces the main idea, the relationship between the perceiver (*judge*) and the perceived (*target*).

When first reading a paragraph, you can ignore examples and other detail like citations, which writers may signal as less important by placing in parentheses. In focused reading, however, such detail may be important.

usually associated with greater accuracy (see Biesanz, West, & Millevoi, 2007, for a thorough review). Moreover, the better we get along with others, the more accurately they can infer our thoughts and feelings (Thomas & Fletcher, 2003). Overall, across all types and levels of acquaintance that have been examined, people form remarkably accurate impressions of one another. (Vazire & Carlson, "Others Sometimes Know Us," p. 332)

The writers use three transitions in this paragraph: *Moreover* is a transition of addition or emphasis, showing that the sentence it introduces will add onto the previous one.

The last sentence acts as a paragraph wrap, summarizing its main idea. It does not use the same words as are in the topic sentence but helps illustrate the paragraph's development.

Repetition

Writers can stress important words, phrases, and concepts throughout a paragraph by repeating them in strategic places or by using pronoun substitutes. Similarly, synonyms enable a writer to emphasize a concept by using a word with the same meaning. Strategic repetition not only stresses important words but also makes the paragraph more coherent and easier to follow. Repetition can help assert the importance of a key concept, like the one introduced in the first sentence below.

Strategies for comprehension like those discussed in this section not only help you read texts but also should become part of your own writing process to enable your readers to follow your prose and understand your meaning.

> How would *acknowledging actual histories* change the work of health professionals and humanitarian aid providers? Even in the initial response to a disaster, *it* would change how services are organized, who is leading the effort, and who sets priorities. *Acknowledging actual histories* may have little impact on the technical details of the initial emergency response, but *it* may make a difference in how relief efforts are subsequently carried out . . . . *Actual histories* can help organizations to see how the best of intentions can undermine indigenous systems and societies . . . . (Pinto, "Denaturalizing 'Natural' Disasters," p. 311)

Balanced phrases in the paragraph above also contribute to comprehension: "how services are organized, who is leading the effort, and who sets priorities." See Chapter 1, "Writing Strong Paragraphs," (p. 11) for strategies for making your own writing more coherent. See also Chapter 9, "Stylistic and Rhetorical Techniques: Repetition," (p. 130) for an example of balanced phrases.

EXERCISE 10.2

Compare one body paragraph from an academic essay in this textbook (see the essays in Part II, Section VI of the Readings, "Voices from the Academy," p. 299) with one from a non-academic essay. You can refer to relevant features listed in Table 1.1 (p. 13), along with others you find appropriate.

EXERCISE 10.3

Although the following paragraphs are briefer than most paragraphs of scholarly essays, the writers have used specific comprehension strategies such as topic sentences, prompts, rhetorical patterns, transitions, repetitions, and conclusions. Identify at least two strategies discussed in this chapter in each paragraph.

> Personal attributes and perceptions of animals are relatively independent of the act of eating. However, it is precisely in this moment—when a person is eating or intending to eat—that we would expect the meat paradox to require urgent resolution. Research has begun to examine the dynamic processes that facilitate meat eating. (Loughnan, Bastian, & Haslam, "The Psychology of Eating Animals," p. 304)

> The French Revolution, which began in 1789, sparked a revolt of Haiti's middle class and an uprising of its slave majority. In 1804, Haiti became the second independent republic in the western hemisphere, after the United States. Further, it was the first example of slaves winning nationhood through their own resistance. (Pinto, "Denaturalizing 'Natural' Disasters," p. 308)

EXERCISE 10.4

Choose a body paragraph from one of the academic essays in Part II, Section VI of the Readings and identify specific comprehension strategies.

Chapter 10 Review Questions

1. Which best describes academic writing?
   a) Writing that is highly technical and inaccessible to non-experts
   b) Writing designed for those familiar with its conventions and knowledgeable about the subject
   c) Writing designed for experts and non-experts alike
2. How can knowledge be defined across the disciplines?
3. What accounts for the length of many academic essays?
4. How can the challenges of academic writing be overcome by the student reader?
5. Define primary sources and secondary sources and explain how they differ. Is one kind of source more important than the other?
6. Why do academic writers, especially in the sciences, use the passive voice? Illustrate the passive construction in a sentence of your own of at least eight words; then, rewrite the same sentence using the active construction.

7. a) In addition to passive constructions, how can academic writers convey objectivity?
    b) Why is it essential that they do so?

8. A systematic comparison between one item and another one is called an _____.

9. Choose the best answer: To find information efficiently in academic essays, you should first
    a) Adopt a "pre-reading" strategy and begin by looking at the title, abstract, and headings.
    b) Read from the beginning, looking for important points.
    c) Read the conclusion first, since the important information will be included there.
    d) Focus on the first sentences of all paragraphs since they will include the main ideas.

10. a) Identify two specific features of titles of academic essays.
    b) How do the titles of academic essays differ from those of non-academic essays?

11. Choose the best answer:
    a) An abstract serves as an introduction to the paragraph that follows.
    b) An abstract serves as an overview or summary of the essay that follows.
    c) An abstract is roughly 10 per cent of the length of the essay that follows.
    d) All the above are true of abstracts.

12. What are the two types of headings typically found in academic essays? What are their functions?

13. Identify the following features of an academic introduction and explain the importance of each:
    a) The literature review
    b) Justification
    c) Essay plan
    d) Hypothesis

14. Answer true or false:
    a) In academic writing, the topic sentence is usually not the first sentence.
    b) A prompt can direct you to the main idea, which usually follows directly.
    c) The concluding sentence of the paragraph should repeat the topic sentence in slightly different words.

15. Explain the importance of transitions and repetition in academic writing.

Key Terms

analogy (p. 138)

descriptive headings (p. 140)

Discussion (p. 140)

essay plan (p. 142)

formal headings (p. 140)

hypothesis (p. 142)

IMRAD (p. 140)

Introduction (p. 140)

justification (p. 142)

Method(s) (p. 140)

paragraph wraps (p. 145)

passive construction (p. 137)

primary sources (p. 136)

prompt (p. 144)

Result(s) (p. 140)

secondary sources (p. 136)

Readings

I — First-Person Singular

The first-person point of view (POV) is familiar to readers of literary works, especially novels and short stories where the narrator is a character in the work. One purpose of using the first person is to help a reader relate to this character. However, as in fiction, use of first-person POV in non-fiction is more complex than this: in various ways, using the "I" voice leads the reader to consider the larger picture.

For example, in "I'll Take My Coffee with Fiction," we learn little about the author because her purpose is to describe (and criticize) a phenomenon she refers to as "click-bait," using her own voice both to entertain and to increase credibility. We learn more about the authors of the essays "Flush" and "Giving up the Ghost," which are examples of a literary memoir: a non-fiction form that uses personal observation and/or experience to reveal a stage in the writer's life or the way he or she was affected by a significant event. However, both essays are carefully crafted reminiscences that touch on universal themes, such as addiction in "Giving up the Ghost." The author of "Flush" uses an unexpected image—the toilet—to humorously juxtapose past and present while touching on topics as diverse as censorship and genetic engineering.

Medical technology—in particular, the use of genetic screening—is the subject of the essay "I'm Glad I Never Had to Decide Whether My Strange, Lonely Boy Ought to Exist," a searchingly honest essay that raises difficult and poignant questions about technology and personal choice. In "Is Scientific Progress Inevitable?" the questions are even broader, as the writer uses a visit to an ancient archaeological site with his daughter to reflect on the relationship between scientific and social progress.

Shannon Rupp, "I'll Take My Coffee with Fiction, Thanks"

Shannon Rupp's first-person essay is less about her than about a phenomenon she has observed; it was occasioned, she tells us, by the recent death of a well-known Canadian short story writer. It is notable for its lively writing style and use of copious examples.

 Preparing to Read

1. As you surf the Internet, do you ever think about the quality of the information you see? Do you consider its purpose? Or do you simply enjoy the diversions offered?

After reading Rupp's essay, consider if the answers to any of these questions have changed.

2. Read the first four paragraphs in order to determine the author's subject, tone (attitude to her subject), and writing style. Consider how they might affect your reading of the essay.

3. Using a reliable source, look up Mavis Gallant and write a one-paragraph summary of her career as a writer.

I'll Take My Coffee with Fiction, Thanks

Shannon Rupp

The Tyee, 6 March 2014
(1520 words)

1   Mavis Gallant showed me what's wrong with most online content. I don't think that was ever her goal, of course. But that's what I like about good fiction: it's a bunch of made-up stories that tell you important things when you least expect it.

2   The master short story writer exited on Feb. 18 at 91, after a life well-lived in Paris, reminding me that I hadn't read her in decades. As a nod to her passing, I read "Madeline's Birthday"—her first *New Yorker* publication—and it was so good I read two more in a collection of her early work, *The Cost of Living*.

3   That's a radical departure from my life-long morning ritual of guzzling coffee and reading news. But the pull of Gallant's elegant prose had me skipping headlines for literature morning after morning. Albeit with a twinge of guilt.

4   Given my line of work, I'm expected to be attentive to the tsunami of infotainment that smacks me every morning. I wouldn't call it news so much as a sort of factoid soup from which I sift out what is accurate and possibly meaningful.

5   It's like panning for gold. And as the dwindling crew of miners overworks the increasingly shallow veins, the nuggets washing down are getting smaller and smaller. I'm constantly tinkering with my online news feeds: dropping publications fielding obvious click-bait and dumping reporters who sound like shills. Social media are a never-ending editing job.

6   It's tedious. And lately it seems to reward me with little more than the junk quizzes you find on sites that have "buzz" in the name: "What Game of Thrones Character Are You?" screams the headline. Why would anyone care? More than that, don't readers realize those quizzes are data-scraping tools?

7   Then a few mornings ago, *The Globe and Mail* was pushing a story about how a chain of donut shops is changing two dozen items on its menu of sugar-laden junk foods. Given the real news about the hazards of processed foods and sugar, that story amounts to journalistic malpractice. While this sort of shilling isn't new in old media, spotting it on this cold, dark morning was more irritating than usual. Was it because I'd just forced myself to put down Gallant in exchange for the Velveeta of news stories—a news-like product politely described as tasteless.

8   That donut story gave me the same sort of queasy feeling as eating the donuts themselves and, with that, I dumped *The Globe* and their shilling ways from my feeds.

I'm nobody's traffic

9   The problem with the wealth of "free" media online is that it is often way too expensive. It sucks my time, my private information, and frequently distracts me from finding the real news. While I don't spend any more time with online news sources than I ever did with the paper ones—about 90 minutes a day—I feel far less satisfied.

10   These sites are no longer reporters, they're repeaters. At best, they latch onto something sensational and everyone posts it over and over again, sometimes for days, hoping to pull traffic.

11   A former editor for a technology site, ReadWrite.com, offered some insight into the clutter storm a few weeks ago when he advised other sites to avoid copy editing. That's right: avoid it. He had a tragic tale about how his traffic plunged by half after they hired copy editors to post typo-free stories that (presumably) also benefited from a sober second set of eyes.

12   "[Copy editors] also slowed the publishing process to a screeching near-halt. And, even more importantly: No. One. Cared," Abraham Hyatt wrote.

13   He's highlighting something that much of the media world doesn't want to discuss. There's a difference between readers and "traffic" just as there's a difference between journalism and click-bait. Traffic—the mob—is valuable to the sort of faux news sites that are data scraping and selling it to marketers. It's a shabby way to treat your audience, but then it's a shabby audience they're after. They lure the gullible with schlock and novelty because they're not in the business of journalism; they're in the business of marketing.

14   Hyatt told me a lot about the sort of publication he used to run. And since I'm nobody's "traffic," I dropped ReadWrite too.

15   I'm a reader. I was anxious to get back to Gallant and I had to find the time somewhere, so I began cutting my news perusing. Ruthlessly. Not least because I'm beginning to feel unclean hanging out in the Internet sewers.

16   Do I need to know that Kim Novak, 81, is being mocked viciously for the bad plastic surgery job she revealed when she presented at this year's Oscars? Or that a 10-foot python spent five hours subduing and swallowing a three-foot crocodile? That one comes with the kind of horror movie photos beloved of 11-year-old boys. At least the story might add to biologists' knowledge of the species. But those pictures? Eeuuww. Gross.

17   I saw the outline of that Australian croc in the stretched out body of a snake at least 15 times—a nightmare image I will never be able to scrub from my brain. Thank you, Australian Broadcasting, *The Guardian*, *The Telegraph*, *The Independent*, USA *Today*, and CNN. And a word, BBC: I really expected better from you.

18   As for the Canadian outlets, I'd like to say our people are above such things. But no. They're just slow repeater sites, coming late to this Battle of the Reptiles. Or maybe it was the Triumph of the Plucky Snake—it's hard to believe he ate the whole thing.

19   Don't tell me to ditch my iPad. Going offline isn't the option it was even a few years ago, when it was all the rage. That's because so many print outlets also fill their pages with infotainment found on the interwebs—only they do it a week late.

The difference between meaning and memes

20 Good short stories feel substantial next to the flimsy click-bait that passes for journalism. And as the morning fiction reading became a habit, I was reminded of Oscar Wilde's quip, circa 1880, about the difference between journalism and literature: "Journalism is unreadable and literature is unread."

21 I once dismissed his view as snobbery, since the man was a wordsmithing genius. At the time, most news writers seemed pretty good to me, but I was reading journalism 100 years after Wilde's time. Now that we've entered a publishing landscape that echoes Wilde's era—lots of tiny outlets and pamphleteers all screaming for the mob's attention—it's clear he was onto something.

22 But the most persuasive reason for cutting my consumption of news-like-products in favour of smart prose is this provocative headline on a piece in the *Columbia Journalism Review*: "Who cares if it's true?" They looked at the surprising news that BuzzFeed, one of the most successful purveyors of meaningless drivel, has decided to hire copyeditors.

23 The writer, an editor at *The Washington Post*, argues that accuracy is growing more important in new media, which is increasingly mindful of the embarrassment that comes with circulating fake videos as if they're real. Meanwhile old media have grown more relaxed about repeating whatever garbage is trending. He sees it as a merging of values and standards.

24 I see it as a mind-meld between the worst TV writers of 50 years ago and social media gurus today who serve up the equivalent of old TV schlock: odd characters and dumb catchphrases. Does that Plucky Snake that ate the whole thing have his own Twitter handle yet? I'm afraid to look.

25 *Slate* magazine shares my concern about the online crapfest, although they are understandably ambivalent. Their most popular story ever turned out to be the hilarious John Travolta alternate name generator currently bouncing around. It's a salute to the actor's monumental mispronunciation of Broadway songstress Idina Menzel's name when he introduced her at the Oscars. She became Adele Dazeem.

26 Now everyone on the "interwebs" wants to be "Travoltafied." (I'm Stephen Reezz.)

27 Generally, *Slate* attracts serious readers and has been known to run 18,000-word pieces. So, as editor David Plotz told the Nieman Journalism Lab, he was "bemused" by the enthusiasm for the name generator. Especially as it was outpacing stories about the growing conflict in Ukraine and other significant copy.

28 He needn't feel shame. That name generator is a witty joke that captures the triviality of the Oscars like no other commentary I saw. And it's why *Slate* has a permanent spot on my iPad while other sites are being unfollowed with giddy abandon.

29 Which brings me back to the power of Gallant. Her truthful fiction acts as an intellectual palate cleanser, removing the bad taste of all the junk content I ingest accidentally. She showed me that the current media debate isn't really between old media and new, or digital and print, or even literature and journalism: it's the difference between meaning and memes.

30 All that, and no data scraping. At about 20 bucks a book, fiction is a remarkable bargain and a much better way to greet the morning.

Comprehension

1. Paraphrase paragraph 23, in which Rupp explains the argument of *The Washington Post* editor.

2. In your own words, explain why the online magazine *Slate* "has a permanent spot on [Rupp's] iPad" (par. 28).

3. Rupp uses many colloquialisms, slang, and other informal language in her essay, some of which may not be found in an ordinary dictionary. Determine their meaning by context; after writing a short definition, look the words up on a reliable Internet site:
   - shill (pars. 5 and 7),
   - Velveeta (par. 7),
   - click-bait (par. 13), and
   - wordsmithing (par. 21).

Organization and Style

1. Identify two examples and briefly explain the use of the following stylistic features in Rupp's essay:
   - word play (pun),
   - metaphor or simile, and
   - sentence fragment.

2. a. Analyze Rupp's informal writing style, referring at least twice to her diction, paragraph/sentence structure, tone, or other features or techniques that strike you as significant.

   b. Do you think her informal style might be appropriate given her topic? Explain.

Critical Thinking

1. What does the author do for a living? Using critical thinking, give a one- or two-sentence description of what you believe her job is. (Note that she doesn't directly tell us.)

2. Although Rupp introduces Mavis Gallant in her first paragraph, the argument she presents refers little to Gallant's prose. Do you think her approach was more effective than if she had described what she likes about Gallant's stories, giving examples from her writing? Explain your reasoning.

3. Write a response to Rupp's essay in which you use your own experiences, observations, and critical thinking to argue for or against her topic. Ensure that you refer specifically to her essay.

Madeline Sonik, "Flush"

"Flush" is a personal essay, part of a collection that was nominated for two major non-fiction awards in 2011. Although the essay is ostensibly about the author's life, Sonik extends her vision beyond the personal to take in many larger issues relevant to her audience: like Ian Brown (see "I'm Glad I Never Had to Decide," p. 165), Sonik enables us to question issues that affect us or those we know. Through juxtaposition, Sonik raises questions about technology, censorship, pollution, and generational stereotypes.

Although there are many differences between this essay and both non-academic and scholarly essays (beginning with its one-word title), there are also similarities; for example, like writers of scholarly and some non-academic essays, Sonik uses research. She seamlessly synthesizes facts and statistics with her personal narrative.

 Preparing to Read

Have you ever considered your life as a "story"? What would you include in such a story? What would you exclude? Why?

Flush

Madeline Sonik

Afflictions and Departures, 2011
(3980 words)

1   I arrived the year the toilet made its cinematic debut. Moments before the famous murder scene in Alfred Hitchcock's *Psycho*, Janet Leigh, the victim, flushes incriminating evidence down the loo. The first toilet to appear on the silver screen is strikingly white, and the flush strikingly loud. The appearance of this toilet is an indication of advancing times. Three years before, the commercial censors ban an episode of *Leave It to Beaver*, because a toilet bowl is shown. In 1960, I have not yet seen *Leave It to Beaver*, know nothing of June Cleaver's Princess dresses or her simple string of pearls. In the next few years, I will discover these things, but it will be decades before I understand the significance of the time into which I am born, this great evolutionary leap, this fundamental cultural turning point, and the way it will influence and shape my life. The year I am born is the year in which moving picture meets the appliance of moving bowel.

2   They say, "you can't go back," and although in 1960 I've never heard them say it, I already know my mother's uterus is out of reach to me, the pink, fleshy walls of her womb, the warm sack of fluid where I swam. I have been violently expelled from Eden, a wayfarer, a refugee, set in a cot, fed with a bottle, left to scream. And Janet Leigh flushes the toilet, and the flush sounds like death, like the first sound a baby hears when she enters the noisy, sordid world. But is the world any more sordid than it ever was? If only I had consulted my omniscience in those first few moments when I may have still been bound

with heaven, perhaps I would have learned the reason I chose this moment to be born.

3   Fast forward 45 years: suffering from jet lag in England, unable to read or write, I switch on television. The program *No Angels* is playing. In the first 30 minutes, a drunken man shits his pants; a nurse has sex with a stranger in a car; and a young doctor experiences a premature ejaculation. In Canada, I have not watched TV for years, but I'm certain there's nothing comparable to this. Thirty-two years ago when I lived here, there was the lewd and bawdy *Benny Hill Show*, *George and Mildred*, and *Man About the House*. Having emigrated from North America, I was shocked by all of these programs with their blatant sexual and earthy content, though today I wouldn't even bat an eye if I saw them in Canada. Television "toilet humour" is what my father would have called it. And if he'd lived long enough to witness it, I imagine, he would have paid me, just as he had done with cigarette commercials, each time I switched such offending programs off.

4   It may be that Britain signals the shape of things to come for North American TV and cinema (Alfred Hitchcock was born in Leytonstone, London, after all), or it may be that all the continents of the world are on some kind of inevitable slippery slope. The censors refused to pass *Psycho* . . . not because of the toilet, which was troubling enough, but because Janet Leigh's nipple was visible in the shower scene. Hitchcock didn't edit. He knew they wouldn't review the film again. He lingers in the bathroom, in a coming attraction teaser, gazing at the toilet, a master of suspense. When the white porcelain toilet flushes, the world changes. In Detroit, Michigan, in Crittenton General Hospital, there are women flushing toilets too. They have been routinely prepped and given enemas, some will soon be mothers for the first time; others, like

my own, will have been through it all before. Obstetric ultrasound technology is in its infancy, so none of these women will know the sex of their children. The booties they have made and purchased are predominantly yellow. It will be six years before the fetal heart is "interrogated" and found to sound like "horses' hoofs when running" and another year before placental blood flow will be described as "rushing wind." It will be almost eight years before "the human eye pierces the 'black box' of the womb" and eighteen years before it's described this way in the foreword to an international ultrasound symposium proceeding. But in 1960, the human eye has long pierced the "idiot box." Ninety per cent of Americans have TV sets in their homes and watch programs like *Gunsmoke*, *My Three Sons*, and, of course, *Alfred Hitchcock Presents*. In Britain, Granada TV launches *Coronation Street*. This will become the longest-running soap opera in the world and will remain the most popular show in England for over four decades.

5   Meanwhile, labouring women in North America are anaesthetized and sent into a haze of "twilight sleep"—these procedures numb their bodies, steal their minds, and depress their infants. In 1960, it is better simply, to forget—to accept amnesia with equanimity and afterwards be wheeled from delivery room to ward, transferred to bed, and remain there, catheterised. Moving picture will not meet the appliance of moving bowel for the new mothers at Crittenton General, at least not yet, as ultrasonic fetus has still to make its real-time debut, and the paralyzing drugs their bodies have absorbed will prevent anything resembling its natural functioning. When catheters are finally removed, these invalid mothers will still be bedridden. The only violent flush will be their crimson faces, as nurses slide bedpans under their sheets and

encourage them to pee. Hitchcock once said, "The length of a film should be directly related to the endurance of the human bladder," but he said this not knowing the capacity of a mother's traumatized bladder to endure.

6   The portable television era began four years ago, and more than 500 television stations are broadcasting in the US, but few of these women have access to sets in the hospital. Instead, once they are mobile, they shuffle to the end of the long corridor, buy cigarettes from the dispensing machines, and painfully perch at the end of waiting room chairs to take in their favourite programs. These include soap operas like *The Edge of Night* and dramas like *Perry Mason*. Knowing the sex of their children now, friends and relatives have procured them appropriate coloured wool, so they can begin knitting gender-specific sweaters for their babies. They will speak to each other about their babies, gossip about other women, and drink prune juice by the gallon. They will watch commercials about *Spic and Span* and *Cheer*, and think about ways to get their homes, dishes, hair, husbands, laundry, children, pets, and possessions really, really clean. Since the early 50's there has been an obsession with chemical cleanliness. Arrays of diverse cleansing products have mushroomed in the marketplace, and become increasingly specialized. For example, a farsighted company, knowing the toilet is destined to come out of the water closet and need to be cleaned, has purchased *Ty-D-Bol* this year, but the famous little singing man in a boat, who serenades the goggled-eyed housewife from the bright blue tide waters, is only a glimmer in an ad man's eye. In 45 years, 70,000 new chemical compounds will have been dispersed into the world, and the *Ty-D-Bol* sailor moored, in spite of his popularity, and having nothing to do with water pollution. The toilet flushes, and the world changes. We have not yet begun to question the contents of what goes down the drain.

7   These new mothers at Crittenton General don't speculate. They smoke and chat about the here and now, about the nurseries they have assembled, about in-law problems. The environment consists only of hospital beds, tables and chairs, and the pictures of babies on the walls. It is nine years before *Time* magazine runs its article on the chocolate-coloured Cuyahoga lake that has a history of spontaneous chemical combustion, and ten years before the first "Earth Day." In the future, historians will label this time "the gold rush" of nuclear reactors, when companies such as General Electric, Combustion Engineering, and Westinghouse are bursting to fill the world with the heat and light of nuclear fission, and almost everyone thinks it's a wonderful idea. Three Mile Island is nineteen years in the future, and no one in this hospital has ever even heard of the city of Chernobyl. But in England, there are still people who recall "the days of toxic darkness" when the combination of coal smoke and fog killed over 12,000. There are those who still reflect upon the creepy, insidious nature of this event that stole lives away, without anyone realizing until undertakers ran short of caskets and florists short on flowers.

8   But there is no shortage of flowers here: pink roses and carnations announce the birth of daughters; blue irises and delphiniums announce the birth of sons. Arthur Kornberg produced DNA in a test tube in 1957, but the genetic engineering of cut flowers is over three decades away, so all of these bouquets are destined to an early end. Blue carnations have not yet been developed, and although the smell is lovely, the dozen roses my father brings my mother have not yet been engineered to hold their scents.

9   Although I can't recall, I imagine my sleep is deep and dreamless when my father and his

flowers arrive. When I open my eyes, I stare at the nursery ceiling, instead of looking into my mother's bewildered face. I imagine hearing the Midwestern accents of the busy nurses, instead of my mother's British lilt. I imagine wondering, what the hell I'm doing here. *The Dick Van Dyke Show* is a year away, and the controversial episode in which Rob suspects he and Laura have been given someone else's child in the hospital will not be aired until 1963. Since DNA testing is still the jurisdiction of science fiction, there are no definitive ways to discover answers to questions of mix-ups, or unquestionable questions about paternity. It is still mother who knows best.

10   These new mothers are submissive in spite of the feminist movement, which is about to explode, and despite Betty Friedan, who is already thinking about "the problem that has no name." They will take the babies they are given, without question, and only later, when these babies reach adolescence, begin to ask themselves what went wrong. Hemorrhoids, episiotomies, and paralyzing drugs make the first bowel movements for these women a torturous experience, far more painful than the contractions of childbirth they cannot recall. The bathrooms in this hospital are small, box-like, cold. The toilets are clinical and high off the ground. Small, fat women like my mother teeter upon them. The room smells like a mixture of chemical disinfectant and urine. If I were to make a film of my life now, I think I would begin it here: a tiny female child, cradled in her mother's arm, hovering over a hospital toilet.

11   "Drama is life with the dull bits left out," Hitchcock said, but it is more than the dull bits we extract. The General Principles of the Hays Code, which governed motion picture production from 1930 until the year of my birth, stated: "No picture shall be produced that will lower the moral standards of those who see it. Hence the sympathy of the audience should never be thrown to the side of crime, wrongdoing, evil, or sin; Correct standards of life, subject only to the requirements of drama and entertainment, shall be presented; Law, natural or human, shall not be ridiculed, nor shall sympathy be created for its violation."

12   Forty-three years from the date the Hays Code is defunct, digital formatting will make it easy to create professional-looking movies on a computer. George Lucas will use digital cameras to film the last of the *Star Wars* movies, and a 32-year-old doorman, Jonathan Caouette, will use his "iMovie" program, spend just a little over $200, and produce an award-winning documentary about his troubled, down the toilet, past.

13   If I were to make a film of my life now, I wonder what I would include and what I would cut. Caouette included old videos of life with his mentally ill mother and his eccentric grandparents, of himself in foster care, in drag, in the persona of a battered woman, and as a young gay man throwing up in a toilet after receiving news of his mother's lithium overdose. What he does not include are videos of his son and of the woman he impregnated. He omitted these intentionally because they present aspects of his life out of keeping with its general trajectory.

14   There are years of my life, between the ages of 14 and 19, that haunt me from the cutting room floor. Like Caouette's omissions, these years are out of synch and do not follow a linear story line. They drop me in another continent; leave me in a cultural time warp, where only the toilet remains constant and true.

15   The spectre first appears in Cleveland. My five-year-old brother, four years my senior, pulls the channel selector off the television and flushes it down the toilet. The toilet is utterly

blocked. My father, unwilling to pay a plumber, will fix it himself. Besides a wicked sense of humour, my father also possesses an eight-millimetre movie camera. He sets it up on a tripod to film this event. In years to come, we will sit in darkness watching my father shut off the water supply, siphon out the tank, remove the nuts that hold the bowl to the floor flange. We've heard the story a hundred times—seen it a hundred more—my father succeeds in removing the blockage. An expression of joy imbues his face. He sets the toilet down on the floor flange. As he moves to secure it, the film catches an alteration. We know what has occurred, though my father does not yet. We know that the toilet bowl has cracked and that the cost of replacing it will be significantly more than a plumber.

16   Four years after making this movie, my father is in debt, drinking hard liquor, and chain smoking. We travel to Chicago, to install an intercom system in our expensive, new house under construction. There are lines and vents of rough plumbing for three bathrooms, but the absence of toilets makes my bladder heavy. My father fiddles with hard square speakers and web-thin cords. I don't want to disturb him. I don't want to risk his rage. But he is not angry when I tell him. He places me on his shoulders, carries me to the dark stairless pit that opens into the basement and begins to descend a rickety ladder. Although I can't recall where I've seen it, I am thinking of Alfred Hitchcock's movie *Vertigo*—or rather, the word "vertigo," which I learned as a result of seeing the film. It bombed in 1958 because, some say, it was too dark for the light-craving audiences of *Auntie Mame* and *Houseboat*. Hitchcock once said: "Give them pleasure—the same pleasure they have when they wake up from a nightmare." And that is exactly the kind of pleasure I am experiencing on my father's shoulders, the kind

of pleasure that I have already experienced too much of in my life.

17   Although I am only seven, I already have trouble sleeping at night: I fear the dark, I fear spiders, I fear the invisible monsters lurking beneath my bed and the Princess lamp that once violently wobbled, for no apparent reason, on my bedside table. At home, I never fall asleep in bed, but always on a stair leading down into the living room, where my parents spend the evening fighting. As I teeter on my father's shoulders now, I think of my sleeping habits, and wonder how with such "vertigo" I have managed to survive. When my feet touch clay, my father directs me to a hole in the corner the construction workers made. I am humiliated, disgusted, incredulous. Only twice, so far, since I could use a toilet have I ever experienced not using one. Both times were bad.

18   Rewind to 1965. There I am, in the school ground, playing tag. I need a toilet, but the school doors are locked. I know I should go home, but my brothers aren't ready to leave, and I'm afraid to walk past the ravine alone. I continue playing, trying to forget the overwhelming pressure of my full bladder, hoping my mind can control this. No one is more surprised than me when I wet myself. The kids in the playground laugh. My brothers, mortified, escort me home. My mother gives me a bath and tries to assure me that no one at school will remember, but I know she is wrong. I make her promise to buy me a blond wig, sunglasses and a bright red sweater. I make her promise to re-enrol me in kindergarten as someone completely new. I will not calm down until she promises, and on Monday, when she does not buy me my disguise and insists I go to school exactly as I am, I know I will never completely trust her again.

19   Fast forward to 1966: our car breaks down on a highway. I go into the grassy field behind the car to pee. It is a hot summer day and we

have been waiting for a tow truck for an eternity. I am embarrassed, but my parents assure me no one will see. Fast forward to the day after: my rear end is the colour of a Japanese sun and itches with a potency I have never known. I wonder what curse has befallen me, if I unintentionally touched my private parts while I was sleeping and brought this plague upon myself. I can't bring myself to speak of this, but when the blisters form and break, the pain drives me to my mother who, on examining my backside, summons our family doctor. He diagnosis my condition as poison ivy related. For the next week, I lie in my bed on my stomach, my ravaged naked bottom on display.

20   "You can't trust anyone over 30," Berkeley dissident Jack Weinberg told a reporter in 1964, and although I would not even hear this phrase until I was studying American history at The University of Western Ontario in 1981, something in the collective ethos had infected me. Both of my parents are over 30 when I'm born and they continue getting older. The white porcelain toilet flushes—or it doesn't. The world changes just the same.

21   My father's drinking keeps him out late, gets him in car accidents, fistfights, and finally an unemployment line. A month later, he gets a job as an Encyclopaedia Britannica salesman. This is the year Neil Armstrong lands on the moon. His small step is one giant leap for mankind, while my father's small step drags him around our affluent neighbourhood. Nobody's hungry for knowledge. He can't give encyclopaedias away. It's 1969, *The Saturday Evening Post* stops its presses after 147 years, The Beatles record their last album, and Paul McCartney is rumoured dead. Charles Manson and his followers kill Sharon Tate, Nixon succeeds Johnson, and *The Brady Bunch* and *Sesame Street* make their network debuts.

22   On Christmas day, we move from our large, beautiful house to a small, shabby one in Windsor. My brothers share a bedroom and we all have to share one toilet. This would not be half so bad if my father did not have chronic constipation. He spends a large percentage of his time, when he's home, in the bathroom reading books on World War II. When he's not in the bathroom, he's in the basement, smoking and drinking and building a bar. There are no corporate rehabilitation programs, and although some health professionals view it as such, the vast majority do not consider alcoholism a disease. Every middle-class home has a wet bar. Cocktail hour begins at five. The only hope for a person like my father is to start a business of his own and to run it into the ground.

23   Fast forward to 1974. I am drunk and kneeling over a toilet at the Fire Side Inn restaurant at my father's funeral reception. Two hours earlier, my father was interred in the mausoleum at Green Lawn Cemetery, the same place his father was interred in 1961, and his mother will be interred in 1983. The year my father dies is three years after Dr Denis Burkitt publishes the results of his study comparing diet and the incidence of colon cancer in North America and Africa, and brings the term "fibre" into common usage. It is three years after it has become stylish to eat bran cereals for breakfast and to bring raw broccoli and carrot sticks to parties as finger food. In years to come, there will be passionate debates about the role of dietary fibre in cancer prevention, but right now, fibre seems to be a preventative panacea, and my father never liked eating high-fibre foods. It has not yet been postulated that cigarette smoking and alcohol increase the incidence of this cancer, nor that fat and lack of exercise are extremely unhealthy "lifestyle choices." In fact, the concept of "lifestyle choices" is new, and has not yet been exploited by weight loss businesses or dismissed by economists. In years to come, the

colon will become the third most common site for cancer, and in 31 years, an estimated 104,950 new cases of colon cancer will be diagnosed in the United States alone.

24   But right now, as I lean over the toilet, I see my father. I am not thinking of his unhealthy lifestyle, or his bowel obsession, which began with his constipation several years ago. I am thinking of his split personality, his dichotomy, the kind, sober him and the mean drunk. I am projecting into the future and wondering how I will ever be able to reconcile the past. What kind of person was he? What was my experience of him? What will I choose to remember and what will I choose to flush away?

25   The year I am born, Jack Parr walks off the *Tonight Show* because the NBC censors edit out a segment in which he tells a joke about a toilet. The joke is innocuous—about travellers in England looking for a wayside chapel, and seeing a sign announcing "W.C." Parr doesn't even say the words "Water Closet." For weeks newspapers carry stories about this national controversy. Things will never be the same.

26   Fourteen years later some kind of amnesia falls over me. I awake in England, or at least partially awake. My mother, in her panic, has sold, given away, or burned everything we owned in Windsor and has moved to England. She has had to make major decisions about what to take with her and what to leave behind. She has decided that my father was a terrible bastard and that she's well rid of him. She has had to throw out her entire life in North America as bad business, to return to the place of her birth and the home of her brother and sister in-law. Because I am 14, she takes me with her. Everything is different here: the accents, the currency, the electrical outlets. In 1974, the school system in England is impenetrable to a North American high school student; there are no equivalencies, no opportunities of entry. One night, my aunt tells me she's found a job for me, and the next day, I begin working in a hotel as a chamber maid. I clean toilets every day of my life, toilet after toilet, for the next five years, until the white porcelain toilet flushes and I decide to make a final cut.

Organization and Style

1. Sonik uses many literary devices in her essay. Discuss her use of two of the following: imagery, diction (word choice), figurative language, juxtaposition (placing contrastive elements next to each other). (See pp. 125, 128, and 138 for details on the above literary devices.)

2. Sonik does not use the conventional chronological method to order events. Comment on her alternation of the present and past and the way it relates to her theme, referring to specific passages.

3. Discuss Sonik's use of humour, referring to specific passages.

Critical Thinking

1. What do the quotations from Alfred Hitchcock contribute to her essay?

2. Analyze Sonik's use of (a) television or (b) the toilet as a metaphor or symbol that reveals the essay's themes.

3. Discuss the ways that the author's examples from both her distant past and her more recent past illuminate the generational differences highlighted in the essay. How do they comment on or reveal aspects of social change?

4. Compare and contrast "Flush" with one of the non-academic essays in this textbook; or, compare and contrast "Flush" with either "Giving up the Ghost," p. 170, "I'm Glad I Never Had to Decide," p. 165, or "Is Scientific Progress Inevitable?" p. 162. Use at least two bases of comparison.

Andrew Irvine, "Is Scientific Progress Inevitable?"

"Is Scientific Progress Inevitable?" is an essay in the book *In the Agora: The Public Face of Canadian Philosophy*, co-edited by Andrew Irvine, in which Canadian writers discuss the intersections between philosophy and current topics, such as the limits of scientific advancement. The Agora was a marketplace in ancient Athens where people discussed important topics of the day; the essays in *In the Agora* are intended for a similar purpose.

Irvine uses personal experience in his essay to help him introduce his topic; he has not, unlike Ian Brown, p. 165, or Madeline Sonik, p. 155, written a personal essay but a reflective one.

 ## Preparing to Read

1. Using reliable sources, investigate the concept of medicine wheels. In your own words, explain what they are, why they might have been erected, and how they were once used.

2. Do you believe that the progress of science is inevitable? Why or why not?

Is Scientific Progress Inevitable?

Andrew Irvine

In the Agora: The Public Face of Canadian Philosophy, 2006
(1175 words)

1   When my daughter was nine, I took her to see an Aboriginal medicine wheel in rural Saskatch-ewan. Built between 1500 and 4500 years ago, some 150 of these stone structures are still scattered throughout the Canadian prairies and the American Midwest. Most are found within 200 kilometres of the confluence of the Red Deer and South Saskatchewan Rivers. Many have spokes like a wagon wheel. Others have series of concentric circles. Some are in the shape of turtles or people.

2   The medicine wheel we visited rests atop the rolling Moose Mountains, a two-and-a-half-

hour drive southeast of Regina. Constructed by the Plains Indians, it consists of a central stone cairn and five stone spokes laid out at various angles from the cairn. At the end of each spoke is a smaller cairn. An elliptical ring of stones, approximately 62 by 50 feet, surrounds the central cairn.

3 It is difficult to take children much younger than 9 or 10 to this wheel since they need to be able to control a horse to reach it. You also need permission from the Pheasant Rump Reserve and a guide to show you the way.

4 Once you reach the site, it's easy to be impressed. For one thing, the view is tremendous. As *everyone* knows, Saskatchewan is flat. This means that from a good rise of land there is nothing between you and the horizon. Just as on the ocean, on a clear day the only thing blocking your view is the curvature of the earth. Also, it's a rare thing in North America to come face to face with any man-made object as old as England's Stonehenge or Egypt's pyramids. The mere fact that some of these structures have stood undisturbed for thousands of years is enough to remind you of the shortness of your own life and the fragility of human existence.

5 Another thing of which we are reminded is the fragility of science. We often think of science as something inescapably linked to progress, and of progress as continually marching forward. We assume that there is something inevitable about the increase of knowledge and the benefits this knowledge brings. Yet nothing could be further from the truth. The advancement of knowledge in general—and of scientific knowledge in particular—is much more like a Saskatchewan wheat field than a solid rock structure: without appropriate care and nurturing, it could very easily shrivel up and die.

6 This point was brought home as we looked at the Moose Mountain medicine wheel. It is likely that there is no single explanation as to why these stone structures were built. Some may have been built to commemorate the dead; others as ceremonial sites to help communities observe important occasions; and yet others simply as landmarks on an otherwise barren prairie. Whatever their original purpose, there is no denying that all of the sites have had important spiritual connections to Native communities, both past and present.

7 But some of the wheels may also have been built with a more scientific purpose in mind. Two structures in particular, the Moose Mountain medicine wheel and the larger but similar Bighorn wheel in Wyoming, more than 700 kilometres away, have spokes marking several important astronomical sightings. The two wheels have so many similarities that one archeologist has commented that they could have been built from the same set of plans.

8 Perhaps most striking, the longest spoke in both wheels lines up directly with the point of sunrise at the summer solstice. As every ancient people could observe throughout the year, sunrise and sunset shift along the horizon. As spring comes closer, the sunrise moves farther north each morning. This continues until 21 June, the summer solstice, when the sun's northern motion stops. Six months later the winter solstice marks the end of the sun's opposite motion southward along the horizon. Other small cairns mark the positions of three of the northern hemisphere's brightest stars: Aldebaran in the constellation Taurus, Rigel in Orion, and Sirius in Canis Major.

9 Today, the alignments between the cairns and these various astronomical sightings are off by a few degrees, but if corrections are made for how the stars have shifted over the centuries since the cairns were built, the alignments become nearly perfect.

10 The importance of the astronomical sciences to many ancient cultures has been well

documented. It's not at all improbable that this knowledge would also have been important to the Plains Indians. Whenever we speak of a "blue moon" or the "dog days of summer" we are reflecting the significance the night sky had to ancient cultures. On the prairies, the summer solstice was marked by important ceremonies such as the sun dance; it would also have helped regulate the nomadic movements of a people with no written calendar. It is also interesting that many medicine wheels have spokes or cairns that point to other, similar structures 15, 30, even 70 kilometres away.

11   Today, the astronomical knowledge underlying these structures has been all but lost to the original inhabitants of the plains. Even so, this knowledge was once of great importance to Aboriginal communities, as evidenced by the fact that even today they recognize and celebrate these monuments as sacred sites.

12   Just as importantly, these monuments remind us that scientific knowledge is not inevitable, that it can just as easily decline as advance. They tell us that scientific progress is linked in complex, unpredictable ways to social progress, and vice versa.

13   When I think about these issues, I'm reminded of the words of the philosopher Sidney Hook. As he neared the end of his life, having witnessed the social and political turbulence of almost the entire twentieth century, he was convinced that nothing about human existence is inevitable. As he put it,

14   Looking back on a life longer than I ever expected . . . I am confident that one of my strongest beliefs will remain unaltered. This is the overwhelming conviction that what has happened need not necessarily have happened. The great events of our time, or of any time, good or bad, victories or disasters, need not have occurred. I am not saying that anything *could* have happened at any time. We do not live in a magical world or one of absolute chance. . . . Yet the more closely we explore the tangled web of causation of any historical event, the more likely it is that we will conclude that it didn't have to be.

15   In other words, there is no guarantee that social progress will continue unabated or that scientific knowledge will continue to increase. Unless we continue to nurture what is important, to look for ways to improve what we already have, life has no guarantees.

16   We know that science has the potential to alleviate hunger, disease, and even war. But without the will to protect these accomplishments and the desire to improve on them, life will remain unpredictable. Scientific knowledge remains a rare and valuable commodity in the history of the world, and this is as true today as it was thousands of years ago.

⚫ Comprehension

1.   Summarize paragraphs 12 and 15, which discuss the nature of scientific knowledge.

⚫ Organization and Style

1.   How does the author connect the scene he witnesses at the top of the Moose Mountains with his perceptions about science and scientific knowledge (pars. 4–6)?

2. How does Irvine use language, imagery, and/or style to evoke his experience at the Moose Mountain medicine wheel? Refer to specific paragraphs in the essay to support your points.

Critical Thinking

1. Who was Sidney Hook and why might he be an appropriate source for Irvine (pars. 13–15)?

2. Write a critical response, using one of the following statements as a prompt:

    a. "We assume that there is something inevitable about the increase of [scientific] knowledge and the benefits this knowledge brings. Yet nothing could be further from the truth" (par. 5).

    b. "We know that science has the potential to alleviate hunger, disease, and even war. But without the will to protect these accomplishments and the desire to improve on them, life will remain unpredictable" (par. 16).

3. Write an analytical/reflective essay about a specific incident or observation—such as one involving the natural world—that led you to reflect on its larger significance or a universal truth. You can begin, as Irvine does, with narration or description.

Ian Brown, "I'm Glad I Never Had to Decide Whether My Strange, Lonely Boy Ought to Exist"

Ian Brown, a former features writer with *The Globe and Mail*, has written a personal essay about his life with his severely disabled son. However, his essay is not *just* about him and his son. The best personal essays use a personal situation to enable a reader to relate to an experience and, usually, universalize an important issue—in this case, the ethics of genetic engineering. Although Brown also includes the words of members of the medical community, he keeps reminding the reader that he's involved—that the issue is complex and that it evokes complex, even contradictory, feelings.

Preparing to Read

1. What are some of the issues related to genetic testing? Genetic engineering? (For example, do you believe guidelines need to be put in place by governments?) You could approach this as a brainstorming or clustering activity (see p. 3).

2.   To explore your own attitude toward these issues, freewrite for five to ten minutes, starting with a relevant prompt, such as "I believe that self-selecting your future child's physical traits is . . . ."

I'm Glad I Never Had to Decide Whether My Strange, Lonely Boy Ought to Exist

Ian Brown

The Globe and Mail, 27 August 2011
(2316 words)

1   New prenatal tests can check fetal DNA for everything from gender to serious medical conditions. But as the father of one disabled son asks, who has the right to decide which life isn't worth living?

2   In the early years of my son's life, before I understood how far outside the norm his disabilities took us, I was always astonished to hear a parent say, "I wouldn't change my disabled child for anything."

3   My wife, Johanna—an exceptionally compassionate person, and a terrific mother—never made such statements.

4   "I hear parents of other handicapped kids saying all the time, 'I wouldn't change my child, I wouldn't trade him for anything,'" Johanna once said to me. We were lying on our backs in bed, talking in the night, which we did on the rare occasions Walker fell asleep. Talking into the darkness, you could say anything. "But I would. I would trade Walker, if I could push a button, for the most average child in the world, who got Cs in school. I would trade him in an instant.

5   "I wouldn't trade him for my sake, for our sake. But I would trade him for his sake. I think Walker has a very, very hard life."

6   Trading him still isn't possible, but choosing him is getting closer. A new raft of ultra-accurate, at-home, fetal-DNA tests are flying off North American drugstore and Internet shelves these days, and a massive debate is close behind.

7   The DNA-testing industry (which is growing so fast that the US Federal Drug Administration is investigating the tests) has no sooner offered us the opportunity to select the number and gender of the babies we can have—to say nothing of the chance to guarantee they are free of some debilitating syndrome—than doctors and bioethicists are up in arms, accusing medical researchers of promoting genetic cleansing.

8   These arguments come along every few years now. The more science lets us interfere in the beginnings of life, to engineer what kind of babies we can make, the more we seem to need to debate who we want to be as human beings. Maybe this should tell us something.

9   In my house, such debates always bring on an identity crisis. Walker suffers from CFC, an impossibly rare affliction (150 known cases, globally) caused by a completely random genetic mutation. He's 15 now, looks 10 and has the mind of a two-year-old. He always will.

10   He is an often charming and fantastic companion, but he can't speak, or live on his own (or even with us, anymore), or manage the toilet,

or eat without a tube, or go for long without smashing his ears flat and ugly with his fists.

11 We raised him on our own for 10 years, and the experience almost shattered everything I valued—my family, my marriage, my healthy daughter's life, my finances, my friendships, life as I wanted to live it.

12 There was no genetic test for his syndrome when he was born (there still isn't). For a long time, not a day went by when I didn't wish there'd been one. Today, I'm glad no test existed then—that I never had to decide, based on a piece of paper damp with my wife's blood, whether my strange and lonely boy ought to exist.

13 Still, wouldn't he have been better off, thanks to a simple genetic test, not living his shadowy, pain-filled, so-called life? I understand the question. I understand the appeal of the DNA test, its trouble-free promise. But the answer is complicated.

14 Pregnant women can now self-administer a simple blood test as early as the seventh week of pregnancy, and know, with 95-per-cent accuracy, the gender of the child they will be having. This, in turn, gives them the opportunity to abort the fetus if it's not the gender they want. A set of fertility clinics in Los Angeles, New York, and Mexico recently reported that 85 per cent of their clients wanted to select for sex (for purposes of "family balancing")—and that three-quarters of those clients came from overseas. (Some manufacturers of gender-testing kits refuse to sell them in India and China for that reason.)

15 The smorgasbord of genetic choices doesn't stop there. Women who use fertility drugs to have children now find a growing number of perinatologists willing to reduce healthy twins to a singleton in utero—purely for the convenience of the woman, as there is rarely any medical need today to perform the procedure.

16 And couples who buy donor eggs and sperm from commercial fertility clinics can now select for hair colour, ethnicity, temperament, athleticism, and intellectual prowess—even for the length of the donor's eyelashes. If you think that's creepy, recall that at the beginning of the twentieth century, cosmetic surgery was considered creepy too.

17 We do these things not just because we need to, but because we can. Ethics follow technology, not the other way around.

18 Of course, there are more humane and significant uses for the new tests. Duchenne muscular dystrophy afflicts only boys, and a test can accurately identify the genders of potential candidates and evade the burden of a troubled life. Fetal-DNA researchers are reportedly close to marketing a cheap, accurate blood test for Down syndrome (which 800,000 people in North America live with); similar screens will soon identify even more serious genetic diseases in utero, such as cystic fibrosis (70,000 people worldwide), and sickle-cell anemia (20 per cent of the sub-Saharan population).

19 Geneticists even predict the imminent arrival of the holy grail of the medical testing business, "the $1000 genome"—the (fairly) cheap sequencing of all the most important exons (nucleic-acid sequences) in a fetus' DNA.

20 That will vastly expand would-be parents' understanding of the sicknesses their fetus is heir to (provided geneticists can figure out how to read the data—there are, after all, 4000 known single-gene diseases), and increase the odds they will take abortive action if a serious syndrome is revealed, thereby avoiding a great deal of pain and trouble and medical expense. Danish newspapers have predicted a Down-syndrome-free society by 2030.

21 Needless to say, there are a lot of people who find this revolution in genetic choice alarming

and inhuman. Margaret Somerville, the well-known medical ethicist at McGill University, recently lambasted the prospect of widespread prenatal testing as a symptom of our diminished respect for human life. She called it nothing short of a "search and destroy" mission to wipe out disabled people.

22   But Dr Somerville is an ethicist. The geneticists I know keep clear of the ethical debate. David Chitayat, a clinical pediatrician and geneticist at Toronto's Hospital for Sick Children, thinks Dr Somerville is talking nonsense.

23   "We're not doing screening to eliminate Down syndrome," Dr Chitayat explained rather testily the other day, when I phoned to see if he could help me sort out my complicated feelings. No amount of screening, he points out, will eliminate the genes that cause Down syndrome. But he stoutly defends the right of parents to a choice in the matter.

24   In his view, the value of all life, even the life of the disabled, is counterweighed by the downside of any serious genetic syndrome—the physical toll it takes on the child and the family, the cataclysmic lack of government funding for lodging and care, and the isolation and parental guilt a serious syndrome causes.

25   "Dr Somerville can do what she wants," he said, "but the decision to screen and to act is an individual decision. Let's say this is true—that severely disabled people teach us something. That is one thing. But to tell someone this is what they have to do because they cannot screen, that they have to have a disabled child? Does she know how many husbands leave when a disabled child is born into a family? Or what the impact is on other children? It's an individual decision in the context of the family about what is good and what's bad. The family decides."

26   "Would you have taken the test and had an abortion," I once asked my wife, "if there had been one?" It was his loneliness I couldn't bear, the boy's own sad sense of how different he was. Somehow he knew that.

27   "If there had been a test when I was pregnant that revealed what Walker's life would have been like, I would have had the abortion."

28   "But then you wouldn't have had Walker," I said.

29   Suddenly Johanna began to move around the kitchen a little faster. "You can't say that after I've known Walker—would I have done something to get rid of him? It's one thing to abort an anonymous fetus. It's another to murder Walker. A fetus wouldn't be Walker."

30   "What do you think the world would be like without people like Walker?" I asked. It was an obnoxious thing to ask. "Without kids like him, I mean, kids who have real setbacks." Fetal-DNA testing makes this more and more of a possibility.

31   I'll always remember her answer. "A world where there are only masters of the universe would be like Sparta," she said. "It would not be a kind country. It would be a cruel place."

32   By then she was crying.

33   I suspect the reason we can't stop debating the value of genetic testing, despite its many virtues, is that we don't care to choose our fates.

34   Genetic control threatens what Harvard University political scientist Michael Sandel, in his book *The Case Against Perfection*, calls our "lively sense of the contingency of our gifts—our sense that none of us is wholly responsible for his or her success, [which] saves a meritocratic society from the smug assumption that that success is the crown of virtue."

35   We aren't really scared of the slick and dreamless future Dr Somerville conjures out of

her distaste for quasi-therapeutic abortion. We aren't even that afraid of what perfections we might attempt with genetic technology. We're afraid of what the new biotechnology will do to us—that its "stance of mastery and control," as Carl Elliott, a brilliant bioethicist in Minnesota, has written, "leaves insufficient cultural space for the alternate ways of living a human life."

36 I have no objection to genetic testing. If you can avoid it, I don't want your child to face the daunting, aimless future Walker may have, especially after his mother and I are gone.

37 But I have an objection if the results of those tests are the only measure you accept of what constitutes a valuable life. I object if you say that my son is a mistake, that we don't want more of him, and deny what he is: an exotic, living form of freedom; a way of being liberated from the grind of the survival of the fittest; free of all the orthodoxies by which we normals measure a "successful" life—the Harvard acceptance, the hot partner, the good job, the fit body, the millions.

38 Disability is by nature anti-establishment. It's the very lack of so-called normal expectations, the absence of the possibility that Walker and I can ever "achieve" much or even disappoint each other, that frees us from the established and the status quo, to be who we actually are with each other, rather than what society says we are supposed to be. A rare and often impossible form of love lies in that small hollow.

39 Genetic tests are a way to try to eliminate the imperfect, and all the pain and fear that comes with imperfection. (Especially our own.) But imperfection is not just pain and agony.

40 On his good days, Walker is proof of what the imperfect and the fragile have to offer—a reminder that there are many ways to be human, and that judgment is our least valuable human capacity.

41 In terms of physical human evolution, he is a mistake, an error. But he is peerless as a way of developing what Charles Darwin himself in *The Descent of Man* deemed the evolutionary advantages of "the social instincts . . . love, and the distinct emotion of sympathy."

42 I see him for three days every two weeks, now that he lives mostly in an assisted-living home. When he does come home, I try to take him for a walk down Bloor Street, the big city artery nearest our house, him in his chair and me on foot.

43 I lean down and push the chair with my elbows, so I can talk in the ear hole of his soft foam helmet. "Look, Walkie," I say, "look, the white micro-miniskirt is back this summer!" Or: "That Hungarian butcher has had that same side of meat hanging there for a year—let's never eat in there."

44 I say all sorts of things, whatever comes to view. I am pretty sure he understands none of it, rationally. But he knows we are having a conversation, and he knows he is on one end of it. The wriggling, blasting laugh of pleasure our yakking always gives him reminds me again and again how important it is to make that gesture—to engage another, to try to reach the other, no matter how remote the likelihood of any return or result or reward.

45 It doesn't matter that Walker will never pass his genetic test. What matters is that I pass his test, that I had a chance to be a human being, a friend, a chatting buddy, a decent if doltish dad, and that I seized it.

46 I am ashamed to say I regret many things in my life. But I never regret those pointless but utterly unpredictable strolls, those strange, lifting afternoons on the hot city sidewalk with the test-failing boy. They're just one more way of measuring what we might be.

Comprehension

1. a. Explain the significance of the statement "Maybe this should tell us something." (par. 8)
   b. Explain the reason for quotation marks in paragraph 14.
   c. Explain the capitalization of "Conversation" and "Other" in paragraph 44.

2. Paraphrase one of the following two important paragraphs in the essay and summarize the other one: 37, 38.

Organization and Style

1. Brown interweaves his personal perspective with facts and expert opinion. Taking one passage of at least three paragraphs, analyze his success. (Hint: the first or last paragraph should include a transition between personal perspective and facts/experts.)

2. How much of the essay would you consider the introduction? Analyze its effectiveness.

Critical Thinking/Research

1. Analyze Brown's writing style, commenting on its effectiveness. For example, you could consider sentence/paragraph length and variety, word choice, voice, tone, and other devices. (Remember that Brown is writing for readers of a national newspaper.)

2. Did the essay change your view about any aspect of genetic testing or engineering? Identify one passage that you considered particularly successful in support of his thesis and explain why you have chosen it.

3. To get a sense of the debate, use reliable sources, such as your library's database, to access two essays that argue one side of the other of an issue related to genetic testing—for example, "designer babies," fertility clinics, or embryo screening. Critically analyze the two essays, evaluating the strengths/weaknesses of their arguments.

Lynn Cunningham, "Giving up the Ghost: When It Comes to Quitting Smoking, You're on Your Own"

Lynn Cunningham is a journalist and former instructor at Ryerson University. In "Giving up the Ghost," she writes of her personal experience with quitting smoking. In its blunt honesty, the essay sometimes reads like the confessions of an addictive personality. However, Cunningham does not just talk about herself: her narrative contains an argument, which is hinted at in the essay's subtitle. Thus, like many personal essays, Cunningham's universalizes her situation, making it relevant to her readers.

Preparing to Read

1. In a couple of paragraphs and using reliable sources, summarize current scientific findings on the types, causes, and prevalence of addiction today.
2. What does it mean "to give up the ghost?" Based on the title (and subtitle), what do you expect the essay to be about?

Giving up the Ghost: When It Comes to Quitting Smoking, You're on Your Own

Lynn Cunningham

The Walrus, 2014
(3640 words)

1   I had expected an austere, sanatorium-like atmosphere, with staff in crisp lab coats, the walls plastered with rules and bumper sticker-type slogans: *Rehab is for quitters*, maybe. Instead, the place skews toward homey, or at least as homey as a medical facility can be, with nary a motivational poster to be seen. My room features a Murphy bed, a small desk, a wall-mounted TV, and an inoffensive print; brown and beige are the dominant colours. The space is reminiscent of an upscale dorm or a highway motel, except for the syringe disposal receptacle in the bathroom.

2   But matters of decor are not top of mind on this Friday in January, as I stand outside the entrance of the building. Instead, I'm focused on cigarettes—or, more precisely, smoking as many of them as possible in the time left before 4:30 p.m., when nine other people and I will hand over our packs and lighters, and put our faith in the Mayo Clinic's Nicotine Dependence Centre.

3   A half-century ago, I lit up for the first time. It was 1964, the same year that United States surgeon general Luther Terry released a depth-charge report unequivocally drawing a direct link between cigarettes and lung cancer, chronic bronchitis, emphysema, and coronary heart disease. Or, as *The New York Times* headline succinctly put it, "Cigarettes Peril Health." Being 14 at the time, I didn't read *The Times*, but the news filtered into my hometown of Guelph, Ontario—the site of an Imperial Tobacco factory, where, it was said, workers got free cartons. My friends and I mordantly joked that every cigarette we smoked would shorten our lives by ten minutes. Because we were immortal, this didn't seem like a big deal.

4   At school, I belonged to the science club and entered fairs with projects like "The Miracle of Rayon." I was an A student in home economics; my pocket money came from babysitting. In short, I was something of a nerd, and desperately wished for an edgier image, which I believed smoking bestowed.

5   At the time, nearly half of Canadian adults were smokers, and in that *Mad Men* era you could light up just about anywhere—planes, banks, movie theatres, even doctors' offices and hospital rooms. To object to someone smoking was rather like being the cranky neighbour yelling at kids for playing hockey in the street. These days, though, the 16 per cent of us who still smoke daily are the ones beyond the pale—which is to say a car's length or two from building entrances, if we're obeying the omnipresent signs.

6   I could claim that an extremely belated road-to-Damascus experience led me to rehab, but the fact is, for years now, you have had to be either terminally dense or a Big Tobacco executive (not mutually exclusive categories) to deny the health risks. It wasn't even the pariah status, the death-ray glares of disapproval that lighting up automatically incurs. True, that contempt—and its flip side, a self-image hovering below zero—was one of the reasons I'd quit numerous times over the past five decades. I had stopped for as little as a week and as long as seven years, the latter an interregnum that went up in flames during an evening that featured a lot of fun and too much wine; suddenly, cadging a cig seemed like a good idea. Within a week, I was back to a pack and a half a day.

7   This time, there were two things that influenced me to kick the habit. One was my kid, 23 years old and a smoker since he was 15. I know he's not immortal, even if he doesn't, and my guilt about being a noxious role model is intense. The second, at the risk of seeming to have skewed priorities, was the money. I was smoking two large packs a day—50 cigarettes, about 30 more than what's currently defined as heavy smoking—which translated to a ludicrous $8,750 a year. On the cusp of retirement, with its decreased income, I realized I couldn't afford to keep smoking if I still wanted to live indoors.

8   Cigarettes are expensive, but, as I learned, so is quitting. Knowing that a period of policed abstinence and sharp-eyed supervision would be critical to getting me through the first few days, I started looking for a residential cessation program. I anticipated finding dozens of choices. Seek live-in treatment for drugs or booze, and you can generally be accommodated speedily in a free, non-profit 12-step program. If you can hang on for a while, your stay at a private facility will be covered by most provincial health care plans; with a decent extended health plan, you may not even have to wait.

9   Nicotine addiction is both more common and more deadly than dependence on alcohol or other drugs, and, according to one study, costs the Canadian economy $17 billion a year. But being strung out on tobacco is treated almost exclusively through outpatient programs and other measures of debatable utility, such as the helpline number tucked into every pack. (I called once, three weeks into an attempt. The woman on the other end of the phone said, essentially, Carry on, and wished me luck.) I discovered that there is just a handful of residential cessation programs in North America. One, located outside Ottawa, I crossed off my list as soon as I encountered the New Agey phrase *smudging materials*.

10   So, here I am at the Mayo, in unprepossessing Rochester, Minnesota, a city that's never been on my bucket list. About once a month, the Nicotine Dependence Centre takes over the fourth floor of the Colonial Building, on the eastern edge of the clinic's considerable downtown campus. There's a simple reason why the program isn't offered more frequently, and it unites all ten of us would-be quitters: unlike most people, we can afford the $5,500 (US) price tag for the eight days, plus airfare and the cost of the patches, gum, and other nicotine replacements that are central to the clinic's treatment model. (Nicotine itself, while highly addictive, is not carcinogenic, nor does it cause the myriad other health issues associated with cigarettes.) In my case, the total comes to more than $7,000 (US). Not a pack's worth of the cost is reimbursed by my provincial health plan or my employee benefits.

11   The truth is that we don't fund cigarette rehab because we don't consider smoking a true addiction. Today, people are said to be hooked

on everything from Facebook to Oreos, but being an Internet fanatic or cookie monster is not the same as experiencing the panicky tightening in the gut, the I'd-do-anything-for-a-hit feeling, that strikes when you're running short of fill-in-the-blank—smack, booze, Oxys, cocaine, cigs. Unlike those other substances, though, cigarettes are both legal and, when used as intended, apt to kill their consumers. It's impossible to contemplate these dissonant facts without engaging in some conspiracy theorizing. Might there be a connection between cigarettes' still-lawful status, despite their indisputably lethal nature, and the $7.3 billion in tobacco-related tax revenue the federal and provincial governments reaped last year? After all, if everyone actually quit, that's a lot of dough forgone.

12   Behind these counterintuitive policies is the big lie that smoking is merely a bad habit. As the industry's disingenuous slogan of the 1980s and 1990s had it, "My pleasure, my choice." But it's not just Big Tobacco that advances this perspective. Last February, *The Globe and Mail* columnist Margaret Wente articulated a common outlook: "If addiction is a disease, it's a peculiar one." Her point was that, unlike those with so-called real diseases, addicts get themselves into trouble and can jolly well get themselves out. "The disease model of addiction implies that the victim is helpless," she wrote. "It denies the role of personal agency, which is probably the most important force of all when facing down your demons."

13   This is reminiscent of how wartime post-traumatic stress disorder was once chalked up to LMF—lack of moral fibre. It's the attitude of those who unhelpfully recount how they just got up one day and pitched their cigs, the implication being that you could do the same if you weren't such a gormless loser. And it's a point of view that even permeates anti-tobacco campaigns, which over the decades have morphed from concern for the addict—"Smoking kills"—to stigma-driven shock and shame. Think of that American Cancer Society poster featuring the ravaged older woman, puffing away, with the slogan, "Smoking is very glamorous." Cruise the Internet a bit and you'll find images that are even more jolting. One substitutes a cigarette filter for a woman's nipple (i.e., smoking is bad for breastfeeding babies); another, aimed at teenagers, equates smoking with being forced to perform oral sex. In these ads, there is no acknowledgement of cigarettes' extraordinary addictive power. We don't expect drug users just to just kick the habit, but that idea permeates cigarette discourse. The message is as clear as a No Smoking sign: when it comes to quitting, you're on your own.

14   In the minutes before Friday's 4:30 p.m. relinquishing of our cigs and lighters, everyone chain-smokes furiously outside the Colonial Building. We aren't acquainted yet, but there's lots of nervous banter as we mainline our nicotine, huddled in twos and threes. Do any of us really believe the butts we've just ground out will be our last? Still, once inside, we all participate in the disposal ritual—everything's tossed into an ordinary plastic bag, which doesn't strike me as sufficiently ceremonious—and then we have our initial group therapy session. Besides me, there are six men and three women, two of whom are also Canadian.

15   A decade ago, I realized I was drinking too much—more than a bottle of wine a night—and tottered off to Alcoholics Anonymous. There, we called them *drunkalogs*—tales of humiliating things done while under the influence of booze. At the exotic end of the spectrum were exploits like attempting to steal a plane or losing a rental car; more common were heartbreaking accounts of domestic upheaval, workplace

flame-outs, [and] sordid affairs. In smokers' rehab, our versions are more quotidian. Illicit puffs in airport washrooms figure prominently, with a couple of the guys trading stories about their favourite spots at Chicago O'Hare. An entertainment entrepreneur spins a hilarious story about smoking up a hotel room and simply leaving the several-hundred-dollar fine in cash when he checked out. The parents of younger children describe John le Carré-level diversionary tactics to prevent their kids from learning their secret. I recount having missed a plane in Dublin a few years ago because I was indulging my addiction rather than lining up for the security check, a dumb-ass move that cost me $500 in rebooking fees; it's too painful to confess to the group that I missed the moment of my mother's death because I'd nipped out for a hit. None of these anecdotes addresses the matter of compromised health, but they don't really have to, since one of us, a fellow in his late fifties, has barely finished chemo for lung cancer.

16   The absence of the titillating or outlandish in our stories perhaps explains the dearth of motivational books or movies for the would-be non-smoker. Prior to my trip to the Mayo, a diligent search for butting-out memoirs, something along the lines of Mary Karr's *Lit*, or Augusten Burroughs' *Dry*, turned up just one. *Lighting Up* features an overexcited subtitle—*How I Stopped Smoking, Drinking, and Everything Else I Loved in Life Except Sex*—that fails to suggest the mix of chaos and catharsis that makes a good taking-the-cure account. On the flick front, finding nothing about tobacco at all, I thought I'd screen some of the booze-and-drugs rehab movies I'd watched when I decided to quit drinking—*28 Days*; *Clean and Sober*; *My Name Is Bill W.* What I hadn't noticed ten years ago was that everyone in these movies smokes all the time. In fact, being a nicotine fiend is

kind of a thing among reformed drinkers. Bill Wilson of AA fame apparently smoked like a chimney. Caroline Knapp, the author of the acclaimed memoir *Drinking: A Love Story*, died of lung cancer at 42. As Burroughs observed, "Everybody in recovery smokes." You can see the problem. Popular culture basically doesn't acknowledge smoking as a dangerous addiction, nor does it lend it the patina of romantic dissolution that might garner users more sympathy—or better treatment options.

17   I used to wonder why I am the only member of my family with addiction issues. Then I realized a strong vein of clinical depression runs through our history, and addiction is often a co-occurring condition. My father struggled through many dark days; one of my sisters committed suicide; my cousins knock back antidepressants, and so do I. I saw my first psychiatrist at 18, when even taking a shower began to seem too hard. I can't recall when my drinking shifted from recreational to alcoholic, but it spiked during a period of high drama: My kid (step-grandson, actually)—who, tragically, has fetal alcohol syndrome—was a rebel without a cause by the time he was 13. My husband had his own alcohol issues. There was also my then-undiagnosed bipolar disorder, which co-occurs with alcoholism up to 50 per cent of the time. At the Mayo, we don't spend a lot of time comparing our psychological profiles, but I quickly realize that I'm not alone. Three of the others are addicts-turned-teetotalers; another takes a pharmacopoeia of medications that rivals my own.

18   Scientists trying to understand people like us have found that the brain of the zebrafish, a freshwater member of the minnow family, is a good substitute for the human organ when it comes to studying addiction. The Centre for Tobacco-Free Living, a public-information space at the Mayo, features a big tank labelled

Zebrafish, in recognition of their key role in research. But the tank's occupants are imposters—the real zebrafish were so small they kept getting sucked into the filter. It's not hard to see a metaphor here, with the doomed creatures representing smokers trapped and enslaved by Big Tobacco. This interpretation, embraced by the Mayo program, is comforting: it's not my fault.

19   Still, I have to acknowledge that being a cigarette addict isn't all tubercular coughing and grimy ashtrays. Smoking doesn't come with the perils associated with other types of dependence—jail time, homelessness, personal chaos. Plus, there's that first-puff-of-the-morning kapow, the immediate rush of nicotine to the brain, a high that doesn't fade no matter how long you've smoked—no chasing the dragon, trying to recapture the sensation of your initial hit. It makes for great anecdotes, like the time I realized the only other occupant of a New York theatre's gritty little smoking area (except for a bodyguard) was Pierre Trudeau, then on his second stint as prime minister. And then there's the camaraderie of smokers at events, puffing away alfresco and joking that we are the most interesting people there. (Or were. Recently, experiences like this past New Year's Eve have been more typical: inside, the other guests were playing a boisterous game of Rob Ford charades—*hammered on the Danforth*; *I have more than enough to eat at home*—while I shivered alone on the porch with my Rothmans Special.)

20   But these golden moments account for just a fraction of the half-million-odd cigarettes I've consumed in my life. According to Dr Richard Hurt, the founder of the Mayo program, I've mostly lit up because the numerous nicotine receptors in my brain have been calling out for another hit. Why some people smoke and not get hooked is what those zebrafish are helping to illuminate. Clearly, I'm not addiction-proof, and neither are the members of my Mayo posse.

21   In our discussions throughout the week, there is a major hitch—the word *cigarette* comes up constantly, just as we're all trying to bat away the constant fantasy of lighting up. Still, between Friday afternoon and the end of Sunday, the chance that anyone could sneak away for a fix is about zero, since the only way off the ward is in the company of a staff member. We call it lockdown, although there's no bolted door or elevator code, just a lot of eyes; each night, an unnaturally alert person occupies a desk with a view of all the room doors, just in case. Sunday afternoon finds all ten of us trooping through the maze of tunnels that anchors downtown Rochester, shepherded by our wellness coach and making self-conscious jokes about holding on to the rope. There's an unspoken acknowledgement that, for many of us, this is not our first time in such a situation, whether because of previous rehab stints or in-patient treatment for mental-health troubles. In a movie, some of us might be sullen or transgressive; in real life, we're just happy to get a decent cup of coffee in town.

22   By Monday, we're allowed out in pairs, and on Wednesday, we can go solo. This presents limited risk, since—thanks to the clinic—the entire downtown seems to be a non-smoking zone. Other than the escalating freedom, the days are largely the same, starting with a 6:30 a.m. reveille, followed by breakfast and morning check-in visits from Dr Hurt. From 9 a.m. to 5 p.m., there are classes and lectures: stress reduction, relapse prevention, nutrition, wellness, [and] group therapy. Everyone fixedly chews nicotine gum or puffs inhalers. One woman cries, but it's because she gets the news that a beloved pet has died.

23   In fact, the most dramatic day is the last. Not because of the sadness of saying goodbye—

we liked one another fine, but everyone's been too busy not smoking to be particularly social. Instead, on the final day, we almost can't get home. A nasty storm causes airline delays and cancellations across a swath of the Eastern US. It's a cosmic test that, a week before, would have seen us all puffing away determinedly. Instead, we take over a group therapy room, pull out our computers and phones, and attempt to get away from the spot where, a few days earlier, we were wishing aloud we could stay at forever. Some scramble for the Twin Cities to catch alternate flights; I make it as far as Chicago. For the first time in many years, I don't end up chain-smoking outside the terminal.

24   The next day, we all check in by email. Everyone made it home, and no one smoked.

25   In 1992, my husband was diagnosed with lung cancer. He lost one-third of his left lung, but was spectacularly lucky, and is still alive today. Not surprisingly, he quit smoking, and so did I—for a while. But even his near miss wasn't enough to cure me.

26   Recently, I tried to determine the odds of a heavy smoker like me getting lung cancer. One source says the chance of dying from the disease is 18.5 per cent for women who smoke 25 or more cigarettes a day; another that a female smoker has a 13 per cent chance of succumbing to it. Lung Cancer Canada's news is more dire: "For long-time smokers, the chance of dying from a smoking-related cause is, on average, 1 in 2."

27   I haven't yet developed cancer, but a test in rehab revealed that I have early-stage chronic obstructive pulmonary disease, which encompasses both emphysema and bronchitis. The Canadian Lung Association website explains dispassionately that "COPD makes airways swollen and partly blocked by mucus. It also damages . . . the tiny air sacs at the tips

of your airways. This makes it hard to move air in and out of your lungs." Those people you see lugging around oxygen tanks? Odds are they have COPD. The unequivocal message from the doctor was that if I kept smoking, I would eventually have my own oxygen tank, which would accompany me until my deeply unpleasant death.

28   Perversely, I'm happy about this news—it is another compelling reason to stay off cigarettes, and there are moments when I need to marshal every one of them. One such time comes four months after my Mayo sojourn. Up until that point, it seemed that the urge—the need—to smoke had been successfully eradicated. Then an administrative foul-up leads to a three-week wait for a vital piece of ID for my kid; without it, he can't get a new passport, and hence can't accompany me on a planned trip to Paris. While definitely a First-World problem, it's the kind of situation that would normally have me chain-smoking obsessively. The image of the oxygen tank keeps me, if only just, from snatching a cigarette out of a stranger's mouth. Eventually, the crisis passes.

29   Well, sort of. By the time I land at Charles de Gaulle, I have started drinking again, for the first time in ten years—half a glass of Chardonnay in the airport lounge, a mini-bottle of Merlot on the plane. And today, although I'm not consuming anything close to the quantity of wine I once did, I haven't stopped.

30   Initially, I thought that I might have grown out of my unwholesome attraction to alcohol—that I can have a casual drink now and then, without returning to full-blown alcoholism. This is, of course, a delusion. Maybe I am simply incapable of quitting more than one vice at a time.

31   That bout of investigating lung cancer data turned up one more bit of relevant info. Remember how my teenage pals and I joked about each

cigarette reducing our lives by ten minutes? Turns out, we may have been right—except we underestimated the toll. In a 2000 *BMJ* paper, researchers calculated that each cigarette could knock 11 minutes off a smoker's lifespan.

32   I have smoked away a decade of my life.

 ## Comprehension

1. a. What does the author mean when she refers to "the big lie" about smoking?
    b. Who are the perpetrators of "the big lie?"
    c. Explain why Cunningham considers the "lie" unfair to today's smokers (see pars. 12–13).
2. Cunningham uses several challenging words in her essay.
    a. Choose three words you are unfamiliar with from the following list and try to determine their meaning from the context before looking them up in a dictionary to confirm meaning.
    b. Use each of these words in a sentence:
        •   mordantly (par. 3),
        •   pariah (par. 6),
        •   disingenuous (par. 12),
        •   quotidian (par. 15), and
        •   eradicate (par. 28).

Organization and Style

1. Show how Cunningham uses the first two paragraphs to create reader interest.
2. a. Analyze the way that the author uses facts and statistics in her essay so that they don't intrude in her narrative (refer to at least two specific passages); or
    b. Compare Cunningham's use of facts with Madeline Sonik's use of facts in "Flush," p. 155 (remember that to compare is to find similarities and/or differences, see p. 14).
3. a. Analyze the author's use of tone (see tone, p. 128), drawing on at least two specific passages in which different tones are used; or
    b. Analyze the author's use of humour and its contribution to the essay, referring to specific examples.

Critical Thinking

1. Although Cunningham's essay focuses mostly on her smoking addiction, she also discusses her addiction to alcohol. Referring to two relevant passages, show how they contribute to her essay.
2. In two or three sentences, summarize Cunningham's argument and analyze its validity; in other words, do you think that it makes sense? Why or why not?
3. After having read the essay, reconsider the title, "Giving up the Ghost." Do you consider it an apt title for this essay? Explain.

II   Are the Generations Alike or Unalike?

Though the term "generation gap" was popularized in the 1960s, it resonates in many different ways for today's generations, especially for "Gen(eration) X" and "Gen(eration) Y," which are often seen as opposites—for example, in their approach to economic realities.

In this section, "Generation Spend" examines the growing problem of youth indebtedness and proposes solutions. "Generation Velcro" and "In Defence of the iGeneration" both take contrastive points of view on Gen Y. The author of "Generation Velcro" puts forth the provocative claim that the technological abilities of Generation Y come with a high price, possibly its very survival; the author of "In Defence of the iGeneration" argues that technological know-how is a strength, especially when combined with adept collaborative skills.

The other two essays in this section focus on relationships between different generations. The authors of "Vancouver Hockey Riot Is a Symptom of a Larger Problem" argue that the response of some youths to the Vancouver Canucks 2011 Stanley Cup final game loss stems from feelings of hopelessness, the legacy of previous generations. In "The Birth of Power Dressing," the author explores the historical connections between fashion and membership in high-status groups, a phenomenon that connects the generations over the centuries.

Erica Alini, "Generation Spend"

 Preparing to Read

1. If you are unfamiliar with the reality TV show *Til Debt Do Us Part*, do a search to determine the show's purpose and premise.
2. How would you describe your own spending and saving habits? How do they differ—if at all—from those of your friends and family? Are you concerned about your financial future? What circumstances might influence that concern?

Generation Spend

Erica Alini

Maclean's, 15 November 2010
(1161 words)

1   "If I want something I want it, no matter what," says Kezia, one of the protagonists of a new Slice TV series *Princess*, where *Til Debt Do Us Part* host Gail Vaz-Oxlade tries to put young, female serial shoppers through personal finance rehab. A makeup artist who normally makes "probably" around $30,000 a year, Kezia would shed up to $355 a month on her hairdo, and eat out "probably" four times a week. "I don't ever look at my credit card statements,"

the pretty (dyed) blond says, gazing dreamingly at the camera. "As soon as they come, I throw them away."

2   Twenty-five-year-old Kezia belongs to a new species of consumer whose capacity to spend will surpass that of the boomers sometime in the next decade. Variously referred to as Generation Y or Generation Next, they are loosely defined as the age group going from kids in their early teens to young adults. In the US, 8- to 24-year-olds are expected to spend $224 billion of their projected $348 billion annual income, according to Harris Interactive, a market research and consulting firm. Yet the percentage of those who have no savings at all is over 50 per cent. The stats in Canada are equally troubling. For young adults, the proportion between the ages of 25 and 34 who say they are impulsive spenders and can't save is 30 per cent, a figure very similar to the 31 per cent found among the so-called Generation X (or 35- to 49-year-olds), according to a recent study by the Royal Bank of Canada.

3   The recession was supposed to teach some important lessons about saving and living frugally, but Generation Y seems poised to fall into similar spending habits that left their parents with crippling debt. Whereas the financial crisis raised the national savings rate in the US from a low of less than 2 per cent in 2007 to over 8 per cent in mid-2009 (it is now at around 5 per cent), in Canada it edged up from 2.8 per cent on average three years ago to a still very modest 4.4 per cent overall this year. Despite this small effort to repair household balance sheets, 4 in 10 Canadians say they struggle to put a nickel in the piggy bank, according to RBC. It's an unsettling trend for those preaching financial good sense.

4   How then to raise a breed of conscientious spenders and good savers (if not by example)?

Part of the answer, say experts, is coming from financial institutions trying to stage a digital catch-up to the marketing industry that has so effectively targeted young spenders. Most savings products, says Dilip Soman at the University of Toronto's Rotman School of Management, have "supremely boring advertising." On the other end of the spectrum of the battle for young wallets, however, are marketing firms with a sophisticated arsenal of advertising tools. Their methods range from social networking sites like Facebook and Twitter to guerrilla-style campaigns that use the power of peer pressure to encourage spending, (In one campaign for Neutrogena, for example, 4000 high school girls were recruited to work as "brand evangelizers," pitching the product to classmates and friends in exchange for prizes including concert tickets.)

5   Simple financial behaviours like saving, or making rational decisions about limited resources, must be embedded in a language young people understand—the same language that speaks to them about PlayStations and Coach bags, say experts. A group of US researchers has had good results, for instance, by having young people interact with digital, retirement-age avatars of themselves as they make hypothetical savings decisions. In one case study, the expression on the avatars' faces would display a smile or an unhappy grimace depending on the positive or negative impact of the savings decisions on the participants' future financial situation. In all cases, the study says, participants who interacted with their aged avatars showed a greater propensity to forgo the instant pleasure of spending for the delayed pleasure of having and using savings in the future.

6   Another way to go about this is finding "smart ways of leveraging social networking," says Alessandro Previtero at the University of

Western Ontario's Richard Ivey School of Business. He says young people might find it easier to set and reach financial targets if they use something like StickK.com, a website designed by a team at Yale that helps people achieve their goals (from losing weight to quitting smoking) by, among other things, getting their friends involved. Much like friends on Facebook, supporters on StickK.com receive regular updates on status changes—in this case, a person's progress toward the stated goal. If constructive use of peer pressure helps people shed their extra pounds or their pack of cigarettes, it could also help them save, says Previtero.

7   And whether the lesson comes from social networking or old-fashioned parenting, teaching youngsters how to set financial goals is key, says Patricia Domingo, an investment retirement planner at RBC. She recalls setting up a savings account and a guaranteed investment certificate for a 15-year-old who made $8000 designing and selling a website. The parents, she said, sat him face to face with the family financial adviser so he'd be forced to think about what he should do with the money.

8   Other healthy practices, says Greg Holohan, an investment executive at ScotiaMcLeod, include openly discussing family income, utility bills, and even investment strategies with the kids; encouraging them to use their allowance or summer job money to pay for some of their needs; and refusing to pay for everything. A good strategy, he says, might also be to tell the young ones that they have to pay for part of their college and university costs, but then reward them afterward by paying them back and giving them a tidy sum to start with as they enter the job market.

9   Deborah Beedie, an account executive in Dundas, Ont., thinks she got it right. "Our kids can probably tell you how much we make, what we have in terms of investments, and what bills come up when," she says of sons Michael, 20, and Scott, 14. Whenever Scott gets his weekly allowance of $14 (one dollar per every year since he was born), he has to decide how much to put in one of three jars labelled "savings," "spending," and "other." Michael, a junior at Dalhousie University, had tuition, books and rent paid for, but must use summer job money to sustain his social life and contribute to food expenses. Apparently, he now has the grocery store mapped out according to product pricing and won't even go near the middle of the alley where, he says, the more expensive stuff is on display.

10   Whether it's trying to protect your kid from slick online marketing or the corner street dealer, says Beedie, all you can do is "have a value system that you can transmit"—leave the kids autonomy but know what they're up to, and hope for the best.

⬤ Comprehension, Organization, and Style

1. Identify two compare–contrast paragraphs and summarize the content of one of them.

2. What kinds of experts does the writer focus on for support? Take one expert and analyze his or her contribution to the essay.

3. Analyze one paragraph, considering how the writer's strategies increase comprehension and readability (see Chapter 1, pp. 11–16).

Critical Thinking

1. Do you think Kezia (pars. 1–2) is a good representative of the Gen Y consumer? Why or why not?
2. Of the various solutions to make Gen Y consumers more financially responsible, which do you believe is the most promising? Give reasons to justify your answer.

Dorothy Woodend, "Generation Velcro"

"Generation Velcro" is an "opinion piece": its author uses personal experience and other evidence to express a viewpoint. To use personal experience successfully when writing for an audience, the writer must generalize from the personal situation to one that is relevant to individual readers. Non-academic writers often begin with a "hook," a technique to "catch" the reader's interest, such as asking a question or relating an anecdote. Having intrigued the reader, the author can apply the question or anecdote to universal issues like technological dependency and parental responsibility. In "Generation Velcro," Woodend skilfully employs an appealing style and occasional humour to highlight her serious concerns about today's youth.

Preparing to Read

1. Do you believe that our society is too dependent on technology? Could you get by with less technology in your life? Using these questions as a prompt, freewrite for five minutes; or
2. List the pros and cons of current technology in people's lives. Share your list with another student's and discuss one or two of the specific items on each list.

Generation Velcro

Dorothy Woodend

The Tyee, 21 November 2008
(1262 words)

1   The other day I took my seven-year-old son Louis to buy some running shoes. "Pick something with Velcro," I said, as he trotted off to roam the racks.

2   A clerk, hovering nearby, gave me a jaundiced look: "You know we get high school kids in here who have to buy Velcro because they never learned to tie their shoes. Every year their parents would just buy them Velcro because it was easier than making them learn how to tie laces."

3   I stared at him and he went on.

4   "The other day we had to special order a pair of shoes for this kid's high school graduation

because he couldn't tie his laces, and he needed a pair of Velcro formal shoes."

5   I put the shoes Louis had chosen back on the shelf, and picked out a pair of lace-up running shoes. It wasn't just that I'd been shamed into compliance by the salesman, but something Jane Jacobs had written about in her last book about the coming dark ages hit home. The loss of knowledge, she said, once vanished, is so difficult to regain—even if it's something as mundane as tying your shoes.

6   In case you think this episode is an isolated example, the other day I heard a youth worker, whose job it is to help teens at risk, say that almost none of them know how to tie their shoes. I'm sure this isn't a causal relationship—wear Velcro, go to jail—but it made me think. What else have we lost, or failed to pass along, to the generation of kids about to inherit an increasingly compromised planet?

7   Is this generation heading into a coming dark age with little more than the ability to update their Facebook statuses and watch Youtube, all with laces untied?

Failing memories

8   When I talk to my mother, ensconced on her farm in the Kootenays, about people quietly preparing for coming disaster, she says the first thing people in her neighbourhood say is "Well, my freezer is full." Then they metaphorically pat themselves on the back for having the forethought to freeze a supply of broccoli and peaches.

9   "But what happens if the power goes off?" I ask.

10   She shrugs and says, "The one thing I'm worried about is being able to get seeds." (In case you didn't know, Monsanto has been qui-

etly buying up heritage seed companies for the past while.) Then she says, "I'm thinking about starting a farm school." I tell her it's not a bad idea.

11   In the *Vancouver Sun*, Meeru Dhalwala recently wrote a column about wanting to start a vegetable garden, but not having even the slightest notion of where to start. For those of us even just a generation removed from the family farm, already the loss of knowledge is enormous. I don't know how to butcher an animal, build a house, or make my own soap, although my grandparents certainly did. To a lesser extent my mother still does. If I told my son to go outside, start a fire, and cook himself some food, he wouldn't have the very first clue.

12   While this generation can text-message, download, update, and surf online simultaneously, this constant deluge of information is in fact something of a mirage. Information is not knowledge, nor even close to wisdom. And it is actually getting harder to learn and remember things. In *The Overflowing Brain*, Torkel Klingberg, a professor of cognitive neuroscience at Sweden's Karolinska Institute writes, "If we do not focus our attention on something, we will not remember it." The inability to concentrate in a world of competing bits of information and constant multitasking have led to brains that can no longer keep up. Suddenly, I see why a podcaster has sought out my mother's repository of practical knowledge.

13   "We're counting on you, old lady," I tell her.

Is our society "self aware?"

14   In North America now, less than two per cent of people call themselves farmers and the median age of farmers in Canada is already

pushing mid-50s. What happens when too many people who actually know stuff age and then buy the farm, as they say?

15   Which brings me back to the question that has me tied up in shoe knots.

16   If the lights start to go out sometime in the near future, and the Walmart closes its doors, who would really be useful? The answer changes, but basically it comes down to people who know how to do things—farmers, carpenters, doctors—people with a body of knowledge that can be applied directly, physically to the real world. It certainly won't be film critics or bond traders.

17   In *Dark Age Ahead*, Jane Jacobs writes that, "A society must be self-aware. Any culture that jettisons the values that have given it competence, adaptability and identity becomes weak and hollow."

18   James Kunstler shares Jacobs's dim view of the North American future, but he apparently has even less hope for the ability of the current population to do the work that needs doing. Kunstler writes often about the great tattooed, hedonistic, neo-Darwinian masses of Americans, who bear almost no resemblance to the hardworking, industrious people of the 1930s, who, when FDR announced his plans to turn the nation around, basically set to the task at hand.

19   I keep coming back to Kunstler's operatic outpourings of fury and despair, maybe because there is a bitter tang of something that isn't even approached in mainstream media. Kunstler opines that Americans in the 1930s and 40s bear little resemblance to the current crop, and if required to roll up their sleeves and dig ditches, they might not be up to task.

20   My grandfather came of age in the Great Depression. His mother died of cancer when he was 7 years old, and he basically went to work at the age of 12. The same is true of my grandmother, who never made it past Grade 7 because she had to cook meals in the rooming house run by her mother. Their lives and their stories are unremarkable in some ways, in that they weren't all that unusual. They were born to work and they spent their entire lives doing just that, farming, day in and out, merely to survive. They were almost completely self-sufficient, both in food and in skills.

Life without Velcro

21   Louis, on the other hand, along with all of his Velcro-shod, video-game-playing friends, has been kept safely inside since he was born. He is probably ill-prepared for the world if it becomes much more harsh. Am I, then, a failure? If your first impulse is always to protect your children, are you actually doing them a disservice? If suffering breeds character, does a complete lack of suffering foster utter helplessness?

22   This is why the public imagination was seized by the tragic story of 15-year-old Brandon Crisp, who ran away after a fight with his parents about video games. How could a young boy die so easily? Brandon discovered in the most terrible way that the real world bears little resemblance to a video game. It gets dark and cold, and if you fall out of a tree, you die.

23   Every day, while Louis struggles with his laces, wailing that he can't do it and I should do it for him, I say: "You need to learn to do this yourself; you can't depend on anyone to do it for you."

24   My own words echo oddly inside my brain, already assuming some larger meaning. It is as much my responsibility to teach him, as it is his to learn.

Organization and Style

1. Identify Woodend's thesis, explaining why Woodend might want to use this type of thesis. (See pp. 8–9 for different types of thesis statements.)

2. Discuss Woodend's tone (attitude toward her subject, see p. 128), referring to specific passages.

3. Comment on Woodend's use of personal experience. You could consider its use in her introduction and conclusion and/or its use to support a point or provide a transition.

Critical Thinking/Research

1. Respond to or critically analyze one of the following statements from the essay:
   a. "The inability to concentrate in a world of competing bits of information and constant multitasking have led to brains that can no longer keep up" (par. 12); or
   b. "If suffering breeds character, does a complete lack of suffering foster utter help-lessness?" (par. 21)

2. Using reliable sources, discuss the significance of (a) Jane Jacobs (pars. 5 and 17) or (b) James Howard Kunstler (pars. 18–19) to Woodend's essay. Include a short biography that addresses Jacobs' or Kunstler's credibility and show how Woodend uses her or him to support her points.

3. Analyze Woodend's argument, considering argumentative strategies, use of evidence, and reasoning. Refer specifically to the text for support.

Adrian Mack and Miranda Nelson, "Vancouver Hockey Riot Is a Symptom of a Larger Problem"

This essay was published in *The Georgia Straight* the day after riots following the loss of the Vancouver Canucks in the final game of the 2011 Stanley Cup finals. The essay was one of many attempts of a shocked community to account for the behaviour of some of its citizens.

Billing itself as "Canada's Largest Urban Weekly," *The Georgia Straight* focuses on social and cultural issues, often with a youth-oriented slant. Beginning as an "underground" newspaper, it has recently won several awards for its news and investigative features.

 ## Preparing to Read

Using objective, reliable sources, summarize the events surrounding the riot and its aftermath.

Vancouver Hockey Riot Is a Symptom of a Larger Problem

Adrian Mack and Miranda Nelson

The Georgia Straight, 16 June 2011
(1172 words)

1   We've heard a lot of reasons (excuses?) batted around as to why last night's post-Cup riot happened. A very outraged man on the radio this morning blamed the whole thing on faulty parenting. Others look at the idiocy of city politicians for inviting 100,000 people into the downtown core, TransLink for ramping up service to a peninsula with limited escape routes, and the provincial order to close downtown liquor stores at 4 p.m., ensuring that those in attendance would be drunk before they even arrived. You can also look to the mainstream media for hyping up this series to unheard-of proportions and constantly reminding the populace of the infamous 1994 Stanley Cup riots.

2   But maybe what we have is just a sick culture. Maybe as a society, we've simply become borderline psychotic. You only need to ride a bus to see what an angry group of people we've become. We're rude, we're snotty, we don't talk or engage with each other. We've created the stupidest generation: a barely literate group of narcissists who don't know how to take care of themselves, but are like military-trained experts when it comes to tagging themselves in Facebook photos.

3   From all reports, there was a small group of young hooligans determined to riot and smash 'n' grab no matter what the outcome of the game was. Several sites have been set up to post pictures, Facebook screencaps, and video of morons proudly declaring their involvement in the

violence. Should we be surprised? And doesn't it seem a little obvious that there was never going to be a good outcome, regardless of who won? At 4:30 p.m. the streets of the downtown core were already simmering with the dangerous and hair-trigger emotions of the mob, and all that emotion—good or bad—was going to be purged, somewhere, somehow. In the weeks leading up to the final, the magnitude of our bizarre, tribal attachment to a hockey team became more and more clear. And it exceeds far beyond a natural and healthy spirit of competitiveness or an appreciation of the beauty of the game itself. It's pathological. It's monstrously unhealthy. And it speaks to a monumental emptiness at the heart of our culture.

4   So, why are there so many hungry souls out there, ready and willing to bring chaos down on the so-called most liveable city on the planet? In reality, matters have only gotten much worse politically and economically since 1994, and Generation Y has been delivered into a beyond-callous world facing a perfect storm of crises. They know it. What does the future look like for the average 20 year old? It's a depressing, empty place where they can't get decent-paying (let alone secure) jobs or ever have a hope of owning property. Can you imagine how much more fearful and angry they would be if they fully comprehended the seriousness of peak oil?

5   And yet despite the terminal condition of a socio-economic superstructure hurtling towards the edge of a cliff while wondering if it even has enough gas to get there, the market rolls on, plundering the public coffers and starving the arts and education, producing a society that is spiritually malnourished but not sensitive enough to ask why. Meanwhile, we have dissonant messages relentlessly beamed into our heads: wealth is good, the poor have nobody but themselves to blame, personal devices make

you happy, war is peace, "Save money, live better," Don Cherry deserves your attention and respect, and have some pride in your Canucks. Because what else have you got going for you?

6   The market practices institutional violence on every single one of us, every day, just by virtue of existing. It's not the game of hockey that's the problem; it's the capitalistic appropriation of our national pastime. It's the myriad of advertisers trotting out the "I am Canadian!" sentiments in order to sell products. It's the message we are force-fed that if we don't pay attention to the spectacle, we are somehow disenfranching ourselves. That's the way advertising has always worked: make people insecure about a fictional problem, and then sell them the fix.

7   This isn't to excuse the rioters, and we should remember and praise those who were there, and who resisted, and who did the right thing. There's a powerful clip on YouTube . . . of two men—one in a Canucks jersey, one not—trying to prevent assholes from smashing out the windows of The Bay downtown. They have some initial success, but then the non-jerseyed man pushes a rioter back and gets beaten for his efforts.

8   But we can't just blame a few "bad apples." This riot didn't happen on its own. Society as a whole ensured that it was the only outcome, starting with the assumption that our over-amped if not war-like passion for something as inconsequential as a hockey game is appropriate to begin with, let alone officially sanctioned. But hey, it's a . . . goldmine for advertisers and a hell of a vacuum to suck in a growing population of bored, distracted, disassociated, and quietly despairing Lower Mainlanders marinated in the hegemony of cheap sensation, and governed by institutions hostile to art, truth, and beauty. It's a problem that, as always, starts at the very top.

9   The wrong questions will inevitably get asked in the wake of all this, and the wrong solutions applied. Expect "tougher policing" and a ramped up culture of intolerance in a city that already turns a blind-eye to a tsunami of social ills. The VPD—which was quick to blame the violence on "criminals, anarchists, and thugs"—is encouraging anyone with high-resolution pictures to email them to the department, but is that really what we want to become? Yes, last night's violence was inexcusable and the offenders should be prosecuted, but the slope towards becoming a Big Brother-like society where we tattle on our neighbours is already slippery enough. Wouldn't it be preferable to live in a society in which we actually *knew* our neighbours to begin with? To know and trust the people around us to act like responsible individuals? To enjoy a culture of mutual respect rather than suspicion, hyper-competition, and meaningless interaction mediated through our phones and iPads? All we're doing right now is gawking at city-sanctioned spectacles—or plugging in our headphones so we can ignore each other.

10   There was a beautiful outpouring of love and support for our fair city this morning as hundreds of volunteers took to the streets to help clean up the terrible mess from last night. We do have the capacity to be kind, gentle, thoughtful individuals, and, hopefully, we can begin to repair the damage to our tarnished reputation. Unfortunately, there's no simple Band-Aid solution that will fix a sick society. The symptoms are clearly manifesting but, without facing up to the fact that there is an overarching problem, there is absolutely no chance for us to heal. But perhaps the first step towards solving this systemic problem is to acknowledge the fact that there is actually something wrong with us.

Comprehension

1. In your own words, explain the meaning of the following statement: "[A hockey game is] a . . . goldmine for advertisers and . . . a vacuum to suck in a growing population of bored, distracted, disassociated, and quietly despairing Lower Mainlanders marinated in the hegemony of cheap sensation, and governed by institutions hostile to art, truth, and beauty." (par. 8)

Organization and Style

1. Comment on the authors' style and voice (see Chapter 10, p. 137), paying particular attention to any possible biases and/or use of non-objective language.

2. Analyze the authors' final two paragraphs, showing whether they function as an effective conclusion to their argument.

Critical Thinking

1. Who or what do the authors ultimately blame for the riots? Discuss the accuracy and validity of their conclusions, referring to specific passages in the essay.

2. Respond to one of the following statements in the essay:
   a. "The market practices institutional violence on every single one of us, every day, just by virtue of existing" (par. 6); or
   b. "[T]he terminal condition of [our] socio-economic superstructure . . . [has produced] a society that is spiritually malnourished but not sensitive enough to ask why" (par. 5).

Ulinka Rublack, "The Birth of Power Dressing"

The articles in *History Today* are written by experts for a wide readership. Although they focus on scholarly subjects, they are not considered scholarly, as sources are not cited. Their main purpose is to make history relevant to non-specialists, utilizing a variety of techniques to enhance reader interest. For example, Rublack begins by narrating a personal experience and, in paragraph 3, ties it into the historical period she introduces in this and the following paragraph.

"The Birth of Power Dressing," like most humanities essays, uses primary (original) sources extensively for support; these include written texts like books and contemporary historical documents as well as visual ones, like paintings and other art.

Preparing to Read

1. What are your associations with clothes—for example, school uniforms, consumerism, branding?
2. Do you think you and/or your friends pay too much attention to clothes? Why or why not?

The Birth of Power Dressing

Ulinka Rublack

History Today, January 2011
(3917 words)

Dressing up

1   I shall never forget, while staying in Paris, the day a friend's husband returned home from a business trip. She and I were having coffee in a huge sunny living room overlooking the Seine. His key turned in the door. Next, a pair of beautiful, shiny black shoes flew down the corridor. Finally, the man himself appeared. "My feet are killing me!" he exclaimed. The shoes were by Gucci.

2   We might think that these are the modern follies of fashion, which now beset men as much as women. My friend certainly valued herself partly in terms of the wardrobe she had assembled and her accessories of bags, sunglasses, stilettoes, and shoes. She had modest breast implants and a slim, sportive body. They were moving to Dubai. In her spare time when she was not looking after children, going shopping, walking the dog, or jogging, she would write poems and cry.

3   Yet neither my friend nor her husband would be much out of place in the middle of the fifteenth century. Remember men's long pointed Gothic shoes? In the Franconian village of Niklashausen at this time a wandering preacher drew large crowds and got men to cut off their shoulder-length hair and slash the long tips of their pointed shoes, which were seen as wasteful of leather. Learning to walk down stairs in them was a skill. Men and women in this period aspired to an elongated, delicate, slim silhouette. Very small people were considered deformed and were given the role of grotesque fools. Italian doctors already wrote books about cosmetic surgery.

4   When, how, and why did looks become deeply embedded in how people felt about themselves and others? The Renaissance was a turning point. I use the term in its widest sense to describe a long period, from c.1300 to 1600. After 1300 a much greater variety and quantity of goods was produced and consumed across the globe. Textiles, furnishings, and items of apparel formed a key part of this unprecedented diffusion of objects and increased interaction with overseas worlds. Tailoring was transformed by new materials and innovative techniques in cutting and sewing, as well as the desire for a tighter fit to emphasise bodily form, particularly of men's clothing. Merchants expanded markets in courts and cities by making chic accessories such as hats, bags, gloves, or hairpieces, ranging from beards to long braids. At the same time, new media and the spread of mirrors led to more people becoming interested in their self-image and into trying to

imagine how they appeared to others; artists were depicting humans on an unprecedented scale, in the form of medals, portraits, woodcuts and genre scenes, and print circulated more information about dress across the world, as the genre of "costume books" was born.

Dressed to thrill

5   These expanding consumer and visual worlds conditioned new ways of feeling. In July 1526, Matthäus Schwarz, a 29-year-old chief accountant for the mighty Fugger family of merchants from Augsburg, commissioned a naked image of himself as fashionably slim and precisely noted his waist measurements. He worried about gaining weight, which to him signalled ageing and diminished attractiveness. Over the course of his life, from his twenties to his old age, Schwarz commissioned 135 watercolour paintings showing his dressed self, which he eventually compiled into a remarkable album, the *Klaidungsbüchlein* (*Book of Clothes*), which is housed today in a small museum in Brunswick. From the many fascinating details the album reveals, we know that, while he was courting women, Schwarz carried heart-shaped leather bags in green, the colour of hope. The new material expression of these emotions, which were tied to appearances, heart-shaped bags for men, artificial braids for women, or red silk stockings for young boys, may strike us as odd. Yet the messages they contained (of self-esteem, erotic appeal, or social advancement and their effects, which ranged from delight in wonderful craftsmanship to concern that a look had not been achieved or that someone's appearance was deceiving) remain familiar to us today.

6   When cultures throw up new words, historians can be fairly sure that they have struck on new developments. The word "fashion" gained currency in different languages during the Renaissance. *Moda* was adapted from Latin into Italian to convey the idea of fashionable dressing as opposed to costume, which denoted more stable customs relating to dress. In sixteenth-century France, the word "mode" began to supersede the Old French expression *cointerie* to mean "in style." The French term was adapted in seventeenth-century German as *à la mode*. The English word "fashion" came from the Latin word for "making." It was first used 1550 to refer to a temporary mode of dress in the physician Andrew Boorde's *Book of Knowledge*. Boorde depicted an almost naked Englishman on a woodcut, cheerily announcing: "Now I will wear I cannot tell what, all fashions be pleasant to me." Boorde thought that the English would never be role models for other nations if they assimilated other fashions. His book was also the first in Europe to include woodcut depictions of people in different dress from across Europe. Yet the new preoccupation with fashion reached beyond the continent. In 1570 the Chinese student Chen Yao wrote of how hairstyles, accessories, and styles in his region of China changed "without warning. It's what they call fashion" (the word he used was *shiyang*, which literally translates as "the look of the moment").

7   Many people reacted with shock to these cultural transformations. Stability, or a return to old customs, signalled order, whereas change, and especially constant change, seemed threatening and corrupting. Moralists warned that there should be clear principles concerning who should wear what in terms of their profession and bodily needs in different climates. Once the right kind of clothing had been identified there would be no need ever to change. Elites naturally tried to preserve the signalling of high rank through fine clothing. Sumptuary laws, dating from Roman times and so called

after the Latin word *sumptus*, meaning expense, had multiplied during the Renaissance. These sought to limit the amount of money wealthy people could spend on apparel, so as to limit competitive spending. They also typically set out what kinds of materials and sometimes even colours each rank could wear. Like Andrew Boorde, many worried about the introduction of foreign styles. Moralists across Europe really believed that dress shaped people's mentalities, so that fine foreign clothing, for instance, would make a person more affected and licentious. Such commentators were concerned about the money that would be taken from one country to another and about people losing their virtuous, "national" customs of behaviour; the worst was when people mixed fashions from different cultures and thus became completely unidentifiable in any national, political, or moral sense.

8   Alongside these reactions was the dawning realization that clothing made one historical. Matthäus Schwarz was in his early teens when he started talking to old people about what they had worn in the past and began to make drawings of his own apparel. People began to be aware that future generations would look at them with a sense of historical distance and incredulity, simply on account of what they looked like. Rather than revering their ancestors, they might be laughing at their funny shoes. This uncomfortable realization raised the question which underlies all cultural history: how were these changing customs to be explained?

9   One answer suggested by contemporaries, such as the Strasbourg-born poet and satirist Sebastian Brant (1457–1521), was that humans were like apes because they imitated others. Such a view was neither sophisticated nor uplifting. It presented two choices: either to join the apes and take part in the folly of human life or to turn rigidly moral and refuse the dance.

The latter position was as ridiculous as the former because those opting out of fashion appeared archaic, particularly at a moment when beauty and inventions were highly esteemed. Cities such as Florence were praised for the beauty of their women and sumptuary laws were suspended, often for months, when important foreign dignitaries visited. People stored finery for such moments or forged links with those from whom they could borrow garments. Consequently, inventories that record the kind of clothing people possessed when they married or died often provide an incomplete account of the goods they had access to via networks of friends and family.

Colour and class

10   Lending and borrowing sustained much of early modern life, especially among poorer sections of society. Women in particular relied on such connections, because they were paid less than men or were engaged in unsalaried labour. At the same time unmarried women were expected to look attractive in their efforts to gain a partner, so sumptuary legislation sometimes made allowances for accessories they might wear. For example, a 1530 Imperial Police Ordinance permitted daughters and unmarried peasant women to wear hairbands of silk.

11   There was general disdain of slovenly dress, a strong theme, for example, in the writing of the Dominican priest Thomas Aquinas (1225–74), who thought that wives needed to look their best to keep their husbands faithful. New colours excited people, and since outfits were usually composed of many individual elements, such as detachable sleeves, those lower down the social scale might be able to afford one section in a fashionable colour, perhaps purchasing it second hand. Yellow, for example, became a

fashionable colour at the beginning of the six- teenth century. Inventories from the Swiss city of Basel at this time show that the colour was first adopted by wealthy men and women, but within a few years it became popular with prostitutes, journeymen, apprentices, and maidservants, as well as minor officials and artisans. In 1512 the widow of the town piper in Basel is registered as owning a yellow bodice and her husband's yellow and green hose. By 1520 just about everyone in the city wore yellow and the colour appeared in many innovative combinations—yellow-brown, yellow-red, yellow-green, and yellow-black.

12   Fashion gained favours for men and women alike. Matthäus Schwarz had three expensive outfits tailored for himself to please Archduke Ferdinand I of Austria, whom he met twice during the Imperial Diet of Augsburg of 1530, presided over by the archduke and his brother, the Holy Roman Emperor, Charles V. Mem- bers of the emperor's entourage were certain to write about how civilized or not a city ap- peared to be. Such diaries and travelogues were frequently published. Visitors were keen to see craft workshops and examples of urban ingenu- ity on display; they would dance, dine, be waited upon and bestow gifts. Few people wanted to seem "behind the times," especially since Ital- ians had ingrained in European society the no- tion that a refined civilization was a superior one. But what bearing did Schwarz's appearance have on the imperial party in 1530? Schwarz, who had slimmed in advance and had grown a beard like Ferdinand himself, used fashion to produce an image of himself which made the archduke like and trust him. In 1541 Schwarz himself received a particularly special reward from the emperor, whom he had also had a chance to impress in person; he was ennobled. Of course he had been loyal to the Catholic Habsburgs during the Ref- ormation and had worked as head accountant for the firm that did most to finance them. Schwarz celebrated this achievement and had himself depicted in a coat lined with marten skin, a fur which was restricted to the highest elites. Such fur was homogenously coloured dark brown and came in rectangular pieces measuring up to 60 centimetres. It materialized the rich man's garb in relation to that of the poor man, whose coat, in contrast, was likely to have been made of scraps of different furs.

13   What was new in the Renaissance is the dynamic ability of fashion to reach down the social scale. Schwarz was not an aristocrat, but a wine merchant's son. In the depictions he has left us (as well as the book of clothes he also commis- sioned two surviving oil paintings of himself) we see a burgher who knew how to create effective and lasting self images. Real life was less glamor- ous. In April 1538, at the age of 41, Schwarz mar- ried Barbara Mangolt, the not very exciting and not very young daughter of a local manager in the Fugger firm. In the picture of himself mark- ing the occasion Schwarz is shown in his home from behind wearing a dark coat trimmed with green half-silken taffeta. The text accompanying the image reads simply: "20 February 1538 when I took a wife this coat . . . was made." After this he got fat, had a stroke, and afterwards looked his age. Politics, too, did not work out the way he hoped because the Reformation made headway, and in the 1550s German trade entered a pro- found credit crisis. Schwarz left long gaps in be- tween images of himself in his album. It was dif- ficult to find a fitting end. When he had decided on his final image in September 1560, he could not help but look back at the paintings of himself in his prime to note, sardonically, that he looked so different now from then. Social expectation did not permit older people to be so playful with dress. Now his days in bright red were over and he wore mostly black and white.

14 Schwarz's extraordinary record of his clothes has wider meanings. It shows why it is too simplistic to treat fashion, as the French sociologist Gilles Lipovetsky does, as an engine of western modernity since the Middle Ages, in his view because it broke with tradition, encouraged self-determination, individual dignity and opinion-making. It did this in part, and importantly so, but not in uniform ways and not in the West alone. Clothes already formed an important part of what we might call people's "psychic landscapes." Wardrobes could become repositories of fantasies and insecurities, as well as reflecting expectations of what a person might look like and behave. These cultural arguments and tensions lie at the heart of our struggle to understand the Renaissance. People's interaction with material goods and visual media added further complexities to their lives. Images could sometimes be manipulated in highly controlled visual displays designed to achieve a specific response from large public audiences evoking, for example, divine magnificence at papal rituals. But they could also be used to explore more openly what was local, regional, and foreign, to manage conflicting emotions, or to reflect ways in which an individual tried to appear to others.

New ideas of luxury

15 When we study the Renaissance, therefore, we need to trace the process by which increasing numbers of people outside courts became attached to material possessions and tried to work out how virtue and decorum might be maintained amid selfish, vain, and competitive human tendencies. In southern and northern Europe this process was crucial to people's attempts to give meaning to life. Even English Puritans were able to acknowledge that possessions could be God's temporal blessings as "ornaments and delights." Protestants, however, developed a particular notion of new, "justifiable luxury" as opposed to corrupt "old luxury." According to this view, "old luxury" was the preserve of a narrow elite trapped in a vicious circle of self-congratulation and greed, which cultivated extravagant, effeminate and over-sensuous tastes. Protestants saw examples of papal, oriental, and monarchical splendour as excessive and guilty of creating a false world of fantastic illusion which overwhelmed onlookers and engendered envy even among elites. Furthermore, such manifestations of conspicuous consumption suggested an emotional style pertaining to uncontrollable passions rather than manageable emotion. "Old luxury" was perceived as doomed and, as in ancient Rome, set to lead to a republic's decline, as well as evincing the misery of human nature after the fall.

16 "New luxury" could, by contrast, be declared virtuous. Together with the defence of new decencies, it could be identified with a republican spirit, public gain, gentility, and politeness. This notion enshrined clear codes of honourable, often more frugal, consumption based on self examination of whether one needed something or was being over-indulgent.

17 In the seventeenth and eighteenth centuries, bourgeois consumption qualified as "good," if it did not encourage travesty—men as effeminate gallants, for instance, or women in breeches. In a rare miniature exploring sexual identities beyond the clear divisions of masculine and feminine so rigorously upheld by society, the Dutch artist Adriaen van der Venne depicts a vomiting cat next to an ordinary couple having fun by cross dressing. The cat symbolises sexuality, the act of vomiting a satire on the couple's subversive act. Bourgeois

consumption was meant to establish men as respectable heterosexuals, who would marry and take on public roles, women as distinctly feminine as well as destined for fidelity in marriage. The appearance of small flower patterns and pastel colours, meanwhile, created a softer, more delicate style, which took its cues from Persian designs and was an alternative to the hypermasculinity of much of the sixteenth century, with its bold stripy patterns, daring slashes, and frequently loud colours. Meanwhile, black, in its different shades, continued for some time as the international shade indicating sumptuous restraint for both sexes. New models of luxury consumption endorsed measured innovation and the notion of aesthetic pleasure to reinforce cultural competence. Sensations such as surprise and delight could be regarded as refined, because they were not linked to simple utility or physical pleasure. Necessity pointed to functional utility, whereas luxury suggested honourable decorum and progressive, though "polite," creativity. Such evaluations were connected to the notion that consumers should obtain a high degree of product information and an understanding of intricate cuts and constructions of clothing from artisans, shops, and tradesmen, or books and magazines—hence the cultivation of taste based on knowledge and civil sociability rather than the kind that advertised conspicuous wealth. Bourgeois classes could positively cherish fashion as a forward-looking social tool. It could now be presented in a positive light as fuelling the wealth of nations and engendering emotional well-being.

French dressing

18 Molière's 1661 comedy *L'École des Maris* (*The School for Husbands*) is a perfect example of the trend. This short, entertaining play was a pan-European success. It was not just performed, but published with plentiful captivating engravings. Its whole plot turns on two brothers who had totally different ideas about dress; each had been promised orphaned girls for marriage, if they looked after them. The younger brother, Sganarelle, wants his girl to dress in brown and grey wool and to remain indoors. Likewise, he himself only dresses functionally and traditionally. His older and more relaxed brother, Aristide, by contrast, considers social pleasures, such as the theatre and good company, as the meaning of life. To him, fine clothes are a further fount of pleasure that he acknowledges as a source of female self-esteem. As Aristide sees it, women feel well-treated by men who provide money to clothe them nicely, making them feel honoured and happy. Hence, in Molière's play, commerce and sociability were presented overtly as guaranteeing female civility and emotional contentment.

19 Molière was writing during the reign of Louis XIV and thus did not advertise this life in any way as republican. Rather, it was linked to the notion of a good monarchy as opposed to a tyranny. Sganarelle exemplified tyranny in the way the household was run, which contemporaries thought of as a microcosm of the state. Tyranny was presented as resulting from a deep fear of rebellion; in the household this would be typified as adultery. For Sganarelle, the overly restrictive nature of his domestic regime resulted in him losing his woman to a fop. On the other hand, Molière gives Aristide's girl, Leonore, a voice to defend women's rights to enjoy dress and how these link to the values of a civilized society, which should encourage self-regard, in contrast to the treatment of women by barbarous Turks. Leonore argues for women's liberty and against their

subjection to men's will and suspicions. She speaks of trust enabling women's natural virtue to manifest itself:

> 20 Yes, all these stern precautions are inhuman. Are we in Turkey, where they lock up women? It's said that females are slaves or worse, And that's why Turks are under Heaven's curse. Our honour, Sir, is truly very frail If we, to keep it, must be kept in jail . . .
>
> All these constraints are vain and ludicrous: The best course, always, is to trust in us. It's dangerous, Sir, to underrate our gender.Our honour likes to be its own defender.

The Renaissance watershed

21 Debates about fashion that started in the Renaissance did not end with Molière. The idea that the defence of decorous fashion was compatible with a good Christian existence evolved as did complex debates about clothing of the kind we are familiar with today. But the development of fashion in this period marks a historical watershed. How one dressed began to be seen as the right of an individual and this conviction helped gradually to erode sumptuary legislation. Interest in what one wore was increasingly informed by lure of what craftsmen were able to produce. Different kinds of half-silks, beautiful dyes, and lovely patterned textiles seemed delightful to explore and purchase. Yet these choices could also cause confusion and cultural arguments. Women were worried about what colours would be considered seemly and students angered their mothers by asking for money for clothes. Family exchanges now included children bargaining with parents over what they might wear, while parents desperately sought to exercise control. Take the case of Paul Behaim, son of a Nuremberg merchant, who in 1574, aged 17, travelled to Italy with two friends. Having left unsettled debts in Leipzig, where he had been a student, he knew that he now needed to display to his widowed mother a more frugal attitude while simultaneously arguing his case. In his first letter home, he wrote:

> 22 Dear Mother . . . I have used the money from the sale (of a horse) to have the simplest coarse green clothing made for myself—a doublet with modest trim, pleatless hose (like those Gienger [the tutor] wears at home), and a hooded coat . . . . Lest you think things are cheap here, all this has cost me approximately 17 or 18 crowns, even though it was as plain and simple as it could be. I could not have been more amazed when I saw (that bill) than you will be when I send it to you. In all these ways, then, clothing has changed the ways in which we feel and behave.

23 The Renaissance is in some ways a mirror which leads us back in time to disturb the notion that the world we live in was made in a modern age. Messages reflected in clothing about self-esteem, erotic appeal, or social advancement of the wearer are all familiar to us today. Since they first surfaced, we have had to deal more intensely with clever marketing, as well as with questions about image and self-image and whether clothes wear us or we wear them. In short, dress has changed in history and it changes history.

Comprehension

1. In your own words, explain Andrew Boorde's contribution to our understanding of clothing in the sixteenth century.
2. What were "sumptuary laws" (par. 7)? Explain the need for such laws in Europe.
3. Explain how religion and religious values came to play a role in shaping perception of material possessions in the Renaissance.

Organization and Style

1. Discuss strategies that the author uses to make the topic relevant and interesting to a reader without a background in the history of clothing; refer to specific strategies and passages in the text.

Critical Thinking

1. Analyze the importance Rublack gives to Matthäus Schwarz throughout her essay (he is first mentioned in paragraph 5).
2. Show how Rublack uses Molière's play *The School for Husbands* (par. 18) as "a perfect example of the trend" referred to in the previous paragraph.
3. Many of the references in Rublack's essay are to men. Does this surprise you? What accounts for this fact, do you think?
4. What similarities does the essay suggest between our perceptions of fashion today and those of the Renaissance? What differences are suggested?

Renée Wilson, "In Defence of the iGeneration"

Like many writers, Wilson began thinking about her topic after reading an essay that aroused her curiosity and critical thinking faculties. Using recent studies, along with her own experience and observations, she challenges the seemingly accepted views of those of her generation, adding to the debate. In turn, her essay could challenge other readers and critical thinkers, further adding to the debate concerning today's generation of students.

Preparing to Read

1. The author calls her essay "a scientific and anecdotal rumination." What is a rumination?
2. Access the article Wilson refers to in paragraph 1. After scanning it, summarize or paraphrase the thesis in one sentence. Also, see question #4 under "Critical Thinking."

In Defence of the iGeneration

Renée Wilson

This Magazine, 2013
(3151 words)

Abstract

A scientific and anecdotal rumination on why to-day's kids are more than alright—they're the best generation yet.

1   I had only been a college professor for three years when Gregory Levey's controversial and much-discussed magazine piece "Lament for the iGeneration" was published in 2009. I interpreted it as a cautionary tale: if we're in the hands of the next generation, we're really screwed. Levey, a Ryerson communications professor, basically argued he's pretty sure education has tanked; the iGeneration (those born in the 1990s) can't handle post-secondary learning; and that the gap between the schools and the kids is too huge to mend. Dismal stuff, but I understood where Levey was coming from—kind of.

2   I was terrified when I first started teaching. I didn't have any teacher training. I got hired via email. There was no mentoring, no lesson plans, and no prep. One day I was writing a magazine column in my crap clothes from home, and the next I was dressed like a grown up stammering through a lesson at the helm of a full class. I just wanted them to like me. I guess that's why I took it personally when they paid more attention to Facebook than they did to me during a lecture. It was an out-of-body experience to have to tell them to turn their computers off and listen to me. I felt the same frustration Levey described in his article: "Radical advances in technology over the past decade have made today's young minds incompatible with traditional learning. It isn't just what they know or don't know. It's also how they know things at all."

3   Seven years later, I still die inside a little bit when, inevitably, I have to give the speech about shutting down screens when I'm directly addressing them. I hate that I have to say it, but now I don't take it personally. I still worry that they won't get the crux of the lesson if they don't give me their full attention, but I know they're not mentally flitting around out of disrespect. Asking them to drop their tech would be like asking you to wear your shoes on the wrong feet. It's do-able, of course, but does it ever feel wrong. What I found is that this generation multi-task very well, and that the cynicism surrounding the iGeneration is dead wrong. Not only are the kids alright, they could be the best generation yet.

4   My cynical generation is great at slapping critical labels on the iGeneration. We do it all the time. "Everyone dumps on the youngest generation," says Giselle Kovary, co-founder and Managing Partner of Toronto-based Ngen People Performance Inc., which specializes in managing generational differences in the workplace. "But this generation is scary smart."

5   The generation born in the 1990s has pretty much always known things we haven't: Facebook (est. 2004), YouTube (est. 2005), Twitter (est. 2006), Google (est. 1996) and Wiki (est. 2001). Social networking to them is what colour TV was to GenX: It's hard to remember life before it—and just like TV used to be the big scare, we are obsessed over what the Internet does to children of the iGeneration, especially now that they're growing up. All of this freaky attachment to tech is seriously messing with the "social" part of their brains, some experts say. Everyone—including iGeneration itself—is

extremely sensitized to the way young people interact with technology. The list of scientific studies on the topic is as expansive as the more amateur commentary making its way through social media circuits.

6 The conclusions that such technology-attached-brain studies and commentaries reach are overwhelmingly scary. They ring not of advancement and exciting future possibilities, but of one word: beware. Take, for instance, the conclusions of one cautionary book. "Besides influencing how we think, digital technology is altering how we feel, how we behave, and the way in which our brains function," says Gary Small in his book *iBrain: Surviving the technological alteration of the modern mind*, which he co-wrote with his wife, Gigi Vorgan, in 2008. "As the brain evolves and shifts its focus toward new technological skills, it drifts away from fundamental social skills, such as reading facial expressions during conversation or grasping the emotional context of a subtle gesture."

7 In other words, the iGeneration's techno brains are morphing them into socially-inept robots. It's easy—perhaps too easy—to agree with this assessment, but I don't buy it. In my seven years in the classroom, I've witnessed how much more mature this generation is than I ever was as a student. On the upside, this techno brain phenom has resulted in a cohort that can think on its feet, make snap decisions and, on the flip side of all the negative studies about them turning into social morons, there's just as much research to show that students who use tech to communicate are actually fantastic collaborators. It's like they're wired for it. They are fearless about pushing buttons—literally and figuratively—and, as one article put it, it's "as if they've been programmed how to know what to do."

8 I'm in constant contact with my students, partly because they demand it and partly be-cause it's just easier that way. Why wait a week to get an answer from me, when they can fire off a quick message, get the direction they need and then press on with an assignment? Isn't that just working smarter? I've talked a student through a class project at 8 p.m., while she was still at school and I was grocery shopping. I've conducted a class from my hotel room at Disney World during March Break without a single hiccup. The students didn't think twice about passing me around on an iPad to answer questions. What's more, they all showed up to class, even though they knew I wouldn't be there in body.

9 "This generation is known for its innovation and creativity," laughs Kovary over the phone. "Think outside of the box? Um, they don't even know there is a box." This generation only knows a world where the next-best version is released quarterly. What they've internalized is that there's no need to wait until every detail is perfect. Instead, you make adjustments as needed, in real time. This freedom of approach is what, perhaps, makes them the gutsiest of all generations. As Kovary adds, the iGeneration doesn't get stuck in the older generation's static world, or even in the status quo. Change is okay. In fact, it's great.

10 If the box no longer exists, neither does any sort of social or geographical barrier. Enter the now ubiquitous crowdsourcing movement. What once was a small world has become a teeny, tiny world and no generation is more adept at taking advantage of that than the iGeneration. When I was a kid (Ugh. Did I just say that?), I wanted to be a travel agent. (Don't laugh. Who saw Expedia coming in the '80s?). But I didn't know anyone in the field, I couldn't find a college or university program, and that dream died. Today, those obstacles don't exist. The iGeneration doesn't blink at the thought of finding valuable life, job, or education

connections through technology or social media. Just as those from other generations might ask their spouse, mentor, or close friend, the iGeneration will source hundreds of "friends" and "followers" for love advice, career advice, and even thoughts on what to eat for lunch.

11   It can seem gutsy to put out a public SOS on Facebook or Twitter, but that's the way the iGeneration rolls. "They will crowdsource, no matter what the challenge," says Kovary. "Their 'pack' is 700 people." While critics lambasted the generation for its "me-me-me" focus, the truth is that collaboration comes naturally to this extended pack. Their willingness to source what other people have to say almost makes relying on others second nature.

12   In one class, for instance, I blindfolded my students and told them to make their way around the classroom, being sure to touch each of the four walls before returning to their chairs, in an unconventional attempt to teach them about deadlines (newsflash: I set them because I can see what's coming). Almost the entire group instinctively worked as a team, made a human chain and executed the task in a pack. In the end, I made my point about deadlines (my due date is preventing you from ramming into the proverbial desk you didn't see) and they reinforced the notion that there is power, and trust, in a pack.

13   Perhaps surprisingly, rather than creating a generation of followers and drifters—as is so often suggested—this ask-everybody-and-anybody-everything-and-anything attitude has created a cohort of peers. This extends to all areas, including business, and pretty much anything, where top-down leadership was once instinctive. Now, says Kovary, everyone within a corporation is a peer. "If a senior manager says 'email me,' [this generation] will," she adds. "If you're going to tout open communication, get ready!"

14   Whereas other generations were meant to maintain respectful distance, connecting with people—all people—is the iGeneration's natural expectation. Or as 23-year-old Katie Fewster-Yan puts it, because her generation is able to make so many easy connections with people, the top-down model of leadership seems unappealing, even obsolete. Instead, she suggests the term micro-leaders. She is co-founder of Ruckus Readings. Ruckus is a Toronto-based reading series that promotes spoken word literature, one of many, she admits, that exists in Toronto—an exercise in diversifying options, instead of competing for an audience. "Since it's so easy to connect with people," she adds, "You can really choose to follow the ones you're drawn to."

15   For Fewster-Yan, this has nothing to do with a sense of entitlement (another common, and tired, criticism of today's twentysomethings.) In fact, she mostly feels like she has the inverse of entitlement: that her resume is one small sheet in a massive stack of overqualified resumes, not even entitled to minimum wage despite her university education. She guesses that, more than anything, is why many of the iGeneration start things on their own, like she did with Ruckus Readings. It's not that they feel entitled to be happy or immediately successful or even that they should jump frog over others with more experience. Rather, there is a general sense that the old model of "shimmying in at the bottom, hanging tight, and working your way up" is broken. And why, in this new world of change and crowdsourcing wouldn't it seem that way? "I think of plenty of people as role models," says Fewster-Yan, "but I see them more as exemplary peers than superiors."

16   Or, as 22-year-old Chanelle Seguin says, "The best part is that the older generations are learning from the iGen." Seguin is the sole staff

reporter at the *Pincher Creek Echo* in Alberta, where she is responsible for writing and designing the weekly community newspaper. In addition to putting in a solid eight hours at the paper, she also works part-time at Walmart to pay off the line of credit she needed to move from Ontario to Alberta for the reporting gig. Plus, she is a volunteer Girl Guide leader, is planning to coach hockey, and is working on her own sports magazine start-up, *Tough Competition*.

17 She says her generation was forced to become leaders. They had to teach themselves how to use Facebook, Twitter, smartphones, Bluetooth—and the list goes on. Her generation doesn't, she adds, follow the same way other generations did. In that way, she admits, they kind of deserve the selfish moniker everyone slaps on them. "We are almost selfish," says Seguin, "because we lead ourselves and don't consider following anyone."

18 Even so, don't ask for an iGeneration's undivided attention because you're not going to get it. It would be like asking a GenX to go back to changing channels without a clicker, or trying to convince a Traditionalist that debt is good. It just feels wrong. The iGeneration is of the "do it now, fix it later" mentality. But why wouldn't they be? They've come of age at a time when technology changes quarterly. Change is good. Rapid change means things are getting cooler.

19 Some have labelled this trait as the desire for immediate gratification, or a lack of stick-with-it-ness, but I think they're wrong. I think it's a matter of momentum. They can't stay static because everything around them, the social life-sustaining technology that triggers their all-consuming dopamine, is in perpetual change. Science tells us that brain function from age 15 to 25 is dopamine induced, which is why this is life's most emotionally-powerful span. It isn't until later, sometime from age 25 onward, that

the ability to control impulses kicks in. Dopamine is the feel-good chemical, it's that little Russell Brand voice in your head that whispers, "Go ahead, luv, have another piece of cake."

20 The iGeneration is swimming in it. Science also tells us that hits of dopamine, for the iGeneration, come from things like Facebook status likes and re-Tweets. It's easy to confuse this with narcissism. While nearly all researchers peg key human development on ages birth to three years, prominent figures in adolescent research beg to elaborate. They say people ultimately become who they are during adolescence. The prefrontal cortex—the steady-Eddie part of our brain—starts developing just before adolescence and doesn't stop until we're in our mid-twenties, which means from puberty until then everything feels really intense. We can blame this intensity on dopamine, a neurotransmitter that helps control the brain's reward and pleasure centres and gushes when we do something that feels good. This entire process is about preparing young people to shape their own notion of who they are as people, as they strive for self-actualization.

21 In Jennifer Senior's article, "Why You Truly Never Leave High School," published in January in *New York* magazine, the power of dopamine is explored. She quotes studies on the "reminiscence bump"—the term used for the fact that, "when given a series of random prompts and cues, grown adults will recall a disproportionate number of memories from adolescence." This explains BOOM radio, mullets in 2013, why NKOTB can still sell out, and why otherwise placid grandparents can still bust a mean jive at a wedding reception. Societal circumstances change with the generations, but basic brain development doesn't. The drastic variable with the iGeneration, though, is the breakneck speed of technology. According to *iBrain*, we haven't

seen this kind of leap since humankind first learned how to use a tool.

22 Every human being experiences the same stages of brain development, in that we're all in prefrontal cortex development from puberty to our mid-twenties. The difference today is that dopamine hits are coming from tech, and tech is everywhere, and tech equals perpetual change. According to Joel Stein's article, "The Me Me Me Generation," published in May [2013] in *Time* magazine, in order to retain this generation in the workforce, companies must provide more than just money; they must also provide self-actualization. "During work hours at DreamWorks (for example)," Stein writes, "you can take classes in photography, sculpting, painting, cinematography, and karate."

23 This whole self-actualization thing is a bit *much* for GenXers and Boomers to stomach, especially in the workplace. I get it. And it took me a few runs at it, but I now see that self-actualization is truly the only way to reach the iGeneration in the classroom. I don't fancy myself Michelle Pfeiffer's character in *Dangerous Minds*, and I certainly have nothing on *Dead Poets Society*'s captain-my-captain, but when I handed out marshmallows to students in a magazine writing class I knew I grabbed them tighter than Facebook in that lesson. I had found a way to tap into their value system. It was all about them (ahem, self-actualization), yes, but I knew every student also had a story to tell.

24 Still, I had completely underestimated the power of my "marshmallow" lesson. I was humbled when one student's composition described how it made him feel when he and his sister roasted marshmallows by candle flame because, as "apartment kids," they never had the privilege of a backyard campfire. In [the] "marshmallow" [experiment], I expected a literal description of the taste of a marshmallow. Perhaps I underestimated the trust they had in me, and in their classmates, to share such personal stories. Educators need to find out what iGeneration's values are by sneaking up on them with unconventional lessons.

Traditionalists: 1922–1945
IN A WORD: STABLE
CATCH PHRASE: "If it ain't broke, don't fix it."
CHARACTERISTICS: stayed in the same company, doing the same job, forever; stayed married forever; change only happens for a good reason; maintaining the status quo is just fine

Baby Boomers: 1946–1964
IN A WORD: CAUTIOUS
CATCH PHRASE: "Change fatigue"
CHARACTERISTICS: many lost their jobs during the recessions of the '80s and '90s; had to endure "flavour of the month" leadership changes resulting in lack of enthusiasm for new changes; very politically savvy; must poke holes in a project before committing to it

Generation X: 1965–1980

IN A WORD: CYNICAL

CATCH PHRASE: "What's in it for me?"

CHARACTERISTICS: skeptical of leader's motivations and intentions; if they see what's in it for them, they will act as great champions for change; witnessed corporate downsizing, the dot-com bubble burst, and the scandals on Wall Street; expect change to happen

Generation Y: 1981–2000

IN A WORD: FLEXIBLE

CATCH PHRASE: "Do it now. Fix it later."

CHARACTERISTICS: have grown up in a world where technology changes every three-to-six months; don't long for the past; constantly seeking the newest, latest improvement; can become frustrated when faced with a reluctance to change; can't stand lip-service; no need to wait until every detail is perfect; make adjustments as needed, in real time

Summarized from Upgrade Now, *a guidebook for how to work harmoniously in a multi-generational workforce, by Adwoa Buahene and Giselle Kovary of Ngen People Performance Inc.*

25   I remember another lesson, where I had students write a hate letter to anyone or anything. Dear Money. Dear Coffee. Dear Dad. Anything. One girl, a Harley-Davidson employee, addressed her letter as: Dear Chrome-Loving Douche Bag. Of course, when I read it aloud to the class, there was an extended laughter pause, but the content of the letter revealed a real revulsion, and fear of, a middle-aged man who flirted with her during a sale. It's bizarre. I've had some of the best Canadian journalists come speak in my classes, and I still catch students sneaking Facebook during the session. Yet, the Douche-Bag letter warranted undivided attention.

26   In a world so saturated with noise, it's like the iGeneration is thirsty for honesty and direct, transparent communication. If you spin an inauthentic response, they will quickly abandon ship. I have to admit, there's something endearing about a generation who wants to cut through the bullshit—much of it knee-jerk criticism of themselves.

⬤ Comprehension

1. Summarize paragraph 19, in which the author discusses studies on the effects of dopamine on the brain.

Organization and Style

1. Who do you think is Wilson's target audience, and how is her language and style suited (or not suited) to this audience? In addition to diction and/or tone, you could consider her use of analogies and personal experience.

2. Explain, using examples, Wilson's use of the compare and contrast rhetorical pattern in the essay.

Critical Thinking

1. Consider issues that might arise when making generalizations about large groups of people, such as two generations. (For background, see p. 44, which discusses deductive reasoning.) Choose one such generalization Wilson makes about the iGeneration from the following choices:

   a. "Whereas other generations were meant to maintain respectful distance, connecting with people—all people—is the iGeneration's natural expectation";

   b. ". . . [D]on't ask for an iGeneration's undivided attention because you're not going to get it"; or

   c. "In a world so saturated with noise, it's like the iGeneration is thirsty for honesty and direct, transparent communication."

   In one or two paragraphs, explore its validity. Questions you might consider:

   • Is the claim true to your own experience?
   • Do you think most readers would agree with it? Why (not)?

2. Consider the purpose of the sidebar on pp. 200–1.

   a. How does it relate to the essay itself?

   b. Do you think the sidebar tends to promote a more positive or more negative view of generational differences? Explain why or why not.

3. Analyze the various kinds of evidence used in this essay in order to determine their importance and effectiveness. Provide at least two specific examples of each type to illustrate your points:

   • scientific studies,
   • experts and authorities, and
   • personal experience/anecdotal evidence.

   Explain which of these you believe is the most effective and why.

4. After summarizing Wilson's teaching methods as far as you can determine from the essay, respond to the following questions:

   • Are they typical of your experience in college so far? Consider both similarities and differences?
   • Would you like to have her as a teacher? Justify your response.

5. Do you believe that Wilson has offered an effective challenge to the essay she is responding to (see par. 1)? Support your answer by at least two references to each essay.

Technological advancements have seldom come without a cost, at least to some individuals. For example, the invention of the printing press in 1440 made it easier to transmit ideas to an educated population, but it also made it easier for opponents of the church and state to disseminate their radical ideas, and so represented a threat to authority. During the European Industrial Revolution, Luddites were a group who protested the widespread use of labour-saving machines that they believed were putting them out of work. The essential question collectively addressed by the essays in this section is whether the costs of technology today outweigh its benefits.

The author of the essay "Distraction" argues that technology-induced distraction "kills—you and others." While less extreme in his approach, the author of "Stop Believing in the 'World-Changing' Power of Every New Gadget" agrees that our need for more and better technology creates an unhealthy dependence. The author of "The Future of Machines with Feelings" uses humour and exaggeration to express a similar viewpoint.

Challenging common perceptions about technology, the author of "You DO Like Reading off a Computer Screen" asserts that computer screens are meant for reading and that reading computer text and reading print text are quite compatible. "Fully Destructible" challenges a more controversial position by demonstrating that, far from being a retreat from the natural world, some video games cause us to reflect on and appreciate nature.

"The UnAtomic Age" and "Stop Killing the Good Guys!" address specific aspects of technology—nuclear energy and antibiotics, respectively—proposing alternatives.

Jim Harris, "The UnAtomic Age"

Although "The UnAtomic Age" begins by referring to the 2011 Fukushima tragedy, its author goes on to consider the fiscal price of nuclear reactors to governments and taxpayers before considering alternatives to nuclear energy. Jim Harris's argument is heavily dependent on the extensive use of statistics.

 ### Preparing to Read

1. Read the short biography of the author at the end of the essay. Consider if or how this information might affect a reader's approach to the essay.
2. What period of time does "The Atomic Age" refer to? (You might have to do some research to answer this question.) From the title, do you think the author will focus mostly on the problems created by nuclear energy, on solutions to the problem, or both?

The UnAtomic Age

Jim Harris

Alternatives Journal, 2014
(2487 words)

1   Since the 2011 Fukushima catastrophe, the global decline in nuclear power has steepened. More than 20 countries are phasing out nuclear plants, have stopped the construction of new reactors, or passed laws prohibiting nuclear power. The number of reactors and nuclear electricity output is falling worldwide.

2   Japanese citizens are still feeling the horror of Fukushima. Some 400,000 people were evacuated—and a staggering 100,000 people are still displaced three years later. In all, 800 square kilometres of land is too radioactive for human habitation. More than 225,000 tonnes of radioactive soil sits in plastic bags about the area, and 272 tonnes of radioactive water still flow into the Pacific Ocean every day.

3   The cost of the damage caused by the Fukushima Daiichi power plant meltdown is estimated at US$250 billion and could end up doubling. And guess who is going to bear that cost? Japanese taxpayers.

4   The fact that no company will insure nuclear power suggests that it is a financial catastrophe in waiting. In Canada, the Harper government has passed legislation that will limit the nuclear industry's liability to $1-billion. So if a Fukushima-scale catastrophe happened in Canada, the nuclear industry would be responsible for less than 0.4 per cent of the cost. Taxpayers would be on the hook for the other $249-billion. Certainly, the financial burden of catastrophic fallout would be unaffordable.

5   While the federal government obviously doesn't have a grip on adequate liability, the nuclear industry also consistently and dramatically underestimates the costs of construction, operation, and decommissioning of nuclear plants. In the United Kingdom, the decommissioning costs of Sellafield nuclear site have hit £70-billion (CAD$128-billion). If, for instance, the cost of decommissioning the Darlington nuclear reactors in Southeastern Ontario were the same, every Ontario resident would have to bear $10,000 in additional taxes. The real message is that we just cannot afford nuclear energy.

6   Nuclear power has never been profitable when all costs are included. No private corporation will agree to construct and operate nuclear reactors without government guarantees of paying for construction cost overruns, covering or capping accident liability, and paying for the long-term disposal of nuclear waste.

7   The Darlington reactors went 4.5 times over budget, costing provincial taxpayers $14.3-billion. Every Ontario electricity user pays a global adjustment charge on her or his hydro bill, as well as a debt retirement charge. Much of both charges are associated with nuclear power. A study by Navigant showed that 42 per cent of the global adjustment charge is due to nuclear. When Ontario Hydro was broken up in 1998, its $19.4-billion nuclear debt was called "stranded debt" and has been paid for by Ontario taxpayers. As of 2010, Ontarians had paid $19.6-billion to retire this debt—and $14.8-billion was still owing. In other words, the total debt payments have already exceeded the original value of the debt!

8   Energy efficiency is the cheapest form of power generation because it creates more usable energy within the grid—someone somewhere can use every kWh of power that I don't. Ontario can secure energy efficiency in homes and buildings for 2.3 cents per kilowatt-hour (kWh). Homeowners that insulate their attics and walls, install weather stripping or energy

efficient lights, or swap out an old 150-litre hot water tank for an on-demand system to lower their home energy use. A staggering 24 per cent of electricity in North America is used simply for lighting, and LEDs reduce usage by 80 per cent compared to incandescent bulbs.

9   Alternatively, Ontario could source cheap hydroelectric power from Quebec for three cents per kWh, or install combined heat and power (CHP—also known as cogen or cogeneration) for 6 cents per kWh.

10   Ontario's residential utility customers currently pay 8.6 cents per kilowatt-hour (kWh) for the first 750 kWh per month, then 10.1 cents a kWh thereafter. Homes that use electricity on "time-of-use rates" pay 7.5 cents per kWh during off-peak hours (7pm to 7am): 11.2 cents per kWh for mid-peak (7am to 11am and 5pm to 7pm): and 13.5 cents per kWh from 11am to 5pm.

11   By contrast, Moody's Credit Rating puts the cost of electricity generated by new nuclear power plants at 15 cents per kWh. According to Jack Gibbons of the Ontario Clean Air Alliance (OCAA), refurbishing Darlington's four nuclear reactors will cost 19 to 37 cents per kWh. The Ontario Power Generation (OPG) lowballs the cost at eight to 14 cents per kWh.

12   But it's notable that Ontario's past nuclear decisions have followed a predictable pattern: lowball costs are used to secure project approval, and then overruns are simply passed on to taxpayers. Nuclear projects in Ontario, on average, have gone 2.5 times over budget—so it's reasonable to multiply OPG's 8 cents per kWh by 2.5 and 4.5 (Darlington's overruns) and get a more realistic range of 20 to 36 cents per kWh, in line with Jack Gibbon's more accurate and trustworthy estimate.

13   A wise saying applies here: Never ask a barber if you need a haircut. Given that 50 per cent of Ontario's electricity comes from nuclear reactors, perhaps we shouldn't ask the OPG or Ontario Power Authority (OPA) about the province's energy future. It is particularly telling that no company anywhere in the world will build a nuclear reactor, unless, it is shielded from liability and can pass cost overruns on to taxpayers.

14   Why then are both the Ontario Liberals and Conservatives advocating spending billions of dollars refurbishing old nuclear reactors? The NPD supports it too because of unionized power workers, but its party leaders are cagey about categorical statements. Only the Green Party of Ontario remains steadfastly opposed to nuclear refurbishment.

15   OPG admitted in June 2014 that the Darlington refurbishment project is already $300-million over budget—before any actual construction work has begun. Will Ontario's new Liberal majority government continue to pursue nuclear refurbishment or stop throwing good money after bad?

16   McKinsey & Company, one of the world's preeminent management consulting firms, has identified $2-trillion worth of energy efficiency initiatives not currently being pursued worldwide, which have an internal rate of return of 17 per cent or better. Government and business leaders should be aggressively pursuing these highly profitable opportunities rather than embarking on nuclear refurbishment.

17   But even smart people have problems predicting the future. In the 1980s, AT&T commissioned a study by McKinsey & Company that predicted the market for cell phones by the year 2000 would be 100,000 users. That year, 107 million phones were sold.

18   How could the leading phone company and management consulting firm have been so off? For the same five reasons that we should be investing in renewable energy and energy efficiency projects instead of refurbishing nuclear reactors.

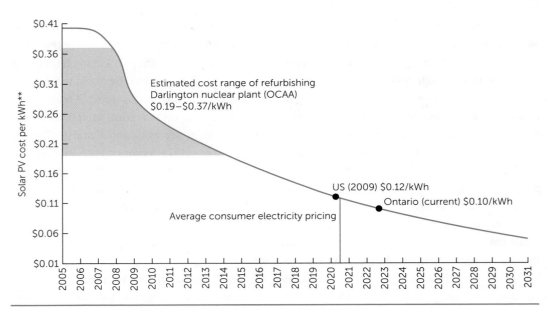

FIGURE 1   The Declining Cost of Solar (Projected past 2009*)

Grid parity is the point at which the cost of buying electricity from an alternative energy source is less than or equal to purchasing power from the traditional grid. When an energy source reaches grid parity it becomes economically competitive without the need for government subsidies. For solar photovoltaic electricity, grid parity is projected to occur around 2020.

*Projection is based on 2009 dollars (exchange rate: US$0.955). Other values assume USD/CAD$ at parity.

**PV data from 2009. *DOE NREL Solar Technologies, Market Report*, Jan. 2010. Projection by Ramez Naam.

Faster, better, smaller, cheaper

19   In 1965, computer tech pioneer Gordon Moore predicted that a CPU (central processing unit—the 'brains' of a computer) would double in power every two years while the price point to produce it stayed the same. Practically, this means that transistor-based technologies—computers, tablets, cell phones, etc.—get faster, better, smaller, and cheaper. The same is true of solar photovoltaics (PV), the cost of which has fallen 100-fold since 1977, and 80 per cent since 2008 (see the chart above).

20   Nobel Laureate and former US Secretary of Energy Steven Chu predicted in 2011 that solar power will be at grid parity by 2020—meaning solar power will be dramatically cheaper than nuclear power. Renewable energy (excluding hydro) currently represents only 8.5 per cent of the world's generating capacity—causing some critics to dismiss it. But in 2013, renewables created a staggering 44 per cent of new global energy capacity.

21   Here's another stunning fact: more solar energy can fall on Earth in a single hour than all the energy used globally in a year. On June 9, 2014, Germany produced a record 50.6 per cent of its electricity in the middle of the day from solar power! Germany is not noted for a sunny climate, and 90 per cent of the world's population lives in countries with substantially more sunlight—so the potential of solar power in the future is fantastic. The annual

solar energy that Earth receives dwarfs all remaining fossil fuels.

22 By 2030 renewable energy—primarily wind and solar power—will make up 66 per cent of the power supply according to *Bloomberg New Energy Finance*. But I believe the timeline for renewable dominance is actually closer at hand than that. In 2013, 29 per cent of the electricity capacity added in the US was solar. In fact, more solar was installed in the US in 18 months from June 2012 to December 2013 than in the prior 30 years combined.

23 But according to Ontario's Long Term Energy Plan, the Darlington nuclear reactor refurbishment won't be completed until 2025. If it proceeds, Ontario taxpayers will be locked into the most expensive form of electricity for the next 40 years. So while other provinces, states, and countries will be basking in the endless supply of low-cost solar power, Ontario businesses, manufacturers, and homeowners will be burdened with billions in high costs to pay for nuclear power.

24 As the famous energy consultant Wayne Gretzky said, "I never go where the puck is, I go to where it's going to be." The critical question seems to be: Where is the world's energy future going?

A crowdsourced power grid

25 Back when AT&T commissioned McKinsey to study cell phones, the technology was horrifically expensive and therefore ownership was very exclusive—only a small group of wealthy individuals or corporations could afford them. But as the technology plummeted in price—driven by Moore's Law—millions of individuals became buyers. This completely revolutionized the industry.

26 The same thing is happening in the renewable energy sector. Feed-in-Tariff (FIT) programs around the world are driving the adoption of wind and solar power. FIT programs ensure that homeowners, farmers, private investors, community, and Aboriginal groups are paid a fixed price for the electricity they generate and feed into the grid. Rather than the governments or electric utilities laying out billions of dollars of capital for big, expensive centralized power plants (as with coal, nuclear, or gas operations), individuals, communities, and local groups are investing in small-scale renewable energy.

27 As of 2010, more than 50 countries have FIT programs, which also have some ancillary benefits. They increase consumers' consciousness about energy and as a result, those people become more efficient at using and conserving it. Homeowners who are being paid a premium for electricity generation become conscious of the value of electricity and use less.

28 The resulting energy consciousness thereby lowers demand. FIT programs also reduce transmission line loss, which can reach as high as 22.5 per cent at peak demand because locally produced electricity does not have to be transported hundreds or thousands of miles from a centralized facility. Likewise, the FIT approach increases grid reliability because generation is distributed over a wider geographic area and is therefore more fault-tolerant.

Developing economies of scale

29 Nokia rose to dominance in the cell phone industry by producing inexpensive phones. In fact, Western nations have developing nations to thank for cheap cell phones. China, India,

and other developing nations in Latin America and Africa couldn't afford the wire line infrastructure required to provide billions of land line phones to emerging middle-class and poor consumers. So these heavily populated areas leapfrogged the West and moved directly to cellular mobile technology. Their massive economies of scale dramatically reduced the price of mobile technology.

30 China has announced it will triple its current installed solar capacity to 70 GW by 2017. China already has the second-largest installed capacity of solar—by 2017, it will be the leading country globally.

31 And [solar energy's] potential is already huge: A PV farm in the Sahara covering just 0.3 per cent of the desert could power all of Europe.

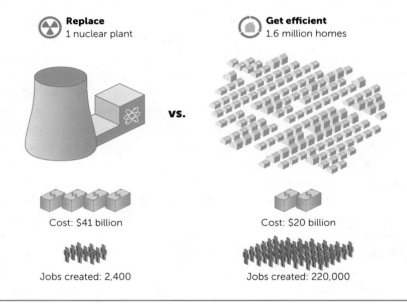

Replace
1 nuclear plant

Get efficient
1.6 million homes

VS.

Cost: $41 billion

Cost: $20 billion

Jobs created: 2,400

Jobs created: 220,000

FIGURE 2   Energy Efficiency Costs Less & Creates More Jobs

You want to save money and create jobs? Get efficient. For half the cost of replacing one nuclear power plant, we can retrofit 1,600,000 homes for energy efficiency and create 220,000 new jobs—that's 90 times more jobs than you'd get from a power plant replacement.

Source: EnergySavvy, Inc.

An explosion of exponential growth

32 Imagine a pond that starts with one lily pad, and the number of lilies doubles every day. At the end of day two, there are two lilies, then four lilies after three days, eight after four days, 16 after five days, and so on. However, on day 14, one day before the entire pond is covered, 50 per cent of the water will still be open. On day 13, 75 per cent of the pond will be uncovered, and on day 11, nearly 95 per cent is visible.

33 If you began warning people on day 11 that the pond was about to be covered over with lilies, they'd look at you like you're crazy. The key lesson is that most people—most strategic

planners, most OPA and OPG energy planners—cannot see exponential growth until it overwhelms their plans.

34   Solar power might only be a small percentage of the global energy mix at the moment. But global solar capacity has been growing by 40 per cent a year, compounded annually for the last 20 years!

35   People really don't understand the power of exponential growth. The amount of computational power in a wristwatch is greater than all the computer power on the first lunar landing module. The average computer notebook today has more raw computing power than IMB's largest mainframe 15 years ago.

36   Exponential growth is a game-changer. Whole industries are blindsided by it. The exponential growth in bandwidth resulted in Netflix blindsiding Blockbuster into bankruptcy. More than 33 per cent of all international long-distance calls are now facilitated by Skype, which blindsided the telecom industry's traditional profit. The exponential growth of social media has vaulted the valuation of Facebook, Twitter, and LinkedIn into the billions. The exponential growth of digital music compression transformed music consumption.

37   In industry after industry, exponential growth of a new technology or trend has dramatically changed the playing field.

Jobs, jobs, jobs

38   In 2013, 1,350,000 Canadians were out of work and another 914,000 were underemployed. At a time where we need to create two million jobs for Canadians, government policy should be focused on job creation as a first priority.

39   In 2011, EnergySavvy.com produced a study about the value proposition of expanding US nuclear capacity versus household-scale energy efficiency, summed up by the infographic below. If Canada's political leaders cared about jobs, they'd get busy promoting energy efficiency, building retrofits and mass transit.

40   Green Party of Ontario leader Mike Schreiner points out that energy efficiency could create 14 times more jobs than building new nuclear plants. You'd think all political parties would favour an overriding focus on energy efficiency, because it creates jobs in every community and insulates homeowners and businesses from inevitable rises in energy prices.

41   By pursuing the lower-cost options of energy efficiency and buying power from Quebec, Ontario can assure taxpayers better electricity rates going forward without the threat of debt, provide better environmental choices and less risk, and create more jobs. To defeat nuclear refurbishment in Ontario, we need to delay the decision to proceed, and leave it to market forces and the falling price of solar power to eliminate this unnecessary and overly expensive option.

Jim Harris is an author and thinker concerned with change and leadership. He speaks internationally at 40 conferences a year and is the program director of the Centre of Excellence on Sustainability and Innovation at the Schulich Executive Education Centre at York University's School of Business. Under Harris's leadership (2003 to 2006), the Green Party of Canada increased its voter support, membership, potential voter pool, and budget by a factor of 7, 14, 45, and 100 respectively. He was personally trained by Al Gore to give his Inconvenient Truth slide show.

Comprehension

1. Summarize one of the following sections of the essay in 70–90 words: "Faster, Better, Smaller, Cheaper," "A Crowdsourced Power Grid," or "Jobs, Jobs, Jobs."

2. Explain the meaning of the following statements as they apply to the part of the essay in which they occur:
   - "A wise saying applies here: Never ask a barber if you need a haircut" (par. 13) and
   - "As the famous energy consultant Wayne Gretzky said, 'I never go where the puck is. I go to where it's going to be'" (par. 24).

Organization and Style

1. Consider the writer's use of facts and statistics to give information and support to his thesis. Choose any two consecutive paragraphs from the first section of the essay and analyze the use of facts and statistics. You can use these or other questions to help with your answer:
   - What is the function of facts/statistics?
   - What do they contribute to the passage in which they occur?
   - Do they seem reliable? (Remember that non-academic writers don't usually cite their sources.)
   - Are facts/statistics overused?

2. Find a paragraph in which the following kind of evidence plays a significant role and explain how it is used to support the author's point:
   - analogy,
   - examples, and
   - experts.

Critical Thinking/Research

1. What is the Darlington refurbishing project referred to in Harris's essay? Using at least two reliable sources (no more than one should be an industry source), briefly explain the nature of this project; include any relevant updates since 2014 (when the essay was published).

2. Identify the essay's purpose and intended audience (see Chapter 4, p. 34) and comment, with specific references to the essay, on how it achieves its purpose and appeals to its audience.

3. Which do you consider the most important of the "five reasons" Harris proposes for investment in renewable energy sources? Justify your reasoning.

Navneet Alang, "Stop Believing in the 'World-Changing' Power of Every New Gadget"

Rather than just cater to our expectations and give us more of what we think we want, good journalism should probe and question our underlying motivations. In his short but incisive essay, Navneet Alang explores what he considers a deeply rooted social phenomenon behind the need for the latest tech improvements.

 Preparing to Read

1. What are your expectations—and/or those of your friends/peers—regarding the latest tech updates? For example, do you pay them much attention, or do you consider them mostly "hype?" Discuss in groups or write a short response to these or similar questions.

2. How did you respond when you read this essay's title? Did you form any first impressions about the essay or about its author? Use a reliable Internet site to get information about the writer, including his qualifications for writing about his topic.

Stop Believing in the "World-Changing" Power of Every New Gadget

Navneet Alang

The Globe and Mail, 25 October 2013
(876 words)

1   Earlier this week, the citizens of the world gathered in front of their glowing blue screens, waiting with bated breath to hear tales of revolutionary ideas, magical new technology, and innovative new gadgets. What they got instead was slightly better productivity software.

2   How strange then that this quite ordinary announcement still generated an enormous amount of chatter online and garnered the top spot in many news lineups. It's almost as if we are in a collective cultural hangover. Drunk off the effects of what were legitimately revolutionary products, we now expect the same again, treating each new update to the iPad and iPhone as if it were as important as the first.

3   This is not "Apple is doomed, can't innovate, Jobs woulda" over-reactive whining. That would be ungenerous to Apple Inc. who, earlier this week, unveiled some genuinely compelling updates to their iPads, MacBooks, and their iLife and iWork suites. Nonetheless, they were hardly Earth-shattering revelations. Rather, they were just the usual new features and redesigns we've come to expect from most technology companies—or, for that matter, makers of kitchen appliances, too.

4   What's worrying about the continued, outdated fervour over Apple news is that it's a symptom of a broader misguided faith in digital technology's power to solve the problems of the

contemporary world. To explain that, we need to start at the beginning.

5   Even the most dogmatic technophobe or Apple-hater cannot deny the effects Apple's products have had on modern life. You can get into arguments about who released what feature first, but the iPod, iPhone, and iPad each had consequences that extended far beyond "technology." Whether the mainstreaming of mobile pocket computing—or the myriad changes in news, reading habits, media consumption or location-based services—for a while Apple seemed to both direct and exemplify the tenor of the so-called new digital age.

6   As a result, we quickly learned that an Apple announcement wasn't just a question of fetishizing the latest tech trinket (though it was that, too); it was about seeing where culture might be heading next. We'd tune into Steve Jobs' talks because just a few short years ago, checking Yelp while walking down the street or video chatting from the bus seemed impossibly futuristic. What new things might we possibly be doing next?

7   Now, after a few sub-revolutionary events, we've gotten some insight into just how rare and hard that kind of sea-change is. The story of the iPhone's creation is one of many moving parts and untested designs that had to come together in a strange, serendipitous, alchemic mixture. What is clear is that, when a technological change is profound enough to affect culture, it isn't due to any one thing, but because of a swirling mass of many shifting factors coming together at the right time—and it isn't something that happens very often.

8   It's possible that Apple is cooking up similar revelations in wearable computing, TV, or something else. But for the time being, they've become a company that is interested in preserving their massive profits and operat-ing margins. That's fine; Apple is doing what a public corporation should by protecting value. What is perhaps less than ideal, however, is that both we and the media-at-large continue to treat each morsel of Apple news as if it is going to have similar ramifications to the launch of the iPhone, when in fact, it's just the sort of inane consumer updates best left to trade publications, rather than being headline news or kitchen-table conversation.

9   But if that kind of empty fetishizing of technology is one more unfortunate side effect of a broader consumerist culture, I'd venture it also expresses a specific kind of yearning. Having seen how radically digital technology has changed our lives, it seems we continue to want it do so, and in more ways. Think of proposed tech solutions to education, city governance, homelessness, or nutrition. All of them seen to evince a desire to take tech's capacity to change something like book publishing or news subscriptions and apply it to everything. It's a phenomenon that writers like Evgeny Morozov or Ian Bogost call "solutionism": the idea that for every problem, there's a tech solution, regardless of whether it's an improvement, or if it's even true.

10   That kind of hope for a neat, digital answer to the messiness and complexity of the world's problems is an eminently human response. We want things to get better and, lately anyway, we've seen things change so drastically simply because of the phones we carry around with us. As a result, we are constantly expecting the proverbial Apple to hit us on the head and usher in something else similarly world-changing.

11   As it turns out, though, such radical techno-cultural upheaval is a very rare thing. Maybe we've lived through an accelerated period of change, and now need to tend to the nitty-gritty of our newly digitized lives. More to the point,

looking to large corporations or some nebulous thing called "technology" for where culture is heading next may not be the best idea. And perhaps a good first step to changing things would be treating Apple events for what they have now become—not culturally significant moments, but just one more company doing its best to peddle its wares.

Comprehension

1. Alang uses the word "fetishizing" twice in his essay. From its context, come up with a definition of "fetishizing" and comment on its importance in the paragraphs in which it occurs (6 and 9).

2. a. Summarize paragraph 7, in which Alang explains the creation of the iPhone.
   b. Paraphrase the author's definition of "solutionism" (par. 9).

Organization and Style

1. After identifying the author's introduction and thesis statement (see Chapter 1, p. 8), analyze his effectiveness in fulfilling basic functions of introductions and theses.

2. Show how Alang use language to attract the reader's interest and make the author appear reasonable and fair. Come up with at least two examples of diction that reflect these purposes.

Critical Thinking

1. Who do you think Alang is writing to in his essay (i.e., who is his audience)? Referring specifically to the text, support your answer.

2. Identify two examples of concessions (see Chapter 4, p. 48) that the author makes and explain how they help his argument.

3. Discuss in groups or respond in writing to the following statement from the essay: "[W]e are constantly expecting the proverbial Apple to hit us on the head and usher in something else similarly world-changing" (par. 11).

Nik Harron, "Fully Destructible: Exploring a Personal Relationship with Nature through Video Games"

For many journalists, a new perception or an old idea re-examined becomes the impetus for an article. Harron begins by referring to the common perception about video gaming as an energy-intensive but personally isolating experience; then he introduces his new insight. The result is an argumentative essay designed to raise awareness or draw attention to something previously overlooked.

Preparing to Read

1. After reading the first two paragraphs, respond in writing (or discuss in groups) to the author's depiction of video games and video-game culture. Is it accurate in your view?

2. Who is Rachel Carson and why might her book *Silent Spring* be relevant to Harron's topic? Use reliable sources to answer these questions.

Fully Destructible: Exploring a Personal Relationship with Nature through Video Games

Nik Harron

Alternatives Journal, 2014
(3007 words)

1   In his book *The Grasshopper: Games, Life, and Utopia*, Bernard Suits defines the act of playing games as "the voluntary attempt to overcome unnecessary obstacles." It's easy to dismiss playing games as an impediment to the real-world experiences required to develop an environmental ethos.

2   Video games seem especially emblematic of Western society's retreat from nature and a widespread, willful neglect of real and profound environmental challenges during the past 40 years. As the population has shifted toward a predominately urban and media-saturated experience, many recreational activities have been virtualized and much community-scale interaction has been lost. The criticism levelled at a screen-dominated electronic culture—its physically disposable nature, the pollution, and habitat destruction associated with its manufacture, and its profligate use of energy—would seem to apply especially to gaming, a non-productive and potentially socially isolating activity.

3   But like any modern technology, video games have both positive and negative aspects. While urban environments restrict access to nature and the virtualized environments of many video games seem like caricatures of the physical world (for now), gaming provides an interactive experience that can support learning and awareness of the otherwise inaccessible natural world. The artful construction of the simulated environments in video games—which aspects of reality are simulated, at what fidelity, and where they sit on the spectrum between realistic and fantastical—can offer experiences that are not feasible with traditional media or even direct contact with nature.

4   The first commercially successful video game was *Pong*, released a mere decade after Rachel Carson's *Silent Spring*. During the four decades since, video games have evolved from simplistic, twitchy tests of reaction times and endurance, created over months by individual programmers. They now encompass cinematic virtual experiences with budgets comparable to Hollywood films, crafted over years by hundreds of people. In a similar fashion, the environments in video games have matured to cover the gamut from *Pong*'s formless void to believable, simulation-driven spectacles that use the same special effects technologies as modern films.

5   However, in recent years an "indie" developer scene has been rethinking the expensive realism and large-scale production values that constitute a video game. Limited budgets are driving individuals and small teams of developers to experiment with minimalistic styles and explore themes and taboos that would normally be considered beyond the purview of mere games, such as mortality, morality, economics, and abuse. Humans develop and learn by playing, and that includes video games.

6   A player's experience and abilities within a game are defined in many ways through the design of the digital environment, constraining the gameplay mechanic—the actions available to the player to overcome the game's obstacles. The mechanic dictates how the simplified reality within the game supports a specific type of play, including the ability to replay scenarios and explore alternative approaches. The basic simulation technology underlying the environments of many video games is either cellular automata (2D) or box modelling (3D). Essentially, the reality being simulated is broken down into a 2D or 3D grid of boxes. The state of each box in the grid is determined algorithmically at each moment by a calculation that takes into account the initial state of the box, as well as that of adjacent boxes. The variables tracked in a simulation can be as simple as whether or not the box is black or white, on or off, or something much more complex.

7   Box modelling is at the core of many climate simulations used in scientific research. These models track a large number of variables (temperature, air pressure, solar influx, wind speed, and direction, etc.) but the basic process is the same as that of video games. Environmental scientists rely on digital simulations to gain insight into climate change. But unlike video games, a key element that research simulations cannot

provide is a first-hand experience of what it is like to be in that altered, forecasted world. Just as scientific modelling can inform rational policy decisions on a global scale, video games can inform environmental ethics at an individual one.

Proteus

First-person 3D exploration in a procedurally generated open world—created by Ed Key and David Kanaga (2013); Linux, OS-X, Windows, PS Vita, PS3.

www.visitproteus.com

8   In Greek legend, Proteus was the god of "elusive sea-change," gifted with the power of prophecy. The ever-mutable son of Poseidon could also change form to escape captors and not be forced to reveal the future. The video game *Proteus* reveals the mystery of the player's inevitable future by metaphorically exploring an individual lifetime within nature's grander cycles.

9   Imagine a bright, cartoon island full of creatures and plants that live out their entire lives through four seasons, from spring to winter. The player emerges from the ocean as the eponymous character to explore a randomly generated landscape (novel structures and terrain created by a complex algorithm). The game literally consists of strolling and observing the cycles and rhythms of nature in an idyllic landscape.

10   *Proteus* generated controversy within the gaming community. Some critics accused its minimalist graphics and gameplay—the only actions available to the player are walking and sitting—as not constituting a game. It was derided as a walkabout. But its surprisingly engaging, non-violent, and stripped-down exploratory experience quickly made it a fan favourite. *Proteus* has succeeded because of its minimalism, not in spite of it. The deceptively simplistic

graphics have a non-threatening 8-bit cuteness that forces players to interact with the digital environment on a symbolic level, concentrating on the core experience over the details.

11   Time in *Proteus* is highly compressed. The year is broken up into four seasons. Each night and day cycle lasts about 15 minutes and the game can be played to completion in roughly an hour if a player spends only one day in each season. (A season can also last as long as the player cares to linger.) The changing weather and the rising and setting of the sun and moon are highlighted, and players can rapidly traverse the small environment and flexibly explore its ever-changing vista.

12   As a landscape painter who has focused on observing and depicting nature for 25 years, this opportunity to repeat and quickly modify my viewpoint has led me to a new understanding of what constitutes an engaging scene. It has also driven home the notion that how I choose to observe my surroundings is intimately tied to my connection with them.

13   The cycle of the seasons allows players to quickly experience how the landscape's entire ecosystem changes with natural cycles. Creatures and plants that emerged in spring grow old and pass away while retaining their recognizable identities. Watching a flock of 'birds' dying on the ground—when just minutes before they flew through the sky—can provoke a profoundly emotional response and evoke a strong sense of impending mortality.

14   Players consciously choose when the transition between seasons occurs. During the first night of each season, a vortex of glowing lights appears within a circle of standing stones and is a portal that the player must step into to advance to the next season. Approaching the centre of the circle allows players to speed up time to watch days and nights passing in a quick time lapse. Stepping into the centre triggers a fade to white and the season advances.

15   This magical interlude is not a singular marvel within the game. Several locations on the island are associated with transcendental experiences and once-in-a-real-lifetime events. Spectacular meteor storms or sky-spanning auroras occur with relative frequency. Alongside the understanding of nature's cycles, the game captures a deep sense of nature's wonder and mystery.

16   ***Spoiler alert:*** Winter in *Proteus* concludes with the player's death and teaches a powerful lesson about the lack of separation between human life and the environment that sustains it. Death creeps up, and in the moment of realization that life is coming to an end, a feeling of calm pervades alongside an understanding that mortality is simply another observable pattern on the island.

17   I did experience a brief moment of panic when I first realized the game was ending beyond my control. Yet this feeling quickly transformed into a sense of loss—not for myself, but for the undisturbed nature that I was leaving behind. Death in *Proteus* is a profoundly selfless moment that identifies the larger rhythms and cycles of nature, in stark contrast to sheltered urban living.

Flower

First-person flight simulation with linear world design created by ThatGameCompany (2009); PS3, PS4, PS Vita.

www.thatgamecompany.com/games/flower

18   The Journey in *Flower* begins inside of a dingy, drab apartment in the middle of an unnamed city. Gameplay starts by clicking on a lone flower on a shelf below a window, which transports the player to a colourful, open, lush, grass-filled landscape completely devoid of

human presence. You assume the role of the wind and fly around, bending the grass and pulling petals from flowers into your breeze. As a player collects petals, new areas of the landscape can be explored.

19 Playing *Flower* is an exhilarating experience. The initial beauty of the landscape and the sense of freedom is a stark contrast to a claustrophobic urban existence. The player is returned to the apartment after levels are completed, indicated by a new flower on the shelf that turns the formerly drab apartment noticeably brighter and more colourful.

20 **Spoiler alert:** *Flower* consists of six levels that form a coherent, environmentally focused narrative. The first level presents nature unspoiled. The second continues this theme, but tasks you with making the landscape bloom. The third finds you powering wind turbines and sustainably integrating technology with the environment. The fourth begins innocently enough, depicting a nocturnal agrarian landscape crossed by power lines, presumably connected to the wind turbines. You interact with the crops, metaphorically pollinating the fields with light until a downed power line marks a dramatic turn in the emotional mood of the game. The claustrophobic and harrowing fifth level forces you to navigate a ruined and increasingly hostile environment overcome by technology, represented by the twisted black metal girders of collapsed transmission towers. The final, triumphant level sees you freeing the city from the mechanistic towers that choke it, reestablishing a sense of control and optimism that the city can be redesigned as a sustainable and life-affirming space.

21 Jenova Chen, director of California-based ThatGameCompany, is focused on designing games that allow players an emotionally charged, ego-free experience that is characterized by extreme engagement and focus. His earlier games, *Cloud* and *Flow*, dealt with weather manipulation and living as a microscopic organism. Similarly, *Flower* creates a sense of identification with elemental nature and makes its threats visceral and personal.

22 Wordlessly, the design of *Flower*'s landscapes and levels convey an environmental narrative, beginning with a sense of wonderment at the cheerful biome and the freedom to explore it. When the player reestablishes control and liberates the city, the joy engendered by the initial, unspoiled nature of the first level is reaffirmed. In this way, the game confronts the feeling of being powerless to affect large-scale environmental change, focusing instead on pure emotion as a connection point with nature that can motivate positive action. If this is escapism for the urban-bound dweller, it is more an embrace of nature's phenomena as an integral part of sustainability than a rejection of the city. By providing such a simple but dramatic surrogate for experiencing nature, *Flower* nurtures a strong sense of stewardship.

Minecraft

First- or third-person 3D exploration roleplaying game in a procedurally generated, fully modifiable open world created by Markus "Notch" Persson and Jens "Jeb" Bergensten (2009); Linux, Android, iOS, Windows, OSX PS3, PS4, PS Vita, Xbox360, Xbox One, Java.

www.minecraft.net

23 The player awakes without any tools, resources, or knowledge about how they got to a deserted landscape populated only by wildlife. She or he is free to explore without limitations. As night falls, however, the charming and harmless landscape becomes overrun with hostile "mobs"—zombies, pigmen, skeletons,

and giant spiders, to name a few—and players must learn to extract resources from the environment to build protective structures and craft items to survive.

24 *Minecraft*'s sales, awards, and critical reception make it arguably the most successful indie game of all time. Its landscape is composed entirely of one-metre cubes, and an algorithm generates its hills, lakes, rivers, forests, ravines, sprawling cave systems, and mountains as the player explores. For all intents and purposes, the world of *Minecraft* is infinite—the total surface area is more than 9 million times that of Earth—and it is comprised of several biomes, ranging from desert to plains and swamps to mountains. There are dozens of types of minerals to be mined and collected. Nearly 200 individual items can be crafted, and they can also be combined to build larger, more elaborate machines and structures limited only by imagination. The simulation technology underlying the game is sophisticated enough to allow a recapitulation of the entire history of technological civilization, from primitive wood and stone tools, through agriculture, right up to factory-sized computers capable of running algorithms and displaying animated outputs on giant screens.

25 *Minecraft* can be played either as a single player or while connected to online servers that allow several people to collaborate or compete within the same world. Many players choose to import real-world ethics and phenomena that are not encoded into the multiplayer game; social innovations such as economic models and cities, or group activities such as sports, can emerge. Some players choose a non-violent or vegan approach, making moral decisions to limit how their own actions exploit the game's landscape. As one of the first truly open-world games, *Minecraft* forces players to explore and modify the landscape to achieve their own set of goals without any instructions or guidelines. It poses a fascinating question: What would you do if you could rewind time and find yourself on an unspoiled Earth?

26 Initially, I simply explored. When threatened by the mobs, I built a modest home to spend the night in safety. I explored simple technologies and harvested coal to craft torches, and began to explore the caves underfoot to pass the time until sunrise. It didn't take long to become dissatisfied with a modest life in harmony with my surroundings. The desire to create something larger took hold.

27 Without questioning the consequences of my actions, my extractive activity ramped up very quickly. I set about clearcutting forests for fuel and strip-mining the landscape for building materials. I worked my way up through the stone and metal ages, constructing a sprawling castle and terracing the hills to grow food for the people I imagined would live there. My preconceived notions of civilization dictated what should exist within the landscape, and I wanted it all to be plausible. Roads emerged to connect structures, and I laid large areas to waste as the need for raw materials outstripped the surface supply.

28 A fully destructible world is normally considered a desirable feature in a video game (and a no-brainer sell line in game advertising). Before *Minecraft*, however, this idea had only been realized in limited ways, such as specific structures that could be destroyed or damaged, but never an entire landscape. Within *Minecraft*, everything is mineable, everything is craftable.

29 I joined a multiplayer server, and together we ramped up our activity to an industrial level. When it became hard to find areas on the map that were close enough to travel to conveniently,

we built mass transit systems to move avatars and materials to construction sites. Similar to the real world, we chose to build our structures in unspoiled areas and hid evidence of our resource extraction from view, mining in remote locations or underground.

30 At the peak of our "civilization," we built what is known as a "mob factory," a massive structure designed to exploit the natural ecosystem by automatically slaughtering thousands of animals, then conveniently sorting and conveying their raw material to a central collection point. One of the primary goals was to amass gunpowder—the by-product of killing an explosive creature known as a "creeper"— and combine it with sand to make TNT. Why did we need the TNT? To strip-mine sand in large quantities to make even greater amounts of TNT, because it seemed the easiest way to extract large amounts of minerals by blasting out quarries. Without questioning our actions, we had taken an unspoiled world and recapitulated the time line of our disastrous, real-world society.

31 Eventually our moderator installed software on the server to generate satellite-view maps of our civilization. What we had done was sobering. At ground level, our wastelands had their own Burtynsky-like charm, but from a cartographer's view, they were horrifying. We had cut down entire forests and our quarries were huge, ugly scars; we had begun to sprawl across the landscape. While the world was infinite, it had become impossible to explore it within any practical timeframe without running across evidence of human activity. In seeking to overcome our natural limits, we had—in a very real sense—ruined our natural world.

32 The experience of actually despoiling undisturbed terrain—albeit virtual—forced a hard re-examination of the choices I had made within the game, and by extension my choices in the real world. I had an awareness of environmental challenges and how they came to be before playing *Minecraft*, but the experience of unwittingly mirroring history made me more mindful. It has become harder to simply blame history for our predicament because I now understand how possible it is to damage an environment through an escalating series of small, unthinking decisions that make specific sense at the time.

33 I still play *Minecraft*, but my activities have changed. I spend more time simply exploring and appreciating the landscape. Now when I build my own structures, they are ruins rather than contemporary habitats. Two major features of my crafted world are a massive, forested underground cave and a giant canyon, both much grander in scale than what the game would otherwise create. The game has become about finding, creating and fostering sacred spaces that evoke a sense of wonder, beauty, and dramatic naturalism.

Comprehension

1. Identify, then paraphrase, the author's thesis.
2. What is Harron's purpose in comparing the process of climate simulations and the "gameplay dynamic" of video games? Summarize paragraph 7 where the comparison is explained.

Organization and Style

1. Identify one paragraph in which the following rhetorical patterns (see Chapter 3, p. 30) are used:
   • definition,
   • chronology,
   • description,
   • process analysis, and
   • cause–effect.
   Choosing two of these patterns, explain what they contribute to the essay as a whole.

Critical Thinking

1. In the section "Minecraft," analyze the author's extensive use of first person (personal experience), explaining what it contributes to this section as well as the entire essay.
2. Why do you think the author did not include a formal conclusion? Do you think the essay is complete without one? Write a 2–3 sentence concluding paragraph.
3. Do you think Harron was successful in drawing attention to his perspective on video games? Respond to or critically analyze his argument. (Responses often include personal experiences and/or observations, whereas analyses do not.)

Cory Doctorow, "You DO Like Reading off a Computer Screen"

"You DO Like Reading off a Computer Screen" tackles a familiar concern of today's authors, publishers, and readers: the future of print books. However, while other writers often argue simple positions—yes, there is a future, or, no, there isn't—Doctorow argues more complexly that "long-form narratives," such as novels, are fundamentally different from other computer texts, giving rise to different cognitive processes. Perhaps more notable than Doctorow's thesis, however, is his use of a distinctive style to reflect his content (see "Organization and Style," below).

 ## Preparing to Read

1. Doctorow is a prominent Canadian writer, speaker, and blogger and is considered one of his generation's most vocal advocates of the "open Internet." Using reliable sources, write a short biography of Doctorow that includes his achievements and the genres in which he writes, along with his major areas of interest.
2. Do you often or even occasionally read long works of fiction or non-fiction onscreen? List some of the pros and cons of reading longer works this way.

You DO Like Reading off a Computer Screen

Cory Doctorow

Content: Selected Essays on Technology, Creativity, Copyright, and the Future of the Future, 2008 (1202 words)

1 "I don't like reading off a computer screen"—it's a cliché of the e-book world. It means "I don't read novels off computer screens" (or phones, or PDAs, or dedicated e-book readers), and often as not the person who says it is someone who, in fact, spends every hour that Cthulhu sends reading off a computer screen. It's like watching someone shovel Mars Bars into his gob while telling you how much he hates chocolate.

2 But I know what you mean. You don't like reading long-form works off a computer screen. I understand perfectly—in the ten minutes since I typed the first word in the paragraph above, I've checked my mail, deleted two spams, checked an image-sharing community I like, downloaded a YouTube clip of Stephen Colbert complaining about the iPhone (pausing my MP3 player first), cleared out my RSS reader, and then returned to write this paragraph.

3 This is not an ideal environment in which to concentrate on long-form narrative (sorry, one sec, gotta blog this guy who's made cardboard furniture) (wait, the Colbert clip's done, gotta start the music up) (19 more RSS items). But that's not to say that it's not an *entertainment medium*—indeed, practically everything I do on the computer entertains the hell out of me. It's nearly all text-based, too. Basically, what I do on the computer is pleasure-reading. But it's a fundamentally more scattered, splintered kind of pleasure. Computers have their own cognitive style, and it's not much like the cognitive style invented with the first modern novel (one sec, let me google that and confirm it), *Don Quixote*, some 400 years ago.

4 The novel is an invention, one that was engendered by technological changes in information display, reproduction, and distribution. The cognitive style of the novel is different from the cognitive style of the legend. The cognitive style of the computer is different from the cognitive style of the novel.

5 Computers want you to do lots of things with them. Networked computers doubly so—they (another RSS item) have a million ways of asking for your attention, and just as many ways of rewarding it.

6 There's a persistent fantasy/nightmare in the publishing world of the advent of very sharp, very portable computer screens. In the fantasy version, this creates an infinite new market for electronic books, and we all get to sell the rights to our work all over again. In the nightmare version, this leads to runaway piracy, and no one ever gets to sell a novel again.

7 I think they're both wrong. The infinitely divisible copyright ignores the "decision cost" borne by users who have to decide, over and over again, whether they want to spend a millionth of a cent on a millionth of a word—no one buys newspapers by the paragraph, even though most of us only read a slim fraction of any given paper. A super-sharp, super-portable screen would be used to read all day long, but most of us won't spend most of our time reading anything recognizable as a book on them.

8 Take the record album. Everything about it is technologically pre-determined. The technology of the LP demanded artwork to differentiate one package from the next. The length was set by the groove density of the pressing plants and playback apparatus. The dynamic range likewise. These factors gave us the idea of the 40-to-

60-minute package, split into two acts, with accompanying artwork. Musicians were encouraged to create works that would be enjoyed as a unitary whole for a protracted period—think of *Dark Side of the Moon*, or *Sgt. Pepper's*.

9   No one thinks about albums today. Music is now divisible to the single, as represented by an individual MP3, and then subdivisible into snippets like ringtones and samples. When recording artists demand that their works be considered as a whole—like when Radiohead insisted that the iTunes Music Store sell their whole album as a single, indivisible file that you would have to listen to all the way through—they sound like cranky throwbacks.

10   The idea of a 60-minute album is as weird in the Internet era as the idea of sitting through 15 hours of *Der Ring des Nibelungen* was 20 years ago. There are some anachronisms who love their long-form opera, but the real action is in the more fluid stuff that can slither around on hot wax—and now the superfluid droplets of MP3s and samples. Opera survives, but it is a tiny sliver of a much bigger, looser music market. The future composts the past: old operas get mounted for living anachronisms; Andrew Lloyd Webber picks up the rest of the business.

11   Or look at digital video. We're watching more digital video, sooner, than anyone imagined. But we're watching it in three-minute chunks from YouTube. The video's got a pause button so you can stop it when the phone rings and a scrubber to go back and forth when you miss something while answering an IM.

12   And attention spans don't increase when you move from the PC to a handheld device. These things have less capacity for multitasking than real PCs, and the network connections are slower and more expensive. But they are fundamentally multitasking devices—you can always stop reading an e-book to play a hand of solitaire that is interrupted by a phone call—and their social context is that they are used in public places, with a million distractions. It is socially acceptable to interrupt someone who is looking at a PDA screen. By contrast, the TV room—a whole room for TV!—is a shrine where none may speak until the commercial airs.

13   The problem, then, isn't that screens aren't sharp enough to read novels off of. The problem is that novels aren't screeny enough to warrant protracted, regular reading on screens.

14   Electronic books are a wonderful adjunct to print books. It's great to have a couple of hundred novels in your pocket when the plane doesn't take off or the line is too long at the post office. It's cool to be able to search the text of a novel to find a beloved passage. It's excellent to use a novel socially, sending it to your friends, pasting it into your sig file.

15   But the numbers tell their own story—people who read off screens all day long buy lots of print books and read them primarily on paper. There are some who prefer an all-electronic existence (I'd like to be able to get rid of the objects after my first reading, but keep the e-books around for reference), but they're in a tiny minority.

16   There's a generation of web writers who produce "pleasure reading" on the web. Some are funny. Some are touching. Some are enraging. Most dwell in Sturgeon's 90th percentile and below. They're not writing novels. If they were, they wouldn't be web writers.

17   Mostly, we can read just enough of a free e-book to decide whether to buy it in hard copy—but not enough to substitute the e-book for the hard copy. Like practically everything in marketing and promotion, the trick is to find the form of the work that serves as enticement, not replacement.

18   Sorry, got to go—eight more e-mails.

 Comprehension

1. Summarize paragraphs 6 and 7 in two sentences.

Organization and Style

1. Doctorow uses several allusions in his essay. Using at least one reliable Internet source per allusion, briefly explain the significance of two of the following to the essay:
    *   Cthulhu (par. 1);
    *   Stephen Colbert (par. 2);
    *   Andrew Lloyd Webber (par. 10); and/or
    *   "Sturgeon's 90th percentile" (par. 16).
2. a. Analyze Doctorow's style. Your analysis could include word choice, paragraph or sentence structure, voice, tone, and/or stylistic devices such as imagery.
    b. Explain how the author uses his writing style to reinforce his main points, referring specifically to the text.
3. Identify two examples of comparisons (they could involve similarities, differences, or both); explain what is being compared and the effectiveness of the comparison.

Critical Thinking/Research

1. What kind of reader was this essay written for? How do you know this? Refer to specific passages to support your claims.
2. Do you find Doctorow's argument convincing? Analyze its effectiveness, considering such factors as use of logic, kinds of evidence, and argumentative strategies and techniques. In your analysis, bear in mind his audience (see question 1).
3. Write a comparative analysis of this essay and another essay on the same or a similar topic (for example, the uses of today's technology). Essays on e-books versus print books can be found in many Canadian newspapers and magazines.

Bryan Appleyard, "Distraction"

Using the familiar non-academic approach of introducing the problem he intends to analyze via a personal experience, Appleyard goes on to express what might be considered a common viewpoint today, at least among the older generations: that our technology is distracting us and, Appleyard warns, "Distraction kills."

Preparing to Read

1.   Respond to one of the following prompts:
   • Distraction is a major problem in my life and/or in the lives of my peers; or
   • Distraction is more/no more prevalent in the lives of today's youth than in those of past generations.

Distraction

Bryan Appleyard

The Sunday Times, 20 July 2008
(1885 words)

1   On Wednesday I received 72 emails, not counting junk, and only two text messages. It was a quiet day but, then again, I'm not including the telephone calls. I'm also not including the deafening and pointless announcements on a train journey to Wakefield—use a screen, jerks—the piercingly loud telephone conversations of unsocialized adults and the screaming of untamed brats. And, come to think of it, why not include the junk emails? They also interrupt. There were 38. Oh and I'd better throw in the 400-odd news alerts that I receive from all the websites I monitor via my iPhone.

2   I was—the irony!—trying to read a book called *Distracted: The Erosion of Attention and the Coming Dark Age* by Maggie Jackson. Crushed in my train, I had become the embodiment of T.S. Eliot's great summary of the modern predicament: "Distracted from distraction by distraction." This is, you might think, a pretty standard, vaguely comic vignette of modern life—man harassed by self-inflicted technology. And so it is. We're all distracted, we're all interrupted. How foolish we are! But, listen carefully, it's killing me and it's killing you.

3   David Meyer is professor of psychology at the University of Michigan. In 1995, his son was killed by a distracted driver who ran a red light. Meyer's specialty was attention: how we focus on one thing rather than another. Attention is the golden key to the mystery of human consciousness; it might one day tell us how we make the world in our heads. Attention comes naturally to us; attending to what matters is how we survive and define ourselves.

4   The opposite of attention is distraction, an unnatural condition and one that, as Meyer discovered in 1995, kills. Now he is convinced that chronic, long-term distraction is as dangerous as cigarette smoking. In particular, there is the great myth of multitasking. No human being, he says, can effectively write an email and speak on the telephone. Both activities use language and the language channel in the brain can't cope. Multitaskers fool themselves by rapidly switching attention and, as a result, their output deteriorates.

5   The same thing happens if you talk on a mobile phone while driving—even legally with a hands-free kit. You listen to language on the phone and lose the ability to take in the language of road signs. Worst of all is if your caller describes something visual, a wallpaper pattern, [or] a view. As you imagine this, your visual channel gets clogged and you start losing your sense of the road ahead. Distraction kills—you or others.

6   Chronic distraction, from which we all now suffer, kills you more slowly. Meyer says there is evidence that people in chronically distracted jobs are, in early middle age, appearing with the

same symptoms of burn-out as air traffic controllers. They might have stress-related diseases, even irreversible brain damage. But the damage is not caused by overwork, it's caused by multiple distracted work. One American study found that interruptions take up 2.1 hours of the average knowledge worker's day. This, it was estimated, cost the US economy $588 billion a year. Yet the rabidly multitasking distractee is seen as some kind of social and economic ideal.

7 Meyer tells me that he sees part of his job as warning as many people as possible of the dangers of the distracted world we are creating. Other voices, particularly in America, have joined the chorus of dismay. Jackson's book warns of a new Dark Age: "As our attentional skills are squandered, we are plunging into a culture of mistrust, skimming, and a dehumanizing merger between man and machine."

8 Mark Bauerlein, professor of English at Emory University in Atlanta, has just written *The Dumbest Generation: How the Digital Age Stupefies Young Americans and Jeopardizes Our Future*. He portrays a bibliophobic generation of teens, incapable of sustaining concentration long enough to read a book. And learning a poem by heart just strikes them as dumb.

9 In an influential essay in *The Atlantic* magazine, Nicholas Carr asks: "Is Google making us stupid?" Carr, a chronic distractee like the rest of us, noticed that he was finding it increasingly difficult to immerse himself in a book or a long article—"The deep reading that used to come naturally has become a struggle."

10 Instead he now Googles his way through life, scanning and skimming, not pausing to think, to absorb. He feels himself being hollowed out by "the replacement of complex inner density with a new kind of self-evolving under the pressure of information overload and the technology of the 'instantly available.'"

11 "The important thing," he tells me, "is that we now go outside of ourselves to make all the connections that we used to make inside of ourselves." The attending self is enfeebled as its functions are transferred to cyberspace.

12 "The next generation will not grieve because they will not know what they have lost," says Bill McKibben, the great environmentalist.

13 McKibben's hero is Henry Thoreau, who, in the nineteenth century, cut himself off from the distractions of industrializing America to live in quiet contemplation by Walden Pond in Massachusetts. He was, says McKibben, "incredibly prescient." McKibben can't live that life, though. He must organize his global warming campaigns through the Internet, and suffer and react to the beeping pleading of the incoming email.

14 "I feel that much of my life is ebbing away in the tide of minute-by-minute distraction . . . I'm not certain what the effect on the world will be. But psychologists do say that intense close engagement with things does provide the most human satisfaction." The psychologists are right. McKibben describes himself as "loving novelty" and yet "craving depth," the contemporary predicament in a nutshell.

15 Ironically, the companies most active in denying us our craving for depth, the great distracters—Microsoft, Google, IBM, Intel—are trying to do something about this. They have formed the Information Overload Research Group, "dedicated to promoting solutions to email overload and interruptions." None of this will work, of course, because of the overwhelming economic forces involved. People make big money out of distracting us. So what can be done?

16 The first issue is the determination of the distracters to create young distractees. Television was the first culprit. Tests clearly show that a switched-on television reduces the quality and quantity of interaction between

children and their parents. The Internet multiplies the effect a thousandfold. Paradoxically, the supreme information provider also has the effect of reducing information intake.

17　Bauerlein is 49. As a child, he says, he learned about the Vietnam war from Walter Cronkite, the great television news anchor of the time. Now teenagers just go to their laptops on coming home from school and sink into their online cocoon. But this isn't the informational paradise dreamt of by Bill Gates and Google: 90 per cent of sites visited by teenagers are social networks. They are immersed not in knowledge but in "gossip and social banter."

18　"They don't," says Bauerlein, "grow up." They are "living off the thrill of peer attention. Meanwhile, their intellects refuse the cultural and civic inheritance that has made us what we are now."

19　The hyper-connectivity of the young is bewildering. Jackson tells me that one study looked at five years of email activity of a 24-year-old. He was found to have connections with 11.7m people. Most of these connections would be pretty threadbare. But that, in a way, is the point. All Internet connections are threadbare. They lack the complexity and depth of real-world interactions. This is concealed by the language. Join Facebook or MySpace and you suddenly have "friends" all over the place. Of course, you don't. These are just casual, tenuous electronic pings. Nothing could be further removed from the idea of friendship.

20　These connections are severed as quickly as they are taken up—with the click of a mouse. Jackson and everyone else I spoke to was alarmed by the potential impact on real-world relationships. Teenagers are being groomed to think others can be picked up on a whim and dropped because of a mood or some slight offence. The fear is that the idea of sticking with

another through thick and thin—the very essence of friendship and love—will come to seem absurd, uncool, [and] meaningless.

21　One irony that lies behind all this is the myth that children are good at this stuff. Adults often joke that their 10-year-old has to fix the computer. But it's not true. Studies show older people are generally more adept with computers than younger. This is because, like all multitaskers, the kids are deluding themselves into thinking that busy-ness is depth when, in fact, they are skimming the surface of cyberspace as surely as they are skimming the surface of life. It takes an adult imagination to discriminate, to make judgments; and those are the only skills that really matter.

22　The concern of all these writers and thinkers is that it is precisely these skills that will vanish from the world as we become infantilized cyber-serfs, our entertainments and impulses maintained and controlled by the techno-geek aristocracy. They have all noted—either in themselves or in others—diminishing attention spans, inability to focus, a loss of the meditative mode. "I can't read *War and Peace* anymore," confessed one of Carr's friends. "I've lost the ability to do that. Even a blog post of more than three or four paragraphs is too much to absorb. I skim it."

23　The computer is training us not to attend, to drown in the sea of information, rather than to swim. Jackson thinks this can be fixed. The brain is malleable. Just as it can be trained to be distracted, so it can be trained to pay attention. Education and work can be restructured to teach and propagate the skills of concentration and focus. People can be taught to turn off, to ignore the beep and the ping.

24　Bauerlein, dismayed by his distracted students, is not optimistic. Multiple distractions might, he admits, be a phase, and in time, society will self-correct. But the sheer power of the forces of distraction is such that he thinks this will not happen.

25   This, for him, puts democracy at risk. It is a form of government that puts "a heavy burden of responsibility on our citizens." But if they think Paris is in England and they can't find Iraq on a map because their world is a social network of "friends"—examples of appalling ignorance recently found in American teenagers—how can they be expected to shoulder that burden?

26   This may all be a moral panic, a severe case of the older generation wagging its finger at the young. It was ever thus. But what is new is the assiduity with which companies and institutions are selling us the tools of distraction. Every new device on the market is, to return to Eliot, "Filled with fancies and empty of meaning/Tumid apathy with no concentration."

27   These things do make our lives easier, but only by destroying the very selves that should be protesting at every distraction, demanding peace, quiet, and contemplation. The distracters have product to shift, and it's shifting. On the train to Wakefield, with my new 3G iPhone, distracted from distraction by distraction, I saw the future and, to my horror, it worked.

◉ Comprehension

1.   In your own words, define what Appleyard calls "chronic distraction" (see pars. 4–6).
2.   Near the end of his essay, Appleyard refers to the views of two experts, whose opinions differ on the likelihood of our being able to overcome the problem of distraction:
     a.   Summarize the two views; and
     b.   Ask yourself, which view do you think Appleyard finds the most convincing and why?
     (Part "b" could be considered a "Critical Thinking" question.)

◈ Organization and Style

1.   Analyze paragraphs 1–5 for their rhetorical effectiveness (that is, the strategies and techniques the author uses to try to persuade his readers). You could consider such features as language/diction, voice, tone, sentence structure, repetition, and the like.
2.   Analyze the role of experts and authorities in the essay. Using one such expert as an example, explain how his or her ideas or comments help Appleyard support his claims.

◉ Critical Thinking/Research

1.   a.   Does Appleyard believe that it is only today's youth who are distracted?
     b.   Who or what does Appleyard ultimately blame for the problems caused by distraction?
     Explain your answers by referring directly to the text.
2.   Using critical thinking, evaluate one of the following claims from the essay. Remember that in an argument, general statements need to appear reasonable and valid, so

some of your evaluation should explain why or why not the claim appears reasonable and valid:

- "[Teenagers] are 'living off the thrill of peer attention. Meanwhile, their intellects refuse the cultural and civic inheritance that has made us what we are now'" (par. 18); and
- "It takes an adult imagination to discriminate, to make judgments; and those are the only skills that really matter" (par. 22).

3. Access the website of the Information Overload Research Group (IORG) referred to in paragraph 15).

   a. In 2–3 sentences, identify its purpose and target audience; and

   b. After familiarizing yourself with the site's design and major features, explain whether you agree with Appleyard's assessment of the site (see par. 15).

4. In a critical analysis, you objectively evaluate the arguments on both sides; in a critical response, you combine analysis with your own ideas, observations, and experiences.

   a. Write a critical analysis that compares Appleyard's argument with that of Wilson (see p. 195). Use specific passages to support your claim concerning the effectiveness of each argument; or,

   b. Write a critical response that compares arguments presented by these writers.

Scott Feschuk, "The Future of Machines with Feelings"

Literary and non-academic writers often use humour to both entertain their readers and explore serious topics. Scott Feschuk, writing in the mass-market Canadian magazine *Maclean's*, imagines a future in which machines will be capable of reading our moods and catering to our emotions. Understanding humour may depend on our ability as readers to understand the writer's attitude to his or her subject, as is certainly the case with the essay below. Feschuk's essay was written in response to a longer essay that appeared in *The New Yorker*.

 ## Preparing to Read

1. What are your own beliefs, feelings, or impression about machines that are able to "read" and respond to human emotions? Do you believe that such machines will have an important role in our future? Discuss in groups or respond to this topic in writing.

2. Using reliable sources, come up with a one-paragraph biography of Rana el Kaliouby, first mentioned in paragraph 6.

The Future of Machines with Feelings

Scott Feschuk

Maclean's, 24 January 2015
(729 words)

1   Is something missing from your relationship with your smartphone? Do you crave deeper intimacy with your cable box? Are you dreaming of the day you finally bond with your refrigerator?

2   Hope is on the way, weirdo. According to an article in *The New Yorker*, researchers are imbuing machines and devices with the capacity "to read our feelings and react in ways that have come to seem startlingly human." Scientific consensus: we are only a few short years away from living in a world in which we can disappoint our dishwasher.

3   Some of these software programs instantly analyze our facial expressions. Others monitor our gestures or the inflection in our voices. For the most part, they can swiftly calculate when we're happy, or sad, or confused. Some programs still struggle with the meaning of raised eyebrows—but they've got it narrowed down to "surprise" and "hilarious Nicole Kidman Botox impression."

4   Experts believe that emotionally responsive devices will soon be "ubiquitous," which is great news if you've always wanted a blender as your BFF. "Ten years down the line," a researcher said, "we won't remember what it was like when we couldn't just frown at our device, and our device would say, 'Oh, you didn't like that, did you?'" Doesn't that sound awesome helpful cool inevitable?

5   The pace of progress in this field will surely lead to tough questions, such as "Will these devices infringe on privacy rights?" and "How can I stop my toaster from rolling its eyes at my bunny slippers?" And then there's the biggest unknown: how will this invasive yet intriguing technology ultimately be used? Will it be harnessed for the betterment of society as a whole? Or for a second reason that isn't as totally naive as that first one?

6   To find our way to an answer, let's consider the work of Rana el Kaliouby, a brilliant scientist who is featured in *The New Yorker* article. Kaliouby wanted to develop technologies that could help autistic children better respond to the range of human emotions. She had noble goals and big dreams. Now, after many years, she has these technologies at her disposal—and so naturally she's ditched the autism plan and is helping huge corporations test market their TV commercials.

7   That's only one application of this technology. Companies have already filed patents for "emotion-sensing vending machines" and for an ATM capable of gauging whether a customer is "relaxed" enough to be receptive to advertising. Anheuser-Busch is even working on a "responsive" beer bottle—although they could probably save a ton of money by just telling every Bud Light drinker that the bottle turns brown when they're horny.

8   Kaliouby is totally psyched about the potential of the "emotion economy"—so maybe we should be, too. Think of all that will change. Now when hackers swipe data from the cloud, they'll get your credit card information, your buck-naked selfies, and evidence that you cried at the ending of *Transformers 2*. And who among us doesn't look forward to a day when corporations can quietly monitor the emotional state of their employees?

9   Smithers: Sir, our facial probes indicate happiness is down eight per cent this morning.

10   Burns: Release the YouTube video of that bulldog bouncing on a trampoline!

11   Or consider the humble cable box. In the US, the industry is reportedly working on models capable of scanning a room, identifying its occupants and tracking actions, such as eating, reading, and, ahem, "cuddling."

12   This data could be used to determine the ads you see. Just have a fight with your spouse? Your cable box may choose to show you an ad for a marriage counsellor. Just have a fight with your cable box? Your cable box may choose to show you a huge pixelated middle finger and 12 consecutive hours of *The Nanny*.

13   Meanwhile, Kaliouby's start-up company is keen to partner with corporations to identify your emotional state and "monetize those moments," which doesn't sound creepy or gross at all.

14   Confused about what she has in mind? Kaliouby offers an example. When your phone senses you're having a sad moment maybe that would be a good time for Kleenex to send you a coupon? Wouldn't that be super? And why stop there? Hello, we are a huge faceless corporation that totally cares your dog just died. Here's a coupon for 20 cents off a new dog! All better now?

Comprehension

1.   Using a reliable dictionary, define "ubiquitous" (par. 4) using your own words and explain why understanding its meaning might be important in understanding the author's thesis.

2.   In some humorous writing, writers do not express their meaning directly but require their readers to "read between the lines" (see irony, p. 128). Briefly explain the author's meaning in the last two questions in paragraph 5 and the last question in paragraph 8.

Organization and Style

1.   The author includes many direct quotations in his short essay. What are his reasons for doing so? Why might the exact words be important? Refer to at least two examples in your answer.

2.   Whom do you think Feschuk is writing to? Identify and comment on specific stylistic features that point toward his audience. For example, you could consider diction and other linguistic resources, examples, use of humour, and the like.

Critical Thinking

1.   How do you think Feschuk feels about the kinds of machines he describes? For example, do you believe that he would welcome such machines, that they make him uneasy, or that he doesn't care one way or the other? Defend your answer by referring to specific passages in his essay.

2.   Satire is a genre of literature that uses humour, irony, and exaggeration to poke fun at a target. Do you believe that "The Future of Machines with Feelings" is a satire or has satiric elements? Show how the essay fits or does not fit this definition of satire, referring specifically to the text. If you believe that it does, what is its target?

Aviva Romm, "Stop Killing the Good Guys!"

Medical technology is generally praised for providing many benefits in our lives today. However, that doesn't mean that scientists, medical professionals, or citizens should uncritically accept every scientific advancement. As the author of "Stop Killing the Good Guys!" asserts, "more is not always better," and the overuse of what has been called a medical wonder, antibiotics, comes with drawbacks. Aviva Romm, writing in the popular online site *The Huffington Post*, uses an informal style suited to general readers but also includes citations to increase her credibility.

 Preparing to Read

1. In paragraph 1, Romm states that the average American has been treated between 10 to 20 times with antibiotics by the age of 18. Recall your own experiences with antibiotics and your assessment of their value. (You could do this as a freewriting exercise or in groups.)

2. After reading the first two paragraphs, comment on the author's credibility. Does she appear knowledgeable and reliable? Identify at least two specific passages that suggest (or do not suggest) this.

Stop Killing the Good Guys!

Aviva Romm

The Huffington Post, 8 January 2015
(1583 words)

1 There's no doubt that antibiotics are a good thing. They save lives every day. We can, in part, attribute our longer lifespans, reduction in infant mortality and childhood deaths from life-threatening infections, and the near elimination of childbirth-related maternal deaths from infections in hospitals to antibiotics. As a medical doctor, I am grateful to be able to prescribe them for serious bacterial and other appropriate infections, for example Lyme disease. As with many things, however, more is not always better. And this is certainly the case with antibiotics.

2 The average child in the United States will receive between 10 and 20 courses of antibiotics by the time he or she is 18 years old. (2) We are so accustomed to antibiotics being prescribed for childhood illnesses that we assume that they are as safe as they are common. But this is far from the truth. We are now learning the hard way that the common overuse of antibiotics, both as medicines and in our foods (they are given to cattle and poultry to keep them "healthy" until they are slaughtered for food; antibiotics also promote growth in these animals by the same mechanisms that their chronic use increases the risk of obesity in humans) is responsible for two major health problems: global antibiotic resistance to serious infections and damage to the human microbiome.

3 This growing awareness that antibiotic overuse is dangerous for both public and personal health requires us to drastically and

immediately rethink and adjust our antibiotic use. In doing so we can prevent our children from developing life-long chronic illnesses associated with microbiome damage, some of which rival the seriousness of the bacterial infections that used to threaten them, and we can reduce the major global threat of antibiotic resistance we all face.

Antibiotics, your child's microbiome, and chronic disease

4   Antibiotics kill bacteria. The problem is that they not only kill off the bad guys (and as you'll see below, because of antibiotic resistance, they are doing this less effectively!); they kill off the good ones, too. When we give antibiotics to children at a young age or frequently enough, some of the good guys may never fully recover. These good gut flora, and their composite, our microbiome, are essential for more functions that protect and support our health than we'd ever imagined until recently. We now know that microbiome damage directly and significantly increases the risks of our children developing long-term health problems including food, environmental, and seasonal allergies, eczema, asthma, ulcerative colitis, Crohn's disease, obesity (even when they're not over-eating), diabetes, and cardiovascular disease. (1) (4)

5   Antibiotics are given to between 30 and 50 per cent of all women during pregnancy or labour. (2) Mom's exposure to antibiotics perinatally also negatively affects the breast milk microbiome, which is part of what is supposed to help colonize baby's gut with beneficial flora. (5) Additionally, 34 per cent of babies in the US are born by Caesarean. These babies miss out on the important inoculation their gut flora is meant to receive through natural exposure to mom's vaginal flora, thus compounding the problem. Our babies thus begin their antibiotic exposure even before birth, and as a result, damage to their formative microbial populations begins before they've had a chance to establish their optimal gut flora. If your baby was born by Caesarean section, or if you did need to have antibiotics in labour, no need to be worried! Start your baby on a probiotic in the day or so after birth. Data has shown that while we can't necessarily restore the native flora baby might have had, we can prevent eczema, allergies, and asthma with early probiotic treatment. (6)

6   By age 24 months, 69 per cent of children in the US have received at least one systemic antibiotic course, though the average is 2.3 courses for ear infections, bronchitis, sore throat, and other common childhood illnesses. Yet according to the Centres for Disease Control, and other official reports, at least 50 per cent and as many as 70 per cent of the antibiotics prescribed for children for these and other symptoms/conditions are unnecessary and inappropriate. (3)

7   Reactions to antibiotics are responsible for at least 140,000 hospital visits annually in the US. (3) One in every five emergency department visits due to a medication reaction is due to antibiotics, and in kids under 18 years old they are the most common cause of drug reactions. When a child takes an antibiotic that is not needed, not only is she or he getting no benefit; she or he is exposed to all the risks of harm and the use of that medication adds to antibiotic resistance.

8   Why are antibiotics overprescribed? There are four main reasons:

1.   Doctors think that parents expect an antibiotic prescription when they bring their child in for a sick visit—and many do—

leading to 50 to 70 per cent of the antibiotics that are prescribed. (4)

2. Doctors are afraid to get sued should an infection that they didn't treat with an antibiotic turn out to be more serious than anticipated.

3. Doctors don't feel that they have time to explain the problems with antibiotics to parents in the time allocated for a child's sick visit, whereas it is quick and easy to prescribe an antibiotic.

4. Doctors aren't knowledgeable about alternatives to antibiotics and want to prescribe something they think will help.

9 The Centres for Disease Control and Prevention (CDC) has been on a several decade-long campaign to get physicians to reduce their antibiotic overprescribing. While there has been about a 20 per cent decrease in antibiotic prescribing over the past 20 years as a result, the rates of overprescribing remain shockingly high, according to the CDC and other researchers. (3)

Antibiotic resistance: A global health threat

10 We are in the midst of a global health crisis—antibiotic resistance, which is a direct result over the overprescribing and inappropriate prescribing of antibiotics, and the overuse of antibiotics in the meat industry.

11 Antibiotic resistance is not something that develops just in the individual—that is, it's not just that you become resistant to that antibiotic—it means that the bacteria themselves have learned to outwit the antibiotic so that the antibiotic is no longer effective in treating anyone who is infected with the resistant strain.

12 Each year in the US alone, over 2 million Americans acquire serious infections with bacteria that are now resistant to some or all of the antibiotics that we have to treat those organisms, and at least 23,000 people die each year as a result of antibiotic resistance. (3) Global leaders in public health have declared that these "nightmare bacteria" pose a catastrophic threat to every person in the world!

Five steps to preventing antibiotic overuse in your child

1. Promote health in your children: Preventing recurrent upper respiratory infections including coughs, colds, [and] sore throats is an important and logical step you can take to prevent antibiotic overuse. Less need for them = less use of them! A healthy diet of natural foods with plenty of good quality protein, good quality fats, plenty of fresh vegetables, and low sugar, reduction of chronic stress, playing outside and getting dirty to get exposure to natural probiotics in the soil, and regular hand-washing with soap and water (don't use antibacterial soaps—these also contribute to antibiotic resistance), along with a multivitamin that contains adequate iron, vitamin D, essential fats, and zinc, all support optimal immunity. The gut can also be nourished and the microflora supported with a probiotic.

2. Choose organic for your meats and dairy: While it may not be feasible for you to serve your family an entirely organic diet for economic reasons, at least use only antibiotic-free meats and poultry, and organic dairy. These are where the heavy

antibiotic exposures come from in the diet—so it's where you can make your money count most toward reducing antibiotic exposures.

3. Know your options—Get Smart: The CDC has a website called Get Smart that is dedicated to preventing antibiotic resistance through preventing antibiotic overuse. You can find information on the primary infections for which antibiotics are overused, how to know when your child really does need an antibiotic, and how to avoid unnecessary use. Included is also information on comfort measures and medical alternatives for common symptoms ranging from cough and sore throat, to fever and ear infections. I don't necessarily agree with all of the CDC's alternative treatment recommendations, particularly the liberal use of Tylenol and ibuprofen, which have their own potentially serious side effects, but the overall information is very useful and also provides solid information to bring to your child's doctor's appointment to share with the pediatrician in case there is disagreement over whether the antibiotic is necessary and appropriate.

4. Know your rights: Doctors are not infallible, nor are we omniscient. And not all doctors are aware of the importance of avoiding antibiotic overprescribing, so some may insist on the prescription in spite of the CDC's guidelines. If you cannot reach agreement with your pediatrician, you have the right to seek another opinion or to change doctors. You should not be coerced into giving unnecessary antibiotics to your child. If your pediatrician is, however, insistent, find out why—she may have a different perspective on your child's symptoms and of course the CDC guidelines are just that—clinical judgment is also important.

5. Use natural treatments for the symptoms of common childhood illnesses whenever possible.

References

1. Bailey L.C. et al. (2014, September 29). Association of antibiotics in infancy with early childhood obesity. *JAMA Pediatrics*.

2. Blaser, M. (2011, August). Stop the killing of beneficial bacteria. *Nature. 476*, 393–94.

3. CDC. (2013). Antibiotic resistance threats in the United States. US Dept. of Health and Human Services, Centres for Disease Control and Prevention.

4. Dooling K.L. et al. (2014, September 29). Overprescribing and inappropriate antibiotic selection for children with pharyngitis in the United States, 1997–2010. *JAMA Pediatrics*.

5. Williams, F. (2013). *Breasts: A natural and unnatural history*. New York, NY: W.W. Norton.

6. Osborn D.A. & Sinn J.K. (2007, October 17). Probiotics in infants for prevention of allergic disease and food hypersensitivity. *Cochrane Database Syst. Rev.* (4):CD006475.

Comprehension

1. Summarize paragraph 3 in one sentence.

Organization and Style

1. Whom would you consider the intended audience of Romm's essay? Support your answer by referring to specific passages.
2. Analyze the essay's organizational and/or stylistic features, showing how the author has helped facilitate the reading process; for example, you could consider the order of points, along with structural and linguistic features. If appropriate, you could also consider how Romm could have improved the essay's readability.
3. Identify and explain the importance of two of the following rhetorical patterns in the essay:
    *   cost–benefit analysis;
    *   problem–solution;
    *   reasons; and
    *   cause–effect.

Critical Thinking

1. In paragraph 1,
    a. give one example of the author's effective use of deductive reasoning (see Chapter 4, p. 44). (Hint: look for a general claim or assumption that appears valid.); and
    b. In the same paragraph, give one example of the effective use of inductive reasoning (see Chapter 4, p. 44). (Hint: look for a point that is supported by factual evidence.)
2. The essay lacks a conventional or traditional conclusion. Do you believe that such a conclusion helps or is needed? Why or why not?

IV What Does It Take to Be a Leader?

While most of us acknowledge the importance of leadership in today's world, finding an adequate definition of "leadership" can be problematic. Bill Gates, co-founder of Microsoft, defined leadership as the ability to empower people; others stress a leader's vision or goal-oriented thinking rather than focus on what a leader does. Mark van Vugt, a leadership scholar, divides leadership into specific sub-categories: planning, communication, group decision-making, competence recognition, social learning, and conflict management.

All the essays in this section demonstrate the varied and complex applications of this term. Focusing on competence recognition, the essay "Do You Have the Brain of a CEO?" attempts to answer the question, what qualities make a successful CEO? Two other essays, "Steal Your Success" and "Raising Young Einsteins," take opposing views on the value of innovation. In "Steal Your Success," the author argues that it is often overrated and that most companies succeed by imitation. The author of "Raising Young Einsteins" begins with the assumption that innovation is essential to success but that Canadian youth are falling behind other countries in innovation; she argues that a new teaching model is needed. Although the fields of business, technology, and science are often associated with leadership, the author of "The Genius of the Generalist" argues that the skills of the generalist are needed now more than ever before. The author of "Thinking 'Bigger than Me' in the Liberal Arts" defines leadership partly as the ability to "adopt a different perspective" and include others in one's vision or art.

Natasha Milijasevic, "The Genius of the Generalist: Why Environmental Studies Is Essential to the Workforce We Need Now"

In "The Genius of the Generalist," Natasha Milijasevic synthesizes summary and direct quotations, taking on more of a mediating role than most of the authors of other non-academic essays in this textbook (see "Steal Your Success" on p. 256 for an essay that uses a similar approach). In such essays, writers provide essential summaries but rely more on direct quotations, often placing key points in the words of their sources. In this way, they give immediacy and relevance to the issues raised in the text.

Preparing to Read

1. What associations do you have with the word "generalist"? For example, is it primarily a positive or a negative term? Reflect on the connotations of the word and the reason you have specific associations.

The Genius of the Generalist: Why Environmental Studies is Essential to the Workforce We Need Now

Natasha Milijasevic

Alternatives Journal, 2014
(3348 words)

"The future will belong to the nature-smart—those individuals, families, businesses, and political leaders who develop a deeper understanding of the transformative power of the natural world and who balance the virtual with the real. The more high-tech we become, the more nature we need."

—Richard Louv

1   Predicting the best career options for the next four years, or the next 20, seems next to impossible these days. Today's post-secondary students are overwhelmed with choice, anxiety, and the worst job prospects in three generations. The current youth unemployment rate for Canadians ages 15 to 24 was 13.2 per cent in July 2014. That number doesn't include the rampant underemployment that sees educated young Canadians stuck in down-market service jobs well after graduation. At the same time, companies are complaining about skills shortages. It's no wonder that Canadian students (and their parents) are frustrated and uncertain about how to approach this rite of passage into adulthood and acquire employable skills.

2   Overwhelmingly, science, technology, engineering, and mathematics—the so-called STEM disciplines—lead to the best-remunerated professions for new post-secondary graduates. According to PayScale Inc., an online compensation information company, the average salary for a computer software engineer in 2013 was $65,885 per year, while a mining or petroleum engineer could expect to make $79,068 and $85,188, respectively. In contrast, graduates in environmental disciplines could expect to make comparably less straight out of school, if they can find employment at all. The average salary for an environmental consultant last year was $51,038, while environmental scientists made $50,749. This pattern is reflected south of the border as well; a July 2014 issue of *Forbes* reported that the highest paying jobs in the US in 2013 were in drilling, petroleum, or mining engineering.

3   We can't intensify our extraction of resources while also hoping to rely on technology to innovate us out of our planet's ecological mess. The educational biases of our time continue to accelerate outcomes that are dire yet predictable. We certainly need technologists

and other specialists. But our societal focus on specialized education to the exclusion of other disciplines exacerbates a distressing imbalance.

4   It was not always this way.

5   In Western classical antiquity, a well-rounded education was considered essential to participation in civic life. Those fortunate enough to receive an education would learn multiple languages, musical instruments, poetry, mathematics, theology, and philosophy. Such individuals were referred to as polymaths, Greek for "having learned much," and they could draw on diverse bodies of knowledge to solve problems.

6   Prominent Renaissance author Baldassare Castiglione described the idealized human of his time as broadly articulate and ethical courtiers, who benefited their fellow citizens by bringing their fluency in a variety of subjects to civic debates and diplomatic engagements. This polymath ideal contributed to a wealth of scientific discoveries over the centuries following the Renaissance—the printing press, pocket watch, and telescope, among others. But as knowledge grew, information expanded exponentially, and specialized knowledge and skill areas also increased. Universities splintered into silos of specialized faculties. In the twentieth century, organizations including corporations also evolved to have departments like marketing, finance, and manufacturing, all operating as distinct entities. As organizational structures became compartmentalized, thinking became compartmentalized. Over the same time period, our planet's ecology became dirtier, hotter, and increasingly imbalanced.

7   The drive to rebalance priorities compels many to study environmental disciplines.

8   "I have found peace and connection in nature since I was a child," says Caitlin Langlois Greenham, who waded into the job market in 2007 with a bachelor of science in environmental biology and technology from North Bay's Nipissing University and a joint diploma in environmental protection and compliance from Canadore College. "Unfortunately, my courses at school gave me an apolitical view of nature, where people were perceived as separate. I wanted to learn about the reality of the integration between nature and the people living within it."

9   Greenham's desire for a more practical integrative experience led her to work for several years in environmental education with community groups, and later compelled her to return to continue an environmental education. To honour her desire to see environmental problems through various lenses (including a political one), she began a master of environmental studies and a post-graduate diploma in environmental education at Toronto's York University in 2010.

10   "My master's integrated people with nature for me, through a focus on permaculture, food justice, and popular education," says Greenham. "The participatory education projects I was able to engage in were wonderful." Putting her education into practice included participatory permaculture design with Toronto's High Park Children's Garden and contributing to the Growing Food and Justice for All Initiative, an organization that strives to empower low-income and communities of colour through sustainable and local agriculture.

11   Like others of the so-called Generation Y cohort, Greenham cobbles together a living through several jobs—urban farming, community organizing, and teaching permaculture practices. She is the co-founder of Sage Rising, a decentralized urban herb farm comprised of shared yard spaces in downtown Toronto, and she also works with the North York Harvest

Food Bank, where "we invite people to garden together and share the harvest while they wait to access the food bank."

12 Asked about the value of being an environmental studies graduate, Greenham says, "we live in a specialized society, but we need generalists—bridge-people—who can make connections between community and business, health and the environment." Being a generalist diversifies your portfolio of employable skills and strategic problem-solving abilities. "If you return to the ecological metaphor, animals that are generalists, like squirrels and raccoons, are the ones who have prospered in urban spaces!"

13 Using different lenses and frameworks often leads to creative solutions, especially when harnessing the power of community and social Justice.

14 "My environmental education has provided me with an understanding of how important connections—of trust and respect—made at the grassroots level are key determinants of social, environmental, and political change," explains Rolie Srivastava, also a graduate of York's master of environmental studies program. "The value you bring is in your understanding of multiple systems, your ability to connect between them, and then to apply your knowledge and skills as required."

15 Originally from Winnipeg, Srivastava focused her' master's research in the early 1990s on biodiversity conservation. She worked for the International Development Research Centre (IDRC) during her degree, and later examined the illegal trafficking of flora and fauna, eventually setting up an international medicinal plants network and database accessible to partners across continents, organizations, researchers, and traditional healers.

16 Srivastava is currently a social networks researcher at the Centre for Sustainable Food Systems at Wilfrid Laurier University in Waterloo, Ontario. She helps enable linkages and information sharing between local, regional, and provincial organizations working in food security and distribution. She says her education taught her how to establish sound, meaningful personal relationships to organize change, whether face-to-face or virtually.

17 Cam Collyer, a program director at the national advocacy and empowerment organization Evergreen, also highlights the value of an integrative systems approach when tackling environmental challenges. "One of the things I liked about environmental studies is that I was able to learn about a variety of issues—energy, biology, policy, to name a few. I studied the great nature writers. It helped me gain a range of perspectives and experiences which I still use to this day."

18 Collyer works out of Evergreen Brick Works, the NGO's multi-use conservation complex in Toronto, directing children's programs including camps, weekend activities, and school visits. He also manages the Toyota Evergreen Learning Grounds, a national greening effort. Collyer studied at Trent University in the 1990s before completing a postgrad degree at Queen's University specializing in Outdoor and Experiential Education. "I encourage students to explore a range of topics within environmental studies so that they can understand the issues: the natural sciences, the levers of change, the policy mechanisms, the history of ecological issues, [and] the on-the-ground perspective."

19 He also tries to channel his former professors' highly motivating activist natures. "It's not merely an academic path that changes the world," he says. "My education was a direct background for my career, but it also taught me engagement and network building." And Collyer believes those networks offer both career

and personal resilience. "Engagement in society provides us with perspective and builds empathy and compassion. A sense of engagement, coupled with strong social networks, helps us navigate life's highs and lows, create opportunities, and stimulate our development."

20   Just as a liberal arts education is said to be a rock in the foundation of liberty in democratic societies, so too has an environmental education become a core element of resilient societies. A common narrative emerges from conversations with environmental studies graduates from the 1980s, 90s, 2000s, and 10s. Environmental education teaches how to be in the world, how to connect and partner with others to achieve a goal, how to synthesize disparate worldviews and consider innovative possibilities as solutions. This is a modern take on a classically integrative education.

21   Julie Forand started her adult life as a ski racer but in 2006, she began pursuing a diploma in fashion at Vancouver's Art Institute. After six years of working in the fashion industry in Montreal, she yearned to make a more positive social impact and enrolled at Ontario College of Applied Design (OCAD). "I went to OCAD for Industrial Design with a minor in sustainability in hopes of working to make supply chains more environmentally and socially responsible," says Forand. "The people I met in and out of the classroom were a source of energy for me."

22   Forand became heavily involved with the Sustainable Design Awards, a student-led initiative to inspire a grassroots post-secondary focus on ecological, social, cultural, and economic sustainability. In 2013, she started a business as an extension of her OCAD thesis; Sprout Guerrilla is an eco-packaging and design company that aims to encourage urban sustainability interventions. The company's DIY moss graffiti kits have become a popular way for customers to green their interior and exterior spaces.

23   "You don't have to study something in particular to have an impact, you just need to be mindful, and create your own environmental education," says Forand. "Get involved! Whether it's extracurricular activities, volunteering—anything to help you create your path around the causes you are most passionate about."

24   Extracurricular activities have flourished alongside the growth of environmental studies degrees. Initiatives have spawned across Canadian university campuses, including efforts to establish more pedestrian-friendly streets or green terraces and roofs, or healing gardens where students can help plant flowers and vegetables—or simply come to relax.

25   Environmental studies graduates like Jonas Spring are also moving such ideas off-campus. Spring received a bachelor of sciences in agroecology from the University of British Columbia in Vancouver and a landscape design certificate from Ryerson University in Toronto in the 2000s. "What I learned about agricultural systems I now apply to the cultivation of natural urban systems," says Spring.

26   After graduation, Spring started EcoMan, a Toronto-based landscape design company that reimagines the gardening business by embedding stewardship principles into every service it provides. "My professors taught me that urban ecologies are micro-ecologies," says Spring. "I use a systems approach, aggregating specialized knowledge while taking a birds-eye perspective to come up with a strategy."

27   EcoMan designed and maintained the green roof at Mountain Equipment Co-op's Toronto location. "On a green roof, you essentially have an island ecology, because it's isolated from other ecosystems," explains Spring. "You have to plan for and accommodate wind

or bird-borne seeds that will rapidly colonize the green roof if they take hold. Something that might take 100 years in a forest may take only a few years on a green roof."

28 Spring takes inspiration from nature and designs solutions with lifecycle management in mind, thinking ahead to how the urban environment will interact with the plants selected. His work highlights the idea that we can't solve ecological problems with the same technocratic thinking that created them.

29 Innovation theorists say that governments, corporations, and citizens need to be more balanced—right- and left-brained, integrative—in order to truly address the problems we face today. Canadian business philosopher Roger Martin writes that successful people use integrative thinking to creatively resolve the tension in opposing models and form entirely new and better ones. Martin argues that integrative thinking has always been an advantage, but especially in our modern era of overwhelming information and complexity.

30 An environmental education provides individuals with holistic problem-solving and personal-engagement skills. Noel Padilla, manager of sustainability at the Ontario Lottery and Gaming Corporation (OLG), has helped his organization achieve its recent sustainability targets by using his knowledge and stakeholder management skills. OLG has reduced its energy consumption and paper use, as well as established volunteer green teams to address office-specific environmental issues in partnership with non-governmental organizations like the World Wildlife Fund (WWF).

31 "I'm blessed in that my career is a direct extension of my studies and early career experiences in the Philippines," says Padilla. "When I immigrated, I did not have to formally upgrade my education." Padilla arrived in Canada in 2008 with three degrees from the University of the Philippines—an undergrad in metallurgical engineering, a master of public administration and a PhD in community development.

32 "Mining is one of the dirtiest industries there is, but it opened my eyes and led me to seek out a job at the Ministry of Environment and Natural Resources in the Philippines," he explains of his early interest in sustainability. "Part of my mandate was to develop the country's natural resources, but also mitigate the pollution created through this activity."

33 Padilla went back to school after almost a decade of working in the government, focusing his PhD dissertation on sustainable community development. "I wanted to close the loop, so to speak," he says. "My undergraduate studies were focused on industry, my master's was focused on government; therefore, I felt a need to have the perspective of the communities in which I worked, which are equal partners with industry and government in achieving sustainable development." After graduating he worked with farmers in the Philippines to establish sustainable agricultural and forestry practices while meeting government goals for both industry and conservation—a challenging objective. He now applies his experience guiding communities, industry, government, and NGO partners toward a common goal in Canada.

34 Padilla especially values the work experience that led him to deepen his knowledge and commitment to creating change. "Don't confine your learning to the classroom—participate in outside initiatives," he advises students. Environmental studies students and graduates are passionate people driven by a noble goal, and Padiila encourages them to let employers *see* that energy. "Make sure your interest and enthusiasm come through when you are looking for work."

35 With dismal employee satisfaction ratings across the corporate world, screening for enthusiasm and commitment in the recruiting process might be a remedy to a long-standing problem. According to a 2013 Deloitte study, "passionate" workers tend to view new challenges as opportunities to learn additional skills, and they have a drive, commitment, and agility that make them resilient to rapid change. Passionate workers also possess a strong connective disposition—as do the environmental studies graduates interviewed for this article.

36 "I was always interested in the interaction between people and nature," says Laurel Bernard, who credits her passionately naturalist parents with her early interest in conservation. Bernard was raised in Nova Scotia and [earned] a bachelor of science and master of biology from the University of New Brunswick in Fredericton. Her thesis focused on the habitat and breeding success of Black Terns in the Saint John River valley. After graduating in 1999, she assisted her supervisor in the field, working closely with the provincial Ministry of Natural Resources. This experience led to a project assistant job with the Nature Conservancy of Canada (NCC), where Bernard now works as director of stewardship.

37 "Get as much experience in the field as you can because you need the practical skills as well as the education," she says. A true environmental education provides this kind of integrative knowledge—an academic background combined with experience in nature and society. "Sometimes I meet job candidates who know how to identify so many birds and flowers because of their love of the outdoors and the practical skills they cultivated through hiking, canoeing, and outdoor navigation. Somebody who is keen, self-directed, and self-motivating is the kind of person that I look for."

38 Few fields allow job candidates to boast about their favourite hikes and wildflowers in an inter-

view. "You have to be pretty rugged for some of our field positions; it helps if you don't mind being outside In all kinds of weather," says Bernard. "We have employees whose passion for outdoor photography drew them to the outdoors—and resulted in amazing photos of some of our NCC properties."

39 The market now demands both theoretical capacity and applied experience, even in students' first jobs out of school. With high competition for few job openings, the prospect of training a new candidate often leads employers to opt for those with the most practical skills.

40 Irena Stankovic completed a master of applied science at Ryerson University in 2014 after receiving an undergraduate degree in political science and economics. She entered her postsecondary degree with clear intent: to find work embedding corporate social responsibility into commercial real estate. "I needed an education in that context, so I researched and reached out to a handful of leaders in that area, asking for information interviews on how to differentiate myself on the job market."

41 Stankovic found her dream job working as a sustainability coordinator for Triovest Realty Advisors in 2013, while completing her thesis about integrating sustainability in the Canadian commercial real estate and construction industry. "My willingness to learn how to integrate theory into practice made me stand out against other candidates," says Stankovic. To keep up with the requirements of her chosen field, Stankovic became a certified LEED (Leadership in Energy and Environmental Design) accredited professional. This designation has helped her better understand the requirements for energy and waste management, water conservation, and sustainable procurement in the construction and real estate sectors.

42 "Sustainability is becoming important to investors and tenants in commercial real estate,"

says Stankovic, who now helps develop and apply strategies with positive environmental impacts that extend to the company's stakeholders. "Triovest is joining the ranks of Canadian leaders who are seeing the value in integrating sustainability into day-to-day operations."

43 Integrating environmental approaches with a strategic organizational direction is a growing priority in many industries. "We believe strongly in environmental education," says Frances Edmonds, director of environmental programs for Hewlett Packard (HP) Canada. "I hire and mentor many students myself, including co-op students from Waterloo's Environment and Business program. We are committed to bringing up the next generation of students and providing them work experience in the intersection between business and environment."

44 HP has demonstrated a long-term dedication to sustainability. "We created the HP Eco Advocate program and champion the WWF living Planet at Work program to educate not only our workforce, but those of other companies, even ones we don't do business with," Edmonds adds. "We take the environmental expertise we have, make it freely available via the web, and invite the employees of our customers and other organizations to green their own business."

45 When polled in 2013, more than 90 per cent of HP employees said being a sustainability leader is important both to their business and their customers' business. Because the majority of the company's carbon footprint is created by customer organizations, everyone within HP is encouraged to become environmentally literate and work with their customers to reduce the collective environmental impact of HP's products and services.

46 In preparing for a career in a company like HP, "it is really important to understand how business works and how to apply environmental principles to reducing footprint within the business," says Edmonds. She envisions a future where sustainability is built into every job function. "Sustainability is a team sport. We need people of all designations to be thinking about this, and collaborating, to move the needle forward as fast as we can."

Comprehension

1. What is the "polymath ideal" (par. 6)? Explain why this ideal is absent today from education and corporations, according to the author.

2. Using the mixed format method for integrating sources (see p. 70), combine a summary of paragraph 20 with 3–5 words of direct quotation (use the most significant words in the paragraph for the direct quotation). Aim for a word count of about 30.

Organization and Style

1. Like many non-academic essays, "The Genius of the Generalist" does not contain a clear thesis statement early in the essay:

    a. Scan the first third of the essay (up to par. 15) to try to locate the thesis; and

    b. In your own words, come up with a one-sentence thesis statement applicable to the essay.

2. After breaking the essay into four or five logical divisions, provide brief content (descriptive) headings for each section.

3. With reference to at least three consecutive paragraphs, show how Milijasevic integrates summary and direct quotations into her essay.

Critical Thinking

1. Although many non-academic writers rely on expert evidence for support, Milijasevic relies more on anecdotal evidence (i.e., those whose experience with or observations on the subject give them credibility).

   a. What do the examples of anecdotal sources have in common and how do they differ? In order to answer these questions, refer to at least three such anecdotal sources.

   b. Do you believe that the use of anecdotal evidence was effective given the author's topic and approach to the topic? Why or why not?

2. Which do you think is seen as more valuable to those Milijasevic uses as sources in her essay: education or practical experience? Support your points with textual references.

3. Collaboratively or individually, consider the function today of the "generalist" in areas other than the environmental sciences. How might the skills of the generalist be applied to other disciplines? How can these skills benefit society as a whole?

Steven J. Tepper, "Thinking 'Bigger than Me' in the Liberal Arts"

Academic and non-academic writers need to be attuned to cultural shifts and variations and often study their significance. In "Thinking 'Bigger than Me' in the Liberal Arts," Steven J. Tepper argues to draw attention to a contemporary trend which, though once praised, he now sees as problematic. Using both experts and academic studies, Tepper attempts to support his claim that "iCreativity" undermines the fundamental idea of creativity as process.

 ## Preparing to Read

1. Have you ever published your creative endeavours online, such as on YouTube or other online collaborative communities? If so, reflect on the experience and/or your observations about others' experiences. If you have not, have you ever considered it? What might lead you to do so?

2. Who is Steven J. Tepper? Using reliable sources, write a 2–3 sentence biography of him. How does Tepper try to establish his credibility in the first paragraph?

Thinking "Bigger than Me" in the Liberal Arts

Steven J. Tepper

The Chronicle of Higher Education, 19 September 2014
(1429 words)

1   A decade ago, arts leaders faced a crisis in America. National data indicated significant declines in attendance at venues for virtually every art form—classical music, dance, theatre, opera, jazz, museums. Bill Ivey, a former chairman of the National Endowment for the Arts, and I offered a counternarrative[1] in 2006: We saw a renaissance in creativity and cultural engagement, made possible, in part, by new technology. Guitar sales had tripled in the course of the decade; 25 per cent of college students in one study indicated that they had produced their own music and posted it online. "Pro-ams" were on the rise—people who were not making money at their art but were part of robust creative and collaborative communities. More than 100 hours of content uploaded to YouTube every minute suggested the emergence of new forms of online creativity.

2   I now believe the pendulum has swung too far.

3   Much of the cultural activity we celebrated in 2006 could be categorized as "iCreativity," emphasizing personal expression, identity, individual customization, convenience, and choice. Too often that has turned into what I will call "me experiences." Market researchers call this the era of IWWIWWIWI (I Want What I Want When I Want It). In both culture and education, what we need are more "bigger-than-me experiences."

4   Self-confidence is great, but not at the expense of considering others. A survey of high school students that has been repeated for the past 60 years presents a startling picture. In 1950, 12 per cent of students agreed with the statement, "I am a very important person." By 1990 that had risen to 80 per cent. Other scholars have found[2] that student scores on an index of empathy have been going down over the same period. Moreover, recent research in cognitive science suggests[3] that media overload (often implicated in iCreativity) may reduce compassion, empathy, moral reasoning, and tolerance. For many young people, if they cannot insert themselves into an experience—capture it in what some observers call "life-catching"—and share it online with friends—then it is not worth the effort.

5   "Me experiences" are different from "bigger-than-me experiences." "Me experiences" are about

TABLE 1	"Me Experiences" versus "Bigger-than-Me Experiences"

In college society, creativity has become defined as self-expression. There's much more to it.

ME	BIGGER THAN ME
Voice: What do I have to say?	Insight: What do I need to know?
Expression	Reflection
Doing	Undergoing
Pleasure (Hedonic)	Purpose (Eudaimonic)
Identity	Identification
Egoistic Imagination	Empathic Imagination
Entertainment	Enlightenment
Everyday	Sublime

Source: Steven J. Tepper.

voice; they help students express themselves. The underlying question they begin with is, "What do I have to say?" BTM experiences are about insight; they start with, "What don't I know?" Voice comes after reflection. "Me experiences" are about jumping into a project and making something—an idea, an artifact, a piece of media. BTM focuses on John Dewey's notion of "undergoing"—making something happen in the world, which requires, first, a shift in our own subjectivity. We must anticipate problems, struggle with ideas, [and] seek some resolution. It's a process.

6   "Me experiences" aim at maximizing pleasure, rewards, and positive affect. Getting an A on an exam; getting a dozen "likes" on a Facebook or Instagram post; being the centre of attention. On the other hand, "bigger-than-me experiences" pursue positive relations with others, feeling a sense of purpose, helping solve a collective problem. They also promote an attribute central to creativity: imagination. In "me experiences," the ego shapes imagination, providing us with material to envision who we are and what we might become. "Bigger-than-Me experiences" help us develop our empathic imagination—putting ourselves in another's shoes, adopting a different perspective, and trying to identify with a different place, time, or people.

7   Many of us believe deeply in fostering a sense of "bigger than me" in liberal arts education. But it is easy to drift away from that—trying to meet students where they are; encouraging them to make stuff through new media (often without deep reflection); giving them choices so that they can find a topic that fits an existing interest; and filling our classes with "doing" rather than "undergoing" as we rush from assignment to assignment and grade to grade.

8   As educators, how do we nurture "bigger-than-me experiences" in the generation committed to "me?" One way is to radically change students' temporal experience. For example, Jennifer Roberts, an art historian at Harvard University, required her students[4] to sit in front of a painting for three hours at the Museum of Fine Arts. At first, they resisted the assignment, but then they discovered so much about the painting that they never would have experienced in the typical pace and focus of education.

9   A second strategy is to require students to become immersed in the perspective and experience of someone very different from themselves. A good example comes from an assignment in Ted Solis' music-as-culture class at Arizona State University's School of Music. He requires student teams—from all performance levels and musical disciplines—to work together to learn the musical technique of another culture. Then the teams create a new performance in that tradition, using only their voices and bodies, not their preferred studio instruments. Learning and performing without notation, and combining playing and moving, push them beyond their comfort zones.

10   In her book *Hiking the Horizontal*, the choreographer Liz Lerman describes creating a similar experience of "free fall" with students in a history class. She had them retell a sequence of events—for example, "write a story about what happened in school last Friday"—in which they came to realize that their memories were different from everyone else's in the group. Students experience the "rug being pulled out from under them" as each inconsistency reveals a lack of shared understanding about even the most basic and mundane aspects of life.

11   A third strategy is to invert fundamental roles and social relationships. Terry McDonnell, a sociologist at the University of Notre Dame, and Amelia Winger-Bearskin, an artist, teamed up

to challenge notions of privacy and surveillance. Students from one class were each told to "spy on" a student from another class (with that student's permission). Their task was to collect as much information about the other student as possible, identify his or her routines, and photograph or record video of the subject in public. The two classes met at the end of the semester, with the "spies" presenting fake Facebook pages of the other students based on all of the information they collected. McDonnell reports, "The students reflected on how easy it was to collect this information, the 'kinds' of people this 'representation' made them out to be, how true or biased the representation was, feelings of paranoia, and how fragile their notions of privacy were."

12   Finally, "bigger-than-me experiences" can emerge when an idea or object or text is introduced or explored in a completely different context or form. In his famous essay "The Loss of the Creature," Walker Percy argues that genuine learning happens when students are spared the distortion of preconceptions, expert opinion, previous associations, and other people's expectations. In the classroom, that requires surprising students by placing something unfamiliar in a familiar context. A biology student might, one day, find a Shakespeare sonnet on her dissecting boards; an English-poetry student might find a dead dogfish on his desk. Both could be asked to poke, read, explore, and learn about those objects before meaning is filtered through the educational complex.

13   Katharine Owens, an associate professor of policy and government at the University of Hartford, gets her students to cut through existing policy frames by asking them to describe a public-policy problem through the form of a haiku. The radical change in format forces them to see the problem in a new way. By playing with

unusual juxtapositions, changing the context of learning, and adding an element of surprise to the classroom, we can help students break with routine, get outside of themselves, and have "bigger-than-me experiences."

14   It is not a coincidence that many of the above examples of fostering creativity come from the arts. In spite of the perception that the arts primarily promote individual expression and voice, many of the core competencies developed through arts training create opportunities for "bigger-than-me experiences." In arts classes, students hone their empathic imagination, routinely shift contexts, ask "what if" questions, try out multiple perspectives, and, in the words of Lerman, experience the "free fall" of recognizing that reality is up for grabs and their assumptions about the world might not be shared.

15   Our pedagogical challenge in an era of iCreativity lies somewhere between "me [experiences]" and "bigger-than-me experiences." Or, as C. Wright Mills said, at the "intersection of biography and history." We need to inspire students to find their voices and make learning personal, but we must also help them realize that authentic growth comes as much from escaping as from discovering the self.

Notes

1.   http://chronicle.com.ezproxy.library.uvic.ca/article/Cultural-Renaissance-or/6435/

2.   http://psr.sagepub.com.ezproxy.library.uvic.ca/content/15/2/180

3.   www.dailymail.co.uk/health/article-1205669/Is-multi-tasking-bad-brain-Experts-reveal-hidden-perils-juggling-jobs.html

4.   http://harvardmagazine.com/2013/11/the-power-of-patience

Comprehension

1. What is the potential problem with self-confidence, according to the author (see par. 4)?
2. Using the information in paragraph 5, come up with concise definitions of "me experiences" and "bigger-than-me experiences."
3. According to the author, why might arts classes be well suited to the development of "bigger-than-me experiences?"

Organization and Style

1. a. Identify, then paraphrase the thesis statement.
   b. Identify, then summarize the paragraph in which Tepper makes the transition between pointing out the problem with "me experiences," as he sees it, and solutions to the problem.
2. Discuss the role of experts in Tepper's essay, drawing on two examples in order to show how they are used to support the author's points.

Critical Thinking

1. Do you think that Tepper is offering mostly constructive criticism in his essay, or is he more concerned with pointing out the failures or inadequacies of the present generation? Support your answer by specific references to the text.
2. Taking one of the four strategies discussed in paragraphs 8–13, come up with a concrete application of your own that would produce a "bigger-than-me experience" in the classroom. (This could be done individually or as a collaborative project that is tried out in class.)

Joanna Pachner, "Do You Have the Brain of a CEO?"

Joanna Pachner begins her essay "Do You Have the Brain of a CEO?" with a title and opening designed to intrigue the reader, but her use of first-person experience has a more complex aim (though attracting interest is one aim). Synthesizing personal experience with the evidence of experts, she provides a look at leadership qualities and the tests that are given to detect them.

 ## Preparing to Read

1. By the time you get to college, there is a good chance you have been interviewed for a job. What was the experience like? How do/did you judge your performance? Reflect

orally or in writing on this experience. (You could respond to one of these questions as a freewriting prompt.)

2. List 2–3 strengths you feel you would bring to a job that you would like to do (i.e., have applied for or might consider applying for); list 2–3 weakness for the same job. Show your list to someone who knows you well enough to comment on the accuracy of the items on the list (for example, a friend, family member, or someone you have worked closely with on a project). Briefly summarize in writing the friend's comments, focusing especially on any perceptions of strengths/weaknesses different from your own.

Do You Have the Brain of a CEO?

Joanna Pachner

Canadian Business, 2014
(3622 words)

1   About half an hour into my session with industrial psychologist Pamela Ennis, she performs a neat trick. As part of my leadership assessment, I've been walking her through my CV; as we reach 2001, when I returned to Toronto after a job in California, she suddenly asks: What leadership training do I think I would most benefit from?

2   "Making presentations," I say. I generally recoil from stages and speaker panels.

3   Ennis flips back through the legal pad on which she's been scribbling and points to the note she had written at the top of the first page. I feel vaguely disappointed at being such an open book. But her point goes beyond my avoidance of the spotlight. There comes a time in a career, she explains, when further advancement becomes more dependent on how others perceive you than on your actual performance. I tend to be a "storyteller," she says (a reference, I assume, to my rambling career summary). "You have to project yourself with greater forcefulness, presence, and gravitas, or others might underestimate your considerable abilities."

4   Sounds like a polite way of saying that I don't impress—an inauspicious sign for my leadership prospects, the feasibility of which I'm here to assess.

5   A legion of Canadian corporations recently acquired new CEOs: Guy Laurence joined Rogers (which owns this magazine) last December, one month after BlackBerry brought in turnaround artist John Chen to fix its ailing smartphone business; at TD Bank, Bharat Masrani spent a year (some might say his entire career) preparing to take over for Ed Clark, while across the street at CIBC, internal candidate Victor Dodig was given just six weeks before he replaced Gerald McCaughey. Odds are, each of these executives at some point underwent a leadership evaluation—a combination of interviews and psychometric tests, typically conducted by industrial-organizational psychologists, to gauge candidates' behavioural, cognitive, and personality traits. I began to wonder: What can a management shrink glean that's not revealed through standard HR vetting? More important, what qualifies as CEO material these days—and do I have it?

6   Filling a C-suite is a risky and expensive exercise, in search fees and the board's time, as well as in subsequent on-boarding and business disruption. A mistake multiplies those costs. An analysis by New York HR consultant Nat Stoddard pegs the price of a CEO mis-hire at a

large-cap company at more than US$50 million, based not only on salary and severance outlay but also factors like lost productivity and opportunities. It takes more than a year, on average, to remove a CEO dud. Turnover in the C-suite is at a historical high—Forbes estimates CEO tenure at the largest US companies to be less than five years—so it's no surprise organizations are increasingly tapping psychological assessments for insights before making selections. A study by Aberdeen Group in Boston found that almost three-quarters of the 516 companies the firm polled incorporate such assessments into the hiring process. "While recommendations go a long way, a lot of that information is provided qualitatively and may be based on the fact the person has clout," says Zach Lahey, an Aberdeen analyst.

7   Many executives go through the process several times over their careers, starting when they first show leadership potential, then as they apply for increasingly senior positions. The Ontario Teachers' Pension Plan, for example, started using leadership assessments a couple of years ago to help pinpoint areas where senior staff need improvement and to verify impressions of outside candidates. "We're in an intellectual capital business, and it has a lot to do with people's ability to fit into certain jobs," says CEO Ron Mock. While an executive may have successfully led a team of self-motivated portfolio managers, the traits that made the person effective may not translate into a higher-level strategy-setting role. "The thinking in this field [industrial psychology] has advanced quite a long way," says Mock, "especially in assessing people's future potential and their ability to change and adapt."

8   By the time a CEO candidate is subjected to a psych assessment, he or she has been thoroughly vetted and is assumed to possess the functional expertise to do the job. At that point, it's about fit. Say the company's heir apparent is being passed over but will remain on the executive team: Which of the two final candidates can best finesse that situation? Or, the company has a new board of directors: Does this individual have the ability to quickly gain their trust? "It's like a flight simulator for leadership," says Leslie Pratch, a Chicago-based psychologist whose book *Looks Good on Paper? Using In-Depth Personality Assessment to Predict Leadership Performance* came out in June. "You're not actually flying a jet, but you can see how you would respond in that situation without exposing yourself and the client."

9   What many boards seek today are people able to adapt to changing conditions and lead amid volatility. Pratch calls such executives "active copers"—always striving to overcome difficulties instead of becoming overwhelmed by frustration. It's not so much a skill as an orientation to the world, she says, "the ability to see change as an opportunity rather than as a threat." There's also a greater emphasis on balanced leaders, people brains and expertise but also the emotional and social intelligence to motivate and persuade all stakeholders. "It's like farming: You've got to take care of the land and know its strengths as well as its limitations," says Tim Gilmor, an organizational psychologist in Toronto. Ultimately, when Gilmor assesses leader candidates, he's looking for the individual's character. "People don't fail in jobs for lack of technical competence," he says. "They fail because their qualities of character were not a match for the role in the organization."

10   Before starting the process, I do a mental checklist: openness to change? Yup. I thrive amid the chaos of new ideas. Emotional intelligence? I find EQ to be such a vague concept; I feel optimistic but less confident. The character

issue is most intriguing, because that's not just about ethics, but values. Can a shrink interpret those accurately from a multiple-choice test?

11 When you're about to undergo a psychological evaluation, it's tempting to analyze your analyst in return. Pamela Ennis' midtown Toronto office is replete with flowers (a feminine vibe to disarm big egos?). The room is devoid of technology, aside from a standard office phone (to minimize distraction or a personal quirk?). When Ennis volunteers before our meeting that "on the one-on-one stuff, I'm considered to be hands-down the best in the business," is it an anxiety-alleviating technique or a big, fat boast?

12 Ennis, an attractive blond in her early 60s with a penchant for bright colours and a way of enunciating every word that suggests she's a practised public speaker, provides executive coaching, testing, and team-building services to many of Canada's largest private and public organizations. But her specialty is leadership assessment. Earlier in her career, she worked at the Centre for Addiction and Mental Health in Toronto, where she helped develop Ontario's Reduce Impaired Driving Everywhere (RIDE) program, but she was drawn to the application of psychology in management. A brief stint at an executive search firm was followed by a partnership with a former boss that also didn't stick. She started her own practice at 27. "I like to be in control of my outcomes," she says.

13 I do as well. I know what to expect: Prior to meeting in person, Ennis asked me to complete a series of eight questionnaires at my leisure. (Like most in her field, she insists that I don't reveal the specific tests.) Today, I'm to meet Ennis for an interview of about 90 minutes, after which I'll do a series of short timed tests in her office. Ennis will then interpret the results and present the findings in a report that's typically sent to the client firm and given to the candidate

during a second in-person session. "It's a developmental process," says Richard Davis, CEO of Kilberry Leadership Advisors in Toronto, who specializes in evaluating top-of-house executives at large North American corporations. "It's important the person should come out of it better than they came in."

14 Ennis warned me to keep my sense of humour: Some tests date back to the 1950s and are dotted with references to typing pools and door-to-door salesmen. One Saturday afternoon, I put my attitudes, personality, critical thinking, interpersonal skills, and knowledge of sales tactics and management through dozens of multiple-choice questions. Some tests seemed intentionally repetitive, offering similar choices in varied orders or in slightly different wording (do I prefer "to experience the unusual" or "have a variety of experiences?"). Ennis assured me that each test has a unique purpose and embedded subscales—as many as six—that only a trained practitioner can interpret. "There are all kinds of snake-oil salesmen and saleswomen who purport to have 'the one test,'" she says, "but you have to look at hard-core competencies, personality characteristics, motivational factors."

15 When I show up for our one-on-one meeting, I know the review has begun before I even shake Ennis' hand (which I make sure to do firmly, maintaining eye contact). Assessors will often ask their assistants to report on how candidates handle the process of arranging their appointments—were they courteous or difficult? "I'll usually size someone up within the first four to five seconds," says one management psychologist who asked not to be named. "Then it's a matter of validating that impression." Along with discussing the candidate's career, some will ask open-ended questions: What does this opportunity mean to you? What are your

strengths and weaknesses? But the answers matter less than how you reply, how well and how quickly you explain yourself, and how self-aware you seem. Of particular interest is the person's comfort in this unusual context. "The individual is now in a position where they have to comply when they're not in control," says the psychologist. "Many [powerful executives] have trouble with that."

16   I spend almost an hour describing my career while Ennis takes notes, rarely asking questions other than to prompt me to move on. This technique, I've learned from Davis, leads candidates to eventually drop their guard and reveal how events in their lives fit together. "You can almost see it emerging in people's minds," says Davis, "how they've made decisions and the way they were in high school, what that means about them and their connection to the opportunity." The patterns I detect strike me as negative: The longest I've stayed in a job is three years (I'm a drifter); I've turned down top positions to stay independent (I'm afraid of success). But I don't have time to mull as Ennis guides me to another room for the timed tests, which measure abstract reasoning and problem solving.

17   Psychologists differ in the value they place on tests. "When I started to do this about 12 years ago, it was the Wild West of test development," says Davis. Over the past half-decade, there's been some consolidation. The Hogan Personality Inventory and a few cognitive tests, such as Raven's Matrices and Watson-Glaser Critical Thinking Test, have become standard tools. The Myers-Briggs—which divides participants according to, among other things, their tendencies toward extroversion versus introversion and thinking versus feeling—remains popular, even though some practitioners question its validity. Projective tests, such as the famous Rorschach, are more controversial, and are used to assess how people handle ambiguity. Then there are so-called assessment centres, workplace simulations that involve daylong exercises in off-site facilities where candidates are put in scenarios they might encounter in their jobs: A disgruntled employee comes into your office. Can you see beyond their superficial complaint to the real issue? Psychologists tend to disdain such drills. "For a high-level role, they're pretty useless," says Pratch. "By this point, you know how to treat subordinates or organize your time."

18   Leadership assessments aren't infallible. Research shows that people can game their test results, though many psychologists argue they can spot fakers using metrics like "infrequency scales," which highlight inconsistencies in a subject's responses. Besides, everyone I've talked to stresses that a psychological assessment is just one data point weighed in a hiring decision. To prove assessments' value, psychologists tend to cite cases in which a hiring committee rejected their advice, and seasoned practitioners have lots of war stories. Early in his career, Davis was hired to assess a potential C-level hire for a Fortune 100 retailer. "Within five minutes of starting the interview, I knew he would be a disaster," Davis says. The person was a terrible fit culturally with the client company, yet throughout the process, the CEO, clearly a fan of the candidate, repeatedly contacted Davis, trying to influence his views. When Davis gave the candidate a strong thumbs-down, the retailer hired him anyway. The executive lasted four months. It was a public embarrassment for the company. "After that, the CEO became my best client," says Davis.

19   Such failures are traumatic for everyone—most of all, the hire. Some psychologists will even tell a candidate if they think the person is a poor fit for a job, but only if they believe he or she can absorb that kind of feedback. Those

least able to accept constructive criticism often tend to exhibit other red-flag characteristics, such as narcissism or a sense of infallibility. "Perfectionism is the most under-recognized trait that reliably predicts malfeasance," Davis wrote in a *Harvard Business Review* blog post titled, "Can You Predict Leadership Failures?" Additionally, when people get their first exposure to power they can be transformed by it, says Gilmor. "You can see more of the dark side emerge because they get the adrenalin rush. This is where you need to watch for the exploitive personality showing up." Gilmor has evaluated people he considered downright dangerous. "I've seen companies broken up because they hired a chief gardener and didn't recognize that he had a black thumb."

20 Three weeks after our first meeting, I'm back in Ennis' office. I'm nervous. Ennis has told me that she believes leaders are born, not made, and there is some research to back that view. For example, of the 16 Myers-Briggs personality types, four dominate leadership roles; the most common in big business and politics is the extroverted, intuitive thinker, or, to use the test's lingo ENTJ. "The whole North American leadership-development industry is predicated on the idea that if you send people to enough courses, you can make them leaders, but it's not true," Ennis says. "The environment can dial up or down what we've got, but it cannot replace what's not there in the first place." In short: You either have it or you don't, and I'm about to find out if I do.

21 The first thing Ennis tells me is that I'm smart—though she stresses that she's not talking IQ but analytical skills and "intellectual functioning." Mine are "absolutely first-rate" and in the "superior range" compared with other senior executives she's assessed. I mentally fist-pump.

22 There's more good news. I'm strong at both big-picture strategy and operational detail, which is a valuable mix in leadership roles. My Myers-Briggs profile (introversion-intuition-thinking-judgment, or INTJ) suggests, among other things, that I trust my own insights, regardless of authority or popular opinion—another vital leadership quality, says Ennis. This confidence in my own judgment, combined with resilience and responsibility for my actions, means I have emotional intelligence in spades. Additionally, I work very well under pressure (as those timed tests testify), apparently a rare skill. "Everybody thinks they do, because it's a sexy thing to say," says Ennis, "but all the research indicates that most folks crash and burn."

23 It's pleasing to hear about my strengths, but it's my shortcomings—or, as Ennis terms them, "exposures"—that I find more intriguing. A big one she identifies is impatience with slackers and the tendency to work around them. I know she's right, but I've never really thought of it as a fault. Ennis explains: A leader needs to know how to motivate and inspire all types. "It's gratifying for you to coach up-and-coming Joannas," she says. "It's a strain to coach people who are about 50 IQ points less bright than you and need constant reinforcement." I also need to boost my persuasion abilities. "A key leadership skill at the executive level is dealing with difficult people," Ennis says, "those irrational or hostile individuals determined to foil you. You need to know how to keep a sanguine look on your face while you're thinking, 'You're going to play that game? Bring it on. I will eviscerate you with such finesse, you won't even know you were cut open.'" It's chilling to hear this genial lady transform into Machiavelli. She then brightly informs me that the Ivey Business School offers a course on this.

24 The next one stings: "You're not the most empathic of individuals." I register strongly as a "thinker" on the Myers-Briggs scale, which means that when making decisions, I'm all business, giving little credence to subjective or emotional factors. And because I'm an introvert, I can be perceived as aloof. "You're very emotionally intelligent; socially intelligent is where you need some development," Ennis advises. It's slightly comforting to learn that most CEOs rank low on empathy. "They understand it intellectually, so they pay attention and ask questions about not just what people think but how they feel."

25 Nothing I hear comes as a big surprise, which is a common reaction. "The overwhelming majority of people who sit in this chair say, 'You nailed me,'" says Ennis. More than 95 per cent of the assessment is based on her interpretation of the tests, and she intentionally doesn't ask the candidates for any self-analysis. "If I come to you independently and my assessment resonates with your sense of self, then we can both be confident of it," she says. The interview is helpful, but secondary, she says. "An interview focuses on the present and past. I'm trying to look at future potential." And predicting rather than just describing is where a leadership assessment's true value lies.

26 I leave Ennis' office energized, believing I have vast potential, and just need to direct it in the right ways. Mock at the Ontario Teachers' Pension Plan had a similar reaction when he underwent an assessment with Ennis. "I thoroughly enjoyed the process," he says. It motivated him to ensure that his team filled the gaps in his skill set. "You have to be aware of your blind spots that could become impediments," Mock says. "I told my team, 'If you see them coming out, you tell me.'"

27 People who study leadership deal with a lot of misconceptions. For example, we tend to think of leaders as the best and the brightest, but that's usually not the case. "You have to be smart enough," says Ennis. "But the most brilliant of us do not necessarily lead companies or countries." Secondly, a born leader can be a lousy manager, and Ennis believes companies put insufficient focus on developing management skills such as coaching and delegating without losing control. Conversely, people who aren't natural-born leaders can successfully lead organizations by compensating for their shortcomings once they're aware of them.

28 Enlightened companies recognize this fact, which is why leadership assessments are increasingly used to identify talent worth grooming. When Ennis started her practice, the vast majority of her engagements involved vetting senior job candidates. "Now the pyramid has shifted," she says, "and two-thirds are developmental assessments of high-potential people." Canadian Tire, for example, appraises middle managers it's considering moving into executive ranks. "When we see potential, we want to help close their knowledge gaps and understand their underlying natural inclinations, what's in that person's DNA," says Olga Giovanniello, the retailer's vice-president of HR. Sometimes, an evaluation indicates that a person wasn't ready for a promotion or that their real value lies in a different role. "It's not that it's a surprise, but it helps you explain the why," says Giovanniello.

29 At the end of my assessment review, I press Ennis for a verdict: Do I have what it takes to be a leader? She hedges; there are long pauses. "I think you'd be a great leader . . . leading four to five people who are just like you: self-motivated, technically competent, not whiny," she tells me with a warm smile. "If you can hand-pick your A-team, they're gonna love you." However, she cautions me that taking on a top job would come at a high cost for me. The intense demands of

time and other people's needs would challenge someone with my strong independent streak. She has successful CEO clients with similar profiles to mine, but she stresses that I'd have to really want the job.

30 The ability to lead is ultimately an aptitude—an innate quality that needs polishing to shine. "A leader is an individual who can see the possibilities and creates the environment where people allow themselves to be led because they want to follow," says Ennis. "This type of person tends to be self-directed and independent, and might question authority, so in their early careers, there are attempts to rein them in or drum them out." Psychological assessments' fundamental promise for employers is to help identify such people, so they can be encouraged to take on the challenge before they leave for a competitor. As I drive home, I realize I've received this encouragement in the past and have demurred to retain control over my work, obligations, and time—to be the CEO of my own career. Ennis has helped me to see that I made those choices for good reasons—and that I have the potential to make different choices in the future.

 ## Comprehension

1. Summarize paragraph 19; paraphrase the following direct quotation from the same paragraph: "Perfectionism is the most under-recognized trait that reliably predicts malfeasance."

 ## Organization and Style

1. Analyze the essay's opening paragraphs, 1–4. What are their functions? Do they fulfill all the functions of introductions as discussed in Chapter 3, p. 27? Why do you think Pachner chose to begin her essay this way?

2. Analyze the author's writing style—in particular, her use of language, which could include diction and tone—with specific examples from her essay. In your answer, explain how this style reflects (or fails to reflect) her intended audience.

3. Analyze paragraph 18 and one other paragraph that is at least seven sentences long for their coherence and readability. For example, you could discuss the use of topic sentences, prompts, transitions, rhetorical patterns, paragraph/sentence structure, diction, and the like.

Critical Thinking

1. a. Comment on Pachner's use of personal experience, showing how it contributes (or fails to contribute) to the essay's effectiveness, including its readability; or

    b. Compare the use of personal experience in "Do You Have the Brain of a CEO?" to its use in "Is Scientific Progress Inevitable?" Remember that comparisons could involve similarities, differences, or both.

2. From the evidence Pachner provides, summarize in a brief paragraph (3–4 sentences) the answer to the question in paragraph 5: "[W]hat qualifies as CEO material these days?"

Joe Castaldo, "Steal Your Success"

Journalists, and, for that matter, many academic writers, often look for a fresh perspective on an old topic. This can take the form of a new approach to a common perception or accepted practice. Using experts, along with the views of entrepreneurs, Joe Castaldo asks whether the much praised concept of "innovation" truly reflects the reality of most successful businesses today.

 Preparing to Read

1. Does the title of the essay surprise you?
   a. Based on the title, what do you think the essay will be about?
   b. After reading the first two paragraphs, come up with a one-sentence statement that summarizes the author's topic.

Steal Your Success

Joe Castaldo

Canadian Business, July 2014
(1861 words)

1   In May, HootSuite CEO Ryan Holmes responded to new competition with some old poetry. His competitor, Salesforce, announced a product called Social Studio, a tool for businesses to manage and analyze all of their social media feeds. It happened to be a direct challenger to HootSuite, a Canadian firm that counts half of the Fortune 500 as users of its own social media dashboard. Holmes wasn't bothered by Salesforce's assault. "Reminds me of my favourite Kipling quote," he tweeted, along with a link to the passage in question: "They copied all they could follow / but they couldn't copy my mind / so I left them sweating and stealing / a year and a half behind."

2   Holmes shouldn't be so cavalier about a deep-pocketed imitator gunning for his customers. The history of business shows that copycats can be just as successful—if not more so—than originators. "People have been almost intentionally blind and simply do not want to see the evidence in front of them," says Oded Shenkar, a professor at the Fisher College of Business at the Ohio State University and an imitation-in-business researcher. "Innovation" has somehow become the defining buzzword of our times. Tech companies are obsessed with disruption and profess to be on a mission to change the world. Bestselling business books often centre on the importance of innovation in one way or another. Shenkar likens it to a religion in North America, one that is never questioned. Innovation, invention, and getting to market first [are] often considered crucial to success. But one of the most important skills a business person or entrepreneur can learn is how to copy effectively.

3   Think of just about any company today, and you'll find evidence of imitation. McDonald's founder Ray Kroc was inspired by White Castle. Johnson & Johnson first introduced disposable

diapers in the US, but it was crushed by Procter & Gamble, whose Pampers line was cheaper. Walmart founder Sam Walton was an original thinker to be sure, but he was also a ruthless copycat. In the early days, he skulked around other discount stores to figure out how they worked. He met with executives from long-forgotten chains like Mammoth Mart and Zayre to glean intelligence. Walton frequently visited Kmart locations, too. "They were the laboratory, and they were better than we were," he once recounted. In his autobiography, he wrote, "Most everything I've done, I've copied from somebody else."

4   Academic literature supports the notion that we're putting too much emphasis on novelty and invention. A 2003 paper in *Management Science* found that while we assume new, innovative products will yield profit, there is a "lack of strong and direct empirical support in the published literature." A 2007 study in the *Journal of the Academy of Marketing Science* attempted to quantify the advantage of being first to market and found the benefits are "not as dramatic as some have implied." Originators captured 7 per cent of the market for their products, according to research from American business professors Peter Golder and Gerard Tellis. And yet a study from way back in 1986 found that a company that is second or even third to market [could] outperform the originator.

5   Yet imitation is derided and seen as distasteful. During his years of research, Shenkar found executives from US companies were reluctant to even use the word in reference to their businesses. Brazen copycats, such as the founders of Rocket Internet, are often ridiculed. Run by three brothers in Germany, Rocket Internet is essentially a factory that churns out copies of popular US companies for new markets. Linio is Amazon for Mexico; Zalora is a knock-off of Zappos, but for Malaysia. CityDeal was a Groupon replica for Germany that Groupon later purchased for an undisclosed sum. Some parts of Silicon Valley prefer to heap scorn on Rocket Internet. Tech writer Sarah Lacy of PandoDaily wrote that the company's founders are the "worst kinds of copycats," who "flit from shameless rip-off to shameless rip-off." But their sites generate a reported $3 billion in annual revenue.

6   The act of borrowing an idea to start a business didn't bother Canadian entrepreneur Eric Pateman. "I don't have a problem with that at all," he says. "You don't need to reinvent the wheel. You just need to make it your own." Pateman was on vacation in Paris when he came across a company called Edible Paris that organized culinary-themed trips and tours in the city. Pateman, then a consultant in the hospitality industry, wasn't looking for a business idea at the time, but his accountant had been giving him a hard time about how much money he was spending in restaurants. Pateman thought if he started a similar business, he'd be able to write off his dining bills. He later talked with the founder of Edible Paris—another Canadian, as it turns out. "She was more than comfortable telling me to take the idea back to Canada and run with it," he says.

7   Pateman even borrowed the name and set up shop as Edible Vancouver in 2005. He later renamed it Edible Canada, and the company now ranks No. 183 on the PROFIT 500. He didn't stick to his Parisian counterpart's model entirely, of course, adding things like whisky tours to his offerings and eventually opening a bistro and retail store. Pateman travels regularly in search of new ideas and encourages his staff to do the same. (He became enamoured of the concept of flavoured tonic water on a recent trip to Spain.) "That's how you get better," he says. "You never know what you're going to find."

8   Some concepts are easier to import and maintain than others. Beyond the Rack, a members-only flash-sale website founded in 2009 in Montreal, is essentially a knock-off of Gilt Groupe in New York. Both companies buy excess inventory or end-of-line apparel from upscale clothing brands at a discount and hold online sales for members. Chris Arsenault, managing partner at iNovia Capital in Montreal, participated in three financing rounds for the Canadian company. He wasn't bothered by the fact that Beyond the Rack was a clone. "There [are] probably 500 of these in the world," Arsenault says. "But what made the success of one versus the failure of others was the understanding of what makes this type of business tick."

9   Although flash-sale sites cater to fashionistas, it's not fashion knowledge that dictates success in the space. Instead, email marketing plays a huge role in enticing people to buy. "What differentiated Beyond the Rack is that it's probably the most efficient, most knowledgeable email marketing company out there," Arsenault says. (Both founders have marketing backgrounds.) Logistics is equally important to ensure timely delivery. The company struggled with that at first, but later recruited the ex-head of logistics from Amazon.

10   Beyond the Rack also made for an effective copy because it had home-field advantage against Gilt Groupe. Securing inventory is crucial for flash-sale sites, and inventory is locked up by geography. Beyond the Rack was able to strike agreements with Canadian retailers for product early on to hobble would-be competitors. "It was very hard for any of these flash-sale companies to be as successful outside their country as they are inside their country," Arsenault says. Today, around 10 million people have signed up with Beyond the Rack.

11   Edward Yao, co-founder of group-buying website TeamBuy, didn't have quite the same advantage. Yao got the idea for the company after coming across the group-buying concept in China, and later found out about Groupon and its competitor, Woot. He launched TeamBuy, the first such site in Canada, with a partner shortly afterward. It was an easy idea to copy, which wasn't necessarily a good thing. "It was a double-edged sword," Yao says. "As soon as we realized how easy it was, we knew it was inevitable that it was going to be a crowded space." That meant Yao and his team had to hustle to establish relationships with small businesses, develop an image and build enough brand awareness to get ahead of competition, particularly Groupon. He borrowed concepts directly from Groupon and Woot, such as limiting deals to 24 hours, which encourages people to participate. Groupon did eventually set up shop in Canada. Yao, who has since left the company, estimates TeamBuy is number one in some markets, whereas Groupon is tops in others.

12   Imitation can make securing financing easier, too. Most investors are not looking for pure copycats to back, but they do feel more comfortable investing in a concept that's been proven to work. Investing is all about limiting risk, and an entirely new concept requires more money and time to educate the market with little assurance of success. "If you need to change the behaviours of people, that's a generational project. And it's very, very tough to change the behaviours of people," says Boris Wertz, founder of Version One Ventures in Vancouver.

13   For Mark Skapinker, a co-founder at Brightspark Ventures, the originality of a concept is not paramount when considering an investment. "The main issue for us is whether the company can create huge value," he says. Often companies are attacking the same problem

but have slightly different approaches. Protecode, which Skapinker backs, detects whether commercial software products are using open-source code correctly in order to avoid legal issues. Black Duck Software, an American firm, does the same thing and was founded a few years earlier. However, Black Duck's audits are conducted after the fact, whereas Protecode works in real time—a subtle difference that Skapinker believes gives Protecode an edge.

14 Indeed, the best imitators will take a concept and improve it ever so slightly. The consequences of failing to do so can be severe. Consider the BlackBerry Storm, the company's delayed response to the iPhone. BlackBerry couldn't match the experience of using the iPhone's touch screen interface, let alone improve upon it. Naturally, the Storm bombed. Imitation is a skill that entrepreneurs and existing companies need to approach with a standardized process, according to Shenkar at Fisher College. The first step is recognizing that imitation is not only acceptable but also crucial for a

company to keep thriving. "You basically have to admit that imitation is as important as innovation," Shenkar says. Successful copying then requires a system of scouring the landscape for interesting ideas, understanding what makes them work, and determining how and if the concepts can be adopted. "Once you acknowledge that imitation is a sophisticated, complex endeavour, you can begin to do it right," he says.

15 The world still needs people willing to do the hard work of coming up with radical new ideas and putting them into practice, of course. But entrepreneurs should realize that great ideas are often borrowed, and there's no shame in that. Arsenault likens it to evolution versus revolution. "With revolution, 99 per cent of the time you will die before it arrives. You serve as that company that had a great idea, but it didn't work out because it was too complicated," he says. "Which company do you want to be in? The one that failed—or the one that picked up someone else's product and made something else out of it?"

 ## Comprehension

1. a. Summarize paragraph 9.
   b. Paraphrase paragraph 12.

 ## Organization and Style

1. Castaldo uses various kinds of evidence in his essay. Choosing two of the following kinds of evidence, show how they contribute to the essay, referring to specific passages for support: experts, academic studies, and/or illustrations (examples that are fully developed to support a point).

2. Analyze the essay's introduction (the first two paragraphs) (see Chapter 3, p. 27) for its effectiveness in both attracting the reader's interest and providing a structure for the essay. For example, you could consider the opening, the thesis, organization, language and word choice, and the like.

3.   Divide the essay into sections that reflect the topic of each section. Come up with brief headings that could be used to summarize each topic.

💡 Critical Thinking

1.   a.   Why do you think the author used the word "steal" in his title when, clearly, mostly of his examples do not refer to dishonest activities?
     b.   Find two near-synonyms of "steal" in the essay that better represent the practices Castaldo describes. Show how the connotation (see Chapter 6, p. 104) of each word better suits the author's subject and purpose.
2.   After identifying where the author has addressed the other side of the issue, consider whether he has devoted enough space to this other viewpoint, supporting your claims.

Rachel Mendleson, "Raising Young Einsteins"

Unlike the previous essay, "Steal Your Success," Rachel Mendleson's "Raising Young Einsteins" focuses on innovation rather than imitation. As well, while the author of the former essay supports his thesis by examples from the business community, Mendleson applies the "Hole in the Wall" concept to the larger community of teachers and learners.

"Raising Young Einsteins" focuses on the ideas of Sugata Mitra. Like most researchers, Mitra does not draw conclusions based on only one experiment but tests his concept by repeating it under different conditions. In this way, the essay shows the stages of inductive reasoning (see Chapter 4, p. 44), beginning with a hypothesis, or prediction, and concluding with the results of the experiment and its possible applications.

 ## Preparing to Read

Where does most of your learning take place: in groups or by yourself? Do you think that most people learn the same way or by both and perhaps other methods? Reflect on the answers to these questions by freewriting on the topic or by discussing them orally with your peers.

Raising Young Einsteins

Rachel Mendleson

Canadian Business, 14 July 2011
(1953 words)

1   Sugata Mitra insists that he did not have "a particularly altruistic motivation" when he first discovered that the poorest children in New Delhi could teach themselves to browse the Internet. It was 1999, and Mitra, at the time chief scientist at a major Indian software firm, says he was "a little irritated" by the fact that new educational technology was most often piloted in India's best schools, which also benefitted from the best teachers, and therefore needed it the least. What would happen, he wondered, if disadvantaged children had access to the Internet? Would it enhance their learning, even if no one showed them how to use it?

2   To find out, Mitra punched a hole in the wall of his office, which was located on the edge of one of the city's slums, and installed a computer and a touch-pad mouse, as well as a video camera so he could observe. Within minutes, a group of children gathered around, running their fingers across the mouse pad and observing the effect on the screen. Almost immediately, they were browsing. "People said it will get stolen, it will get broken, but none of that happened," says Mitra. "Then all hell broke loose, because the media said, 'How is this possible?' It took years and years to show that it will always happen this way."

3   The revelation that disadvantaged children can teach themselves to use complex technology is an important one, and not just for impoverished communities. Consider how much time politicians, educators, and researchers spend talking about how to teach the next gen-

eration to be innovative. Also, consider how befuddled experts seem about how to accomplish that goal. Though neither well defined nor understood, innovation is widely believed to directly influence a company's (and country's) bottom line. And yet, when it comes to instilling this trait in our youth, the evidence suggests that Canada's on a slow slide to mediocrity. In 2009, Canada ranked 24th out of 35 countries in granting university degrees in science and engineering, a key benchmark for innovation. Our academic performance on the international stage, once a point of pride among educators, is also cause for concern. Despite maintaining stable, above-average scores, Canada's relative ranking on the OECD's prestigious Programme for International Student Assessment, which is administered to 15-year-olds around the world, is slipping. From 2000 to 2009, Canada's position in reading dipped from No. 2 to No. 5; in math and science, Canada's rank dropped to ninth and seventh respectively, down from fifth in both subjects. "There are other countries that are looking at the need to develop science and technology—innovation—in their kids," says Reni Barlow, head of Youth Science Canada. "As a result, though our numbers and our performance [are] still good, we're being passed by other countries that are now outperforming us."

4   If innovation is even half as important as everyone says it is, then the extent to which we encourage our kids to become creative, independent thinkers, and foster their passion for technology, science, and math—the traditional springboards for invention and discovery— could mean the difference between building a country that leads and one that follows. This seems like a good reason to put some serious effort into arming the next generation with the necessary skills and ambition to bring revolutionary ideas to fruition. But how? It's a vexing

question with no obvious answer, which could explain why one of the most promising solutions was discovered almost by accident, in a place you'd least expect. Experts tend to focus on universities and colleges as the place where we need to teach innovative thinking. Some might be bold enough to suggest starting in high school. But perhaps we need to start much, much younger. As Mitra's findings suggest, the secret might not lie in research labs, or even traditional classrooms, but in giving kids some technology, an intriguing challenge, and then leaving them alone to figure things out.

5   Mitra's initial conclusion—that if left to their own devices, uneducated children could learn to use technology—was indeed surprising, particularly in a place and time when the use of computers and the Internet were limited primarily to those who could afford expert training. So he set out to replicate the results, conducting another so-called Hole In the Wall experiment in a poor rural village, where the kids didn't even speak English. After two months, Mitra says he was expecting to find them "doing something fascinating like playing games." But when he arrived, the children informed him that they needed a faster processor and a better mouse. "I couldn't believe my ears," he says. "I asked them how they knew [about those things], and they said, 'You left a machine which works only in English, so we taught ourselves how to use English.' And then gradually, they began to understand what it was all about." In addition to playing games, browsing, and sending emails, the children had picked up some 200 English words.

6   As Mitra got similar results again and again (to date, Hole In the Wall experiments have been conducted in more than a hundred communities in India, Southeast Asia and Africa), he began to wonder about what else kids with digital resources could teach themselves.

Soon, he started to understand "the power of what a group of children can do if you lift the adult intervention." The learning typically went something like this: a small group of "experts" (the handful of kids who spent the most time at the computer) would be surrounded by a larger group who offered suggestions and proposed new ideas. These kids were in turn surrounded by a much larger group of observers. Quite often, the younger kids took on the teaching roles. And in a matter of months, hundreds of children would become computer literate.

7   By 2007, he had observed kids teaching themselves to email and play games so often that he wanted to test the capability of what appeared to be a self-organizing learning system. He came up with the most outrageous proposal he could think of: "Can 12-year-old Tamil-speaking children in a Tsunami-hit Indian village teach themselves the biotechnology of DNA replication in English from a roadside computer?" He set up the Hole In the Wall, gave the children the assignment, and allowed them to play. After three months, the kids initially told him they'd understood nothing. However, when he pressed further, he got a truly shocking response. "They said, 'Apart from the fact that improper reproduction of the DNA molecule causes genetic disease and deformities, we haven't understood anything else,'" says Mitra, who published his findings in the *British Journal of Educational Technology* last year. Their learning outcomes, meanwhile, were on par with those of similarly aged children in a nearby state school. "What is it that they can't teach themselves?" asks Mitra. "I think I'm on the edge of that answer now, and it's a crazy answer: groups of children with digital resources can teach themselves anything."

8   In recent years, Mitra has put the lessons from the Hole In the Wall to work in Western

primary schools. The method, which he has tried in classrooms in the UK, Italy, and the US, begins by dividing kids into groups of four, and giving each group a computer with Internet access. Unlike conventional group work, the kids are told that they can talk across groups, swap members, and observe what other groups are doing. (As Mitra tells the kids, this isn't cheating. "It's sharing," he says. "That's how people find out things.") The children are then given a tough question—anything from "Do trees have feelings?" to "Who was Pythagoras, and what did he do?"—and left to figure it out. When they present their findings 30 or 40 minutes later, they are interested and engaged. Consistently, they touch on concepts and ideas thought to be well above grade level. "We are not capable of understanding the size and the power of the Internet," says Mitra, who is now a professor at Newcastle University in the UK. "What I think I'm finding with these groups of children is that they plunge into this ocean, and they can swim."

9   In settings where teachers are required to adhere to a more stringent curriculum, Mitra's approach is perhaps best seen as a springboard for learning. When students at an international school in China were asked to delve into the question "How does an iPad know where it is?" they began to explore triangulation. "I went to the math teacher and said, 'You walk into your boring trigonometry class now, but you'll find that they're working a lot harder,'" he says. According to Emma Crawley, a primary school teacher in Gateshead, England, who has been using Mitra's method since 2009, empowering kids to direct their own learning makes them more confident, and more likely to start asking their own tough questions. "They kind of take things upon themselves a lot more. They develop an interest outside of the classroom," says

Crawley. "It can be used for anything really. We haven't seen how far it can go."

10   In many ways, Mitra's experiments simply reinforce what we already know (or suspect) about the necessary pre-conditions for innovation. In a recent conversation with *Canadian Business*, high school students en route to the prestigious Intel International Science and Engineering Fair highlighted the importance of having the freedom to come up with their own experiments. "You can really take your own direction. You really just go for it, and it takes you in many different areas," says Megan Schlorff, 18, who earned a place on Team Canada for her idea for generating wind electricity in developing regions. Working in groups is "the most important thing," says her teammate Adelina Corina Cozma, 15, whose computer-based communication system for people with autism went on to win several awards at the May event. "Being in an environment with like-minded individuals gives you a perfect [opportunity] to share ideas and just build on top of new ideas," she says.

11   It is no coincidence that the school system in Finland, the darling of the international educational community for its superior test scores, is built on an experience-based model, where science and math are taught through doing, and labs take precedence over textbooks. On top of having one of the best cohorts of teachers in the world (even primary school teachers are required to hold master's degrees), Finland has made hands-on subjects a priority. Whereas shop and music classes are becoming increasingly rare in Canada, in Finland, students spend a significant chunk of their weeks studying something inventive, like cooking, metalwork, or carpentry, and get 75 minutes of recess a day. As one Helsinki principal recently told *The New Republic*: "The children can't learn if they don't play. The children must play."

12 Perhaps the most pertinent lesson from [the] Hole In the Wall [experiment] is to give kids a break from the textbooks, standardized tests, and sit-up-and-pay-attention instruction for which North American classrooms are known. If the aim is to inspire the next generation to come up with creative solutions to the world's biggest problems (and show them that science and math are neither boring nor hard) an unconventional approach seems like a logical starting point.

13 "Experimentation in learning methods should be encouraged," says Paul Cappon, president and CEO of the Canadian Council on Learning. "Students learn best when they are engaged; when they perceive the significance of study in their real daily lives." Mitra's take is a little more blunt. "The Old World [idea of] innovation," he says, "where you sit in a quiet room and close your eyes and breathe deeply and ideas form in your mind—I don't believe a word of that."

Comprehension

1. What is OECD (see par. 3—you might have to do research to answer this question)? Why do you think the author does not identify it by its full name? (Hint: consider the essay's target audience.)

2. Summarize the main differences between the experience-based model, as described in paragraph 11, and the traditional approach that the author says is typical of North American classrooms (see par. 12).

Organization and Style

1. Show how the author uses facts and statistics in paragraph 3 to argue the need to "put some serious effort into arming the next generation with the necessary skills and ambition . . . ." (par. 4).

2. From the information given in the essay, write a one-paragraph biography of Mitra. You can also use one reliable source outside the essay to supplement your biography. (Note that Mendleson does not include all the biographical details in one paragraph.)

3. Analyze the author's use of summary and/or paraphrase, and direct quotations in paragraph 9 and one other paragraph.

Critical Thinking/Research

1. a. Write a rhetorical analysis that compares "Raising Young Einsteins" and "Steal Your Success" (p. 256), using at least two bases of comparison. (Remember that comparisons could involve similarities, differences, or both.); or

   b. Write a rhetorical analysis that compares "Raising Young Einsteins" and "In Defence of the iGeneration" (p. 195), using at least two bases of comparison. (One of the bases of your comparison could be the technological skills of the current generation as discussed by each author.)

For both questions, you could consider style, purpose, kinds of sources, rhetorical patterns and other organizational methods, appeals and other argumentative strategies, and the like. (See Chapter 3 for a checklist for writing a rhetorical analysis.)

2. Using at least two reliable sources, discuss the conceptual importance of the "Hole In the Wall" experiment and its relevance to today's researchers and professionals. For example, you could consider how the results of the experiment have been applied across different fields and disciplines.

3. What are the differences between the kind of group-focused learning described in the essay and more traditional individual-focused learning? Do you believe that Sugata Mitra's dismissal of individual-focused learning in the last sentence of the essay accurately portrays this method of learning? Using some of the ideas found in the essay, address one the following:

   a. Objectively analyze the pros and cons of the two methods.

   b. Argue for one or the other as a better learning method in general (i.e., for most people).

   Use specific argumentative strategies (see Chapter 4, p. 47) to support your claims.

What Is Critical Thinking?

Critical thinking (see pp. 108–14) is integral to successful essays. Common uses of critical thinking include challenging assumptions we take for granted, probing unexpected connections, and proposing unconventional arguments. In this way, critical thinking encourages readers to question what they read but to remain open to new viewpoints. The author of "Does Peace Have a Chance?" challenges the common perception that war is inevitable, while the author of "Slip-Sliding Away, Down the Ethical Slope" challenges our traditional way of thinking about dishonesty, which is summed up in his thesis that doing right is harder than doing wrong. The author of "Debunking the Myths" exposes the flaws in common arguments of climate change deniers, challenging their validity.

The authors of "Bullshit" and "The Selfish Metaphor" explore connections within our culture—between *insincere rhetoric* and culture and between *language* and culture, respectively. The former argues that while seldom discussed, "bullshit" is endemic to our culture and secretly works to undermine it. In "The Selfish Metaphor," the author explores the cognitive bases of our thought processes as they are embedded in language, helping to explain why opinions can be hard to change.

The author of "When a Cellphone Beats a Royal Flush" turns the tables on what seems a surprising fact: that more people currently own cellphones than have access to a toilet; using critical thinking, the author explains why this is entirely reasonable. "The Undiscovered Province" "modestly" proposes that Aboriginal self-government can best be achieved by creating a new province out of Aboriginal lands. The author of "Burning Mistry" does not target the act of book burning per se, as a reader might expect, but the dubious morality of a government that refuses to condemn it.

Robert Gibson, "Bullshit"

Non-academic writers often make extensive use of experts, such as researchers, teachers, or others actively involved in their field. Robert Gibson uses such an expert, Harry G. Frankfurt, an emeritus philosophy professor, to help organize his essay. Although not involved in research themselves, such writers serve a valuable function in spreading others' ideas to their readers while making their own contribution to the subject.

Preparing to Read

This brief essay appeared in a Canadian online magazine aimed at readers with an interest in the environment. For more information, access the journal website and summarize the purpose of the journal, using information on or accessible from its main page.

What does the word *bullshit* mean to you? In one sentence, define it using your own words; come up with two or three other words of similar meaning, considering some of the differences among them.

Bullshit

Robert Gibson

Alternatives Journal, 7 December 2010
(637 words)

1   Back in 2005, Princeton University Press published an engaging essay by Harry G. Frankfurt, an emeritus professor of moral philosophy. The title of the little book, which spent many weeks on *The New York Times* bestseller list, was *On Bullshit*.

2   Frankfurt began his essay by observing that although bullshit is a particularly salient feature of our culture, it gets almost zero serious attention.

3   Bullshit is one of the many occupants of the space between truth and lies. Among the others are nonsense and codswallop, bunkum, hooey, humbug, bafflegab, chicanery, and duplicity. Some are mean-spirited. Some are fun. Most are on the slope between highly irritating and largely harmless.

4   In this bunch, bullshit avoids attention because it is not obviously nasty and because it is too common and too easily accommodated to be immediately worrisome. Frankfurt says it is nevertheless deeply insidious because it undermines the expectation and practice of truthfulness.

5   Frankfurt defines bullshit as speech (or writing or even certain actions) that aims to influence perceptions and choices, but has no real concern for truth. The particulars of what is said may be true or untrue, but for the bullshit-

ter that is irrelevant. Bullshit aims only to serve an immediate end—to puff up the reputation of the speaker and/or to promote a product or a position. That is all.

6   Advertising is mostly bullshit—intentional misrepresentation by exaggeration and omission. But so is much of what passes for debate these days. Even reasoned deliberation often takes the form of various stakeholders arguing one-sidedly for their favoured positions. The underlying model is decision making in an essentially adversarial forum where each player takes a stand and argues for it. Compromises may be made, alliances negotiated, and agreements reached. It is even possible that some mutual lear ning and appreciation will emerge. But the focus is on winning, not understanding.

7   Environmentalists who claim to know for sure that we have only 10 years to save the planet are bullshitting. So are cornucopians who claim that technological progress will save us. Neither of them is seeking to present a well-founded summary of the full story. Their focus is persuasion, not truth. And in their world, the concept of truth fades.

8   Bullshit is not a recent invention. Over two millennia ago, Plato condemned rhetoric as manipulative oratory, and yet it continued to be a focus of education until the twentieth century. The old bullshit served established elites and the many conflicting versions of the One True Faith,

enforced by burning heretics and enslaving unbelievers.

9   The old bullshit survives today in the intolerant fundamentalisms of overwhelmed people grasping for certainty. In a big, complex, diverse and dynamic world, the simple faiths of the Tea Parties, and Talibans require massive ignorance. But the old bullshit is probably still less dangerous than the exaggerations and omissions of the post-modern bullshitters serving narrow interests. Their battles for influence based on swayed opinion threaten to bury the struggle for truthful communication, perhaps even truthful understanding.

10   More power, then, to the merry bands of bullshit exposers—the Yes Men, Adbusters, and Ecobunkers—who have been busily poking spanners in the spinworks. More power as well to the independent scientists, non-aligned journalists and collaborative researchers who have been quietly delivering reliable reports on the state of life on our planet.

11   Most deserving of celebration, however, are the activists who refuse to stoop. There is nothing easier today than to step down into the trough and fight one-sided bullshit with other-sided bullshit. Maybe sometimes the green poop will prevail, but the smell remains and the substance is corrosive.

12   In his other short book, *On Truth*, Harry Frankfurt notes that establishing and sustaining an advanced culture is impossible if we are debilitated by error or ignorance. Bullshit is an agent of debilitation. The only viable response is to rise above it.

◉ Comprehension

1. a. How is "bullshit" different from a lie? How is it similar, according to Frankfurt?
    b. What makes "bullshit" more dangerous than the other kinds of "untruths" mentioned in paragraph 3?
2. Using context, if possible, define the word *cornucopians* (par. 7); explain the phrase *spanners in the spinworks* (par. 10).
3. Summarize paragraph 11 in one sentence.

◉ Organization and Style

1. What organizational method (rhetorical pattern) is used in paragraph 6, paragraph 8, and paragraph 12?

◉ Critical Thinking/Research

1. How does the term *rhetoric*, as used by Plato (par. 8), differ from other uses of this term today?
2. Recall one debate you have listened to—it could be a debate among your friends, in school, or on TV or the Internet. How did it resemble what is described in paragraphs 6–7? Was it different in any way? Briefly summarize the debate, and in point form or in separate paragraphs, list/describe similarities and differences.
3. Using a reliable source, such as a newspaper or magazine, access a review of Frankfurt's book *On Bullshit* and summarize the writer's opinions about the book.

Doug Saunders, "When a Cellphone Beats a Royal Flush"

In paragraph 2 of the essay that follows, *The Globe and Mail* columnist Doug Saunders cites a surprising statistic concerning the number of cellphone users versus toilet users. While most people might respond by expressing shocked dismay, Saunders reasons that preferring a cellphone over a toilet might be a rational choice for those in developing countries. Using critical thinking, Saunders tries to account for the statistic.

 Preparing to Read

Do you consider a cellphone a luxury or a necessity? Why?

When a Cellphone Beats a Royal Flush

Doug Saunders

The Globe and Mail, 26 March 2011
(752 words)

1   About a third of the world's people have no toilet. This is both unsanitary and inconvenient. In villages, it's often customary for the women to rise at 5 a.m. and pay a visit to the field, and the men to make their pilgrimage an hour later. In cities, there are open cesspits, fetid back alleys, and plastic-bag "flying toilets."

2   Nowadays, it's increasingly familiar to see people composing text messages while engaging in such demeaning public activities. As we learned this week, 4.3 billion people have access to a toilet, and 4.6 billion people personally own a cellphone. This means there are 300 million people in the world, equivalent to the population of the United States, who have a cellphone in their pocket but no access to a toilet.

3   To many of us, this sounds absurd: A toilet is a basic necessity, whereas a mobile electronic device still seems like a frill or a minor luxury. People with family incomes below $2 a day shouldn't be buying $20 devices, should they?

4   That was certainly how it was taken when most people read those figures from World Water Day, which marks a worthy campaign to get proper sanitation to more people in poor countries.

5   But let's not discount cellphones for the very poor, or question their priorities. Why would someone want to have a cellphone before a toilet? I have met a good many people, on four continents, who have a stick of beeping silicon in their pocket but no slab of wet porcelain in their house, and while none are happy with the lack of sanitation, none would consider their phone to be anything less than vital.

6   There are a number of reasons why a cellphone is as important as a toilet, if not more so, for those at the bottom of the barrel:

7   *Toilets are about sitting still, phones are about movement.* A toilet in your house will

prevent disease and bring dignity and value to life. But life for the very poor is about constant change and risk. Poor people have to move house much more frequently than those with higher incomes; they have cash-flow problems and need to seize on ever-changing minuscule income opportunities.

8   They tend to make their livings from multiple sources—as economist Deepa Narayan has found, poor villagers manage by building "joint portfolios" of farming, small businesses, and casual labour in the city, to hedge their risk across several platforms. As the four economists who wrote the recent study "Portfolios of the Poor" noted, the world's poorest people endure the "triple whammy" of "low incomes; irregularity; and unpredictability; and a lack of tools."

9   Most of the world's poor now live in motion, with part of the family in the village and part on the margins of a city. There are more than 200 million Chinese families divided between village and city; they rely on instant mobile communications to avoid catastrophe and to find opportunities to escape their plight.

10   Poverty, in short, is vulnerable to sudden change. A phone at least provides a few more potential lifelines.

11   *Phones can mean debt, but toilets can mean eviction.* As anyone who's received a cellphone for Christmas knows, it's a gift that requires constant payments. In poor countries, cellphone use costs upward of $2 a month—so they can contribute to dangerous levels of indebtedness.

12   But they can also be ways out of debt. In Africa, small-hold farmers frequently use cellphone crop-information services such as Ghana's Esoko to locate buyers, get the best prices, and find out what to plant based on futures markets—a useful service for a Western farmer but a lifesaver for a poor sub-Saharan one.

13   On the other hand, when an aid agency hooks up a toilet to your shack, there's the risk that your property value will be raised above the poor-family level: great if you own, but potentially tragic if you rent.

14   *A phone won't stop your children from getting dysentery, but a toilet won't overthrow your dictatorship.* Yes, the people of Eastern Europe managed to overthrow their autocrats in 1989 without cellphones. But they used very similar networks built on well-established connections. Among the new classes of the Middle East, the cellphone has become vital for communicating new opportunities—not just in income, but in politics.

15   Increasingly, it's the tool people are using for dramatic reform. It doesn't have the comforts of a toilet, but it can help you flush away that stinking mess.

⬤ Comprehension

1.   Explain what the author means in paragraph 11.

📌 Organization and Style

1.   What is the primary organizational method in the essay? Identify one paragraph that uses the cause–effect method and another that uses the problem–solution method.

2.   Discuss the author's use of humour in his essay.

3.   Give three examples of informal diction (words or phrases) in the essay. For each, provide a substitute that would be suitable for an academic essay.

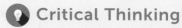 Critical Thinking

1. Analyze the author's argument, commenting on any argumentative strategies and their effectiveness.
2. Think of a situation involving two alternatives and argue in support of the "least likely" alternative (for example, that a high-school education is more beneficial than a college or university education).

Mary Midgley, "The Selfish Metaphor"

This article, which appeared in the popular science magazine *New Scientist*, considers the role that metaphorical thinking can play in scientific thought. *New Scientist* is designed for readers interested in a wide variety of science-related topics, so it is not an academic journal, though its authors often refer to academic studies.

 Preparing to Read

1. What is a metaphor and how is it used in literary writing?
2. Have you ever considered how common metaphors can affect our perception?
3. Can you think of a metaphor that has an everyday use? For example, how is the Internet "web-like"?
4. Access the *New Scientist* website and scan recent articles in order to determine the kinds of articles published.

The Selfish Metaphor

Mary Midgley

New Scientist, 29 January 2011
(1311 words)

1   Selfish genes, survival of the fittest, competition, hawk, and dove strategies. Like all theories, Darwinism has its own distinct vocabulary. So distinct, in fact, that we end up asking how else we can talk about evolution? After all, isn't competitive evolution the only possible context for explaining the biological facts? The drama implied by competition, war, and selfishness passes unnoticed because people are used to this rather hyped-up way of talking even about current scientific beliefs.

2   The trouble with metaphors is that they don't just mirror scientific beliefs, but they also shape them. Our imagery is never just surface paint. It expresses, advertises, and strengthens our preferred interpretations. It also usually carries unconscious bias from the age we live in—and this can be tricky to ditch no matter how faulty, unless we ask ourselves how and

why things go wrong, and start to talk publicly about how we should understand metaphor.

3   Evolution has been the most glaring example of the thoughtless use of metaphor over the past 30 years, with the selfish/war metaphors dominating and defining the landscape so completely it becomes hard to admit there are other ways of conceiving it. In *How The Leopard Changed Its Spots*, biologist and complexity theorist Brian Goodwin suggested the kind of correction needed, remarking mildly that humans are "every bit as co-operative as we are competitive; as altruistic as we are selfish. These are not romantic yearnings and Utopian ideals; they arise from a rethinking of our nature that is emerging from the sciences of complexity." But that was in 1991—and few were listening.

4   From the merest glance at a wider context, it becomes clear that competition cannot be the ultimate human reality, still less (as philosopher Daniel Dennett argued) the central creative force behind the universe. Entities complex enough to compete cannot exist at all without much internal cooperation. To create cells, organelles must combine; to create armies, soldiers must organize. Even the evolutionary biologist Richard Dawkins pointed out on the 30th anniversary of publication of his iconic book, *The Selfish Gene*, that genes are actually cooperative rather than egoistic.

5   So why has this imagery become so prevalent? Because it expresses deep conflicts originating in seventeenth-century England which are still unresolved in the western world. The central clash is between communal and separatist views of human nature. It rose out of the English Civil War, which shifted the world picture from a feudal, communal pattern toward the more individualistic, pluralistic model we

officially follow today. Ideals of personal allegiance, heroic warfare and the divine right of kings began to yield to civilian visions based on democracy, technology, and commerce.

6   That individualistic, post–Civil War world view has always been seen as scientific. This was largely because Newtonian physics viewed matter atomistically, as composed of hard, billiard-ball-like particles bouncing off each other in complex patterns—patterns which, under God, shaped that huge clock, the classical universe. Billiards, fashionable at the time, may have helped shape this view, while the vision of a vast, regular, unchanging cosmic machine was certainly reassuring.

7   The reality, however, was that society was changing unpredictably and would need other, very different kinds of metaphors and images—ones better able to reveal shifts and clashes of interest. To fill this need, philosopher Jean-Jacques Rousseau devised a kind of social atomism, along with the colourful individualistic metaphors it inspired and still inspires. Through this lens, people no longer appeared as parts of a machine: they were still atoms, but distinct, active, independent units.

8   But the philosopher Thomas Hobbes's claim that the natural state of humans was "a war of all against all" (put forward in a bid to stop people supporting misguided governments) accidentally launched a wider revolt against the notion of citizenship. The slogan made it possible to argue later that there is no such thing as society, that we owe one another nothing. This thought also inspired campaigns for admirable things like easier divorce and universal suffrage and it is still strong today, even though physicists themselves no longer see their particles as radically disconnected.

9 In the eighteenth century, economists eagerly applied individualism to commerce, arguing that free competition always serves the general good. Its champions could thus believe they were being scientific while still acting as good citizens. And its emphasis on conflict reassured them they were still heroes, that bourgeois life had not corrupted their machismo. So atomistic thinking, originally drawn from physics, acquired a social meaning in economics and was then returned to science as ideas of competition began to dominate nineteenth-century biology. The resulting jumble of atomistic ontology, laissez-faire economics and warlike noises came together fully in the theories of nineteenth-century "social Darwinists" like Herbert Spencer.

10 Charles Darwin actually hated much of it, flatly rejecting the crude, direct application of natural selection to social policies. In *The Descent of Man* he insisted that humans are a deeply social species whose values cannot be derived from selfish calculation. Yet, as a man of his age, he still shared Spencer's obsessive belief in the creative force of competition. He ruled that natural selection was indeed the main cause of evolutionary changes, and—apart from sexual selection—he could not suggest any other possible source.

11 He was sure, however, that natural selection could not be their sole cause. He must be right: natural selection is only a filter and filters cannot be the sole cause of the coffee that comes from them. "Evolutionary coffee"—genuine new developments—could not emerge unless the range of selectables has somehow been shaped to make it possible. If that range were indefinite only randomness could follow, however much time elapsed.

12 Biologist D'Arcy Thompson pointed this out in *On Growth And Form* in 1917, noting the striking natural tendencies which contribute to evolution—the subtle, natural patterns such as Fibonacci spirals that shape all manner of organic forms, and the logic underlying patterns such as the arrangement of a creature's limbs. Thompson's work was little noted in the twentieth-century's concentration on natural selection, but more recently biologists such as Brian Goodwin, Steven Rose, and Simon Conway Morris have developed his work, showing how natural selection is supplemented by a kind of self-organization within each species, which has its own logic.

13 Now the old metaphors of evolution need to give way to new ones founded on integrative thinking—reasoning based on systems thinking. This way, the work of evolution can be seen as intelligible and constructive, not as a gamble driven randomly by the forces of competition. And if non-competitive imagery is needed, systems biologist Denis Noble has a good go at it in *The Music of Life*, where he points out how natural development, not being a car, needs no single "driver" to direct it. Symphonies, he remarks, are not caused only by a single dominant instrument nor, indeed, solely by their composer. And developing organisms do not even need a composer: they grow, as wholes, out of vast and ancient systems which are themselves parts of nature.

14 Recognizing the cultural origins of evolution's metaphors and that we are slowly, painfully, creating new ones takes the drama out of things, but it does mean we will learn how to think about metaphors and their philosophical underpinning. We will discover we need them to serve us as thinking tools, not to turn us into slaves of our own conceits.

Comprehension

1. Summarize paragraph 2 in a sentence.
2. Why does the author use the domain of 30 years in describing the use of the selfish metaphor?
3. Why does the English Civil War represent a turning point in the world view of the English, according to the author?
4. Of what use does Herbert Spencer make of the selfish metaphor? What is "social Darwinism"?

Organization and Style

1. Identify two organizational methods (rhetorical patterns) used in paragraphs 5–9.

Critical Thinking/Research

1. In addition to the selfish metaphor, identify one other metaphor used by the author and analyze its purpose and effectiveness.
2. Using a reliable source:
   a. Summarize in two or three sentences the contribution of one of the following figures in the history of ideas: Jean-Jacques Rousseau or Thomas Hobbes.
   b. Explain in one or two sentences the importance of Rousseau and Hobbes to Midgley's essay.

Robert J. Sternberg, "Slip-Sliding Away, Down the Ethical Slope"

The topic of student cheating has garnered a great deal of attention in recent years—not only in academic journals like *The Chronicle of Higher Education*, published for the college and university communities, but also in magazines and major newspapers. In his short argumentative essay, Sternberg challenges a common perception that underlies students' unethical behaviour.

 Preparing to Read

1. What do you believe causes students to cheat? Make a list of possible reasons that can result in unethical student behaviour.
2. Read the first two paragraphs of the essay and, in groups, discuss answers to the questions posed by the author.

Slip-Sliding Away, Down the Ethical Slope

Robert J. Sternberg

The Chronicle of Higher Education, 9 January 2011 (893 words)

1 "You see your roommate at his computer, writing a paper. You notice him transferring text from an online document to the paper he is writing without attribution. He changes a few words here and there so he cannot be accused of plagiarism. Is there a problem here? What, if anything, should you do?"

2 "Professor Johnson is known for not giving back exams because he uses pretty much the same questions from year to year. Your roommate comes back to your room with a big smile. A fraternity brother has managed to slip out a copy of last year's exam and has given it to him. Your roommate figures he can get an edge on this year's exam by studying last year's. 'Not my fault,' he says, 'that Professor Johnson reuses his test questions.' Is there a problem here? What, if anything, should you do?"

3 In presenting problems such as these to various student groups, I have been taken aback by the number of those who either do not see an ethical breach or, if they do, feel that it is minor or not of concern to them. It's a problem that goes much deeper than the occasional incident—we find cheating on the rise even before students get to college, and many cheaters are more concerned with getting caught than with actually committing the act.

4 When it comes to unethical behaviour such as cheating, our society has, I believe, engaged in a fundamental misperception. It derives from our conviction that, through religious training or other ethical training—at home, for example—students have been brought up to know right from wrong and thus to behave ethically. The misperception is that it is easy to do the right thing, and that doing the wrong thing requires extra mental or other effort. In fact, the opposite is true: It is often hard to do the right thing, which is why there is cheating.

5 To behave ethically is not a one-step process: Do the right thing. It is a sometimes arduous eight-step process. To behave ethically, you must:

1. Recognize that there is a situation that deserves to be noticed and reflected upon.
2. Define the situation as having an ethical component.
3. Decide that the ethical component is important enough to deserve attention.
4. View the ethical component as relevant to you personally.
5. Ascertain what ethical rule applies to the situation.
6. Figure out how to apply the ethical rule.
7. Prepare for possible adverse consequences, such as retaliation, if you should act ethically.
8. Act.

6 All of those steps can be relatively difficult to execute, and, unfortunately, behaving ethically can be as challenging for parents as it is for students. Parents may cross the line by going from helping their children with homework, papers, science projects, and writing college-application essays to essentially doing the work. It is then little wonder that students reach college and hire others to do their work for them. This point came home in a *Chronicle Review* article, "The Shadow Scholar," by an individual who anonymously writes student papers for pay. Of course, it is not clear that professors are immune: Just as students are outsourcing the writing of papers, so are some professors now outsourcing

the grading of papers. One wonders whether our society will eventually eliminate the middlemen—college students and faculty—and simply have the outsourced writers and the outsourced graders work together directly.

7   More realistically, educators need to stop assuming that ethical behaviour is the normal course of action for a well-educated individual, and that cheating and other forms of unethical behaviour are not the norm. Rather, they have to assume that behaving ethically is often challenging, as any fired whistle-blower can tell you.

8   Schools need to teach students the steps involved in ethical behaviour and the challenges of executing them. And they need to do so with real-life case studies relevant to the students' lives. The steps toward ethical behaviour are not ones that students can internalize by memorization, but only through active experiential learning with personally relevant examples.

9   There is a larger question our society must face: Have we abrogated what should be a fundamental responsibility of higher education?

The financiers who helped to create the financial meltdown of 2008 were, for the most part, bright and well educated. Many were graduates of this country's finest colleges and universities. Is it possible that, in placing so much emphasis on grades and test scores, we are failing to select for and teach the qualities that will produce not just ethical individuals but also ethical leaders?

10   We have come, in large part, to use standardized-test scores and other objective measurements to provide opportunities to students who score well—opportunities that are much scarcer for others. But is it enough to look for such narrowly defined academic skills? Is it not time to search for and develop the wisdom and positive ethical skills that we need in order to steer this country *up* the slippery slope rather than *down*?

11   Once started on that slide, it is hard to stop before the crash at the bottom. Just ask any disgraced politician, executive, clergyman, or educator. While unethical behaviour may start in schools with plagiarism or stolen exams, we know all too sadly, and all too well, that it doesn't end there.

Comprehension

1. Identify, then paraphrase, the author's thesis.
2. According to the author, how can schools best address the problem of unethical student behaviour?

Critical Thinking/Research

1. Is this essay just concerned about stopping students from cheating? What other, larger concerns does Sternberg raise? Do you believe they are important ones?
2. In groups, come up with a real-life scenario, like those that begin the essay, in which unethical behaviour might be involved and share them with other members of the class.
3. In the short-term, what specific steps can be taken by instructors or administration to reduce the incidence of cheating at the post-secondary level?
4. Summarize the results of at least two studies that deal with problems of unethical student behaviour published in the last ten years; or, summarize at least two commentaries/editorials on the same topic, making sure the essays are from reliable sources.

John Horgan, "Does Peace Have a Chance?"

In the journalistic essay "Does Peace Have a Chance?" John Horgan takes issue with a common perception concerning the aggressive tendencies of humans, questioning the logic behind the perception primarily through the use of facts and statistics.

 Preparing to Read

1. Who is John Horgan? Do an Internet search to answer this question.
2. Reflect on your own position in the debate. Do you believe that war and/or aggression is innate in humans? You could try to answer this question by brainstorming, dividing your ideas into two columns (yes and no); then, look back at your points and decide which are the strongest.

Does Peace Have a Chance?

John Horgan

Slate, 4 August 2009
(1191 words)

1　The West Point War Museum, right across the Hudson River from my home, offers a brisk tour of the history of weaponry, from Paleolithic stone axes to Fat Man, the atomic bomb dropped on Nagasaki in 1945. A sign at the museum's entrance states, "Unquestionably, war-making is an aspect of human nature which will continue as nations attempt to impose their will upon each other." Actually, this assertion is quite questionable. A recent decline in war casualties—especially compared to historical and even prehistorical rates—has some scholars wondering whether the era of international war may be ending.

2　Counting casualties is fraught with uncertainty; scholars' estimates vary according to how they define war and what sources they accept as reliable, among other factors. Nevertheless, a clear trend emerges from recent studies. Last year, 25,600 combatants and civilians were killed as a direct result of armed conflicts, according to the 2009 Yearbook of SIPRI, the Stockholm International Peace Research Institute, to be released 17 August. Two thirds of these deaths took place in just three trouble spots: Sri Lanka (8400), Afghanistan (4600), and Iraq (4000). In contrast, almost 500,000 people are killed each year in violent crimes and well over 1 million die in automobile accidents.

3　SIPRI's figure excludes deaths from "one-sided conflict," in which combatants deliberately kill unarmed civilians, and "indirect" deaths from war-related disease and famine. If these casualties are included, annual war-related deaths from 2004 to 2007 rise tenfold to 250,000 per year, according to "The Global Burden of Armed Violence," a 2008 report published by an international organization set up in the aftermath of the Geneva Declaration. Even this much higher number, the report states, is "remarkably low in comparison to historical figures."

4   For example, Milton Leitenberg of the University of Maryland's School for International and Security Studies has estimated that war and state-sponsored genocide in the first half of the twentieth century killed as many as 190 million people, both directly and indirectly. That comes to an average of 3.8 million deaths per year. His analysis found that wars killed fewer than one-quarter of that total in the second half of the twentieth century—40 million altogether, or 800,000 per year.

5   Even these staggering figures are low in comparison with prehistoric ones, if considered as a percentage of population. All the horrific wars and genocides of the twentieth century accounted for less than 3 per cent of all deaths worldwide, according to one estimate. That is much less than the probable rate of violent death among our early ancestors.

6   The economist Samuel Bowles of the Santa Fe Institute recently analyzed dozens of archaeological and ethnographic studies of hunter-gatherer societies like the ones our ancestors are thought to have lived in for most of our prehistory. Warfare and other forms of violence led to 14 percent of the deaths in these simple societies, Bowles concludes.

7   In his influential book *War Before Civilization*, the anthropologist Lawrence Keeley of the University of Illinois estimates that violence accounted for as many as 25 per cent of all deaths among early societies. Keeley includes not only hunter-gatherers but also tribal societies such as the Yanomamo in Amazonia and the Enga in New Guinea, which practice simple horticulture as well as hunting. These early people racked up such murderous totals with clubs, spears, and arrows rather than machine guns and bombs—and Keeley's stats don't even include indirect deaths from famine and disease.

8   Our prehistory seems to have grown more bellicose as time went on, however. According to anthropologist Brian Ferguson, there is little or no clear-cut evidence of lethal group aggression among any societies prior to 12,000 years ago. War emerged and rapidly spread over the next few thousand years among hunter-gatherers and other groups, particularly in regions where people abandoned a nomadic lifestyle for a more sedentary one and populations grew. War arose, according to this perspective, because of changing environmental and cultural conditions rather than because of "human nature," as the West Point War Museum suggests.

9   This view contradicts what many people believe about war. Since 2006, when I first started teaching a college course called "War and Human Nature," I've asked hundreds of students and other people whether humans will ever stop fighting wars. More than four in five—young and old, conservative and liberal, male and female—answer "No." Asked to explain this response, they often say that we have always fought wars, and we always will, because we are innately aggressive.

10   Of course, all human behaviour ultimately stems from our biology. But the sudden emergence of war around 10,000 BCE and its recent decline suggest it's primarily a cultural phenomenon and one that culture is now helping us to overcome. There have been no international wars since the US invasion of Iraq in 2003 and no wars between major industrialized powers since the end of World War II. Most conflicts now consist of guerilla wars, insurgencies, and terrorism—or what the political scientist John Mueller of Ohio State University calls the "remnants of war."

11   Mueller rejects biological explanations for this trend, noting in one paper that "testosterone levels seem to be as high as ever." At least part of the decline, he says, can be attributed to a surge in the number of democracies since

World War II, from 20 to nearly 100 (depending on how democracy is defined). Since democracies rarely, if ever, wage war against each other, we may well see a continuing decline in the magnitude of armed conflict.

12 Harvard psychologist Steven Pinker identifies several other cultural factors contributing to the modern decline of violence, both between and within states. First, the creation of stable states with effective legal systems and police forces has eliminated the endless feuding that plagued many tribal societies. Second, increased life expectancies make us less willing to risk our lives by engaging in violence. Third, as a result of globalization and communications, we have become increasingly interdependent on—and empathetic toward—others outside of our immediate "tribes."

13 If war is not inevitable, neither is peace. "This past year saw increasing threats to security, stability, and peace in nearly every corner of the globe," warns the SIPRI 2009 Yearbook.

Global arms spending—especially by the United States, China, and Russia—has surged, and efforts to stem nuclear proliferation have stalled. An al-Qaeda operative could detonate a nuclear suitcase bomb in New York City tomorrow, reversing the recent trend in an instant. But the evidence of a decline in war-related deaths shows that we need not—and should not—accept war as an eternal scourge of the human condition.

14 In fact, this fatalistic view is wrong empirically and morally. Empirically, because war clearly stems less from some hard-wired "instinct" than from mutable cultural and environmental conditions; much can be done, and has been done, to reduce the risks it poses. Morally, because the belief that war will never end helps perpetuate it. The surer we are that the world is irredeemably violent, the more likely we are to support hawkish leaders and policies, making our belief self-fulfilling. Our first step toward ending war is to believe that we can end it.

⬤ Comprehension

1. To what does Horgan attribute the increase in group violence after 10,000 BCE?
2. Why does Horgan believe it would not affect his thesis if a single act of terrorism occurred tomorrow (par. 13)?

📌 Organization and Style

1. a. Explain Horgan's use of personal experience in his essay.
   b. Explain his use of compare–contrast. Do you believe he overuses personal experience or compare–contrast? Justify your answer.

💡 Critical Thinking/Research

1. Why do you think Horgan does not address the opposing view other than simply acknowledging it in paragraphs 1 and 9?
2. Which paragraph do you believe is the most effective in the essay? Explain its effectiveness and the ways it strengthens the essay as a whole.

Danny Chivers, "Debunking the Myths: Myths about the Basic Science"

Not all periodicals target only an academic or only a non-academic audience. For example, some academic journals include shorter articles of interest to educated non-specialists. Similarly, many non-academic magazines, such as *New Internationalist*, target educated non-specialists who do not need to be drawn into the essay by a catchy opening or eye-grabbing graphics; such articles are written primarily to inform, and their authors may use endnotes, usually a feature of academic writing.

 Preparing to Read

1. To get an awareness of a typical reader of *New Internationalist*, in which "Debunking the Myths" appeared, access its website and navigate to a page that explains the magazine's purpose (such as an "About Us" page). In a couple of sentences, create a profile of a typical reader of the magazine, using criteria you deem the most relevant.

2. Scan the essay, including the sidebar (p. 288), to determine the essay's main purpose.

Debunking the Myths: Myths about the Basic Science

Danny Chivers

New Internationalist, May 2011
(3230 words)

Myths about the Basic Science

CO₂ isn't a greenhouse gas

1   This is basic, well-established science that is difficult to deny—but some people still like to have a go. Carbon dioxide's heat-trapping properties were first discovered by John Tyndall in the 1860s.[1] The warming powers of CO_2 can be demonstrated simply by filling a plastic bottle with the gas, shining a lamp on it, and measuring its temperature compared to a bottle filled with ordinary air. The BBC does it in a two-minute video [at] news.bbc.co.uk/2/hi/8394168.stm

When the climate changed in prehistoric times, the warming came first, then the CO₂ rose afterwards

2   Evidence from ancient ice cores, tree rings, coastlines, and the ocean's depths provide

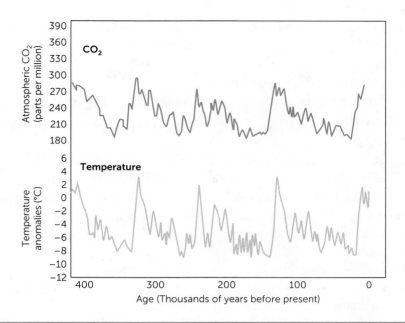

FIGURE 1   Historic CO_2 and temperature data from the Vostok ice core

Source: Petit et al. "Climate and atmospheric history of the past 420,000 years from the Vostok ice core, Antarctica." (June 1999) *Nature* 399, 429–36.

us with a pretty decent picture of how temperatures, sea levels, and the amount of CO_2 in the air have changed over the last few tens of millions of years. The results are fascinating—the Earth has swung periodically between colder and warmer periods over the eons (see Figure 1). These huge changes were initially triggered by tiny fluctuations in the Earth's temperature—the sun might go through a slightly warmer or cooler phase,[2] or kinks in the Earth's orbit might take the planet out a little further or in a little closer.[3] The planet would then warm or cool gradually, over hundreds or thousands of years. Then suddenly this would transform into rapid change, switching the planet from cool to warm or vice versa.

3   Why the sudden flip into rapid change? Well, as the planet warms up, carbon dioxide and methane are released from plants, soils, and oceans. These gases create a greenhouse effect which leads to more warming and thus the release of more CO_2 and so on until the whole climate has changed completely. This explains why temperatures started to rise first, and then CO_2 followed.

4   Imagine that a group of gibbons escape and run amok at a zoo. They cause plenty of chaos by themselves, but the zookeepers don't round them up quickly enough and so the gleeful gibbons started releasing the chimpanzees from *their* cages, who then start letting the other animals loose, until the whole thing spirals completely out of control. Looking back on this afterward, it's true that the zoo was already in chaos *before* the chimpanzees escaped; but it doesn't mean that it's therefore fine to release as many chimpanzees into your

own zoo as you like, without expecting any consequences . . .

Many scientists don't agree with the consensus on climate change

5   According to a 2009 survey, 97 per cent of published climate scientists believe that humanity is changing the climate.4 The basic underlying science linking humanity's greenhouse gas emissions with climate change is as well-established as the link between smoking and lung cancer, or HIV and AIDS—some people still deny these connections, but no one takes them seriously. There is disagreement and debate around the precise effects of climate change; but the facts that it's happening, it's serious, and it's caused by humans are well-established and agreed by all but a small handful of scientists.

6   Unfortunately, this small group gets a huge amount of attention, making them seem more numerous than they really are—and a lot of this is to do with the funding and support they receive. This isn't to say that the climate contrarians are simply in it for the money. I'm sure most of them believe in the things they say. But they wouldn't have such prominence and status without the backing of certain wealthy and powerful individuals, political groups, media outlets, and corporations with a (short-term and profit-driven) interest in preventing action on climate change. The mainstream media have a tendency to set up head to head "debates" between climate scientists/campaigners and climate change deniers, which creates the false impression that the science is still disputed. It's about as useful as watching a debate on how to solve the African AIDS crisis between an experienced Ugandan health campaigner and

someone who believes that HIV is spread by evil pixies and can be cured by eating spaghetti.

Myths about temperature rise

The world isn't really warming up

7   The first graph [Figure 2] shows the global air temperature over the last 150 years; the second [Figure 3] adds in the ocean temperature since 1950.

8   So the temperature changes we are feeling on land are small fry (if you'll pardon the expression) compared to the heating of the oceans. Meanwhile, cyclical weather patterns like El Niño and La Niña move heat back and forth between the oceans and the air in an irregular fashion—a major reason why atmospheric temperatures aren't rising in a nice neat line. For example, a strong El Niño shifted a lot of heat from the seas into the air in 1998, causing a spike in air temperatures. When temperatures in the following years reverted back, climate deniers started going on about how global warming had "stopped." Of course it hadn't—it was just that the heat was being stored in the ocean rather than the atmosphere, as Figure 3 clearly shows. The top ten hottest years in recorded human history all happened in the last twelve years, with 2005 and 2010 tied for the hottest ever.7

The world cooled down between 1940 and 1970

9   This isn't true, but is based on something genuinely interesting. Global warming did plateau for a bit between the 1940s and

the 1970s due to the phenomenon of "global dimming"—a type of industrial pollutant called sulphate aerosols were partially blocking the sun's rays. This lasted for a while until the ongoing build-up of greenhouse gases—combined, ironically enough, with a reduction in sulphate pollution from power stations—eventually swamped the dimming effect and the temperature began to rise once more.[8] You can see this flattened period on the graph in Figure 2.

The temperature data are fixed/flawed/manipulated

10 To somehow tamper with or subvert the data from around 7,000 different measurement stations and satellites, which are processed via three different major organizations with hundreds of staff, would require an utterly fantastic level of conspiracy. Nonetheless, in 2010 a procession of (mostly online) commentators claimed that a series of hacked emails from the Climate Research Unit at the UK's University of East Anglia contained evidence of just such a conspiracy (which they imaginatively dubbed "Climategate"). Three separate independent enquiries trawled through the emails and found evidence of nothing more than a few scientists occasionally being a bit rude about some of their colleagues, using some unhelpful jargon and having the odd moan about incessant public requests for information.[9] However, there was one useful outcome: much more of the raw temperature data has since been made public, to avoid similar accusations in the future.[10]

But it's cold today . . .

11 Although the average global temperature is rising, that doesn't mean that everywhere is get-

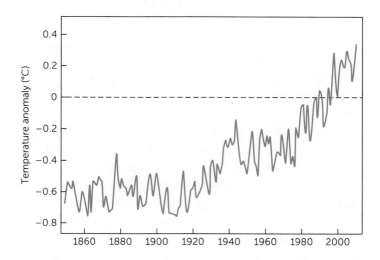

FIGURE 2 Global warming since 1850, an average computed from 10 different sources. The "0" line is the 1990–2000 average temperature

Source: Appears in "Debunking the myths" by Danny Chivers, *New Internationalist*; May 2011; 15.

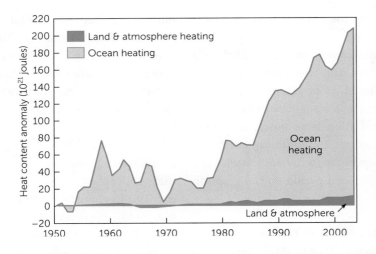

FIGURE 3   Total Earth heat content from 1950.

Sources: Murphy et al. 2009[5] and Domingues et al. 2008[6.] Appears in "Debunking the myths" by Danny Chivers, *New Internationalist*; May 2011; 15.

ting hotter at the same rate. The global climate system is complicated; some places are heating faster than others, and some may even cool down depending on ocean currents and wind patterns.

12 The difference between *climate* and *weather* is important here. Climate change is a gradual, long-term process; weather is about short-term, day-to-day changes due to local patterns of wind, evaporation, and ocean currents, and is more unpredictable. A few weeks of cold weather in one location tells us little about long-term global temperature change—that's why we need all those thousands of temperature measurement stations taking decades' worth of readings. Those measurements are telling us that every time there's a bit of unusually cold weather somewhere in the world, it's being outweighed by many more examples of unusually hot weather elsewhere, and so the overall trend is of a warming planet.

Myths about other things that might be causing it

Volcanoes produce more CO₂ than humans

13 This one's just nonsense—humanity is responsible for at least 60 times the CO_2 of volcanoes.[11] This point was firmly underlined when the Icelandic volcano Eyjafjallajokull erupted in March 2010; the resulting ash cloud led to the grounding of planes across Europe for several weeks, preventing far more carbon dioxide than the volcano was emitting. It created a net saving of around 50,000 tonnes of CO_2 per day.[12]

It's caused by the sun

14 The sun does occasionally go through periods of increased activity, where it puts out a bit of extra heat. However, all the extra sun

activity of the last 150 years can only account for a small amount of the warming we've seen in that time—the rest must be due to something else. Sun activity has remained roughly level since the 1960s, and has, in fact, been cooler than usual since 2003—see Figure 4. This is all well-measured and noncontroversial.[13] So it can't be due to the sun alone.

It's caused by cosmic rays/ something else

15   There are other "theories" out there, but with little or no evidence to back them up. Of course, in order to overturn the existing theory of human-made global warming, they'd need to have a mountain of contrary evidence that explains why the current scientific explanation isn't correct. For example, if you decided that the *real* reason why leaves fall off trees in winter is that they're being tugged off by mischievous squirrels, you'd need a bit more evidence than a photo of a squirrel sheepishly clutching an oak leaf. None of the other supposed explanations for climate change can provide the evidence (for example, the "cosmic rays" idea comes from a handful of largely discredited scientific papers about the possible effect of cosmic rays on cloud formation[15]).

Myths about the effects of climate change

The Antarctic ice is growing, not shrinking

16   This is true for certain areas of Antarctica—and, intriguingly, it actually gives us *more* evidence for global warming. Increased

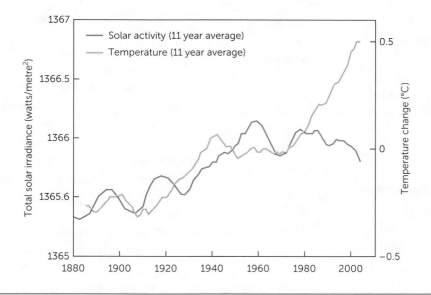

FIGURE 4   Global temperature (grey) and total solar irradiance (blue)

Source: Data from NASA, Solanki, and PMOD[14]. Appears in "Debunking the myths" by Danny Chivers, *New Internationalist*; May 2011; 15.

evaporation caused by higher temperatures has led to more snowfall in some parts of Antarctica, and thus thicker ice cover in these areas (usually inland). Closer to the sea (which is warming faster than the air) the ice is retreating.

Climate change has good effects, not just bad ones!

17   True—up to a point. Warmer winters in some countries will mean fewer people die from cold. Increased temperatures have made it easier to grow crops in some regions. Sadly, these small pockets of positive effects are hugely outweighed by the negative ones.[16] We have built almost all our settlements in places that are comfortable and fertile in our current climate, and our ways of growing food are carefully adapted to the weather we've been used to for thousands of years. Rapid changes in the Earth's climate are already starting to throw this out of kilter—hence increasing deaths from storms, floods, and famines. Even if climate change makes some places more comfortable to humans, do we expect everyone to migrate to the limited number of places where this is so?

Climate change is a problem, but there are bigger problems that we need to tackle first

18   This argument offers a false choice—we can (and should) tackle the problems of climate change, poverty, healthcare, etc. all at the same time. Many of these problems have the same root causes—the relentless pursuit of profit and economic growth over people's real needs—so it makes sense to work on them all together. Climate change is making many of the world's problems much worse—Kofi Annan's Global Humanitarian Forum[17] found that climate change threatens all eight of the Millennium Development Goals[18] and is making it much harder to tackle global poverty and disease. Any progress we make in these areas will be swept away by climate change, unless we act to prevent its worst effects.

We can't trust the computer models

19   While the "big picture" climate change predictions (increased temperatures, more evaporation, melting ice caps, and rising seas) are based on observed results and the prehistoric record, the more detailed projections (how much climate change, where, and by when) are based on computer models. These models are constantly checked and improved, and tested against real-life scenarios to make sure they're as accurate as possible, but there are always going to be some uncertainties. This is why climate scientists talk in terms of probabilities and risks; no one knows all the details of what's going to happen as the climate changes, but these models can show us the most likely trends and give us some useful indications and warnings.

20   Some use this uncertainty to argue against taking action to tackle climate change and spending money on climate solutions, saying that it might not be as bad as we think. The problem with this argument is that we *do*

know it's going to be bad. We know because it's *already* bad—people are suffering in floods and droughts, we're losing species left, right, and centre, and over 300,000 people are dying every year as a result of climate change.[19] We don't need the models to tell us that if we keep on pumping out the polluting gases that caused this mess, things are going to keep getting worse.

Other distraction tactics

It's too late, we need to adapt to climate change instead

21 We're already committed to a certain level of climate change, and so some adaptation will be absolutely vital. If we're serious about climate justice then the nations most responsible for causing climate change should be providing funds and technology to the people on the receiving end, to help them cope with rising sea levels and more serious floods, storms, and droughts.

22 However, adaptation cannot be a replacement for reducing greenhouse gas emissions. "Adapting" to more serious levels of climate change would involve coping with mass food shortages, the loss of dozens of major cities, finding new homes for hundreds of millions of people and countless deaths from starvation, conflict, and disease. Runaway climate change could leave us with a largely uninhabitable planet.

23 Even if it were possible, adaptation on this scale wouldn't be cheaper or easier than cutting CO_2 emissions—even conservative estimates like the British government's Stern Review place the costs of climate impacts far higher than the costs of prevention. It's like saying "it's just too much effort to hit the brakes, I'm sure my car can adapt to that brick wall."

24 Leading climate scientists are telling us that we still have a decent chance of avoiding runaway climate change, but only if we act fast. Telling ourselves it's too late is just another form of denial—an excuse to avoid action.

It's all about population growth

25 It's true that the more people there are on the planet, the fewer resources there are to go around. However, birth rates in most Northern nations are low; most population growth is occurring in poorer countries. The current per capita consumption rate in these countries is very small—for example, the average Canadian uses the same amount of energy per year as 20 Tanzanians. The wealthiest 20 per cent of the world's people use over 70 per cent of the energy. With regard to climate change it is far more urgent to reduce consumption levels in the North than birth rates in the South.

26 High birth rates are strongly associated with poverty, hunger, and a lack of access to healthcare. They are also connected to a lack of women's rights and restricted access to health information and contraception. If we want the world's population to stabilize sooner rather than later, we need to support people around the world—especially women—to claim more rights, greater dignity, and full control over their lives. However, we also need to urgently reduce emissions in the North!

How to talk to a climate change denier

If they're just misinformed, or don't want to believe it for personal reasons, then you may have a chance of changing their mind. Don't expect to win them over all in one go—be sensitive, explain the facts as simply and clearly as you can and try not to get frustrated. Remember that the reality of climate change is a huge and scary thing to get our heads around—it's a complex, decentralized, and enormous threat that can't be easily blamed on any one single organization or person. Accepting it fully means we need to make genuine changes in our lives and start working actively to stop it, which is a significant responsibility to take on.

Try being gently challenging rather than staying on the defensive—do they have a coherent argument as to why climate change isn't happening, or isn't serious? Most people don't—they have a collection of soundbites or excuses that they use to justify not thinking about the problem properly. Don't be too confrontational though—the aim is to make them seriously think the matter through and change their minds by themselves, rather than for you to "win the argument." Be sympathetic rather than accusatory—make it clear that the fault doesn't lie with the person you're speaking to, but the public misinformers and their corporate funders.

If you're debating with a "hardline" denier—someone with a strong vested interest, or who's being paid to spout an anti-science line—you need to be aware that you're not likely to win them over! The only time it's worth doing this is when there are other people watching—for example, at a public debate, on an Internet message board, or in a media interview. In these cases, remember that it's the audience, not the denier, that you're trying to win over—and so coming across well is just as important as having the right arguments.

Stay calm, confident, and polite. Counter their nonsense as best you can, but don't just be reactive—ask them which bits of the basic science they disagree with. Do they not believe CO_2 is a greenhouse gas, or that the planet is warming up? Ask them what evidence they have for these extraordinary claims that contradict 150 years of science and tens of thousands of temperature measurements. If they claim it's not a big problem, give them some real-life examples of what floods, droughts, and storms are already doing to people all over the world. Professional deniers love to pick at details but often struggle when challenged on the overall picture, because their cherry-picked criticisms don't add up to anything coherent.

Scientists exaggerate the risks of climate change to get more funding

27 This is completely back to front—if a scientist found real evidence that contradicted the accepted theory of human-made climate change, do you think they'd have any difficulty finding funding? Successful climate change deniers can already rake in hundreds of thousands of dollars just to present their opinions, without the backing of any reputable science.[20]

28 A survey of climate scientists by the Union of Concerned Scientists in 2007 found that 58 per cent of respondents had experienced political pressure to water down their scientific findings.[21] The 2007 Intergovernmental Panel on Climate Change (IPCC) report was stripped of many "undesirable" passages by politicians before it could be published, including warnings about the likely impacts of climate change on North America and references to the risk of runaway climate change.[22] More recently, the outspoken IPCC chair Rajendra Pachauri has endured a barrage of false claims of fraud and corruption from climate deniers.[23] There is plenty of pressure on climate scientists to change their research—but nearly all of it is pushing them to tone down their message, and not to speak out.

Notes

1. Tyndall, J. (1861). On the absorption and radiation of heat by gases and vapors, and on the physical connexion of radiation, absorption, and conduction. *Philosophical Transactions of the Royal Society of London, 51.*

2. http://nin.tl/bk59Hd

3. http://nin.tl/d4vx46

4. Doran, P.T. & M. Kendall Zimmerman (2009). Examining the scientific consensus on climate change. *EOS, Transactions of the American Geophysical Union, 90,* 22.

5. Murphy et al. (2009). An observationally based energy balance for the Earth since 1950. *Journal of Geophysical Research, 114.* See also www.skepticalscience.com "It hasn't warmed since 1998."

6. Domingues et al. (2008). Improved estimates of upper-ocean warming and multi-decadal sea-level rise. *Nature, 453.*

7. National Oceanic and Atmospheric Administration.

8. See for example Stanhill, G. & S. Cohen (2001). Global dimming: A review of the evidence for a widespread and significant reduction in global radiation with discussion of its probable causes and possible agricultural consequences. *Agricultural and Forest Meteorology, 107.*

9. The House of Commons Science and Technology Committee. (2010, March 31). The Science Assessment Panel (2010, April 14), and The Independent Climate Change Email Review chaired by Sir Muir Russell (2010, July 7).

10. Met Office press release. (2009, December 5). *Release of Global-Average Temperature Data.* http://nin.tl/dyuKWv

11. Figures from UNESCO/SCOPE/UNEP report *The Human Perturbation of the Climate Cycle.* Available at http://nin.tl/bc7rhm Gigatonnes of carbon converted into billions of tonnes of CO_2 by my own calculation (multiplied by 3.67).

12. http://nin.tl/9N4i5B

13. IPCC. *Fourth Assessment Report.* Working Group 1, Section 2.7.

14. http://nin.tl/ gYpVgj

15. http://nin.tl/ekctai

16. There's an excellent list of the positive and negative effects of climate change, with links to the relevant scientific research, at http://nin.tl/bBzYPb

17. Global Humanitarian Forum. (2009). *The Anatomy of a Silent Crisis*. Available online at http://nin.tl/awh8nC

18. A set of globally-agreed targets to improve health and fight poverty and hunger. See www.un.org/millenniumgoals/

19. Global Humanitarian Forum. (2009). *The Anatomy of a Silent Crisis*.

20. (2010, January 11). Global warming skeptic takes his message to Noosa. *The Noosa Journal*. See also www.prwatch.org/node/8686

21. Union of Concerned Scientists and Government Accountability Project. (2007, February). *Atmosphere of Pressure: Political Interference in Federal Climate Science*.

22. Harrabin, R. (2007, April 6). *The Today Programme*. BBC Radio 4; Wasdell, D. (2007, February). Political corruption of the IPCC report?

23. Vidal, J. (2010, September 3). If Rajendra Pachauri goes, who on Earth would want to be IPCC chair? *The Guardian*.

● Comprehension

1. Summarize paragraph 2 of the essay; paraphrase paragraph 1.

● Organization and Style

1. a. Analyze the essay's organization as a whole, commenting on specific structural features and their functions.

   b. Choose one paragraph or two successive paragraphs from the section "Myths about the Effects of Climate Change" and discuss the strategies for coherence (for example, paragraph structure, strategic repetition, word choice, use of prompts or transitions, and the like).

2. a. Identify three examples of analogies (comparisons) in the essay.

   b. Evaluate the effectiveness of one of the analogies, supporting your answer by referring to the text.

3. Although "Debunking the Myths" is not an academic essay, and its audience would not be composed mostly of scholars and researchers, Chivers uses features of academic as well as non-academic essays. Identify two such features commonly used in academic essays (see Chapter 10, pp. 136–9) and comment on their function(s) in this essay.

4. Write a 3–5 sentence introduction or conclusion to "Debunking the Myths," ensuring that it fulfils the functions of effective introductions/conclusions as discussed on p. 7 and p. 17.

Critical Thinking

1. a. Explain how the myth described in paragraph 18 represents the "false choice" fallacy.

   b. Referring to the chart of logical fallacies, on p. 46 (Table 4.2), identify one other fallacy that Chivers claims is used by some climate change deniers.

2. Analyze the author's challenge to one of the myths in the sub-section "We Can't Trust the Computer Models" and one other sub-section of comparable length in the essay, commenting on the author's use of argument and, if applicable, argumentative strategies (see Chapter 4, pp. 47–52).

3. Referring to the sidebar, "How to Talk to a Climate Change Denier,"

   a. What does Chivers suggest the argumentative purpose (see Chapter 4, p. 47) should be if one is arguing with a climate change denier?

   b. Explain how awareness of the audience can be used to argue effectively with a climate change denier, according to Chivers.

Alberto Manguel, "Burning Mistry"

Many journalistic essays are inspired by specific events. Responding to the event, the writer may compare it to similar incidents and comment on its significance, moving from the particular to universal issues. Alberto Manguel begins "Burning Mistry" by referring to two incidents of book burning, one recent, one from the distant past, which leads into a discussion of the effects of censorship and the value of literature.

Preparing to Read

1. Who are Alberto Manguel and Rohinton Mistry? Using reliable sources, briefly summarize their careers as writers and their contributions to literature.

2. In an individual or group activity, come up with titles of books that have been considered too controversial or objectionable to be taught in schools or included in public libraries. What are the grounds for censoring literature? Are they justifiable in some instances? Why or why not?

Burning Mistry

Alberto Manguel

Geist, May 2011
(1093 words)

1   In one of the earliest instances of book burning we know (but certainly not the first), in the year 213 BCE, the Chinese emperor Shih Huang-ti issued an edict ordering that all the books in his realm should be destroyed. In one of the latest instances (but certainly not the last), in September 2010, Rohinton Mistry's *Such a Long Journey* was burned at the gates of Mumbai University by students belonging to the right-wing Shiv Sena party. Between the Chinese emperor's edict and the Mumbai students' action lie twenty-two centuries of books set on fire. If proof were needed of the essential power and value of literature, this long line of burning pages should suffice. Nothing less vigorously alive could elicit such fear.

2   Fear of what? we ask. Among other things, of the truth. Over half a century ago, Jorge Luis Borges suggested that one of the reasons for Huang-ti's action was the fact of his mother's adultery, which the emperor wished to erase from Chinese memory by erasing Chinese history itself. (Borges noted that his case was similar to that of a certain king of Judea who, wishing to kill one child, ordered that all children should be killed.) The burners of Mistry's novel complained that *Such a Long Journey* depicted right-wing politicians, and particularly the Shiv Sena party, in a less than flattering light, and assumed, like their remote Chinese ancestor, that by reducing the story to ashes they would eliminate the fact. No doubt somewhere, in the hundreds of thousands of pages that constituted the corpus of Chinese literature prior to the third century BCE, a mention might have been found of the emperor's mother's peccadillo, but if Huang-ti's reason was indeed to erase such a fact from public memory, his colossal task of destruction had the contrary effect, since the towering flames signalled, even to those quite uninterested in the affairs of the Chinese court, that there was something rotten in the Middle Kingdom.

3   The Shiv Sena students have now achieved much the same thing. As a keen reader of Mistry's books (having once written an afterword for a school edition of *Such a Long Journey*), I think I have a fair recollection of the events and characters in the novel. I must confess, however, that I had not paid particular attention to the presence in it of the Shiv Sena party, and had to go back to the book to refresh my memory. Yes, there is a mention (on page 298 of the first edition) of "dutiful Shiv Sena patrols and motley fascists who roamed city streets with stones at the ready, patriotically shattering windows that they deemed inadequately blacked-out." Mistry writes in a deceptively plain style, with great elegance and quiet humour, and his fiction is infused by a belief in what Robert Louis Stevenson called "the ultimate decency of things." But if I were to offer a selection of outstanding examples of Mistry's writing, I suspect the Shiv Sena passage would not be one of them: there are far subtler, stronger, deeper lines in the novel than this efficiently documentary one. (Here is one, for instance, describing what a father thinks of a hammer that belonged to his own father and that he hopes his son will one day inherit: "He will add his gloss to the wood.") However, now that the irate students have drawn my attention to the appearance of their grouplet in the book, the passage carries for me all the vigour of a political manifesto. We readers should always remember that it is often the censor who draws our attention to the hidden virtues of a text.

4   But there were two other consequences to the book burning that are, if not more outrageous than the act itself, then certainly as distressing. One was the response of the Mumbai University authorities. The other was the lack of response of the Canadian government.

5   In India, when the leader of the Shiv Sena students was interviewed by a television journalist, he said that Mistry was lucky to live in Canada: if he lived in Mumbai, they would burn him as well as his book. He then added that his group demanded the removal of *Such a Long Journey* (prescribed reading for years in the university's MA and BA courses) from the syllabus. After several days, the vice-chancellor of Mumbai University, Dr Rajan Welukar, did as he was told. The decision, he said, was not his, but that of the outgoing Board of Studies who, with one foot on the stirrup, declared that *Such a Long Journey* should no longer be taught. Dr Welukar responded, of course, in accordance to a time-honoured bureaucratic tradition, according to which, in such cases, the person responsible must always pass on the blame, preferably to someone departing or departed. Fortunately, India's readers reacted otherwise. In colleges and universities across the country, in individual blogs and in the public press, readers expressed their outrage at both the burning and the banning.

6   In Canada, where indignation is rarely expressed above a polite "Oh, you shouldn't," the response was more subdued. *The Globe and Mail* dutifully reported the incident, the *National Post* noted it briefly, CBC Radio mentioned it on an international program dealing with Canadian matters abroad, PEN Canada, the Writers' Trust, and the Toronto Reference Library issued statements of protest, and Mistry's publisher sent out a stern press release. From the government of the True North, Strong and Free, came not a whisper. We must not forget that India has become a vital economic partner for Canada and it would not do to bring up anything that might upset business negotiations, whether in the electronic or the tourist trade. The silence of Harper's government should therefore not surprise us, nor that of the Honourable Michael Chan, Minister for Tourism and Culture of Ontario, Mistry's province: as the minister's title indicates, one industry takes precedence over the other.

7   However, for those with the long view, there is consolation in the fact that book burnings never quite succeed in their purpose. Huang-ti's determination to condemn to oblivion the three thousand years of books that preceded him failed, as these things always do. Today we can still read the sayings of Confucius and the parables of Chuang Tzu and the medical books of the Yellow Emperor, just as we will continue to read *Such a Long Journey*, to revisit its passionate pages or to discover what made it so powerful that a fanatical mob and a cowardly vice-chancellor believed that it merited the flames.

Comprehension

1. What does the author mean in the last sentence of paragraph 6, where he refers to Michael Chan's title?
2. According to Manguel, what is the ultimate effect of book burning?

Organization and Style

1. Identify two examples of irony and explain what they contribute to the essay. (Writers employ irony through their use of language: irony reveals a second, deeper meaning under the literal surface; see p. 128.)

Critical Thinking

1. Manguel begins with a comparison, which is recalled elsewhere in the essay. Analyze its validity and effectiveness by referring to specific passages.

2. What is Manguel's purpose in comparing the passage of Mistry's prose on page 298 of his book to another passage in the same book (see par. 3)?

3. Discuss the ways that Manguel attempts to establish his credibility. Why is it essential that he does this?

Bruce M. Hicks, "The Undiscovered Province"

In non-academic essays, especially ones in which writers do not usually cite their sources, credibility of the writer is crucial. Scan the essay to determine Hicks's credibility. Then, using a reliable website, determine the writer's credentials, such as his background, vocation, and publishing history.

 Preparing to Read

1. What do you know about the "Idle No More" protest movement in Canada? Are you interested in, or concerned about, issues related to Aboriginal self-government and cultural autonomy?

2. Should issues related to Aboriginal self-government be of concern to all Canadians, regardless of racial or cultural background? You could discuss this in groups or free-write about it using this prompt: "Canadians should (not) have a voice in Aboriginal self-government . . ."

The Undiscovered Province

Bruce M. Hicks

This Magazine, Jan./Feb. 2010
(1205 words)

1   The Royal Proclamation of 1763 included a clause prohibiting British colonists from purchasing "Lands of the Indians," so as not to commit more of the "frauds and abuses" that characterized colonial takeovers of Aboriginal territory. To my reading, this measure was intended to make clear to the English colonists that Aboriginal Peoples enjoyed equal status. As we know, that's not quite how it worked out.

2   In 1987, after the premiers met at Meech Lake and agreed to open the Constitution, I posed to several prominent people involved in the process that the easiest way to respect that commitment, and to lessen the offense of their putting Quebec before Aboriginals, would be to create an 11th province out of the remaining Aboriginal and territorial lands. Twenty-two years later, First Nations are still fighting to get even a modicum of self-government.

3   When Canada was patriating the Constitution in 1982, Aboriginal leaders were able to create enough domestic and international pressure on the federal and provincial governments that the first ministers committed to making the next round of constitutional change about Aboriginal issues. They even enshrined in the Constitution a requirement for first ministers to have one, and then two more meetings with Aboriginal leaders.

4   But the election of the Progressive Conservative party under Brian Mulroney in Ottawa, and the defeat of the separatist Parti Québécois in Quebec at the hands of the Liberals under Robert Bourassa, suddenly moved the now infamous "Quebec round" ahead of Aboriginal people. While the constitutional requirement of first ministers' meetings with Aboriginal leaders to amend the Constitution was met, it seems with hindsight that these meetings were simply pro forma, as Bourassa and Mulroney already had plans for the Meech Lake Constitutional Accord.

5   The accord failed, in part, due to a single Aboriginal member of the Manitoba legislature named Elijah Harper who refused to give unanimous consent so it could be adopted by the Manitoba legislature by the Mulroney government's declared deadline for ratification: 23 June 1990.

6   A year later, the Mulroney government appointed a Royal Commission on Aboriginal Peoples. Among its recommendations was a list of powers that Aboriginal nations needed to protect their language, religion, culture, and heritage.

7   The underlying concepts are similar to the powers that the Fathers of Confederation from Lower Canada had identified as necessary for the preservation of the francophone language, religion, culture, and heritage. Letting provincial governments have the powers necessary to protect language, culture, and religion was the key to Confederation and then the innovation of federalism was chosen for the new Dominion of Canada. Even though Canada was based on this idea of division of powers to allow for regional cultural autonomy, the federal and provincial governments have rejected similar devolution of powers to Aboriginal communities or provincehood for the northern territories. The federal and provincial governments claim the population is too few and too dispersed to manage all these powers. And, of course, small provinces and Quebec do not want to start adding multiple provinces, beginning with three in the North, as their own relative influence would diminish.

8   But what about one province for all Aboriginal Peoples?

9   Aboriginal lands, including the three northern territories, are legally held in reserve on behalf of Aboriginal Peoples. The federal government acts as trustee over the land, and this creates a rather distasteful paternalistic dimension to Aboriginal–non-Aboriginal relations. What if our government simply takes all this land held in reserve and returns it to Aboriginals? Make all that land the 11th province of Canada.

10   The structure of government for this new province is unimportant and frankly not the business of the people who don't live on this land. The constitutional change would be simpler than one would imagine. It would not require the unanimous consent of the provinces. According to the Constitution Act, 1982, the agreement of only seven provinces, representing the majority of the population, is needed for the federal parliament to create a new province. But it also states that this is "notwithstanding any other law or practice," and for the federal parliament to take all remaining Aboriginal land and designate it the "final" province, given constitutionally entrenched treaty rights and federal jurisdiction over "Indians, and land reserved for Indians," it may even be possible to do part of the change without provincial consent.

11   This change does not even have to significantly alter the existing structures of Aboriginal communities—unless, of course, they decide to alter them on their own once they have obtained provincehood. In many of the current provinces there are three levels of government managing provincial powers, namely the provincial government, regional governments, and

Nunavut Commissioner Helen Mamayaok (L) and Canadian Governor General Roméo Leblanc (C) look on as the Nunavut flag is unveiled in a ceremony in the arctic town of Iqaluit, 1 April 1999. On that day the territory of Nunavut came into being.

Kevin Frayer/The Canadian Press

municipal governments. So, for example, the Government of Nunavut could continue as a regional government within the new Aboriginal province and the Sambaa K'e Dene Band could continue to operate similar to a municipal government, with authority delegated from the Aboriginal province. As the Aboriginal province would have all of the powers that Aboriginals have identified as central to the preservation of their languages, religions, and cultures, it can delegate powers as needed locally or act provincially as expedient.

12 With the exception of the creation of a provincial government, this is pretty close to the position the federal government has been taking vis-à-vis territorial governments and local band councils. The big change will be that in the future, instead of Aboriginals demanding from the federal government the right to handle their own affairs, they would be dealing with their own provincial government—a government they elect and that is accountable to them.

13 For those concerned about corruption within band councils, their own provincial government would regulate these matters and being concerned about how monies transferred to the local governments are handled, it would undoubtedly do so more effectively than the federal government, and without the racism or paternalistic interference. Equalization payments to the province would replace the now direct transfer to Aboriginals and their band councils, thus eliminating the demoralizing stigma of dependency. What is more, some of the Aboriginal land held in reserve is resource-rich, providing an independent source of revenue.

14 Critics of nationalism most strongly reject the idea of a province based on ethnicity. But based on its territory and its land base, the new 11th province would not be exclusively Aboriginal. Many non-Aboriginals live on these lands and within the broader Aboriginal grouping there are First Nations, Inuit, and Métis, subdivided by hundreds of individual Aboriginal nations. This would be a civic nation like Quebec, and a province like any other, though the provincial leadership will likely be Aboriginal.

15 This largely Aboriginal province will be bigger in territory, richer in resources, and competitive in population size to the average Canadian province. It can negotiate with the more influential provinces, where many of its off-reserve citizens live or work, namely Alberta, B.C., Quebec, and Ontario. And, like the other civic nation of Quebec, its premier, by virtue of representing a cultural group that is in the minority across Canada, would have a powerful voice at the table of first ministers.

16 With provincehood would come an increase in Aboriginal members in the Senate and House of Commons. Aboriginal Peoples would finally be truly engaged in Canada's political process and this is essential for full citizenship and equality.

Comprehension

1. In one sentence, paraphrase Hicks's proposal as it is presented in paragraph 9.
2. In which paragraphs does Hicks address the views of opponents? Summarize one of these paragraphs.

Organization and Style

1. Before discussing the practical implications of his proposal, Hicks refers to several historical/political events:

    a.   What is the purpose of his timeline (pars. 1–6)?

    b.   Taking one such event, analyze its importance to the essay as a whole and the writer's thesis.

Critical Thinking/Research

1. Using a reliable source, summarize the significance of two of the following:

    *   Patriation of the Constitution, 1982;
    *   The Meech Lake Constitutional Accord; and/or
    *   Elijah Harper.

2. What is the function of the comparisons between Quebec-related issues and Aboriginal issues? Analyze the validity of these comparisons in the essay.

3. Analyze the persuasiveness of Hicks's argument. You could consider such factors as order and effectiveness of points, kinds and organization of evidence, essay structure, specific argumentative strategies, and/or fallacies.

VI Voices from the Academy

The academic essays that make up this section all use the research of other scholars; their audience is usually other experts. Academic essays can be divided into three groups according to their main purpose:

1. to argue a viewpoint;
2. to review studies on a topic; and
3. to conduct an experiment.

The first essay, "The Psychology of Eating Animals," is annotated to show common features of academic writing.

Like non-academic writers, academic writers sometimes try to raise awareness about a neglected topic or convince their readers to take action, using research sources, reason, and argumentative strategies to do so. The author of "Denaturalizing 'Natural' Disasters: Haiti's Earthquake and the Humanitarian Impulse" acknowledges the human impulse to do good but asks whether, by itself, this enables us to solve the kinds of problems fostered by repressive colonial practices. The authors of the editorial "Canadian Lifestyle Choices: A Public Health Failure" assert that the federal government's health policies have helped create an overweight, unhealthy generation of Canadians. The author of "'Coming up Next': Promos in the Future of Television and Television Studies" argues that promotional spots for television shows have more complex functions and subtle influences than is commonly believed.

Several essays in this section review what has already been written on their topics, revealing gaps or suggesting directions for future research. The essay "The Impact of Pets on Human Health and Psychological Well-Being: Fact, Fiction, or Hypothesis?" examines the research to answer the question whether having pets provides physical and psychological benefits. The authors of the essays "How to Think, Say, or Do Precisely the Worst Thing for Any Occasion" and "Others Sometimes Know Us Better than We Know Ourselves" review research in the field to explain seemingly contradictory aspects of human nature. "How to Think, Say, or Do . . ." accounts for counter-productive human behaviour, while "Others Sometimes Know Us Better . . ." helps make sense of the paradoxical truth that we often misunderstand aspects of our own personalities.

A final purpose of academic essays is to test and potentially disprove previous research. Using an experiment, the authors of "'He Loves Me, He Loves Me Not . . .': Uncertainty Can Increase Romantic Attraction" challenge the logical, but sometimes inaccurate, perception that we like people who we believe like us. Similarly, the authors of "How Random Is the Toss of a Coin?" design an experiment the results of which contradict the "common-sense" belief that a coin toss has a 50/50 outcome.

Steve Loughnan, Brock Bastian, and Nick Haslam, "The Psychology of Eating Animals"

"The Psychology of Animals" represents a common type of academic essay that, using logical and clear organization, reviews related studies on a topic. The essay annotations that follow illustrate many of the features and conventions of academic essays as discussed in Chapter 10. Understanding these conventions will help you read all the essays in Section VI. Other annotations refer to effective writing strategies discussed in Chapter 1 and other chapters. Paying attention to these strategies will help with coherence and clarity in your writing.

The Psychology of Eating Animals

Steve Loughnan, Brock Bastian, and Nick Haslam

Current Directions in Psychological Science, 2014
(2496 words)

An abstract is a condensed summary of the article and usually includes the topic and purpose, the method, the results, and the conclusions.

→ **Abstract**

Most people both eat animals and care about animals. Research has begun to examine the psychological processes that allow people to negotiate this "meat paradox." To understand the psychology of eating animals, we examine characteristics of the eaters (people), the eaten (animals), and the eating (the behaviour). People who value masculinity, enjoy meat and do not see it as a moral issue, and find dominance and inequality acceptable are most likely to consume animals. Perceiving animals as highly dissimilar to humans and as lacking mental attributes, such as the capacity for pain, also supports meat eating. In addition to these beliefs, values, and perceptions, the act of eating meat triggers psychological processes that regulate negative emotions associated with eating animals. We conclude by discussing the implications of this research for understanding the psychology of morality.

1   Most people eat meat. They do so fully aware that it comes from animals, at the cost of their lives. The rate at which we eat animals is truly staggering. The average American consumes approximately 120 kg (264 lb) of meat annually (Food and Agriculture

Organization of the United Nations, 2013), an appetite fed by the slaughter of 10 billion land animals (90 per cent are chickens; Joy, 2010). Globally, the average person consumes an estimated 48 kg (106 lb) of meat annually, requiring over 50 billion land animals (Food and Agriculture Organization of the United Nations, 2013). We have eaten meat for millennia, and our meat consumption predates human civilization (Rose & Marshall, 1996).

2   The avidity of our meat consumption seems to imply that we do not care about animals. This is clearly not correct. Most people find animal suffering emotionally disturbing and morally repugnant (Allen et al., 2002; Plous, 1993). As our meat consumption grows, so too do our expenditures on pets (American Pet Products Association, 2013) and the legal rights we afford animals (Tischler, 2012). This reflects the "meat paradox": Most people care about animals and do not want to see them harmed but engage in a diet that requires them to be killed and, usually, to suffer (Herzog, 2010; Joy, 2010; Singer, 1975). Despite this suffering and premature death conflicting with people's beliefs about how animals should be treated, most people continue to eat meat. This paradox may not apply to all forms of meat eating (e.g., the eating of roadkill), may apply differently to meat producers, and may not always be experienced subjectively as a conflict. However, it highlights the moral dilemma involved in eating animals, a dilemma that all people resolve.

3   We will examine the psychological factors that support eating animals by focusing on characteristics of the eaters (people), the eaten (animals), and the eating (the act of consumption). We finish by discussing how psychological resolution of the meat paradox can inform our understanding of morality.

The Eaters

4   The surest way to eliminate moral tension associated with eating animals is to not eat them. Vegetarians experience no conflict between their beliefs about animal harm and their dietary practices. Studies of vegetarianism have revealed that moral concern regarding the raising and slaughter of animals is a principal motivation for eliminating meat consumption (Amato & Partridge, 1989; Ruby, 2012). In addition to motivating dietary change, valuing animal welfare helps sustain and moralize vegetarian diets (Rozin, Markwith, & Stoess, 1997). Vegetarians avoid the meat paradox through a behavioural choice driven by moral concern for animals.

5   Nevertheless, vegetarians seldom exceed 10 per cent of any national population—most people consume meat. The primary motivation omnivores report is that meat tastes good (Lea & Worsley, 2003). Its appetitive qualities likely reflect an evolved preference for foods high in fat, protein, and calories (Stanford, 1999). However, meat can also elicit disgust, arguably because it poses a higher risk of carrying dangerous pathogens than plant material (Fessler & Navarrete, 2003). This oral disgust can also be a moral disgust for some,

---

Margin notes:

Many academic essays include a literature review in their introductions where the authors summarize the results of studies related to their own. Other academic essays, like this one, summarize results throughout the essay.

An essay plan acts as the thesis, outlining the essay's topics in the order in which they will appear.

The authors don't define words they expect their audience to know; however, the meaning of "ambivalent" can be determined by context. Because the term "authoritarianism" is used in a specialized context in paragraph 6, the concept is defined.

A clear topic sentence linking meat and identity announces the paragraph's main idea. It is developed through two related subpoints: male identity and "valued identities." As in student essays, topic sentences in academic essays help create coherence.

A transition begins the last paragraph of this section.

The authors use balanced phrasing (first sentence) and repetition for emphasis (e.g., "moral concern," "moral worth," "considerable variability," and "this variability"). These strategies increase coherence and reader comprehension.

providing an emotional base for their moral avoidance of meat (Rozin et al., 1997). People's feelings toward meat are therefore ambivalent, and the balance of pleasure and disgust helps determine who eats meat and who rejects it (Rozin, 1996, 2004; Rozin et al., 1997).

6   Some meat eaters find their consumption less morally problematic than others. Two political ideologies underlying this individual difference are authoritarianism, the belief that it is acceptable to control and aggress against subordinates (Altemeyer, 1981), and social dominance orientation (SDO), the endorsement of social hierarchy and inequality (Sidanius & Pratto, 2001). Research has found that omnivores are higher in both factors than vegetarians and that omnivores who value inequality and hierarchy eat more red meat than those who do not (Allen & Baines, 2002; Allen, Wilson, Ng, & Dunne, 2000).

7   People may also eat meat because it expresses their identity. At a personal level, meat consumption is tied to male identity, and its consumption makes some males feel like "real men" (Rothgerber, 2013). The association is so close that meat has become metaphorically "male" (Rozin, Hormes, Faith, & Wansink, 2012), such that meat eaters are perceived as more masculine than vegetarians (Ruby & Heine, 2011). Rejecting meat can also help express valued identities. A recent cross-cultural study of vegetarianism found that Indian vegetarians value their in-group and respect authority more than omnivorous Indians do (Ruby, Heine, Kamble, Cheng, & Waddar, 2013). This finding indicates that the decision to reject meat may be tied to a sense of belonging to a cultural group and endorsement of group values.

8   In sum, the psychological characteristics of eaters may influence their appetite for eating animals. People for whom meat is a moral issue of animal welfare are inclined to eschew it; people who accept or endorse domination and inequality eat meat eagerly. Hedonic and identity-related motives also play important roles.

The Eaten

9   Understanding how people think about animals—the eaten—offers insights into the psychology of meat eating that complement those based on understanding the characteristics of eaters. In particular, an animal's perceived mind and its perceived similarity to humans are key factors influencing people's willingness to eat it.

10   Eating animals is morally troublesome when animals are perceived as worthy of moral concern. The more moral concern we afford an entity, the more immoral it becomes to harm it. People show considerable variability in the extent to which they deem animals worthy of moral concern (Bastian, Loughnan, Haslam, & Radke, 2012). This variability is partially determined by the extent to which animals are perceived to be capable of suffering. The idea that an animal's pain sensitivity can determine its moral worth dates back to Jeremy Bentham (Bentham, 1789/1907), who argued that "the question is not, Can they *reason*? nor, Can they *talk*? but, Can they *suffer*?" ("Limits Between Private Ethics and the Art of Legislation," note 122). Psychologists have corroborated Bentham's point by finding that the perceived capacity for subjective experience—including the capacity for

pain—partially underlies the extent to which entities are deemed worthy of moral concern (Waytz, Gray, Epley, & Wegner, 2010). If perceived pain sensitivity partially underlies moral concern, reducing animals' capacity to suffer might facilitate eating them.

11   Several recent studies have found this to be the case. We (Bastian, Loughnan, et al., 2012) asked people to rate the extent to which each of 32 animals possessed a set of mental capacities and their willingness to eat each animal. We found a strong negative relationship between attributed mind and edibility. Eating a more "mindful" animal was also judged as more morally wrong and more subjectively unpleasant. These findings hold across diverse samples, with other research showing that American, Canadian, Hong Kong Chinese, and Indian consumers report less willingness to eat "mindful" animals and more disgust at the thought of doing so (Ruby & Heine, 2012).

12   These findings may reflect that omnivores reduce animals' minds to justify the fact that they are eaten. Alternatively, omnivores may simply choose to eat "mindless" animals. To test whether animals are viewed as relatively lacking minds *because* they are eaten, we asked American participants to rate the extent to which a tree kangaroo was capable of feeling pain and deserved moral concern (Bratanova, Loughnan, & Bastian, 2011). Participants were told either that the animal was considered food by locals in Papua New Guinea or simply that it was an animal living there. Even though participants had never eaten tree kangaroo and did not belong to the group that did, tree kangaroos framed as "food animals" were judged less capable of suffering and less deserving of moral concern. Simply being categorized as food undermines an animal's perceived mind.

13   The perception of animals as relatively mindless may also contribute to the belief that they are dissimilar to humans. Plous (1993) showed that an animal's perceived capacity to experience pain was strongly related to its perceived similarity to humans. People not only judge humanlike animals as more pain sensitive but also experience greater autonomic arousal when watching them being mistreated (Plous, 1993) and recommend harsher sentences for people who abuse humanlike animals (Allen et al., 2002). By implication, seeing an animal as dissimilar should dampen our emotional reactions to its suffering. Indeed, people who see animals as dissimilar to humans attribute them lesser minds and consequently see them as less worthy of moral concern (Bastian, Costello, Loughnan, & Hodson, 2012). This decreased moral concern may be reflected in an increased willingness to allow animals to be harmed (e.g., for meat or for entertainment; Bastian, Costello, et al., 2012).

14   Attributing animals lesser minds and reducing their perceived capacity to suffer is a powerful means of resolving the meat paradox. Another, hitherto unexamined, possibility is that people might accept that animals can suffer but deny that animals suffer when humanely killed. By limiting animals' capacity to suffer, people can judge them less worthy of moral concern. Interestingly, reducing the perceived minds of meat animals occurs when people are *not* seeking to justify their own consumption—for example, when they categorize an animal as food (Bratanova et al., 2011) or when they contemplate the differences between humans and animals (Bastian, Costello, et al., 2012). These findings indicate that the psychological processes that support eating animals cannot be reduced to

Researchers often cite their own studies, along with those of other researchers. See References for additional experiments in which the authors of this study were involved.

Here the authors draw conclusions based on general claims, using deductive reasoning. They also use inductive reasoning extensively by citing many experiments to support their claims.

self-serving, motivated reasons; how we construe animals and the human/animal boundary is critical to our willingness to eat them. In short, the way animals are perceived is intimately tied to eating meat.

The Eating

15   Personal attributes and perceptions of animals are relatively independent of the act of eating. However, it is precisely in this moment—when a person is eating or intending to eat—that we would expect the meat paradox to require urgent resolution. Research has begun to examine the dynamic processes that facilitate meat eating.

16   In one study, we (Loughnan, Haslam, & Bastian, 2010) randomly assigned participants to consume either beef or nuts, and, subsequently, to report their moral concern for animals and rate a cow's capacity to suffer. We found that participants who had recently consumed beef, but not nuts, restricted their moral concern for animals and rated the cow as less capable of suffering. This response may have served to alleviate any post hoc negative feelings participants experienced as a result of eating meat. A similar emotion-regulation process may occur in anticipation of eating meat. In another study, participants came to the laboratory and were led to expect to sample meat or fruit (Bastian, Loughnan, et al., 2012). Participants who anticipated meat consumption attributed cows and lambs lesser minds, consistent with previous research showing that both situational and chronic meat consumption lowers mind attribution (Bilewicz, Imhoff, & Drogosz, 2011; Loughnan et al., 2010). Importantly, people in the meat condition who ascribed diminished mentality to the animals reported less negative emotional arousal when anticipating meat consumption. This finding suggests that people can alleviate unpleasant feelings aroused by meat consumption by attributing animals lesser minds.

17   The tension omnivores experience when reminded that their behaviour may not match their beliefs and values, and the resolution of this tension by changing those beliefs, fits with the theory of cognitive dissonance (Harmon-Jones & Mills, 1999). Whereas some people (e.g., vegetarians) reduce this negative state by changing their actions, others may do so by strategically changing their beliefs, specifically about animals' minds, suffering, and moral standing. Dissonance theory could help explain why the act of eating, which makes the meat paradox highly salient, motivates these psychological changes.

Conclusions

18   Eating animals has been commonplace for millennia. Nevertheless, it can generate a significant tension between people's aversion to animal harm and their desire for meat. We have examined some factors that enable people to negotiate this paradox. Meat eaters tend to care less about animal welfare, to value masculinity, and to accept social hierarchy and inequality. They tend to reduce mind attribution to animals and see them as dissimilar to humans. In preparation for eating meat, and after it, they attribute diminished mental

---

Academic writers do not just report on the findings of research: they interpret them and synthesize them with other findings. Here the authors use verbs like "may have served" and "may occur" to suggest the speculative nature of their conclusions.

In the "conclusion" or "discussion" section of academic essays, the writers usually begin by summarizing their results or main points. They may also suggest directions for future research (see the last two sentences of paragraph 18).

capacities to animals. These factors combine to reduce animals' moral standing, making their passage from farm to fork less troubling. There are a number of pathways through which people may adjust their perceptions of animals in ways that appear more consistent with their consumption of them. One putative pathway is that people change their perceptions to reduce negative affect associated with the act of meat eating. Still, no work has directly captured these negative affective reactions to the tension between concern for animal suffering and consumption of animals. Future research could employ physiological or neuroimaging measures of affective reactions (cf. Plous, 1993) that would allow researchers to capture rapid, nonconscious, or disavowed emotions associated with meat.

19   Although we believe that the psychology of eating animals is a worthy topic in its own right, it can also be viewed as an extended case study on human morality. Psychological approaches to understanding morality have typically focused on domain-general cognitive and emotional processes (e.g., Greene, 2007; Haidt, 2001) and broad, encompassing moral categories (e.g., Haidt & Joseph, 2007) or dimensions (e.g., Gray, Young, & Waytz, 2012; Janoff-Bulman, Sheikh, & Hepp, 2009; for a discussion, see Rozin, 2006). By examining a single moral behaviour, we can illuminate how emotions (pleasure, disgust, guilt), cognitions (categorization, attribution, justification), and personality characteristics (values, beliefs, identities) combine when people face everyday moral problems. In doing so, researchers have shown how emotion regulation, mind perception, and moral judgment are intimately connected. Adopting a similar approach to understanding other domains of everyday morality—narrow in its focus but deep in its attention to the complexity of the phenomenon—may prove equally fruitful.

20   In 1996, Paul Rozin made an appeal in this journal for psychologists to take meat eating seriously (Rozin, 1996). The field has heeded his call and responded by laying bare many of the psychological factors at play when people eat meat. We now have a clearer idea about who eats animals, what they think of animals, and how their psychology changes when they engage in meat eating. In doing so, we have begun to unearth the psychological roots of an ancient, widespread, and increasingly controversial behaviour.

Declaration of Conflicting Interests

21   The author declared no conflicts of interest with respect to the authorship or the publication of this article.

References

Allen, M., & Baines, S. (2002). Manipulating the symbolic meaning of meat to encourage greater acceptance of fruits and vegetables and less proclivity for red and white meats. *Appetite, 38*, 118–130.

Allen, M., Hunstone, M., Waerstad, J., Foy, E., Hobbins, T., Wikner, B., & Wirrel, J. (2002). Human-to-animal similarity and participant mood influence punishment recommendations for animal abusers. *Society & Animals, 10*, 267–284.

Another important function of the "conclusion" or "discussion" section of academic essays is the attempt to extend or broaden the conclusions.

Such statements are common in academic essays where writers need to assure their readers that they are unbiased.

Writers of academic review essays, like this one, synthesize many studies on their topic. In American Psychological Association (APA) style, the studies appear alphabetically by the last name of the first author. For more about APA formats, see p. 85.

Allen, M., Wilson, M., Ng, S., & Dunne, M. (2000). Values and beliefs of vegetarians and omnivores. *Journal of Social Psychology, 140,* 405–422.

Altemeyer, B. (1981). *Right-wing authoritarianism.* Winnipeg, Canada: University of Manitoba Press.

Amato, P., & Partridge, S. (1989). *The new vegetarians: Promoting health and protecting life.* New York, NY: Plenum Press.

American Pet Products Association. (2013). *US pet industry spending figures and future outlook.* Retrieved from www.americanpetproducts.org/press_industrytrends.asp

Bastian, B., Costello, K., Loughnan, S., & Hodson, G. (2012). When closing the human-animal divide expands moral concern: The importance of framing. *Social Psychological and Personality Science, 36,* 100–107.

Bastian, B., Loughnan, S., Haslam, N., & Radke, H. (2012). Don't mind meat? The denial of mind to animals used for human consumption. *Personality and Social Psychology Bulletin, 38,* 247–256.

Bentham, J. (1907). *An introduction to the principles of morals and legislation.* Oxford, England: Clarendon Press. (Original work published 1789). Retrieved from www.econlib.org/library/Bentham/bnthPMLCover.html

Bilewicz, M., Imhoff, R., & Drogosz, M. (2011). The humanity of what we eat: Conceptions of human uniqueness among vegetarians and omnivores. *European Journal of Social Psychology, 41,* 201–209.

Bratanova, B., Loughnan, S., & Bastian, B. (2011). The effect of categorization as food on the perceived moral standing of animals. *Appetite, 57,* 193–196.

Fessler, D., & Navarrete, C. (2003). Meat is good to taboo: Dietary proscriptions as a product of the interaction of psychological mechanisms and social processes. *Journal of Cognition and Culture, 3,* 1–40.

Food and Agriculture Organization of the United Nations. (2013). *FAOSTAT food supply—livestock and fish primary equivalent per capita* [Data set]. Retrieved from http://faostat3.fao.org/faostat-gateway/go/to/download/C/CL/E

Gray, K., Young, L., & Waytz, A. (2012). Mind perception is the essence of morality. *Psychological Inquiry, 23,* 101–124.

Greene, J. (2007). Why are VMPFC patients more utilitarian? A dual-process theory of moral judgment explains. *Trends in Cognitive Sciences, 11,* 322–323.

Haidt, J. (2001). The emotional dog and its rational tail: A social intuitionist approach to moral judgment. *Psychological Review, 108,* 814–834.

Haidt, J., & Joseph, C. (2007). The moral mind: How five sets of innate intuitions guide the development of many culture-specific virtues, and perhaps even modules. In P. Carruthers, S. Laurence, & S. Stich (Eds.), *The innate mind* (Vol. 3, pp. 367–391). New York, NY: Oxford University Press.

Harmon-Jones, E., & Mills, J. (1999). *Cognitive dissonance: Progress on a pivotal theory in social psychology.* Washington, DC: American Psychological Association.

Herzog, H. (2010). *Some we love, some we hate, some we eat: Why it's so hard to think straight about animals.* New York, NY: Harper Collins.

Janoff-Bulman, R., Sheikh, S., & Hepp, S. (2009). Proscriptive versus prescriptive morality: Two faces of moral regulation. *Journal of Personality and Social Psychology, 96,* 521–537.

Joy, M. (2010). *Why we love dogs, eat pigs, and wear cows: An introduction to carnism.* San Francisco, CA: Conari Press.

Lea, E., & Worsley, A. (2003). Benefits and barriers to the consumption of a vegetarian diet in Australia. *Appetite, 6,* 127–136.

Loughnan, S., Haslam, N., & Bastian, B. (2010). The role of meat consumption in the denial of mind and moral status to meat animals. *Appetite, 55,* 156–159.

Plous, S. (1993). Psychological mechanisms in the human use of animals. *Journal of Social Issues, 49,* 11–52.

Rose, L., & Marshall, F. (1996). Meat eating, hominid sociality, and home bases revisited. *Current Anthropology, 37,* 307–338.

Rothgerber, H. (2013). Real men don't eat (vegetable) quiche: Masculinity and the justification of meat consumption. *Psychology of Men & Masculinity, 14,* 363–375.

Rozin, P. (1996). Towards a psychology of food and eating: From motivation to module to model to marker, morality, meaning, and metaphor. *Current Directions in Psychological Science, 5,* 18–24.

Rozin, P. (2004). Meat. In S. Katz (Ed.), *Encyclopedia of food* (pp. 666–671). New York, NY: Scribner.

Rozin, P. (2006). Domain denigration and process preference in academic psychology. *Perspectives on Psychological Science, 1,* 365–376.

Rozin, P., Hormes, J., Faith, M., & Wansink, B. (2012). Is meat male? A quantitative multi-method framework to establish metaphoric relationships. *Journal of Consumer Research, 39,* 629–643.

Rozin, P., Markwith, M., & Stoess, C. (1997). Moralization and becoming a vegetarian: The transformation of preferences into values and the recruitment of disgust. *Psychological Science, 8,* 67–73.

Ruby, M. (2012). Vegetarianism: A blossoming field of study. *Appetite, 58,* 141–150.

Ruby, M., & Heine, S. (2011). Meat, morals, and masculinity. *Appetite, 56,* 447–450.

Ruby, M., & Heine, S. (2012). Too close to home. Factors predicting meat avoidance. *Appetite, 59,* 47–52.

Ruby, M., Heine, S., Kamble, S., Cheng, T., & Waddar, M. (2013). Compassion and contamination: Cultural differences in vegetarianism. *Appetite, 71,* 340–348.

Sidanius, J., & Pratto, F. (2001). *Social dominance: An intergroup theory of social hierarchy and oppression.* Cambridge, England: Cambridge University Press.

Singer, P. (1975). *Animal liberation: Toward an end to man's inhumanity to animals.* New York, NY: HarperCollins.

Stanford, C. (1999). *The hunting apes: Meat eating and the origins of human behaviour.* Princeton, NJ: Princeton University Press.

Tischler, J. (2012). A brief history of animal law, part II (1985–2011). *Stanford Journal of Animal Law and Policy, 27,* 57–59.

Waytz, A., Gray, K., Epley, N., & Wegner, D. (2010). Causes and consequences of mind perception. *Trends in Cognitive Sciences, 14,* 383–388.

Andrew D. Pinto, "Denaturalizing 'Natural' Disasters: Haiti's Earthquake and the Humanitarian Impulse"

Academic writers often analyze issues of concern to readers, using formats similar to those of student essays. Like many such essays, "Denaturalizing 'Natural' Disasters" is cross-disciplinary: while the author is a physician specializing in community medicine, the essay touches on the disciplines of history, geography, economics, ethics, and political science. Pinto uses argumentative strategies to draw attention to a problem overlooked by governments and the mainstream media.

An increasing number of "open-access" journals, like *Open Medicine*, provide access to users without requiring passwords or view fees. The *Open Medicine* website includes the journal's mission statement, along with the purpose of open-access journals.

 Preparing to Read

Are you aware of the social and economic problems that have beset Haiti prior to the devastating 2010 earthquake? Using a reliable source, briefly summarize the facts surrounding the disaster and its aftermath.

Denaturalizing "Natural" Disasters: Haiti's Earthquake and the Humanitarian Impulse

Andrew D. Pinto

Open Medicine, November 2010
(2017 words)

1   On 12 January 2010, at 16:53 local time, Haiti experienced a catastrophic magnitude-7.0 earthquake 25 kilometres west of the capital, Port-au-Prince. The United Nations Office for the Coordination of Humanitarian Affairs estimates that more than 220,000 people died and 2.3 million were displaced.[1] This earthquake was more than twice as lethal as any previous of a similar magnitude in the last century.[2] In striking contrast, the magnitude-8.8 earthquake that struck Chile on 27 February 2010 resulted in fewer than 800 deaths, despite its higher magnitude.[3]

2   Why was Haiti's experience so different? Most commentators have pointed to physical factors, such as the shallow epicentre of the earthquake, its proximity to a major population centre, poor building construction, and the lack of an adequate emergency response system.[2,4] These undoubtedly played a role in the extraordinarily high mortality rate. However, although many have noted Haiti's poverty and internal strife, only a few commentators have identified these as key determinants of the level of devastation caused by the earthquake.[5,6] Even fewer have suggested looking at the historical record or where Haiti stands in the current world order for an explanation.

3   What is considered "natural," in the context of disasters such as Haiti's, is seen as independent of human actions. Any analysis of such events must "denaturalize" them by examining the historic, political, and economic contexts within which they occur.[7,8] Specifically, health professionals and policy-makers need to understand the unnatural determinants of the problems facing the country and how these affect any form of response. Without such an understanding, the humanitarian impulse informing international efforts to support Haiti's recovery and development may serve to merely reinforce the historic relationship between wealthy countries and Haiti and may fuel continued underdevelopment.

Foundations of a disaster

4   Knowledge of Haiti's history is integral to an informed understanding of the earthquake and its outcome. Only a brief review is possible here; more detailed accounts are available elsewhere.[9,10] Soon after Spanish colonizers led by Christopher Columbus arrived in 1492 on the island they christened Hispaniola—present day Haiti and the Dominican Republic—the annihilation of the island's indigenous peoples began. Paul Farmer has argued that the triple assault of imported disease, malnutrition and maltreatment set a precedent for the subjugation of human life in Haiti at the hands of wealthy nations.[9] Plantations of sugar cane became fields of misery for tens of thousands of trafficked African slaves, while Spain and France reaped the profits.[11]

5   The French Revolution, which began in 1789, sparked a revolt of Haiti's middle class and an uprising of its slave majority. In 1804, Haiti became the second independent republic in the western hemisphere, after the United States. Further, it was the first example of slaves winning nationhood through their own resistance.[12]

6   In abolishing slavery and resisting colonial rule, Haiti was not easily tolerated by European powers or by the slave-owning United States. With its economy ruined by its revolutionary war, Haiti was forced to agree to unfair trading relationships with nations that refused to recognize its sovereignty. In 1825, France sent an armada to retake Haiti; the French invasion was averted only when the young nation agreed to pay 150 million francs as compensation for the loss of the slave trade. This indemnity was not paid off by Haiti until 1947.[10] Similar instances of gunboat diplomacy by the United States, Germany, and Britain drained Haiti's national coffers throughout the nineteenth century.[9]

7   Foreign interference and political destabilization have continually undermined governance in Haiti. For example, the United States occupied Haiti from 1915 to 1934; although the Americans have claimed that their occupation improved Haitian economic and governance infrastructure,[13] contemporary accounts note that the presence of a military force enabled the passing of a constitution that permitted foreign ownership of land.[14] The US Marines also left behind a well-trained army that went on to rule Haiti, installing and deposing leader after leader. "Papa Doc" Duvalier and his son "Baby Doc" would be the last and most horrific of these leaders, using *tonton macoutes* death squads to establish and entrench their rule between 1957 and 1986. Although foreign aid continued to flow to this regime, the national debt grew dramatically.[15] Historians agree that the Duvaliers were supported by the West throughout the Cold War, ostensibly to help fight against communism but also to support the interests of foreign companies who benefited from low-cost Haitian labour.[16]

8   Against significant odds, Jean-Bertrand Aristide was elected in the nation's first democratic elections in 1990, overwhelmingly supported by the poor and working class. His government was short lived, as his popular reforms threatened the status quo for Haiti's oligarchs and foreign interests. He was ousted in a coup after only eight months and sent into exile. After years of Aristide and his supporters lobbying the US government, and the intervention of numerous advocates, he was reinstated as president in 1994. He was re-elected in 2000, only to again be exiled during a coup in 2004. External forces played a role in both coups, leaving Haiti's political health tenuous ever since.[9,17,18]

The humanitarian impulse

9   With this historical background in mind, one can examine the response of the global community to the 2010 earthquake. Many individuals around the world generously donated funds, propelled by the humanitarian impulse, an innate, visceral urge to help fellow human beings who are suffering.[19] By 14 November, over US$3.4 billion in donations poured into international aid agencies.[20] As with the 2004 Indian Ocean tsunami, the magnitude of the devastation and the natural aspect of the disaster led to a desire to help by the global community.

10   The immediate response by the international community succeeded in many ways. Many humanitarian non-governmental organizations (NGOs) and governmental development agencies should be given credit for what they accomplished in the face of enormous devastation. Numerous rescue attempts were mounted in the immediate aftermath, and emergency medical services were operational within hours of the earthquake. In the six months following the disaster more than 4.3 million families received food assistance and more than 900,000

vaccinations of children and adults were carried out. Over 1 million people received daily water rations, and thousands of latrines were built. As a result, no major epidemics have yet occurred in any of the camps for internally displaced persons,[21] although cholera has recently begun to spread throughout the country.

11   However, some aspects of the post-earthquake response have been problematic, reflecting the history of Haiti's relationship with external actors. Media coverage of the disaster and the response often played into the stereotype of Haiti as a cursed nation.[22] There was scant recognition of the legacy left by Haiti's colonial powers and of the role these nations were now playing in the relief effort. The US military assumed the leadership of the humanitarian response almost immediately. It began by coordinating flights at the request of the Haitian government, but its role soon extended to many aspects of the relief efforts. There were examples of medical supply flights being turned away in favour of military flights.[23] Some observers have argued that too great an emphasis was placed on security, at the expense of relief operations.[24] Others have noted a focus on the protection of private property, which may have detracted from efforts to ensure access to food and water for those in need.[25] Concern about the poor coordination of the response[26] has led some commentators to take issue with the role of NGOs and with their agendas for participating in the relief efforts.[27,28] Finally, the focus on the immediate humanitarian response appears to have prevented a consideration of how the groundwork for future development could be best laid.[6]

12   At the time of publishing, the vast majority of those displaced are still living in tents or other temporary structures and over 95 per cent of the rubble has yet to be cleared.[1] The provision of essential social services by the Haitian government, including accessible education, primary health care, and a functioning police force and judiciary, is unlikely in the near future. Concerns about the trafficking of children and the sexual exploitation of women are growing.[29] Less than 10 per cent of the $5.3 billion pledged for Haiti at an international donors' conference in March 2010 has been provided.[30] Media attention has long since shifted away from Haiti, and no clear plan is evident for addressing the nation's long-term concerns, such as economic independence and a political environment free of foreign interference.

Humanitarianism based on actual histories

13   The humanitarian impulse is too often fitful and fragmented. Furthermore, the involvement of high-income countries in the root causes of the devastation caused by "natural" disasters in low-income countries is rarely examined. The political philosopher Thomas Pogge questions simplistic conceptions of injustice when they are seen primarily as issues of distribution.[31] He adds a relational element to the conception of justice. Investigations of relational justice seek to identify the causes of disparities, challenging us to look at the conditions and actions that have created them. In Pogge's reimagining of justice, wealthy nations must address their role in creating the historic conditions that have led to the profound global economic disparities we see today. He calls on wealthy nations to recognize their complicity in the exploitation of human and natural resources, the degradation and oppression of good, governance structures within poorer nations and to understand the consequences of their support for corrupt

and illegitimate regimes.[32] These actual histories should replace the more palatable fictional histories that attempt to explain away wealthy nations' past contributions to the persistent poverty in the world.[33]

14 How would acknowledging actual histories change the work of health professionals and humanitarian aid providers? Even in the initial response to a disaster, it would change how services are organized, who is leading the effort, and who sets priorities. Acknowledging actual histories may have little impact on the technical details of the initial emergency response, but it may make a difference in how relief efforts are subsequently carried out, particularly in the long term. Some may argue that disasters on the scale of the Haitian earthquake wipe out the existing civil society leadership. However, even in such conditions, the affected communities can and should be involved from the start. Actual histories can help organizations to see how the best of intentions can undermine indigenous systems and societies and can help them to understand the difference between providing temporary charity and contributing to self-sustaining, just communities.[34,35]

15 Appeals for funds can be combined with educational initiatives to explain to policy-makers and the public why an event has occurred and how it relates to social, economic, and political forces. Resilience should be emphasized over victimhood. Such campaigns could also be linked to advocacy efforts; for example, calls for economic justice could be supported[36] or efforts could be made to ensure that elections after a disaster are fair and free of foreign interference.

16 Acknowledging the actual histories that have led to Haiti's underdevelopment would require wealthy nations to probe their own political, social, and economic involvement—through action or inaction—in Haiti's underdevelopment. This would also require companies and consumers to ask themselves how they have benefited from Haiti's underdevelopment. The answers to these questions need to meaningfully inform humanitarian efforts in Haiti for these efforts to address the root conditions that enabled an earthquake to level Port-au-Prince.

Conclusion

17 Although a laudable humanitarian impulse has driven relief efforts in Haiti, it alone is insufficient for the task of rebuilding the nation. Any lasting efforts to improve life for Haiti's citizens must be informed by an understanding of the disaster's foundational causes. A humanitarian response based on actual histories could resemble the work of NGOs like Partners in Health, which has worked toward just, effective, and sustainable humanitarianism in Haiti for years. Even better would be a response that explicitly supported Haitian organizations, civil society, and government institutions to lead the recovery effort.[37]

18 The analysis presented here is certainly applicable beyond Haiti. In numerous countries where humanitarians operate, respecting history and seeing the connection between historic actions and present conditions is essential. Ultimately, standing in solidarity means making a long-term commitment to transforming how we relate to Haiti and similar nations around the world.

References

1. United Nations Office for the Coordination of Humanitarian Affairs. *Haiti: 6 months after . . .* 2010. Available: http://www.reliefweb.int/rw/RWFiles2010. nsf/FilesByRWDocUnidFilename/SNAA-8AD4 A6-full_report.pdf/$File/full_report.pdf (accessed 2010 Nov 9).

2. Bilham R. Lessons from the Haiti earthquake. *Nature* 2010;463(7283):878–879.

3. Bajak F. Chile-Haiti earthquake comparison: Chile was more prepared. *The Huffington Post* 2010 Feb 27. Available: http:// www.huffingtonpost.com/2010/02/27/chile-haiti-earthquake-co_n_479705. html (accessed 2010 Nov 5).

4. Why Haiti's quake was so devastating. *CBC News* 2010 Jan 13. Available: http://www.cbc.ca/world/story/2010/01/13/f-earthquake-devastation-comparison.html (accessed 2010 Nov 5).

5. Henley J. Haiti: a long descent to hell. *The Guardian* 2010 Jan 14. Available: http://www.guardian. co.uk/world/2010/jan/14/haiti-history-earthquake-disaster (accessed 2010 Nov 5).

6. Flegel K, Hebert PC. Helping Haiti. *CMAJ* 2010; 182(4):325.

7. Schrecker T. Denaturalizing scarcity: a strategy of enquiry for public-health ethics. *Bull World Health Organ* 2008;86(8):600–605.

8. Smith N. There's no such thing as a natural disaster. *Understanding Katrina: perspectives from the social sciences.* New York: Social Science Research Council. 2006 June 11. Available: http://understandingkatrina.ssrc.org/Smith/ (accessed 2010 Nov 5).

9. Farmer P. *The uses of Haiti.* 2nd ed. Monroe (ME): Common Courage Press; 2003.

10. Hallward P. *Damming the flood: Haiti, Aristide, and the politics of containment.* London: Verso; 2007.

11. Mintz SW. Can Haiti change? *Foreign Aff* 1995;74 (1):73–86.

12. Prou ME. Haiti's condemnation: history and culture at the crossroads. *Lat Am Res Rev* 2005; 40(3):191–201.

13. Haggerty RA. Haiti: a country study. In: Metz HC, editor. *Dominican Republic and Haiti: Country studies.* Federal Research Division, Library of Congress; 2001. Available: http://memory.loc.gov/frd/cs/httoc.html (accessed 2010 Nov 5).

14. Gruening E. The issue in Haiti. *Foreign Aff* 1993; 11(2):279–289.

15. Chatterjee P. Haiti's forgotten emergency. *Lancet* 2008;372 (9639):615–618.

16. Shamsie Y. Export processing zones: the purported glimmer in Haiti's development murk. *Rev Int Pol Econ* 2009;16(4):649–672.

17. Farmer P. Political violence and public health in Haiti. *N Engl J Med* 2004;350(15):1483–1486.

18. Dupuy A. Haiti election 2006: A pyrrhic victory for René Préval? *Lat Am Perspect* 2006;33(148): 132–141.

19. Sondorp E, Bornemisza O. Public health, emergencies and the humanitarian impulse. *Bull World Health Organ* 2005;83(3):163.

20. Financial Tracking Service. Table A: List of all commitments/contributions and pledges as of 14 November 2010. *Haiti—Earthquakes—January 2010.* New York: Office for the Coordination of Humanitarian Affairs; 2010. Available at: http://ocha.unog.ch/fts/reports/daily/ocha_R10_E15797_asof___1003150208. pdf (accessed 2010 Nov 14).

21. International Federation of Red Cross and Red Crescent Societies. *Haiti. From sustaining lives to sustainable solutions: the challenge of sanitation. Special report, six months on.* 2010. Available: http://www.ifrc.org/Docs/reports/199600-haiti-sanitation-report-july-2010-EN.pdf (accessed 2010 Nov 5).

22. British Broadcasting Corporation. White House calls Robertson's Haiti comment 'stupid.' 2010 Jan 15. Available: http://news.bbc.co.uk/2/hi/americas/8460520.stm (accessed 2010 Nov 7).

23. Médecins Sans Frontières—Canada. *Haiti: MSF cargo plane with full hospital and staff blocked from landing in Port-au- Prince.* 2010 Jan 17. Available: http://www.msf.ca/news-media/news/2010/02/haiti-msf-cargo-plane-with-full-hospital-and-staff-blocked-from-landing-in-port-au-prince/ (accessed 2010 Nov 7).

24. Associated Press. Haiti gets a penny of each U.S. aid dollar. *CBS News* 2010 Jan 27. Available: http://www.cbsnews.com/stories/2010/01/27/world/main6146903.shtml (accessed 2010 Nov 7).

25. Goodman A. With foreign aid still at a trickle, devastated Port-au-Prince General Hospital struggles to meet overwhelming need. *Democracy Now!* 2010 Jan 20. Available: http://www.democracynow.org/2010/1/20/devastated_port_au_prince_hospital_struggles (accessed 2010 Nov 7).

26. Lynch C. Top U.N. aid official critiques Haiti aid efforts in confidential email. *Foreign Policy* 2010 Feb 17. Available: http://turtlebay.foreignpolicy.com/posts/2010/02/17/top_un_aid_official_critiques_haiti_aid_efforts_in_confidential_email (accessed 2010 Nov 7).

27. Growth of aid and the decline of humanitarianism. *Lancet* 2010;375(9711):253.

28. Zoellick RB. How to rebuild Haiti. *Politico* 2010 Feb 1. Available: http://www.politico.com/news/stories/0110/32284.html (accessed 2010 Nov 7).

29. Gupta J, Agrawal A. Chronic aftershocks of an earthquake on the well-being of children in Haiti: violence, psychosocial health and slavery. *CMAJ* 2010 Aug 3. Available: http://www.cmaj.ca/cgi/rapidpdf/cmaj.100526v1 (accessed 2010 Nov 12).

30. Katz JM. Clinton: Donors still holding out on Haiti pledges. *The Boston Globe* 2010 Aug 6. Available: http://www.boston.com/news/world/latinamerica/articles/2010/08/06/clinton_donors_still_holding_out_on_haiti_pledges/ (accessed 2010 Nov 7).

31. Pogge T. Relational conceptions of justice: responsibilities for health outcomes. In: Anand S, Peter F, Sen A, editors. *Public health, ethics and equity.* Oxford (UK): Oxford University Press; 2004.

32. Pogge T. Real world justice. *J Ethics* 2005; 9(1–2):29–53.

33. Pogge T. World poverty and human rights. *Ethics Int Aff* 2005;19(1):1–7.

34. Yamin AE. Our place in the world: conceptualizing obligations beyond borders in human rights-based approaches to health. *Health Hum Rights* 2010; 12(1):3–14.

35. Ruger JP. Global health justice. *Public Health Ethics* 2009;2(3):261–275.

36. Willsher K. France urged to repay Haiti billions paid for its independence. *The Guardian* 2010 Aug 15. Available: http://www.guardian.co.uk/world/2010/aug/15/france-haiti-independence-debt (accessed 2010 Nov 7).

37. Schwartz D. The next challenge in Haiti. *CBC News* Available: www.cbc.ca/world/story/2010/03/26/f-haiti-rebuild.html (accessed 2010 Nov 7).

Comprehension

1. What is the significance of the quotation marks around *natural* in the title and in paragraph 3? What is the meaning of *denaturalize* and *unnatural* in the same paragraph? Why is it important to understand the precise way the author is using these words?

2. How does the author use the ideas of Thomas Pogge in paragraph 13? Paraphrase the last sentence in this paragraph.

Organization and Style

1. In the introduction, identify the study's justification and the thesis statement.

2. a. Identify two different rhetorical patterns used in paragraphs 6 and 7.

   b. Identify the main rhetorical pattern used in the section "Foundations of a disaster."

3. In the section "The Humanitarian Impulse,"

   a. Identify one paragraph in which the first sentence is the topic sentence.

   b. Identify one paragraph that does not have a clear topic sentence.

Critical Thinking/Research

1. Do the last two paragraphs form a successful conclusion to Pinto's argument? Analyze their effectiveness, considering the role of any argumentative strategies discussed on pp. 47–50.

2. Using "Denaturalizing 'Natural' Disasters" and one other reliable source, such as a reference work like an encyclopedia, discuss the role of colonialism in Haiti's history from its independence to the present.

Daniel M. Wegner, "How to Think, Say, or Do Precisely the Worst Thing for Any Occasion"

The author of this essay uses the format of the critical review to explore a puzzling, apparently contradictory, aspect of human behaviour. Although the essay appeared in the respected peer-reviewed journal *Science*, it was not written for highly trained experts but for those with a general knowledge of and interest in science. Readers could infer by the work's title, its abstract, and the first paragraphs that it was not an experimental study.

 Preparing to Read

Have you ever said or done the precise thing you did not want to do? How did you respond at the time (for example, become upset, laugh it off)? Freewrite for five to ten minutes about this time, trying to recall your reaction. If appropriate, this could be a group or class exercise in which individuals shared their experiences.

How to Think, Say, or Do Precisely the Worst Thing for Any Occasion

Daniel M. Wegner

Science, 3 July 2009
(3085 words)

In slapstick comedy, the worst thing that could happen usually does: The person with a sore toe manages to stub it, sometimes twice. Such errors also arise in daily life, and research traces the tendency to do precisely the worst thing to ironic processes of mental control. These monitoring processes keep us watchful for errors of thought, speech, and action and enable us to avoid the worst thing in most situations, but they also increase the likelihood of such errors when we attempt to ex- ert control under mental load (stress, time pressure, or distraction). Ironic errors in attention and memory occur with identifiable brain activity and prompt recurrent unwanted thoughts; attraction to forbidden desires; expression of objectionable social prejudices; production of movement errors; and rebounds of negative experiences such as anxiety, pain, and depression. Such ironies can be overcome when effective control strategies are deployed and mental load is minimized.

1   There are many kinds of errors. We can fall short, overreach, or skitter off the edge, of course, but we can also miss by a mile, take our eyes off the prize, throw the baby out with the bath water—and otherwise foul up in a disturbingly wide variety of ways. Standing out in this assortment of would-be wreckage, though, is one kind of error that is special: the precisely counterintentional error. This is when we manage to do the worst possible thing, the

blunder so outrageous that we think about it in advance and resolve not to let it happen.

2　　And then it does. We see a rut coming up in the road ahead and proceed to steer our bike right into it. We make a mental note not to mention a sore point in conversation and then cringe in horror as we blurt out exactly that thing. We carefully cradle the glass of red wine as we cross the room, all the while thinking "don't spill," and then juggle it onto the carpet under the gaze of our host. Normally, our vigilance for such pitfalls helps us avoid them. We steer away from ruts, squelch improper comments, and protect carpets from spills by virtue of our sensitivity to error. Knowing the worst that could happen is essential for control. But sometimes this sensitivity backfires, becoming part of a perverse psychological process that makes the worst occur.

3　　Observers of human psychology have suggested that the mind can indeed generate just such ironic errors. Edgar Allan Poe called this unfortunate feature of mind the "imp of the perverse."[1] Sigmund Freud dubbed it the "counter will."[2] William James said too that "automatic activity in the nerves often runs most counter to the selective pressure of consciousness."[3] Charles Baudouin pronounced it the "law of reversed effort,"[4] and Charles Darwin joined in to proclaim "How unconsciously many habitual actions are performed, indeed not rarely in direct opposition to our conscious will!"[5] Hieronymus Bosch illustrated this human preoccupation with the worst, depicting a world in which error, sin, and ruin are the usual consequence of human endeavor (Fig. 1).

FIGURE 1 This detail from *The Last Judgment* by Hieronymus Bosch illustrates the artist's apocalyptic vision of some of the worst that humans can think, say, or do.

Photo: Hieronymus Bosch (c.1450–1516) Erich Lessing/Art Resource NYART101554

Intentions and ironies: Best and worst

4   Do we do the worst thing more often than other things? Fortunately for the proprietors of china shops, we do not. However, accumulating evidence on ironic processes of mental control[6] reveals conditions under which people commit precisely counterintentional errors. The prototypical error of this kind occurs when people are asked to keep a thought out of mind (e.g., "don't think about a white bear"). The thought often comes back. When asked to signal any return of that thought, people may indicate that it comes back about once per minute[7]—often to echo for yet longer periods[8] and, at the extreme, to return for days.[9, 10] Some people are better at such thought suppression than others,[11, 12] of course, and some try more than others,[13] but keeping a thought out of mind remains a challenge for most of us even when we have only arbitrarily tried to suppress it.

5   Why would thought suppression be so hard? It does seem paradoxical: We try to put out of mind what we are thinking now, while still remembering at some level not to think of it later. The ironic process theory[6] suggests that we achieve this trick through two mental processes: The first is a conscious, effortful process aimed at creating the desired mental state. The person engaged in suppressing white bear thoughts, for example, might peruse the room or otherwise cast about for something, anything, that is not a white bear. Filling the mind with other things, after all, achieves "not thinking of a white bear."

6   As these distracters enter consciousness, though, a small part of the mind remains strangely alert to the white bear, searching for indications of this thought in service of ushering it away with more distractions. Ironic process theory proposes that this second component of suppression is an ironic monitoring process, an unconscious search for the very mental state that is unwanted. The conscious search for distractions and the unconscious search for the unwanted thought work together to achieve suppression—the conscious search doing the work and the unconscious search checking for errors.

7   The control system underlying conscious mental control is unique, however, in that its monitoring process can also produce errors. When distractions, stressors, or other mental loads interfere with conscious attempts at self-distraction, they leave unchecked the ironic monitor to sensitize us to exactly what we do not want. This is not a passive monitor, like those often assumed in control system theories, but rather is an active unconscious search for errors that subtly and consistently increases their likelihood via processes of cognitive priming.[14] For example, when people are asked not to think about a target word while under pressure to respond quickly in a word association task, they become inclined to offer precisely that forbidden target word[15]. Indeed, with time pressure people more often blurt out a word while suppressing it than when they are specifically asked to concentrate on it.

8   Fortunately, the ironic return of suppressed thoughts is not inevitable, or we would be plagued by every thought we had ever tried to put out of mind. We can stop thinking of things quite successfully when we have time to devote to the project and become absorbed in our self-distractions. The ironic rebound of suppressed thoughts after suppression is mainly evident when people abandon the attempt to suppress or are encouraged to revisit the suppressed thought.[16, 17] The ironic return of suppressed thoughts during suppression is found only sporadically when people are simply reporting their thoughts but is readily observed with measures of thought that are sensitive to automatic, uncontrollable indications of the thought.[18]

9   For example, when people are asked to name the colours in which words are displayed and encounter a word they have been asked not to think about, they name the word's colour more slowly—apparently because their attention is rapidly drawn to the word's meaning and so interferes with colour-naming.[15, 19] Such automatic attention to suppressed thoughts surfaces in colour-naming when people are under mental load (such as holding a five-digit number in mind) and can be found as an effect of load in many paradigms.[20, 21] Colour-naming research reveals, though, that ironic monitoring processes are not limited only to suppression; they also occur during intentional concentration. People intentionally concentrating on particular words under load show slowed colour-naming for words that are not concentration targets because these non-targets now pop more easily to mind.[19] Perhaps this is why concentrating under pressure, such as during last-minute studying, seems to accentuate the clarity of every stray noise within earshot.

10   The ironic monitoring process also influences memory. Memories we try to forget can be more easily remembered because of the ironic results of our efforts, but they do this mainly when mental loads undermine conscious attempts to avoid the memories.[22, 23] People attempting to forget many items at once can do so with some success,[24, 25] perhaps because monitoring multiple control projects dilutes ironic monitoring effects.[26] Functional magnetic resonance imaging studies show a similar disparity in brain activity: People trying to forget many targets show a suite of changes in brain activity associated with forgetting,[27] whereas those trying not to think of a single target show specific monitoring-related activity of the anterior cingulate and dorsolateral prefrontal cortex.[28, 29] The brain regions subserving ironic and intentional processes are differentiable when people do targeted mental control tasks.

Taboos and faux pas: Worst thoughts and utterances

11   Ironic lapses of mental control often appear when we attempt to be socially desirable, as when we try to keep our minds out of the gutter. People instructed to stop thinking of sex, for example, show greater arousal (as gauged by finger skin conductance) than do those asked to stop thinking about a neutral topic. Indeed, levels of arousal are inflated during the suppression of sex thoughts to the same degree that they inflate during attempts to concentrate on such thoughts.[8] In research on sexual arousal per se, male participants instructed to inhibit erections as they watched erotic films found it harder than they had hoped, so to speak—particularly if they imbibed a mental load in the form of a couple of alcoholic drinks.[30] Ironic effects also may underlie the tendency of homophobic males to show exaggerated sexual arousal to homoerotic pictures.[31]

12   The causal role of forbidden desires in ironic effects is clear in experimental research on the effects of imposed secrecy.[32] People randomly paired to play "footsie" under the table in a laboratory study reported greater subsequent attraction to their assigned partner when they had been asked to keep their contact secret from others at the table, and survey respondents revealed similar effects of tainted love: a greater desire for past romantic partners with whom relationships had first started in secret.[33] This desire seems to arise as an ironic emotional effect of suppression: People who are asked not to think about a specific old flame show greater psychophysiological arousal than do others when later allowed to think about that relationship.[34]

13   Like forbidden romance, other occasions for social deception are a fertile source of ironic

effects. People admonished to keep an item private in conversation, for example, become more likely to mention it; speakers asked to keep a target hidden from an addressee more often leaked its identity by making inadvertent reference to it—for example, describing the target in Fig. 2 as a "small triangle" and thereby revealing that the occluded object was a larger one.[35] Interviewees with eating disorders who role-played not having a disorder for the interviewer also showed ironic effects. During the interview, they reported intrusive thoughts of eating and revealed preoccupation with the topic by rating the interviewer, too, as the likely victim of an eating disorder.[36]

14 Another challenge for mental control is keeping a lid on our social prejudices. There is substantial evidence that racism, sexism, homophobia, and other prejudices can be expressed automatically after all, even when we try to control them.[37, 38] But the ironic process theory holds that unconscious urges to express such prejudices will be especially insistent when we try to control them under load. This possibility was initially documented in research that asked British participants to suppress their stereotypes of skinheads (white supremacists) and found that such stereotypes then rebounded—even leading experimental participants to sit far away from a skinhead in a waiting room.[39] Ironic effects have since surfaced showing that expressions of prejudice against racial, ethnic, national, and gender groups are often prompted by attempts to be "politically correct" under mental load.[40, 41, 42] The desire to be fair and unprejudiced, exercised in haste or distraction, can engender surprising levels of bias and prejudice.

Yips and worries: Worst movements and emotions

15 Pressures to avoid the worst are not always a matter of doing what is socially desirable—they can arise in attempts to achieve self-imposed goals as well. The desire to succeed at a task defines the worst thing that could happen in that situation as failure at this task. So, when people grasp a string with a weight attached and try to keep this pendulum from swinging in one direction, they often find that the pendulum swings

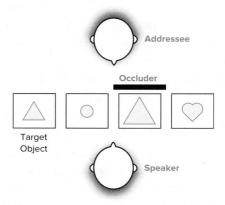

FIGURE 2 Speaker who is asked to describe the mutually visible target becomes more likely to mention a clue to the hidden target that is irrelevant to the addressee (e.g., saying "small triangle" rather than "triangle") when instructed to conceal the identity of the target from the addressee. [Adapted from Lane, L.W. et al. (2006).[35]]

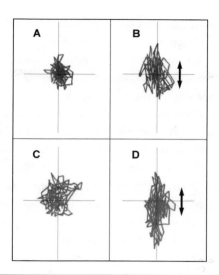

FIGURE 3 Sample tracings of 30-s videos from below a handheld pendulum on a string when pendulum holder is asked to (A) hold it steady, (B) keep it from swinging parallel to the arrow, (C) hold it steady while counting backward from 1000 by threes, or (D) keep it from swinging parallel to the arrow while counting backward from 1000 by threes. [Figure based on data from Wegner et al. (1998).43]

in just the way they hope to avoid.43 And, as predicted by ironic process theory, the pendulum is even more likely to swing in the unwanted direction when its holder is distracted by counting backward from 1000 by threes (Fig. 3).

16   Sports psychologists and coaches are familiar with ironic movement errors, counterintentional movements induced by the very desire to prevent them. Former major league baseball players Chuck Knoblauch, Steve Blass, and Rick Ankiel were famed for sporadic wild throws as well as for the desire to avoid them, Ankiel even calling his chronic error "the Creature".44 In golf putting, the ironic tendency has a name (the "yips"), and golfers who are instructed to avoid a particular error (e.g., "don't overshoot") indeed make it more often when under load.43, 45 Eye-tracking cameras reveal that soccer players who are instructed to avoid kicking a penalty shot to a particular part of the goal more often direct their gaze to the very area to be avoided.46 Perhaps the common sensation we get as we look over

a precipice—that we are teetering toward the edge—is an accurate perception of our subtle ironic movements. (It may be best when poised at the brink, by the way, not to count backward from 1000 by threes.)

17   Worries and fears are also fertile ground for ironic effects. Unwanted emotions associated with thoughts not only provide a reason to avoid those thoughts but also prompt an unwanted emotional punch when the thoughts return. Emotions we put out of mind are experienced with unusual intensity when the emotional thoughts recur after suppression.19, 34, 47 Depressed mood is especially recalcitrant, recurring after suppression when reminders, negative events, or increased mental loads are encountered.48 And when anxious thoughts are suppressed under mental load, their return can rekindle anxiety with particular vigor.49

18   Worry about falling asleep yields similar ironic effects: People urged to fall asleep as quickly as possible, but who are also given a mental load

(in the form of Sousa march music), are particularly likely then to have trouble sleeping.[50] The common observation that dreams centre on unpleasant and emotionally disturbing topics makes sense in this light: When people are instructed to suppress thoughts of neutral or emotional topics before sleep, they report more frequent dreaming about those topics.[51–53] If we spontaneously choose to avoid unpleasant or worrisome thoughts in daytime, it makes sense that such thoughts would then populate our dreams.

19   Puzzling ironies arise too in response to pain. Usually, people exposed to painful stimulation report higher levels of felt pain when they direct their attention toward the pain. However, suppression of laboratory-induced pain can result in some ironic effects, including ironic increments in suppressed pain and ironic decrements in attended pain.[54–56] Such effects are unreliable and have not been examined under variations in mental load, so conclusions are not yet clear.[57, 58] Caution should also be exercised in considering ironic effects of thinking about death. People suppress thoughts of death spontaneously or use strategies other than direct suppression, so ironic effects of suppressing thoughts of one's own death are not always evident.[59] Research on such effects is complicated when natural attempts people make to gain mental control obscure the effects of experimental manipulations of control striving.

Putting the worst behind us

20   The ubiquity of ironic effects suggests we should consider it something of a treat when we control ourselves successfully. According to ironic process theory, however, successful control is likely to be far more prevalent than ironic error because people often use effective strategies for control and deploy them under conditions that are not mentally loading. Ironic effects are often small, and the experimental production of ironic errors often depends on the introduction of artificial loads, time pressures, or other means of magnifying ironic effects. Even such amplifiers of ironic error may be overcome, however, in certain individuals with talents for mental control. People who are susceptible to hypnotic suggestion, for example, and who are given suggestions to control thoughts show heightened mental control without ironic effects.[60, 61]

21   The rest of us, however, who go through life without special talent for mental control, sometimes must turn to other tactics to overcome ironic error. Strategies people use to relax excessive striving for control, for example, show promise in reducing the severity of ironic effects. Potentially effective strategies include accepting symptoms rather than attempting to control them[62] and disclosing problems rather than keeping them secret.[63] Therapies devised for improving mental control—or for helping people to relax it—remain largely untested, however, and there are enough ambiguities surrounding the translation of laboratory research into effective treatments that recommendations for clinical practice at this time are premature. Current research indicates only that, under certain conditions, we may be better able to avoid the worst in what we think, do, or say by avoiding the avoiding. Failing that, our best option is to orchestrate our circumstances so as to minimize mental load when mental control is needed.

Acknowledgments

Thanks to K. Gray, A. Heberlein, A. Jenkins, A. Knickman, K. Koh, and T. Wegner for helpful comments. This work was supported by National Institute for Mental Health grant MH 49127.

References and Notes

1. E. A. Poe, "The imp of the perverse," *Graham's Lady's and Gentleman's Magazine* (July 1845), vol. 28, pp. 1–3.

2. S. Freud, in *The Standard Edition of the Complete Psychological Works of Sigmund Freud*, J. Strachey, Ed. (Hogarth, London, 1950), vol. 1, pp. 115–128.

3. W. James, *Mind* 4, 1 (1879).

4. C. Baudoin, *Suggestion and Autosuggestion* (Dodd, Mead, New York, 1921).

5. C. Darwin, *On the Origin of Species by Means of Natural Selection* (Broadview, Peterborough, Canada, 2003).

6. D. M. Wegner, *Psychol. Rev.* 101, 34 (1994).

7. D. M. Wegner, D. J. Schneider, S. Carter, T. White, *J. Pers. Soc. Psychol.* 53, 5 (1987).

8. D. M. Wegner, J. W. Shortt, A. W. Blake, M. S. Page, *J. Pers. Soc. Psychol.* 58, 409 (1990).

9. H. Trinder, P. M. Salkovskis, *Behav. Res. Ther.* 32, 833 (1994).

10. P. Muris, H. Merckelbach, R. Horselenberg, *Behav. Res. Ther.* 34, 501 (1996).

11. R. D. V. Nixon, J. Flood, K. Jackson, *Pers. Individ. Dif.* 42, 677 (2007).

12. D. F. Tolin, J. S. Abramowitz, A. Przeworski, E. B. Foa, *Behav. Res. Ther.* 40, 1255 (2002).

13. D. M. Wegner, S. Zanakos, *J. Pers.* 62, 615 (1994).

14. E. T. Higgins, in *Unintended Thought*, J. S. Uleman, J. A. Bargh, Eds. (Guilford, New York, 1999), pp. 75–123.

15. D. M. Wegner, R. E. Erber, *J. Pers. Soc. Psychol.* 63, 903 (1992).

16. J. S. Abramowitz, D. F. Tolin, G. P. Street, *Clin. Psychol. Rev.* 21, 683 (2001).

17. E. Rassin, H. Merckelbach, P. Muris, *Clin. Psychol. Rev.* 20, 973 (2000).

18. D. M. Wegner, in *Advances in Experimental Social Psychology*, M. Zanna, Ed. (Academic Press, San Diego, CA, 1992), vol. 25, pp. 193–225.

19. D. M. Wegner, R. E. Erber, S. Zanakos, *J. Pers. Soc. Psychol.* 65, 1093 (1993).

20. A. C. Page, V. Locke, M. Trio, *J. Pers. Soc. Psychol.* 88, 421 (2005).

21. L. S. Newman, K. J. Duff, R. F. Baumeister, *J. Pers. Soc. Psychol.* 72, 980 (1997).

22. C. N. Macrae, G. V. Bodenhausen, A. B. Milne, R. L. Ford, *J. Pers. Soc. Psychol.* 72, 709 (1997).

23. S. Najmi, D. M. Wegner, *Conscious. Cogn.* 17, 114 (2008).

24. M. C. Anderson, C. Green, *Nature* 410, 366 (2001).

25. D. M. Wegner, F. Quillian, C. E. Houston, *J. Pers. Soc. Psychol.* 71, 680 (1996).

26. R. M. Wenzlaff, D. E. Bates, *Pers. Soc. Psychol. Bull.* 26, 1200 (2000).

27. M. C. Anderson et al., *Science* 303, 232 (2004).

28. J. P. Mitchell et al., *Psychol. Sci.* 18, 292 (2007).

29. C. L. Wyland, W. M. Kelley, C. N. Macrae, H. L. Gordon, T. F. Heatherton, *Neuropsychologia* 41, 1863 (2003).

30. H. B. Rubin, D. R. Henson, *Psychopharmacology (Berlin)* 47, 123 (1976).

31. H. E. Adams, L. W. Wright Jr., B. A. Lohr, *J. Abnorm. Psychol.* 105, 440 (1996).

32. J. D. Lane, D. M. Wegner, *J. Pers. Soc. Psychol.* 69, 237 (1995).

33. D. M. Wegner, J. D. Lane, S. Dimitri, *J. Pers. Soc. Psychol.* 66, 287 (1994).

34. D. M. Wegner, D. B. Gold, *J. Pers. Soc. Psychol.* 68, 782 (1995).

35. L. W. Lane, M. Groisman, V. S. Ferreira, *Psychol. Sci.* 17, 273 (2006).

36. L. Smart, D. M. Wegner, *J. Pers. Soc. Psychol.* 77, 474 (1999).

37. A. G. Greenwald, M. R. Banaji, *Psychol. Rev.* 102, 4 (1995).

38. J. A. Bargh, in *Dual Process Theories in Social Psychology*, S. Chaiken, Y. Trope, Eds. (Guilford, New York, 1999), pp. 361–382.

39. C. N. Macrae, G. V. Bodenhausen, A. B. Milne, J. Jetten, *J. Pers. Soc. Psychol.* 67, 808 (1994).

40. M. J. Monteith, J. W. Sherman, P. G. Devine, *Pers. Soc. Psychol. Rev.* 2, 63 (1998).

41. A. D. Galinsky, G. B. Moskowitz, *J. Exp. Soc. Psychol.* 43, 833 (2007).

42. C. N. Macrae, G. V. Bodenhausen, *Annu. Rev. Psychol.* 51, 93 (2000).

43. D. M. Wegner, M. Ansfield, D. Pilloff, *Psychol. Sci.* 9, 196 (1998).

44. J. Merron, "Ankiel can't seem to conquer 'The Creature'" (2003), http://assets.espn.go.com/mlb/s/2003/0615/ 1568307.html.

45. D. L. Beilock, J. A. Afremow, A. L. Rabe, T. H. Carr, *J. Sport Exerc. Psychol.* 23, 200 (2001).

46. F. C. Bakker, R. R. D. Oudejans, O. Binsch, J. Van der Kamp, *Int. J. Sport Psychol.* 37, 265 (2006).

47. E. H. W. Koster, E. Rassin, G. Crombez, G. W. B. Naring, *Behav. Res. Ther.* 41, 1113 (2003).

48. C. G. Beevers, R. M. Wenzlaff, A. M. Hayes, W. D. Scott, *Clin. Psychol. Sci. Pract.* 6, 133 (1999).

49. D. M. Wegner, A. Broome, S. J. Blumberg, *Behav. Res. Ther.* 35, 11 (1997).

50. M. E. Ansfield, D. M. Wegner, R. Bowser, *Behav. Res. Ther.* 34, 523 (1996).

51. D. M. Wegner, R. M. Wenzlaff, M. Kozak, *Psychol. Sci.* 15, 232 (2004).

52. F. Taylor, R. A. Bryant, *Behav. Res. Ther.* 45, 163 (2007).

53. R. E. Schmidt, G. H. E. Gendolla, *Conscious. Cogn.* 17, 714 (2008).

54. D. Cioffi, J. Holloway, *J. Pers. Soc. Psychol.* 64, 274 (1993).

55. L. Goubert, G. Crombez, C. Eccleston, J. Devulder, *Pain* 110, 220 (2004).

56. J. D. Eastwood, P. Gaskovski, K. S. Bowers, *Int. J. Clin. Exp. Hypn.* 46, 77 (1998).

57. A. G. Harvey, B. McGuire, *Behav. Res. Ther.* 38, 1117 (2000).

58. A. I. Masedo, M. R. Esteve, *Behav. Res. Ther.* 45, 199 (2007).

59. J. Arndt, J. Greenberg, S. Solomon, T. Pyszczynski, L. Simon, *J. Pers. Soc. Psychol.* 73, 5 (1997).

60. B. J. King, J. R. Council, *Int. J. Clin. Exp. Hypn.* 46, 295 (1998).

61. R. A. Bryant, S. Wimalaweera, *Int. J. Clin. Exp. Hypn.* 54, 488 (2006).

62. P. Bach, S. C. Hayes, *J. Consult. Clin. Psychol.* 70, 1129 (2002).

63. J. W. Pennebaker, *Psychol. Sci.* 8, 162 (1997).

Comprehension

1. a. In your own words, define the following:
    - *counterintentional errors* (pars. 1 and 4); and
    - *ironic process theory* (pars. 5 and 6).

    b. Find a synonym or near-synonym for *counterintentional error* in the introductory section.

2. Define *mental load* (par. 9, etc.) and explain the importance of this concept in Wegner's essay.

3. Summarize one paragraph from "Taboos and Faux Pas: Worst Thoughts and Utterances."

Organization and Style

1. Consider the range of examples in paragraph 3. What disciplines are referred to in this paragraph, and what is its main function?

2. Discuss the ways that the author attracts our interest in his essay as well as the strategies he uses to maintain it throughout. Refer to specific passages.

3. Discuss strategies used to make information understandable to a reader with minimal knowledge of science or psychology (i.e., an educated non-specialist). Refer to specific passages.

Critical Thinking

1. Who appears to be the most important researcher in this field (see pars. 1–5)?

2. a. Does Wegner consider "counterintentional errors" a major problem in most people's lives?

    b. Can these errors be overcome by most people? Explain why or why not.

Harold Herzog, "The Impact of Pets on Human Health and Psychological Well-Being: Fact, Fiction, or Hypothesis?"

"The Impact of Pets" illustrates the need for clear organization in academic review articles. Diverse studies on a topic need to be carefully categorized and logically connected to one another. Using critical thinking, the author begins by questioning the common perception that pets provide physical and psychological benefits for their owners. In his review, he underscores a vital principle: findings can be taken as reliable only if experimental results can be replicated.

 Preparing to Read

Have you and/or your family owned a pet? Consider the pros and cons of pet ownership from your own perspective (you could freewrite on the topic).

The Impact of Pets on Human Health and Psychological Well-Being: Fact, Fiction, or Hypothesis?

Harold Herzog

Current Directions in Psychological Science,
August 2011
(2300 words)

1   Many people are deeply attached to companion animals. In the United States, over two-thirds of households include a pet, most of which are regarded by their owners as family members. Considering that the lifetime costs of owning a pet are about $8000 for a medium-sized dog and $10,000 for a cat (cats tend to live longer than dogs), devoting resources on a crea-ture with whom you share no genes and who is unlikely to ever return the favour seems to make little evolutionary sense. Aside from the expense, there are other downsides to companion animals. In the United States, a person is 100 times more likely to be seriously injured or killed by a dog than by a venomous snake, and over 85,000 Americans are taken to emergency rooms each year because of falls caused by their pets. Further, people can contract a cornucopia of diseases from companion animals, including brucellosis, roundworm, skin mites, *E. coli*, salmonella, giardia, ringworms, and cat-scratch fever. And, pets are second only to late-night noise as a source of conflict between neighbors.

2   Although not culturally universal, pet keeping exists in most societies, and an array of theories have been offered to explain why people bring animals into their lives (Herzog, 2010). Among these are the misfiring of parental instincts, biophilia (a hypothetical biologically-based love of

nature), social contagion, the tendency for the middle class to emulate the customs of the rich, the need to dominate the natural world, social isolation in urban societies, and the desire to teach responsibility and kindness to children. While the reasons that pet keeping has become a widespread cultural phenomenon are unclear, it is evident that companion animals are vitally important in the lives of many people.

The "pet effect"

3   When asked what they specifically get from their relationships with pets, people typically mention companionship, having a play partner, and the need to love and care for another creature. But fueled by media reports and books with titles like *The Healing Power of Pets: Harnessing the Amazing Ability of Pets to Make and Keep People Happy and Healthy* (Becker, 2002), the public has come to accept as fact the idea that pets can also serve as substitutes for physicians and clinical psychologists. The idea that living with an animal can improve human health, psychological well-being, and longevity has been called the "pet effect" (Allen, 2003).

4   Most pet owners believe that their companion animals are good for them. Personal convictions, however, do not constitute scientific evidence. Claims about the medical and psychological benefits of living with animals need to be subjected to the same standards of evidence as a new drug, medical device, or form of psychotherapy. Over the past 30 years, hundreds of studies have examined the impact of pets on human health and happiness. Here I argue that, contrary to media reports, an examination of this body of literature indicates that the pet effect remains an uncorroborated hypothesis rather than an established fact. (Note that the main focus of this article is on the effects of pets on the physical and mental health of their owners, not the efficacy of animals as therapeutic agents for disorders such as autism and attention-deficit/hyperactivity disorder.)

The evidence that pets are good for people

5   The first demonstration of an association between pets and health was an early study of 92 heart-attack victims in which 28 per cent of pet owners survived for at least a year as compared to only 6 per cent of non-pet owners (Friedmann, Katcher, Lynch, & Thomas, 1980). These findings generated a flurry of research on the positive impact of interacting with companion animals (see review by Wells, 2009a). For example, stroking dogs and cats, watching tropical fish in an aquarium, and even caressing a pet boa constrictor have been reported to reduce blood pressure and stress levels. The most convincing of these studies was a clinical trial in which hypertensive stockbrokers were randomly assigned to either pet or no-pet conditions. Six months later, when put in a stressful situation, subjects in the pet group showed lower increases in blood pressure than did those in the non-pet control condition (Allen, Shykoff, & Izzo, 2001). Researchers have also reported that psychological benefits accrue from living with animals. These include studies showing that pet owners have higher self-esteem, more positive moods, more ambition, greater life satisfaction, and lower levels of loneliness (El-Alayli, Lystad, Webb, Hollingsworth, & Ciolli, 2006).

6   Epidemiologists have also connected pet ownership to better health and well-being (see review by Headey & Grabka, 2011). For example, among 11,000 German and Australian adults, pet owners were in better physical condition than non-pet owners, and they made 15 per cent fewer doctor

visits, a potential savings of billions of dollars in national health expenditures. And an epidemiological study of Chinese women found that pet owners exercised more, slept better, felt more physically fit, and missed fewer days from work than women without pets. Further, these effects were particularly strong for individuals who reported that they were very closely attached to their pets.

Now the bad news

7   Pet owners are, of course, delighted to read about research that confirms the view that living with a dog or cat makes for a happier and longer life. But while the media abounds with stories extolling the health benefits of pets, studies in which pet ownership has been found to have no impact or even negative effects on human physical or mental health rarely make headlines. For instance, there was no media coverage of a recent study of 425 heart-attack victims that found pet owners were *more* likely than non-pet owners to die or suffer remissions within a year of suffering their heart attack (22 per cent versus 14 per cent; Parker et al., 2010). Indeed, replication has been a persistent problem with research on the effects of pets on human health. Straatman, Hanson, Endenburg, and Mol (1997), for instance, found that performing a stressful task in the presence of a dog had no short-term effect on blood pressure. And a study of 1179 older adults found no differences in the blood pressure or risk of hypertension of pet and non-pet owners (Wright, Kritz-Silverstein, Morton, Wingard, & Barrett-Connor, 2007). (The pet owners in the study did, however, exercise less than non-owners and were more apt to be overweight.)

8   The impact of pets on psychological well-being has also been called into question. A Pew Research Center survey of 3000 Americans found no differences in the proportion of pet owners and non-owners who described themselves as "very happy" (in Herzog, 2010). Researchers in England administered the UCLA–Loneliness scale to people who were seeking a companion animal. When retested 6 months later, the individuals who had acquired pets were just as lonely as they were before they got their companion animal. In addition, they were no happier than participants who had not gotten a pet (Gilbey, Mc-Nicholas, & Collis, 2007). Another recent study found that older adults who were highly attached to their dogs tended to be more depressed than individuals who were not as attached to their companion animals (Miltiades & Shearer, 2011).

9   Nor has pet ownership fared well in recent epidemiological studies. A study of 40,000 Swedes found that while pet owners were physically healthier than non-pet owners, they suffered more from psychological problems including anxiety, chronic tiredness, insomnia, and depression (Müllersdorf, Granström, Sahlqvist, & Tillgren, 2010). A Finnish study of 21,000 adults reported that pet owners were at increased risk for hypertension, high cholesterol, gastric ulcers, migraine headaches, depression, and panic attacks (Koivusilta & Ojanlatva, 2006). In an Australian study of 2551 elderly adults, dog ownership was associated with poorer physical health and with depression (Parslow, Jorm, Christensen, & Rodgers, 2005). Finally, in a longitudinal study of nearly 12,000 American adults, cat or dog ownership was unrelated to mortality rates (Gillum & Obisesan, 2010).

Reasons why pet-effect research is inconclusive

10   For many people, pets are profoundly pleasurable and a source of psychological support. The fact is, however, that empirical studies of the effects of pets on human health and

well-being have produced a mishmash of conflicting results. While pets are undoubtedly good for some people, there is presently insufficient evidence to support the contention that, as a group, pet owners are healthier or happier or that they live longer than people who do not have companion animals in their lives. Why are the results of studies on the pet effect so inconsistent? Ioannidis (2005) argues that conflicting results and failures to replicate are especially prevalent in areas of science in which studies are characterized by small and homogeneous samples, a wide diversity of research designs, and small effect sizes. He also believes that research topics that are particularly "hot" are especially prone to replication problems. All of these criteria apply to research on the effects of pets on human health.

11   Design problems are common in studies of human–animal interactions. Meta-analyses enable scientists to look for patterns in the results of multiple studies on the same topic, but there have been no meta-analyses of studies of the effects of pets on owner happiness or health. However, for a meta-analysis in a related area (the effectiveness of animal-assisted therapy), Nimer and Lundahl (2007) had to comb through 250 studies to find 49 that met even minimal standards for methodological rigor.

12   There is also the problem of how to interpret differences between pet owners and non-owners. Most studies reporting positive effects of pets are not true experiments in which the subjects are randomly assigned to "pet" and "non-pet" groups. Rather, they involve correlational or quasiexperimental designs that compare people who choose to live with pets with people who do not. Hence, while it might be the case that pets *cause* their owners to be healthier and happier, it is equally possible that the causal arrow points the other direction—that people who are healthier, happier, and wealthier to begin with are more likely to have the energy and financial resources required to bring companion animals into their lives and to keep them for extended periods. (Of course, the caution against conflating correlation and causality also applies to studies in which pet ownership has been found to be associated with poorer mental or physical health.)

13   In addition, many studies of human–animal interactions are based on self-reports of pet owners. While these can be useful, self-reports sometimes produce results that are at odds with more objective indices of health. For example, Wells (2009b) investigated the impact of acquiring a pet on individuals suffering from chronic fatigue syndrome. She found that while the pet owners in the study claimed their animals provided them with a host of psychological and physical benefits, their scores on standardized measures (the Chalder Fatigue Questionnaire, the General Health Questionnaire (12), and the Short Form (37) Health Survey) indicated that they were just as tired, depressed, worried, and stressed as chronic fatigue sufferers who did not get a pet.

14   A problem called the "file drawer effect," which plagues many areas of research, also skews the scientific literature on human–animal relationships. This is the tendency for negative results to wind up in the researcher's filing cabinet rather than in the pages of a scientific journal. At a session at a 2009 conference on human–animal interactions, for example, one researcher reported that separation from their pets had no effect on the psychological adjustment of college students, another found that interacting with animals did not reduce depression in psychiatric nursing home residents, and a third found no differences in the loneliness of adult pet owners and nonowners. So far, none of these studies have appeared in print.

15 Finally, erroneous positive results are more common in areas of science in which researchers have vested interests—financial or otherwise—in a study's outcome. Researchers are often drawn to the study of human–animal relationships because they are pet lovers who are personally convinced of the healing powers of the human–animal bond. Hence, investigators in this field need to be particularly vigilant in designing studies that reduce the chances of unconsciously biasing research results. This can be especially problematic in studies on the impact of pets on human health in which it is often difficult or impossible to eliminate placebo effects via traditional methods such as single- and double-blind experimental and control groups.

Why psychologists should study human–animal relationships

16 In short, despite the growing body of research on the bonds between people and pets, the existence of a pet effect on human health and happiness remains a hypothesis in need of confirmation rather than an established fact. This conclusion should not be taken as a condemnation of pet keeping. Indeed, companion animals have always been part of my own life, and I understand the joys that come with living with members of other species. Nor am I arguing that behavioural scientists should avoid studying the impact of animals on human health and well-being. In fact, we need more rather than less research on this topic.

17 Rozin (2006) cogently observed that in their quest to explain general principles of behaviour, psychologists have neglected huge domains of human life such as food, work, and religion. I would add our attitudes, behaviours, and relationships with other species to the list of topics that most people find fascinating but that psychologists have, for the most part, ignored. The study of our interactions with animals is interesting, important, and challenging. Whether, and under what circumstances, pets make people happier and healthier is unclear. It is, however, clear that animals play a role in nearly every aspect of human psychological and cultural life. And our attitudes and behaviours toward and relationships with other species offer a unique window into many aspects of human nature.

Declaration of Conflicting Interests

The author declared no potential conflicts of interest with respect to the research, authorship, and/or publication of this article.

References

Allen, K. (2003). Are pets a healthy pleasure? The influence of pets on blood pressure. *Current Directions in Psychological Science, 12,* 236–239.

Allen, K., Shykoff, B.E., & Izzo, J.L. (2001). Pet ownership, but not ACE inhibitor therapy, blunts home blood pressure responses to mental stress. *Hypertension, 38,* 815–820.

Becker, M. (2002). *The healing power of pets: Harnessing the amazing ability of pets to make and keep people happy and healthy.* New York, NY: Hyperion Books.

El-Alayli, A., Lystad, A.L., Webb, S.R., Hollingsworth, S.L., & Ciolli, J. L. (2006). Reigning cats and dogs: A pet-enhancement bias and its link to pet attachment, pet–self similarity, self-enhancement, and well-being. *Basic and Applied Social Psychology, 28,* 131–143.

Friedmann, E., Katcher, A., Lynch, J., & Thomas, S. (1980). Animal companions and one-year survival of patients after discharge from a coronary care unit. *Public Health Reports, 95,* 307–312.

Gilbey, A., McNicholas, J., & Collis, G.M. (2007). A longitudinal test of the belief that companion animal ownership can help reduce loneliness. *Anthrozoös, 20,* 345–353.

Gillum, R.F., & Obisesan, T.O. (2010). Living with companion animals, physical activity and mortality in a US national cohort. *International Journal of Environmental Research and Public Health, 7,* 2452–2459.

Headey, B., & Grabka, M. (2011). Health correlates of pet ownership from national surveys. In P. McCardle, S. McCune, J.A. Griffin & V. Maholmes (Eds.), *How animals affect us: Examining the influence of human–animal interaction on child development and human health* (pp. 153–162). Washington, DC: American Psychological Association.

Herzog, H. (2010). *Some we love, some we hate, some we eat: Why it's so hard to think straight about animals.* New York, NY: Harper.

Ioannidis, J.P.A. (2005). Why most published research findings are false. *PLoS Medicine, 2,* 696–701.

Koivusilta, L.K., & Ojanlatva, A. (2006). To have or not to have a pet for better health? *PloS One, 1,* 1–9.

Miltiades, H., & Shearer, J. (2011). Attachment to pet dogs and depression in rural older adults. *Anthrozoös, 24,* 147–154.

Müllersdorf, M., Granström, F., Sahlqvist, L., & Tillgren, P. (2010). Aspects of health, physical/leisure activities, work, and sociodemographics associated with pet ownership in Sweden. *Scandinavian Journal of Public Health, 38,* 53–63.

Nimer, J., & Lundahl, B. (2007). Animal-assisted therapy: A meta-analysis. *Anthrozoös, 20,* 225–238.

Parker, G., Gayed, A., Owen, C., Hyett, M., Hilton, T., & Heruc, G. (2010). Survival following an acute coronary syndrome: A pet theory put to the test. *Acta Psychiatrica Scandinavica, 121,* 65–70.

Parslow, R.A., Jorm, A.F., Christensen, H., & Rodgers, B. (2005). Pet ownership and health in older adults: Findings from a survey of 2,551 community-based Australians aged 60–64. *Gerontology, 51,* 40–47.

Rozin, P. (2006). Domain denigration and process preference in academic psychology. *Perspectives on Psychological Science, 1,* 365–376.

Straatman, I., Hanson, E.K.S., Endenburg, N., & Mol, J.A. (1997). The influence of a dog on male students during a stressor. *Anthrozoös, 10,* 191–197.

Wells, D.L. (2009a). The effects of animals on human health and well-being. *Journal of Social Issues, 65,* 523–543.

Wells, D.L. (2009b). Associations between pet ownership and self-reported health status in people suffering from chronic fatigue syndrome. *Journal of Alternative and Complementary Medicine, 15,* 407–413.

Wright, J.D., Kritz-Silverstein, D., Morton, D.J., Wingard, D.L., & Barrett-Connor, E. (2007). Pet ownership and blood pressure in old age. *Epidemiology, 18,* 613–617.

⊚ Comprehension

1. In your own words, explain the "file drawer effect" (par. 14).

2. Why does the author believe that more, rather than fewer, research studies on the effects of pets are needed (see par. 16)?

⚒ Organization and Style

1. Identify the bases of comparison in paragraphs 5–6 and 7–9. Why is it important that the same order of points is used in these two sections?

2. Identify two strategies for comprehension the writer uses in his article, referring to at least one specific example for each.

💡 Critical Thinking

1. How does the author justify his study?
2. Of the reasons Herzog gives for the inconsistency of results in the section "Reasons why pet-effect research is inconclusive," which do you believe is the most important? Explain.

Simine Vazire and Erika N. Carlson, "Others Sometimes Know Us Better than We Know Ourselves"

This article is a critical review that evaluates the current state of knowledge on a topic of interest. (See Loughnan et al., p. 300; Herzog, p. 323; and Wegner, p. 314.) Such essays use analysis and synthesis in order to determine how much has been done and how much research needs to be done, concluding with suggestions for practical applications.

Because these kinds of academic essays deal with interrelated research areas, differing methodologies, and (usually) a large number of studies, organization is crucial to their success. In this case, the authors use questions as headings to suggest specific subtopics while providing a coherent structure for each section (see "Organization and Style" question 1).

Preparing to Read

1. Have you ever thought about how well you know yourself, or whether others' opinions about you might be more accurate than your own perceptions? Write down five positive or neutral personality traits that best describe you; then, have a close friend or family member write down five positive or neutral traits he or she believes describe you. Compare the results.

2. If you have ever taken personality tests like the "Big Five" or the Myers-Briggs Type Indicator (versions may be available online from reliable websites), compare the test results with your own perceptions. Can you account for any differences in test results and your own beliefs about yourself? (See the essay "Do You Have the Brain of a CEO?" by Joanna Pachner in Section IV for more on personality tests.)

Others Sometimes Know Us Better than We Know Ourselves

Simine Vazire and Erika N. Carlson

Current Directions in Psychological Science,
April 2011
(2352 words)

Abstract

Most people believe that they know themselves better than anyone else knows them. However, a complete picture of what a person is like requires both the person's own perspective and the perspective of others who know him or her well. People's perceptions of their own personalities, while largely accurate, contain important omissions. Some of these blind spots are likely due to a simple lack of information, whereas others are due to motivated distortions in our self-perceptions. Perhaps for these reasons, others can perceive some aspects of personality better than the self can. This is especially true for traits that are very desirable or undesirable, when motivational factors are most likely to distort self-perceptions. Therefore, much can be learned about a person's personality from how he or she is seen by others. Future research should examine how people can tap into others' knowledge to improve self-knowledge.

> "Do we understand each other?"
> Gracie wants to know . . . .
> "Better than we understand ourselves,"
> I tell her.
>
> -*Straight Man*, Richard Russo, p. 106

1   Who knows you best? Most of us have the powerful intuition that we know ourselves better than others know us (Pronin, Kruger, Savitsky, & Ross, 2001). Indeed, there are several good reasons to think that we are the best judge of ourselves: We have privileged knowledge about our own histories, our thoughts and feelings, and our private behaviours. Yet, we all know people who seem to be deluded about themselves—which raises the uncomfortable possibility that we, too, might be so deluded.

2   When it comes to our own personalities, there is increasing evidence that our blind spots are substantial. Moreover, others can sometimes see things about our personalities that we cannot. The aim of this paper is to review the latest evidence concerning the accuracy of self- and other-perceptions of personality and show that a complete picture of what a person is like requires both the person's own perspective and the perspective of others who know him or her well. This conclusion has implications for researchers and practitioners who rely on self-reports and for people who want to get to know others—or themselves.

How could we not know?

3   The first step in establishing that others know things about our personality that we do not is to show that there are gaps in our self-knowledge. Why do we sometimes misperceive our own personality? Some blind spots may be due to a simple lack of information. We have all experienced the supervisor who, unbeknownst to him, has a persistent frown when listening intently and, as a result, is a lot more intimidating than he realizes. A simple dose of feedback could bring his self-perception in line with his behaviour (or even better, bring his behaviour in line

with his self-perception). Blind spots can also be due to having too much information—we have access to so many of our thoughts, feelings, and behaviours that we often have a hard time mentally aggregating this evidence and noticing patterns (Sande, Goethals, & Radloff, 1988). For example, most of us can probably think of many times when we have acted friendly or unfriendly, making it difficult to know how friendly we are in general. In other words, it is difficult for us to see the forest for the trees.

4   In many cases, however, blind spots are not so innocent—they are the result of motivated cognitive processes. One motive that has a strong influence on self-perception is the motive to maintain and enhance our self-worth (Sedikides & Gregg, 2008). There is a great deal of research documenting the lengths people will go to in order to maintain a positive view of themselves, leading to flawed self-assessment (Dunning, 2005). While our desire to protect our sense of self-worth influences our self-perception, it is not clear that these biases are always in the positive direction. Indeed, there are important individual differences in self-enhancement (Paulhus, 1998) and some people seek to confirm their overly negative self-views (Swann, 1997). What is beyond doubt is that self-perception is not simply an objective, neutral process. Motivated cognition influences and distorts self-perception in a multitude of ways that help to create and maintain blind spots in self-knowledge. As a result, we cannot judge our own personality as dispassionately as we might a stranger's.

5   One vivid example of blind spots in self-knowledge comes from research on the discrepancies between people's explicit and implicit perceptions of their own personality. Implicit personality is typically measured by tapping into people's automatic associations between themselves and specific traits or behaviours. The logic behind these measures is that people form automatic or implicit associations (e.g., between the concepts "me" and "assertive") based on their previous patterns of behaviour. Thus, the traits that people automatically associate with themselves in implicit tests may predict behaviour above and beyond the traits they consciously endorse in explicit measures of personality. Indeed, this is exactly what has been found. In one study, people's implicit self-views of their personality predicted their behaviour even after controlling for what could be predicted from their explicit self-views (Back, Schmukle, & Egloff, 2009). This pattern was strongest for extraversion and neuroticism, traits that are non-evaluative and that people are typically willing to report honestly, which suggests that people have implicit knowledge about their pattern of behaviours that they cannot report on explicitly.

6   Are these implicit blind spots merely an efficient way to process information—it may be easier to form implicit associations than to constantly update our explicit self-views—or are they the result of motivated cognition? If processing self-knowledge implicitly were merely a matter of efficiency, we should be able to increase the congruence between our explicit and implicit self-views simply by focusing our attention on the behavioural manifestations of our implicit personality. Contrary to this prediction, participants who watched themselves on video did not bring their explicit self-views more in line with their implicit personality, despite the fact that strangers who watched the same videos were able to detect the implicit aspects of the targets' personalities (Hofmann, Gschwendner, & Schmitt, 2009). Thus, it seems that our motives sometimes lead us to ignore aspects of our personality that others can detect. As a result, our conscious self-perceptions provide a valuable but incomplete perspective on our personality.

How do they know?

7   The second step in establishing that others may know things about our personality that we do not is to show that others are adept at detecting personality. As it turns out, many aspects of personality are remarkably transparent to others, even when we are not intentionally broadcasting them. For example, many traits can be judged accurately from people's physical appearance, their Facebook profiles, or a brief interaction (Kenny & West, 2008). This evidence suggests that our day-to-day behaviour is infused with traces of our personality and that others make good use of these cues when inferring our personality (Mehl, Gosling, & Pennebaker, 2006). In addition, we (intentionally and unintentionally) broadcast our personality in our living spaces, music collections, and online habitats (Gosling, 2008). In other words, others have plenty of fodder for detecting our personality, while we see ourselves through the distorted lens of our own motives, biases, wishes, and fears.

8   Of course, not all others are created equal— the relationship between the judge and the target matters. While too much intimacy can lead to the same biases that distort self-perceptions (e.g., one's self-worth can be threatened as much by the knowledge that one's spouse is incompetent as it is by the thought of one's own incompetence), closeness is usually associated with greater accuracy (see Biesanz, West, & Millevoi, 2007, for a thorough review). Moreover, the better we get along with others, the more accurately they can infer our thoughts and feelings (Thomas & Fletcher, 2003). Overall, across all types and levels of acquaintance that have been examined, people form remarkably accurate impressions of one another.

9   These findings show that we are astute judges of each others' personalities, likely due to the importance of interpersonal perception for our social species. As a result, other people— especially those who spend a lot of time around us and who we open up to—almost inevitably become experts on our personality. This conclusion should cast serious doubt on the longstanding assumption among researchers that we necessarily know our own personality better than others know us. It seems likely that, at least for some aspects of personality, others might be in a better position to see us clearly than we are.

Who knows what?

10   The goal of this article is not to bring readers to despair of self-perceptions. Rather, the goal is to make the case that others sometimes see aspects of our personality that we are blind to. Perhaps the most important evidence is the body of research that directly compares the accuracy of self- and other-perceptions of personality. Here we focus on studies that measure accuracy using a correlational approach—that is, by comparing judgments by the self and others to a criterion. The available evidence suggests that self- and other-perceptions are roughly equally good at predicting behaviour in a laboratory (e.g., behaviour in a group discussion; Kolar, Funder, & Colvin, 1996; Vazire, 2010), predicting real-world behaviour (e.g., behaviour when out with friends; Vazire & Mehl, 2008), and predicting outcomes (e.g., discharge from the military; Fiedler, Oltmanns, & Turkheimer, 2004). However, the overall equality in levels of accuracy obscures a more interesting pattern: Self- and other-ratings of a person's personality do not simply provide redundant information. Instead, they capture different aspects.

11   Vazire (2010) recently proposed the self-other knowledge asymmetry (SOKA) model to map out the aspects of personality that are known uniquely to the self or uniquely to others.

According to this model, the differences between what we know about ourselves and what others know about us are not random but are driven by differences between the information available to the self and others and motivational biases that differentially affect perceptions of the self and others (Andersen, Glassman, & Gold, 1998).

12   Specifically, Vazire (2010) proposed that the self has better information than others do for judging internal traits—traits defined primarily by thoughts and feelings, such as being anxious or optimistic—but that others have better information than the self for judging external traits—traits defined primarily by overt behaviour, such as being boisterous or charming. In addition, Vazire argued that self-perception on highly evaluative traits (e.g., being rude, being intelligent) is severely distorted by biases. As a result, self-ratings on evaluative traits often do not track our actual standing on those traits (but instead might track individual differences in self-esteem or narcissism). In contrast, when perceiving others on highly evaluative traits, we are able to form impressions that are mostly accurate (assuming we have enough information). This is not to say that others see us more harshly than we see ourselves. In fact, there is evidence that close others may in fact have more positive impressions of us than we do, but that their perceptions are nevertheless more accurate. This can happen if people who have the most positive ratings from their friends also tend to actually have the most positive personalities (even if nobody's personality is quite as delightful as their friends portray it). In this case, friends' ratings would be overly positive in an absolute sense, but more accurate in their rank order, and thus friends' ratings would be a very good predictor of actual behaviour (e.g., those whose friends say they are the most friendly are likely to behave the friendliest).

13   To test these hypotheses, Vazire (2010) compared self- and friend-ratings of personality to how people behaved in videotaped laboratory exercises and how they performed on intelligence and creativity tests. Consistent with Vazire's first hypothesis, self-ratings of internal, neutral traits (e.g., anxiety, self-esteem) were better than friends' ratings at predicting behaviour (Fig. 1). Consistent with her second hypothesis, friends' ratings of evaluative traits (e.g., intelligence, creativity) were better than self-ratings at predicting performance in these domains.

14   Consistent with the SOKA model, other research has shown that close others are often better than the self at predicting very desirable or undesirable outcomes, such as college GPA, relationship dissolution, and coronary disease. Together, these findings suggest that those who know us well sometimes see things that we do not see in ourselves, particularly when it comes to aspects of our personality that are observable to others and that we care a lot about (and thus cannot see objectively).

What do we do now?

15   The appropriate conclusion from the empirical literatures seems to be that to know people's personalities, we need to know both how they see themselves and how they are seen by others who know them well. The fact that self-perception is an important part of personality is not new; the novel finding is that others also know a lot about us that we don't know. How can we tap into others' knowledge to improve our self-knowledge? Direct, honest feedback might be very useful, but it is rare, and probably for good reason. A more realistic strategy is to take the perspective of others when perceiving our own personality (i.e., meta-perception). Research suggests that

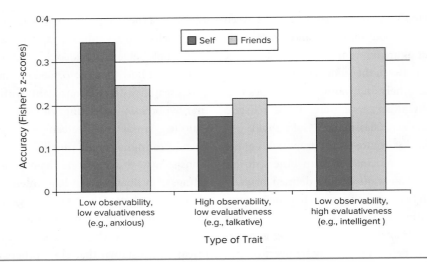

FIGURE 1   Accuracy of Self- and Friends-Ratings for Different Traits

Average accuracy scores (transformed to Fisher's z-scores for purposes of comparison) for self- and friends-ratings of personality traits that are less observable and less evaluative (left), more observable and less evaluative (middle), and less observable and more evaluative (right). Adapted from Vazire (2010).

although we overestimate the degree to which others share our perception of ourselves, we are able to detect the impression we make on others, even when meeting someone for the first time (Carlson, Furr, & Vazire, 2010). We also seem to know how we are seen differently by people who know us in different contexts (e.g., parents versus friends; Carlson & Furr, 2009). In short, it seems that we have some awareness of how others see us, but we do not always make use of this information when judging our own personality. Thus, we may be able to improve our self-knowledge by placing more weight on our impressions of how others see us—particularly, as Vazire's (2010) research suggests, when it comes to observable, evaluative traits (e.g., funny, charming).

16   Finally, introspection has historically attracted a great deal of attention as a route to self-knowledge. Unfortunately, recent research shows that many aspects of ourselves are hidden from conscious awareness, limiting the effectiveness of introspection in the pursuit of self-knowledge (Wilson, 2009). Perhaps a more promising avenue for increasing self-knowledge is to reduce the self-protective motives (e.g., defensiveness) that prevent us from seeing ourselves objectively. Recent work suggests that self-affirmation reduces defensive responding and makes us more open to negative information about ourselves (Critcher, Dunning, & Armor, 2010). Along the same lines, training in mindfulness meditation (i.e., non-judgmental attention to one's current experience) improves people's emotion-regulation skills, memory, and attention and can improve their ability to differentiate between their transient emotional experiences and their global dispositions (Williams, 2010). Thus, these techniques may reduce the two major obstacles to self-knowledge: lack of information and motivational biases.

17   In short, little is known about successful routes to improving self-knowledge. Clearly, much remains to be learned about how we can know ourselves better. What is now evident, however, is

that, as a fortune cookie admonishes, "There are lessons to be learned by listening to others."

Acknowledgments

18   We thank Krystle Disney, John Doris, Sam Gosling, Sanjay Srivastava, and Tim Wilson for their helpful suggestions concerning this article.

Declaration of Conflicting Interests

19   The authors declared that they had no conflicts of interest with respect to their authorship or the publication of this article.

References

Andersen, S.M., Glassman, N.S., & Gold, D.A. (1998). Mental representations of the self, significant others, and nonsignificant others: Structure and processing of private and public aspects. *Journal of Personality and Social Psychology, 75,* 845–861.

Back, M.D., Schmukle, S.C., & Egloff, B. (2009). Predicting actual behavior from the explicit and implicit self-concept of personality. *Journal of Personality and Social Psychology, 97,* 533–548.

Biesanz, J.C., West, S.G., & Millevoi, A. (2007). What do you learn about someone over time? The relationship between length of acquaintance and consensus and self-other agreement in judgments of personality. *Journal of Personality and Social Psychology, 92,* 119–135.

Carlson, E.N., & Furr, R.M. (2009). Evidence of differential metaaccuracy: People understand the different impressions they make. *Psychological Science, 20,* 1033–1039.

Carlson, E.N., Furr, R.M., & Vazire, S. (2010). Do we know the first impressions we make? Evidence for idiographic meta-accuracy and calibration of first impressions. *Social Psychological and Personality Science, 1,* 94–98.

Critcher, C.R., Dunning, D., & Armor, D.A. (2010). When self-affirmations reduce defensiveness: Timing is key. *Personality and Social Psychology Bulletin, 36,* 947–959.

Dunning, D. (2005). *Self-insight: Roadblocks and detours on the path to knowing thyself.* New York, NY: Psychology Press.

Fiedler, E.R., Oltmanns, T.F., & Turkheimer, E. (2004). Traits associated with personality disorders and adjustment to military life: Predictive validity of self and peer reports. *Military Medicine, 169,* 207–211.

Gosling, S.D. (2008). *Snoop: What your stuff says about you.* New York, NY: Basic Books.

Hofmann, W., Gschwendner, T., & Schmitt, M. (2009). The road to the unconscious self not taken: Discrepancies between self- and observer-inferences about implicit dispositions from nonverbal behavioral cues. *European Journal of Personality, 23,* 343–366.

Kenny, D.A., & West, T.V. (2008). Zero-acquaintance: Definitions, statistical model, findings, and process. In N. Ambady & J.J. Skowronski (Eds.), *First impressions* (pp. 129–146). New York, NY: Guilford Press.

Kolar, D.W., Funder, D.C., & Colvin, C.R. (1996). Comparing the accuracy of personality judgments by the self and knowledgeable others. *Journal of Personality, 64,* 311–337.

Mehl, M.R., Gosling, S.D., & Pennebaker, J.W. (2006). Personality in its natural habitat: Manifestations and implicit folk theories of personality in daily life. *Journal of Personality and Social Psychology, 90,* 862–877.

Paulhus, D.L. (1998). Interpersonal and intrapsychic adaptiveness of trait self-enhancement: A mixed blessing? *Journal of Personality and Social Psychology, 74,* 1197–1208.

Pronin, E., Kruger, J., Savitsky, K., & Ross, L. (2001). You don't know me, but I know you: The illusion of asymmetric insight. *Journal of Personality and Social Psychology, 81,* 639–656.

Russo, R. (1988). *Straight man.* New York, NY: Vintage.

Sande, G.N., Goethals, G.R., & Radloff, C.E. (1988). Perceiving one's own traits and others': The multifaceted self. *Journal of Personality and Social Psychology, 54,* 13–20.

Sedikides, C., & Gregg, A.P. (2008). Self-enhancement: Food for thought. *Perspectives on Psychological Science, 3,* 102–116.

Swann, W.B., Jr. (1997). The trouble with change: Self-verification and allegiance to the self. *Psychological Science, 8,* 177–180.

Thomas, G., & Fletcher, G.J.O. (2003). Mind-reading accuracy in intimate relationships: Assessing the roles of the relationship, the target, and the judge. *Journal of Personality and Social Psychology, 85,* 1079–1094.

Vazire, S. (2010). Who knows what about a person? The self-other knowledge asymmetry (SOKA) model. *Journal of Personality and Social Psychology, 98*, 281–300.

Vazire, S., & Mehl, M.R. (2008). Knowing me, knowing you: The accuracy and unique predictive validity of self-ratings and other-ratings of daily behavior. *Journal of Personality and Social Psychology, 95*, 1202–1216.

Williams, J.M. (2010). Mindfulness and psychological process. *Emotion, 10*, 1–7.

Wilson, T.D. (2009). Know thyself. *Perspectives on Psychological Science, 4*, 384–389.

◉ Comprehension

1. Identify specific words or phrases in the first three paragraphs that show this essay is intended more for a wider audience than experts in perceptual psychology.

2. Define *implicit personality* (par. 5) and briefly explain its importance to personality researchers.

3. a. Explain how Vazire tested her hypotheses that the self is a better judge of internal traits but not as good a judge of external traits of the individual.

   b. Explain the results of the testing (pars. 12–13).

◉ Organization and Style

1. Analyze the organizational strategies used in the section "How Do They Know?" to increase comprehension. (You can consider paragraph structure and development; strategies for coherence, such as repetition, transitions, and word choice; and use of sources.)

2. In your own words, explain the importance of the graph on p. 334.

◉ Critical Thinking

1. Why is direct feedback rarely used to help us understand our own personalities (par. 15)?

2. After reading the concluding section, "What Do We Do Now?" do you think the authors are optimistic about the opportunities that exist for gaining self-knowledge? Explain your answer by referring to at least three specific points in this section.

Erin R. Whitchurch et al., "'He Loves Me, He Loves Me Not . . .': Uncertainty Can Increase Romantic Attraction"

This scholarly essay presents the findings of an experiment designed to explore an aspect of human relationships—using the medium of Facebook. Articles based on lab experiments usually adhere to a very specific structure: they are divided into introductory, methods, results, and discussion (IMRAD) sections. (See Chapter 10, p. 140 for a detailed discussion on IMRAD; see also "How Random Is the Toss of a Coin?" p. 352, which uses the same structure.) Each section has a specific function; for example, in the "Results" section, the researchers present the numerical data, usually with the help of tables or charts. In the "Discussion" section, they summarize their results and suggest how their findings can be used.

The article's abstract takes the reader through the stages of the experiment, beginning by defining an important term; it includes brief mention of the study's method before summarizing its results and conclusions.

 Preparing to Read

Read the first three paragraphs of the essay, noting their organization and layout.
1. Was the meaning of the paragraphs clear?
2. Were ideas logically developed?
3. Why might clarity and accessibility of information be important in essays like this one?

"He Loves Me, He Loves Me Not . . . ": Uncertainty Can Increase Romantic Attraction

Erin R. Whitchurch, Timothy D. Wilson, and Daniel T. Gilbert

Psychological Science, February 2011 (2783 words)

Abstract

This research qualifies a social psychological truism: that people like others who like them (the reciprocity principle). College women viewed the Facebook profiles of four male students who had previously seen their profiles. They were told that the men (a) liked them a lot, (b) liked them only an average amount, or (c) liked them either a lot or an average amount (uncertain condition). Comparison of the first two conditions yielded results consistent with the reciprocity principle. Participants were more attracted to men who liked them a lot than to men who liked them an average amount. Results for the uncertain condition, however, were consistent with research on the pleasures of uncertainty. Participants in the uncertain condition were most attracted to the men—even more attracted than were participants who were told that the men liked them a lot. Uncertain participants reported thinking about the men the most, and this increased their attraction toward the men.

1 Substantial research shows that people like others who like them—which is known as the reciprocity principle (Aronson & Worchel, 1966; Gouldner, 1960; Kenny, 1994; Luo & Zhang, 2009). It is rewarding to be liked by others, and these social rewards generate positive feelings. Further, people assume that those who like them have benevolent intentions and will treat them well (Montoya & Insko, 2008). Thus, if we want to know how much Sarah likes Bob, a good predictor is how much she thinks Bob likes her.

2   But what if Sarah is not sure how much Bob likes her? He seems interested, but in the words of a popular book and movie, maybe he is "just not that into" her (Behrendt & Tuccillo, 2009). How much will Sarah like Bob under this condition of uncertainty? Research on reciprocity suggests that she should like him less than if she were certain that he liked her, because the less certain she is, the fewer social rewards she should experience and the less sure she can be that he has good intentions toward her. In other words, according to the reciprocity principle, Sarah should like Bob more when she is certain that he likes her than when she believes he might not.

3   Recent research on the pleasures of uncertainty, however, suggests otherwise. Under some circumstances, uncertainty about the nature of a positive event can produce more positive affect than certainty about the nature of that event (Bar-Anan, Wilson, & Gilbert, 2009; Kurtz, Wilson, & Gilbert, 2007; Lee & Qiu, 2009; Wilson, Centerbar, Kermer, & Gilbert, 2005). When people are certain that a positive event has occurred, they begin to adapt to it, primarily by reaching an understanding of what the event means and why it occurred (Wilson & Gilbert, 2008). Thus, whereas people may be very pleased that someone likes them, once they are certain of this fact they construct explanations as to why, and as a result the news loses some of its force.

4   In contrast, when people are uncertain about an important outcome, they can hardly think about anything else. They think about such an event but do not yet adapt to it, because they do not know which outcome to make sense of and explain. The affective consequences of such uncertainty depend on the valence of the thoughts people have about the potential outcomes. Often these thoughts are negative, because one of the possible outcomes is undesired and people's attention is drawn to that possibility (e.g., "the biopsy might show that I have cancer"). In such a case, uncertainty will lead to an increase in negative affect. Sometimes, however, the potential outcomes are positive or neutral, such as the possibility that a new, attractive acquaintance is very fond of us (positive) or has no special impression of us (neutral).

5   There may thus be an exception to the reciprocity principle: People might like someone more when they are uncertain about how much that person likes them than when they are certain, as long as they have some initial attraction toward the person. Uncertainty causes people to think more about the person, we suggest, and, further, people might interpret these thoughts as a sign of liking via a self-perception effect (e.g., "I must like him if he keeps popping into my thoughts"; Bem, 1972). In short, people's uncertainty about how much another person likes them—such that they pick petals off a flower to try to find out whether that person loves them or loves them not—may increase their liking for that person.

6   Prior studies of the pleasures of uncertainty have examined the effects of uncertainty about such things as the source of a gift, and the dependent measure in prior studies was overall mood, not interpersonal attraction (e.g., Kurtz et al., 2007). We are unaware of any studies that have examined the effects of uncertainty on interpersonal attraction.[1] In the present study, female college students learned that male college students at other universities had looked at Facebook profiles of several college women, including the participants' profiles, and had rated how much they liked each woman. Participants then looked at the profiles of four of the men. Some participants were told that they were viewing the men who had liked them the most, some were told that they were viewing the men who had

given them average ratings, and some (in the uncertain condition) were told that they were viewing either the men who had liked them the most or the men who had given them average ratings. We predicted that participants in the uncertain condition would be most attracted to the men.

Method

Participants

7   Participants were 47 female undergraduates at the University of Virginia who participated in return for partial course credit.

Procedure

8   Participants signed up at least 48 hours in advance of their session, with the understanding that their Facebook profiles would be viewed by students at other universities. When participants arrived for the experimental session, the experimenter explained that the study was exploring the effectiveness of Facebook as an online dating website and that several male students from two collaborating universities had viewed the Facebook profiles of approximately 15 to 20 female college students, including the participants', and had rated the degree to which they thought they would get along with each woman if they got to know her better. Each participant was told that she would see the Facebook profiles of four of the men. In the liked-best condition, participants learned that they had been randomly assigned to see the four men who had given them the highest ratings (e.g., "of all the people who saw your profile, these are the four who thought they would like you the best"). In the average-liking condition, participants learned that they had been randomly assigned to see the four men who had

given them average ratings (e.g., "of all the people who saw your profile, these four did not rate you as the highest or the lowest; they are people who liked you about average"). In the uncertain condition, participants read:

> 9   For reasons of experimental control neither you nor the experimenter knows the condition you have been randomly assigned to. The profiles you will see might be the participants who saw your profile and liked you the most. Or, the profiles you see might be the participants who saw your profile and gave you an average rating.

10   Participants then examined four fictitious Facebook profiles that convincingly portrayed likeable, attractive male college students (two Caucasian, one African American, and one Asian), ostensibly from the University of Michigan and the University of California, Los Angeles. Next, participants completed several filler tasks and dependent measures.

11   *Time 1 mood.* After completing a filler task, participants rated the degree to which the adjectives *positive*, *pleased*, *disappointed*, and *sad* described how they felt at that moment. Ratings were made on 21-point dot scales (1 = *not at all*, 21 = *extremely*).

12   *Attraction to the male students.* After completing additional filler tasks, participants rated each man according to how much they liked him, how much they wanted to work with him on a class project, and how similar they were to him (1 = *not at all*, 8 = *extremely*); how much they would be interested in him as a casual acquaintance and as a friend (1 = *not at all*, 10 = *extremely*); and how much they would be interested in him as "someone I would hook up with" and as "a potential boyfriend/girlfriend" (1 = *not at all*, 10 = *extremely*). A factor analysis revealed that all of these items except interest in

the man as a casual acquaintance had a loading of at least .40 on a primary liking factor. We therefore averaged the standardized ratings of all items except the casual-acquaintance item to form an attraction index (α = .86).

13   *Time 2 mood.* After rating their attraction to the men, participants rated their mood again on the same measures that they had received earlier.

14   *Reported thoughts.* Finally, participants rated the extent to which thoughts about the men had "popped into their head" during the previous 15 min (1 = *not at all*, 9 = *extremely often*) and then were thoroughly debriefed.

Results

Attraction

15   An analysis of variance revealed a significant effect of condition on participants' attraction toward the men, $F(2, 44) = 15.06, p < .001$ $\eta^2 = .41$. As Table 1 shows, participants in the liked-best condition were more attracted to the men than were participants in the average-liking condition, $t(44) = 3.52, p = .001$. This finding replicates the reciprocity effect. As predicted, participants in the uncertain condition were most attracted to the men—even more attracted than were participants in the liked-best condition, $t(44) = 2.07, p = .04$. In other words, women were more attracted to men whose liking for them was uncertain than to men who they knew liked them the best.

Reported thoughts

16   As predicted, participants in the uncertain condition reported having thought about the men the most, followed by participants in the average-liking condition and then participants in the liked-best condition (see Table 1). Although the overall effect of condition was not significant, $F(2, 43) = 2.14, p = .13, \eta^2 = .09$, participants in the uncertain condition reported thinking significantly more about the men than did participants in the liked-best condition, as predicted, $t(43) = 1.99, p = .05$.

Mediation

17   In a mediation analysis, we compared participants in the uncertain condition (dummy code = 1) with participants in the liked-best condition (dummy code = 0). Condition significantly predicted participants' frequency of thought about the men, $b = 1.51 (SE = 0.70)$, $p = .04$, and frequency of thought marginally

TABLE 1	Mean Attraction to the Men, Frequency of Thought About the Men, and Mood by Condition		
	Condition		
Measure	**Uncertain**	**Liked best**	**Average liking**
Attraction	0.57 (0.44)	0.12 (0.60)	−0.62 (0.71)
Reported thoughts	5.07 (2.17)	3.56 (1.67)	4.63 (2.34)
Mood, Time 1	16.64 (3.62)	16.09 (2.04)	13.55 (4.25)
Mood, Time 2	16.89 (2.97)	15.24 (3.11)	13.40 (4.41)

Note: Standard deviations are in parentheses. The attraction index is the average of the standard scores of six items. The mood index is the average of ratings of two positive adjectives and two (reverse-scored) negative adjectives. Higher numbers reflect greater attraction to the men in the profiles, more frequent thought about the men, and more positive moods.

predicted participants' level of attraction (controlling for condition), $b = 0.09$ ($SE = 0.05$), $p = .10$. These results are consistent with our hypothesis that the effect of uncertainty on attraction would be mediated by frequency of thought about the men. However, because a bootstrapping analysis revealed that the 95 per cent confidence interval for the indirect effect ([-.03, .40]) did not quite exclude zero, the evidence for mediation is tentative (Shrout & Bolger, 2002).

Mood

18 We averaged responses to the four mood items after reverse scoring the two negative items (Time 1 $\alpha = .86$, Time 2 $\alpha = .84$). A 3 (condition; between subjects) × 2 (time; within subjects) analysis of variance revealed a main effect of condition, $F(2, 44) = 3.86$, $p = .03$, $\eta^2 = .15$. Participants were in a better mood in the liked-best condition than in the average-liking condition, $t(44) = 2.70$, $p = .01$ (see Table 1). Participants were in an even better mood in the uncertain condition, though the difference between the uncertain and like-best conditions was not significant, $t(44) = 0.92$, $p = .36$.

Discussion

19 This study replicated the effects of reciprocity on attraction: Participants liked the men more when they believed the men liked them a lot than when they believed the men liked them only an average amount. As predicted, however, participants in the uncertain condition were most attracted to the men. Put differently, women were more attracted to men when there was only a 50 per cent chance that the men liked them the best than when there was a 100 per cent chance that the men liked them the best. Also as predicted, women in the uncertain condition reported thinking about the men more than did women in the like-best condition.

20 These results help solve an enigma about whether "playing hard to get" increases one's attractiveness to others. Numerous popular books advise people not to display their affections too openly to a potential romantic partner and to instead appear choosy and selective. Social psychological research, however, has not confirmed this advice. Walster, Walster, Piliavin, and Schmidt (1973), for example, found evidence only for a "selectively hard to get" hypothesis: Men were most attracted to a potential date who expressed interest in them but not other people, and were less attracted to a woman who was "uniformly hard to get" (she was unenthusiastic about dating anyone) or a woman who was "uniformly easy to get" (she was enthusiastic about dating several men).

21 A form of playing hard to get that has not been tested, however, is keeping the person guessing about how one feels about him or her without communicating anything about how interested one is in other people. Ours is the first study to manipulate uncertainty in the absence of any information about choosiness, and by so doing has confirmed a new version of the playing-hard-to-get hypothesis: People who create uncertainty about how much they like someone can increase that person's interest in them.

22 We should note some limitations of the present research. First, the participants rated the men on the basis of a small amount of information, and it is unclear whether people's uncertainty about how much someone likes them would continue to increase attraction once they meet the person and begin relationship. However, many people meet online these days, and this study simulated the kind of information people often get about potential dating partners. Uncertainty at the very beginning of this process appears to confer some benefits.

23   Second, we included only female participants. Previous research has not found gender differences in the pleasure of uncertainty (e.g., Wilson et al., 2005), but this is the first study examining the effects of uncertainty on interpersonal attraction, and it is possible that there are gender differences in this domain.

24   Finally, we did not replicate previous studies that found that participants who were uncertain about a positive outcome were in a significantly better mood than participants who were certain (e.g., Wilson et al., 2005). However, our results were in the same direction, and it is notable that participants in the uncertain condition were in at least as good a mood as participants in the liked-best condition, given that there was only a 50 per cent chance that the former participants had seen the men who liked them the best. Uncertainty increased attraction and had no deleterious effect on people's mood.

25   Clearly, the determinants of interpersonal attraction are complex, and there is no simple formula people can use to get someone to like them. When people first meet, however, it may be that popular dating advice is correct: Keeping people in the dark about how much we like them will increase how much they think about us and will pique their interest.

Declaration of Conflicting Interests

9   The authors declared that they had no conflicts of interest with respect to their authorship or the publication of this article.

Note

1.   Norton, Frost, and Ariely (2007) found that the more information people had about another person, the less they liked him or her, but this effect was mediated by participants' perception of their similarity to the person and not by uncertainty about how much the person liked them. Eastwick and Finkel (2008) found that increasing attachment anxiety toward someone increased attraction to that person. It is possible that perceived uncertainty about reciprocity contributed to the effect.

References

Aronson, E., & Worchel, P. (1966). Similarity versus liking as determinants of interpersonal attractiveness. *Psychonomic Science, 5*, 157–158.

Bar-Anan, Y., Wilson, T.D., & Gilbert, D.T. (2009). The feeling of uncertainty intensifies affective reactions. *Emotion, 9*, 123–127.

Behrendt, G., & Tuccillo, L. (2009). *He's just not that into you: The no-excuses truth to understanding guys.* New York, NY: Gallery.

Bem, D.J. (1972). Self-perception theory. In L. Berkowitz (Ed.), *Advances in experimental social psychology* (Vol. 6, pp. 1–62). New York, NY: Academic Press.

Eastwick, P.W., & Finkel, E.J. (2008). The attachment system in fledgling relationships: An activating role for attachment anxiety. *Journal of Personality and Social Psychology, 95*, 628–647.

Gouldner, A.W. (1960). The norm of reciprocity: A preliminary statement. *American Sociological Review, 25*, 161–178.

Kenny, D.A. (1994). *Interpersonal perception.* New York, NY: Guilford Press.

Kurtz, J.L., Wilson, T.D., & Gilbert, D.T. (2007). Quantity versus uncertainty: When winning one gift is better than winning two. *Journal of Experimental Social Psychology, 43*, 979–985.

Lee, Y., & Qiu, C. (2009). When uncertainty brings pleasure: The role of prospect imageability and mental imagery. *Journal of Consumer Research, 36*, 624–633.

Luo, S., & Zhang, G. (2009). What leads to romantic attraction: Similarity, reciprocity, security, or beauty? Evidence from a speed-dating study. *Journal of Personality, 77*, 933–964.

Montoya, R.M., & Insko, C.A. (2008). Toward a more complete understanding of the reciprocity of liking effect. *European Journal of Social Psychology, 38,* 477–498.

Norton, M.I., Frost, J.H., & Ariely, D. (2007). Less is more: The lure of ambiguity, or why familiarity breeds contempt. *Journal of Personality and Social Psychology, 92,* 97–105.

Shrout, P.E., & Bolger, N. (2002). Mediation in experimental and nonexperimental studies: New procedures and recommendations. *Psychological Methods, 7,* 422–445.

Walster, E., Walster, W., Piliavin, J., & Schmidt, L. (1973). "Playing hard to get": Understanding an elusive phenomenon. *Journal of Personality and Social Psychology, 26,* 113–121.

Wilson, T.D., Centerbar, D.B., Kermer, D.A., & Gilbert, D.T. (2005). The pleasures of uncertainty: Prolonging positive moods in ways people do not anticipate. *Journal of Personality and Social Psychology, 88,* 5–21.

Wilson, T.D., & Gilbert, D.T. (2008). Explaining away: A model of affective adaptation. *Perspectives on Psychological Science, 3,* 370–386.

Organization and Style

1. Summarize the contrastive explanations given in paragraphs 1–3; include the topic or main idea in each paragraph.
2. a. In the "introduction," how do the authors justify their study?
   b. Paraphrase the authors' hypothesis (prediction).
3. In a short paragraph, summarize the results shown in Table 1 (you can also use the information in the text of the "Results" section).

Critical Thinking

1. Referring to the "Discussion" section, answer the following questions:
   a. To what extent does this study confirm the results of previous experiments?
   b. What unique findings does this study contribute to the subject of attraction?
2. Does the mention of limitations of the study (par. 22) weaken or strengthen its results? Explain.
3. Referring to one of the gaps or limitations of the current study, come up with a hypothesis that could be used in a future study in this subject area.

Daniel Rosenfield et al., "Canadian Lifestyle Choices: A Public Health Failure"

Although the *Canadian Medical Association Journal* publishes the results of research, it also publishes editorials in which professionals take a position on a topic of concern to its readers. However, the authors of "Canadian Lifestyle Choices" somewhat unusually utilize a satiric tone to make their argumentative points stand out. Satire criticizes institutions or commonly held beliefs through humour, ridicule, and irony. Writers who use satire to provoke changes have specific targets in mind, which are usually evident to a careful reader.

Preparing to Read

1. After scanning the first sentences of the first few paragraphs, consider why the authors might have decided to use an ironic tone rather than present their points directly (in irony, two levels of meaning are evident, a surface meaning and a deeper one; see p. 128). What role might the topic, purpose, or audience have played in this decision? (You can also consider this question after you have read the entire essay.)

2. When you shop, do you notice food labelling or the nutritional content of your food? Would you pay more attention if it were more prominently displayed? How important do you believe this knowledge would be to a typical Canadian consumer?

Canadian Lifestyle Choices: A Public Health Failure

Daniel Rosenfield, Paul C. Hébert, Matthew B. Stanbrook, Noni MacDonald, Ken Flegel, and Jane Coutts

Canadian Medical Association Journal,
20 September, 2011
(695 words)

1   Recently, we caught up with Mister and Missus Average Canadian. Like classmates at our high school reunions (but Hey, not us of course!), they've changed a lot over the years, thanks in no small part to our federal government's health policies.

2   Back in the day, Mister Average Canadian was a lean, mean, hockey-playing machine who was pretty fit and healthy. The missus was an avid ringette player. In fact, they met at the arena. But 25 years on, they're fat, hypertensive, smoking, diabetic couch potatoes. Years of inaction by the federal government have helped shape the Canadians into people who can barely heft a hockey or ringette stick, let alone play a game.

3   The Canadians sleep easy (well, not quite, because of their obstructive sleep apnea) thanks to a government that lets the products they love onto the market unfettered. Their favourite diet, high in trans fats and sodium, is not affected by regulation of the food industry, because the current government ignored calls from public health officials to ban trans fats and reduce salt and broke up the advisory panels that advocated for those changes.[1] It also dragged its feet to renew and increase graphic labelling on cigarette packages—and thank goodness, because having to look at images of lung and oral cancers is just *such* a downer when you want a hit of nicotine.[2]

4   The Canadians are something of an institution in their neighbourhood—and a growing one; two-thirds of their neighbours, like them, are overweight or obese.[3] It's the inevitable result of a steady diet of processed foods and meals at restaurants that rarely give nutritional information but love to serve up giant portions.

5   Through either convoluted or absent labelling, the Canadians are rarely aware of the nutritional content of their food, either in grocery stores or restaurants. Making healthy food choices can be difficult, and evidence shows that helpful, consumer-friendly labels on all consumer and restaurant food products can help people make healthy food choices.[4] Largely unaware of these benefits, the Canadians had

no idea why groups such as the Canadian Institute for Health Information, Centre for Science in the Public Interest and the Heart and Stroke Foundation called for mandatory food labelling.

6   Because some information can't be avoided, the Canadians do know their systolic blood pressure is closing in on their bowling average of 220. They don't know, however, how that's been helped along by the food industry, which loves loading food up with salt, to make otherwise unpalatable cheap food taste good, prolong shelf life and keep the food industry rich.[5] Also, like many tired parents, the Canadians just want happy children, and the billion-dollar junk-food industry helps by marketing its products to them, promising joy by the salty, sugary, and fatty serving. That lets the Canadians give their children everything they missed when they were young—incidentally putting them on track to outdo their parents in obesity and hypertension. There's little fear of an interruption in that trajectory—their federal government had proposals for regulating sodium that would have saved health care costs and lengthened lives,[6] but decided the financial and flavour consequences were too high and instead disbanded Health Canada's Sodium Working Group.[7]

7   If the Canadians lived in the United Kingdom, their consumption of sodium and trans fats would be on its way down.[8] If they were from California, they would have access to proper food labelling, even in restaurants. If they were from Australia, their government would be introducing legislation to cover entire cigarette packages with generic warning labels. In short, their government would have already implemented some simple policies that have a substantial impact on the public's health.

8   In Canada, individual preference, industry influence, and ideology all militate against evidence-based public health policy. This has created a population-health time bomb—which can and should be defused. As health professionals and role models, we must help our patients make healthy choices and do so ourselves. As health advocates, we need to put more energy into "nudging" governments into developing effective public health policies. The goal should be to make it easy for Canadians to improve their nutrition, make healthy choices and stay fit.

Declaration of Conflicting Interests

The authors declare that they had no conflicts with respect to the publication of this article. See www.cmaj.ca/site/misc/cmaj_staff.xhtml. None declared by Daniel Rosenfield and Jane Coutts.

References

1. Trans Fat Task Force. (2006). *TRANSforming the food supply: report of the Trans Fat Task Force submitted to the Minister of Health.* Ottawa (ON): Health Canada.

2. Hammond D, Fong G.T., McNeill A, et al. (2006). Effectiveness of cigarette warning labels in informing smokers about the risks of smoking: Findings from the International Tobacco Control (ITC) Four Country Survey. *Tobacco Control, 15(3),* 19–25.

3. Statistics Canada. (2004). *Data tables from the Canadian Community Health Survey (CCHS).* Accessed at www.statcan.gc.ca/pub/82-620-m/2005001/4053601-eng.htm.

4. Burton S, Creyer U.H., Kees J, et al. (2006). Attacking the obesity epidemic: An examination of the potential health benefits of nutrition information provision in restaurants. *American Journal of Public Health 96,* 1669–75.

5. The Centre for Science in the Public Interest. (2011). *Testimony of Bill Jeffery, LLB, National Coordinator Centre for Science in the Public Interest before the House of Commons Standing*

Committee on Health Hearing on Healthy Living 3 February 2011 in Ottawa [technical brief]. Accessed at cspinet.org/canada/pdf/english. speakingnotes.cspi.pdf.

6. Bibbins-Domingo K, Chertow G.M., Coxson P.G., et al. (2010). Projected effect of dietary salt reductions on future cardiovascular disease. *New England Journal of Med 362*, 590–9.

7. Schmidt S. (2011 February 4). Sodium reduction panel disbanded. *Ottawa Citizen* Accessed at www.ottawacitizen.com/health/Sodium+reduction+panel+disbanded /4220182/story.html.

8. Food Standard Agency. (2009). *Agency publishes 2012 salt reduction targets*. London (UK): The Agency. Available: Accessed at www.food.gov.uk/ news/press releases/2009/may/salttargets.

Comprehension

1. Identify, then paraphrase, the thesis statement.

Organization and Style

1. In paragraphs 6 and 7, identify the topic sentences.
2. Which paragraph uses compare–contrast? Comment on its placement and its effectiveness. Para 7
3. a. Give two examples of ironic statements in the essay.
   b. Give two examples of humour, such as exaggeration or word play.

Critical Thinking/Research

1. Who are the authors primarily criticizing in their essay? Refer to specific passages that show this.
2. Analyze the use of logical, emotional, and ethical appeals in the essay.
3. Using at least two reliable sources, explain the current debate about the content of salt in Canadian food today. Try to use articles published within the last two years and/ or websites recently updated.

Jonathan Gray, "'Coming up Next': Promos in the Future of Television and Television Studies"

"Coming up Next" is a humanities essay that interprets primary sources from a specific perspective; as is evident in the abstract, the sources that are analyzed in the pages that follow are promos for television shows. The author tries to persuade his audience that these kinds of texts are worth considering.

The concept of the "text" is crucial to an understanding of this essay and the author's approach to his subject. In the abstract, the word *text* and variants on this word—*contextualize* and *textuality*—are referred to. By *texts*, then, the author means something more than books, articles, and other print formats. Come up with a definition of *text* that would include easily recognizable forms like books and movies but would also include advertisements (print or visual).

Preparing to Read

How much attention do you pay to promos of television shows, movies, or other media? What role do they play in your decision to watch or not watch a program or movie, or buy a product? Which are successful in attracting your interest and which are less successful?
1. Identify specific characteristics of successful and unsuccessful promos.
2. Discuss the questions above or similar questions in groups or freewrite on the topic of promos.

"Coming up Next": Promos in the Future of Television and Television Studies

Jonathan Gray

Journal of Popular Film and Television,
August 2010
(2709 words)

Abstract

This article argues for the importance of studying promos. First, it is noted that promos often begin the text, offering viewers their first understandings of and encounters with the text. Second, promos' role in creating notions of the channel as a whole and these notions' role in contextualizing our understanding of any given text are examined. Thus, while promos have often been regarded as annoying hype at worst, or as secondary and peripheral distractions at best, the article argues that they frequently make vital contributions to the production of television's textuality.

1   Campaigns to keep cancelled shows on the air have been commonplace in the world of television for many years. Increasingly, though, they are offset by the large number of people who have never even heard of many of the cancelled shows, let alone watched them. As much as our contemporary media environment is suffused with discussion of video "going viral," the sheer number of available channels on many televisions, mixed with formidable competition from a proliferation of other sources, has made a sterile, unheard-of existence the more regular state of affairs for many television shows. Or, posing as serious a problem for many shows' economic livelihoods is the increased incidence of viewers downloading their programs off iTunes, using online streaming episode players or BitTorrent, or buying the DVD, thereby forgoing the broadcast presentation of the shows and eluding the Nielsen ratings that keep said shows alive. In the face of such obstacles, only foolish, headstrong network executives would feel secure regarding their future advertising revenues, much less the future of their industry as they know it. As such, promotion has become all the more important. Savvy showrunners and executives must now spend as much if not considerably more time and energy telling the world about their shows and bringing audiences to the network presentation of them as they must in creating the shows in the first place.

2   Amanda Lotz observes that the major American networks broadcast an estimated 30,000 promos a year, in the process forgoing

approximately $4 billion worth of ad revenue (108–109). Rarely does a commercial break go by without at least one in-station promo. Stepping away from the television, though, we still experience promos aplenty. Public transit systems are often heavily populated by posters advertising television shows. Billboards along busy highways similarly announce the virtues of this or that show, online pop-up ads frequently accompany our email, Facebook page, or other Web activities with flashy appeals to watch tonight, and online video-sharing sites such as YouTube are flush with trailers and promos. More innovative forms of promos exist, too; for instance, ABC covered beaches with messages in bottles advertising the castaway show *Lost* before it premiered and they circulated laundry bags to advertise the dirty laundry–peddling *Desperate Housewives*. When *Dexter* moved to England, it was accompanied by a website—www.icetruck.tv—that allowed people to send video postcards to friends (or foes?) that seemingly suggested that one of the show's feared serial killers was coming after them next. Many shows have long since learned the value of creating official website that offer production details, clips, discussion forums, surrounding and background materials, and occasionally alternate reality games (ARGs) or other spaces of play for fans or would-be fans. Thus, *Heroes* has an online comic book; many television characters have their own blogs or MySpace or Facebook pages; and *The Office* invites viewers to become workers at the Dunder Mifflin paper company, personalizing their workspaces online. Meanwhile, late-night talk shows regularly host stars talking about their new shows, entertainment magazines and newspaper sections feature interviews that marketing teams have set up, and iTunes offers podcasts with additional information. The industry, in other words, is spending a lot of time, money, and labour to fill the media-scape with promos.

3   Amid such a situation, the promo campaign becomes an important entity for television scholars to examine. If we have proven slow to do so—and I believe we have—cultural critics' prevailing dislike of advertising is probably in large part responsible. Ads, after all, are seen as manipulative and as trying to get something out of us rather than to give something to us; they are seen as peddling stereotypes and as appealing to base instincts rather than addressing or even developing more noble instincts, and thus they are seen as more worthy of critique or scorn than of attention, much less engagement. Quite simply, too, when discussing television, television scholars have often operated as have the DVDs on which we study television, expunging the ads from a show's record as if they never existed. We have become quite skilled at ignoring ads textually, even if we will discuss them at ~~using cavemen, a Cockney lizard, and a pile of money with eyes as "spokespeople," Geico aims to convince us that it is a personable, hip insurance company that, unlike the others, is kind of quirky, yet in a refreshing way. The simplicity of their ads, meanwhile, aims to suggest that all dealings with the company will be short, sweet, and simple. The ads create a brand identity for Geico, by way of creating a narrative of and an experience for Geico. However, shifting to promos~~ length when examining the structure of the *industry*. How, then, might we start to think of promos differently in this, the age of the promo?

[handwritten marginal note: "mis-print"]

Where the text begins: Promos as frames

4   The key binaries that we must move beyond are those of art and promotion, text and ad, show and peripheral. What is an ad, after all, but an attempt to brand something, or, reworded, an attempt to create a text, a narrative for, and

an experience of something? To take the many Geico ads as an example: through using cavemen, a Cockney lizard, and a pile of money with eyes as "spokespeople," Geico aims to convince us that it is a personable, hip insurance company that, unlike the others, is kind of quirky, yet in a refreshing way. The simplicity of their ads, meanwhile, aims to suggest that all dealings with the company will be short, sweet, and simple. The ads create a brand identity for Geico, by way of creating a narrative of and an experience for Geico. However, shifting to promos for television shows, to create a narrative and an experience for a product that *is* a narrative and an experience will now contribute to that text. Cultural critics have long noted the at-times radical disconnect between brand and product—as most evident, for instance, when car ads consistently situate the action in vast expanses of nature to suggest environmental friendliness—and critics have rightfully been concerned about an ad's ability to take over the history, present, and experience of a product with branding (see, for instance, Jhally). With ads and promos for television shows, then, a similar situation exists, wherein the promo exerts strong *textual* pull over the show. Promos are "paratexts," as Gérard Genette called the material surrounding books such as covers, prefaces, and typeface choices—appended to the show without being considered a *bona fide* part of it, yet nevertheless working to create an idea of what that show is, means, and does. Promos quite frequently create a text.

5   This process begins with advance promos and buzz campaigns that hail a specific audience and that promise that audience a very particular set of pleasures, dictating what a text is while also creating a tone, mood, and sensibility for it. They might insist that a text is for men only, for instance, that it is for teens, that it is liberal, that it is post-ironic, that it is a dramedy, that it is just like another beloved show, or so forth. They will introduce us to the cast in specific ways, privileging some over others, drawing on certain star intertexts while downplaying others, and inviting us to identify with some yet not others. And they will sample the world we are being invited to enter, aiming to give us our first interaction with it, yet a carefully framed and managed interaction at that. So, for example, when NBC began advertising its new show *Southland* in the spring of 2009, its ads suggested a gritty, realistic depiction of life in the Los Angeles Police Department. The ads regularly boasted how the show was from *ER*'s producers, thus laying claim to *ER*'s mantle of quality, realistic television. They prominently featured the show's star, Benjamin McKenzie, offering him as the viewer's surrogate on the show, at least while we, like McKenzie's rookie cop character, adjust to this crazy world. Meanwhile, a visit to the show's web site reveals a quiz on LAPD radio codes and a short video on famous crimes in the real Los Angeles's history, both of which further aim to steep the show in realism, suggesting, respectively, that the show would offer specialist knowledge of LAPD life and that it would focus on Los Angeles as a character. Fans or viewers who then went on to watch the show would likely revise their understanding of the text and fill in the larger picture, but the promos still likely played a vital role in establishing the text and in creating initial expectations and the all-important intertextual and evaluative frames through which the viewer would make sense of the show. Advance promos are thus like the front covers and opening chapters of books, establishing the audience's initial contact with and first impressions of texts.

6   The importance of advance promos is best appreciated if we consider the situation of those

who watch the promo yet decide not to watch the show. Clearly, such audiences have based their decision not to watch on something, and that something is thus a form of text that is created largely by the promos and surrounding buzz. If, for instance, one decided not to watch *Southland* since it looked too somber and gritty, because one hated McKenzie on *The OC* and had no interest in a show centred on him, because it seemed too much of a boy's show, or for whatever other reason, one would have already created an image and a text of *Southland*. At this point, whether the promos were accurate in suggesting a somber and gritty, McKenzie-centred, boys-with-guns show is largely immaterial if that is a widespread image of *Southland* and if that is the text with which the public at large becomes familiar. For too long, we in television studies have considered the audience of a television show as limited to those who watch the show, but a show's public standing relies just as much on the opinions of those who have not watched the show, yet who have watched the promos, as on those who have seen the show.

The frame around the frames: Flow and channel idents

7   We must also be able to think beyond the level of the individual show, however, and when we do so, promos become even more important. In a multichannel era, each channel must sell not only its programs but the entire channel. At the 2008 International Radio and Television Society Foundation and Disney's Digital Media Summit that I attended in Burbank, Disney staffers continually repeated Disney president and CEO Bob Iger's instructions to them to think of themselves as selling not *shows* but the three central

brands of Disney, ABC, and ESPN. Selling shows can backfire, since audiences can fall in love with a show yet buy it on DVD, download it via Bit-Torrent, or otherwise avoid the broadcast presentation; if enough audiences do so, its resulting anemic Nielsen ratings may require cancellation. But if networks and cable channels can make viewers fans of the network or channel itself, and if, over and above love for any given show, fans identify with specific channels, such brand loyalty is likely to translate more easily into the kind of metrics on which the television industry relies. With the network or channel as the product for sale, however, on one hand, the shows become a form of promo themselves, and on the other hand, the industry must care all the more about audiences' images and understandings of texts they do not watch. *Southland* promos, as such, do not just send us messages about *Southland*—they also send us messages about NBC.

8   If Iger's philosophy is one for the future of television, it is an industrial version of Raymond Williams's famous statement regarding television as *flow* between show-and-show, show-and-ad, as "perhaps the defining characteristic of broadcasting, simultaneously as a technology and as a cultural form" (86). The "text" for sale is the entire channel. Although television studies need not, of course, follow this philosophy itself, we nevertheless find ourselves in the situation whereby we have often ignored promos, deeming them unimportant textually, yet now we find that the shows that we thought were important are themselves promos. In saying this, I do not mean to suggest that they have thus become devalued, but rather I mean to argue that television is full of promos, and it would be odd for textual studies to focus only on one set (namely, the programs).

9   We might also, therefore, pay renewed attention to channel idents and other promos for the network or channel itself. NBC, for example,

is fond of channel idents involving some of its shows' more personable and likeable characters or actors fooling around. *The Office*'s Pam and Jim will share a joke with the camera, *Heroes*'s Greg Grunberg and Masi Oka will goof around together, or *Chuck*'s titular character will address us directly. Such idents aim to create an intimate, friendly bond between the viewer and both the stars and the characters, while also branding NBC as a place for fresh comedy and for characters with whom we can identify. But what role do these idents play in the network's attempts to crawl out of the Nielsen basement? Television studies' focus on shows and the production, reception, and textual processes surrounding them may have blinded us to asking questions about the production, reception, and textuality of networks or channels as a whole. Promos, as I have argued, can best be thought of textually as frames, and thus closer attention to channel idents would equate to closer attention to the frames that surround television viewing. Such work promises to be all the more helpful in an era when many viewers have multiple choices of where they can watch their beloved shows, since their choice of venue on one hand may be greatly determined by the value added to that venue by branding, and on the other hand may subtly or profoundly change the experience and construction of the television text being watched. As the Mac/PC wars and accompanying ads suggest, viewers often care greatly (or are, at least, asked to care greatly) about interface, about the semiotics of their point of access to content, and about frames. Moreover, Derek Kompare has examined how cable channels use reruns to (re)brand their channel, and Lynn Spigel observes that the reruns are often reframed in the process (often becoming camp); both scholars'

work, therefore, suggests that the textuality and meanings of a channel and of a show are always contingent on one another. To understand a show textually, we may be required to study a channel textually.

Conclusion

10 To examine promos and channel idents more closely may also be a way to bridge an old divide in media studies, between studies of the audience, text, or industry. Often, undergraduate and graduate students are divided up into teams of audience, text, and industry scholars, as if in preparation for intramural sports competitions. The text and audience "teams" have usually enjoyed a healthy relationship, while the industry team has often operated by itself, a natural rival to both the text and audience scholars. Admittedly and refreshingly, though, many scholars have of late challenged these divisions, offering multiple models for a broader scholarship that takes audience, text, industry, and context into account. The closer study of promos could further contribute to this breaking down of barriers, since promos are intrinsically industrial entities, yet also, as I have argued, they are intrinsically textual. To study the promo is to study the logic by which the industry monetizes and publicizes its content *and* to study how texts work *and* to study how audiences work. While the industry funnels millions on millions of dollars into creating promos, while considerable creative care and energy is put into making many promos, and while audiences spend an increasing amount of time with promos—whether as trailers, ARGs, pop-up ads, or so forth—the nature of the business is shifting in a way that renders the promo profoundly important, for both popular and scholarly understandings of television.

Works Cited

Genette, Gérard. *Paratexts: Thresholds of Interpretation.* Trans. Jane E. Lewin. Cambridge: Cambridge UP, 1997. Print.

Jhally, Sut. *The Codes of Advertising: Fetishism and the Political Economy of Meaning in the Consumer Society.* New York: Routledge, 1987. Print.

Kompare, Derek. *Rerun Nation: How Repeats Invented American Television.* New York: Routledge, 2005. Print.

Lotz, Amanda. *The Television Will Be Revolutionized.* New York: NYU Press, 2007. Print.

Spigel, Lynn. "From the Dark Ages to the Golden Age: Women's Memories and Television Reruns." *Screen* 36.1 (1995): 16–33. Print.

Williams, Raymond. *Television: Technology and Cultural Form.* London: Fontana/Collins, 1974. Print.

● Comprehension

1. Identify the essay's thesis and the form it takes. In view of the essay's purpose, why might this form be an appropriate one?
2. In your own words, define *binaries* and *paratexts* from paragraph 4.
3. Why does the author believe that people who choose not to watch a television show might be just as important to the study of television as those who do watch? (par. 6)

● Organization and Style

1. a. What is the purpose of paragraph 2?
   b. What is the main method of development in this paragraph and how does it contribute to the introduction as a whole?
   c. Analyze paragraph organization, mentioning specific strategies that aid in comprehension.

● Critical Thinking

1. Who is the intended audience of this article? Point to specific passages that show you this.
2. Analyze the author's credibility as it is established by specific passages in the essay.
3. Analyze the effectiveness of the conclusion, considering its purpose(s) and the way(s) it satisfies the requirements of successful academic conclusions.

Matthew P.A. Clark and Brian D. Westerberg, "How Random Is the Toss of a Coin?"

Like "'He Loves Me, He Loves Me Not . . .'" (p. 336), "How Random Is the Toss of a Coin?" follows the chronological stages of an experiment. When the experiment has been completed, the researchers discuss the significance of the results. (For more information about how these types of essays are structured, see the introductory notes to the Whitchurch essay on p. 336.)

Like journalistic writers, academic writers ask questions about topics of concern and, with the aid of critical thinking, may re-evaluate previous assumptions, such as the fairness of the coin toss, applying it to their particular research area (medicine in this case). The goal is not necessarily to disprove the old assumption but, perhaps, to cast doubt on its validity. Future researchers might seek to duplicate the findings or vary the method of their experiment to make it applicable to other situations or demographics.

Preparing to Read

Pre-read the essay by scanning the abstract, section headings, and introduction. In one or two sentences, comment on the practical importance of their study. Give specific examples of situations in which the results of a coin toss would be very important.

How Random Is the Toss of a Coin?

Matthew P.A. Clark and Brian D. Westerberg

CMAJ, 2009
(1776 words)

Abstract

Background: The toss of a coin has been a method used to determine random outcomes for centuries. It is still used in some research studies as a method of randomization, although it has largely been discredited as a valid randomization method. We sought to provide evidence that the toss of a coin can be manipulated.

Methods: We performed a prospective experiment involving otolaryngology residents in Vancouver, Canada. The main outcome was the proportion of "heads" coin tosses achieved (out of 300 attempts) by each participant. Each of the participants attempted to flip the coin so as to achieve a heads result.

Results: All participants achieved more heads than tails results, with 7 of the 13 participants having significantly more heads results ($p \leq 0.05$). The highest proportion of heads achieved was 0.68 (95 per cent confidence interval 0.62–0.73, $p < 0.001$).

Interpretation: Certain people are able to successfully manipulate the toss of a coin. This throws into doubt the validity of using a coin toss to determine a chance result.

1   The toss or flip of a coin to randomly assign a decision traditionally involves throwing a coin into the air and seeing which side lands facing up. This method may be used to resolve a dispute, see who goes first in a game or determine which type of treatment a patient receives in a clinical trial. There are only two possible outcomes, "heads" or "tails," although, in theory, landing on an edge is possible. (Research suggests that when the coin is allowed to fall onto a hard surface, the chance of this happening is in the order of 1 in 6000 tosses.[1])

2   When a coin is flipped into the air, it is supposedly made to rotate about an axis parallel to its flat surfaces. The coin is initially placed on a bent forefinger, and the thumb is released from under the coin surface, where it has been held under tension. The thumbnail strikes the part of the coin unsupported by the index finger, sending it rotating upward. All this is done with an upward movement of the hand and forearm. The coin may be allowed to fall to the floor or other surface or it may be caught by the "tosser" and sometimes turned onto the back of the opposite hand and then revealed. The catching method should not matter, provided it is consistent for each toss. The opponent often calls the toss when the coin is airborne, although in the case of randomization for clinical trials, this is unnecessary because one is simply looking for an outcome.

3   The appeal of the coin toss is that it is a simple, seemingly unbiased, method of deciding between two options. Although the outcome of a coin toss should be at even odds, the outcome may well not be. Historically, the toss of a coin before a duel reputedly decided which person had his back to the sun—an obvious advantage when taking aim! In medical trials, a simple statistical manipulation can have a dramatic effect on the treatment a patient receives. Our hypothesis is that with minimal training, the outcome of the toss can be weighted heavily to the call of the tosser, thus abolishing the 50:50 chance result that is expected and allowing for manipulation of an apparently random event.

Methods

4   We included 13 otolaryngology residents from the University of British Columbia who verbally consented to participate. We excluded any residents who had a hand injury that would prevent them from tossing a coin with their dominant hand.

5   The participants were told about the purpose of the study several weeks before the trial. The investigators instructed the residents and demonstrated the toss. The residents were allowed to practise tossing the coin in a consistent manner for a couple of minutes. Each resident then performed 300 coin tosses in which they tried to achieve a heads result each time. The results were recorded by an observer to avoid the possibility of cheating. The two participants who achieved the greatest manipulation of the results (i.e., the highest proportion of heads) were given an incentive (i.e., $20 and $10 coffee vouchers). We felt that the use of an incentive would reproduce real-life situations.

Statistical analysis

6   Because our null hypothesis was that the coin-weighting was unbiased, we assumed that 50 per cent of the tosses would result in heads. We used two-sided binomial testing because we could not assume that if we were trying to increase the proportion of heads, we would not instead reduce this proportion. For a change of at least 10 per cent, we calculated that 263 coin tosses per participant would be required to achieve 90 per cent power to detect this difference with a significance level of 0.05.

7   We performed a comparison of proportions. The statistical calculations were performed on the basis of how many coin tosses an individual would have to perform to show a significant manipulation. Therefore, any participant who achieved this level would have a significant result. We did not use group statistics for this reason.

Results

8   Each of the 13 participants tossed a coin 300 times. All participants tried to achieve a heads

result. Each participant successfully achieved more heads than tails results; this difference was statistically significant for 7 participants (Table 1). The participant who was most successful at manipulating the outcome achieved a proportion of heads of 0.68 (95 per cent confidence interval 0.62–0.73; $p < 0.001$).

Interpretation

9   This study shows that when participants are given simple instructions about how to manipulate the toss of a coin and only a few minutes to practise this technique, more than half can significantly manipulate the outcome. With devoted training, more participants would probably be able to achieve this figure, and the magnitude of the manipulation would probably be increased.

10   With respect to the use of a coin toss to randomly assign patients to a treatment in a clinical trial, our results could be considered clinically significant if only one participant in this study had achieved a nonrandom result. We have shown that a person tossing a coin may have the ability to manipulate the toss and significantly bias the results to their liking. Given that we would never know the manipulation skills or motivation of the person tossing the coin, this method seems unsuitable for randomization procedures in experiments in which bias needs to be minimized.

11   Research by Diaconis and colleagues[2] has suggested a dynamic bias to coin tosses. They suggest that, for natural flips, the chance of the coin landing as it started is about 0.51, with a number of assumptions or required conditions. Diaconis states that, for a fair toss, the coin must be caught in the palm of the hand and not allowed to land on a surface and bounce, because the latter often incorporates a degree of spinning on the coin's edge. Because catching a

| TABLE 1 | Results of coin tosses in which 13 participants attempted to achieve a "heads" result |

Participant	Outcome $n = 300$		Proportion of heads (95% CI)	P value*
	Heads	Tails		
1	162	138	0.54 (0.48–0.60)	0.18
2	175	125	0.58 (0.53–0.64)	0.005
3	159	141	0.53 (0.47–0.59)	0.37
4	179	121	0.60 (0.54–0.65)	0.001
5	203	97	0.68 (0.62–0.73)	< 0.001
6	168	132	0.56 (0.50–0.62)	0.043
7	170	130	0.57 (0.51–0.62)	0.024
8	160	140	0.53 (0.48–0.59)	0.27
9	192	108	0.64 (0.58–0.69)	< 0.001
10	167	133	0.56 (0.50–0.61)	0.06
11	154	146	0.51 (0.46–0.57)	0.69
12	153	147	0.51 (0.45–0.57)	0.77
13	176	124	0.59 (0.53–0.64)	0.003

Note: CI = confidence interval.
*Determined by use of a binomial test.

coin in one's palm and turning it onto the back of the opposite hand allows for manipulation with sleight of hand, the coin must be allowed to just land in the palm of the hand.

12   Diaconis and colleagues[2] assumed that when tossed, the uppermost side of the coin is known by the tosser (and caller). If this is not the case, the true 50:50 probability of the result prevails. But if it is known, the side of the coin that starts off face up is more likely to end that way up because that side spends more time facing up during the flight than does the opposite side. However, because of the large number of tosses required to detect this difference (shown to be 250,000 tosses), this apparent difference is generally irrelevant.

13   Coins have different raised profiles on each side. In theory, one side could be more weighted, thus making the coin toss unfair. This could be achieved by tampering with a coin. With the introduction of the Euro, Polish statisticians claimed that the 1€ coin (from Belgium), when spun on a surface, came up heads more often than tails.[3] This report resulted in a tongue-in-cheek warning in the British press to teams playing against Belgium in the forthcoming soccer World Cup.[4] Of 250 spins, 56 per cent came up heads. However, independent statistical analysis showed that random variation could produce such scatter even with an unbiased coin given this number of spins (acceptable range 43.8 per cent to 56.2 per cent). Other research suggests that even if a grossly weighted coin is used (one side lead, the other balsa wood), no significant bias shows up.[3]

14   The usual method of tossing a coin should not be taken for granted. Gary Kosnitzky, a Las Vegas magician adept in the art of coin magic, can reputedly manipulate coin tosses to give a predictable outcome by use of a method that gives the illusion of a spinning coin. When his coin "spins" in the air, it is not rotating about its axis but is instead fluttering or wobbling and not turning over. This gives the illusion of a normally spinning coin, yet gives a predictable result if caught in the palm of the hand.[5] Admittedly, this is probably an art more practised by the gambler than the researcher, but it serves as a reminder that an apparently fair situation can be manipulated.

15   The most compelling finding that raises concerns about the validity of the coin toss comes from the use of mechanical coin flippers, which can be made to impart exactly the same initial conditions for every toss, namely the starting position, velocity, and force. In these cases, the outcome can be highly, if not entirely, predictable. Coin tossing becomes physics rather than a random event. It is the human element that makes the process random in that each toss tends to be at a different speed, sent to a different height, launched at a different angle, or caught in a different manner. Therefore, the possibility of practising the task to reduce these differing elements can be considered. If you try to toss the coin the same way each time, you should be able to make the outcome significantly different than 50:50.

16   A limitation of our study is the uncertainty about whether the individual results are repeatable. However, we conclude that the validity of using the toss of a coin to provide a random 50:50 outcome is thrown into doubt, both in medicine and everyday life.

Competing interests

None declared.

Contributors

Both authors contributed to the conception of the study design, the acquisition and analysis of the data, and writing and revising the manuscript. Both authors approved the final version submitted for publication. Matthew Clark accepts full responsibility for the work and the conduct of the study, had access to the data and controlled the decision to publish.

References

1. Murray D.B., Teare S.W. (1993). Probability of a tossed coin falling on its edge. *Physical Review E., Statistical Physics, Plasmas, Fluids, and Relational Interdisciplinary Topics* 48(4), 2547–52.

2. Diaconis P., Homes S., Montgomery R. (2007). Dynamical bias in the coin toss. *SIAM Review 49*, 211–35.

3. MacKenzie, D. (2002, January 4) Euro coin accused of unfair flipping. *New Scientist.* Retrieved from: www.newscientist.com/ article/dn1748-euro-coin-accused-of-unfairflipping

4. Denny C., Dennis S. (2002, January 4). Heads, Belgium wins—and wins. *The Guardian* [UK]. Retrieved from www.guardian.co.uk/world/2002/jan/04/euro.eu2

5. Kosnitzky G. (2006). Heads or tails. *Murphy's Magic Supplies*. Rancho Cordova, CA: Murphy's Magical Supplies. See www.murphysmagic.com/Product.aspx?id541336

Acknowledgements

The authors thank Hong Qian for her advice on the statistical analysis.

Comprehension

1. Summarize the steps that the researchers took to ensure the validity of their results (see "Methods"); then, paraphrase the researchers' hypothesis (par. 3).

2. From the context, define what is meant by a "null hypothesis" (par. 6); then, confirm the definition by referring to a reliable Internet source.

3. Why do the authors state that mechanical coin flippers provide "[t]he most compelling finding" about the validity of the coin toss?

Organization and Style

1. What rhetorical pattern is used in paragraph 2? Explain its purpose.

2. Identify an example of anecdotal evidence (see p. 42) in the "Interpretation" section of the essay and explain its purpose.

3. The following are common functions of "Discussion" ("Interpretation") sections of academic essays; identify them by paragraph number(s) in this essay:
   • summarizing the results;
   • comparing the results with results of related studies;
   • suggesting practical applications of the results; and
   • mentioning limitations of the study.

💡 Critical Thinking

1. Why do you think the authors of this study did not provide details about how the coin could be tossed in order to make a "heads" outcome more probable? (See "Methods.")

2. Do you believe Clark and Westerberg successfully refute the findings of Diaconis, Homes, and Montgomery? (see pars. 11–12). Support your answer by direct references to the text.

PART III | Handbook

Academic writing is grammatical writing. For students, competent grammatical skills make an excellent first impression on teachers or employers. These skills do not necessarily stand out on their own—but poor grammar or punctuation may attract the wrong kind of notice, preventing the reader from focusing on your ideas. Correct grammar and punctuation usually go hand in hand with clear organization and expression. In other words, they are one part of a larger process, and mastering a few rules for grammar is likely to improve your skills in other writing areas too. In Chapter 11, we review the basic concepts of the parts of speech, phrases and clauses, and the simple sentence. We end by discussing major errors in sentence construction: fragments, run-on sentences, and comma splices. In Chapter 12, we take a streamlined approach to learning rules for punctuation and apostrophe use. Finally, in Chapter 13, other typical problem areas are addressed: agreement, pronoun use, modifier errors, and parallelism.

11

Grammar Fundamentals

In this chapter, you will learn

- How to recognize the seven major parts of speech and their functions

- How to identify a sentence and distinguish it from a sentence fragment

- How to identify phrases and clauses as well as the two main kinds of clauses

- How to join sentences grammatically and avoid run-on sentences and comma splices

In the academic world, as in the professional world, good grammar is a given. The benefits of good grammar are twofold: for the writer, grammar and punctuation rules help make your writing clearer and communication with your audience easier. Academic and professional readers expect to read grammatical, well-punctuated prose. Even if they can't always explain *why* a sentence is wrong, they may still need to stop and reread an ungrammatical sentence. If they do this too often, they may give up reading or begin to question your content. By contrast, grammatical writing enhances your credibility.

In addition, becoming more conscious of grammatical writing will help make you a better writer by focusing your attention on words, phrases, and sentences—in other words, on the building blocks of prose. People read by processing words, phrases, and sentences before they consider larger entities like ideas or argument. Focusing on grammar and other sentence-level concerns can help you communicate your intended meaning to your intended audience.

EXERCISE 11.1 | Grammar Preview

Most of the following sentences contain a grammatical or punctuation error. Identify and/or explain the errors. Then write out the complete paragraph. The answers can be found at the end of Chapter 13, p. 427.

1. Obsession over one's weight is a common practice in todays society.
2. The desire to be thin and the need to possess the perfect body overshadows everything else.

3.   Advertisements that feature skinny models help fuel this desire; promoting unhealthy expectations for young women.
4.   Expectations that can't be met by the average woman, who weighs 140 pounds.
5.   By contrast, the average model weighs less than 120 pounds, and is almost 6 feet tall.
6.   Body consciousness begins early, it can even be seen in young girls following exposure to Barbie dolls.
7.   At age 13 50 per cent of girls exposed to Barbie dolls don't like the way they look.
8.   Increasing by age 18 to more than 80 per cent.
9.   If we change our cultural ideals, young girls will begin to see themselves as "normal."
10. With a positive self-image, young women will be better able to succeed socially, academically, and in their chosen vocation.

The Parts of Speech and Their Functions

In the following sections, we introduce the parts of speech and their functions. We then turn to the larger units in a sentence—phrases and clauses—before discussing sentence errors.

The parts of speech can be compared to members of an organization. In this analogy, each has both a "job title" and a "job description." They are called by their name (title), but what they do (job description) in the organization (sentence) helps determine the organization's success (i.e., whether it is a grammatical sentence).

Here, then, is the profile of the sentence with its seven principal members. Examples and hints for identifying the parts of speech are given.

The Take-Charge Nouns

A **noun** names people, places, things, qualities, or conditions. A proper noun begins with a capital letter; a common noun does not. You can often identify common nouns, like the singular common noun *singer*, by the fact you can put an article (*a, an, the*) in front of them: *a/the singer*.

> A **noun** names people, places, things, qualities, or conditions.

What Nouns Do

1. Subject of Verb

A noun acts as a **subject** of the verb if it performs the verb's action. (We speak of subjects performing the action of a verb, but many verbs convey a state or condition rather than an action.) See "The Busy Verbs," below. The noun subject is italicized and the verb is underlined below.

> The **subject** performs the verb's action.

Beyoncé, a world renowned singer, <u>supports</u> many humanitarian causes.

Hint: A subject usually precedes its verb. (See p. 404 for exceptions.)

2. Object of Verb

A noun acts as an **object** of the verb (direct object) if it receives the verb's action. The noun object is italicized and the verb is underlined below.

Beyoncé, a world renowned singer, <u>supports</u> many humanitarian *causes*.

Hint: An object usually follows its verb.

3. Object of Preposition

A noun can act as an **object of a preposition** (indirect object). The indirect object is italicized and the preposition is underlined below.

Beyoncé, a world renowned singer, supports many humanitarian causes <u>around</u> the *globe*.

Hint: An indirect object may follow the direct object, if there is one, and is usually preceded by a preposition.

4. Appositive

A noun can act as an appositive, naming or rephrasing a preceding noun or noun phrase. The appositive is italicized and the preceding noun is underlined below.

<u>Beyoncé</u>, *a world renowned singer*, supports many humanitarian causes.

Hint: An appositive follows a noun or noun phrase.

5. Subject Complement

A noun acts as a **subject complement** if it completes the subject after a linking verb. The subject complement is italicized and the linking verb is underlined below.

Beyoncé <u>is</u> a world renowned *singer*.

Hint: Look for subject complements—nouns or adjectives—after verbs like *is*, *are*, *was*, and *were*.

In the examples below, the noun subject is bolded, the object of the verb is italicized, the object of a preposition is underlined, the appositive is in caps, and the subjective complement is bolded and italicized.

The overly eager **student** in the front <u>row</u> always raises his *hand* unnecessarily.

Montréal, the CAPITAL OF QUEBEC, was once the largest *city* in <u>Canada</u>, but **Toronto** now has 1.7 million more *people*.

The Understudy Pronouns

The **pronoun** usually takes the place of a noun (called the antecedent) in a sentence. A **personal pronoun** refers to people, places, and things. A **relative pronoun** refers back to a previous noun/pronoun. An **interrogative pronoun** introduces questions. Indefinite pronouns refer to non-specified groups. Other pronouns include demonstrative, intensive, reflexive, and reciprocal.

When they refer to people and sometimes animals, personal pronouns take forms like *I, you, he, she, we, they*; referring to things and places, they take forms like *it* or *they*. In the possessive case, they can function as adjectives. (See "The Informative Adjectives," pp. 366–7.) The pronouns are bolded and the antecedents are italicized below.

> *Beth* trained in *yoga* for three months, but **she** gave **it** up to pursue a martial arts diploma.

A relative pronoun relates what follows to a preceding noun or pronoun (antecedent); the complete grammatical unit, including the relative pronoun and what follows (which will be at least a verb), is called a relative clause (see p. 376), a type of dependent clause (see p. 375). Relative pronouns include *who, which, that, whose*, and a few others. The relative clause is italicized, the relative pronoun is bolded, and the antecedent is underlined below.

> The "Now Hiring" <u>sign</u> ***that** appeared at 8 am* was taken down by 8:30.

Interrogative pronouns introduce questions and include *how, what, which, when, why, who, whose*, and *where*. Interrogative pronouns are italicized below.

> *Whose* turn it is to cook dinner tonight? ***When*** will it be ready?

A **demonstrative pronoun** (*this, that, these, those*) points to nouns; it can function as an adjective when it precedes a noun. Demonstrative pronouns are italicized below.

> *This* is the easiest path to take to get us home. *That* path will get us lost.

An **indefinite pronoun** refers to a non-specified individual(s) or group(s). Most indefinite pronouns are singular and do not have antecedents; in fact, they may act as antecedents for personal pronouns.

Common singular indefinite pronouns include words ending in *–one, –body*, and *–thing*, such as *everyone, anybody*, and *something*, along with *each, either, much, neither, none, nothing*, and *one*.

A **pronoun** replaces a noun:

- A **personal pronoun** refers to people, places, and things.
- A **relative pronoun** relates what follows to a preceding noun or pronoun.
- An **interrogative pronoun** introduces questions (how, what, which, when, why, who, whose, and where).

A **demonstrative pronoun** (*this, that, these, those*) points to nouns.

An **indefinite pronoun** refers to a non-specified individual or group.

The indefinite pronoun is italicized, the personal pronouns underlined below.

If *anyone* saw any suspicious activity, <u>he</u> or <u>she</u> should contact the supervisor.

For agreement problems involving indefinite pronouns, see pp. 409–10.

Intensive, reflexive, and *reciprocal* pronouns are other kinds of pronouns, showing different kinds of relationships with their noun/pronoun antecedent.

I *myself* met the visitor's plane. [Intensive pronoun, emphasizes subject, *I*]

I embarrassed *myself* when I forgot the visitor's name. [Reflexive pronoun, names receiver of action, which is the same as the doer of the action, *I*]

The visitor and I looked at *each other* a few seconds before laughing. [Reciprocal pronoun, refers to separate parts of a plural antecedent—*visitor and I*. Use *one another* if the antecedent refers to more than two.]

What Pronouns Do

Most pronouns have the same jobs as nouns in the sentence. (See "The Take-Charge Nouns," pp. 361–2.) In this example, the pronoun subjects are bolded, the object of the verb (direct object) is italicized, the object of the preposition (indirect object) is underlined, and the possessive form of the personal pronoun is in caps.

He promised to leave after <u>her</u> so that **he** could follow *her* in HIS car.

The Busy Verbs

> The **verb** conveys an action or a state of being, or combines with a main verb to express conditions like possibility or a complex temporal (time-related) action.

The **verb** conveys an action or state of being, or combines with a main verb to express conditions like possibility or a complex temporal (time-related) action.

If a "sentence" lacks either a subject noun/pronoun or a verb that shows what the subject is doing (its action) or the state of the subject, it could be an incomplete sentence. (See "Sentence Fragments: Errors of Incompletion," p. 376.)

What Verbs Do

1. Action Verb

> An **action verb** conveys an action—physical or mental/emotional.

An **action verb** conveys an action (physical: *jumps, smiles, takes*; or mental/emotional: *thinks, expects, hopes*). An action verb can be followed by an object (direct or indirect) or be modified by adverbs. (See "The Versatile Adverbs," p. 367.) The verb is italicized, the direct object is bolded, and the adverb modifiers are underlined below.

The overly eager student in the front row <u>always</u> *raises* his **hand** <u>unnecessarily</u>.

2. Linking Verb

A linking verb links the subject to the predicate noun/pronoun or adjective that completes the subject (e.g., *be, act, appear, become, feel, look, seem*, along with verbs referring to the senses—*smell, sound, taste*). Forms of *be* include *am, is, are, was, were, being,* and *been*. Linking verbs are followed by subject complements, predicate nouns or adjectives, not objects, and they are not modified by adverbs. The linking verbs are italicized, the predicate noun is bolded, and the predicate adjective is underlined below.

> Tennis player Eugenie Bouchard *became* the top Canadian female **athlete** of 2014, although at 20, she *is* very <u>young</u>.

Most of the verbs listed above can also be used as action verbs, depending on context, but forms of *to be* are always linking verbs.

Hint: Learn the various forms of the verb *to be* so you can recognize a common linking verb.

3. Helping Verb

A helping (auxiliary) verb combines with the main verb to express a condition such as time, necessity, probability, and other relationships. For more about helping verbs and verb tense, see the inside back cover of this textbook. Helping verbs are italicized and the main verbs are bolded below.

> She often *will be* **playing** video games when she *should be* **studying**.

Hint: The helping verb precedes the main verb in a sentence.

BOX 11.1 | Verb Impersonators

A verbal is formed from a complete verb, but does not act as a verb in a sentence. It is an "impersonator" because it can be mistaken for a verb. The *–ing* form of the verb (called the present participle) combines with a helping verb to make a complete verb form. The past participle (*–en, –ed*) can also form a verbal.

> *Complete verb forms:* am hoping, is running, will be competing, has eaten

(continued)

A **linking verb** links the subject to the predicate.

The predicate is the part of the sentence that contains at least a verb that states something about the subject—for example, what it is doing.

Action verbs can be modified by adverbs. Linking verbs are completed by predicate nouns or predicate adjectives.

A **helping (auxiliary) verb** combines with the main verb to express a condition such as time, necessity, probability, and other relationships.

An incomplete verb form, or **verbal**, can be used as a noun, adjective, and adverb. It shouldn't be mistaken for a complete verb form.

However, *hoping*, *running*, *competing*, and *eaten* when used alone are incomplete verb forms and cannot combine with subjects to make grammatical statements: *I hoping*, *she running*, *they competing*, and *we eaten* don't make sense.

But –*ing* and other incomplete verb forms do have their uses in sentences as nouns, adjectives, and adverbs, as illustrated below.

A **participle** usually ends in –*ing*, –*ed*, –*en*, or –*t* and usually acts as an adjective (see "The Informative Adjectives," below). Participles used as adjectives are underlined.

> The <u>Running</u> Man is a novel <u>written</u> by Stephen King.

A **gerund** is formed from the present participle of a verb. A gerund ends in –*ing* and functions as a noun. Gerunds are underlined.

> <u>Running</u> in the morning is healthier than <u>drinking</u> coffee.

An **infinitive** includes *to* along with the base verb form and acts as a noun, adjective, or adverb. A noun infinitive is italicized and an infinitive used as an adverb underlined below.

> He hoped *to run* this morning. She drank two cups of coffee <u>to wake up</u>.

Hint: Do not confuse an infinitive with a prepositional phrase beginning with *to*. The infinitive is italicized and the prepositional phrase is underlined below.

> She put her coffee in a thermos *to keep* it warm; it was good <u>to the last drop</u>.

Verbals often combine with other words to form phrases, which can act as nouns, adjectives, or adverbs in the sentence. See "Phrases," p. 373.

A **participle** usually ends in –*ing*, –*ed*, –*en*, or –*t* and acts as an adjective.

A **gerund** is formed from the present participal of a verb. A gerund ends in –*ing* and functions as a noun.

An **infinitive** includes *to* along with the base verb form and acts as a noun, adjective, or adverb.

An **adjective** gives information about (modifies) a noun or pronoun. It can answer questions like *Which one? What kind?* or *How many?* When an adjective is one word, it usually precedes the noun, unless it follows a linking verb as a predicate adjective.

The Informative Adjectives

An **adjective** modifies (describes or limits) a noun or pronoun.

What Adjectives Do

1. Modifier

One-word adjectives usually come before the word/phrase they modify.

Hint: Look for adjectives before nouns/pronouns. Adjectives are italicized and the nouns/pronouns they modify/complete are underlined below.

The *complex* <u>assignment</u> kept him up all *last* <u>night</u>. [*Assignment* and *night* are nouns.]

Almost <u>everyone</u> in the group has completed the assignment. [*Everyone* is a pronoun.]

Hint: Ask the questions *Which one? What kind?* or *How many?* of a noun/pronoun. *What kind of assignment?* A complex assignment; *Which night?* Last night.

2. Subject Completion

Predicate adjectives follow linking verbs, completing the subject.

> **Hint:** Look after linking verbs to find predicate adjectives.

The <u>assignment</u> was *complex*. [*Was* is a linking verb.]

3. Adjectival Phrases and Clauses

Phrases and clauses as adjectival modifiers usually follow the word/phrase they modify, though they can also precede them as participial phrases. Modifiers are italicized and their nouns are underlined below.

> **Hint:** Look after nouns/pronouns to find most phrasal and clausal adjectival modifiers. (See "Phrases and Clauses," p. 373.)

Adjectival phrase: <u>Posters</u> *of celebrities* adorned the walls.

Adjectival clause: The <u>posters</u> *that adorned the walls* made the room look tiny.

4. Articles as Adjectives

Articles (*a*, *an*, *the*) are considered adjectival as are some pronouns when they precede a noun.

the assignment; *that* circumstance; *their* integrity; *most* children

Nouns can also precede other nouns and act as adjectives (italicized).

a *human* cannonball, the *school's Christmas* play

The Versatile Adverbs

An **adverb** modifies a verb, an adjective, or another adverb. It can also modify a complete sentence.

An **adverb** gives information about a verb, an adjective, and/or another adverb. It answers questions like *How? When? Where? How much?* or *To what degree?*

Hint: Adverbs tend to be more moveable than adjectives, so the best way to identify them is by asking the questions *How? When? Where? How much?* or *To what degree?*

Hint: Most (but not all) adverbs end in *–ly*.

What Adverbs Do

1. Verb Modifier

Adverbs most often modify verbs. The adverb, answering the question *How?*, is italicized, and the verb it modifies is underlined below.

Hockey has <u>changed</u> *greatly* over its 100-year existence.

2. Adjective Modifier

Adverbs often modify adjectives. Below, the italicized adverb modifies the underlined adjective (answers *To what degree?*); the adjective *entertaining* modifies the noun *sport*.

It is still a *very* <u>entertaining</u> sport in spite of these changes.

3. Adverb Modifier

Adverbs can modify other adverbs. Below, the italicized adverb modifies the underlined adverb by answering the question *To what degree?* (The underlined adverb modifies the verb *watched* by answering the question *When?*).

It remains watched *more* <u>often</u> by Canadians than any other sport.

4. Sentence Modifier

An adverb can modify a complete sentence. Below, the adverb *however* modifies the sentence. *Today*, an adverb, modifies *believe*, a verb (answers *When?*).

However, some fans today believe fighting undermines the sport's integrity.

Adverbs like *however*, above, can be recruited to act as joiners (see "The Workhorse Conjunctions," p. 369). When they are used to join sentences, they are punctuated differently than when they act as ordinary adverbs.

The Overlooked Prepositions

A **preposition**, which often refers to place or time, joins the noun/pronoun that follows to the rest of the sentence.

A **preposition** is a small word that often refers to place or time and that is followed by a noun/pronoun object. Thus, prepositions introduce prepositional phrases (see "Phrases," p. 373).

What Prepositions Do

Prepositions join the noun/pronoun to the rest of the sentence, helping it modify another part of speech.

Hint: A preposition is usually followed by a noun/pronoun object. The prepositions are italicized, the objects underlined below.

> You will find the game *on top of* the Xbox *beside* the television.

Hint: To help you recognize prepositions, it's a good idea to become familiar with the most common ones (bolded) among those below. Prepositions can be more than one word (e.g., *on top of* in the sentence above).

about	**at**	down	near	over	under
above	**before**	**during**	next (to)	past	until
across	behind	except	**of**	regarding	up
after	below	**for**	off	since	upon
against	beside(s)	**from**	**on**	than	**with**
along	**between**	**in**	onto	**through**	within
among	beyond	inside	opposite	throughout	without
around	**by**	**into**	out	**to**	
as	despite	**like**	outside (of)	toward(s)	

The Workhorse Conjunctions

Like a preposition, a conjunction is a joiner. It fulfills all the other joining functions in the sentence.

> A **conjunction** joins words, phrases, or clauses in a sentence.

What Conjunctions Do

1. Coordinating Conjunction

A coordinating conjunction joins *equal* grammatical units, such as noun to noun, verb to verb, and independent clause to independent clause (see "Clauses," p. 375). The coordinating conjunctions are italicized and the words they join are underlined.

> A **coordinating conjunction** joins *equal* grammatical units.

> Video games have evolved rapidly *yet* controversially, often resembling horror films in their crude language *and* gory images.

Yet joins two adverbs; *and* joins two nouns.

> Parents try to protect their children from violent content, *but* graphic content seems everywhere.

But joins two independent clauses, or sentence equivalents.

The seven coordinating conjunctions are *for, and, nor, but, or, yet,* and *so* (FANBOYS).

A **subordinating conjunction** joins *unequal* grammatical units, specifically dependent to independent clauses, showing how they are related.

Hint: Memorize the seven coordinating conjunctions, whose first letters spell out FANBOYS: *for, and, nor, but, or, yet,* and *so*.

2. Subordinating Conjunction

A **subordinating conjunction** joins *unequal* grammatical units, specifically dependent to independent clauses (see "Clauses," p. 375), showing how they are related. The subordinating conjunction is italicized, and the dependent clause is underlined; the remainder of the sentence is the independent clause.

> She was the first in her family to get her degree, *though* she was 68 years old.

Note that the subordinating conjunction introduces the dependent clause and is part of it.

Hint: Although there are too many subordinating conjunctions to memorize, learn to recognize the bolded ones below. (Relative pronouns are also included as they, too, introduce dependent clauses; they are discussed on p. 376.)

after	**because**	in case	**though**	**where**	who
although	**before**	in order that	**unless**	**whereas**	whoever
as	even though	once	**until**	wherever	whom
as if	ever since	rather than	what	**whether**	whose
as long as	how	**since**	whatever	which	why
as soon as	**if**	so that	**when**	whichever	
as though	if only	**that**	whenever	**while**	

3. Adverbial Conjunction

An **adverbial conjunction** joins independent clauses.

An **adverbial conjunction** is an adverb (see "The Versatile Adverbs," pp. 367–8) that is used to connect two independent clauses. When an adverb is used this way, a semicolon precedes the adverbial conjunction and a comma follows it. The adverbial conjunction is italicized, and the independent clause it joins to the first is underlined.

> Adverbs have many uses in a sentence; *however,* they must be punctuated with care.

Hint: Since many one-word adverbs and transitional phrases can be used to connect two independent clauses, the best way to identify them is to look at how they are being used. If an independent clause precedes *and* follows the adverb, it is probably an adverbial conjunction and should be preceded by a semicolon. (See "Clauses," p. 375 and "2. Semicolon (;)," p. 385.)

Here are some adverbial conjunctions and transitional phrases. (Commonly used words/phrases are in bold.)

accordingly	hence	meanwhile	still
afterward	**however**	**moreover**	subsequently
also	if not	namely	that is
as a result	**in addition**	**nevertheless**	**then**
besides	**in fact**	next	**therefore**
certainly	in the meantime	**nonetheless**	**thus**
consequently	indeed	on the contrary	undoubtedly
finally	instead	on the other hand	
for example	later	otherwise	
further(more)	likewise	similarly	

4. Correlative Conjunction

A **correlative conjunction** is a pair of conjunctions (e.g., *either . . . or, neither . . . nor, both . . . and, not only . . . but also*) (see p. 422).

A **correlative conjunction** is a pair of conjunctions.

EXERCISE 11.2

Identify the parts of speech (noun, pronoun, verb, adjective, adverb, preposition, or conjunction) in the following sentences. A sample sentence has been done for you.

   Hint: (1) Separate the subject from the predicate; (2) identify nouns/pronouns and verbs; (3) look to see if these words are modified by adjectives or adverbs; and (4) identify joiners (prepositions and conjunctions). Not all the sentences contain all seven parts of speech.

   Researchers once thought that chocolate had little nutritional value.
   1.   Researchers | once thought that chocolate | had little nutritional value.
   2.   *Nouns:* researchers, chocolate; *verbs:* thought, had
   3.   *Adjective:* nutritional; *adverbs:* once, little
   4.   *Joiner (conjunction):* that

   1.   The judge announced her decision yesterday.
   2.   Hockey is certainly a very aggressive sport.
   3.   The puppies romped happily under the mother's watchful eye.
   4.   Most people in North America now access their news on the Internet.
   5.   They attended the rally during class time after the professor gave his permission.

Sentences

As we have seen, above, the parts of speech can have various roles within a sentence—from small ones, like prepositions that join a noun/pronoun to the sentence, to larger ones, like adverbial conjunctions that join two "sentences" (independent clauses). We now turn to the sentence itself and to units larger than single words, phrases and clauses.

What Is a Sentence?

A sentence expresses a completed idea, or thought. On the other hand, an incomplete sentence, or sentence fragment, *sounds* incomplete. However, sound is not the best way to identify a fragment. A sentence can be defined grammatically as *a group of words that contains a subject and a predicate and that needs nothing else to complete it.*

> A **sentence** can be defined grammatically as a group of words that contains a subject and a predicate and that needs nothing else to complete it.

Subject

The subject of a simple sentence is the noun or pronoun that states who or what is acting: the actor. Most, but not all, subjects precede the verb. A simple subject consists only of the main noun/pronoun. A complete subject consists of the main noun/pronoun and its modifiers.

> A **simple subject** consists only of the main noun/pronoun.
>
> A **complete subject** contains the main noun/pronoun along with any modifiers of the subject.
>
> The subject of a simple sentence is the noun or pronoun that states who or what is acting.

The *moon* shines brightly.

The simple subject is *moon*.

The full moon seen through the telescope was extremely bright.

The complete subject is *The full moon seen through the telescope*.

Predicate

The predicate tells you what the subject is doing or shows you the state or condition of the subject. A simple predicate consists only of the main verb; a complete predicate includes other words, such as modifiers and direct or indirect objects.

> The **predicate** tells you what the subject is doing or shows you the state or condition of the subject:
>
> • A **simple predicate** consists only of the main verb.
> • A **complete predicate** includes other words, such as modifiers and direct or indirect objects.

In the first example under "Subject," above, the complete predicate tells you that the moon *shines brightly* (an action). In the second example, the complete predicate tells you that the moon *was extremely bright* (a state).

BOX 11.2 | Matching Verb to Subject

Make sure that the subject of a clause makes sense with the verb. In the following sentence, the verb, *believes*, shouldn't be used with the non-animate subject, *justice system*.

Mismatched subject–verb: The *Canadian justice system believes* citizens should be accountable for our actions.

Matching subject–verb: A basic principle of the Canadian justice system is that *citizens should be accountable* for their actions.

In an **imperative sentence**, the subject is *you*. Although it may not actually be in the sentence, it is understood to be there acting as the subject.

> Shine! = (You) shine!

An **imperative sentence** issues an order or direction and is a complete sentence even if it consists of only one word, a verb.

An imperative sentence issues an order or direction and is a complete sentence—other grammatical sentences must have at least two words. (For more on incomplete sentences, or sentence fragments, see p. 376.)

Phrases and Clauses

Phrases and clauses are grammatical units that are larger than single words. One type of clause, an independent clause, is equivalent to a complete sentence. Phrases and clauses have various functions in the sentence.

Phrases

A phrase is a group of two or more words that lacks a subject and a predicate. Among the functions of phrases *within* sentences, they could act as a subject or a predicate in a complete sentence or could modify a noun or verb.

1. Prepositional Phrases

A **prepositional phrase** begins with a preposition and can act adjectivally (as an adjective modifying a noun/pronoun) or adverbially (as an adverb modifying a verb). In the sentence below, the line separates subject from predicate. Prepositional phrases are italicized below, and arrows show the words they modify.

A **prepositional phrase** begins with a preposition and can act adjectivally or adverbially.

A clerk ◄——*with a jovial smile* | directed me   *to the second room* ◄—— *on the right*.

| Noun | adjectival phrase | verb | adverbial phrase | adjectival phrase |

In the sentence above, *A clerk with a jovial smile* is a noun phrase, the subject of the sentence.

> A clerk with a jovial smile = complete subject, noun
> *clerk* = simple subject, noun
> *with a jovial smile* = prepositional phrase, adjective modifies *clerk*, noun
> *with* = preposition, introduces phrase
> *jovial* = adjective, modifies *smile*, noun
> *smile* = object of preposition, *with*

A **verb phrase** consists of a main verb and any helping verbs.

A **verb phrase** consists of a main verb and any helping verbs.

> It *has been raining* hard since Tuesday.

Has been is a helping verb form; *raining* is the present participle of the verb *rain*, the main verb.

Verbals (see above, p. 365) can combine with other words, such as objects or modifiers, to function as adjectives, nouns, and adverbs in a sentence. There are three types of verbal phrases.

2. Participle (Adjective) Phrases

A **participle (adjective) phrase** is formed from present (*–ing*) or past (*–ed*, *–en*, *–t*) participles of verbs. As an adjective, it can modify a noun or pronoun. The participial phrases are italicized and the pronouns are underlined below.

> *Satiated after a full meal*, <u>he</u> yawned and fell asleep. *Dreaming of more food*, <u>he</u> awoke suddenly.

When you use a participial phrase, make sure that the noun/pronoun that it is intended to modify is in the sentence.

> *Dangling modifier error:* Satiated after a full meal, sleep suddenly arrived.

Satiated after a full meal mistakenly modifies the noun *sleep*, making it appear that sleep was satiated. (To fix this kind of error, see p. 419, "Dangling Modifiers.")

3. Gerund (Noun) Phrases

A **gerund (noun) phrase** is formed from the present (*–ing*) participle of a verb and functions as a noun, for example, as a subject or an object. While other nouns are modified by adjectives, adverbs can modify gerunds. The gerund (noun) is italicized and the gerund phrase subject, including an adverb, is underlined below.

> <u>*Jogging* briskly</u> was part of her daily routine.

Jogging briskly is the complete subject; *briskly* is an adverb modifying the gerund (answers the question *how?*).

4. Infinitive (Noun, Adjective, Adverb) Phrases

An **infinitive (noun, adjective, adverb) phrase** is formed by putting *to* before the base verb form. The infinitive phrase is italicized below.

> She planned *to lose weight*.

To lose weight acts as the noun object of the verb *planned*. (Like most objects, it follows the verb.)

Margin notes:

A **participle (adjective) phrase** is formed from present (*–ing*) or past (*–ed*, *–en*, *–t*) participles of verbs.

A **gerund (noun) phrase** is formed from the present (*–ing*) participle of a verb and functions as a noun, for example, as a subject or an object.

An **infinitive (noun, adjective, or adverb) phrase** includes *to* along with the base verb form and acts as a noun, adjective, or adverb.

EXERCISE 11.3

Identify the underlined words as prepositional, noun, verb, or verbal (participial, gerund, infinitive) phrases. If applicable, identify the word(s) they modify or their function. A sample sentence has been done for you.

<u>The death penalty</u>	is enforced today	<u>in 58 countries</u>	<u>across the globe.</u>
noun phrase (subject)		prep. phrase (adverbial, modifies verb *is enforced*)	prep phrase (adjectival, modifies noun *countries*)

1. <u>Reintroduced in 1976</u>, the death penalty remains hotly debated <u>in the US</u>.
2. Approximately 3,000 inmates currently reside <u>on death row</u>.
3. Most countries, however, <u>have abolished</u> the death penalty.
4. <u>Having murderers pay for crimes with their own lives</u> is considered barbaric by many people.
5. At this time, Canada has no plans <u>to bring back</u> capital punishment.

Clauses

A clause is a group of words that, unlike a phrase, contains a subject and a predicate. An **independent clause** can stand on its own as a complete sentence and needs no other words to complete it. Although a **dependent clause** contains a subject and a predicate, it cannot stand on its own as it does not express a complete thought.

What is the main idea in the following sentence?

> Although an eighteenth-century novel was on the course, it had fewer than 300 pages.

> *Although an eighteenth-century novel was on the course*? Or, *It had fewer than 300 pages*?

> **Answer:** *It had fewer than 300 pages* expresses a complete thought, though it is shorter than the word group that precedes it.

The point is that the sentence is grammatically complete with a subject (the pronoun *it* and a main verb, *had*). On the other hand, *Although an eighteenth-century novel was on the course* hints at an upcoming contrast. But more information is needed—specifically, the second part of the contrast. In fact, you could write several endings to a sentence that began this way.

> Although an eighteenth-century novel was on the course, I decided not to take it.

> . . . , four twentieth-century novels were on it too.

> . . . , it had fewer than 300 pages.

A clause is a group of words that contains a subject and a predicate.

- An **independent clause** is equivalent to a complete sentence.
- A **dependent clause** contains a subject and a predicate but does not express a complete thought.

An independent clause, such as *it had fewer than 300 pages*, can stand alone or complete a sentence that begins (or ends) with a dependent clause.

A dependent clause indicates a specific relationship with the independent clause. The subordinating conjunction *although*, in the example above, begins the dependent clause and shows a contrastive relationship with the independent clause or main idea.

Another kind of dependent clause begins with a relative pronoun (see p. 363) rather than a subordinating conjunction. (See p. 370 for a list of common subordinating conjunctions.) A relative clause—which usually begins with *that*, *which*, *who*, *whom*, or *whose*—follows a noun/pronoun and modifies it. The relative pronoun is bolded, the relative (dependent) clause is underlined, and the noun that the clause modifies is in caps below.

> VIRGINIA WOOLF, **who** wrote *Mrs Dalloway*, is a twentieth-century writer on the course.

> The NOVEL, **which** recalls the memories of a middle-aged woman, explores societal ills in post–World War I England.

In the two examples, above, a dependent clause interrupts the independent clause.

A **relative clause** follows a noun or pronoun and modifies it.

EXERCISE 11.4

Underline independent clauses, put parentheses around dependent clauses, and circle the subordinating conjunction or relative pronoun. A sample sentence has been done for you.

The end of the transatlantic slave trade came in 1807 ((when) importing slaves was finally banned in the US).

1. While drug testing has become more common, athletes are still taking drugs.
2. The battle against cancer will continue until a cure is found.
3. When Nelson Mandela became South Africa's president, a more democratic era began.
4. The game "Baggataway," which was played by many Aboriginal tribes, intrigued British colonizers.
5. Although 10,000 women belong to the Canadian Armed Forces today, only a few are members of the combat force.

Sentence Fragments: Errors of Incompletion

The two definitions of the sentence given below can be used to ensure that you always write in complete sentences and do not use an incomplete sentence, or sentence fragment, in formal writing.

A **sentence fragment** lacks a subject and/or predicate or consists only of a dependent clause, which does not express a complete thought.

1. A sentence is a group of words that includes a subject and a predicate and that needs nothing else to complete it.
2. A sentence is a group of words that expresses a complete thought.

Sentence fragments fail to satisfy these two requirements. They either (1) lack a subject or a predicate or both subject and predicate, or (2) consist of a dependent clause by itself without an independent clause. Consequently, they do not express a complete thought.

Fragment Type 1: Lacks Subject, Predicate, or Both
Example 1

A *noun subject by itself* is an example of a fragment, whether it is a simple subject or a complete one with added detail.

> The moon.

> The full moon.

> The full moon whose beams glittered eerily on the still lake.

To make any of these word groups into a complete sentence, you would need to add a verb so that the moon is doing something or a state about the moon is revealed. The simple subject is italicized and the predicate (verb) is underlined in the examples below. A line separates simple subject from simple predicate.

> The *moon* | <u>rose</u>. [action]

> The full *moon* | <u>looked</u> within reaching distance. [state]

> The full *moon* whose beams glittered eerily on the still lake | <u>recalled</u> a long-forgotten memory. [action]

All the sentences are now complete as they have a subject *and* a predicate; they also express a complete thought.

Example 2

A sentence must include both a subject and *a predicate that consists of a complete verb form.*

> I experienced an odd desire. Looking at the full moon.

Looking is an incomplete verb form. What follows *desire*, then, is a fragment. To turn it into a complete sentence, you would need to add a helping verb plus a subject.

> I experienced an odd desire. *I was looking* at the full moon at the time.

You can use these two definitions of a sentence to help avoid incomplete sentences, or sentence fragments.

1. A sentence is a group of words that includes a subject and a predicate and that needs nothing else to complete it.
2. A sentence is a group of words that expresses a complete thought.

More efficiently, add the phrase *looking at the full moon* to the previous sentence.

I experienced an odd desire as I was looking at the full moon.

OR

Looking at the full moon, I experienced an odd desire.

Example 3

A noun in a group of words doesn't always indicate that a subject is present.

At a *position* near the *Ocean* of *Storms* on the *surface* of the *moon*.

Although there are five nouns (italicized) here, they are all preceded by prepositions (underlined) and are objects of prepositions, not subjects. A subject and a predicate need to be added to make this a grammatical sentence.

I was looking at a position near the Ocean of Storms on the surface of the moon.

At a position near the Ocean of Storms on the surface of the moon *was a gigantic crater.*

Fragment Type 2: Dependent Clause Fragment

A dependent clause fragment contains a subject and predicate but does not express a complete thought. It begins with a subordinating conjunction or relative pronoun and needs to be completed by an independent clause.

This kind of fragment contains a subject and predicate but does not express a complete thought. It begins with a subordinating conjunction or relative pronoun. In the first sentence below, the subordinating conjunction is italicized; in the second sentence, the relative pronoun is italicized.

Looking at the full moon, I experienced an odd desire. *As* a howl came to my lips.

Looking at the full moon, I experienced an odd desire. *Which* found expression as a howl.

To fix dependent clause fragments, simply join the dependent clauses, which give less important information, to the independent clauses, which express the main idea.

Looking at the full moon, I experienced an odd desire as a howl came to my lips.

Looking at the full moon, I experienced an odd desire, which found expression as a howl.

EXERCISE 11.5

Turn the sentence fragments below into grammatical sentences that contain a subject and a predicate, and express a complete thought. A sample sentence has been done for you.

Being careful not to write a sentence fragment.

I am being careful not to write a sentence fragment.

OR

Being careful not to write a sentence fragment can make you a better writer.

1. Although a sewage plant would fix the city's waste problem.
2. A novel about a boy who loses his parents to a disaster at sea.
3. The goalie lost his stick in the mad scramble. Which led to the winning goal.
4. Many people today are obsessed with the Internet. Whether they connect with friends on Facebook or watch videos on YouTube.
5. The relationship between one adolescent and another affects nearly everything in their lives. From clothing choices to self-esteem.

Errors of Joining

Incorrectly joined sentences, like incomplete sentences, are difficult to read. The rules for using commas, semicolons, and colons in Chapter 12 (pp. 385–7) will familiarize you with methods for connecting your sentences. This section focuses on two errors in sentence combining, the run-on sentence (or "fused sentence") and the comma splice (or "comma fault").

Run-On Sentences

In a run-on sentence, the writer follows the first sentence (independent clause) with the second sentence (independent clause) without any punctuation in between. It is left up to the reader to figure out where the first ends and the second begins.

> In a run-on sentence, the writer follows the first sentence (independent clause) with the second sentence (independent clause) without any punctuation in between.

Macs come with iPhoto, Photobooth, and iMovie these add-ons are useful to today's consumer.

The simplest way to fix a run-on sentence is to put a period after the first independent clause and follow with the second independent clause as a new sentence.

Macs come with iPhoto, Photobooth, and iMovie. These add-ons are useful to today's consumer.

However, you can also join independent clauses by using a coordinating conjunction (see FANBOYS p. 370) preceded by a comma or, in some cases, by using a semicolon.

> Macs come with iPhoto, Photobooth, and iMovie, and these add-ons are useful to today's consumer.

> Macs come with iPhoto, Photobooth, and iMovie; these add-ons are useful to today's consumer.

Comma Splices

A **comma splice** is the incorrect use of a comma alone to join two independent clauses.

Commas are used in various ways *within* sentences, rather than to join two complete sentences (comma splice). However, as you will see, *a comma + a coordinating conjunction can be used to join two sentences* (independent clauses). Learning to identify independent clauses will make it easier to avoid comma splices.

How many independent clauses do the following sentences contain?

> 1. Having tried to shut down his computer for several minutes, the frustrated student finally had to resort to unplugging the power source.

> 2. The frustrated student tried to shut down his computer for several minutes, he finally had to resort to unplugging the power source.

> *Answer:* Sentence (1) contains one independent clause, or subject–verb unit: *the frustrated student finally had to resort to unplugging the power source*. There is no subject or complete verb form in the preceding word group, a participial phrase.

Sentence (2) contains two independent clauses, or subject–verb units, which are incorrectly joined by only a comma. The subject of the first is *the frustrated student*; the subject of the sentence is *he*.

As is the case with run-on sentences, above, the simplest way to fix a comma splice is to make the two independent clauses into simple sentences.

> The frustrated student tried to shut down his computer for several minutes.

> He finally had to resort to unplugging the power source.

However, a coordinating conjunction preceded by a comma would probably be better in this case because "but" clarifies the link between the clauses.

> The frustrated student tried to shut down his computer for several minutes, *but* he finally had to resort to unplugging the power source.

See Chapter 12, "Joining Independent Clauses" (p. 384) for other ways to fix the problem.

Hint: Many comma splices occur when the second independent clause ("sentence") begins with a pronoun, such as *he*, *she*, *it*, or *they*. Pronouns often look less important than nouns, but both nouns and pronouns can act as grammatical subjects.

EXERCISE 11.6

Identify the sentence error (fragment, run-on sentence, or comma splice). Correct it by adding punctuation if it is an error of joining. If it is a fragment, add information to turn it into a grammatical sentence. A sample sentence has been done for you.

Multiculturalism connects youth with one another, it provides them with a meeting place, a common ground. [comma splice]

Multiculturalism connects youth with one another. It provides them with a meeting place, a common ground.

Multiculturalism connects youth with one another, for it provides them with a meeting place, a common ground.

1. Massive Multiplayer Online Role-Playing Games (MMORPGS) are the last frontier in escape gaming they literally take you into another world.
2. Women from Afghanistan who share the Muslim religion.
3. We can no longer turn our backs to what is happening in the north, it is time to take action.
4. Modern technology has resulted in astonishing benefits for our communities. Though it has created many new problems as well.
5. It has been more than 40 years since the last pandemic, another one is clearly overdue.

EXERCISE 11.7

Correct any fragments, run-on sentences, and comma splices in the following paragraph (all these errors may not be present).

The life of Aboriginals in Canada has undergone many disruptions. Since the arrival of Europeans in the early 1400s. The introduction of guns greatly affected their lifestyle, it also affected their trades with Europeans. Along with this new lifestyle came diseases and alcohol, these brought on problems that were unknown before the arrival of Europeans. In 1869, John Wesley Powell introduced the concept of "reservations." Which he intended to serve as a "school of industry and a home for [those] unfortunate people." This concept was designed to assimilate the Natives of Canada. Teaching them English and the values of White society.

Chapter 11 Review Questions

1. What are the benefits of learning correct grammar and punctuation?
2. a) Name the seven parts of speech.
   b) Briefly explain one way that can help you identify
      i. A noun acting as a subject
      ii. A noun acting as an object of a verb
      iii. A noun acting as an object of a preposition
3. Most pronouns replace _____. The class of pronoun that refers to people and things is called a _____ pronoun; the class of pronoun that refers to non-specified individuals or groups is called an _____ pronoun.
4. Answer true or false:
   a) *Has eaten* is an example of a complete verb form.
   b) A verbal is one kind of complete verb form.
   c) A verbal can act as a noun in a sentence.
5. Summarize the grammatical functions of adverbs and adjectives.
6. Which of the following words is *not* a conjunction?
   a) because
   b) when
   c) and
   d) between
7. Give two definitions of a sentence and explain which is more useful for a student of grammar.
8. Explain the difference between
   a) A phrase and a clause
   b) An independent clause and a dependent clause
9. Identify two kinds of fragments and make up sentence fragments that illustrate the two kinds; then turn the fragments into complete sentences.
10. a) Define a run-on sentence and illustrate by making one up; turn it into a complete, correctly punctuated sentence or two sentences.
    b) Define a comma splice and illustrate by making one up; turn it into a complete, correctly punctuated sentence or two sentences.

Key Terms

action verb (p. 364)
adjective (p. 366)
adverb (p. 367)
adverbial conjunction (p. 370)
appositive (p. 362)
comma splice (p. 380)
complete predicate (p. 372)
complete subject (p. 372)

conjunction (p. 369)
coordinating conjunction (p. 369)
correlative conjunction (p. 371)
demonstrative pronoun (p. 363)
dependent clause (p. 375)
FANBOYS (p. 370)
gerund (p. 366)
gerund (noun) phrase (p. 374)

helping (auxiliary) verb (p. 365)

imperative sentence (p. 373)

indefinite pronoun (p. 363)

independent clause (p. 375)

infinitive (p. 366)

infinitive (noun, adjective, adverb) phrase (p. 374)

interrogative pronoun (p. 363)

linking verb (p. 365)

noun (p. 361)

object (p. 362)

object of a preposition (p. 362)

participle (p. 366)

participle (adjective) phrase (p. 374)

personal pronoun (p. 363)

phrase (p. 373)

predicate (p. 372)

preposition (p. 368)

prepositional phrase (p. 373)

pronoun (p. 363)

relative clause (p. 376)

relative pronoun (p. 363)

sentence (p. 372)

sentence fragment (p. 376)

simple predicate (p. 372)

simple subject (p. 372)

subject (p. 361)

subject complement (p. 362)

subordinating conjunction (p. 370)

verb (p. 364)

verb phrase (p. 373)

verbal (p. 365)

12

Punctuation and Apostrophes

In this chapter, you will learn:

- How to use correct punctuation to join two ideas (independent clauses)

- How to use commas, semicolons, and colons correctly with a series

- How to use commas after an introductory word, phrase, or clause when an independent clause follows

- How to use commas with parenthetical (non-essential) information

- How to use correct punctuation with quotations

- How to use commas with adjectives, dates, addresses, and numbers

- How to use apostrophes to indicate relationships like possession and to show letters left out in contractions

The choice of using a comma, semicolon, or colon may depend on whether you are writing informally (e.g., for a student newspaper or a blog) or formally (e.g., for your English instructor or an admissions committee).

The rules below apply especially to formal writing, but they are applicable to most kinds of writing. For clearer understanding, we will deal with the rules for joining complete sentences before discussing the rules for separating elements *within* a sentence. Punctuation rules are summarized on p. 395.

A **simple sentence**, which has a subject–predicate unit, is equivalent to an independent clause.

A **compound sentence** consists of two independent clauses joined by a comma and coordinating conjunction, a semicolon, or a colon.

Joining Independent Clauses

Independent clauses are equivalent to a simple sentence: they contain a subject–predicate unit. When two simple sentences are grammatically joined, they produce a compound sentence.

1. Comma (,) + Coordinating Conjunction (cc)

To create a compound sentence from two independent clauses or simple sentences, you can use a coordinating conjunction to join the independent clauses, making sure you precede the joining word by a comma.

> *Simple sentence A:* The first smartphone, made by IBM, was known as Simon.

> *Simple sentence B:* It was demonstrated at a computer industry trade show in 1992.

Sentences joined by a comma and coordinating conjunction (italicized): A, cc B.

> The first smartphone, made by IBM, was known as Simon, *and* it was demonstrated at a computer industry trade show in 1992.

Do not use a comma before a coordinating conjunction if it is joining only two words or phrases. In the example below, *and* is joining two verbs, *made* and *known*. There is only one independent clause with a compound predicate (that is, two verbs making up the predicate).

> The first smartphone *was made* by IBM and *was known* as Simon.

The coordinating conjunctions are *for, and, nor, but, or, yet,* and *so*; their first letters spell out FANBOYS.

Use a comma with a coordinating conjunction to join two independent clauses, not two nouns, verbs, or adjectives, etc.

2. Semicolon (;)

You may use a semicolon instead of a comma + coordinating conjunction if you want to stress that the ideas in the independent clauses are closely related. For example, the second clause could expand on the first or add information; it could also express a contrast with the first one: A; B.

> The first smartphone, made by IBM, was known as Simon; it was demonstrated at a computer industry trade show in 1992. [adds information]

> Smartphones were originally created to benefit modern businesses; the main use of smartphones today is social interaction. [contrast]

3. Semicolon (;) + Adverbial Conjunction (ac)

Adverbial conjunctions are ordinary adverbs, such as *however, therefore, moreover,* and *thus,* along with transitional phrases, such as *for example, in addition,* and *in fact,* that can join independent clauses. They indicate a specific relationship between the clauses. A comma usually follows the adverbial conjunction: A; ac, B.

Use a semicolon to join two independent clauses if you use a word/phrase other than a coordinating conjunction. Adverbs like *however* and *therefore* are examples of common joiners. Follow the joining word/phrase by a comma. For a list of common adverbial conjunctions and transitional phrases, see p. 371.

> Smartphone apps can be created for almost anything; for example, one man created an app that triggered a mini-fridge to shoot a beverage can at the operator.

When these kinds of adverbs occur within clauses, rather than as joiners, they are enclosed by commas (see p. 390). Failing to recognize their two distinct roles in a sentence is responsible for a common writing error.

Hint: If an independent clause precedes *and* follows the adverb, it is probably an adverbial conjunction and needs to be preceded by a semicolon and followed by a comma.

4. Colon (:)

A colon can be used to join independent clauses if the second clause answers or explains the reason for the statement in the first clause.

A colon can be used to join independent clauses if the second clause (the one after the colon) answers or explains the reason for the statement in the first clause (compare "Semicolon," above): A: B.

> There appears to be one disadvantage of smartphones: they can create a dependency, or even an addiction, in some users.

EXERCISE 12.1

Consider the rules for joining independent clauses, and decide which would be the best in each instance. Write out the complete sentence and include the most suitable joining word if you do not choose to use only a semicolon or colon (do not use *and* unless it is the only conjunction that makes the sentence make sense). A list of coordinating conjunctions is on p. 385; a list of common conjunctive adverbs is on p. 371. A sample sentence has been done for you.

The number of single-parent families is increasing.

Many people today believe that a child needs two parents.

Answer 1: The number of single-parent families is increasing, but many people today believe that a child needs two parents.

Answer 2: The number of single-parent families is increasing; however, many people today believe that a child needs two parents.

1. As more air is blown into a balloon, its volume increases. Its surface area also increases.
2. The language of music is universal. People everywhere connect with others through some form of music.
3. Most homeless people who live on the street carry some cash in their pockets. They are more vulnerable to street crime.
4. Global warming and the depletion of our resources are major problems. They are preventable ones.
5. Caffeine affects the central nervous system. Its effects include heightened awareness, decreased reaction time, and improved coordination.

Punctuation within Sentences (Internal Punctuation)

To punctuate within sentences, you will probably use commas most of the time; however, often a semicolon or colon is the better choice or, occasionally, parentheses or dashes. The punctuation rules are discussed under four rule categories below:

1. a series,
2. sentence introductions,
3. non-essential information, and
4. miscellaneous, including adjectives, dates, addresses, and direct quotations.

1. Items in a Series (Three or More Items)

Use commas to separate simple items (three or more) in a series whether they are nouns, adjectives, predicates, independent clauses, or other parallel items.

Use commas to separate three or more items in a series.

> Studies show that bullying is a learned behaviour in primary, middle, and secondary schools.

Omission of Comma before "and"

In informal writing, you can often omit the comma before the coordinating conjunction *and*. But if the second or third element contains a coordinating conjunction, as in the italicized element in the example below, the comma should be included, even in informal writing.

> Contrary to common belief, the victim of cyberbullying is often competent, *popular and even admired*, and high-functioning.

Parallel Elements

When you make a list in formal prose, all the elements should be the same part of speech and have the same grammatical function; that way, the elements will be parallel. (See p. 421 for more information about parallel structure.)

List not parallel: Cyberbullying is relentless, public, and it is usually anonymous. [two adjectives and one independent clause]

List parallel: Cyberbullying is *relentless*, *public*, and, usually, *anonymous*. [three adjectives]

Serial Semicolon

If one or more of the elements in the list contain commas, separate each item by a semicolon rather than a comma.

If one or more of the elements in the list contain commas, separate each item by a semicolon rather than a comma.

Bullying traditionally is divided into verbal bullying, marked by taunts, threats, and teasing; physical bullying, such as shoving, pushing, and theft; and relational bullying, involving gossip, excluding, and spreading rumours.

Colon to Set Up a List

A colon can set up a list if it follows an independent clause. Do not insert a colon before a list if the thought is incomplete.

Incorrect: Cyberbullying has distinct characteristics from those of traditional bullying including: a distinct set of victims, a different environment, and an enhanced sexual component.

Correct: Cyberbullying has distinct characteristics from those of traditional bullying: a distinct set of victims, a different environment, and an enhanced sexual component.

Also correct: Cyberbullying has distinct characteristics from those of traditional bullying, including the following: a distinct set of victims, a different environment, and an enhanced sexual component.

When you use a colon or a semicolon with a list, your sentence should end after the last item in the list. Do not continue the sentence after the list.

Incorrect: Cyberbullying has distinct characteristics from those of traditional bullying: a distinct set of victims, a different environment, and an enhanced sexual component, and should not be thought of as just another kind of bullying.

Correct: Cyberbullying has distinct characteristics from those of traditional bullying: a distinct set of victims, a different environment, and an enhanced sexual component. It should not be thought of as just another kind of bullying.

2. Sentence Introductions

An introductory word, phrase, or dependent clause should be separated by a comma from the independent clause that follows. Exceptions can be made for brief introductions, especially referring to time or place (e.g., *On Tuesdays . . .* ; *In Toronto . . .*). However, in formal writing it is a good idea to make a habit of using a comma after an introduction when an independent clause (main idea) follows.

> *One word introduction: Ultimately,* students will not reach their full learning potential if the educational system fails to emphasize creativity.

> *Phrasal introduction: Through the use of a rigid structure,* the education system tends to stress conformity, not creativity.

> *Dependent clause introduction: When curriculum designers choose to stress factual knowledge above everything else,* the freedom to explore options is threatened.

An introductory word, phrase, or dependent clause should be separated by a comma from the independent clause that follows.

A sentence that includes both an independent clause and a dependent clause is called a **complex sentence**. A **compound-complex sentence** combines two independent clauses (the "compound" part) with at least one dependent clause (the "complex" part). Below is an example of a compound-complex sentence (the compound part is bolded, the complex part italicized).

> *When curriculum designers choose to stress factual knowledge above everything else,* **the freedom to explore options is threatened, and students may become apathetic about their studies.**

A **complex sentence** is made up of an independent and one or more dependent clauses.

A **compound-complex sentence** combines two independent clauses (the "compound" part) with at least one dependent clause (the "complex" part).

For how to punctuate a sentence that consists of one or more independent clauses and ends with a dependent clause, see pp. 375–6.

3. Non-Essential Information

In the process of writing, writers often add detail or emphasis, qualify a point, or suggest a contrast. When this information does not affect the basic meaning of the sentence or clause, it is called **non-essential, (parenthetical) information**.

Use two commas for a non-essential element unless it occurs at the end of the sentence before the period.

Non-essential (parenthetical) information is information that does not affect the basic meaning of the sentence or clause. Use commas to separate this material from the more important information.

Non-essential elements, whether words, phrases, or clauses, are sometimes referred to as parenthetical because, much like the information inside parentheses, they are a word or word group set off from the main or essential part of the sentence.

Separating non-essential from essential information is often important for the reader's understanding: it assists the reading process. Non-essential information can be studied by dividing it into four subcategories: (A) adverbs and transitional phrases that interrupt sentence flow, (B) appositives, (C) adjectival relative clauses, and (D) concluding phrases and clauses.

A. Adverbs and Transitional Phrases That Interrupt Sentence Flow

Adverbs and transitional phrases that interrupt sentence flow should be set off by commas in formal writing. These words may emphasize, qualify, or contrast with preceding words.

> Adverbs and transitional phrases that interrupt sentence flow should be set off by commas in formal writing.

Emphasis: The act of dropping the gloves is, *undoubtedly*, a sign that a hockey fight is imminent.

Qualification: Not all fans, *however*, are in favour of fighting.

Contrast: Many "enforcers" today fight just for the sake of fighting, *not for passion*, some fans believe.

B. Appositives

Appositives are nouns and noun phrases that are grammatically parallel to preceding nouns or noun phrases. They do not modify the noun, but name or restate it. Thus, they do not contain essential information, and as non-essential elements, they are set off by two commas.

> An appositive consists of a noun or noun phrase that follows and is parallel to a preceding noun or noun phrase, which it renames. Two commas set off the appositive from the rest of the sentence.

Last year, Leonard Katz, *acting chairman of the CRTC*, announced that broadcasters could no longer air loud advertising.

What follows the proper noun *Leonard Katz* names him by giving his position. It can be taken out of the sentence without affecting the main idea; it gives additional information.

Nouns can modify other nouns as adjectives. Be careful not to place two commas around nouns acting as adjectives.

Incorrect commas: Last year, acting chairman of the CRTC, Leonard Katz, announced that broadcasters could no longer air loud advertising.

Correct: Last year, *acting chairman of the CRTC* Leonard Katz announced that broadcasters could no longer air loud advertising.

If you try to take *Leonard Katz* out of the sentence, you can see that it is essential information: *Last year, acting chairman of the CRTC announced that broadcasters could no longer air loud advertising* doesn't make sense. (The only comma in the sentence separates the introductory phrase, *Last year*, from the rest of the sentence.)

C. Adjectival Clauses

An adjectival (relative) clause modifies the preceding noun or pronoun (see p. 367) and begins with a relative pronoun, such as *who*, *which*, or *that*. Depending on the writer's intent, it can give additional information or essential information and is punctuated accordingly. In the following example, additional (non-essential) information is given in a clause (italicized).

> Louis Riel, *who stood up to the Canadian government of John A. Macdonald*, remains a hero to many today.

The main idea is that Riel is a hero to many; the description of Riel given in the adjectival clause, though it adds detail, is not essential to the sentence's meaning.

Sometimes, the parenthetical information could be a phrase rather than a clause. In the following sentence, a phrase gives non-essential information.

> Louis Riel, *having stood up to the Canadian government of John A. Macdonald*, remains a hero to many today.

Having stood up to the Canadian government of John A. Macdonald is a participial phrase modifying *Louis Riel*.

When a clause provides essential information, no comma should be used.

> A person who stands up for his or her beliefs is often considered a hero.

Who stands up for his or her beliefs is needed or the sentence will state vaguely, "A person is often considered a hero."

Hint: To test for non-essential material, whether it is words, phrases, or clauses, try taking the material out of the sentence. Is the essential meaning unchanged? Is it clear to the reader who or what you are describing? If so, put commas before and after the non-essential material.

Remember that *two commas* are normally required with non-essential material.

If adjectival (relative) clauses, such as those beginning with *who*, *which*, or *that*, give non-essential information, use commas around the adjectival clause.

D. Concluding Words, Phrases, and Clauses

You should precede a concluding word, phrase, or clause with a comma if it is considered a non-essential element in the sentence. However, if it completes the thought expressed in the independent clause that precedes it, do not use a comma.

> **Non-essential phrase:** The forests provide humans with numerous services and resources, *from lumber for our homes to the oxygen we breathe*. (David Suzuki Foundation, www.davidsuzuki.org/issues/wildlife-habitat/)

Use a comma before a concluding word, phrase, or clause if it is considered a non-essential element in the sentence. However, if it completes the thought of the independent clause, you do not use a comma.

The main idea is complete before the comma; the concluding phrase gives examples of services and resources.

> *Non-essential dependent clause:* Quebec, Ontario, and BC have made the most progress in combating climate change, *whereas Alberta and Saskatchewan rank at the bottom of the list.*

The main idea is complete before the comma. Often, the subordinating conjunctions *although*, *though*, *even though*, *whereas*, and sometimes *while* are preceded by a comma when they introduce a concluding dependent clause because they suggest a contrast with the main idea rather than a continuation of it.

A dependent clause beginning with *although*, *though*, *even though*, and *whereas* is usually separated from the preceding independent clause by a comma. In most cases, however, the dependent clause conclusion is not preceded by a comma.

> *Essential dependent clause:* According to the David Suzuki Foundation, Canada as a whole is making progress on climate change *because the provinces have stepped in with new initiatives.*

The concluding dependent clause completes the thought begun in the preceding independent clause.

EXERCISE 12.2

Add commas where necessary to indicate non-essential (parenthetical) material. A sample sentence has been done for you.

Classmates may avoid students with low social status who may then feel depressed increasing their chances of being bullied.

Classmates may avoid students with low social status, who may then feel depressed, increasing their chances of being bullied. [*who may then feel depressed* is a relative clause modifying *students*; *increasing their chances of being bullied* is the non-essential concluding phrase]

1. Every year, more diesel-powered cars are being announced whereas only a few were produced in the past.
2. After the 1976 Olympics an economic disaster for taxpayers Canadians looked forward to the 2010 Olympics.
3. Young women who believe they can look like the skinny models in advertising will likely continue with their unhealthy eating patterns.
4. Penicillin an antibiotic crucial in treating bacterial infection was possible due to the biodiversity of plants.
5. Researchers are uncertain whether the link between media and aggression is a causal one.

Miscellaneous Uses of the Comma

Direct Quotation

Punctuating a direct quotation depends on how the quotation is integrated into your sentence. If the source is named before the quotation, a comma follows the verb. If the source is named after, a comma follows the quotation, separating it from the source.

> Hicks states**,** "As we know, that's not how it turned out" (334).

> "As we know, that's not how it turned out**,**" Hicks states (334).

Do not put a comma before a direct quotation if the word *that* precedes it or if, otherwise, grammar does not require a comma.

> Joan Petersilia argues that "imprisonment has reached often counter-productive levels" (2).

> Brand recognition is an advertising strategy that builds "social or emotional associations with products or brands" (Connor 1483).

As mentioned, a colon may precede a direct quotation if the thought is completely expressed before the colon (see "Colon to Set Up a List," p. 388).

Adjectives

Coordinate adjectives precede a noun and modify it individually; they are separated by two commas. However, **non-coordinate adjectives** together modify the noun and cannot be separated; commas are not used with non-coordinate adjectives.

One test of whether adjectives are coordinate is to put the word *and* between the adjectives. If you can't do this without changing the meaning, the adjectives are non-coordinate, and a comma should not be used.

> *Coordinate:* The animal that could best portray Canadian values is the powerful, *resourceful* polar bear. [powerful *and* resourceful polar bear]

> *Non-coordinate:* Polar bears often swim in search of *new hunting* grounds or *alternative food* sources. [new *and* hunting grounds? alternative *and* food sources?]

If the source is named before the quotation, a comma follows the verb. If the source is named after, a comma follows the quotation, separating it from the source. Do not precede a direct quotation by a comma unless grammar requires it.

Coordinate adjectives precede a noun and modify it individually. If two or more adjectives precede a noun and modify it individually, use commas between the adjectives. If the adjectives together modify the noun and cannot be separated, they are **non-coordinate adjectives**—in which case, do not use commas.

Dates, Addresses, and Numbers

Dates

Commas are conventionally used with month, day, and year when the elements occur in that order; when the date begins with the day or when the day is left out, commas are not used.

> May 12, 2015, will be her fiftieth birthday; her younger daughter will celebrate her twenty-fifth birthday in November 2015.
>
> BUT
>
> 12 May 2015

Addresses

Commas are conventionally used between elements of addresses. If the sentence continues, a comma is included after the name of the province or state.

> The leader of the opposition resides at Stornoway, 541 Acadia Avenue, Ottawa, Ontario, which was built in 1914.

Numbers

A comma is conventionally used in numbers of four or more digits, separating them into groups of three: *45,000 visitors*; *$1,330,000*. In the metric system, spaces replace commas, e.g, 45 000.

Other Punctuation: Question Marks, Dashes, and Parentheses

Question Marks

Use a question mark at the end of an interrogative sentence.

> Do laws concerning Muslim veils restrict women's rights?

If a direct quotation ends in a question or exclamation mark, include it inside the second quotation mark, but if you continue your sentence, do not include a comma even if a rule appears to require it. The question mark replaces a comma, which would normally be required.

> "Do laws concerning Muslim veils restrict women's rights?" asked the group's spokesperson.

TABLE 12.1 Summary of Major Punctuation Rules

Mark	Rule	Description of Rule
,	Independent clauses	Use a comma before a coordinating conjunction that joins two independent clauses.
	Series	Use commas to separate items in a series, whether words, phrases, or clauses.
	Introductions	Use a comma after an introduction, whether a word, phrase, or dependent clause, when followed by an independent clause.
	Non-essential elements: relative clauses	Use commas around relative clauses, which often begin with *who*, *which*, or *that*, when they give non-essential information.
	Non-essential elements: appositives	Use commas around appositives (nouns or noun phrases) that give non-essential information.
	Non-essential elements: interrupters	Use commas around adverbial interrupters or other parenthetical elements when they give non-essential information.
	Essential elements	Do not use commas if the word, phrase, or relative clause is essential to meaning.
	Coordinate adjectives	Use a comma to separate coordinate adjectives before a noun; coordinate adjectives separately modify the noun.
	Direct quotations	Use a comma before a direct quotation if the preceding or following phrase includes the author's name and a verb. Do not use a comma if to do so will make an ungrammatical sentence.
	Dates, addresses, and numbers	Use a comma if convention requires it (see p. 394).
;	Independent clauses	Use a semicolon in place of a comma and coordinating conjunction between independent clauses to stress that the clauses are closely related.
	Adverbial conjunctions	Use a semicolon before an adverbial conjunction or transitional phrase when it joins two independent clauses; follow the joiner with a comma.
	Series with commas in one or more elements	Use a semicolon to join items in a series if at least one of the items contains commas.
:	Quotations and lists	Use a colon to set up a direct quotation or list if the thought is complete before the colon. Note: Other methods exist for setting up a direct quotation or list.
	Independent clauses	Use a colon between independent clauses if the second clause answers or explains the reason for the statement in the first independent clause. The thought should be complete before the colon. Note: What follows a colon could be just a word or phrase if it answers a question implied in the independent clause preceding the colon.

Dashes and Parentheses

Use dashes to set off important or dramatic words or phrases. While dashes emphasize something, parentheses de-emphasize. Placing words in parentheses shows the reader that the material is not important enough to be included in the main part of the sentence. Using parentheses or dashes could make the sentence more readable, helping the reader understand the sentence better, but too many dashes or parentheses should be avoided as they could distract your reader.

> Many women who wear a burqa do so as a personal choice—not as a religious duty.

> A woman wearing a veil in France could face a fine of 150 Euros (C$195).

Do not put a comma before a parenthesis; if punctuation is required after the parentheses, ensure it goes outside the closing parenthesis unless what is in parentheses is a complete sentence by itself—not part of a sentence.

In parenthetical citation styles, parentheses enclose brief information about a source (see pp. 85–90).

> Supporters of the veil suggest they can "offer women protection and a safe haven" (Leane 1053).

EXERCISE 12.3 | Selah's Vegan Moment

There are 20 marks of underlining in the two paragraphs below. Identify the rule, summarized in the chart above and/or discussed in the preceding pages, that accounts for the mark of punctuation or for the absence of punctuation.

Selah wanted to be cool and healthy, so she thought she would make a New Year's resolution to go vegan. She knew that beans, tofu, and nuts were high-protein options for vegans. Unfortunately, Selah was allergic to nuts; they made her violently ill. She had tried tofu, which consists of mashed soya beans, and found it had a rubbery, mushy texture. She liked beans well enough, but not every day!

She knew several people who were vegans. For example, there was her ex-roommate, Ruth; her boyfriend, Bal; and her best friend, Frieda. They were all healthy people; however, were they cool? Ruth had once exclaimed, "tie-dyed shirts are awesome!" and Bal wore white knee socks with his sandals. Frieda was the least cool of all: she once invited Selah to the movie Vampires from Outer Space—and was on the edge of her seat (literally) the whole time. After she had weighed all these factors to her satisfaction, Selah sighed regretfully and ordered out for pepperoni pizza with extra cheese.

EXERCISE 12.4

Add commas as necessary in the sentences below. There is more than one punctuation rule to be applied in some sentences. A sample sentence has been done for you.

Small amounts of cocaine may cause hyperactivity elevated blood pressure and heart rate and increased sexual interest but large amounts can cause violent unpredictable behaviour.

Small amounts of cocaine may cause hyperactivity, **[1]** elevated blood pressure and heart rate, **[2]** and increased sexual interest, **[3]** but large amounts can cause violent, **[4]** unpredictable behaviour.

[1] Separates items in list

[2] Separates items in list

[3] Separates two independent clauses joined by coordinating conjunction

[4] Separates coordinate adjectives

1. Brain development occurs rapidly at young ages and this development can be affected by music.
2. The first video game *Tennis for Two* was created in 1958.
3. Some instructors treat sites that rate professors as a learning opportunity whereas others think such websites should be banned.
4. To relieve stress explore the world and have fun students should take a break after high school.
5. Some studies suggest that exposure to modern media contributes to low self-esteem in young girls and increases the odds of developing an eating disorder.
6. It was predicted that the movie *The King's Speech* would win the Oscar for Best Picture and it did.
7. Textese a hybrid of spoken and written English is the language of text messaging a recent global phenomenon.
8. On July 19 2005 the same-sex marriage law in Canada was passed but many Christians remained opposed to this law.
9. He always wanted to write a popular critically acclaimed novel; she always wanted to write "the great Canadian novel."
10. Alcohol affects every part of the body and the brain such as the circulatory nervous and gastrointestinal systems.

Apostrophes

An **apostrophe** has two main uses: (1) in formal and informal writing, it is used to indicate possession and other relationships between two nouns or an indefinite pronoun and a noun; (2) in informal writing, it is used in contractions to show that one or more letters have been omitted.

1. Apostrophe Showing Possession and Other Relationships

Use an apostrophe to identify or illustrate ownership, authorship, duration, and similar relationships.

> *Ownership:* The neighbour's property [the property belongs to the neighbour]

> *Authorship:* Margaret Atwood's poem [the poem was written by Margaret Atwood]

> *Duration:* Two days' extension [an extension that lasts two days]

> *Similar relationships:* The professor's classes [the classes are taught by the professor]

Many indefinite pronouns also require an apostrophe when followed by a noun if the relationship between them is one of ownership or the like. However, personal pronoun forms do not include apostrophes.

> *Indefinite pronoun examples: everyone's* beliefs, *somebody's* laptop, *one's* motive [the beliefs of everyone, the laptop of someone, the motive of one]

> *Personal pronoun forms:* hers, theirs; NOT her's, their's

When nouns and pronouns form the possessive and are placed before nouns, they function adjectivally.

> **Hint:** If you have trouble knowing whether something you have written requires an apostrophe, try inverting the two nouns and placing *of* or *of the* in between the rearranged words.

> *If you've written:* the neighbours property . . .

> *Rearranged:* the property *of* the neighbour

> *Corrected:* the neighbour's property

The same can be done with an indefinite pronoun and a noun (see "Indefinite Pronoun Subject," p. 406).

> *If you've written:* ones motive . . .

> *Rearranged:* the motive *of* one

> *Corrected:* one's motive

Forming the Possessive

1. For singular nouns, add *'s*.
2. For plural nouns that end in *–s* or an "s" sound, add an apostrophe after the *–s*.

> the city's businesses [the businesses of the city]

> BUT

> the cities' businesses [the businesses of the cities—more than one city]

Hint: After determining whether the possessive applies to a noun, ask whether the affected noun refers to one or more than one. If it is a singular noun, add *–'s*; if it is plural, add *–s'*.

A few common plural nouns don't end in *–s* and are treated like singular nouns in forming the possessive.

> people's choice, women's sports, men's team, children's toys

If two nouns equally own or partake in something, use an apostrophe with the second noun only.

> Jake and Jeff's presentation. [Jake and Jeff gave the same presentation]

> BUT

> Leat's and Layne's presentations. [Leat and Layne gave separate presentations]

If a singular proper noun ends in *–s*, such as a person's last name, the rule states that you add *–'s* to make it possessive. However, if the last name is at least two syllables, you will sometimes see only an apostrophe added.

> Mr. Burns's lackey; Mr. Smithers's boss [correct]; Mr. Smithers' boss [also correct]

To form the possessive in singular nouns, add –'s; in plural nouns ending in –s, add an apostrophe after the –s.

A few plural nouns don't end in –s and are treated like singular nouns in forming the possessive.

If two nouns equally own or partake in something, use an apostrophe with the second noun only.

Hint: Do not use an apostrophe with a simple plural or with the third-person singular verb form.

> *Incorrect:* There are several backpack's at the front of the room.

> *Correct:* She is looking through the *backpack's* contents to find her calculator. [contents of the backpack]

> *Incorrect:* She look's happy: she must have found her calculator.

> *Correct:* She *looks* happy: she must have found her calculator.

Occasionally, an apostrophe can be used with the plural of a word if the context requires it.

> He received two B's on his transcript; The '60s were a time of youth revolt.

2. Apostrophe for Contractions

An apostrophe is used to show a letter has been omitted, although contractions are used more often with informal writing than with academic (formal) writing.

don't = do not	isn't = isn't	couldn't = could not
it's = it is	who's = who is	

An apostrophe is used to show a letter omitted. Contractions are not often used in academic writing.

Hint: Do not confuse the contraction *it's* or *who's* with the possessive forms *its* and *whose*. If you're uncertain whether the spelling is correct, try substituting *it is* or *who is* in the sentence. If the sentence makes sense, use an apostrophe as required for contractions.

> *If you've written:* Its sad to see the parrot without its mate.

> *Try:* Its [it is?] sad to see the parrot without its [it is?] mate.

> *Corrected:* It's sad to see the parrot without *its* mate.

EXERCISE 12.5

Add apostrophes where needed in the sentences below; also, add −*s* if required. A sample sentence has been done for you.

> Among the premiers promises is his pledge to stimulate the middle-class earning power.

> Among the premier's [possessive] promises is his pledge to stimulate the middle-class' [possessive] earning power.

1. Childrens playground games today often involve acting the role of contemporary superheroes.
2. A students grade point average can affect an employers hiring decision.
3. The medias obsession with celebrities lives contributes to todays obesity epidemic.
4. Two reasons for pet overpopulation today include societys lack of awareness and pet owners refusal to have their pets neutered.
5. Music is part of most peoples day, whether its classical or jazz, rock, or heavy metal.

Chapter 12 Review Questions

1. What is a compound sentence? Make up two examples of compound sentences, using different joiners in each case. Punctuate correctly.
2. a) When could you use a semicolon to join two independent clauses (simple sentences)? Give two rules.
    b) When could you use a colon to join two independent clauses? Give one rule.
3. What is a complex sentence? Give an example, ensuring that your sentence has the right number of subject–predicate units. Punctuate correctly.
4. Answer true or false:
    a) You should always use a comma to separate two items if they are joined by *and*.
    b) You can always omit the last comma before the "and" for a series of three items.
    c) You should use semicolons to separate three items if at least one of the items contains commas.
5. Explain the rule for using a colon to set up an independent clause.
6. What is parenthetical information? How can you determine whether information in a sentence is parenthetical?
7. When would it be correct to use commas around the words *however, therefore, furthermore*, and the like? When would it be correct to precede these same words by a semicolon?
8. Nouns and noun phrases that are parallel to preceding nouns and noun phrases are called _____. They identify or rename the previous noun/phrase and are set off by _____ (number) commas.
9. Explain the rule that determines whether you use commas around relative (adjectival) clauses.
10. Choose the correct statement:
    a) You always precede a direct quotation by a comma.
    b) You place a comma after a direct quotation if the name of the source follows.
    c) You usually place a comma after "that" if a direct quotation follows.
    d) None of these statements are true.
11. Should you normally use a comma when you begin a sentence with a dependent clause and follow with an independent clause? Should you use one when you begin with an independent clause and conclude with a dependent clause?

12. What are coordinate adjectives? What is the punctuation rule for coordinate adjectives?
13. What are the two main uses of apostrophes?
14.   a) What are the rules for using the apostrophe to show possession in singular and plural nouns?

    b) Name four plural nouns that form the possessive like singular nouns.
15. When would you use an apostrophe with the word *its*?

Key Terms

apostrophe (p. 398)
complex sentence (p. 389)
compound sentence (p. 384)
compound-complex sentence (p. 389)

coordinate adjectives (p. 393)
non-coordinate adjectives (p. 393)
non-essential (parenthetical) information (p. 389)
simple sentence (p. 384)

13

Agreement, Pronoun, Modifier, and Parallelism Errors

In this chapter, you will learn:

- How to apply the rules for subject–verb and pronoun–antecedent agreement

- How to use gender inclusive pronouns

- How to identify and correct pronoun reference, consistency, and case errors

- How to identify and correct modifier errors

- Why parallel structure is important and how to fix parallelism errors

Logic and consistency require that a verb in the present tense agrees in number with its subject and that a pronoun agrees in number with the noun it replaces. Although you will probably not need to stop and think about agreement in every sentence you write, the guidelines below are useful in situations where agreement is not straightforward.

The two sections that follow, on subject–verb agreement and pronoun–antecedent agreement, focus on the most common agreement problems. A chart summarizing subject–verb agreement is on p. 406.

Subject–Verb Agreement

Checking for subject–verb agreement involves three steps: (1) finding the subject, (2) using the guidelines below and on p. 406 to determine if the subject is singular or plural; and (3) choosing the corresponding singular (usually ends in –s in the third person) or plural form (usually does not end in –s) of the verb.

The singular third-person form of the verb (*he, she, it*) ends in –s in the present tense. Plural forms of verbs do not.

Finding the Subject

Most subjects precede their verbs and can easily be found, even if the sentence begins with another noun.

> In most sentences, the *subject* comes before the verb.

For instance, in the above example *subject* is the noun subject and *comes* is the verb. The singular form of *come*—ending in *–s*—agrees with the singular *subject*. (*Sentences* is not the subject; it is the object of the preposition *in*.)

> However, there *are* <u>situations</u> where the subject follows the verb.

In the sentence above, the subject, *situations* (underlined), comes after the verb, *are*. The plural form, *are*, agrees with the plural subject, *situations*.

Hint: If a sentence or clause begins with *there is/are*, *there has been/have been*, *there will be*, *here is/are*, and similar forms of *there/here is/are*, find the subject, which will be after the verb, to determine whether the verb should be singular or plural.

In some sentences with either a **question construction** or a **delayed subject construction**, the subject also follows the verb. The verb is italicized and the subject is underlined below.

> *Question: Is* the <u>student</u> with the computer in the back row paying attention?

> *Delayed subject:* Surrounded by empty desks *sits* the <u>student</u> in the back row.

Hint: If the sentence has a question construction or a delayed subject construction, restructure it so that the sentence is a statement and the subject comes first.

> *Change question to statement:* The <u>student</u> with the computer in the back row *is* (not) paying attention.

> *Change to usual word order:* The <u>student</u> in the back row *sits* surrounded by empty desks.

Intervening Nouns

Many problems in subject–verb agreement result from nouns and pronouns that come between the subject and the verb, obscuring the true subject. Ensure that the verb agrees with the true subject, not with an object of a preposition.

In some sentences with either a **question construction** or a **delayed subject construction**, the verb is placed before the subject.

A subject can follow a verb when (1) the sentence/clause begins with *there is/are*, *here is/are*, and variants of these; (2) when it is structured as a question; and (3) when the delayed subject structure is used.

Be careful that the verb agrees with the true subject, not with nouns or pronouns that come between the subject and the verb.

Hint: To help you find the subject, put parentheses around prepositional phrases that come between the subject and the verb.

If you've written: A coalition of organizations, students, and unions oppose the college's planned development.

Identify true subject: A *coalition* (of organizations, students, and unions) *oppose* the college's planned development.

Corrected: A *coalition* of organizations, students, and unions *opposes* the college's planned development.

Rules for Compound Subjects

When a subject is composed of two nouns, two pronouns, or a noun and a pronoun, it is called a **compound subject**. The rule for agreement depends on the word or phrase that joins the two parts of the subject.

> A **compound subject** is composed of two nouns, two pronouns, or a noun and a pronoun. The rule for agreement depends on the word or phrase that joins the two parts of the subject.

1. Nouns/pronouns joined by *and* make up a plural subject, requiring a plural verb form unless they are parts of one idea that can't be separated, as in the second sentence below, or if they are preceded by *each* or *every*, as in the third sentence.

   > The tortoise *and* the hare *are* taking part in this year's fabled Aesop's Run.

   > When asked for a pre-race comment, the tortoise predicted, *"slow and steady wins* the race."

   > *Each* mammal, bird, and reptile *was* asked who would win.

2. A compound subject in which the nouns/pronouns are joined by *or, nor, neither . . . nor,* or *either . . . or* could be singular or plural depending on the second noun/pronoun—the one closest to the verb. If it is singular, the verb form will be singular; if it is plural, the verb will be plural.

   > Neither the hare *nor* the other *animals expect* the tortoise to win, according to the odds-makers.

3. A compound subject in which the nouns/pronouns are joined by phrases like *along with, alongside, as well as, combined with, in addition to, together with,* and the like is singular if the first noun/pronoun is singular and plural if it is plural.

   > "A full *meal along with* two naps *has* caused the hare to lag far behind the tortoise with only one metre left to go," the crow cawed.

Indefinite Pronoun Subject

Common singular indefinite pronouns include words ending in *–one*, *–body*, and *–thing*, such as *everyone*, *anybody*, and *something*, along with *each*, *either*, *much*, *neither*, *none*, *nothing*, and *one*.

When an indefinite pronoun functions as a subject, it usually is considered singular (see p. 3); therefore, the verb should also be singular. The indefinite pronoun is italicized and the verb is underlined below.

> *Everyone* taking the practice quizzes <u>is</u> going to get one bonus mark per quiz, but *no one* <u>is</u> allowed more than ten bonus marks.

Some indefinite pronouns, however, are always plural, and a few can be singular or plural depending on context.

> *Several* of the textbooks *have* been left in the classroom.

Table 13.1 can be used for quick reference for checking subject–verb agreement. It includes the major rules discussed above as well as other rules that will arise occasionally in your writing. Please note that the first five categories in the table have been discussed in the previous section (with examples), while the remaining categories are less common and are introduced here with examples.

TABLE 13.1	Quick Reference Chart for Checking Subject–Verb Agreement

Rule Category	Rule Description
Subject–verb agreement	Verb agrees with its subject in number whether that subject precedes or follows verb
Compound subject joined by *and*	Plural verb form unless compound refers to one concept
Compound subject joined by *or, nor, either . . . or, neither . . . nor*	Verb agrees with second noun/pronoun
Compound subject joined by *as well as, in addition to*, and similar phrases	Verb agrees with first noun/pronoun
Indefinite pronoun as subject	Verb is singular if pronoun is singular
Collective noun subject: refers to a class or group of individuals (e.g., *audience, board, class, committee, couple, crowd, faculty, family, government, group, jury, mob, team*)	Verb is singular unless stress is on individuals within the group rather than group as a unit. The *class* is listening to the speaker (class as unit); the *class* are giving their presentations (class as individual members)
Portions and fractions + *of* (e.g., *all, a lot, a number, any, a variety, half, more, most, much, none, number, part, plenty, some, the majority/minority* + *of*)	Verb number depends on the noun/pronoun that completes the *of* phrase. Only *part of the garden was* destroyed by aphids, but *all of the azaleas were* obliterated. The phrase *the number of* requires a singular verb form.

TABLE 13.1 *(continued)*	
Rule Category	**Rule Description**
Subjects referring to distance, time, money, weight, and mass	Verb is singular if required by context. *Three kilometres* ahead *is* where the trail ends; *45 minutes is* about how long it will take us to get there.
Singular nouns ending in −s (e.g., *athletics, economics, gymnastics, mathematics, news, the Philippines, physics, politics, statistics, the United States*)	Some nouns that end in −s refer to a single concept and, thus, take a singular verb form. The *Philippines is* the third-largest English-speaking country. Some of these nouns take a plural verb form if they refer to a plural concept or set of properties, rather than a single concept. The *politics* of the twenty-first century *are* radically different from those of earlier centuries. Books and other titles and names of businesses that end in −s are considered singular. *Starbucks is* opening a new store.
Relative clauses	The verb in a clause that begins with a relative pronoun like *who, which, that,* or *whose* agrees with the noun/pronoun that the pronoun refers to. The *person who is* standing looks familiar. The *only one* of . . . will require a singular verb form while *one of* . . . will require the plural form. She is the *only one of* the people who *is* standing. She is *one of* the people who *are* standing.
Gerunds as subjects; gerunds are formed from present participles of verbs and end in −*ing*.	Gerunds as subjects are singular and require singular verb forms. *Understanding* grammar rules *is* not too difficult if you know the principles behind them.

EXERCISE 13.1

Choose the correct form of the verb in each sentence. A sample sentence has been done for you.

The cost of "big box" stores (exceeds/exceed) their benefits to local economies.

The cost of "big box" stores exceeds their benefits to local economies. [*Exceeds* agrees with its subject, *cost*.]

1. Truly, arts and culture (is/are) valuable to most Canadians today.
2. Small class sizes and a low student population (means/mean) few opportunities to meet new people.
3. Several decades of experimental data (has/have) shown that violent video games can cause aggression and hostility.

(continued)

4. One-half of the participants in each group (has/have) been asked to complete a questionnaire.
5. The shortcuts that are common in instant messaging (is/are) creeping into young children's vocabulary.
6. With shipping and oil drilling (comes/come) the risk of oil spills.
7. The immediate economic benefit of genetically modified foods (is/are) clearly visible.
8. Overindulging in alcohol and drugs often (leads/lead) to unsafe sex.
9. In the past, there (has/have) been larger amounts of trans-fat consumed in North America than in Southern Europe and Asia.
10. The regular practice of yoga in addition to a healthy diet (inhibits/inhibit) cell deterioration, according to one study.

Pronoun–Antecedent Agreement

The antecedent of the pronoun is the noun or pronoun it replaces.

The **antecedent** of the pronoun is the noun or pronoun it replaces. Many problems in pronoun–antecedent agreement occur when the antecedent is (1) a compound (see "Rules for Compound Subjects," p. 405), (2) a collective noun, (3) an indefinite pronoun, or (4) a generic singular noun. In (1) and (2), you can be guided by the similar rules for subject–verb agreement as discussed on pp. 405 and 406.

Finding the Antecedent

Checking for possible agreement errors begins with identifying the pronoun antecedent, usually a noun or indefinite pronoun, just as the first step in subject–verb agreement is identifying the subject.

Hint: To ensure you have correctly identified an antecedent, try substituting the antecedent for the pronoun that replaces it. The antecedent is italicized and the pronouns underlined in the sentence below.

> The *shrub* looks unhealthy, and it [the shrub] is shedding its [the shrub's] leaves.

Note that pronoun–antecedent agreement includes adjectives, like *its*, above, that are formed from pronouns.

Main Problems in Pronoun–Antecedent Agreement

1. Compound Antecedent

If the elements of the compound antecedent are joined by *and*, the pronoun will usually be plural, but if the elements are joined by *or/nor*, the pronoun will agree with the second element (the one closest to the pronoun).

The professor *and* the students are looking for *their* classroom.

Neither the professor *nor the students* found *their* classroom.

Note that if the nouns *professor* and *students* are reversed, the result would be a somewhat awkward sentence.

Neither the students nor the *professor* found *her* classroom.

The rule provides consistency, but writers should also be conscious of sound and sense and be ready to revise if necessary.

2. Collective Noun Antecedent

A collective noun refers to groups of people, usually acting collectively. When this type of noun acts as an antecedent, the pronoun is singular unless the stress is on individuals within the group; then, the pronoun is plural. If in doubt, use the singular form of the pronoun.

> The *committee* issued *its* recommendations to the government last week. [It acted as a unit.]

> After failing to reach a consensus, the *committee* will meet with *their* constituents to gather more input. [The stress is on individual members.]

Avoid the practice of using a singular verb along with a plural pronoun with nouns like *government* or names of businesses that represent a single entity. Both verb and pronoun forms should be singular.

> *Incorrect:* Fort McMurray, Alberta, *has* experienced an increase in *their* population since the development of the Athabasca Oil Sands project. [A singular verb and plural pronoun are awkwardly used with the singular subject/antecedent, *Fort McMurray.*]

> *Correct:* Fort McMurray, Alberta, *has* experienced an increase in *its* population since the development of the Athabasca Oil Sands project. [A singular verb and singular pronoun are used with the singular subject/antecedent, *Fort McMurray.*]

3. Indefinite Pronoun Antecedent

Most indefinite pronouns are singular and, along with nouns, can act as antecedents for pronouns, which should be singular to match the antecedent. You can often

A **collective noun** refers to groups of people, usually acting collectively. When this type of noun acts as an antecedent, the pronoun is singular unless the stress is on individuals within the group; then, the pronoun is plural.

tell by context whether an indefinite pronoun is singular or plural. You will then use the appropriate pronoun form.

Each of the alligators *is* sunning *itself* on the rock by my brother's foot.

Both of the alligators *are* sunning *themselves* on the rock by my brother's foot.

However, indefinite pronouns that are always singular can cause problems when they need to be replaced by third-person singular pronouns.

Incorrect: To set a good example, *everybody* on the safety committee has been told to clean up *their* work area. [plural pronoun]

The antecedent, *everybody*, is singular; the pronoun that replaces it, *their*, is plural. (*Their* is the possessive form of the pronoun *they*. Agreement applies to these possessive forms as well as to the subjective and objective forms—for example, *they* and *them*). While the practice of using a plural pronoun, like *their*, with a singular indefinite pronoun antecedent is becoming more acceptable in informal contexts, it typically is not acceptable in academic or professional writing.

Indefinite pronouns refer to non-specific individuals without regard to gender. For example, *everyone* usually includes both genders. However, the third-person pronouns *he*, *she*, *him*, *his*, and *her* specify gender. The following sentence is therefore grammatically correct but does not reflect the gender-neutral goal of most writing today.

> Indefinite pronouns refer to non-specific individuals without regard to gender. When they are replaced by personal pronouns, these pronouns should be singular as well as gender neutral.

Incorrect: To set a good example, *everybody* on the safety committee has been told to clean up *his* work area. [gender biased]

The antecedent, *everybody*, is singular and does not specify gender; *his* is also singular but specifies gender. If the committee were composed of males only, the statement would be both grammatical and precise. However, if there were at least one female on the committee, the statement would be imprecise and reflect sexist usage.

Hint: If you need to use an indefinite pronoun as an antecedent, ensure that the pronoun that follows matches the antecedent in number and reflects gender-neutral, or unbiased, usage.

The best way, then, for the indefinite pronoun to be both singular and gender neutral is to use *his or her*.

> The practice of using a plural pronoun, like *their*, with a singular indefinite pronoun antecedent is becoming more acceptable in informal contexts—but not in academic or professional writing.

Correct: To set a good example, *everybody* on the safety committee has been told to clean up *his or her* work area. [singular, gender neutral]

4. Generic Singular Noun Antecedent

Generic nouns refer to non-specific individuals. When used in the singular as antecedents, they should be followed by singular pronouns.

> *Incorrect:* The candidate should read their exam instructions carefully.

> *Correct:* The *candidate* should read *his or her* exam instructions carefully.

> **Hint:** If the *him or her* substitution seems awkward, consider (1) making the singular antecedent plural or (2) omitting the pronoun and revising the sentence.

> *Correct with a plural antecedent: Candidates* should read *their* exam instructions carefully.

> *Sentence revised: Candidates* should read *the* exam instructions carefully.

> When used in the singular as antecedents, generic singular nouns should be followed by singular pronouns and should be gender-neutral.

> If the *him* or *her* substitution seems otherwise awkward, consider (1) making the singular antecedent plural or (2) omitting the pronoun and revising the sentence.

EXERCISE 13.2

Correct any errors in pronoun–antecedent agreement or sexist usage. A sample sentence has been done for you.

> If a predator lacks a food source, they will often try to adapt by changing their main food source.

> If *a predator* lacks a food source, *it* will often try to adapt by changing *its* main food source.

1. Anyone can increase their self-confidence greatly by participating in physical activity.
2. The ad hoc committee on gender equity will be submitting its interim report on April 30.
3. Copy protection is often ignored as it inconveniences the consumer and makes them allies of those who pirate music.
4. In laparoscopic surgery, the surgeon operates through small insertions using information he receives from a camera inside the patient.
5. When people don't express their anger, feelings of frustration can build up until it is released in an unhealthy way.

Pronoun Reference, Consistency, and Case

Care needs to be taken with pronouns, as errors can occur in pronoun reference, consistency, and case. Each of these areas is discussed below.

Pronoun Reference

A **pronoun reference error** can arise when the pronoun's antecedent is unclear or absent. Pronouns replace specific nouns/pronouns, and a reader should always know what antecedent is intended.

Ambiguous Reference

The reader of the following sentence may be unable to tell the antecedent of *it*.

> The committee issued its recommendations to the government, but *it* has decided that they need revisions.

Clearly, *they* refers to *recommendations*, but is *committee* or *government* the antecedent of *it*? Both singular nouns could serve as grammatical antecedents. In the case of ambiguous antecedents, you can replace the pronoun by the intended noun or, to avoid repetition, revise the sentence.

> *Pronoun replaced:* The committee issued its recommendations to *the government*, but *the government* has decided that they need revisions.

> *Sentence revised:* The committee issued its recommendations to *the government, which* has decided that they need revisions.

In the second sentence, *government* is the grammatical antecedent of the relative pronoun *which*.

Broad or Vague Antecedent

Another problem with pronoun reference occurs when the antecedent refers to a concept or group of words rather than a specific noun/pronoun. What is the antecedent of *which* in the following sentence?

> Back in the 1930s, goalies did not have face protection, *which* was a safety hazard.

Although the grammatical antecedent of *which* appears to be *face protection*, the sense indicates that *not* having face protection is the hazard. Sentences where the pronouns *which*, *this*, *that*, or *it* replaces more than a one-word antecedent often need to be rewritten.

> *Revised:* Back in the 1930s, the absence of face protection for goalies was a safety hazard.

Missing (Implied) Antecedent

Be wary of sentence openings that lack grammatical antecedents. In the following sentence, the author's name cannot be the antecedent of *he* because it is in the possessive (i.e., adjectival) form (underlined).

> *Incorrect:* In <u>Michael McKinley's</u> *Hockey: A People's History*, he discusses the origin of Canada's national game.

> *Revised:* In *Hockey: A People's History*, Michael McKinley discusses the origin of Canada's national game.

> *Alternative revision:* In Michael McKinley's *Hockey: A People's History*, the origin of Canada's national game is discussed.

In the following sentence, what does the pronoun *it* refer to?

> By teaching today's youth safe and healthy approaches to sexuality, *it* will elevate their self-esteem.

It appears to refer back to *teaching*. However, *teaching* is not a subject but the object of the prepositional phrase *by teaching*. Avoid beginning a sentence with prepositions like *at*, *by*, *for*, *in*, *on*, or *with* where the object of the preposition serves as an antecedent of a pronoun like *it*.

> *Revised:* Teaching today's youth safe and healthy approaches to sexuality will elevate their self-esteem.

Teaching is now the subject, and no pronoun is needed.

Pronoun Consistency

The principle behind pronoun consistency is simple: Do not unnecessarily change the person of a pronoun. Table 13.2 shows the singular and plural for each person of pronouns. Do not needlessly shift between pronouns in different rows.

Do not unnecessarily change the person of a pronoun—for example, from *you* to *he* or from *us* to *them*.

First-person pronouns refer to the one *doing the speaking*; second-person pronouns refer to the one *spoken to*; third-person pronouns refer to the ones *spoken about*.

TABLE 13.2 Person of Singular And Plural Pronouns		
Pronoun person	**Singular**	**Plural**
First person	I, me, my	we, us, our
Second person	you, your	you, your
Third person	he, she, it, his, her, its	they, them, their

Unnecessary pronoun shift: Whether music is coming from *your* own headset or blasting from *your* neighbour's house, *we* have all experienced music in *our* lives.

Corrected: Whether music is coming from *our* own headset or blasting from *our* neighbour's house, *we* have all experience music in *our* lives.

Similarly, do not unnecessarily shift from a noun (it can be considered third person) to a first- or second-person pronoun.

Unnecessary shift of noun to second-person pronoun: If *students* can learn effective time management, *your* stress levels will be greatly reduced.

Corrected: If *students* can learn effective time management, *their* stress levels will be greatly reduced.

If your readers are students whom you wish to address informally, the following would be acceptable.

Informal address: If *you* can learn effective time management, *your* stress levels will be greatly reduced.

Pronoun Case

The personal pronouns *I/me, we/us, he/him, she/her,* and *they/them,* along with the relative and interrogative pronouns *who/whom* and *whoever/whomever,* use the form that reflects their grammatical function in the sentence or clause. In order to use the correct pronoun case, or form, you may first have to determine the pronoun's function.

Pronoun case is the form the pronoun takes that shows its function in the sentence or clause. Only a few pronouns change their form to reflect their function.

Personal Pronoun Forms

For the personal pronouns *I/me, we/us, they/them, his/hers,* etc.:

1. If the pronoun is the subject of the verb or subject complement after a linking verb, use a subjective form (see Table 13.3, column 2).
2. If the pronoun is the object of the verb or object of a preposition, use an objective form (see Table 13.3, column 3).
3. If the personal pronoun shows ownership or similar relationship, use a possessive form (Table 13.3, column 4).

Table 13.3 shows pronoun person by function. Note that the second-person pronoun does not change its form depending on whether it is a subject or an object.

TABLE 13.3	Pronoun Person by Function		
	1	2	3	4
Pronoun person	Subjective singular/plural	Objective singular/plural	Possessive singular/plural
First person	I/we	me/us	my/our
Second person	you	you	your
Third person	he, she, it/they	him, her, it/them	his, her, its/their

Note the spelling of the possessive singular pronoun *its*—without an apostrophe.

For example:

> *She* asked *them* about *him* and *his* new job.
>
> *She* = subject
>
> *them* = object of verb
>
> *him* = object of preposition
>
> *his* = possessive pronoun (adjective)

A common pronoun case error occurs with compounds in which both elements are pronouns or one is a noun and the other a pronoun. With two pronouns: Omit one of the pronouns, leaving the one in which you are in doubt. It should then be easier to see which form is correct.

> *If you've written:* You and me can work on the grammar project together.
>
> *Incorrect:* [omitting you] *Me* can work on the grammar project together.
>
> *Correct:* *You and I* can work on the grammar project together. [subject of verb]

With a noun and a pronoun: Since the pronoun will have the same grammatical function as the noun, you can look at the noun's function to determine the pronoun.

> *Incorrect:* *Patty* and *him* were wondering if they could do their grammar project with *Mattie* and *I*.

Patty is the subject (*Patty . . . was wondering*): subjective form is *he*. *Mattie* is the object of the preposition *with* (. . . *with Mattie*): objective form is *me*. The other pronouns in the sentence are correct: *they* is the subject of the dependent clause that begins with *if*; *their* is the possessive form, modifying *grammar project* and referring to *Patty and him (he)*.

> *Correct: Patty and he* were wondering if they could do their grammar project with *Mattie and me.*

It might sound more natural to say, *He and Patty . . .* (or, of course, to name the person).

Interrogative Pronoun Forms

For the interrogative pronouns, *who/whom*:

1. If the pronoun is the subject of the sentence that asks a question or the subject complement with a linking verb, use *who*, the subjective form.
2. If it is the object of the verb or object of a preposition in the sentence, use *whom*, the objective form.

Note that *whose* is the possessive form of the interrogative pronoun.

> *Who* wants to work with Mattie and me on the grammar project?

The subjective form, *who*, is used because it is subject of the verb, *wants*.

> With *whom* do Mattie and I want to work on the grammar project?

Whom is object of the preposition, *with*. Note: do not repeat the preposition later in the sentence.

> With *whom* do Mattie and I want to work ~~with~~ on the grammar project?

When the pronoun is separated from the preposition, it may be harder to see that the objective case should be used. Answer the question: Mattie and I want to work with *him* (objective case), not *he* (subjective).

   Hint: You can alter word order so that the preposition precedes the pronoun, or "answer" the question, substituting a personal pronoun for the interrogative one.

> *Incorrect:* Who do Mattie and I want to work with on the grammar project?

> *Correct: Whom* do Mattie and I want to work with on the grammar project?

Relative Pronoun Forms

For the relative pronouns, *who/whom, whoever/whomever*:

1. If the pronoun is the subject of the dependent clause that it introduces or the subject complement with a linking verb in the same clause, use *who/whoever*, the subjective form.
2. If the pronoun is the object of the verb in the dependent clause or the object of a preposition in the clause, use *whom/whomever*, the objective form.

Note that *whose* is the possessive form of the relative pronoun.

In the sentence below, *who* functions as the subject in the clause it begins. *Who* is the subject of the relative (dependent) clause *who was known for her bad temper.*

> Mattie and I didn't really want to work with Hattie, who was known for her bad temper.

Note that the spelling of the possessive singular pronoun *whose* is without an apostrophe.

Hint: One way to test whether *who* or *whom* is correct in a relative clause is to substitute the personal pronoun and, if necessary, rearrange the clause in a natural order.

> *Incorrect:* Mattie and I didn't really want to work with Hattie, who Mattie didn't like.
>
> *Rearrange clause and substitute personal pronoun:* Mattie didn't like *her.* [objective case]
>
> *Correct:* Mattie and I didn't really want to work with Hattie, *whom* Mattie didn't like. [objective case]

EXERCISE 13.3

Fix the sentences below, which all contain one of the kinds of pronoun errors discussed above: pronoun reference, consistency, or case. A sample sentence has been done for you.

> During his career, Jackie Robinson was subjected to racial hatred from many people who he came in contact with.
>
> During his career, Jackie Robinson was subjected to racial hatred from many people whom he came in contact with. [or . . . *with whom he came in contact*]

1. The new regulations mean that every new driver will have to wait two years until you are eligible for a class-five licence.
2. Some athletes get paid more than doctors or lawyers for something that they once did for free.
3. It is essential to educate Internet users about "Internet ethics." This could greatly reduce the incidence of piracy today.
4. The royal couple, who some Canadians regard as celebrities, recently toured the country.
5. In the article, it states that the right hemisphere of the brain processes visual information.

Modifier Errors

Modifiers, adjectives and adverbs, make sentences more interesting and informative. However, modifiers can sometimes stray from the words they are intended to modify or incorrectly modify a part of speech, thereby confusing a reader.

Misplaced Modifiers

Modifiers are usually placed next to the word(s) they modify. A misplaced modifier modifies a word that it is not intended to modify. Misplaced modifiers can be avoided by placing the adjective or adverb as close as possible to the word it is intended to modify. Limiting adverbs, such as *almost, even, just, nearly, not, merely,* and *only,* need to be placed before their modifier.

> *Imprecise:* Senior managers are permitted up to four weeks of vacation, though employees in their first year with the company are *only permitted* five days off.

> *Precise:* Senior managers are permitted up to four weeks of vacation, though employees in their first year with the company are permitted *only five days off.*

Only should modify the adjective *one*, not the verb *permitted*.

Other one-word modifiers should also be placed as close as possible to the word(s) you want them to modify.

> *Imprecise:* She contemplated the article she *had been given thoughtfully.*

> *Precise:* She *thoughtfully contemplated* the article she had been given.

Although it's possible that the adverb *thoughtfully* should really modify the verb *had been given*, context suggests that *thoughtfully* should modify *contemplated*.

Phrases and clauses should also be placed as close as possible to the word they are intended to modify.

> *Imprecise:* Two of my closest *friends* have been in car accidents *with cellphones.*

> *Precise:* Two of my closest *friends with cellphones* have been in car accidents.

In the first sentence, *with cellphones*, an adjectival (prepositional) phrase, seems to modify *car accidents*, but it is the *friends* who have cellphones.

Imprecise: This essay will examine if animals *suffer through empirical evidence.*

Precise: This essay will *examine, through empirical evidence,* if animals suffer.

In the first sentence, *through empirical evidence,* an adverbial (prepositional) phrase, seems to modify the verb *suffer,* but it answers the question *How?* of the verb *examine.*

Alternative: Through empirical evidence, this essay will examine if animals suffer.

If the adverbial phrase is placed at the beginning, it is still clear that it modifies *examine.*

Hint: Misplaced modifiers can occur anywhere in the sentence but are particularly common at the end, seeming almost an afterthought. Ask yourself if readers might misread part of the sentence due to the modifier's placement.

Finally, avoid using long phrases and clauses as modifiers if they disrupt the sentence, such as those separating a subject from its verb or a verb from its object.

Modifier separates subject from verb: Solar energy, using photovoltaic panels that are expensive to manufacture, is nonetheless a clean and limitless energy source.

Consider revising so verb directly follows subject: Using photovoltaic panels that are expensive to manufacture, *solar energy is* nonetheless a clean and limitless energy source.

Dangling Modifiers

A **dangling modifier** has no suitable word to modify. The intended noun/pronoun may be implied, but is not actually in the sentence. Dangling modifiers can occur anywhere in a sentence but are particularly common at the beginning of the sentence before the main idea (independent clause). They are often participial (*–ing, –ed, –en*) phrases or elliptical clauses without suitable words to modify.

Once you identify a dangling modifier, fix it by including the intended information either in the introductory (participial) phrase or in the independent clause.

No word to modify: Looking out the ferry window, several whales were frolicking.

A **dangling modifier** does not have a suitable word to modify and usually appears to modify the closest noun. They can be fixed by including the intended information either in the introductory (participial) phrase or in the independent clause.

Words added to introductory (participial) phrase: As *I looked out* the ferry window, several whales were frolicking.

Words added to independent clause: Looking out the ferry window, *I saw* several whales were frolicking.

- In the first sentence, it appears that the whales are looking out the ferry window.
- The middle sentence fixes the problem by changing the participial phrase, *looking out the ferry window,* into a dependent clause with a subject, *I,* and a complete verb form, *looked out.*
- The last sentence fixes the problem by changing the subject of the independent clause to *I,* giving the phrase an appropriate word to modify; a complete verb form is also needed, *saw.*

An **elliptical clause** is grammatically incomplete (ellipses = omission) but may be acceptable if the context is clear. If the clause is dangling (appears to modify an unintended word), the context is not clear, and the missing words need to be supplied.

In the following sentence, the **elliptical clause**, *though uncommon in the Islamic world,* modifies *men,* making it seem that men are uncommon in the Islamic world.

No word to modify: Though uncommon in the Islamic world, men are permitted up to four wives.

Words added: Though *polygamous marriages are* uncommon in the Islamic world, men are permitted up to four wives.

Alternate revision: Though uncommon in the Islamic world, *men in polygamous marriages* are permitted up to four wives.

Hint: Dangling modifiers can occur anywhere in a sentence but are particularly common at the beginning of the sentence before the main idea (independent clause). They are often participial (*–ing, –ed, –en*) phrases or elliptical clauses without suitable words to modify.

If you're written: As a first-year student, my professors do not accept Wikipedia as a credible source.

Ask who or what is the actor: Who is the first-year student? *My professors??*

Revision: As a first-year student, I am not allowed by my professors to use Wikipedia as a credible source.

Alternate Revision: As I am a first-year student, my professors do not allow me to use Wikipedia as a credible source.

An **elliptical clause** is grammatically incomplete (ellipses = omission) but may be acceptable if the context is clear. If the clause is dangling (appears to modify an unintended word), the context is not clear, and the missing words need to be supplied.

EXERCISE 13.4

Fix the problems with modifiers. A sample sentence has been done for you.

Having learned about feminism in college, short stories by women are often appreciated. [Who learned about feminism in college?]

Having learned about feminism in college, students often appreciate short stories by women.

1. Birth defects are common among addicted mothers, such as chronic lung diseases.
2. Watching Disney movies, heroines are usually long-legged, ample breasted beauties.
3. A healthy lifestyle can help reduce stress by simply staying active and allowing time to relax.
4. Many animals only use their vocal organs during breeding season in order to attract a mate.
5. Studying the use of stem cells, the benefits to society appear numerous.

Parallelism

Using parallel structures will make your prose more coherent and accessible. By contrast, a lack of parallelism might make part of a sentence sound "off kilter," or even confusing.

Making items parallel in a compound (two items) or a series (three or more items) consists of matching grammatical forms or structures. Being conscious of when and how to apply parallelism will enable you to better communicate your meaning.

Stylistically, writers use parallel structures to make their writing memorable or rhetorically effective.

Consider the following list from "The Impact of Pets on Human Health and Psychological Well-Being" on p. 323. Can you spot the one item that has been changed so it does not match the others?

> Parallelism refers to using similar forms for similar elements in a sentence. Parallelism should be used in both compounds and series.

Among [the reasons for keeping pets] are the misfiring of parental instincts, biophilia, social contagion, the middle class often tries to imitate the fashions of wealthy individuals, [and] the need to dominate the natural world . . . (pp. 323–4).

Some of the items are shorter than others, but length does not usually play a role in making elements parallel. You might have noticed that the fourth item is the only one that includes a complete verb form, *tries*. In fact, it is an independent clause with a subject and predicate. The others are just nouns with modifiers or objects. In the original (see par. 2, pp. 323–4), all the items are parallel because they all consist of nouns phrases—none includes a verb.

Parallelism in a Compound (Two Items)

One way to recognize compounds is to look for the word that joins them, often a coordinating conjunction. Then, match the form of the element that follows the joiner to that which precedes it.

A compound consists of two of something, whether single words, such as two nouns or two verbs, two phrases, or two clauses. One way to recognize compounds is to look for the word that joins them, often a coordinating conjunction. The co-ordinating conjunctions (italicized) below join three compounds, including two independent clauses (*so*). The parts of the compounds joined by *and* are underlined.

> She wanted the <u>sunglasses</u> *and* the <u>hat</u>, *so* she <u>placed</u> her bids *and* <u>waited</u> for the results.

In order to create balance by using parallel structures, first isolate the word that connects the two parts. In the first compound above (underlined), *and* joins the nouns *sunglasses* and *hat*. In the second underlined compound, *and* joins the verb *placed* with the verb *waited*. Finally, *so* (preceded by a comma) grammatically joins two independent clauses. All elements are parallel.

Now, consider an unbalanced structure in which the elements in the compound are not parallel.

> Minor league professionals live a nomadic lifestyle with endless bus journeys and living in cheap hotels.

Although the meaning of the sentence is clear enough, it sounds, and is, off balance due to the identical positions of non-parallel elements, *journeys* and *living*. Gerunds, which end in *–ing*, function as nouns in a sentence but are different in form from other nouns and shouldn't be matched with them to achieve parallelism in formal writing. In the sentence below, the noun *hotels* replaces the gerund, *living*, creating parallelism.

> Minor league professionals live a nomadic lifestyle with endless bus *journeys* and cheap *hotels*.

Correlative conjunctions, which are used as joiners to create parallelism, include *either . . . or, neither . . . nor, both . . . and, not . . . but, not only . . . but also.*

When correlative conjunctions (*either/or, neither/nor, both/and, not/but,* and *not only/but also*) are used as joiners, parallelism can be achieved by matching the word(s) following each part of the conjunction.

> *Non-matching elements:* As many athletes lack a good education, the options are *either accepting* the minor league lifestyle *or to get* a low-paying job.

Consider these strategies when trying to make the above sentence parallel:

1. Isolate the joiners: *either . . . or*
2. Identify the words, phrases, or clauses that are being joined: *accepting . . . to get*

3. Match to achieve parallelism: *accepting. . . getting* OR *to accept . . . to get*

    Matching (parallel) elements: As many athletes lack a good educa-
    tion, the options are *either accepting* the minor league lifestyle *or
    getting* a low-paying job.

Comparisons are another kind of compound since they always have two parts:
something is *compared to* something else. Always ensure that the second object being compared is completely expressed. What is missing in this sentence—in other
words, what exact words are being compared?

    Non-matching elements: The salaries of minor league baseball players
    are still very low compared to professional baseball players today.

Consider these strategies when trying to make the above sentence parallel:

1. Isolate the joiner: *compared to*
2. Identify the words, phrases, or clauses that are being joined: *salaries of
    minor league baseball players . . . professional baseball players* (it's illogical
    to compare salaries to baseball players!)
3. Match to achieve parallelism: *salaries of minor league baseball players . . .
    salaries of professional baseball players* (salaries of one group are now com-
    pared to salaries of another)

    Matching (parallel) elements: The *salaries of* minor league baseball
    players are still very low compared to the *salaries of* professional
    baseball players today.

    Alternate revision: The *salaries of* minor league baseball players are
    still very low compared to *those of* professional baseball players today.

Parallelism in a Series (More than Two Items)

Achieving parallelism with items in a series (three or more items) also involves
matching forms. Consider the following sentence.

    Non-matching elements: Music can directly affect your thoughts, emo-
    tions, and how you feel.

The list is composed of three items: *thoughts*, a noun; *emotions*, a noun; *how you
feel*, a dependent clause (note the pronoun subject, *you*, and the verb, *feel*).

    Matching elements: Music can directly affect your thoughts, emotions,
    and feelings.

As sentences get more complex, it may become more difficult to isolate elements that need to be parallel, as in the following sentence.

Although living off-campus has its disadvantages, it offers better stability in social relationships, greater health benefits, and allows for improved academic performance.

To check for parallel structure, first determine where the list begins. Then, ensure that the items in the series have the same form—for example, all are nouns, verbs, prepositional phrases, or dependent clauses.

1. Determine where the list begins (you can use a vertical line to show this): *offers | better stability*
2. Identify the first, second, and third items in the list: *stability* [noun] . . . *benefits* [noun] . . . *allows for* [verb] . . . *performance* [noun]
3. Match all items to achieve parallelism: *stability . . . benefits . . . performance*

   Matching (parallel) elements: Although living off-campus has its disadvantages, it offers better stability in social relationships, greater health benefits, and improved academic performance.

When you match for parallel items, you look at single words if the list consists of only those words; however, if the words have modifiers or objects, you do not usually need to consider them in making the items parallel. For example, the three parallel nouns in the sentence above, *stability*, *benefits*, and *performance*, have modifiers, but they do not affect parallelism in the series.

Non-matching elements: If you live on campus you can make more friends, travel to your classes more easily, and you get the benefits of meal plans.

Consider these strategies when trying to make the above sentence parallel:

1. Determine where the list begins: *campus | you can . . .*
2. Identify the first, second, and third items in the list: *you can make more friends* [independent clause] . . . *travel to your classes more easily* [verb + object and modifiers] . . . *you can get the benefits of meal plans* [independent clause] . . .
3. Match all items to achieve parallelism: *you can make more friends . . . you can travel to your classes . . . you can get the benefits of meal plans.*

Matching elements: If you live on campus you can make more friends, you can travel to your classes more easily, and you get the benefits of meal plans.

A more concise option would be to use three verbs after *can*, which you could make the new starting point for the series. Notice that all items are now composed of verb phrases.

> **Matching elements:** If you live on campus you can | *make* more friends, *travel* to your classes more easily, and *get* the benefits of meal plans.

EXERCISE 13.5

Correct the parallelism errors. A sample sentence has been done for you.

Television can affect children in a variety of negative ways since children often lack judgment, are naturally curious, and easily influenced.

Television can affect children in a variety of negative ways since children often *lack* judgment, *are* naturally curious, and *are* easily influenced.

1. To some extent, the media is a major cause of extreme diets, eating disorders, and of plastic surgery.
2. Highway safety programs increase public safety by either enforcing existing laws that limit speed or lower speed limits.
3. Purchasing goods locally leads not only to a healthy environment but also healthier economies and communities.
4. Dove is educating people about negative pressure from the media, eating disorders, and what beauty really is.
5. The writer effectively portrays the nature of social hierarchies and how they relate to economic inequality.

Chapter 13 Review Questions

1. a) What is subject–verb agreement?
   b) What is pronoun–antecedent agreement? In your answer, explain what an "antecedent" is.
2. When does the subject not precede the verb in the sentence? How can it be found in such cases?
3. What is a compound subject? How is agreement determined with a compound subject (give three rules)?
4. Choose the correct answers: Indefinite pronouns like *everyone*, *somebody*, and *anything* are considered (singular/plural); when they are used as subjects, the verb is (singular/plural).

If these pronouns are replaced by personal pronouns later in the sentence, these pronouns are (singular/plural).

5. What is a collective noun? How can you decide whether the verb or antecedent that it replaces should be singular or plural?

6. Choose the correct answer: Academic writing is gender-neutral writing, and a student should learn to make (*his/her/their* or *his or her*) prose gender-neutral too.

7. What does it mean to say that "the antecedent is ambiguous" and "the antecedent is missing?" How can these two problems be fixed?

8. What does pronoun inconsistency refer to? How can it be avoided in your sentences?

9. The subjective forms of the third-person singular personal pronouns are _____, _____, and *it*. The objective forms of these pronouns are _____, _____, and *it*.

10. How can you determine whether you should use the pronoun *who* or *whom* in a relative clause?

11. Answer true or false:
    a) Misplaced modifiers are often found at the end of a sentence or clause.
    b) Modifiers should be placed within two words of the part of speech they are intended to modify.
    c) A misplaced modifier error could confuse a reader.
    d) A dangling modifier is another name for a misplaced modifier.

12. What are two ways to correct a dangling modifier error?

13. What steps can be used to ensure that both elements in a compound are parallel?

14. Indicate which of the following series contain parallel items:
    a) noun, noun, noun phrase
    b) independent clause, independent clause, dependent clause
    c) verb, verb, gerund
    d) adverb, adverb, noun phrase

15. What steps can be used to ensure that all the elements in a series are parallel?

Key Terms

antecedent (p. 408)
collective noun (p. 409)
compound subject (p. 405)
dangling modifier (p. 419)
delayed subject construction (p. 404)
elliptical clause (p. 420)

misplaced modifier (p. 418)
parallelism (p. 421)
pronoun case (p. 414)
pronoun reference error (p. 412)
question construction (p. 404)

Answers to Grammar Preview

The following is a list of the errors from the grammar preview in Exercise 11.1, (p. 360). The answers are in paragraph form following the list.

Grammatical Errors:

1. Obsession over one's weight is a common practice in todays society. [apostrophe error; see p. 398.]
2. The desire to be thin and the need to possess the perfect body overshadows everything else. [subject–verb agreement error; see p. 372]
3. Advertisements that feature skinny models help fuel this desire; promoting unhealthy expectations for young women. [semicolon error; see p. 385]
4. Expectations that can't be met by the average woman, who weighs 140 pounds. [sentence fragment; see p. 376]
5. By contrast, the average model weighs less than 120 pounds, and is almost 6 feet tall. [comma error; see p. 385]
6. Body consciousness begins early, it can even be seen in young girls following exposure to Barbie dolls. [comma splice; see p. 380]
7. At age 13 50 per cent of girls exposed to Barbie dolls don't like the way they look. [comma error; see p. 389]
8. Increasing by age 18 to more than 80 per cent. [sentence fragment; see p. 376]
9. If we change our cultural ideals, young girls will begin to see themselves as "normal." [no error]
10. With a positive self-image, young women will be better able to succeed socially, academically, and in their chosen vocation. [parallelism error; see p. 421]

Corrected paragraph: Obsession over one's weight is a common practice in today's society. The desire to be thin and the need to possess the perfect body overshadow everything else. Advertisements that feature skinny models help fuel this desire, promoting unhealthy expectations for young women, expectations that can't be met by the average woman, who weighs 140 pounds. By contrast, the average model weighs less than 120 pounds and is almost 6 feet tall. Body consciousness begins early; it can even be seen in young girls following exposure to Barbie dolls. At age 13, 50 per cent of girls exposed to Barbie dolls don't like the way they look, increasing by age 18 to more than 80 per cent. If we change our cultural ideals, young girls will begin to see themselves as "normal." With a positive self-image, young women will be better able to succeed socially, academically, and professionally.

Glossary

abstract An abstract is a condensed summary used in empirical studies. It is placed before the study begins and includes its purpose, method(s), and result(s), and conclusion.

active reading Active reading refers to an approach to reading in which you take an active, rather than a passive role—by approaching a text as a learning experience—first, by considering your purpose for reading, then, by questioning, evaluating, and using critical analysis to develop your understanding of the text at a more complex level.

action verb An action verb conveys an action—physical or mental/emotional.

adjective An adjective gives information about (modifies) a noun or pronoun. It can answer questions like *Which one? What kind?* or *How many?* When an adjective is one word, it usually precedes the noun, unless it follows a linking verb as a predicate adjective.

adverb An adverb gives information about a verb, an adjective, and/or another adverb. It answers questions like *How? When? Where? How much?* or *To what degree?*

adverbial conjunction An adverbial conjunction is an adverb used to connect two independent clauses.

analogy An analogy is a systematic comparison between one item and another one.

analysis Analysis is a skill used when you closely examine something, breaking it down to look more closely at its parts, as you might do with an essay or paragraph, an argument or point.

anecdotal evidence Anecdotal evidence is suggestive rather than conclusive. It is often based on reliable observation.

annotated bibliography An annotated bibliography is an expanded bibliography that includes not only the information of standard bibliographies but also brief summaries of related works.

antecedent The antecedent of the pronoun is the noun or pronoun it replaces.

apostrophe An apostrophe is used to indicate possession and other relationships between two nouns or an indefinite pronoun and a noun, and to show the omission of one or more letters in contractions.

appositive An appositive is a word or phrase that names, specifies, or explains the previous word or phrase.

arguable claim An arguable claim has an opposing viewpoint and objective evidence to support it.

audience An audience is the reader or readers for whom most writing is designed. Being aware of your audience will help you decide what to include or not include or, in the case of argument, what strategies to use to help convince this audience.

brackets Brackets are used to show a change or addition to a direct quotation or to indicate parentheses inside parentheses.

brainstorming Brainstorming is a pre-writing technique in which you list your associations with a subject in the order they occur to you.

circular conclusion A circular conclusion reminds the reader of the thesis and reinforces it.

claim A claim is an assertion that you will attempt to support through evidence, about a topic appearing in the thesis statement and topic sentences.

climax order Climax order is the order of points that proceeds from the weakest to the strongest. Other orders include inverse climax order and mixed order.

clustering Clustering is a pre-writing technique that works spatially to generate associations with a subject and connections among them.

coherent A coherent paragraph is constructed with ideas that are logically laid out with clear connections between them.

collective noun A collective noun refers to groups of people, usually acting collectively. When this type of noun acts as an antecedent, the pronoun is singular unless the stress is on individuals within the group; then, the pronoun is plural.

colloquial language Colloquial language is conversational in style and is a typical feature of some non-academic writing.

comma splice A comma splice is the incorrect use of a comma alone to join two independent clauses.

common ground Establishing common ground is an argumentative strategy in which you show readers that you share many of their values, making you appear open and approachable.

complete predicate   A complete predicate includes a main verb, along with modifiers and objects.

complete subject   A complete subject contains the main noun/pronoun along with any modifiers of the subject.

complex sentence   A complex sentence is made up of an independent and one or more dependent clauses.

compound-complex sentence   A compound-complex sentence combines two independent clauses (the "compound" part) with at least one dependent clause (the "complex" part).

compound sentence   A compound sentence consists of two independent clauses joined by a comma and coordinating conjunction, a semicolon, or a colon.

compound subject   A compound subject is composed of two nouns, two pronouns, or a noun and a pronoun. The rule for agreement depends on the word or phrase that joins the two parts of the subject.

concession   Making a concession is an argumentative strategy in which you concede or qualify a point, acknowledging its validity in order to come across as fair and reasonable.

concise   Concise writing is effective writing in which you use only the words that are essential to express your meaning and do not waste words.

conjunction   A conjunction joins words, phrases, or clauses in a sentence.

connotation   Connotations are "shades" of meaning or associations (often determined by context).

conventions   Conventions are practices that direct the actions and thinking of specific groups. You can consider them a set of instructions that help us communicate with one another.

coordinate adjective   A coordinate adjective precedes a noun and modifies it individually; a comma separates coordinate adjectives.

coordinating conjunction   A coordinating conjunction joins *equal* grammatical units.

correlative conjunction   A correlative conjunction is a pair of conjunctions.

credibility   Credibility is essential for all writing. Appearing credible involves showing knowledge as well as coming across as trustworthy and fair.

critical analysis   A critical analysis focuses on the text you have read. In a critical analysis, you break down the writer's argument, evaluating its effectiveness for its intended audience while considering the use of reason and specific argumentative strategies.

critical response   A critical response focuses on your own opinions or observations about an issue raised in a text. Although a response is usually more informal than an analysis, it should clearly demonstrate critical thinking.

critical thinking   Critical thinking can be defined as a series of logical mental processes, including evaluating and weighing the evidence, that leads to a conclusion.

cumulative sentence   In a cumulative sentence, the writer begins with the main idea and follows with words, phrases, or clauses that extend this idea.

dangling modifier   A dangling modifier does not have a suitable word to modify and usually appears to modify the closest noun. It can be fixed by including the intended information either in the introductory (participial) phrase or in the independent clause.

deductive reasoning   Deductive reasoning is based on a generalization, which is applied to a specific example or subset to form a conclusion.

delayed subject construction   In the delayed subject construction, the verb is placed before the subject.

demonstrative pronoun   A demonstrative pronoun (*this, that, these, those*) points to a noun(s). Other pronouns include indefinite, intensive, interrogative, personal, relative, reflexive, and reciprocal pronouns.

denotation   Denotation is a word's dictionary meaning.

dependent clause   A dependent clause contains a subject and a predicate but does not express a complete thought.

descriptive headings   Descriptive headings summarize section contents.

digital object identifier   A digital object identifier (DOI) is a number–alphabet sequence often found on journal articles and begins with the number 10; it serves as a permanent link for digital material.

Discussion   Discussion is one of the headings of the IMRAD structure; it includes a summary of the results and compares them with similar studies. The section ends by suggesting directions for future research and, often, practical applications of the findings.

documentation style   Documentation style refers to guidelines for documenting sources put forth in style manuals and handbooks for researchers and other academic writers.

dramatic opening   A dramatic opening is a technique for creating reader interest by beginning with a question, illustration, anecdote, quotation, description, or other attention-grabbing technique.

ellipses   Ellipses means omission; they are used to indicate that you have left out words in a direct quotation by replacing the omitted word(s) by three or four spaced dots.

elliptical clause   An elliptical clause is grammatically incomplete but may be acceptable if the context is clear. If the clause is dangling (appears to modify an unintended word), the context is not clear, and the missing words need to be supplied.

emotional and ethical fallacies   Emotional and ethical fallacies appeal to the emotions in a manipulative or unfair way, such as a partisan appeal, guilt by association, name-calling, or bandwagon.

emphasis   Using emphasis helps focus the reader's attention on specific passages through repetition in language or structure, or other techniques, such as diction or rhythm.

essay plan   An essay plan includes the main points or main sections of the essay's development. It may use the first-person voice.

ethos   Ethos is an argument that is founded on morality.

focused reading   In focused reading, you often concentrate on short or medium-length passages and relate them to a main idea or to other sections of the book. You read the text closely line by line and word by word.

formal headings   Formal headings divide an experiment into stages.

freewriting   Freewriting is a pre-writing technique in which you write on a subject without stopping to edit.

general scan   In a general scan, you try to get the essence of the work—for example, by looking at its title, abstract, and headings. This type of scanning is a form of selective reading in which you look for features that will tell you more about the text, ignoring most detail.

gerund   A gerund is formed from the present participle of a verb. A gerund ends in *–ing* and functions as a noun.

gerund (noun) phrase   A gerund (noun) phrase is formed from the present (*–ing*) participle of a verb and functions as a noun, for example, as a subject or an object.

helping (auxiliary) verb   A helping (auxiliary) verb combines with the main verb to express a condition such as time, necessity, probability, and other relationships.

hypothesis   A hypothesis is a prediction or probable outcome of an experiment.

imperative sentence   An imperative sentence issues an order or direction and is a complete sentence even if it consists of only one word, a verb.

IMRAD   IMRAD stands for Introduction, Method(s), Result(s), and Discussion, the sections that compose an empirical study. (Also see *Introduction, Method(s), Result(s),* and *Discussion.*)

indefinite pronoun   An indefinite pronoun refers to a non-specified individual(s) or group(s). Other pronouns include

demonstrative, intensive, interrogative, personal, relative, reflexive, and reciprocal pronouns.

independent clause   An independent clause is equivalent to a complete sentence.

inductive reasoning   Inductive reasoning relies on facts, details, and observations to form a conclusion.

inference   An inference is a conclusion based on what the evidence shows or points to, without the author stating that conclusion. More than one inference might be possible in a given situation, but the most *probable* one is said to be the *best* inference.

infinitive   An infinitive includes *to* along with the base verb form and acts as a noun, an adjective, or an adverb.

infinitive (noun, adjective, adverb) phrase   An infinitive (noun, adjective, adverb) phrase includes *to* along with the base verb form and acts as a noun, an adjective, or adverb.

integrate   When you integrate sources during the composing stage, you combine their ideas and/or words with your own ideas/ words.

interrogative pronoun   An interrogative pronoun introduces questions.

Introduction   Introduction is one of the headings of the IMRAD structure; it announces the topic and includes summaries of previous research; it ends with a hypothesis or research question.

irony   In irony, a second, or "deeper," meaning exists below the literal meaning, which contradicts the literal meaning.

jargon   Jargon is discipline- or subject-specific language used to communicate among members.

journal   A journal is a kind of periodical designed for readers with specialized interests and knowledge. A journal contains original research, reviews, and editorials—but little, if any, advertising. It may be issued in print and/or online format.

justification   Justification is used by academic writers to legitimize their study in the introduction, either directly stating why it is needed or indirectly stressing its significance. A typical justification is that there is a gap in knowledge, which the researcher will try to fill.

linking verb   A linking verb links the subject to the predicate.

literature review   A literature review is a condensed survey of articles on the topic arranged in a logical order usually ending with the article most relevant to the author's study.

logical fallacies   Logical fallacies are categories of faulty reasoning.

logical opening   A logical opening is a technique for creating reader interest by beginning with a generalization and narrowing to the thesis.

logos   Logos is an argument that is founded on reason.

Method(s)   Method is one of the headings of the IMRAD structure; it explains how the experiment was conducted—for example, *who* took part, *how* it was designed, and *what* procedures were used.

misplaced modifier   A misplaced modifier modifies a word that it is not intended to modify. It can be avoided by placing the adjective or adverb as close as possible to the word it is intended to modify.

mixed order   See *climax order.*

non-coordinate adjectives   Non-coordinate adjectives are adjectives that together modify a noun and cannot be separated without changing the meaning. Commas are not used to separate the adjectives.

non-essential (parenthetical) information   Non-essential (parenthetical) information is information that does not affect the basic meaning of the sentence or clause. Use commas to separate this information from the more important information.

noun   A noun names people, places, things, qualities, or conditions.

object   The object receives the verb's action.

object of a preposition   The object of a preposition is the indirect object of the verb.

outline   An outline is a linear or graphic representation of main points and sub-points, showing an essay's structure.

paragraph wrap   A paragraph wrap is a concluding sentence that functions as a paragraph summary.

parallelism   Parallelism refers to using similar grammatical forms for similar elements in a sentence. Parallelism should be used in both compounds and series.

paraphrase   When you paraphrase, you put someone else's ideas in your own words, keeping the length of the original.

participle   A participle usually ends in *–ing, –ed, –en,* or *–t* and acts as an adjective.

participle (adjective) phrase   A participle phrase is formed from present (*–ing*) or past (*–ed, –en, –t*) participles of verbs.

passive construction   In a passive construction, the subject of the sentence is the receiver of the action.

pathos   Pathos is an argument that is founded on emotion.

peer-reviewed journal   A peer-reviewed journal is a publication in which submissions are reviewed (critiqued) by experts before publication. These experts (typically peers) suggest whether the article is good enough for publication.

periodic sentence   In a periodic sentence, the writer builds toward the main idea, which is expressed at the end of the sentence.

periodical   A periodical is a general term for the kind of publication that is issued at regular intervals.

personal pronoun   A personal pronoun refers to people and sometimes animals, things, or places. Other pronouns include demonstrative, indefinite, intensive, interrogative, relative, reflexive, and reciprocal pronouns.

phrase   A phrase is a group of words acting as a unit of speech. Therefore, a group of words modifying a noun is an adjectival phrase while one modifying a verb is an adverbial phrase.

plagiarism   Plagiarism involves the use of outside material—whether you quote directly, summarize, paraphrase, or just refer to it in your essay—without acknowledging it. It also is considered plagiarism if you use the exact words of the source without putting them in quotation marks, or if you follow the structure of the original too closely.

policy claim   A policy claim is an assertion about a topic that proposes an action (e.g., to fix a problem or improve a situation).

precedent   A precedent is a specific example that refers to the way a situation was dealt with in the past in order to argue for its similar use in the present.

précis   *Précis* is a term for a stand-alone summary. It is usually 20–25 per cent the length of the original.

predicate   The predicate tells you what the subject is doing or shows you the state or condition of the subject.

premise   A premise is a statement or assumption on which a conclusion is based.

preposition   A preposition, which often refers to place or time, joins the noun/pronoun that follows to the rest of the sentence.

prepositional phrase   A prepositional phrase begins with a preposition and can act adjectivally or adverbially.

primary sources   Primary sources are original, or first-hand, material in a field of study.

prompt   A prompt, which can be as lengthy as a sentence or two, can help you locate important information.

pronoun   A pronoun replaces a noun (in most instances). Pronouns include demonstrative, intensive, interrogative, personal, relative, reflexive, and reciprocal pronouns.

pronoun case   Pronoun case is the form the pronoun takes that shows its function in the sentence or clause. Only a few pronouns change their form to reflect their function.

pronoun reference error   A pronoun reference error can occur when the noun/pronoun to which the pronoun refers (its antecedent) is unclear or absent.

question construction   In a question construction the verb is placed before the subject.

questioning   Questioning is a pre-writing technique in which you list questions about the topic.

reader-based prose   Reader-based prose is clear, accessible writing designed for a specific reader.

rebuttal   Rebuttal is an argumentative strategy of raising opposing points in order to counter them with your own points.

relative clause   A relative clause follows a noun or pronoun and modifies it.

relative pronoun   A relative pronoun relates what follows to a preceding noun or pronoun. Other pronouns include demonstrative, indefinite, intensive, interrogative, personal, reflexive, and reciprocal pronouns.

Result(s)   Result(s) is one of the headings of the IMRAD structure; it presents the raw data generated by the experiment, often with accompanying tables and figures.

rhetoric   Rhetoric refers to the structure and strategies of language and/or argumentation used to persuade a specific audience.

rhetorical analysis   A rhetorical analysis focuses on the text you have read. In a rhetorical analysis, you break down a work in order to examine its parts and the author's rhetorical strategies, using your critical thinking skills and your knowledge of texts.

rhetorical pattern   A rhetorical pattern is a method for organizing and presenting information in essays and paragraphs. Examples include cause and effect, classification, comparison and contrast, cost–benefit analysis, and definition.

satire   Satire is a genre that mocks or criticizes institutions or commonly held attitudes.

secondary source   Secondary sources comment on, interpret, or analyze primary sources.

selective reading   Selective reading is planned, conscious reading in which you choose strategies that best reflect your reading purpose, what you are reading, and similar factors.

sentence   A sentence can be defined grammatically as a group of words that contains a subject and a predicate and that needs nothing else to complete it.

sentence fragment   A sentence fragment lacks a subject and/or predicate or consists only of a dependent clause, which does not express a complete thought.

signal phrase   A signal phrase introduces a reference in a phrase that names the author(s) and usually includes a "signal verb" and, in APA style, year of publication.

simple predicate   A simple predicate consists only of the main verb.

simple sentence   A simple sentence, which has one subject–predicate unit, is equivalent to an independent clause.

simple subject   A simple subject consists only of the main noun/pronoun.

slanted language   Slanted language is extreme or accusatory language, which can make an arguer seem biased.

spiral conclusion   A spiral conclusion suggests applications or further research.

subject   The subject performs the verb's action.

subject complement   A subject complement completes the subject after a linking verb.

subject index   A subject index is a list of important words in a text, ordered alphabetically and usually placed at the end of the text.

subordinating conjunction   A subordinating conjunction joins unequal grammatical units, specifically dependent to independent clauses, showing how they are related.

summarization   Summarization is a general term for representing the ideas of a writer in a condensed form, using your own words.

summarize   When you summarize, you include the main idea (or ideas) from a source, expressing it in your own words.

support   Support consists of evidence to help prove a claim.

syllogism   A syllogism is a logical three-part structure that can illustrate how deductive conclusions are made.

synthesis   Synthesis is a skill used when you are "putting together" something in order to reach a conclusion. You combine your own ideas with ideas, facts, and/or findings from other sources.

target scan   A target scan looks for specific content, such as a subject or keyword. This type of scanning is a form of selective reading in which you look for features that will tell you more about the text, ignoring most detail.

theme   A theme is an overarching meaning or universal aspect, seen through a work's basic elements, such as plot, setting, character, images, language, and figurative techniques.

thesis   A thesis includes the main point of your essay or what you will attempt to prove. In most formal writing, it is placed at the end of your introduction.

thesis statement   A thesis statement sets down a generalization that is applicable to the entire essay (simple thesis) or includes the essay's main points as well (expanded thesis, or essay plan).

tone   Tone can be defined as the use of language to convey the writer's attitude toward the subject or the audience.

topic sentence   A topic sentence, usually the first sentence, states the main idea in the paragraph.

unified   A unified paragraph focuses on developing only one main idea.

value claim   A value claim is an assertion about a topic that appeals to its ethical nature (e.g., good/bad or fair/unfair).

verb   The verb conveys an action or a state of being, or combines with a main verb to express conditions like possibility or a complex temporal (time-related) action.

verbal   A verbal, or an incomplete verb form, can be used as a noun, adjective, or adverb. It shouldn't be mistaken for a complete verb form.

verb phrase   A verb phrase consists of a main verb and any helping verbs.

warrant   A warrant provides the foundation of a claim, linking the evidence to the claim being made.

APPENDIX
Answers to Exercises

Answers are given for even-numbered questions. Other options than the one(s) shown may exist.

Exercise 11.2

2. Hockey (N) is (V) certainly (ADV) a (ADJ) very (ADV) aggressive (ADJ) sport (N).
4. Most (ADJ) people (N) in (PRE) North America (N) now (ADV) access (V) their (ADJ) news (N) on (PRE) the (ADJ) Internet (N).

Exercise 11.3

2. Approximately 3,000 inmates currently reside <u>on death row</u>. (adverbial prepositional phrase)
4. <u>Having murderers pay for crimes with their own lives</u> is considered barbaric by many people. (noun phrase subject)

Exercise 11.4

2. The battle against cancer will continue (until a cure is found).
4. <u>The game "Baggataway,"</u> (which was played by many Aboriginal tribes), <u>intrigued British colonizers</u>.

Exercise 11.5

2. A novel about a boy who loses his parents to a disaster at sea *has many sad passages*.
   Or,
   Life of Pi is a novel about a boy who loses his parents to a disaster at sea.
4. Many people today are obsessed with the Internet whether they connect with friends on Facebook or watch videos on YouTube.

Exercise 11.6

2. *The reporter spoke to two w*omen from Afghanistan who share the Muslim religion.
4. Modern technology has resulted in astonishing benefits for our communities, *though* it has created many new problems as well.

Exercise 12.1

2. The language of music is universal; *indeed,* people everywhere connect with others through some form of music.
   Or,
   People everywhere connect with others through some form of music *as t*he language of music is universal.
4. Global warming and the depletion of our resources are major problems; *however,* they are preventable ones.

Exercise 12.2

2. After the 1976 Olympics, an economic disaster for taxpayers, Canadians looked forward to the 2010 Olympics.
4. Penicillin, an antibiotic crucial in treating bacterial infection, was possible due to the biodiversity of plants.

Exercise 12.3

Selah wanted to be cool and healthy, [1]so she thought she would make a New Year's resolution to go vegan. She knew that <u>beans, tofu, and nuts</u>[2] were high-protein options for vegans. Unfortunately, [3]Selah was allergic to nuts; [4]they made her violently ill. She had tried tofu<u>, which consists of mashed soya beans,</u>[5]and found it had a rubbery, [6]mushy texture. She liked beans well enough, [7]but not every day!

1. Independent clauses (commas)
2. Series
3. Introductions
4. Independent clauses (semicolon)
5. Non-essential elements: relative clauses
6. Coordinate adjectives
7. Non-essential concluding phrase

Exercise 12.4

2. The first video game, *Tennis for Two,* was created in 1958.
4. To relieve stress, explore the world, and have fun, students should take a break after high school.

6. It was predicted that the movie *The King's Speech* would win the Oscar for Best Picture—and it did. (or comma)
8. On July 19, 2005, the same-sex marriage law in Canada was passed, but many Christians remained opposed to this law.
10. Alcohol affects every part of the body and the brain, such as the circulatory, nervous, and gastrointestinal systems.

Exercise 12.5

2. A student's grade point average can affect an employer's hiring decision.
4. Two reasons for pet overpopulation today include society's lack of awareness and pet owners' refusal to have their pets neutered.

Exercise 13.1

2. Small class sizes and a low student population (means/<u>mean</u>) few opportunities to meet new people.
4. One-half of the participants in each group (has/<u>have</u>) been asked to complete a questionnaire.
6. With shipping and oil drilling (<u>comes</u>/come) the risk of oil spills.
8. Overindulging in alcohol and drugs often (<u>leads</u>/lead) to unsafe sex.
10. The regular practice of yoga in addition to a healthy diet (<u>inhibits</u>/inhibit) cell deterioration, according to one study.

Exercise 13.2

2. The ad hoc committee on gender equity will be submitting its interim report on April 30.
4. In laparoscopic surgery, the surgeon operates through small insertions using information he or she receives from a camera inside the patient.

Exercise 13.3

2. Some athletes get paid more than doctors or lawyers for something that the athletes once did for free.
    Or,
    Some athletes, who once played their sport for free, get paid more than doctors and lawyers do.
4. The royal couple, whom some Canadians regard as celebrities, recently toured the country.

Exercise 13.4

2. Watching Disney movies, we see heroines who are usually long-legged, ample-breasted beauties.

Or, simply,

Heroines in Disney movies are usually long-legged, ample-breasted beauties.

4. Many animals use their vocal organs only during breeding season in order to attract a mate.

Exercise 13.5

2. Highway safety programs increase public safety either by enforcing existing laws that limit speed or by lowering speed limits.

4. Dove is educating people about negative pressure from the media, eating disorders, and the essence of beauty.

Credits

Alang, Navneet. "Stop Believing in the 'World-Changing' Power of Every New Gadget." *Globe and Mail*, October 25, 2013.

Alini, Erica. "Generation Spend." *Maclean's*, Nov. 15, 2010, pp. 45–6.

Appleyard, Bryan. "Distraction." *The Sunday Times*, July 20, 2008.

Brown, Ian. "I'm Glad I Never Had to Decide Whether My Strange, Lonely Boy Ought to Exist." *Globe and Mail*, August 27, 2011. © The Globe and Mail Inc. All Rights Reserved.

Castaldo, Joe, "Steal Your Success." Canadian Business, 2014.

Chivers, Danny. "Debunking the Myths." *New Internationalist*, 2011.

Clark, Matthew P.A. and Brian D. Westerberg. "How Random is the Toss of a Coin?" *CMAJ* 181.12 (2009): 306–8 ©Access Copyright, 2011. This work is protected by copyright and the making of this copy was with the permission of Access Copyright. Any alteration of this content of further copying in any form whatsoever is strictly prohibited unless otherwise permitted by law.

Cunningham, Lynn. "Giving Up the Ghost: When it Comes to Quitting Smoking, You're on Your Own." *The Walrus*, 2014.

Doctorow, Cory. "You DO Like Reading Off a Computer Screen." *Content: Selected Essays on Technology, Creativity, Copyright, and the Future of the Future*. Tachyon Publication, 2008, 51–4.

Feschuk, Scott. "The Future of Machines with Feelings." *Maclean's*, January 24, 2015.

Gibson, Robert. "Bullshit: Disrespect for the Concept of Truth Erodes the Foundations of Any Worthy Culture." *Alternatives Journal*, 37:1 (2011), reprinted with permission from the author and A/J.

Gray, Jonathan. "Coming Up Next': Promos in the Future of Television and Television Studies," *Journal of Popular Film and Television*, 38.2 (2010): 54–7. Copyright © 2010 Routledge.

Harris, Jim. "The UnAtomic Age: Getting Past the Nuclear Era's Fiscal Meltdown," *Alternatives Journal*, 40:4 (2014), reprinted with permissions from the author and A/J.

Harron, Nik. "Fully Destructible: Exploring a Personal Relationship with Nature Through Video Games." *Alternatives Journal*, 49:3 (2014), reprinted with permission from the author and A/J.

Herzog, Harold. "The Impact of Pets on Human Health and Psychological Well-Being: Fact, Fiction, or Hypothesis?" *Psychological Science* 20.4 (2011): 236–9. Copyright © 2011, © SAGE Publications

Hicks, Bruce M. "The Undiscovered Province." *This Magazine* 43.4 (Jan/Feb 2012): 14–15.

Horgan, John. "Does Peace Have a Chance?" *Slate*, August 4, 2009.

Irvine, Andrew. "Is Scientific Progress Inevitable?" *In the Agora: The Public Face of Canadian Philosophy*, by Andrew Irvine and John S. Russell, eds. © University of Toronto Press, 2006, pp. 45–9. Reprinted with permission of the publisher.

Loughnan, Steve, Brock Bastian, & Nick Haslam. "The Psychology of Eating Animals." 23:2 (2009) *Current Directions in Psychological Science* 2014. Copyright © 2014, © SAGE Publications.

Mack, Adrian & Miranda Nelson. "Vancouver Hockey Riot is a Symptom of a Larger Problem." *The Georgia Straight*, June 16, 2012.

Manguel, Alberto. "Burning Mistry". *Geist*, May 2011. © Alberto Manguel c/o Schavelzon Graham Agencia Literaria www.schavelzongraham.com

Mendleson, Rachel. "Raising young Einsteins." *Canadian Business* 2011.

Midgley, Mary. "The Selfish Metaphor." *New Scientist*, January 29, 2011.

Milijasevic, Natasha. "The Genius of the Generalist: Why Environmental Studies is Essential to the Workforce We Need Now." *Alternatives Journal* 40:4 (2014), reprinted with permission of the author and A/J.

Pachner, Joanna. "Do You Have the Brain of a CEO?" *Canadian Business,* 2014.

Pinto, Andrew D. "Denaturalizing 'Natural' Disasters: Haiti's Earthquake and the Humanitarian Impulse." 4.4 (2010) *Open Medicine*, E1 93–8.

Romm, Aviva. "'Stop Killing the Good Guys!' Protect Your Child's Microbiome from Antibiotic Overuse." *Huffington Post*, January 8, 2015.

Rosenfield, Daniel et al. "Canadian Lifestyle Choices: A Public Health Failure." *CMAJ* 183.13 (2011): 1461. ©Access Copyright, 2011. This work is protected by copyright and the making of this copy was with the permission of Access

Copyright. Any alteration of this content of further copying in any form whatsoever is strictly prohibited unless otherwise permitted by law.

Rublack, Ulinka. "The Birth of Power Dressing." 61.1 *History Today*, January 2011, 20–7.

Rupp, Shannon. "I'll Take My Coffee with Fiction, Thanks." *The Tyee*, March 6, 2014.

Saunders, Doug. "When a Cellphone Beats a Royal Flush." *Globe and Mail*, March 26, 2011. © The Globe and Mail Inc. All Rights Reserved.

Sonik, Madeline. "Flush." *Afflictions and Departures*, Anvil Press (2011): 163–74.

Sternberg, Robert J. "Slip-Sliding Away, Down the Ethical Slope." *The Chronicle of Higher Education*, 57.19 (2011): A23. Used with permission of *The Chronicle of Higher Education*. All rights reserved

Tepper, Steven J. "Thinking 'Bigger than Me' in the Liberal Arts." *The Chronicle of Higher Education* 2014.

Vazire, Simine & Erika N. Carlson. "Others Sometimes Know Us Better Than We Know Ourselves." *Current Directions in Psychological Science* 20.2 (2011): 104–8. Copyright © 2011, © SAGE Publications

Wegner, Daniel M. "How to Think, Say, or Do Precisely the Worst Thing for Any Occasion." *Science* 325 (2009): 48–50. Copyright © 2009, American Association for the Advancement of Science.

Whitchurch, Erin R., Timothy D. Wilson, & Daniel T. Gilbert. "'He Loves Me, He Loves Me Not…': Uncertainty Can Increase Romantic Attraction." *Psychological Science* 22.2 (2011): 172–5. Copyright © 2011, © SAGE Publications.

Wilson, Renée. "In Defence of the iGeneration." *This*, 2013.

Woodend, Dorothy. "Generation Velcro." *The Tyee*, November 21, 2008.

Index